Broadway Musicals

SHOW BY SHOW

SEVENTH EDITION

Also by Stanley Green

The World of Musical Comedy

The Great Clowns of Broadway

Encyclopedia of the Musical Theatre

Encyclopedia of the Musical Film

Broadway Musicals of the 1930s (Ring Bells! Sing Songs!)

Starring Fred Astaire

The Rodgers and Hammerstein Story

Hollywood Musicals Year by Year

Broadway
Musicals

SHOW BY SHOW
SEVENTH EDITION

by Stanley Green

REVISED AND UPDATED BY CARY GINELL

APPLAUSE
THEATRE & CINEMA BOOKS

An Imprint of Hal Leonard Corporation

First edition published in 1985 by Hal Leonard Corporation

Seventh edition published in 2011 by
Applause Theatre & Cinema Books
An Imprint of Hal Leonard Corporation
7777 West Bluemound Road
Milwaukee, WI 53213

Trade Book Division Editorial Offices
33 Plymouth Street
Montclair, NJ 07042

Printed in the United States of America

Book composition: Kristina Rolander

Library of Congress Cataloging-in-Publication Data is available upon request.

ISBN 978-1-55783-784-4

www.halleonardbooks.com

To Stanley and Kay Green...who set the stage

Contents

Preface to the Seventh Edition   xxi

Preface to the Sixth Edition   xxiii

Preface to the Fourth Edition   xxv

Preface to the First Edition   xxvi

Introduction   xxviii

Show by Show

1866

    The Black Crook   3

1874

    Evangeline   4

1879

    The Mulligan Guard Ball   4

1891

    Robin Hood   5

    A Trip to Chinatown   5

1898

    The Fortune Teller   6

1900

    Florodora   6

1903

    The Wizard of Oz   8

    Babes in Toyland   8

1904

    Little Johnny Jones   10

1905

    Mlle. Modiste   10

1906

    Forty-five Minutes from Broadway   13

    The Red Mill   13

1907

    Follies of 1907   14

    The Merry Widow   15

1909

    The Chocolate Soldier   16

Contents

1910

    Madame Sherry   17

    Naughty Marietta   17

1911

    The Pink Lady   18

1912

    The Firefly   18

1913

    Sweethearts   19

1914

    The Girl from Utah   19

    Watch Your Step   20

1915

    Ziegfeld Follies   20

    The Blue Paradise   21

    Very Good Eddie   23

1917

    Oh, Boy!   24

    Maytime   24

    Leave It to Jane   27

1918

    Oh, Lady! Lady!!   26

    Sinbad   29

    Ziegfeld Follies   29

1919

    Ziegfeld Follies   31

    Greenwich Village Follies   31

    Irene   32

1920

    Sally   33

1921

    Shuffle Along   34

    Ziegfeld Follies   34

    Music Box Revue   37

    Blossom Time   38

1922

    Ziegfeld Follies   38

    George White's Scandals   40

1923

    Poppy   40

1924

    Andre Chariot's Revue of 1924   42

    Rose-Marie   43

    Lady, Be Good!   44

    The Student Prince in Heidelberg   45

1925

The Garrick Gaieties	46
No, No, Nanette	47
Dearest Enemy	48
The Vagabond King	48
Sunny	50
The Cocoanuts	51
Tip-Toes	52

1926

George White's Scandals	52
Countess Maritza	53
Oh, Kay!	53
The Desert Song	54
Peggy-Ann	54

1927

Rio Rita	55
Hit the Deck!	56
Good News!	56
A Connecticut Yankee	58
Funny Face	59
Show Boat	60

1928

Rosalie	62
The Three Musketeers	63
Blackbirds of 1928	63
The New Moon	64
Hold Everything!	65
Whoopee	66

1929

Follow Thru	67
The Little Show	67
Sweet Adeline	68
Bitter Sweet	68
Fifty Million Frenchmen	69

1930

Strike Up the Band	70
Flying High	71
Fine and Dandy	72
Girl Crazy	72
Three's a Crowd	73
The New Yorkers	74

1931

The Band Wagon	74
Earl Carroll Vanities	76
George White's Scandals	76
The Cat and the Fiddle	77
Of Thee I Sing	78

Contents

1932

Face the Music	79
Flying Colors	80
Music in the Air	81
Take a Chance	82
Gay Divorce	82

1933

As Thousands Cheer	83
Roberta	84

1934

Ziegfeld Follies	85
New Faces	86
Life Begins at 8:40	87
The Great Waltz	87
Anything Goes	88

1935

At Home Abroad	89
Porgy and Bess	91
Jubilee	92
Jumbo	93

1936

Ziegfeld Follies	93
On Your Toes	94
Red, Hot and Blue!	96
The Show Is On	97

1937

Babes in Arms	98
I'd Rather Be Right	98
Pins and Needles	100
Hooray for What!	100

1938

The Cradle Will Rock	101
I Married an Angel	102
Hellzapoppin	103
Knickerbocker Holiday	104
Leave It to Me!	105
The Boys from Syracuse	107

1939

Too Many Girls	108
DuBarry Was a Lady	109

1940

Louisiana Purchase	110
Cabin in the Sky	111
Panama Hattie	111
Pal Joey	112

1941

Lady in the Dark	113
Best Foot Forward	114
Let's Face It!	115

1942

By Jupiter	116
This Is the Army	117

1943

Oklahoma!	119
The Merry Widow	120
One Touch of Venus	120
Carmen Jones	122

1944

Mexican Hayride	122
Follow the Girls	124
Song of Norway	124
Bloomer Girl	125
On the Town	126

1945

Up in Central Park	126
Carousel	127
The Red Mill	128

1946

Show Boat	128
St. Louis Woman	129
Call Me Mister	129
Annie Get Your Gun	130

1947

Street Scene	132
Finian's Rainbow	133
Sweethearts	134
Brigadoon	134
High Button Shoes	136
Allegro	136

1948

Make Mine Manhattan	137
Inside U.S.A.	137
Love Life	138
Where's Charley?	138
As the Girls Go	139
Lend an Ear	139
Kiss Me, Kate	141

1949

South Pacific	143
Miss Liberty	144
Lost in the Stars	144
Gentlemen Prefer Blondes	146

Contents

1950

Call Me Madam	147
Guys and Dolls	148

1951

The King and I	151
A Tree Grows in Brooklyn	152
Paint Your Wagon	152

1952

Pal Joey	154
New Faces of 1952	154
Wish You Were Here	154

1953

Wonderful Town	155
Porgy and Bess	156
Can-Can	156
Me and Juliet	157
Kismet	158

1954

The Threepenny Opera	159
The Golden Apple	160
The Pajama Game	161
The Boy Friend	162
Peter Pan	163
Fanny	164
House of Flowers	165

1955

Plain and Fancy	166
Silk Stockings	166
Damn Yankees	167

1956

My Fair Lady	168
The Most Happy Fella	170
Li'l Abner	171
Bells Are Ringing	171
Candide	172

1957

New Girl in Town	173
West Side Story	175
Jamaica	176
The Music Man	177

1958

Flower Drum Song	178

Contents

1959

Redhead   179
Destry Rides Again   180
Once Upon a Mattress   181
Gypsy   182
Take Me Along   183
The Sound of Music   184
Little Mary Sunshine   186
Fiorello!   186

1960

Greenwillow   187
Bye Bye Birdie   188
The Fantasticks   189
Irma la Douce   190
The Unsinkable Molly Brown   191
Camelot   193
Do Re Mi   194

1961

Carnival   195
Milk and Honey   195
How to Succeed in Business Without Really Trying   196

1962

No Strings   197
A Funny Thing Happened on the Way to the Forum   198
Stop the World—I Want to Get Off   199
Little Me   200

1963

Oliver!   201
She Loves Me   202
110 in the Shade   203

1964

Hello, Dolly!   204
What Makes Sammy Run?   206
Funny Girl   207
High Spirits   208
Fiddler on the Roof   209
Golden Boy   210

1965

Do I Hear a Waltz?   210
Half a Sixpence   211
The Roar of the Greasepaint—The Smell of the Crowd   212
On a Clear Day You Can See Forever   213
Man of La Mancha   215

Contents

1966

Sweet Charity	216
Mame	217
The Apple Tree	218
Cabaret	219
I Do! I Do!	220

1967

You're a Good Man, Charlie Brown	221

1968

Your Own Thing	222
The Happy Time	222
George M!	223
Hair	224
Zorba	225
Promises, Promises	226
Dames at Sea	226

1969

1776	227

1970

Purlie	228
Applause	228
Company	229
The Rothschilds	230

1971

No, No, Nanette	231
Follies	232
Godspell	233
Jesus Christ Superstar	233
Two Gentlemen of Verona	234

1972

Grease	234
Sugar	235
Don't Bother Me, I Can't Cope	235
Pippin	236

1973

A Little Night Music	237
Irene	238
Raisin	239

1974

Candide	239
The Magic Show	240

1975

The Wiz	241
Shenandoah	242
A Chorus Line	243
Chicago	244

1976

Pacific Overtures   245

1977

I Love My Wife   245
Annie   247
The King and I   248

1978

On the Twentieth Century   249
Dancin'   250
The Best Little Whorehouse in Texas   250
Ain't Misbehavin'   251
I'm Getting My Act Together and Taking It on the Road   252

1979

They're Playing Our Song   252
Sweeney Todd   253
Peter Pan   254
Evita   254
Sugar Babies   255
Oklahoma!   255

1980

Barnum   256
42nd Street   257

1981

The Pirates of Penzance   258
Sophisticated Ladies   259
Woman of the Year   260
Joseph and the Amazing Technicolor Dreamcoat   260
Dreamgirls   261

1982

Nine   262
Little Shop of Horrors   262
Cats   263

1983

On Your Toes   264
My One and Only   264
La Cage aux Folles   266
Zorba   268
The Tap Dance Kid   268

1984

Sunday in the Park With George   269

1985

Big River   270
Song and Dance   271
The Mystery of Edwin Drood   271

Contents

1986

    Sweet Charity   272
    Me and My Girl   273

1987

    Les Misérables   275
    Starlight Express   276
    Anything Goes   277
    Into the Woods   277

1988

    The Phantom of the Opera   278
    Chess   279

1989

    Jerome Robbins' Broadway   280
    Grand Hotel   281
    Gypsy   282
    City of Angels   282

1990

    Aspects of Love   283
    Once on This Island   284

1991

    Miss Saigon   285
    The Secret Garden   286
    The Will Rogers Follies   287

1992

    Crazy for You   288
    Five Guys Named Moe   289
    Guys and Dolls   290
    Jelly's Last Jam   292
    Falsettos   293
    The Most Happy Fella   293

1993

    Tommy   294
    Kiss of the Spider Woman—The Musical   295
    She Loves Me   296

1994

    Carousel   296
    Beauty and the Beast   297
    Passion   298
    Grease   298
    Show Boat   299
    Sunset Boulevard   300

1995

    How to Succeed in Business Without Really Trying   302
    Victor/Victoria   303

1996

The King and I 303
A Funny Thing Happened on the Way to the Forum 304
Rent 305
Bring in 'Da Noise, Bring in 'Da Funk 306
Chicago 307

1997

Titanic 307
Jekyll and Hyde 308
The Scarlet Pimpernel 309
The Lion King 310

1998

Ragtime 311
Cabaret 312
Footloose 313

1999

Fosse 314
Annie Get Your Gun 315
Kiss Me, Kate 315

2000

Aida 316
Contact 318
The Music Man 319
The Full Monty 319

2001

Follies 320
The Producers 321
42nd Street 322
Urinetown 323
Mamma Mia! 324

2002

Oklahoma! 325
Thoroughly Modern Millie 325
Into the Woods 326
Hairspray 326
Flower Drum Song 327
Movin' Out 328
Man of La Mancha 329

2003

Nine 329
Gypsy 329
Avenue Q 330
Wicked 332
Wonderful Town 332

Contents

2004

Fiddler on the Roof	333
Pacific Overtures	333
La Cage aux Folles	333

2005

Dirty Rotten Scoundrels	334
Monty Python's Spamalot	336
The 25th Annual Putnam County Spelling Bee	337
The Light in the Piazza	338
Sweeney Todd	338
Jersey Boys	339
The Color Purple	340

2006

The Pajama Game	341
The Drowsy Chaperone	342
The Fantasticks	343
A Chorus Line	343
Mary Poppins	344
Company	344
Spring Awakening	345
The Wedding Singer	346
Tarzan	347
Dr Seuss' How the Grinch Stole Christmas	348
Les Misérables	349

2007

Curtains	350
Legally Blonde	351
110 in the Shade	352
Xanadu	352
Young Frankenstein	353
Grease	354

2008

The Little Mermaid	355
Sunday in the Park with George	356
In the Heights	357
South Pacific	358
Gypsy	359
A Tale of Two Cities	360
Billy Elliot: The Musical	361
Irving Berlin's White Christmas	362
Shrek: The Musical	363

2009

West Side Story 364
Hair 365
Rock of Ages 366
Next to Normal 368
Memphis 369
Finian's Rainbow 370
Ragtime 371
Fela! 372
A Little Night Music 373

2010

The Addams Family 374
Million Dollar Quartet 375
La Cage aux Folles 376
American Idiot 377
Promises, Promises 378
Rain—A Tribute to the Beatles on Broadway 379

Indexes

Show Index 382

Composer/Lyricist Index 386

Librettist Index 397

Director Index 404

Choreographer Index 412

Major Cast Members Index 419

Theatre Index 477

Preface

TO THE SEVENTH EDITION

When I was asked to update the seventh edition of *Broadway Musicals Show by Show*, I felt humble, excited, and a little scared, all at the same time—humble because I realized that this book has been an institution for the past quarter-century, excited at the prospect of writing about musicals that have fascinated me since the sixth edition came out, and scared because I wasn't sure that I would be able to live up to the legacy Stanley and Kay Green set in compiling this book. Upon looking through it, however, I realized how easy a book this is to read. It's like a well-balanced meal: it goes down easily, isn't too filling, and it is good for you. But like a good meal, something that goes down this easily takes a lot of preparation. The Greens' capsule descriptions of Broadway's finest moments include most of the basic information anyone would want to know about a show, and is suitable for seasoned Broadway aficionados as well as newcomers to the scene. I look forward to continuing the tradition and hope that I do the Greens justice as we continue the series.

Musical theatre is currently undergoing a series of changes. Economic constraints and the rising cost of putting on a Broadway show have forced producers to look for lowest-common-denominator properties, to draw the widest possible audience. Hence the onslaught of shows with a built-in brand (*The Addams Family*, *Shrek*) or those that feature familiar faces starring in familiar shows (*La Cage aux Folles*, *A Little Night Music*). But there have been other developments as well, as Broadway struggles to expand and define its audience.

Jukebox musicals have been around for some decades, but ever since the success of *Mamma Mia!* and *Jersey Boys*, the floodgates have opened, with new shows geared to attract baby boomers and Gen-Xers continuing to be produced. With such shows as *Rock of Ages* and *American Idiot*, the trend today is to attract younger audiences to the theatre, and the success of both of these shows proves that the formula is working.

The most pleasant surprise of all is the scope of unique, thoughtful, daring, and amazingly entertaining shows that have come along in the past few years; shows that take chances by focusing on exotic musical styles (*Fela!*), challenging and sometimes disturbing story lines (*Next to Normal*), and innovative use of newer forms of music and dance (*In the Heights*). Despite the usual parade of revivals, Broadway seems to be going through a renaissance, as innovative producers, writers, and composers continue to push the envelope, take chances, and inject quality and uniqueness into their work. With all the distractions available to theatregoers through today's exploding world of technology, it's still nice to know that despite all of this, nothing compares to the excitement and glamour of an evening at the theatre.

As an inveterate fan of musical theatre, I am fortunate to have seen musicals from several different vantage points. First, I'm a fan, and enjoy going to a show just for the sheer enjoyment of it. But I have also seen shows as possible business properties, sizing up their content for the purpose of compiling musical songbooks. I have also seen shows as a theatre critic, analyzing actors' performances, musical content, scenery, set design, costumes, and all the other intricacies that combine to make a musical work. Finally, I have participated in the presentation of musicals from the unique vantage point of the orchestra pit, performing most recently as a flutist in a local production of *Annie*. From there, I was able to observe the unique relationship an audience has with a show. I watch their faces as the story unfolds; I see heartbreak in their eyes when a character suffers a tragedy or faces a dilemma, joy when two people fall in love, and vindication when villains gets their just deserts. As a member of the audience, one develops a very special, personal relationship with the actors on the stage. This relationship is so intimate, it is almost as if the players are becoming a temporary family. I've seen many audience members linger behind after the curtain falls, not wanting to break the spell of belonging to the magical world they had just visited.

The theatre is a very special universe. One can go anywhere in the world at any time in history, see historical figures live onstage, and experience all sorts of emotions through the characters in the production. This is why no technological device, gadget, or computer will ever take the place of live theatre. There is no business like show business. Now, let's go on with the show.

Cary Ginell
April 2011

Preface
TO THE SIXTH EDITION

When Stanley Green gave me a copy of *Broadway Musicals Show by Show* in 1985, I never imagined that 23 years later I would be writing the preface to the sixth edition. A preface is an introduction to a book, nonetheless I feel this book needs no introduction from me. Those of you who have an earlier edition know its merit and for those picking it up for the first time—five editions speak for themselves. However, if a few words from me can open your eyes to its worth–so be it.

I must admit to a personal interest in this, as I knew Stanley for many years, and his wife, Kay (who nobly has taken on the task of keeping this invaluable book up to date), and I have been privileged to share with them their love and knowledge of musical theatre.

Stanley was a man of the theatre–erudite, witty, and an author who endowed his works with his enjoyment and enthusiasm of the subject.

To anyone remotely interested in musical theatre, Stanley's books are a godsend. To begin with, you can take it as fact that they are accurate; in addition, they are a mine of information set out in a way which appeals both to the playgoer and to the theatrical historian.

Broadway Musicals Show by Show is perhaps a misleading title as by no means is every Broadway show to be found between the covers—merely an annual selection of those Stanley thought, to use his own words, were "memorable" in each year. To have produced a fully comprehensive study of the subject would have resulted in a work whose very size would have rendered it indigestible to the average reader. As it is, Stanley has distilled each year to its essence and produced a readable and informative work that fits neatly into anyone's book shelves.

He takes for his starting point *The Black Crook*—staged in 1866 and usually accepted as the first Broadway musical—a farouche extravaganza which for the first time combined dancing and singing with an underlying plot and dialogue (a form of entertainment which could recently have been seen in London's Drury Lane in *The Lords of the Rings*). With the help of this book you can trace the development of the musical from the fantastic into the more compact and disciplined shows subsequently seen on Broadway.

It is human nature that anyone picking up this book will fail to find his or her favorite show but Stanley, and Kay, have steered a fairly even course through the rocky shoals of public opinion and hindsight in their selection of shows with historical or other importance to the development of the musical.

Latterly, however, the production of original new shows has dwindled and statistics show a predominance of revivals. Basically, this must be because the public—bearing in mind the dangerously high level to which tickets prices have risen—reiterate the dicta of Howard Dietz (from *The Band Wagon*) "it better be good, it better be worth the money" with the result that any attempt to upgrade the intelligence of the musical seems doomed to failure; to wit, Stephen Sondheim, who appears to be a prophet with sporadic profit in his own country. Hence the revivals of shows which tried, tested, and sanctified by reputation are seen (justifiably or not) as being worth the price of admission.

It must be faced, however, that theatre and especially musical theatre is designed for entertainment; Mike Todd's condemnation of *Oklahoma!* "no gals no gags" epitomizes what it is assumed the public requires in this respect—something safe, comfortable, and requiring no effort to enjoy; messages (as was said in another context) are for Western Union. This attitude explains the recent success of shows such as *The Producers*, *Spamalot* and *Curtains* which hark back to the style of the farcical musical popular prior to *Oklahoma!*

However, there are signs that this tide may be turning as can be seen from the more recent years' selections, with shows like *The Light in the Piazza* (although that harks back to the composer's grandfather—Richard Rodgers' *Do I Hear A Waltz?* (page 210)), and *Spring Awakening*. There may be a renaissance of new talent and original shows on the horizon.

This book, however, utters no criticism, what you see is what you get: facts that leave you to make up your own mind up whether or not this is a show you would like to see. It is indeed a veritable vademecum which no theatre lover should be without.

Ian MacBey
June 2008

Ian MacBey is a theatre reviewer who also writes for IndieLondon.co.uk as David Munro.

Preface

TO THE FOURTH EDITION

When Stanley died in December of 1990, I never considered continuing any of his projects. However, after being prodded by Rick Walters, the editor at Hal Leonard, to come up with the name of a person who could, and after equal pressure from my friends to do it myself, I decided that I would update Stanley's book for this fourth edition. I have used the Variety listings for number of performances, and the daily newspapers for my sources of information. I generally conformed to the standards Stanley set for a show's inclusion in the book. For a number of reasons, the task has not been easy. I think I have produced a work he would have approved. I am grateful for the strength Susan Green, Rudy Green, and Christie Mastrangeli have given me, and for the encouragement, guidance, and (a great deal of) direction from Rick Walters, all of whom knew all along that I could finish the project.

Kay Green
Brooklyn, New York

September 1993

Preface
TO THE FIRST EDITION

Broadway Musicals Show by Show is a combination history, guide, fact book, and photograph album of the most memorable productions presented both on and off Broadway from *The Black Crook* in 1866 to *Big River* in 1985. There are some 300 entries, including 18 adaptations of foreign works and 14 revivals, comprising musical comedies, musical dramas, operettas (or comic operas), revues, two retrospective "catalogue" shows *(Ain't Misbehavin' and Sophisticated Ladies)*, one all-dancing show *(Dancin')*, and one gospel show *(Don't Bother Me, I Can't Cope)*. Among criteria for selection were length of run (all book musicals remaining over 500 performances are here), seminal importance, people involved, uniqueness of approach or subject matter, quality of the score, and general acceptance as a significant work in the field. Broadway revivals were included if they ran longer than the original productions, if they were notable in their own right, or if they were part of extended tours.

In the section devoted to a show's credits, I have included names in parentheses of writers, producers, directors, and choreographers who made major contributions to a production, but—for whatever reason—did not receive official credit. Cast listings contain the names of only principal actors (except when a future well-known performer had a bit part or was in the chorus). Song listings are usually only of the best-known musical numbers.

Reference books occasionally differ as to number of performances and, in general, I have followed the listings in *The Best Plays* yearbooks, published by Dodd, Mead, and currently edited by Otis Guernsey, Jr. Continuous runs have been credited to productions that went directly from off to on Broadway and those that may have been temporarily closed for vacations or other reasons. Return visits following a tour, however, have not been included under the original engagements. (The 1954 *Threepenny Opera*, which reopened 15 months after its initial Off-Broadway run, is a special case.)

Since shows today need to play much longer to succeed than in the past, I have cited the five longest running musicals of each decade to give a more accurate indication of their success.

Whenever a theatre is mentioned for the first time, I have noted its location, whether it is still in use, and, if so, whether it has changed its name. (Note that the Majestic Theatre that once stood on Columbus Circle is different from the one still in use, which is on West 44th Street.)

The symbols following most entries indicate if the show has been recorded, published in book form, or licensed for amateur and professional use. An original-cast recording is abbreviated by OC, a studio-cast recording by SC, and a subsequent original-cast recording contains the year that the new production was offered on Broadway. In most cases, the record company listed is the one under whose label the album is currently available. A musical whose text and lyrics (and occasionally songs) have been published as a trade book bears the name of the publisher and the year of publication. An asterisk indicates a soft-cover acting edition. In some cases, the musical's text is published in an anthology. Performing rights organizations that license musicals are represented by the following abbreviations: TW for Tams-Witmark (757 3rd Avenue, New York 10017); SF for Samuel French (25 West 45th Street, New York 10036); MTI for Music Theatre International (49 East 52nd Street, New York 10022); R&H for Rodgers & Hammerstein (598 Madison Avenue, New York 10022); DPC for Dramatic

Publishing Co. (4150 North Milwaukee Avenue, Chicago 60641); SO for Shubert Organization (234 West 44th Street, New York 10036); and TM for Theatre Maximus (1650 Broadway, New York 10019).

The following books were used to check facts: *Songs of the Theatre* by Richard Lewine and Alfred Simon (W. H. Wilson); *The City and the Theatre* by Mary C. Henderson (Preston); *The Collector's Guide to the American Musical Theatre* by David Hummel (Scarecrow); *At This Theatre* by Louis Botto (Dodd, Mead); *Musicals!* ("Directory of Musical Properties Available for Production") by Richard Chigley Lynch (American Library Assn.); *The American Musical Theatre* by Gerald Bordman (Oxford); *Show Music on Record* by Jack Raymond (Frederick Ungar); *American Song* ("The Complete Musical Theatre Companion") by Ken Bloom (Facts on File).

I am particularly grateful to my Hal Leonard associates—Keith Mardak (who first proposed that I write this book), Glenda Herro, and Mary Bultman—for their interest, cooperation, and support. My wife, Kay, as always, was indispensable in checking the manuscript, selecting photographs, and offering many helpful suggestions, and Susan Green and Rudy Green, as always, were available for welcome comments.

Stanley Green
Brooklyn, New York

December 1985

Introduction

With its glitter, its imagination, and its rhythmic beat, the Broadway musical has become a distinctive commodity, recognized and admired throughout the world, even though the form itself derived from many sources. The earliest example of musical comedy is generally cited as John Gay's *The Beggar's Opera*, first performed in London in 1728. Labeled a "ballad-opera," it used popular songs of the day as part of a story that satirized both corrupt political leaders and florid Italianate opera, best exemplified by the works of Handel. Later precursors include the English comic operas of Gilbert and Sullivan, the French *opéra bouffe* of Offenbach, and the Viennese operettas of Strauss, Lehar, Straus, and others. In fact, the first use of the term "musical comedy" dates back to the productions of George Edwardes at the Gaiety Theatre, London, at the end of the 19th Century.

America saw the first musical comedy in 1750 when a traveling company offered the premiere North American showing of *The Beggar's Opera* (whose most celebrated spinoff was Kurt Weill's *The Threepenny Opera*). Homegrown examples of the form were also on view during Colonial days, but it was not until 1866 when the first long-run musical smash, *The Black Crook*, was unveiled in New York to dazzle theatregoers with its spectacular scenic effects and its bevy of barelimbed coryphées. From then on, plays embellished with songs became a major attraction for seekers of theatrical entertainment along the Great White Way.

Possibly because their contributions distinguished this particular form of theatre and also because of the high quality of their work, composers were more noted than lyricists during the early years of the 20th Century. Victor Herbert, Rudolf Friml, Sigmund Romberg, Jerome Kern, George Gershwin, and Vincent Youmans were the most prominent figures during the first two decades, as well as George M. Cohan and Irving Berlin, who, because they wrote the words that went with their music, helped prepare the public for a greater awareness of the importance of lyrics. Due recognition was—eventually—given to the contributions of such practitioners as P. G. Wodehouse, Otto Harbach, Oscar Hammerstein II, Ira Gershwin, and B. G. DeSylva, but it was not until the emergence of Lorenz Hart (who shared equal billing with composer Richard Rodgers) and Cole Porter (who wrote his own music) that lyric-writing was elevated to the same level of public appreciation as that given to music-writing.

It took somewhat longer for the book or libretto (Italian for "little book") to be considered in the same league as music and lyrics, since up through the 1920s it was hardly more than a framework designed to provide opportunities to spotlight the singers, dancers, and comedians. That was also a factor in the popularity of the revue which did away with a story line completely in favor of short farcical or satirical sketches. Florenz Ziegfeld was easily the dominant figure of this kind of entertainment with his elaborate annual *Follies* which he guided through 21 editions. Rival showmen George White and Earl Carroll brought out their own annual *Scandals* and *Vanities*, and this form of musical theatre persisted in popularity through the Forties. Revues should not be confused with vaudeville or variety since they are assembled with a unity of style and can even have a unifying theme or concept. Early masters of the form were such directors as Hassard Short, John Murray Anderson, and Vincente Minnelli, and such writers as Howard Dietz and Arthur Schwartz, E. Y. Harburg, Harold Arlen, and Vernon Duke.

Through the influence of Kern and Hammerstein's *Show Boat,* Broadway's first serious attempt at a modern musical play, creators of musicals began showing greater concern for the stories and the way music and lyrics augmented and embellished them. Because of the country's dire economic condition in the Thirties and the increasing threat of war, musicals began to reflect a more adult and cynical attitude toward the world beyond the footlights, particularly to be seen in works involving George S. Kaufman, Moss Hart, Morrie Ryskind, Marc Blitzstein, and Harold Rome. Beginning in the Forties—largely because of the enormous success of Rodgers and Hammersteins's *Oklahoma!*—the emphasis was now on both the integration of songs, dances and story, and also on the adaptation of works of substance as suitable subject matter in the musical theatre. Plays and novels by Ferenc Molnar, Elmer Rice, Shakespeare, James Michener, Alan Paton, Marcel Pagnol, Bernard Shaw, Voltaire, Eugene O'Neill, Edmond Rostand, T.H. White, Thornton Wilder, Sholom Aleichem, Clifford Odets, Cervantes, Christopher Isherwood, and Nikos Kazantzakis—as well as the Bible—provided the bases for some of the most distinguished productions.

Once the library shelves were exhausted, the manner of telling a story through a particular staging device or personal viewpoint became of increasing concern. These so-called concept musicals developed through the emerging influence of such directors as Gower Champion, Harold Prince, Bob Fosse, Joe Layton, Michael Bennett, and Tommy Tune, and since these men—except for Prince—were all choreographers, their shows put greater accent on dancing in communicating the deeper meanings of these frequently metaphorical musicals. Paradoxically, many have avoided the conventional linear story line — with its beginning, middle and end—in favor of a freer, more episodic structure consisting of individual scenes interspersed with songs and dances. What they had created, of course, is a modern, stylized variation on the supposed outdated revue form.

It comes as no surprise that the amount of money involved in bringing a musical to Broadway has escalated appreciably in recent years. This is due not only to inflated production, but also to the increasing necessity of mounting large-scale advertising and promotion costs campaigns. Because of the enormous expenditure—and since movie sales are so infrequent—shows are rarely able to turn a profit without achieving a run of over 1,000 performances, sending out at least one touring company, and having presentations in foreign countries. That's part of the reason why ticket prices are scaled so high. In 1960, *Camelot* was capitalized at $670,000 and an orchestra seat cost $9.40. In 1971, *Follies* cost $700,000 and had a top weekend ticket price of $15.00. By 1981, *Dreamgirls* had production expenses totalling $3.6 million; two years later *My One and Only* was brought in for over $4 million, and *La Cage aux Folles* $5 million. By 1985, ticket prices for most musicals were up to $45.00, with *La Cage* getting $47.50.

The affluent and the expense-account set have always been able to afford not only top prices but scalper prices for tickets. Those of more modest means, however, are finding that the cheapest seats are proportionately more expensive than the high priced. During the 1958-1959 season, for example, it was possible to see such major attractions as *The Music Man* for $2.50 and *My Fair Lady* for $2.30. By 1985, there were hardly any musicals that could be seen from the last row of the top balcony for less than $30.00. (Surprising exception: *La Cage aux Folles,* which offers some seats at $10.00.) Two-fer tickets distributed to neighborhood stores, TKTS booths offering half-price seats, and even lower priced mail-order tickets available to people in certain professions through TDF (Theatre Development Fund, which also operates the TKTS booths) help somewhat to ease the inflationary burden.

The matter of preserving Broadway musicals—other than on original-cast albums—has been of concern to a number of individuals and organizations. Though schools, community groups, and summer theatres may be relied on to revive the blockbuster hits of the past, other performing centers, such as Michael P. Price's Goodspeed Opera House in East Haddam, Connecticut, are dedicated to pumping new life into the long lost and barely remembered. Concert versions of vintage shows, such as those presented by Bill Tynes' New Amsterdam Company at Town Hall and John McGlinn's series at the Carneigie Recital Hall, both in New York, have also been cropping up.

Another hopeful sign is the number of opera companies that have added musical theatre works to their repertoires. Not only does this help break down artificial barriers, it also creates new audiences for such notable examples as the Kern-Hammerstein *Show Boat*, the Gershwin-Heyward *Porgy and Bess*, the Rodgers-Hammerstein *Carousel*, the Weill-Hughes-Rice *Street Scene*, the Weill-Anderson *Lost in the Stars*, the Bernstein-Sondheim-Laurents *West Side Story*, the Bernstein-Wilbur *Candide*, the Sondheim-Wheeler *Sweeney Todd,* and—almost inevitably—the Sondheim–Lapine *Sunday in the Park With George*.

Stanley Green
1985

SHOW BY SHOW

The Black Crook. Four alluring coryphées.

THE BLACK CROOK

Music & lyrics: Miscellaneous writers
Book: Charles M. Barras
Producers: William Wheatley & Henry Jarrett
Directors: William Wheatley & Leon Vincent
Choreographer: David Costa
Cast: Annie Kemp Bowler, Charles Morton, Marie Bonfanti, J.W. Blaisdell, E.B. Holmes, George Boniface
Songs: "You Naughty Naughty Men"; "March of the Amazons"; "Dare I Tell?"
New York run: Niblo's Garden, September 12, 1866; 475 p.

American plays embellished with songs were being offered in New York as early as Colonial days, but *The Black Crook* was the first long-running musical hit, with a record run that was not overtaken until *Adonis* established a new mark in the late 1880's. It also toured throughout the United States and was revived in New York at least fifteen times.

Although the musical score was partly made up of popular numbers of the day and the grafting of songs, dances and plot was crude, *The Black Crook* claims an important place in theatrical history by introducing such staples of the musical-comedy form as elaborate scenic effects, colorful costumes, and rows of barelimbed dancing girls. The production, however, was something of an accident. A Parisian ballet troupe was booked to appear at the Academy of Music in the fall of 1866, but the theatre burned down the previous May. William Wheatley, the manager of Niblo's Garden, a huge auditorium then at Broadway and Prince Street, had already scheduled a spectacular production of a new work, *The Black Crook*, as his fall attraction. With the ballet company now without a booking, he was persuaded that the play would benefit immeasurably from the addition of one hundred or so immodestly garbed female dancers, since it was obvious that Charles M. Barras's embarrassing script — a preposterous melodrama based on the *Faust* legend — could use all the help it could get. Thus, Henry Jarrett, the ballet company's sponsor, became the co-producer of *The Black Crook*, and the dancers crossed the Atlantic in August to join the production.

In the story, set in, around and even underneath the Harz Mountains of Germany, the year is 1600 and Hertzog, a crook-backed sorcerer (hence the play's title) makes a pact with the Arch Fiend, or Devil, that would allow him to live one extra year for every soul he delivers. The sorcerer's first intended victim is the virtuous Rudolphe, who has been imprisoned by the evil Count Wolfenstein. Rudolphe escapes, discovers a buried treasure, saves the life of Stalacta, the fairy queen, who then reciprocates by saving him from Hertzog's nefarious scheme. At the end, the Black Crook, having failed to deliver on his part of the arrangement, is himself carted off to Hell. (The theme of pact-making with the Devil has since shown up occasionally in the musical theatre, most notably in the 1955 success, *Damn Yankees*.)

But the main attraction was unquestionably the imported dancing girls — used primarily for sequences requiring demons, spirits and water sprites — who proved so alluring to post-Civil War audiences that at a ticket scale of 5¢ to $1.50 they kept flocking to view the spectacle. And it surely did not hurt the boxoffice — nor would it ever — when clergymen and editorial writers turned up their blue noses to denounce the sinful display of bare flesh.

In 1954, *The Girl in Pink Tights*, a Broadway musical with a score by Sigmund Romberg (his last) and Leo Robin, was loosely based on circumstances surrounding the production of *The Black Crook*. The cast was headed by Jeanmaire, Charles Goldner, Brenda Lewis, and David Atkinson, and the show ran for 115 performances.
Applause (1985).

EVANGELINE

Music: Edward E. Rice
Lyrics & book: J. Cheever Goodwin
Producer-director: Edward E. Rice
Cast: Ione Burke, James Dunn, W. H. Crane, J. W. Thoman, Connie Thompson
Songs: "Evangeline March"; "Spinning-Wheel Song"; "Thinking, Love, of Thee"; "Sweet Evangeline"
New York run: Niblo's Garden, July 27, 1874; 16 p.

Evangeline (or *The Belle of Acadia*) was among the first successful musicals to have a score specifically written by one song-writing team. It first opened in New York as an interim booking, then played Boston and toured extensively before returning to New York in 1877 at the Fifth Avenue Theatre (then at 24th Street) in a more elaborate production. After playing two months, it again went on tour, during which it was billed as *Rice's Beautiful Evangeline*. In all, it was revived periodically in New York for almost 30 years, with its most successful engagement being the 251-performance run in 1885 at the 14th Street Theatre.

The "American Opera-Bouffe Extravaganza" came about after its two authors had seen a performance in Boston of Lydia Thompson and her troupe of high-kicking British Blondes. Vowing that they could surely write a more tasteful entertainment that would also feature bare-legged dancers, they chose Longfellow's poem as general inspiration, and they enabled the female members of the cast to show their legs by putting them in tights and casting most of them in male roles. Two other attractions: a two-man dancing heifer and the character of the Lone Fisherman, who spent the evening sitting silently in a corner. In the story, our heroine has a number of comic adventures as she journeys from Acadia to Africa to Arizona in search of her beloved Gabriel.

THE MULLIGAN GUARD BALL

Music: David Braham
Lyrics & book: Edward Harrigan
Producers: Edward Harrigan & Tony Hart
Director: Edward Harrigan
Cast: Edward Harrigan, Tony Hart, Nellie Jones, Annie Yeamans, Annie Mack
Songs: "The Mulligan Guard"; "The Babies on Our Block"; "Pitcher of Beer"; "Skidmore Fancy Ball"
New York run: Theatre Comique, January 13, 1879; 153 p.

Edward "Ned" Harrigan and Tony Hart were the first team to offer plays with music populated by newly arrived immigrants living in the slums of New York. They began their series of shows about the Irish Mulligan Guard in 1878, and in all did seven productions featuring the drinking, brawling members of the social and military club. In this production, their most popular, they were concerned with the rivalry between the Mulligan Guard and a Negro group, the Skidmore Guard, who, through an error, both engage the Harp and Shamrock Ballroom for a social affair on the same night. A compromise of sorts is reached when the Skidmore group is given a room on the second floor right above the ballroom, but their dancing becomes so animated that they crash through the floor and land on top of the celebrating Mulligans. This was the first production to play the Theatre Comique, then located on lower Broadway, and the top ticket price was 75¢. Harrigan's use of working-class Americans as characters in his stories influenced the work of Charles H. Hoyt and George M. Cohan.

ROBIN HOOD

Music: Reginald DeKoven
Lyrics & book: Harry B. Smith
Producer: The Bostonians
Director: Harry Dixon
Cast: Tom Karl, Eugene Cowles, Caroline Hamilton, Jessie Bartlett Davis, W.H. MacDonald, Henry Clay Barnabee, George Frothingham
Songs: "Song of Brown October Ale"; "Oh, Promise Me!" (lyric: Clement Scott); "Tinkers' Chorus"; "Ah, I Do Love Thee"
New York run: Standard Theatre, September 28, 1891; 40 p.

The most celebrated American operetta of the 19th century, *Robin Hood* was produced by a touring company that first presented it in Chicago in June 1890. Though hastily put together at a total cost of $109.50, the musical caught on and was remounted in a more stylish production. It made an auspicious New York bow at the Standard Theatre (then on Broadway at 32nd Street), but its run was cut short because of a prior booking. Eight revivals were shown in the city, the last in 1944.

The story remains faithful to the familiar legend about Robin and his merry band of altruistic outlaws who dwell in Sherwood Forest and take from the have-lots and give to the have-nots. In addition to Robin's béloved Maid Marian, the well-known characters include Little John, Friar Tuck, Will Scarlet, and Alan-a-Dale (a traditionally female part originated by Jessie Bartlett Davis, who scored a hit singing the interpolated "Oh, Promise Me!"). This was the third musical created by the team of Reginald DeKoven and Harry B. Smith, who collaborated on a total of 17, including the unsuccessful sequel, *Maid Marian*.

A TRIP TO CHINATOWN

Music: Percy Gaunt
Lyrics: Percy Gaunt & Charles H. Hoyt
Book: Charles H. Hoyt
Producer: Charles H. Hoyt
Directors: Charles H. Hoyt & Julian Mitchell
Cast: Anna Boyd, Lloyd Wilson, George Beane Jr., Lillian Barr, Harry Conor
Songs: "Reuben and Cynthia"; "The Bowery"; "Push Dem Clouds Away"; "After the Ball" (Charles K. Harris)
New York run: Madison Square Theatre, November 9, 1891; 657 p.

In a large American city at the turn of the century, two young couples are encouraged by a coquettish widow to defy a rich merchant by having a merry night on the town at a fashionable restaurant. Complications arise when the merchant also shows up at the restaurant and is stuck with their bill — which he cannot pay because he doesn't have his wallet. If this outline reads like the plot of *Hello, Dolly!*, well it is. It is also the plot of *A Trip to Chinatown*, which came along 73 years earlier and which also set a long-running record for continuous performances. In fact, its tenure at the Madison Square Theatre (formerly the Fifth Avenue) was so extraordinary for its time that the show held the durability record for 28 years.

A Trip to Chinatown (though set in San Francisco, no one takes a trip anywhere near Chinatown) was the creation of Charles H. Hcyt, a prolific writer of American farces. It was also the first musical to boast no less than three song hits: "Reuben and Cynthia," "The Bowery," and the interpolated "After the Ball."
Indiana U. Press (1964)

THE FORTUNE TELLER

Music: Victor Herbert
Lyrics & book: Harry B. Smith
Producer: Frank L. Perley
Director: Julian Mitchell
Cast: Alice Nielsen, Eugene Cowles, Frank Rushworth, Marguerite Silva, Joseph Herbert, Joseph Cawthorn, May Boley
Songs: "Always Do as People Say You Should"; "Romany Life"; "Gypsy Love Song"; "Czardas"; "Only in the Play"
New York run: Wallack's Theatre, September 26, 1898; 40 p.

Like *Robin Hood, The Fortune Teller* was created for a touring company — in this case the Alice Nielsen Opera Company — which accounted for its brief stay at Wallack's Theatre (then located at Broadway and 30th Street). It was the third and most celebrated of the 13 shows written together by composer Victor Herbert and lyricist-librettist Harry B. Smith (whose total Broadway output was an incredible 123 productions). The musical, which did much to establish Herbert as America's preeminent composer of operetta, makes use of the popular theme of mistaken identity. Hungarian heiress Irma loves a dashing Hussar, but is promised in marriage to a wealthy count. To avoid this unwanted union, Irma gets gypsy fortune teller Musette (both roles being played by Alice Nielsen) to substitute for her. Eventually — somehow aided by a Hungarian military victory — Irma and Musette end up with their appropriate inamoratos. In 1946, a Broadway musical, *Gypsy Lady*, combined this score with that of another Herbert-Smith work, *The Serenade*. The plot, however, was relatively original.

FLORODORA

Music: Leslie Stuart
Lyrics: Leslie Stuart, Paul Rubens, Frank Clement
Book: Owen Hall
Producer: Tom Ryley & John Fisher
Directors: Lewis Hopper & Willie Edouin
Cast: Edna Wallace Hopper, Fannie Johnston, Willie Edouin, Sydney Deane, R.E. Graham, May Edouin
Songs: "The Shade of the Palm" (Stuart); "Tell Me, Pretty Maiden" (Stuart); "When I Leave Town" (Rubens); "I Want to Be a Military Man" (Clement)
New York run: Casino Theatre, November 12, 1900; 553 p.

Next to the Gilbert and Sullivan comic operas, *Florodora* was the most successful early British import staged in New York, even exceeding the original London run of 455 performances. The highlight of the show was the appearance of the dainty, parasol-twirling *Florodora* Sextette who, with six male partners, introduced the coquettish number, "Tell Me, Pretty Maiden." In the plotty plot, Florodora is both the name of an island in the Philippines and the locally manufactured perfume. The elderly manufacturer Cyrus Gilfain wants to marry Dolores, whose father had been cheated by Gilfain, but Dolores loves Gilfain's manager, whom Gilfain wants for his own daughter, even though she loves someone else. For some reason, everyone ends up in Wales where the complications get unknotted and the knots get properly tied. The Casino Theatre, which was torn down in 1930, stood at Broadway and 39th Street.

The last Broadway revival of *Florodora* occurred in 1920 and ran for 150 performances. Christie MacDonald, Eleanor Painter, Walter Woolf, and George Hassell were in the cast.
TW.

Florodora. Pictured on the sheet music cover are the ladies of the original Sextette: Daisy Greene, Marjorie Relyea, Vaughn Texsmith, Margaret Walker, Agnes Wayburn, and Marie L. Wilson.

THE WIZARD OF OZ

Music: Paul Tietjens, A. Baldwin Sloane
Lyrics & book: L. Frank Baum
Producer: Fred R. Hamlin
Director-choreographer: Julian Mitchell
Cast: David Montgomery, Fred Stone, Anna Laughlin, Arthur Hill, Bessie Wynn, Grace Kimball
Songs: "Alas for a Man Without Brains" (Tietjens); "When You Love Love Love" (Tietjens); "Sammy" (Edward Hutchinson - James O'Dea); "Hurrah for Baffin's Bay" (Theodore Morse - Vincent Bryan)
New York run: Majestic Theatre, January 20, 1903; 293 p.

The Wizard of Oz was the premiere attraction at the Majestic Theatre on the west side of Columbus Circle (demolished in 1954), and it also marked the legitimate theatre debut of two vaudeville clowns, Dave Montgomery and Fred Stone, as the Tin Woodman and the Scarecrow. In the spectacular production, which L. Frank Baum adapted from his own fairytale, *The Wonderful Wizard of Oz,* a cyclone blows Dorothy and her pet cow all the way from Kansas to the country of the Munchkins. After meeting the Scarecrow, the Tin Woodman, and the Cowardly Lion, Dorothy takes her three new friends on a number of adventures until they finally meet the Wizard in the Emerald City. The Victor Herbert-Glen MacDonough *Babes in Toyland,* a successor to *The Wizard of Oz,* followed it into the Majestic. In 1939, the classic screen version featured Judy Garland, Frank Morgan, Ray Bolger, Bert Lahr, and Jack Haley, and a new score by Harold Arlen and E.Y. Harburg. *The Wiz,* a contemporary black variation, opened on Broadway in 1975. (See page 241.)
TW (film score).

BABES IN TOYLAND

Music: Victor Herbert
Lyrics & book: Glen MacDonough
Producers: Fred R. Hamlin & Julian Mitchell
Director-choreographer: Julian Mitchell
Cast: William Norris, Mabel Barrison, George Denham, Bessie Wynn
Songs: "I Can't Do the Sum"; "Go to Sleep, Slumber Deep"; "Song of the Poet"; "March of the Toys"; "Toyland"; "Never Mind, Bo-Peep"
New York run: Majestic Theatre, October 13, 1903; 192 p.

Because of the popularity of *The Wizard of Oz,* producers Fred R. Hamlin and Julian Mitchell (who was Broadway's most prolific director of musicals with 78 shows to his credit) commissioned Victor Herbert and Glen MacDonough to come up with a successor, if not exactly a sequel, to follow their previous hit into the Majestic Theatre. Once again audiences were delighted with a fantasy about children that included a devastating storm, a frightening journey through the woods, and the eventual arrival at a mythical magical city, in this case substituting Toyland for the Emerald City. The book may have been no more that a serviceable variation, but the score — the second and most successful of the five collaborations between Herbert and MacDonough — was far superior to its predecessor's. Laurel and Hardy appeared in the 1934 screen version, and Ray Bolger and Ed Wynn were in the 1961 version.
MCA SC./Dramatic Publishing Co. (1978)*/DPC.

Babes in Toyland. William Norris and Mabel Barrison, as the two babes, lead Mother Hubbard's children in singing "I Can't Do the Sum." (Byron)

LITTLE JOHNNY JONES

Music, lyrics & book: George M. Cohan
Producer: Sam H. Harris
Director: George M. Cohan
Cast: George M. Cohan, Jerry Cohan, Helen Cohan, Donald Brian, Ethel Levey, Tom Lewis
Songs: "The Yankee Doodle Boy"; " Give My Regards to Broadway"; "Life's a Funny Proposition After All"
New York run: Liberty Theatre, November 7, 1904; 52 p.

George M. Cohan was cocky, straight-shooting, self-assured, quick-witted, fast-moving, naively patriotic — in short, the personification of the American spirit at the beginning of the 20th Century. He was also just about the most multi-talented man ever to hit Broadway, winning fame as an actor, composer, lyricist, librettist, playwright, director, and producer, with an output comprising 21 musicals and 20 plays.

Little Johnny Jones, Cohan's third musical and his first hit, had an initial run of less than two months at the Liberty Theatre (now a movie house on 42nd Street west of Times Square). After extensive revisions during the road tour, the show returned to New York twice in 1905 for a total run of 20 weeks. The musical was prompted by a newspaper article about Tod Sloan, an American jockey then in England. In Cohan's story, jockey Johnny Jones has gone to Britain to ride his horse Yankee Doodle in the Derby. Accused of throwing the race, Johnny discovers that he has been framed by an American gambler (played by the author's father, Jerry Cohan). With the help of a private detective, he clears his name and celebrates by singing and dancing "Give My Regards to Broadway" on a Southampton pier. In the third act, with the locale abruptly switched to San Francisco's Chinatown, Johnny discovers that his fiancée, Goldie Gates (played by Ethel Levey, Cohan's wife at the time) has been kidnapped. When the jockey and the private detective apprehend the abductor, he turns out to be the same villain who had framed our hero in England. In 1982, a revival of Little Johnny Jones with Donny Osmond tarried but one night on Broadway.

MLLE. MODISTE

Music: Victor Herbert
Lyrics & book: Henry Blossom
Producer: Charles Dillingham
Director: Fred Latham
Cast: Fritzi Scheff, Walter Percival, William Pruette, Claude Gillingwater, Josephine Bartlett
Songs: "Kiss Me Again"; "The Time, the Place and the Girl"; "I Want What I Want When I Want It"; "The Mascot of the Troop"
New York run: Knickerbocker Theatre, December 25, 1905; 202 p.

Mlle. Modiste inaugurated the partnership of composer Victor Herbert and librettist-lyricist Henry Blossom (they wrote eight scores together), and was their second in popularity to The Red Mill. The operetta was closely identified with prima donna Fritzi Scheff, who would be called upon to sing "Kiss Me Again" for the rest of her life (indeed, Miss Scheff returned to New York in Mlle. Modiste on five occasions, the last, when she was 50, in 1929). The musical, which opened at the Knickerbocker (then on Broadway and 38th Street), spins a Cinderella tale of a stagestruck Parisian named Fifi, who works in Mme. Cecile's hat shop on the Rue de la Paix. A wealthy American helps Fifi become a celebrated singer, which also helps smooth the way to her winning the approval of her sweetheart's aristocratic, crotchety uncle.
TW.

Mlle. Modiste. Fritzi Scheff in the final scene at the charity bazaar in the gardens of the Château de St. Mar. From the left are Walter Percival (in uniform), William Pruette, and Claude Gillingwater. (Byron)

Forty-five Minutes from Broadway. The dramatic will-tearing scene with Victor Moore and Fay Templeton. (Hall)

FORTY-FIVE MINUTES FROM BROADWAY

Music, lyrics & book: George M. Cohan
Producers: Marc Klaw & A. L. Erlanger
Director: George M. Cohan
Cast: Fay Templeton, Victor Moore, Donald Brian, Lois Ewell
Songs: "I Want to Be a Popular Millionaire"; "Mary's a Grand Old Name"; "So Long, Mary"; "Forty-five Minutes from Broadway"
New York run: New Amsterdam Theatre, January 1, 1906; 90 p.

More of a play with music than a musical comedy — there were only five songs in the score — *Forty-five Minutes from Broadway* was written as a vehicle for Fay Templeton, but it was Victor Moore, in his first leading role on Broadway, who stole everyone's attention. In the story, set in New Rochelle, New York — which is only 45 minutes from Broadway — a nasty millionaire has died leaving a will that no one can find. His nephew (Donald Brian), who has been assigned as his heir, visits his uncle's home with his secretary, Kid Burns (Mr. Moore), and his fiancée. Burns discovers the will — and the fact that everything has been left to housekeeper Mary Jane Jenkins (Miss Templeton). Since the Kid has fallen in love with Mary, his pride won't let him marry his beloved for her money. The only solution: Mary tears up the will. After only a modest run at the New Amsterdam (now a movie house on 42nd Street west of Times Square), the show became a hit on the road, then was revived in 1912 with Cohan himself taking over the Kid Burns part. Moore, however, again played the same character in Cohan's 1907 musical, *The Talk of New York*.
Dramatic Publishing Co. (1978)*/ DPC.

THE RED MILL

Music: Victor Herbert
Lyrics & book: Henry Blossom
Producer: Charles Dillingham
Director: Fred Latham
Cast: David Montgomery, Fred Stone, Augusta Greenleaf, Joseph Ratliff, Allene Crater, Edward Begley
Songs: "The Isle of Our Dreams"; "When You're Pretty and the World Is Fair"; "Moonbeams"; "Every Day Is Ladies Day With Me"; The Streets of New York"; "Because You're You"
New York run: Knickerbocker Theatre, September 24, 1906; 274 p.

The Red Mill was closer to being a musical farce than the kind of operetta usually associated with Victor Herbert. There was ample compensation, however, in the fact that it achieved the longest run of any of the composer's 41 book musicals produced during his lifetime. The show, which was typical of many of the period in depicting Americans as innocents abroad, is concerned with the adventures of Kid Conner and Con Kidder (Montgomery and Stone), two impoverished tourists stranded in Katwyk-aan-Zee, Holland. Their comic predicaments force them to don a number of disguises (including Sherlock Holmes and Dr. Watson), and they also manage to rescue a girl from a windmill by perching her precariously on one of the sails.

A 1945 production (see page 128) ran almost twice as long as the original, with Eddie Foy scoring a hit in the Dave Montgomery part. Also associated with the show were Stone's two daughters, co-producer Paula and featured actress Dorothy. The favorable reception that greeted this version sparked revivals of two other vintage shows as vehicles for major comedians: *Sweethearts* with Bobby Clark (1947) and *Sally* with Willie Howard (1948).
Capitol SC; Turnabout SC/ TW.

FOLLIES OF 1907

Music & lyrics: Miscellaneous writers
Sketches: Harry B. Smith
Producer: Florenz Ziegfeld
Director: Herbert Gresham
Choreographers: Julian Mitchell, Joe Smith, John O'Neil
Cast: Grace LaRue, Mlle. Dazie, Prince Tokio, Emma Carus, Harry Watson Jr., Marion Sunshine & Florence Tempest, George Bickel, Helen Broderick, Nora Bayes (added)
Songs: "Budweiser's a Friend of Mine" (Seymour Furth-Vincent Bryan); "I Think I Oughtn't Auto any More" (E. Ray Goetz-Bryan); "Handle Me With Care" (Jean Schwartz-William Jerome); "Miss Ginger from Jamaica" (Billy Gaston); "Bye Bye, Dear Old Broadway" (Gus Edwards - Will Cobb)
New York run: Jardin de Paris, July 8, 1907; 70 p.

With the *Follies of 1907,* showman Florenz Ziegfeld inaugurated the most cele-brated and durable series of annual revues in the history of the Broadway thea-tre. From 1907 to 1931, there were 21 such entertainments designated as *Follies* (actually, there should have been 22, but the 1926 edition, due to a legal hassle, was initially called *No Foolin',* then *Ziegfeld American Revue*). The title of the first edition came about through the suggestions of sketch writer Harry B. Smith, who had written a newspaper column called "Follies of the Day," and also because Ziegfeld, whose lucky number was 13, wanted the name to have 13 letters. It was not until 1911 that the impresario's ego triumphed over his superstition and thenceforth the series was known as the *Ziegfeld Follies.*

The idea for the series is credited to Ziegfeld's wife, Anna Held, who sug-gested that the producer put together a show based on the French revue style of entertainment that took satirical pot-shots at society, the theatre, and politics. The hallmark of the *Follies* was opulent production numbers, decoratively adorned showgirls, farcical and topical sketches, comic personalities, and a gen-erous amount of songs. The first edition, presented on the roof garden of the New York Theatre (then at 45th Street on the east side of Broadway), used the theme of introducing Pocahontas and Capt. John Smith to modern life. Along the way they were enlightened by scenes involving the likes of John D. Rockefeller, Anthony Comstock, Oscar Hammerstein, Teddy Roosevelt, and Enrico Caruso, plus a "Dance of the Seven Veils" takeoff and 64 "Anna Held Girls" beating snare drums while marching up and down the aisles. The total production cost was $13,000, and the top ticket price was $2.50.

Known as "A National Institution Glorifying the American Girl," the *Ziegfeld Follies* was itself glorified through the years by the presence of such notable per-formers as Fanny Brice, Bert Williams, Ann Pennington, W.C. Fields, Will Rogers, Ray Dooley, Lillian Lorraine, Leon Errol, Eddie Cantor, Nora Bayes, Van and Schenck, John Steel, Ed Wynn, Ina Claire, Marilyn Miller, Ruth Etting, and Eddie Dowling. The *Follies* may not have been the first Broadway revue — that was *The Passing Show* in 1894 — but it was the one that established the model for this type of entertainment, and which spawned such diversified rivals as *George White's Scandals* (13 editions), the Messrs. Shubert's *Passing Shows* (12 edi-tions), the *Earl Carroll Vanities* (11 editions), the *Greenwich Village Follies* (8 edi-tions), and Irving Berlin's *Music Box Revues* (4 editions). There were also four productions of the *Ziegfeld Follies* — in 1934, 1936, 1943, and 1957 — that were presented on Broadway after Ziegfeld's death. For subsequent editions of the *Follies* see pages 20, 29, 31, 34, 38, 85, and 93.

THE MERRY WIDOW

Music: Franz Lehár
Lyrics: Adrian Ross
Book: (Basil Hood uncredited)
Producer: Henry W. Savage
Director: George Marion
Cast: Ethel Jackson, Donald Brian, Lois Ewell, R.E. Graham, William Weedon, Fred Frear
Songs: "A Dutiful Wife"; "In Marsovia"; "Oh, Come Away, Away!"; "Maxim's"; "Vilia"; "Silly, Silly Cavalier"; "I Love You So" ("The Merry Widow Waltz"); "The Girls at Maxim's"; "Love in My Heart"
New York run: New Amsterdam Theatre, October 21, 1907; 416 p.

The epitome of the lighthearted, melodious, romantic European operetta, Franz Lehár's *The Merry Widow* first swirled onto the stage in Vienna in 1905 under the title *Die Lustige Witwe*. The original text by Viktor Leon and Leo Stein was adapted for the highly successful London production by Basil Hood who refused program credit to spare the feelings of the original librettist whose work had been rejected. This version was also used in New York where the musical won such acclaim that it not only made celebrities of Ethel Jackson and Donald Brian, as the Widow and the Prince, it also prompted the introduction of Merry Widow hats, gowns, corsets, and cigarettes.

The first theatrical offshoot was a parody, *The Merry Widow Burlesque,* which opened less than three months after the operetta's première and continued for 156 performances. Producer Joe Weber (of Weber and Fields) even managed to get permission to use the Lehár music. A more lasting influence, however, was the rash of imported continental operettas that remained a major part of the Broadway scene until the outbreak of World War I. Among the most popular of these were Oscar Straus's *A Waltz Dream,* Leo Fall's *The Dollar Princess,* Straus's *The Chocolate Soldier,* Heinrich Reinhardt's *The Spring Maid,* Johann Strauss's *The Merry Countess (Die Fledermaus),* Lehár's *The Count of Luxembourg,* Emmerich Kalman's *Sari,* and Edmund Eysler's *The Blue Paradise* (with interpolated songs by Sigmund Romberg).

Based on *L'Attaché d'Ambassade,* a French play by Henri Meilhac, *The Merry Widow* is set in Paris and concerns the efforts of Baron Popoff, the ambassador of the mythical kingdom of Marsovia, to induce his attaché, Prince Danilo, to marry wealthy widow Sonia Sadoya in order to aid the country's dwindling finances. Though the widow is wary of fortune-hunting suitors and the prince is chary of being taken for one, they find themselves falling in love to the seductive strains of "The Merry Widow Waltz." Danilo eventually proposes marriage — but only after Sonia has teasingly confessed that she has no money.

The Merry Widow has had five Broadway revivals, the last in 1943. That production, with a libretto coauthored by novelist Sidney Sheldon, had a successful run of 322 performances, then returned in October 1944 for an additional 32. The cast was headed by the husband-wife team of Jan Kiepura and Marta Eggerth. (See page 120.) In 1964, the operetta was mounted by the Music Theatre of Lincoln Center (with Patrice Munsel and Bob Wright), and in 1978 by the New York City Opera (with Beverly Sills and Alan Titus). There have been three Hollywood screen versions: a silent in 1925 directed by Erich Von Stroheim; the Ernst Lubitsch treatment in 1934 with lyrics by Lorenz Hart and starring Maurice Chevalier and Jeanette MacDonald; and a 1952 remake with Lana Turner and Fernando Lamas.
Columbia SC; RCA OC (1964); Angel OC (1978)/ TW.

THE CHOCOLATE SOLDIER
Music: Oscar Straus
Lyrics & book: Stanislaus Stange
Producer: Fred C. Whitney
Director: Stanislaus Stange
Choreographer: Al Holbrook
Cast: Ida Brooks Hunt, J. E. Gardner, Flavia Arcaro, William Pruette
Songs: "My Hero"; "Sympathy"; "Seek the Spy"; "That Would Be Lovely";
"Falling In Love"; "The Letter Song"; "Thank the Lord the War Is Over"
New York run: Lyric Theatre, September 13, 1909; 296 p.

Of all the European operettas imported by Broadway producers in the wake of the spectacular success of *The Merry Widow,* by far the most popular was *The Chocolate Soldier.* Originally presented in Vienna in 1908 as *Der Tapfere Soldat,* the musical was adapted from George Bernard Shaw's play, *Arms and the Man,* though the author always regretted having given his permission. (The next musical treatment of a Shaw play, *My Fair Lady,* came along 47 years later.)

Producer Fred Whitney secured the rights to the English-language version even before the operetta had had its première at the Theater an der Wien, and he opened it in New York at the Lyric Theatre (now a movie house on 42nd Street west of Times Square). The satire on heroes and heroism is set in 1885 during the Serbian invasion of Bulgaria. Lt. Bumerli, the chocolate-eating Swiss soldier serving in the Serb army, is more concerned about saving his neck than displaying valor on the battlefield. He hides in the home of Col. Popoff, a Bulgarian, and soon meets Popoff's daughter, Nadina. Though Nadina's hero is the swaggering Major Alexius Spiridoff, it is not long before she drops him for the peace-loving Bumerli. Other Broadway productions of *The Chocolate Soldier* were offered in 1921, 1930, 1931, 1934, and 1947 (the last in a revised version by Guy Bolton). The 1941 movie with Risë Stevens and Nelson Eddy used a different story. RCA SC.

MADAME SHERRY

Music: Karl Hoschna
Lyrics & book: Otto Harbach
Producers: A. H. Woods, H. H. Frazee, George Lederer
Director: George Lederer
Cast: Lina Abarbanell, Ralph Herz, Elizabeth Murray, Jack Gardner, Dorothy Jardon, Frances Demarest
Songs: "Every Little Movement"; "The Smile She Meant for Me"; "I Want to Play House With You"; "The Birth of Passion"; "Put Your Arms Around Me Honey" (Albert Von Tilzer - Junie McCree)
New York run: New Amsterdam Theatre, August 30, 1910; 231 p.

Madame Sherry remains the best remembered of the six productions written by Karl Hoschna and Otto Harbach (who spelled his name Hauerbach until World War I). It was adapted from an English musical of 1903, which had a different score, and which, in turn, had been based on a French musical. Among the reasons for its success were the insinuating number, "Every Little Movement" ("...has a meaning all its own") and the interpolated "Put Your Arms Around Me Honey." In this tangled tale of mistaken identity, Ed Sherry deceives his uncle, wealthy archeologist Theophilus Sherry, into accepting his Irish landlady as his wife and a dancing teacher's pupils as their children. At first Ed is smitten with Lulu, the dancing teacher, but then transfers his affections to Yvonne, his cousin (played by Metropolitan opera diva Lina Abarbanell). Audiences could enjoy matinee performances of *Madame Sherry* for a top ticket price of $1.50.

NAUGHTY MARIETTA

Music: Victor Herbert
Lyrics & book: Rida Johnson Young
Producer: Oscar Hammerstein
Director: Jacques Coini
Cast: Emma Trentini, Orville Harrold, Edward Martindel, Marie Duchene, Peggy Wood
Songs: "Tramp! Tramp! Tramp!"; "Naughty Marietta"; "'Neath the Southern Moon"; "Italian Street Song"; "Live for Today"; "I'm Falling in Love With Someone"; "Ah! Sweet Mystery of Life"
New York run: New York Theatre, November 7, 1910; 136 p.

Victor Herbert's crowning achievement came into being because mounting debts had forced opera impresario Oscar Hammerstein (grandfather of Oscar II) into the area of the more commercial musical theatre. Hammerstein had it staged with all the care of one of his Manhattan Opera productions, with two of his stars, Emma Trentini and Orville Harrold, in the leading roles of Marietta d'Altena and Capt. Dick Warrington.

Naughty Marietta takes place in New Orleans in 1780. Marietta is there to escape from an unwanted marriage in France and Capt. Dick is there to lead his Rangers against a pirate gang led by Bras Piqué ("Tattooed Arm"). Though Marietta is first attracted to Etienne Grandet, the son of the lieutenant governor, when he is revealed as the pirate leader she is happy to sing her romantic duets with Capt. Dick. She is, in fact, sure that he is the man for her because he is able to finish the "Dream Melody" ("Ah! Sweet Mystery of Life") that Marietta recalls from childhood. One historical error committed by the authors is that New Orleans is supposed to be a French posession, whereas in the year in which the story takes place the colony belonged to Spain. (This error was also made in *The New Moon* in 1928, which had the same locale and period.) The 1935 movie version co-starred Jeanette MacDonald and Nelson Eddy.
Smithsonian SC/ Weinberger, London (1959)*/ TW.

THE PINK LADY

Music: Ivan Caryll
Lyrics & book: C. M. S. McLellan
Producers: Marc Klaw & A. L. Erlanger
Director: Herbert Gresham
Choreographer: Julian Mitchell
Cast: Hazel Dawn, Alice Dovey, William Elliott, Frank Lalor, Jed Prouty
Songs: "On the Saskatchewan"; "My Beautiful Lady"; "Hide and Seek"; "Donny Did, Donny Didn't"
New York run: New Amsterdam Theatre, March 13, 1911; 312 p.

After winning success in London, composer Ivan Caryll indited the scores for 14 Broadway musicals. His most celebrated production was *The Pink Lady*, which contained the durable song "My Beautiful Lady" and gave Hazel Dawn a memorable role that allowed her to play the violin. The story, adapted from a French play, *Le Satyr*, takes place in one day, during which we visit a restaurant in the woods at Compiègne, a furniture shop on the Rue Honoré, and the Ball of the Nymphs and Satyrs. Before settling down to marriage with Angele, Lucien Garidel hopes to enjoy one last fling with Claudine (Miss Dawn), known as the Pink Lady because of her monochromatic wardrobe. When they accidentally meet Angele, Lucien covers his embarrassment by introducing Claudine as the wife of a friend. Following comic complications, the day ends with the involved couples properly sorted.
AEI SC.

THE FIREFLY

Music: Rudolf Friml
Lyrics & book: Otto Harbach
Producer: Arthur Hammerstein
Director: Fred Latham
Choreographer: Signor Albertieri, Sammy Lee
Cast: Emma Trentini, Craig Campbell, Roy Atwell, Sammy Lee, Audrey Maple, Melville Stewart
Songs: "Giannina Mia"; "When a Maid Comes Knocking at Your Heart"; "Love Is Like a Firefly"; "Sympathy"
New York run: Lyric Theatre, December 2, 1912; 120 p.

During a performance he was conducting of *Naughty Marietta*, Victor Herbert had a disagreement with the star, Emma Trentini, and stormed off the podium. He also refused to have anything to do with her next vehicle, *The Firefly*, for which he had been contracted. The composer's decision opened the way for Rudolf Friml, who had never written a Broadway score before, to become a leading creator of American operettas. It also began his partnership with librettist-lyricist Otto Harbach, with whom he would be associated on ten musicals. In the Cinderella tale, cut from a similar bolt of cloth as the one used for *Mlle. Modiste*, Nina Corelli, an Italian street singer in New York, disguises herself as a cabin boy to be near Jack Travers, a guest on a yacht sailing for Bermuda. After hearing her sing, a music teacher offers to give her lessons, and within three years she becomes both a renowned prima donna and Mrs. Jack Travers.
TW.

SWEETHEARTS

MUSIC: Victor Herbert
Lyrics: Robert B. Smith
Book: Harry B. Smith & Fred De Gresac
Producers: Louis Werba & Mark Luescher
Director: Fred Latham
Choreographer: Charles Morgan Jr.
Cast: Christie MacDonald, Thomas Conkey, Ethel Du Fre Houston, Edwin Wilson, Tom McNaughton
Songs: "Sweethearts"; "Angelus"; "Every Lover Must Meet His Fate"; "Pretty as a Picture"; "Jeannette and Her Little Wooden Shoes"
New York run: New Amsterdam Theatre, September 8, 1913; 136 p.

Though allegedly based on the real-life adventures of a 15th Century Neapolitan princess, *Sweethearts* was easily among Broadway's most farfetched musical romances, complete with a mythological country, an abducted princess, and a prince in disguise. To keep her from harm during a war, the infant Princess Sylvia of Zilania has been taken to Bruges where she is brought up believing she is the daughter of a laundress. While traveling incognito, Prince Franz falls in love with Sylvia even before they meet. After their true identities are revealed, they assume the throne as King and Queen of Zilania.

Prompted by the successful 1945 revival of Herbert's *The Red Mill* starring comic Eddie Foy Jr., Herbert's *Sweethearts* was resuscitated for comic Bobby Clark (see page 134). Here the secondary role of political operator Mikel Mikeloviz was retailored to Clark's specifications, and the resourceful clown turned the evening into a self-kidding, hilarious romp. The run was almost twice as long as the original. The 1938 Jeanette MacDonald-Nelson Eddy movie version had a different story.
MMG SC/ TW.

THE GIRL FROM UTAH

Music: Jerome Kern, etc.
Lyrics: Harry B. Smith, etc.
Book: James T. Tanner, Harry B. Smith
Producer: Charles Frohman
Director: J. A. E. Malone
Cast: Julia Sanderson, Donald Brian, Joseph Cawthorn, Queenie Vassar, Venita Fitzhugh
Songs: "Same Sort of Girl"; "They Didn't Believe Me" (lyric: Herbert Reynolds); "Gilbert the Filbert" (Herman Finck - Arthur Wimperis); "Why Don't They Dance the Polka?"; "The Land of Let's Pretend"
New York run: Knickerbocker Theatre, August 24, 1914; 120 p.

Based on a 1913 London musical with music by Paul Rubens and Sidney Jones and lyrics by Adrian Ross and Percy Greenbank, *The Girl from Utah* underwent a major sea change by the time it opened on Broadway, with no less than seven songs now credited to Jerome Kern (including his first hit, "They Didn't Believe Me"). Despite the somewhat misleading title, the story is set in London where Una Trance (Julia Sanderson) has fled to avoid marrying a bigamist Mormon. Though the Mormon pursues her, Una eventually finds true love in the arms of Sandy Blair (Donald Brian), a London song-and-dance man. The show was the first musical hit on Broadway following the outbreak of World War I. With its appealing Kern additions (it was the composer's sixth of 39 Broadway shows), the production was a transitional work leading to the soon-to-come American domination of the musical-comedy field.

WATCH YOUR STEP

Music & lyrics: Irving Berlin
Book: Harry B. Smith
Producer: Charles Dillingham
Director: R. H. Burnside
Cast: Vernon & Irene Castle, Frank Tinney, Charles King, Elizabeth Brice, Elizabeth Murray, Harry Kelly, Justine Johnstone
Songs: "Play a Simple Melody"; "They Always Follow Me Around"; "When I Discovered You"; "Settle Down in a One-Horse Town"; "The Syncopated Walk"
New York run: New Amsterdam Theatre, December 8, 1914; 175 p.

In 1911, at the age of 23, Irving Berlin had the entire country ragtime crazy with "Alexander's Ragtime Band." Three years later, he wrote his first Broadway score (out of a total of 21) which was the first to feature ragtime. It also introduced audiences to another Berlin skill in the contrapuntal "Play a Simple Melody." The songs accompanied a vehicle for dancers Vernon and Irene Castle (it would be the couple's last professional appearance together) that was so flimsy the program credit line read, "Plot, if any, by Harry B. Smith." That plot had to do with a will leaving $2 million to anyone who had never been in love, but by the second act the story was discarded and the evening was turned into a facsimile of a Fifth Avenue nightclub floor show. Also discarded was W.C. Fields. Then primarily a juggler, Fields had sailed from Australia to join the cast during the Syracuse tryout, only to be fired after one performance. The reason: producer Dillingham was fearful that Fields would be such a hit that audiences wouldn't pay attention to the Castles.

ZIEGFELD FOLLIES

Music: Louis A. Hirsch
Lyrics: Gene Buck
Sketches: Gene Buck, Rennold Wolf, Channing Pollock
Producer: Florenz Ziegfeld
Directors: Julian Mitchell, Leon Errol
Choreographer: Julian Mitchell
Cast: W.C. Fields, Ed Wynn, Ann Pennington, Mae Murray, Bernard Granville, George White, Bert Williams, Ina Claire, Justine Johnstone, Leon Errol, Carl Randall, Will West, Melville Stewart
Songs: "Hello, Frisco!"; "Hold Me in Your Loving Arms"; "I Can't Do Without Girls"; "A Girl For Each Month of the Year" (lyric: Wolf, Pollock)
New York run: New Amsterdam Theatre, June 21, 1915; 104 p.

To take the American public's mind off the grave news about World War I (the *Lusitania* had recently been torpedoed), Ziegfeld's ninth annual edition of his *Follies* was the most extravagant and spectacular to date. With its brilliant cast and the equally brilliant scenic designs created by Joseph Urban (his first of 12 *Follies*), this production ushered in an eight year period that is regarded as the pinnacle of the series. Among the show's pleasures: the opening underwater sequence ("The stage setting is the greatest Mr. Ziegfeld has ever presented," according to the program); the first-act finale called "America," with everyone and everything in red, white and blue and Justine Johnstone as the Spirit of Columbia; "The Silver Forest" scene with the girls parading about as months of the year; Ina Claire singing the hit song, "Hello, Frisco!"; the "Gates of Elysium" sequence with real elephants on the stage; and W.C. Fields's comic poolshooting routine (during the road tour Ed Wynn horned in on the act only to have Fields almost knock him unconscious with a cue).

THE BLUE PARADISE

Music: Sigmund Romberg, Edmund Eysler
Lyrics: Herbert Reynolds
Book: Edgar Smith
Producers: Messrs. Shubert
Director: J.H. Benrimo
Choreographer: Ed Hutchinson
Cast: Vivienne Segal, Cecil Lean, Cleo Mayfield, Ted Lorraine, Robert Pitkin, Frances Demarest, Teddy Webb
Songs: "Auf Wiedersehn" (Romberg); "One Step Into Love" (Romberg); "Vienna, Vienna" (Eysler); "A Toast to Woman's Eyes" (Romberg)
New York run: Casino Theatre, August 5, 1915; 356 p.

The fourth longest running book musical of the 1910's, *The Blue Paradise* gave Sigmund Romberg his first chance to compose the kind of sentimental, romantic songs with which he would become identified. (His total Broadway output — including shows for which he shared the writing assignment — was a record 57 productions.) Adapted from *Ein Tag im Paradies,* a Viennese operetta by Edmund Eysler, the musical also provided Vivienne Segal with her professional debut when she took over the female lead during the Washington tryout. In the story, Mizzi (Miss Segal), the flower seller at the Blue Paradise, a Viennese garden restaurant, must bid a tearful "Auf Wiedersehn" (Romberg's first song hit) to her sweetheart Rudolphe (Cecil Lean) as he leaves to make his fortune in America. With fortune made, Rudolphe returns many years later, only to discover that time had transformed sweet little Mizzi into a virago.

The Blue Paradise. Ted Lorraine and Vivienne Segal come to the aid of Teddy Webb, who has apparently bitten off more than he can swallow. (White)

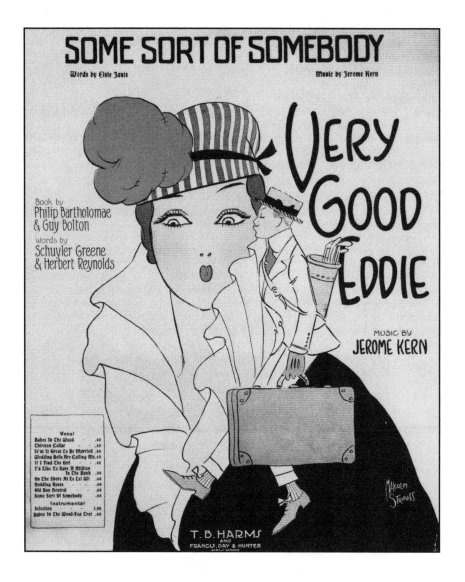

VERY GOOD EDDIE

Music: Jerome Kern
Lyrics: Schuyler Greene
Book: Philip Bartholomae & Guy Bolton
Producers: Elisabeth Marbury & F. Ray Comstock
Director: (uncredited)
Choreographer: David Bennett
Cast: Ernest Truex, Alice Dovey, Oscar Shaw, Helen Raymond, John E.
Hazzard, John Willard, Ada Lewis
Songs: "Some Sort of Somebody" (lyric: Elsie Janis); "Isn't It Great to Be Married?"; "On the Shore at Le Lei Wi" (music with Henry Kailimai; lyric: Herbert Reynolds); "Thirteen Collar"; "Babes in the Wood" (lyric with Kern); "Old Boy Neutral"; "Nodding Roses" (lyric with Reynolds)
New York Run: Princess Theatre, December 23, 1915; 341 p.

When, in 1914, producer F. Ray Comstock was having difficulty filling his 299-seat Princess Theatre (then on 39th Street near 6th Avenue), theatrical and literary agent Elisabeth Marbury suggested that they jointly sponsor a series of modern musical comedies, all with music written by Jerome Kern and librettos by Guy Bolton. The aim was to offer scaled-down shows with casts of no more that 30 (including chorus) and with the action taking place in only two different locations, thus allowing for one set in the first act and another in the second. The stories, all occurring in contemporary America, would have believable if bubbleheaded characters caught in comic situations that evolved naturally out of the action, and the songs would have more than a passing relevance to what was going on in the plot.

The first effort, *Nobody Home,* which opened in April 1915, was something of a compromise since it was based on an English musical, *Mr. Popple of Ippleton*, and it had interpolated numbers. The action, however, took place in New York City, and the story was filled with the same kind of romantic complications and misunderstandings that would be the concern of subsequent shows at the theatre. The second offering did, in fact, indicate greater assurance in fulfilling the goals that the Princess management had initially outlined. *Very Good Eddie* not only adhered to the general plan but also set the style and standard for three subsequent Kern musicals written with Bolton and P.G. Wodehouse — *Oh, Boy!*, *Leave It to Jane*, and *Oh, Lady! Lady!!* — that formed the seminal quartet known as the Princess Theatre Musicals.

Very Good Eddie — no comma in the title since it was an appraisal of character rather than an expression of approval — takes place at first aboard the Hudson River dayliner *Catskill*, which is carrying two honeymooning couples. Eddie Kettle (Ernest Truex) is short and timid and his wife Georgina (Helen Raymond) is tall and domineering, Percy Darling (John Willard) is tall and domineering and *his* wife Elsie (Alice Dovey) is short and timid. Georgina and Percy are accidentally left on shore before the boat sails, thereby resulting in embarrassing predicaments for Eddie and Elsie. Matters get straightened out in the second act at the Rip Van Winkle Inn where Eddie now asserts his authority over his suddenly subservient spouse.

In 1975, the Goodspeed Opera in East Haddam, Connecticut, revived the musical which then had a Broadway run almost as long as the original production. There were some changes in the score, and the final scene — in the renamed Honeymoon Inn — found both couples switching partners according to size and temperament after discovering that the minister who married them had no legal right to perform the ceremony.
DRG OC (1975)/ TW.

OH, BOY!

Music: Jerome Kern
Lyrics: P. G. Wodehouse
Book: Guy Bolton & P. G. Wodehouse
Producers: William Elliott & F. Ray Comstock
Directors: Edward Royce, Robert Milton
Choreographer: Edward Royce
Cast: Marie Carroll, Tom Powers, Anna Wheaton, Hal Forde, Edna May Oliver, Marion Davies, Justine Johnstone, Dorothy Dickson & Carl Hyson
Songs: "You Never Knew About Me"; "The Land Where the Good Songs Go"; "An Old-Fashioned Wife"; "A Pal Like You"; "Till the Clouds Roll By"; "Rolled into One"; "Nesting Time in Flatbush"
New York run: Princess Theatre, February 20, 1917; 463 p.

For *Oh, Boy!*, their third Princess Theatre Musical and the third longest running book musical of the 1910's, Jerome Kern and Guy Bolton were joined by British humorist P. G. Wodehouse, who helped give the characters the flavor of transplanted silly-ass Englishmen. Again the settings were modern and modest, the songs fitted the story, and the comic tale involved romantic and marital mixups. When George Budd (Tom Powers) arrives home to his Long Island apartment after eloping with Lou Ellen Carter (Marie Carroll), he finds his country club friends having a party in his digs. The newlyweds separate while Lou Ellen prepares her parents for the news of her marriage, and George becomes innocently involved with Jackie Sampson (Anna Wheaton), a madcap actress, who has climbed through his bedroom window to avoid the advances of a lecherous judge. After further complications, during which the judge turns out to be Lou Ellen's father and Jackie is alternately passed off as both George's wife and his Quaker aunt, the couple is reunited at the Meadowsides Country Club.

MAYTIME

Music: Sigmund Romberg
Lyrics & book: Rida Johnson Young
Producers: Messrs. Shubert
Director: Edward Temple
Choreographer: Allan K. Foster
Cast: Peggy Wood, Charles Purcell, Ralph Herbert, William Norris, Gertrude Vanderbilt
Songs: "The Road to Paradise"; "Will You Remember?"; "Jump Jim Crow"; "Dancing Will Keep You Young" (lyric: Cyrus Wood)
New York run: Shubert Theatre, August 16, 1917; 492 p.

Maytime established Sigmund Romberg as Victor Herbert's successor as the leading creator of sentimental operettas. The musical, with such pieces as "Will You Remember?" and "The Road to Paradise," became New York's most popular attraction during World War I, even though, ironically, it was based on a German operetta, *Wie Einst im Mai*. In Washington Square, New York, in 1840, wealthy Ottilie Van Zandt (Peggy Wood) and poor Richard Wayne (Charles Purcell) are unable to marry because Ottilie's father has other plans for her. Richard becomes rich and Ottilie, fallen upon hard times, must sell her house which is turned into a dress shop. Their grandchildren (played by the same actors) prove that love will find a way — even if it takes 60 years.

The second longest running book musical of the decade, *Maytime* was seen in three New York theatres following its engagement at the Shubert (on 44th Street west of Broadway). During the run, Purcell was succeeded by future Metropolitan Opera tenor John Charles Thomas. The 1937 movie version, with Jeanette MacDonald and Nelson Eddy, changed the story and the score.

Maytime. Peggy Wood and Charles Purcell in the romantic climax of Act IV.

LEAVE IT TO JANE

Music: Jerome Kern
Lyrics: P. G. Wodehouse
Book: Guy Bolton & P. G. Wodehouse
Producers: William Elliot, F. Ray Comstock, Morris Gest
Director-Choreographer: Edward Royce
Cast: Edith Hallor, Robert Pitkin, Oscar Shaw, Georgia O'Ramey
Songs: "Wait Till Tomorrow"; "Just You Watch My Step"; "Leave It to Jane"; "The Crickets Are Calling"; "The Siren's Song"; "There It Is Again"; "Cleopatterer"; "The Sun Shines Brighter"; "I'm Going to Find a Girl"
New York run: Longacre Theatre, August 28, 1917; 167 p.

Except for the technicality that *Leave It to Jane* never played the Princess Theatre, in every other respect it qualifies as a Princess Theatre Musical. Its score was by Kern and Wodehouse, its book was by Bolton and Wodehouse, and it was presented by the Princess management. In fact, this version of George Ade's 1904 play, *The College Widow*, had been scheduled to follow *Oh, Boy!* into the Princess but that show was doing so well that *Jane* was shifted to a larger house (the Longacre is on 48th Street east of Broadway), with the top ticket price reduced from $3.50 to $2.50. *Leave It to Jane* takes place at good old Atwater College, where everyone is concerned about the Thanksgiving Day football game with rival Bingham. It is left to flirtatious Jane Witherspoon (Edith Hallor), the president's daughter, to induce All-American halfback Billy Bolton (Robert Pitkin), who is to play for Bingham, to switch colleges and play for Atwater under an assumed name. He does and wins both the game and Jane. Over 40 years later, the musical was successfully revived at a Greenwich Village theatre. DRG OC (1959)/ TW.

OH, LADY! LADY!!

Music: Jerome Kern
Lyrics: P. G. Wodehouse
Book: Guy Bolton & P. G. Wodehouse
Producers: William Elliott & F. Ray Comstock
Directors: Edward Royce, Robert Milton
Choreographer: Edward Royce
Cast: Vivienne Segal, Carl Randall, Harry C. Browne, Carroll McComas, Edward Abeles, Florence Shirley, Margaret Dale, Constance Binney
Songs: "Not Yet"; "Do Look at Him"; "I Found You and You Found Me"; "Moon Song"; "When the Ships Come Home"; "Before I Met You"; "Greenwich Village"
New York run: Princess Theatre, February 1, 1918; 219 p.

Using a minstrel-show catch line for a title, the last Kern-Wodehouse-Bolton Princess Theatre Musical was the exclamatory successor to *Oh, Boy!* In a plot that amounted to virtual self-plagiarism, the characters were again caught up in a series of amatory mixups and misunderstandings. Willoughby "Bill" Finch (Carl Randall) is about to marry Molly Farrington (Vivienne Segal) when May Barber (Carroll McComas), his former fiancee from East Giliad, Ohio, shows up at Molly's Long Island home. Though May is there only to deliver Molly's lingerie, her appearance — and that of a comic jewel thief — cause complications that result in the wedding being called off. In Act II the lovers are reunited at a party in Greenwich Village. Curiously, the best known song written for *Oh, Lady! Lady!!* was never used in the show. The heroine was originally to have sung "Bill," but the lyric did not accurately describe the show's Bill, and "Do Look at Him" was substituted. A slightly altered "Bill," of course, later turned up in *Show Boat*. TW.

Oh, Lady! Lady!! Vivienne Segal and Carl Randall. (White)

Sinbad. Showgirl Hazel Cox and Al Jolson. (White)

SINBAD

Music: Sigmund Romberg, etc.
Lyrics: Harold Atteridge, etc.
Book: Harold Atteridge
Producers: Messrs. Shubert
Director: J. C. Huffman
Choreographers: Jack Mason, Alexis Kosloff
Cast: Al Jolson, Kitty Doner, Mabel Withee, Forrest Huff, Grace Washburn, Alexis Kosloff
Songs: "Beauty and the Beast"; "Rock-a-Bye Your Baby With a Dixie Melody" (Jean Schwartz-Sam Lewis, Joe Young); "Why Do They All Take the Night Boat to Albany?" (Schwartz-Lewis, Young); " 'N Everything" (B. G. DeSylva-Gus Kahn)
New York run: Winter Garden, February 14, 1918; 388 p.

At a time when it was not uncommon for musicals to be built around the talents of one individual, no shows were more vehicular than those created to spotlight the exuberant personality of "Mammy" singer Al Jolson. Though they had large casts, such extravaganzas as *Robinson Crusoe, Jr.* (1916), *Sinbad*, *Bombo* (1921), and *Big Boy* (1925) were virtually one-man shows. All the Jolson entertainments were presented by the Messrs. Shubert, directed by J. C. Huffman, had easily ignored books by Harold Atteridge, were full of interpolated songs, and — except for *Bombo* — played the Winter Garden (on Broadway between 50th and 51st Streets).

In *Sinbad*, in which the star wore his customary black-face makeup, Jolson appeared in ancient Bagdad as a comical chap named Inbad who poses as Sinbad the Sailor. Between adventures, he literally stopped the show to introduce his own musical specialties, including "Avalon" (added after the opening) and George Gershwin's first hit, "Swanee" (added during the road tour).

ZIEGFELD FOLLIES

Music & lyrics: Miscellaneous writers
Sketches: Gene Buck, Rennold Wolf
Producer: Florenz Ziegfeld
Director-choreographer: Ned Wayburn
Cast: Marilyn Miller, Eddie Cantor, W. C. Fields, Will Rogers, Harry Kelly, Ann Pennington, Lillian Lorraine, Savoy & Brennan, Fairbanks Twins
Songs: "Syncopated Tune" (Louis A. Hirsch-Gene Buck); "Blue Devils of France" (Irving Berlin); "I'm Gonna Pin a Medal on the Girl I Left Behind" (Berlin); "Any Old Time at All" (Hirsch-Buck)
New York run: New Amsterdam Theatre, June 18, 1918; 151 p.

The star-filled 1918 *Follies* — the 12th annual edition — put the focus on World War I in most of its sketches, production numbers, and songs. These included a "Yankee Doodle" dance by Marilyn Miller (in her *Follies* debut); Will Rogers' topical monologues; a skit with Eddie Cantor playing a would-be aviator in a recruiting office; a stirring parade of showgirls representing the allied nations; a first-act finale of living statues created by Ben Ali Haggin titled "Forward, Allies"; and a sketch showing women on the home front performing jobs usually done by men (a reassuring note in the program contained the information that all members of the male chorus were rejected for military service). Popular pastimes of the day were covered in W. C. Fields' golf routine and a grand finale with everyone indulging in the current passion for jazz dancing. One of six *Follies* staged by the prolific Ned Wayburn, the revue also had the services of a 19-year-old rehearsal pianist named George Gershwin.

Ziegfeld Follies (1918). W.C. Fields, Will Rogers, Eddie Cantor, and Harry Kelly serenade Lillian Lorraine with ''Any Old Time at All.'' (White)

Ziegfeld Follies (1919). Showgirls as ingredients in ''The Follies Salad'' — Spice, Oil, Paprika, Sugar, Lettuce, and Chicken. (White)

ZIEGFELD FOLLIES

Music & lyrics: Irving Berlin, etc.
Sketches: Gene Buck, Rennold Wolf
Producer: Florenz Ziegfeld
Director-choreographer: Ned Wayburn
Cast: Marilyn Miller, Eddie Cantor, Bert Williams, Eddie Dowling, Ray Dooley, Johnny Dooley, Delyle Alda, John Steel, Van & Schenck, Mary Hay
Songs: "My Baby's Arms" (Harry Tierney-Joseph McCarthy); "Tulip Time" (David Stamper-Gene Buck); "Mandy"; "A Pretty Girl Is Like a Melody"; "You'd Be Surprised"; "You Cannot Make Your Shimmy Shake on Tea" (Berlin-Rennold Wolf)
New York run: New Amsterdam Theatre, June 16, 1919; 171 p.

With more song hits than any previous *Follies*, the 13th edition even gave the entire series a theme song in Irving Berlin's "A Pretty Girl Is Like a Melody." Rivalling the 1918 production as the premier revue in the series, it offered showgirls clad as salad ingredients and classical music; Ben Ali Haggin's tableaux depicting the 13th Folly and a scene showing Lady Godiva astride a white horse; and a first-act finale offering a minstrel show with Eddie Cantor and Bert Williams as "Tambo" and "Bones," Marilyn Miller as George Primrose, and a tambourine-banging, high-strutting line of Mandys. The grand finale was a grand tribute to the Salvation Army's morale-boosting contributions to the war. The chief nonmilitary topic was the imminent arrival of Prohibition whose effects were shown in a nightclub scene with showgirls parading around as Coca-Cola, Sarsaparilla, Grape Juice, Lemonade, and Bevo. The production cost was now over $100,000, and the top ticket price was $3.50 at night, $2.00 for matinees. Smithsonian OC.

GREENWICH VILLAGE FOLLIES

Music & lyrics: Miscellaneous writers
Sketches: John Murray Anderson, Philip Bartholomae
Producer: The Bohemians Inc. (Al Jones & Morris Green)
Director: John Murray Anderson
Cast: Bessie McCoy Davis, Ted Lewis Orchestra, Cecil Cunningham, Harry K. Morton
Songs: "When My Baby Smiles at Me" (Billy Munro-Andrew Sterling); "I Want a Daddy who Will Rock Me to Sleep" (A. Baldwin Sloane-Arthur Swanstrom, John Murray Anderson); "(I'll See You in) C-U-B-A" (Irving Berlin)
New York run: Greenwich Village Theatre, July 15, 1919; 232 p.

A stylishly mounted, somewhat less elaborate variation on the *Ziegfeld Follies* format was the *Greenwich Village Follies* (Ziegfeld even threatened to sue over the use of the *Follies* name), which came along in 1919 and lasted through eight editions up to 1928. The guiding light was director John Murray Anderson, who made his professional debut with the first of the series and staged six in all. (Murray's total Broadway credits were 28 musicals.) Despite the title, all editions of the *Greenwich Village Follies* were moved uptown during their runs, with the 1919 production switched to the Nora Bayes Theatre (then on West 44th Street) soon after its Greenwich Village opening. The show, which called itself "A Revusical Comedy of New York's Latin Quarter," took satirical aim at the ballet, free love, Prohibition, and the arts in general. Among the distinguishing characteristics of the series were female impersonations and arty "ballet ballads" based on literary works. In 1925, Hassard Short took over as director (Anderson had replaced *him* at the *Music Box Revue*) and in 1928 it was J. C. Huffman.

IRENE

Music: Harry Tierney
Lyrics: Joseph McCarthy
Book: James Montgomery
Producers: Carle Carlton & Joseph McCarthy
Director-Choreographer: Edward Royce
Cast: Edith Day, Walter Regan, Bobbie Watson, Dorothy Walters, John Litel, Hobart Cavanaugh, Eva Puck
Songs: "Alice Blue Gown"; "Castle of Dreams"; "Irene"; "Skyrocket"; "The Last Part of Ev'ry Party"
New York run: Vanderbilt Theatre, November 18, 1919; 670 p.

By remaining at the Vanderbilt Theatre (then on 48th Street east of 7th Avenue), for one year eight months — and by running 11 performances longer than *A Trip to Chinatown* — *Irene* set a Broadway endurance record that it held onto for 18 years. What made it such a hit for its day (at one time it claimed 17 road companies) resulted from what critics hailed as its intelligent book, diverting comedy, brisk pacing, melodious songs that fitted logically into the story, and talented performers. The show, in fact, won not only critical applause but also gratitude for relieving what Alexander Woollcott termed "Broadway's desperate plight with only 17 or 18 musical comedies in view." Actually, the plot was little more than another version of the Cinderella tale, which has served as the basis for many other musicals including *Mlle. Modiste, The Firefly, Sally, Sunny, Annie Get Your Gun, My Fair Lady, Annie,* and *42nd Street.*

In this variation, a chatty upholsterer's assistant, Irene O'Dare (Edith Day), is sent to a Long Island mansion to mend some cushions. There she meets the instantly smitten Donald Marshall (Walter Regan), who persuades his friend, a male couturier known as Madame Lucy (Bobbie Watson), to hire Irene to pose as a socialite and show off his latest creations. Even though her humble origin is revealed, Irene makes a hit at an elegant party wearing and singing about her Alice blue gown, and ends in Donald's arms.

The show was designed as a star vehicle for Edith Day (who left the cast after only five months to head the London company) and it was the first — of seven — Broadway musicals with songs by Harry Tierney and Joseph McCarthy. During the New York run, Irene Dunne became the fourth actress to play Irene, and Jeanette MacDonald joined the cast as a Long Island belle. Busby Berkeley played Madame Lucy on the road. As for Miss Day, though she appeared on Broadway in two subsequent musicals, her career flourished mostly in London where she was known as the Queen of Drury Lane.

Prompted by the successful revival of *No, No, Nanette* in 1971, *Irene* was brought back two years later by the same producer, Harry Rigby, who had first thought of bringing back *Nanette.* (See page 238.) The new production was also plagued at the outset by the same kind of problems that had affected the previous show, including the replacement of a major cast member (George S. Irving for Billy DeWolfe as Madame Lucy) and the director (Gower Champion for Sir John Gielgud). Though greeted by mixed reviews in New York, the musical remained a year and a half at the newly built Minskoff Theatre, located on the west side of Broadway between 44th and 45th Streets. Debbie Reynolds, who was succeeded during the run by Jane Powell, made her Broadway debut as Irene. Her occupation, however, was changed to that of a piano tuner so that the title song might be used for a male chorus tapping away on top of four uprights as they sing of the charms of Irene. Only five numbers were retained from the original score, with others either pop tunes of the period (though all had lyrics by Joseph McCarthy) or new songs. A screen version was filmed in 1940 with Anna Neagle and Ray Milland.

M-E London OC (1920); Columbia OC (1973)/ TW.

SALLY

Music: Jerome Kern
Lyrics: Clifford Grey, etc.
Book: Guy Bolton
Producer: Florenz Ziegfeld
Director-choreographer: Edward Royce
Cast: Marilyn Miller, Leon Errol, Walter Catlett, Irving Fisher, Mary Hay, Stanley Ridges, Dolores
Songs: "Look for the Silver Lining" (lyric: B.G. DeSylva); "Sally"; "Wild Rose"; "Whip-Poor-Will"; "The Lorelei" (lyric: Anne Caldwell); "The Church 'Round the Corner" (lyric: P.G. Wodehouse)
New York run: New Amsterdam Theatre, December 21, 1920; 570 p.

Just as *Irene* was a Cinderella tale created to show off the talents of singer Edith Day, so *Sally* was a Cinderella tale created to show off the talents of dancer Marilyn Miller (then spelling her first name "Marilynn") in her first starring role. Producer Florenz Ziegfeld commmissioned the Princess Theatre triad of Kern, Bolton and Wodehouse to come up with a suitable vehicle and the team settled on an unproduced musical they had written called *The Little Thing.* Early in the preparations, Wodehouse withdrew from the project, and in the altered script, initially known as *Sally of the Alley,* Sally Green first appears as a dishwashing drudge at the Alley Inn in Greenwich Village dreaming of fame and singing "Look for the Silver Lining." Invited by one of the waiters, really the exiled Duke of Czechogovinia (Leon Errol), Sally goes to an elegant ball in the guise of Mme. Nookerova, a celebrated ballerina. In *Irene* fashion, her true identity is discovered, but here the heroine not only wins the affluent young tenor she is also signed for the *Ziegfeld Follies* and dances a Butterfly Ballet by Victor Herbert. *Sally* was the third longest running Broadway musical of the Twenties. An unsuccessful revival was presented in 1948 with Bambi Linn as Sally and Willie Howard as the duke. Miss Miller was also in the 1929 movie version.
M-E London OC (1921)/ TW.

Sally. Marilyn Miller as a Russian ballerina. (White)

SHUFFLE ALONG

Music: Eubie Blake
Lyrics: Noble Sissle
Book: Flournoy Miller & Aubrey Lyles
Producer: Nikko Producing Co. (Al Mayer)
Director: Walter Brooks
Choreographer: Lawrence Deas
Cast: Flournoy Miller, Aubrey Lyles, Noble Sissle, Gertrude Saunders, Roger
Matthews, Lottie Gee, Lawrence Deas, Eubie Blake
Songs: "I'm Just Wild About Harry"; "Love Will Find a Way"; "Bandana Days";
"If You've Never Been Vamped by a Brownskin"
New York run: 63rd St. Music Hall, May 23, 1921; 504 p.

Developed from a vaudeville sketch, *Shuffle Along* became the first successful
musical written, directed, and acted by black people. Little money was spent on
costumes or scenery, but white audiences were happy to travel a bit north of the
theatre district to enjoy the show's earthy humor, fast pacing, spirited dancing,
and infectious rhythms. The plot is concerned with the race for mayor of
Jimtown, in Dixieland, between the venal Steve Jenkins (Flournoy Miller) and the
virtuous Harry Walton (Roger Matthews), about whom, we are repeatedly advised, everyone is just wild. Though Steve wins, Harry eventually has him and his
equally corrupt police chief, Sam Peck (Aubrey Lyles), thrown out of office. During the run, Paul Robeson joined the cast briefly as a member of a vocal quartet,
and Josephine Baker was added to the touring company as a chorus girl. There
were three titular successors to *Shuffle Along: Keep Shufflin'* (1928), *Shuffle
Along of 1933* (1932), and another *Shuffle Along* (1952). All of them availeth not.
New World OC.

ZIEGFELD FOLLIES

Music, lyrics & sketches: Miscellaneous writers
Producer: Florenz Ziegfeld
Directors: Edward Royce, George Marion
Choreographer: Edward Royce
Cast: Fanny Brice, W. C. Fields, Raymond Hitchcock, Ray Dooley, Mary
Milburn, Van & Schenck, Florence O'Denishawn, Vera Michelena, Mary
Eaton, Channing Pollock, Mary Lewis
Songs: "Strut, Miss Lizzie" (Henry Creamer-Turner Layton); "Second Hand
Rose" (James Hanley-Grant Clarke); "Sally, Won't You Come Back?"
(David Stamper-Gene Buck); "My Man" (Maurice Yvain-Channing
Pollock)
New York run: Globe Theatre, June 21, 1921; 119 p.

The 15th annual *Ziegfeld Follies* was among the Great Glorifier's most elaborate
revues, with another star-filled cast and a number of memorable scenes and
songs. It was also the first of two editions to play the Globe Theatre (now the
Lunt-Fontanne on 46th Street just west of Broadway), since *Sally* was still pack-
ing them in at the New Amsterdam, the *Follies'* customary home. The show got
off to an unexpected display of social consciousness with a scene celebrating
the arrival of immigrants from all over the world. More accustomed forms of
spectacle and spoofing then took over, with an array of chorus girls depicting
various types of roses; a takeoff on both the Barrymore clan and *Camille* with
Fanny Brice, W. C. Fields, and Raymond Hitchcock; and a W. C. Fields sketch
about the frustrations of subway travel. Two of the show's highlights involved
Miss Brice alone, first her comic lament "Second Hand Rose," then her masochistic wail, "My Man," which, though a French song, became a personal expression about the singer's recently convicted gangster husband.

Shuffle Along. Flournoy Miller and Aubrey Lyles. (White)

Music Box Revue (1921). Irving Berlin with "The Eight Little Notes," including Miriam Hopkins at the upper right. (White)

Music Box Revue (1924). Oscar Shaw and Grace Moore singing "All Alone." (White)

Music Box Revue (1924). Bobby Clark and Fanny Brice as Adam and Eve. (White)

MUSIC BOX REVUE

Music & lyrics: Irving Berlin
Sketches: Miscellaneous writers
Producer: Sam H. Harris
Directors: Hassard Short, William Collier
Choreographers: Bert French, I. Tarasoff
Cast: William Collier, Wilda Bennett, Paul Frawley, Sam Bernard, Ivy Sawyer, Joseph Santley, Florence Moore, Brox Sisters, Chester Hale, Irving Berlin, Miriam Hopkins
Songs: "In a Cozy Kitchenette Apartment"; "My Little Book of Poetry"; "Say It With Music"; "Everybody Step"; "The Schoolhouse Blues"; "They Call It Dancing"; "The Legend of the Pearls"
New York run: Music Box, September 22, 1921; 440 p.

The *Music Box Revues* were the only annual revue series to be created with the express purpose of providing a showcase for the songs of just one composer. The project stemmed from Irving Berlin's suggestion to producer Sam H. Harris that the Music Box would be an ideal name for a theatre designed specifically for musicals. Harris and Berlin built the theatre (located on 45th Street west of Broadway) and opened it with the appropriately titled *Music Box Revue*. The initial edition — there would be three more — was an elaborate and colorful show that greatly benefited from the ingenious staging of Hassard Short (whose credits would total 40 Broadway musicals) and a collection of appealing Berlin ballads (including "Say It With Music," sung by Wilda Bennett and Paul Frawley, which was used as a theme for the entire series). Among the visual pleasures were scenes showing chorus girls parading as a pageant of fans, displaying themselves as courses in a restaurant meal, and succumbing to the craze for syncopation in "Everybody Step." Berlin himself appeared in a scene with an octet dubbed "The Eight Little Notes" (the eighth was future film star Miriam Hopkins). As Alexander Woollcott wrote in *The Times*, the show's creators "crowded the stage with such a sumptuous and bespangled revue as cannot possibly earn them anything more substantial than the heart-warming satisfaction of having produced it at all."

None of the subsequent *Music Box Revues* ran as long as the first, yet all were well received. The 1922 edition featured the buffoonery of Bobby Clark and Paul McCullough and the antics of long-legged Charlotte Greenwood, as well as the singing of John Steel ("Lady of the Evening" was his most popular number) and Grace LaRue (who recalled the charms of "Crinoline Days"). The McCarthy Sisters were also on hand to stir things up with "Pack Up Your Sins and Go to the Devil" and "Bring on the Pepper." In 1923, Grace Moore sang "Tell Me a Bedtime Story," "The Waltz of Long Ago," "An Orange Grove in California," and — added during the run — "What'll I Do?" (the last two as duets with John Steel). It was also in this revue that Robert Benchley delivered his classic "Treasurer's Report." For the final edition, in 1924, John Murray Anderson took over as director, with Hassard Short replacing him at the *Greenwich Village Follies*. Clark and McCullough were back, with Clark doing an Adam and Eve sketch with Fanny Brice. On her own Miss Brice was an immigrant pleading "Don't Send Me Back to Petrograd" and a flat-footed gazelle proclaiming "I Want to Be a Ballet Dancer." Grace Moore returned to sing "Tell Her in the Springtime," "Rockabye Baby," and, in a duet with Oscar Shaw, the interpolated "All Alone."

Sam Harris, who produced 32 musicals on Broadway, was also associated with Irving Berlin on *The Cocoanuts, Face the Music,* and *As Thousands Cheer.* Ironically, because of its relatively small size, (1,010 seats), the Music Box is no longer considered economically feasible as a showplace for large-scale musical productions.

BLOSSOM TIME

Music: Sigmund Romberg, based on Franz Schubert
Lyrics & book: Dorothy Donnelly
Producers: Messrs. Shubert
Director: J. C. Huffman
Choreographer: F. M. Gillespie
Cast: Bertram Peacock, Olga Cook, Howard Marsh, Roy Cropper
Songs: "Serenade"; "Three Little Maids"; " Song of Love"; "Tell Me Daisy"
New York run: Ambassador Theatre, September 29, 1921; 516 p.

For the first Broadway musical with songs based on themes from classical compositions, Sigmund Romberg was assigned by the producing Shuberts to adapt melodies by the composing Schubert. The fanciful biographical libretto — a variation on a Viennese operetta, *Das Dreimaederlhaus* — deals with the composer's supposed unrequited love for one Mitzi Kranz. When, at Schubert's request, his friend Baron Schober sings the composer's "Song of Love" to Mitzi, she becomes enamored of the baron, and poor Schubert, no longer inspired, is unable to complete his "Unfinished Symphony." Four road companies of *Blossom Time* were sent out soon after the opening at the Ambassador Theatre (on 49th Street west of Broadway), and the operetta had five revivals in New York, the most recent in 1943.

Broadway has also offered musicals with scores derived from works by such composers as Offenbach in *The Love Song* (1925) and *The Happiest Girl in the World* (1961); Tschaikowsky in *Nadja* (1925) and *Music in My Heart* (1947); Chopin in *White Lilacs* (1928) and *Polonaise* (1945); Grieg in *Song of Norway* (1944); Fritz Kreisler in *Rhapsody* (1944); Villa Lobos in *Magdalena* (1948); Borodin in *Kismet* (1953); and Rachmaninoff in *Anya* (1965).
SO.

ZIEGFELD FOLLIES

Music: Louis A. Hirsch, David Stamper
Lyrics: Gene Buck
Sketches: Miscellaneous writers
Producer: Florenz Ziegfeld
Director: Ned Wayburn
Choreographers: Ned Wayburn, Michel Fokine
Cast: Will Rogers, Gilda Gray, Gallagher & Shean, Evelyn Law, Andrew Tombes, Florence O'Denishawn, Lulu McConnell, Mary Eaton, Nervo & Knox, Mary Lewis, Alexander Gray, Jack Whiting
Songs: "My Rambler Rose"; "Mr. Gallagher and Mr. Shean" (Ed Gallagher-Al Shean, Ernest Ball); " 'Neath the South Sea Moon"; "Oh! Gee, Oh! Gosh, Oh! Golly, I'm in Love" (Ole Olsen-Chic Johnson, Ernest Brewer)
New York run: New Amsterdam Theatre, June 5, 1922; 541 p.

Because of a Summer Edition that began June 25, 1923, and followed without a break, the 1922 *Follies* had the longest run of any revue in the series produced during Ziegfeld's lifetime. Now proclaiming itself "A National Institution Glorifying the American Girl," the 16th annual edition ended the eight-year period generally annointed The Great *Follies*. Humorist Will Rogers made his fourth *Follies* appearance in the show, and hits were also scored by shimmy dancer Gilda Gray and the team of Gallagher and Shean. Among the lavish scenes were "Lace Land," with girls parading in lace before lace costumes in front of lace draperies, and a dance featuring Greek statues coming to life in an art museum. Eddie Cantor, Ann Pennington, and Ilse Marvenga joined the Summer Edition cast.

GEORGE WHITE'S SCANDALS

Music: George Gershwin
Lyrics: B. G. DeSylva
Sketches: George White, Andy Rice
Producer-director-choreographer: George White
Cast: W. C. Fields, Winnie Lightner, Paul Whiteman Orchestra, Lester Allen, George White, Jack McGowan, Pearl Regay, Dolores Costello
Songs: "Cinderelatives"; "I Found a Four-Leaf Clover"; "I'll Build a Stairway to Paradise" (lyric: DeSylva, Ira Gershwin); "Argentina"; "Blue Monday Blues"
New York run: Globe Theatre, August 28, 1922; 88 p.

Of all the revues that enjoyed more than one annual edition, the *George White's Scandals* series was the nearest to the *Ziegfeld Follies* in fame and longevity. Beginning in 1919, George White, who had danced in two *Follies*, turned out 13 editions in 21 years. His series was faster paced, more youthful, less ornately mounted than their model, with a greater emphasis on dancing and new dance steps. They also differed from the *Follies* in having one songwriter or team of songwriters responsible for an entire score, e.g. George Gershwin who, with various lyricists, composed the music for five editions between 1920 and 1924. The 1922 *Scandals* introduced Gershwin's first Broadway hit, "I'll Build a Stairway to Paradise," performed as the first-act finale, and "Blue Monday," an "Opera ala Afro-American." Though it was not well received and was removed after opening night, the work was a forerunner of the composer's later full-length opera, *Porgy and Bess*. For subsequent editions of the *George White's Scandals* see pages 52 and 76.

POPPY

Music: Stephen Jones, Arthur Samuels
Lyrics: Dorothy Donnelly, etc.
Book: Dorothy Donnelly (Howard Dietz, W. C. Fields uncredited)
Producer: Philip Goodman
Director: Dorothy Donnelly
Choreographer: Julian Alfred
Cast: Madge Kennedy, W. C. Fields, Robert Woolsey, Alan Edwards, Luella Gear
Songs: "Two Make a Home"; "Alibi Baby" (music: Samuels; lyric: Howard Dietz); "On Our Honeymoon"; "What Do You Do Sunday, Mary?" (music: Jones; lyric: Irving Caesar)
New York run: Apollo Theatre, September 3, 1923; 346 p.

Poppy was a tour-de-force for W. C. Fields, though initially he received featured billing while Madge Kennedy, who played the eponymous heroine, was solo starred. Fields, however, won stardom when Miss Kennedy's understudy took over her role, and he was co-starred with Miss Kennedy for the tour. In the part of Professor Eustace McGargle, the bulbous-nosed comedian established the character of the bogusly elegant, ornately speaking conman by which he was identified in his later career. Set in 1874 in a Connecticut town, *Poppy* presented Fields as a carnival grifter, juggler, card shark, and shell-game artist who attempts to pass off his foster daughter, Poppy, as a long-lost heiress — only to discover that she really is an heiress. The Apollo Theatre, where *Poppy* was shown, still stands on 42nd Street west of Broadway. Fields appeared in two film versions of the musical: in 1925 (renamed *Sally of the Sawdust*), a silent directed by D. W. Griffith, and in 1936.

Poppy. W. C. Fields demonstrates his latest musical creation, the kadoola-kadoola. (White)

ANDRE CHARLOT'S REVUE OF 1924

Music, lyrics & sketches: Miscellaneous writers
Producer: Arch Selwyn
Director: Andre Charlot
Choreographer: David Bennett
Cast: Beatrice Lillie, Gertrude Lawrence, Jack Buchanan, Douglas Furber, Herbert Mundin, Jessie Matthews, Constance Carpenter
Songs: "Parisian Pierrot" (Noël Coward); "You Were Meant for Me" (Eubie Blake-Noble Sissle); "Limehouse Blues" (Philip Braham-Douglas Furber); "March With Me!" (Ivor Novello-Furber); "There's Life in the Old Girl Yet" (Coward)
New York run: Times Square Theatre, January 9, 1924; 298 p.

London impresario Andre Charlot entered New York's crowded revue field with a sly, sophisticated, witty, intimate show made up of songs, dances, and sketches from his West End revues. He also introduced New York audiences to three performers — Beatrice Lillie, Gertrude Lawrence, and Jack Buchanan — whose careers would flourish on both sides of the Atlantic. The show, which played the Times Square Theatre (now a movie house on 42nd Street west of Times Square), offered such highlights as Miss Lillie as a dignified but disoriented Britannia in "March With Me!," Miss Lawrence crooning "Parisian Pierrot" and "Limehouse Blues," and Jack Buchanan's version of the tired businessman trying to get some peace and quiet at home.

The success of his first endeavor on Broadway prompted Charlot to follow it up with *The Charlot Revue of 1926*, which opened November 10, 1925, at the Selwyn Theatre (right next to the Times Square). The triad of Lillie, Lawrence and Buchanan was again on hand, with Miss Lillie as Wanda Allova in a ballet takeoff, Lillie and Lawrence in a sketch as two precocious babies in their prams, Miss Lawrence singing Noël Coward's moralistic "Poor Little Rich Girl," and Lawrence and Buchanan in a duet of "A Cup of Coffee, a Sandwich and You." A third *Andre Charlot Revue* opened in January 1927 as featured attraction of the "International Edition" of the *Earl Carroll Vanities*. Jessie Matthews and Herbert Mundin headed the cast.

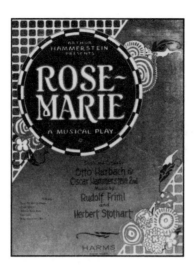

ROSE-MARIE

Music: Rudolf Friml*, Herbert Stothart#
Lyrics & book: Otto Harbach & Oscar Hammerstein II
Producer: Arthur Hammerstein
Director: Paul Dickey
Choreographer: David Bennett
Cast: Mary Ellis, Dennis King, William Kent, Dorothy Mackaye, Eduardo Ciannelli, Pearl Regay, Arthur Deagon
Songs: "Rose-Marie"*; "The Mounties"*#; "Indian Love Call"*; "Why Shouldn't We?"#; "Totem Tom-Tom"*#; "The Door of Her Dreams"*
New York run: Imperial Theatre, September 2, 1924; 557 p.

With such settings as Saskatchewan, the Kootenay Pass in the Canadian Rockies, and the Chateau Frontenac in Quebec, *Rose-Marie* offered audiences at the Imperial Theatre (on 44th Street west of Broadway) an entirely new locale for an opulent, romantic musical. It was, in fact, the idea of doing the first musical with a Canadian setting that prompted producer Arthur Hammerstein to send nephew Oscar Hammerstein II and his lyricist-librettist partner, Otto Harbach, to research a rumored annual ice carnival in Quebec that he felt would make a spectacular stage background. Though the writers were unable to locate the carnival, they did devise an original tale that would take advantage of Canadian locales: singer Rose-Marie La Flamme (Mary Ellis) and fur trapper Jim Kenyon (Dennis King) are in love, but a jealous suitor tries to pin a false murder rap on Jim. True to tradition, the Mounties get their man — who turns out to be a woman — and Rose-Marie and Jim go off into the sunset. The fact that the story deals with a murder was considered something of a novelty for a musical as was the conscientious effort, though it was not entirely successful, to integrate the musical pieces into the story (the program listed only the above five songs that "stand out independent of their dramatic association").

Rose-Marie was composer Rudolf Friml's biggest hit and the fourth longest running musical of the Twenties. In 1936, Jeanette MacDonald and Nelson Eddy were seen in a popular — though completely altered — screen version. The second one, with Howard Keel and Ann Blyth, came out in 1954. RCA SC/ TW.

LADY, BE GOOD!

Music: George Gershwin
Lyrics: Ira Gershwin
Book: Guy Bolton & Fred Thompson
Producers: Alex A. Aarons & Vinton Freedley
Director: Felix Edwardes
Choreographer: Sammy Lee
Cast: Fred & Adele Astaire, Walter Catlett, Cliff Edwards, Alan Edwards, Kathlene Martyn
Songs: "Hang on to Me"; "Fascinating Rhythm"; "So Am I"; "Oh, Lady Be Good!"; "The Half of It Dearie Blues"; "Little Jazz Bird"; "Swiss Miss" (lyric with Arthur Jackson)
New York run: Liberty Theatre, December 1, 1924; 330 p.

With their first of 14 Broadway musicals written as a team, George and Ira Gershwin established the jazzy, pulsating sound of the Broadway musicals of the Twenties. The show also made Fred and Adele Astaire Broadway's leading song-and-dance team. Originally titled *Black Eyed Susan*, *Lady, Be Good!* had a simple-minded story about Dick and Suzie Trevor, a carefree vaudeville team who are dispossessed but continue their dancing and singing at the homes of wealthy friends. Along the way Suzie poses as a Spanish heiress to collect a large inheritance but the ruse is found out. Somehow, she and Dick come into money anyway and somehow she saves Dick from a disastrous marriage. As Stark Young wrote in the *Times,* it is "a drama of outcasts, rents, social shining, loving resolutions, and well-ending marital fortunes." Though the score had enough hits — especially "Fascinating Rhythm" and "Oh, Lady Be Good!" — one eventual hit, "The Man I Love," was dropped from the show during the pre-Broadway tryout.

M-E OC; Smithsonian OC/ TW.

Lady, Be Good! Fred Astaire surrounded by a dozen ostrich-plumed lovelies. (White)

THE STUDENT PRINCE IN HEIDELBERG

Music: Sigmund Romberg
Lyrics & book: Dorothy Donnelly
Producers: Messrs. Shubert
Director: J. C. Huffman
Choreographer: Max Scheck
Cast: Howard Marsh, Ilse Marvenga, Greek Evans, George Hassell, Roberta Beatty
Songs: "Golden Days"; "To the Inn We're Marching"; "Come Boys, Let's All Be Gay, Boys" ("Students March Song"); "Drinking Song"; "Deep in My Heart, Dear"; "Serenade"; "Just We Two"
New York run: Jolson's 59th Street Theatre, December 2, 1924; 608 p.

Bucking the popularity of fast-moving, up-to-date musical comedy and the plotless revue, *The Student Prince in Heidelberg* (the complete title was used throughout the New York run) set the record as the longest running musical of the decade. That fact is all the more impressive since the theatre in which it played, on 59th Street and 7th Avenue, was some distance from the theatre district (the playhouse, later renamed the New Century, was demolished in 1962).

Based on *Old Heidelberg*, a popular turn-of-the-century play which had been adapted from the German *Alt Heidelberg*, the sentimental operetta is set in 1860 in the German university town where Prince Karl Franz (Howard Marsh) has gone with his tutor, Dr. Engel (Greek Evans), to complete his education. There he meets Kathie (Ilse Marvenga), a waitress at the Inn of the Three Golden Apples, and it isn't long before they are professing their love through the melting strains of, "Deep in my heart, dear, I have a dream of you. . ." The prince, however, is soon called away to assume the throne. Two years later, King Karl Franz returns to Heidelberg in a vain effort to recapture the golden days of his youth. *The Student Prince* toured the United States between 1925 and 1933, was revived on Broadway in 1931 and 1943, and joined the repertory of the New York City Opera in 1980. A silent film verson, with Ramon Novarro and Norma Shearer, was made in 1927; a Technicolor version, with Edmund Purdom (using Mario Lanza's singing voice) and Ann Blyth, was made in 1954. A previous Broadway musical, *The Prince of Pilsen* of 1903, also had a Heidelberg student prince as a leading romantic character.

M-E London OC (1926); Odyssey SC/ TW.

The Student Prince in Heidelberg. Howard Marsh and Ilse Marvenga. (White)

THE GARRICK GAIETIES

Music: Richard Rodgers
Lyrics: Lorenz Hart
Sketches: Miscellaneous writers
Producer: Theatre Guild
Director: Philip Loeb
Choreographer: Herbert Fields
Cast: Sterling Holloway, Romney Brent, Betty Starbuck, Libby Holman, June Cochrane, Edith Meiser, Philip Loeb, Sanford Meisner, Lee Strasberg
Songs: "April Fool"; "Manhattan"; "Do You Love Me?"; "Sentimental Me"; "On with the Dance", "Old Fashioned Girl" (lyric: Edith Meiser)
New York run: Garrick Theatre, June 8, 1925; 211 p.

The Garrick Gaieties was an impudent, high-spirited modestly mounted revue created by and featuring young members of the Theatre Guild company to help raise money for tapestries at the Guild's new Guild Theatre on West 52nd Street. The entertainment, however, served equally as a showcase for the talents of the songwriting team of Richard Rodgers and Lorenz Hart, whose score included their first hit, "Manhattan." This was not their first professional show — that was *Poor Little Ritz Girl* in 1919 — but it did provide the stimulus for a partnership that lasted through 26 Broadway musicals until 1943.

Though originally scheduled for only two performances at the Garrick Theatre (then on 35th Street east of Broadway), the revue caught on and had a successful commercial run. Besides the songs, highlights were satirical jibes at the theatre in general and the Theatre Guild in particular whose usually pretentious offerings provided ready targets. A second edition of the *Gaieties* opened the following year with almost the same cast, and a Rodgers and Hart score that included "Mountain Greenery" and an operetta burlesque called "The Rose of Arizona." A third edition, in 1930, was shown at the Guild Theatre (currently named the Virginia). The cast included Sterling Holloway, Edith Meiser, and Philip Loeb, plus newcomers Imogene Coca and Ray Heatherton. A brief return engagement the same year gave Rosalind Russell her first Broadway assignment.

NO, NO, NANETTE

Music: Vincent Youmans
Lyrics: Irving Caesar
Book: Otto Harbach & Frank Mandel
Producer-director: H. H. Frazee
Choreographer: Sammy Lee
Cast: Louise Groody, Charles Winninger, Josephine Whittell, Wellington Cross, Eleanor Dawn, Georgia O'Ramey, Mary Lawlor, John Barker
Songs: "Call of the Sea"; "Too Many Rings Around Rosie"; "I Want to Be Happy"; "No, No, Nanette" (lyric: Otto Harbach); "Tea for Two"; " 'Where Has My Hubby Gone?' Blues"; "You Can Dance With Any Girl at All"
New York run: Globe Theatre, September 16, 1925; 321 p.

Thanks to its worldwide reception, *No, No, Nanette* was probably the most popular musical of the Twenties. It was also the quintessential example of the kind of song-and-dance show of that period that was affectionately satirized in Sandy Wilson's spoof, *The Boy Friend*. In the story, based on a 1919 play, *My Lady Friends*, Jimmy Smith (Charles Winninger), a married bible publisher and guardian of the play's doubly admonished heroine (Louise Groody), has been giving financial support to three comely young ladies living in three different cities. When the Smiths and their friends, including Lucille and Billy Early (Josephine Whittell and Wellington Cross) — plus the three recipients of Jimmy's largesse and a sassy housemaid named Pauline (Georgia O'Ramey) — all turn up at the Smiths' Chickadee Cottage in Atlantic City, no end of comical embarrassments ensue.

The musical's initial production underwent a difficult break-in period on the road. When it first opened in Detroit in April 1924, the reviews were encouraging but the attendance wasn't. Producer H.H. Frazee then took drastic steps. He ordered composer Vincent Youmans and lyricist Irving Caesar (who had replaced Otto Harbach for most of the songs) to come up with two hits — and they obliged with "Tea for Two" and "I Want to Be Happy." He also took over the direction himself and replaced most of the principals in the cast. The result was that the show clicked so well in Chicago that it remained for a year. By the time *No, No, Nanette* arrived in New York a second road company had been touring since January 1925 (with Cleo Mayfield, Cecil Lean, Donald Brian, and Ona Munson), and a London facsimile had been running for six months. Three years later, an affirmative successor yclept *Yes, Yes, Yvette*, did not fare so well, despite the contributions by *Nanette* veterans H.H. Frazee, Irving Caesar, Charles Winninger, and choreographer Sammy Lee.

In 1971, a new production of *No, No, Nanette* opened in New York after experiencing an equally difficult tryout tour (see page 231). Harry Rigby, who conceived the idea of the revival, was bought out by his co-producer Cyma Rubin, Burt Shevelove replaced Busby Berkeley as director, and Jack Gilford and Susan Watson took over the roles of Jimmy and Nanette. Once more, however, the production was whipped into proper shape, and — helped by a sudden nostalgia craze — it went on to a lengthy and profitable run. One of the major attractions of this version was the appearance of Ruby Keeler, who returned to Broadway after an absence of over 41 years to play the part of Sue Smith, Jimmy's wife. During the New York engagement, leading roles were assumed by Penny Singleton (Sue), Benny Baker (Jimmy), and Martha Raye (Pauline). The first road company was headed by June Allyson, Dennis Day, and Judy Canova; the second by Evelyn Keyes, Don Ameche, and Ruth Donnelly.

Movie versions of *No, No, Nanette* were made in 1930 and 1940. Bernice Claire and Alexander Grey were in the first, Anna Neagle and Victor Mature were in the second.

Stanyan London OC (1925); Columbia OC (1971)/ TW.

DEAREST ENEMY

Music: Richard Rodgers
Lyrics: Lorenz Hart
Book: Herbert Fields
Producer: George Ford
Directors: John Murray Anderson, Charles Sinclair, Harry Ford
Choreographer: Carl Hemmer
Cast: Helen Ford, Charles Purcell, Flavia Arcaro, Detmar Poppen
Songs: "Here in My Arms"; "I Beg Your Pardon"; "Cheerio"; "I'd Like To Hide It";
     "Bye and Bye"; "Sweet Peter"; "Old Enough to Love"; "Here's a Kiss"
New York run: Knickerbocker Theatre, September 18, 1925; 286 p.

Dearest Enemy, the first of eight book musicals written together by songwriters Rodgers and Hart and librettist Herbert Fields, found the trio going back to the unlikely subject of the American Revolution for inspiration. Set in 1776 in the mansion of Mrs. Robert Murray — of the Murray Hill Murrays — the saga tells how the wily patriot and her lady friends manage to divert Gen. Howe's British troops long enough for Gen. Putnam's men to link up with the forces under the command of Gen. Washington. The attraction between Irish-American lass Betsy Burke (Helen Ford) and British Captain Sir John Copeland (Charles Purcell) provides a romantic alliance — cemented by their duet, "Here in My Arms" — that is resumed after the war.

The only previous Broadway musical dealing with the American Revolution was *A Daughter of the Revolution* in 1895. Later works concerned with the conflict were *Virginia* (1937), *Arms and the Girl* (1950), *Ben Franklin in Paris* (1964), and the most successful of all, *1776* (1969).
R&H.

THE VAGABOND KING

Music: Rudolf Friml
Lyrics: Brian Hooker
Book: Brian Hooker, Russell Janney, W. H. Post
Producer: Russell Janney
Director: Max Figman
Choreographer: Julian Alfred
Cast: Dennis King, Carolyn Thomson, Max Figman, Herbert Corthell
Songs: "Song of the Vagabonds"; "Some Day"; "Only a Rose"; "Huguette
     Waltz"; "Love Me Tonight"; "Love for Sale"; "Nocturne"
New York run: Casino Theatre, September 21, 1925; 511 p.

Originally, producer Russell Janney planned this operetta to have a score by the youthful team of Richard Rodgers and Lorenz Hart who had already transformed the venerable novel and play, *If I Were King*, into an amateur musical. When he was unable to get financial backing, however, Janney turned to the more experienced team of Rudolf Friml and Brian Hooker. *The Vagabond King* is concerned with the amours and adventures of the 15th Century outlaw Francois Villon (Dennis King) during the reign of King Louis XI. In this attractively mounted, picaresque tale, the poet-vagabond is appointed King of France for a day (it was a week in the original story) in order to save both his neck and Paris by leading his rabble of low degree against the Duke of Burgundy's forces. As a fitting capper to his successful endeavors, Villon even wins the hand of the aristocratic Katherine de Vaucelles (Carolyn Thomson). There were two screen versions: King and Jeanette MacDonald were co-starred in 1930; Oreste and Kathryn Grayson in 1956.
RCA SC/ Samuel French (1929)*/ SF.

Dearest Enemy. Discovered swimming in the nude, Helen Ford keeps Charles Purcell at bay with an umbrella as he tries to return her shoe. (White)

The Vagabond King. Dennis King leads his followers in the "Song of the Vagabonds." (White)

Sunny. Esther Howard, Joseph Cawthorn, Dorothy Francis, Clifton Webb, Marilyn Miller, Paul Frawley, Mary Hay, and Jack Donahue. (White)

SUNNY

Music: Jerome Kern
Lyrics & book: Otto Harbach & Oscar Hammerstein II
Producer: Charles Dillingham
Director: Hassard Short
Choreographers: Julian Mitchell, David Bennett, Alexis Kosloff, John Tiller, Fred Astaire
Cast: Marilyn Miller, Jack Donahue, Clifton Webb, Mary Hay, Joseph Cawthorn, Paul Frawley, Cliff Edwards, Pert Kelton, Moss & Fontana, Esther Howard, Dorothy Francis, George Olsen Orchestra
Songs: "Sunny"; "Who?"; "Let's Say Good Night Till It's Morning"; "D'Ye Love Me?"; "Two Little Bluebirds"; "I Might Grow Fond of You"
New York run: New Amsterdam Theatre, September 22, 1925; 517 p.

In another variation on the Cinderella story, *Sunny* tells the saga of Sunny Peters (Marilyn Miller), a spirited bareback rider appearing with a circus in Southampton, England, whose heart has been stolen away by Tom Warren (Paul Frawley), an American tourist. In pursuit of this glittering prize, Sunny stows aboard the ocean liner taking him back to the United States. In order to be allowed to land, Sunny weds Tom's friend, Jim Deming (Jack Donahue), but once the agreed-to divorce has been granted Sunny and Tom are happily reunited at a fashionable Southern resort. (In the London version, in which Jim was played by popular star Jack Buchanan, Sunny decided that he was really the man for her. This denouement has also been used in American revivals.)

Sunny was the alliterative successor to *Sally*, a musical that also had Marilyn Miller singing and dancing to Jerome Kern melodies. Here, however, the composer was collaborating for the first time with Otto Harbach and Oscar Hammerstein II. Miss Miller repeated her role in the first movie version in 1930; Anna Neagle followed 10 years later.

Stanyan London OC (1926)/ Chappell, London (1926)*/ TW.

The Cocoanuts. Groucho Marx auctioning off Florida land assisted by brothers Chico, Zeppo, and Harpo. (White)

THE COCOANUTS

Music & lyrics: Irving Berlin
Book: George S. Kaufman (Morrie Ryskind uncredited)
Producer: Sam H. Harris
Director: Oscar Eagle
Choreographer: Sammy Lee
Cast: The Marx Brothers, Margaret Dumont, John Barker, Mabel Withee, Frances Williams, Brox Sisters, Basil Ruysdael, George Hale
Songs: "Lucky Boy"; "Why Am I a Hit With the Ladies?"; "A Little Bungalow"; "Florida by the Sea"; "The Monkey Doodle-Doo"
New York run: Lyric Theatre, December 8, 1925; 276 p.

The Cocoanuts was the second of three musicals that the Marx Brothers starred in on Broadway, the others being *I'll Say She Is* and *Animal Crackers*. As might be expected, it offered a gag-filled, loosely constructed spree in which the madcap team was allowed enough room to improvise and add new routines, such as the now classic Groucho-Chico exchange based on the misunderstanding of the word "viaduct" for "Why a duck?" The story is set in Cocoanut Beach, Florida, where Groucho, as Henry W. Schlemmer, runs a hotel and is also a shady real-estate developer trying to cash in on the Florida land boom. Complications arise when jewel thieves posing as hotel guests steal the gems from rich dowager Margaret Dumont, and try to pin the blame on the fiancé of the dowager's daughter. Adding to the mayhem were Chico and Harpo, as hotel guests and Zeppo as a desk clerk. The 1929 screen version of *The Cocoanuts* was the Marx Brothers' first feature-length movie.

The Marx Brothers were leading characters in two later Broadway musicals: the biographical *Minnie's Boys* (1970) and the second half of the "Musical Double Feature," *A Day in Hollywood/A Night in the Ukraine* (1980).
St. Martin's Press (1979).

TIP-TOES

Music: George Gershwin
Lyrics: Ira Gershwin
Book: Guy Bolton & Fred Thompson
Producers: Alex A. Aarons & Vinton Freedley
Director: John Harwood
Choreographer: Sammy Lee
Cast: Queenie Smith, Allen Kearns, Andrew Tombes, Harry Watson Jr., Jeanette MacDonald, Robert Halliday, Gertrude McDonald
Songs: "Looking for a Boy"; "When Do We Dance?"; "These Charming People"; "That Certain Feeling"; "Sweet and Low-Down"; "Nice Baby"; "Nightie Night"
New York run: Liberty Theatre, December 28, 1925; 194 p.

Tip-Toes was something of a creative successor to *Lady, Be Good!*, since it shared the same songwriting team (whose new hit was "That Certain Feeling"), librettists, producers, and choreographer, and it even played the same theatre. There was also a thematic similarity in that the new story was again concerned with down-on-their-luck vaudevillians who become involved with high society. Tip-Toes Kaye (Queenie Smith) and her uncles Al and Harry (Andrew Tombes and Harry Watson Jr.) are stranded in Palm Beach where the uncles try to pass off Tip-Toes as a blueblood to win a rich husband. She falls for glue king Steve Burton (Allen Kearns) and sticks with him even after — as a test, of course — he admits to being penniless. A 1928 screen variation, made in England, featured Dorothy Gish and Will Rogers.
M-E London OC (1926)/ TW.

GEORGE WHITE'S SCANDALS

Music: Ray Henderson
Lyrics: B. G. DeSylva & Lew Brown
Sketches: George White, William K. Wells
Producer-director-choreographer: George White
Cast: Willie & Eugene Howard, Frances Williams, Harry Richman, Tom Patricola, Ann Pennington, McCarthy Sisters, Fairbanks Twins, Buster West, Portland Hoffa
Songs: "Lucky Day"; "Black Bottom"; "Birth of the Blues"; "St. Louis Blues" (W.C. Handy); "Rhapsody in Blue" (music: George Gershwin); "The Girl Is You and the Boy Is Me"
New York run: Apollo Theatre, June 14, 1926; 424 p.

Possibly the foremost edition in the series, the 1926 *Scandals* — the eighth of that title — had by far the longest run. Its attributes included a strong score by DeSylva, Brown and Henderson (the second *Scandals* for the trio), plus a sure-fire combination of mirth (mostly resting on the capable if stooped shoulders of Willie Howard) and production numbers (George White's new dance sensation was the successor to the "Charleston" called the "Black Bottom"). The first-act finale offered a musical debate between the blues and the classics, with such examples of the former as "Birth of the Blues" (sung by Harry Richman), "St. Louis Blues," and the "Rhapsody in Blue" (with lyrics!). The producer was so confident of the show's success that he charged $55.00 per ticket for the first eight rows on opening night (the top price reverted to $5.50 after that).

COUNTESS MARITZA

Music: Emmerich Kalman
Lyrics & book: Harry B. Smith
Producer: Messrs. Shubert
Director: J. C. Huffman
Choreographers: Carl Randall, Jack Mason
Cast: Yvonne D'Arle, Walter Woolf, Odette Myrtil, Carl Randall, Harry K. Morton, Vivian Hart, George Hassell
Songs: "Play, Gypsies — Dance, Gypsies"; "I'll Keep on Dreaming"; "The One I'm Looking For"; "The Call of Love"
New York run: Shubert Theatre, September 18, 1926; 321 p.

One of the few transplanted mid-Twenties operettas to retain its original European score, *Countess Maritza* was the last successful show written by Harry B. Smith. It was also his 115th Broadway production! Originally presented as *Grafin Mariza* two and a half years earlier in Vienna, the work has a certain kinship with *The Merry Widow* in that it offers a heroine constantly on her guard against fortune hunters and a hero who is afraid of being considered one. Set in Hungary, the plot finds the impecunious Count Tassilo (Walter Woolf) working under an assumed name as the overseer on the estate of his beloved countess (Yvonne D'Arle), and leading the merry peasants in the stirring strains of "Play, Gypsies — Dance, Gypsies." After he is dismissed when Maritza erroneously pegs him for a gold digger, the countess — too proud to admit her mistake verbally — proposes to Tassilo via a letter.

OH, KAY!

Music: George Gershwin
Lyrics: Ira Gershwin
Book: Guy Bolton & P. G. Wodehouse
Producers: Alex A. Aarons & Vinton Freedley
Director: John Harwood
Choreographer: Sammy Lee
Cast: Gertrude Lawrence, Oscar Shaw, Victor Moore, Harland Dixon, Fairbanks Twins, Gerald Oliver Smith, Betty Compton, Constance Carpenter
Songs: "Dear Little Girl"; "Maybe"; "Clap Yo' Hands"; "Do Do Do"; "Someone to Watch Over Me"; "Fidgety Feet"; "Heaven on Earth" (lyric with Howard Dietz); "Oh, Kay!" (lyric with Dietz)
New York run: Imperial Theatre, November 8, 1926; 256 p.

Following her Broadway appearances in the *Charlot Revues*, Gertrude Lawrence was besieged with offers to star in an American musical comedy. By accepting the leading role in *Oh, Kay!*, Miss Lawrence became the first British actress to originate a part on Broadway before repeating it in London. The production reunited the Princess Theatre librettists, Guy Bolton and P.G. Wodehouse, whose book for *Oh, Kay!* retained something of the Anglo-American flavor of their previous *Oh, Boy!* and *Oh, Lady! Lady!!* The action takes place at the home of Jimmy Winter (Oscar Shaw) in the imaginary town of Beachampton, Long Island. Jimmy is about to wed when he discovers that he has fallen in love with Kay Denham, who is posing as a cook in his house to be near the hooch that her brother, a titled English bootlegger, has stashed in Jimmy's cellar. Though Kay and Jimmy make their feelings clear in the duet "Maybe," and Kay plaintively pleads for someone to watch over her, the couple must survive obstacles, both legal and matrimonial, before settling down to a life of musical-comedy bliss. A revival of *Oh, Kay!*, somewhat revised, was produced Off Broadway in 1960. Smithsonian part OC; Columbia SC; DRG OC (1960)/ TW.

THE DESERT SONG

Music: Sigmund Romberg
Lyrics: Otto Harbach & Oscar Hammerstein II
Book: Otto Harbach, Oscar Hammerstein II & Frank Mandel
Producers: Laurence Schwab & Frank Mandel
Director: Arthur Hurley
Choreographer: Bobby Connolly
Cast: Vivienne Segal, Robert Halliday, Eddie Buzzell, Pearl Regay, William O'Neal
Songs: "The Riff Song"; "Romance"; "French Military Marching Song"; "I Want a Kiss"; " 'It' "; "The Desert Song"; "Let Love Go"; "One Flower Grows Alone in Your Garden"; "One Alone"
New York run: Casino Theatre, November 30, 1926; 471 p.

Possibly the decade's most enduring operetta, *The Desert Song* marked Sigmund Romberg's first association with librettists-lyricists Otto Harbach and Oscar Hammerstein II (Romberg and Hammerstein would do four other musicals together). Though a swashbuckling romance created along familiar lines, the work was equally inspired by such recent events as the Riff uprising in French Morocco, the accomplishments of Lawrence of Arabia, and the sizzling Rudolph Valentino films *The Sheik* and *The Son of the Sheik.* The operetta is primarily concerned with Margot Bonvalet (Vivienne Segal), a French woman who is abducted into the Sahara — to the emotional strains of "The Desert Song" — by the mysterious Red Shadow (Robert Halliday), the masked leader of the rebellious Riffs. To the surprise of all, he turns out to be Pierre Birabeau, the simpering son of the Governor of Morocco (thus providing a variation on the *Naughty Marietta* story). During the out-of-town tryout, when the show was called *Lady Fair,* Miss Segal was rushed in to replace another actress in the leading female role. *The Desert Song* had an unsuccessful New York revival in 1973. Film versions were released in 1929, 1943, and 1953.
M-E London OC (1927); Columbia SC/ SF.

PEGGY-ANN

Music: Richard Rodgers
Lyrics: Lorenz Hart
Book: Herbert Fields
Producers: Lew Fields & Lyle D. Andrews
Director: Robert Milton
Choreographer: Seymour Felix
Cast: Helen Ford, Lester Cole, Lulu McConnell, Betty Starbuck, Edith Meiser
Songs: "A Tree in the Park"; "A Little Birdie Told Me So"; "Where's That Rainbow?"; "Maybe It's Me"
New York run: Vanderbilt Theatre, December 27, 1926; 333 p.

A daring work for its day, *Peggy-Ann* was loosely adapted from a 1910 Marie Dressler vehicle, *Tillie's Nightmare.* Most of the show was set in a Freudian dreamworld in which Peggy-Ann of Glens Falls, New York, travels to New York City's Fifth Avenue, takes a trip on a yacht, gets married in her step-ins, is thrown overboard by a mutinous crew, and attends the horse races in Havana. At the end, she awakes happily in the arms of her Glens Falls boyfriend. Among the staging innovations: no songs were sung within the first fifteen minutes, the scenery and costumes were changed in full view of the audience, and the first and last scenes were played in almost total darkness. The show was the fourth of five Rodgers and Hart musicals that were presented on Broadway during 1926; the fifth, *Betsy,* opened just one night after *Peggy-Ann.*

RIO RITA

Music: Harry Tierney
Lyrics: Joseph McCarthy
Book: Guy Bolton & Fred Thompson
Producer: Florenz Ziegfeld
Director: John Harwood
Choreographers: Sammy Lee, Albertina Rasch
Cast: Ethelind Terry, J. Harold Murray, Bert Wheeler, Robert Woolsey, Ada May, Vincent Serrano
Songs: "Rio Rita"; "The Rangers' Song"; "The Kinkajou"; "If You're in Love You'll Waltz"; "Following the Sun Around"
New York run: Ziegfeld Theatre, February 2, 1927; 494 p.

Rio Rita was Florenz Ziegfeld's premiere attraction at his Ziegfeld Theatre, then located on the northwest corner of 6th Avenue and 54th Street. In the spectacular production, Capt. James Stewart (J. Harold Murray) leads his Texas Rangers in the stirring "Rangers' Song" as they chase a bank robber known as the Kinkajou. The pursuit takes Capt. Jim across the Rio Grande into the town of Santa Luca where he falls in love with tempestuous Rita Ferguson (Ethelind Terry), whose name is fluvially linked only in the show's title and in song. Their romance hits a snag when Capt. Jim suspects Rita's brother to be the Kinkajou, but he eventually turns out to be a Mexican general (Vincent Serrano) who also has eyes for Rita. (This was still another variation on the outlaw-in-disguise theme of such previous offerings as *Naughty Marietta* and *The Desert Song*.) The 1929 film version, with Bebe Daniels and John Boles, was the first successful screen adaptation of a Broadway musical.
M-E London OC/ TW.

Rio Rita. Ethelind Terry, Vincent Serrano, and J. Harold Murray. (White)

HIT THE DECK!

Music: Vincent Youmans
Lyrics: Clifford Grey & Leo Robin
Book: Herbert Fields
Producers: Lew Fields & Vincent Youmans
Director: Alexander Leftwich
Choreographer: Seymour Felix
Cast: Louise Groody, Charles King, Stella Mayhew, Madeline Cameron, Brian Donlevy, Jack McCauley
Songs: "Join the Navy"; "Harbor of My Heart"; "Lucky Bird"; "Looloo"; "Why, Oh Why?"; "Sometimes I'm Happy" (lyric: Irving Caesar); "Hallelujah"
New York run: Belasco Theatre, April 25, 1927; 352 p.

Vincent Youmans' *Hit the Deck!* was second only to *No, No, Nanette* as the most popular of the composer's 12 Broadway musicals. Based on the 1922 play *Shore Leave*, the show was about a Newport, Rhode Island, coffee-shop owner known as Looloo (Louise Groody, the previous Nanette), who is so totally smitten with sailor Bilge Smith (Charles King) that she follows him all the way to China and even spends her inheritance to salvage a scow for him after his Navy hitch is over. The production, one of the few musicals to play the Belasco Theatre (on 44th Street east of Broadway), introduced audiences to two enduring songs: "Sometimes I'm Happy" and "Hallelujah." The second of three movie versions, retitled *Follow the Fleet*, and released in 1936, featured Fred Astaire and Ginger Rogers and new songs by Irving Berlin.
TW.

GOOD NEWS!

Music: Ray Henderson
Lyrics: B. G. DeSylva & Lew Brown
Book: Laurence Schwab & B. G. DeSylva
Producers: Laurence Schwab & Frank Mandel
Director: Edgar MacGregor
Choreographer: Bobby Connolly
Cast: Mary Lawlor, John Price Jones, Gus Shy, Inez Courtney, Zelma O'Neal, George Olsen Orchestra
Songs: "Just Imagine"; "He's a Ladies Man"; "The Best Things in Life Are Free"; "The Varsity Drag"; "Lucky in Love"; "Good News"
New York run: 46th Street Theatre, September 6, 1927; 551 p.

The fifth longest running musical of the Twenties, *Good News!* was the first of a quartet of breezy, youthful DeSylva, Brown and Henderson musical comedies that capitalized on popular sports, fads, occupations, and innovations. (The others: *Hold Everything!, Flying High,* and *Follow Thru.*) In this caper about America's flaming youth, the setting is Tait College, where students spend their time dancing "The Varsity Drag," where the burning issue is whether football hero Tom Marlowe will be allowed to lead the team despite his failing grade in astronomy, and where hero can console heroine Connie Laine by assuring her "The Best Things in Life Are Free." Helping to establish the collegiate atmosphere of the entertainment were the members of George Olsen's Orchestra who, before playing the overture, marched down the theatre aisles sporting diamond-pattern sweaters and barking football cheers. In the fall of 1974, Alice Faye and Gene Nelson opened on Broadway in a revival that lasted two weeks. June Allyson and Peter Lawford were in the 1947 screen version.
Samuel French (1932)*/ SF.

Hit the Deck! Charles King and Louise Groody. (White)

A CONNECTICUT YANKEE

Music: Richard Rodgers
Lyrics: Lorenz Hart
Book: Herbert Fields
Producers: Lew Fields & Lyle D. Andrews
Director: Alexander Leftwich
Choreographer: Busby Berkeley
Cast: William Gaxton, Constance Carpenter, Nana Bryant, June Cochrane, William Norris, Jack Thompson
Songs: "My Heart Stood Still"; "Thou Swell"; "I Feel at Home With You"; "On a Desert Island With Thee"
New York run: Vanderbilt Theatre, November 3, 1927; 418 p.

Long before winning notice with their songs for *The Garrick Gaieties*, Rodgers and Hart — along with librettist Herbert Fields — had tried unsuccessfully to interest producers in their version of Mark Twain's *A Connecticut Yankee in King Arthur's Court*. By 1927, however, they had little trouble getting Lew Fields to present it at the Vanderbilt Theatre following the run of the trio's first dream fantasy, *Peggy-Ann*, and it became their biggest hit of the 1920s.

The curtain rises on a hotel room in modern-day Hartford, where Martin (William Gaxton), about to be married, gets bopped on the head by his intended spouse. He dreams of being a stranger at the court of King Arthur, where he sings "Thou Swell" and "My Heart Stood Still" with Dame Alisande (Constance Carpenter), and becomes a confidant of the king by industrializing the realm. Upon awakening Martin realizes that he is marrying the wrong girl and turns to Alisande's modern-day double, Alice Carter. (A more serious approach to the Arthurian legend was Lerner and Loewe's *Camelot* in 1960.)

A Connecticut Yankee was revived in 1943 with Dick Foran, Vivienne Segal, Julie Warren, and Vera Ellen. Five of the original songs were retained and six new ones were added, including Miss Segal's showstopper, "To Keep My Love Alive." For the present-day scenes all the characters appeared in military uniforms. This production, which ran 135 performances, opened just five days before Lorenz Hart's death.
AEI OC (1943)/ TW.

A Connecticut Yankee. Yankee William Gaxton is frightened by one of King Arthur's knights.

FUNNY FACE

Music: George Gershwin
Lyrics: Ira Gershwin
Book: Paul Gerard Smith & Fred Thompson
Producers: Alex A. Aarons & Vinton Freedley
Director: Edgar MacGregor
Choreographer: Bobby Connolly
Cast: Fred & Adele Astaire, Victor Moore, William Kent, Allen Kearns, Betty Compton, Dorothy Jordan
Songs: "Funny Face"; "High Hat"; "He Loves and She Loves"; " 'S Wonderful"; "Let's Kiss and Make Up"; "My One and Only"; "The Babbitt and the Bromide"
New York run: Alvin Theatre, November 22, 1927; 244 p.

The second musical the Gershwin brothers wrote for Fred and Adele Astaire, *Funny Face* was another popular lighter-than-air concoction that —like *Lady, Be Good!*—gave the dancing siblings plenty of room for their specialties. In the plot, Frankie Wynne (Adele), the ward of Jimmie Reeve (Fred), persuades aviator Peter Thurston (Allen Kearns), to steal her incriminating diary from Jimmie's wall safe. By mistake, Peter steals a bracelet, which sets off a mad chase that takes the dramatis personae — including two comic burglars — to Lake Wapatog, New Jersey, then on to the Paymore Hotel and the Two-Million Dollar Pier in Atlantic City.

When tried out under the title of *Smarty,* with Robert Benchley as coauthor, the musical was greeted with such disfavor that drastic alterations were quickly made. The name was changed, Benchley was replaced by librettist Paul Gerard Smith, Victor Moore was added as one of the burglars, Allen Kearns took over the male romantic lead, and seven songs were dropped in favor of five new ones (including "He Loves and She Loves," which replaced "How Long Has This Been Going On?"). *Funny Face* became both a hit and the first attraction at the newly built Alvin Theatre (named for the show's producers), which, renamed the Neil Simon, is on 52nd Street west of Broadway.

In 1983, six songs from *Funny Face* were used in the score of *My One and Only,* which had a different book. The 1957 film, *Funny Face,* starring Fred Astaire and Audrey Hepburn, kept four of the original songs but also changed the story.

M-E OC; Smithsonian OC.

Funny Face. Fred Astaire leading the boys in the "High Hat" number. (White)

SHOW BOAT

Music: Jerome Kern
Lyrics & book: Oscar Hammerstein II
Producer: Florenz Ziegfeld
Director: Zeke Colvan (Oscar Hammerstein II uncredited)
Choreographer: Sammy Lee
Cast: Charles Winninger, Norma Terris, Howard Marsh, Helen Morgan, Jules Bledsoe, Edna May Oliver, Eva Puck, Sammy White, Tess Gardella, Charles Ellis, Francis X. Mahoney
Songs: "Make Believe"; "Ol' Man River"; "Can't Help Lovin' Dat Man"; "Life Upon the Wicked Stage"; "You Are Love"; "Why Do I Love You?"; "Bill" (lyric with P.G. Wodehouse); "After the Ball" (Charles K. Harris)
New York run: Ziegfeld Theatre, December 27,1927; 572 p.

Both Jerome Kern and Oscar Hammerstein II had felt for some time that the Broadway musical theatre was suffering from too much sameness and tameness. After reading Edna Ferber's sprawling novel of life on the Mississippi, they became convinced that it was the story best suited to help them make the kinds of changes they felt were needed. Their efforts resulted in a recognized landmark in the history of the theatre, one that broke ground in steering a course away from lightweight musical comedy and overweight operetta. Their characters were more three-dimensional, the music was more skillfully integrated into the libretto, and their plot dared to deal with such unaccustomed subjects as unhappy marriages, miscegenation, and the hard life of black stevedores (as expressed through "Ol' Man River").

The saga covers the period from the mid 1880s to the then current 1927, and is primarily concerned with the fortunes of impressionable Magnolia Hawks (Norma Terris)—whose father Cap'n Andy Hawks (Charles Winninger) runs the show boat *Cotton Blossom*—and ne'er-do-well riverboat gambler Gaylord Ravenal (Howard Marsh). Meeting on the Natchez levee, the couple fall in love at first sight (singing "Make Believe"), then become actors on the showboat, marry, and move to Chicago (revealing their devotion in "Why Do I Love You?"). After they separate when Ravenal loses his money gambling, Magnolia has a tearful meeting with her father while singing at the Trocadero on New Year's Eve. She goes on to become a musical-comedy star, as does her daughter Kim, and years later she and Ravenal are reunited aboard the *Cotton Blossom*. A secondary plot involves Magnolia's mulatto friend, the tragic Julie La Verne (Helen Morgan), and her devotion to *her* man, Steve Baker (though the song she sings about him is called "Bill").

In 1932, Ziegfeld brought the musical back with basically the original cast, except that Howard Marsh was succeeded by Dennis King and Jules Bledsoe by Paul Robeson (for whom the part of the stevedore Joe had originally been intended). The 1946 *Show Boat* was a successful revival, running 418 performances. Twenty years later, the musical was remounted by the Music Theatre of Lincoln Center, with Barbara Cook, Stephen Douglass, David Wayne, Constance Towers, and William Warfield. The fourth Broadway revival, in 1983, was by the Houston Grand Opera. The lavish 1994 Hal Prince production is the most successful *Show Boat* so far.

Three movie versions were filmed: a part-talkie in 1929 with Laura LaPlante and Joseph Schildkraut; the 1936 reproduction with Irene Dunne, Allan Jones, Helen Morgan, Charles Winninger, and Paul Robeson; and the 1951 reconstruction with Kathryn Grayson, Howard Keel, Ava Gardner, Joe E. Brown, and William Warfield.

CSP part OC (1932); Columbia OC (1946); RCA OC (1966); EMI SC/ Chappell, London (1934), *RCA (1994, Toronto), Capitol (1994, Broadway)/ R&H.

Show Boat. A dramatic scene with Helen Morgan surrounded by Francis X. Mahoney, Charles Ellis, Eva Puck, Norma Terris, Charles Winninger, and Edna May Oliver. (White)

Show Boat. Edna May Oliver (right) is unable to stop the wedding of Howard Marsh and Norma Terris. Others in foreground are Charles Winninger, Sammy White, and Eva Puck. (White)

Rosalie. Marilyn Miller and ladies of the ensemble. (White)

ROSALIE

Music: George Gershwin, Sigmund Romberg
Lyrics: Ira Gershwin, P. G. Wodehouse
Book: William Anthony McGuire & Guy Bolton
Producer: Florenz Ziegfeld
Director: William Anthony McGuire
Choreographers: Seymour Felix, Michel Fokine
Cast: Marilyn Miller, Jack Donahue, Frank Morgan, Margaret Dale, Bobbe Arnst, Oliver McLennan
Songs: "Say So!" (music: Gershwin); "West Point Song" (Romberg - Wodehouse); "Oh Gee! Oh Joy!" (music: Gershwin); "How Long Has This Been Going On?" (Gershwin - Gershwin); "Ev'rybody Knows I Love Somebody" (Gershwin - Gershwin).
New York run: New Amsterdam Theatre, January 10, 1928; 335 p.

Although Florenz Ziegfeld is said to have agreed to produce the musical only because it was named after his mother and the score did not represent either Gershwin or Romberg at his best, *Rosalie* became one of the hits of the season — thanks chiefly to twinkling star Marilyn Miller, dancing comedian Jack Donahue, and a stylishly mounted production. The story was "inspired" by two recent events: Lindbergh's solo flight to Paris and the visit of Rumania's Queen Marie and her daughter to the United States. After West Point ace Richard Fay has flown to the mythical kingdom of Romanza to be near the princess he loves, the royal family goes on a state visit to America. Luckily for Richard, he has been appointed leader of the guard of honor; luckily for Richard and Rosalie, the king abdicates so that his daughter might be free to marry a commoner.

The reason the two composers shared the assignment is that Romberg could not undertake it alone because he was then also creating the music for *The New Moon.* Though he was occupied with *Funny Face* at the time, Gershwin agreed to join the project to help relieve the work load. The 1936 movie version, with Eleanor Powell and Nelson Eddy, scrapped all their songs and came up with a new score by Cole Porter.
TW.

THE THREE MUSKETEERS

Music: Rudolf Friml
Lryics: Clifford Grey
Book: William Anthony McGuire
Producer: Florenz Ziegfeld
Directors: William Anthony McGuire, Richard Boleslawsky
Choreographer: Albertina Rasch
Cast: Dennis King, Vivienne Segal, Lester Allen, Vivienne Osborne, Yvonne D'Arle, Reginald Owen, Joseph Macaulay, Harriet Hoctor, Douglass Dumbrille, Detmar Poppen, Clarence Derwent
Songs: "March of the Musketeers" (lyric with P.G. Wodehouse); "Ma Belle"; "Your Eyes" (lyric: Wodehouse); "One Kiss"; "My Sword and I"; "Queen of My Heart"
New York run: Lyric Theatre, March 13, 1928; 318 p.

Just as *The Vagabond King* had offered Dennis King as the dashing Francois Villon singing Rudolf Friml songs in a tale of adventure and intrigue in the days of Louis XI, so *The Three Musketeers* offered King as the dashing d'Artagnan singing Friml songs in a tale of adventure and intrigue in the days of Louis XIII. In this operetta version of the popular Alexandre Dumas novel, the story covers d'Artagnan's first meeting with Musketeers Athos, Porthos, and Aramis (Douglass Dumbrille, Detmar Poppen, and Joseph Macaulay), his romance with Constance Bonacieux (Vivienne Segal), and his noble efforts to save the honor of Queen Anne (Yvonne D'Arle), whom the wily Cardinal Richelieu (Reginald Owen) tries to blackmail. A revised version of the musical had a brief stay on Broadway in 1984.
M-E London OC (1930)/ Chappell, London (1937)*/ TW.

BLACKBIRDS OF 1928

Music: Jimmy McHugh
Lyrics: Dorothy Fields
Sketches: (uncredited)
Producer-director: Lew Leslie
Cast: Adelaide Hall, Bill Robinson, Aida Ward, Tim Moore, Elizabeth Welch, Mantan Moreland, Cecil Mack, Hall Johnson Choir
Songs: "Diga Diga Doo"; "I Can't Give You Anything but Love"; "Porgy"; "Doin' the New Low-Down"; "I Must Have That Man"
New York run: Liberty Theatre, May 9, 1928; 518 p.

Proclaiming itself "A Distinctive and Unique Entertainment with an All-Star Cast of 100 Colored Artists," *Blackbirds of 1928* was the brainchild of impresario Lew Leslie who had first exhibited a *Blackbirds* revue in London in 1926. Florence Mills scored such a hit in that production that Leslie planned to build a show around her in New York, but she died before rehearsals began. Leslie then secured Adelaide Hall and Bill Robinson (who joined the cast during tryout and had only one number, "Doin' the New Low-Down"), and assigned Jimmy HcHugh and Dorothy Fields to write the songs. Among the musical offerings were their first hit, "I Can't Give You Anything but Love," a spirited jungle number, "Diga Diga Doo," and a capsule version of the play, *Porgy,* thus preceding the Gershwin opera by six years. Leslie sponsored *Blackbirds* revues on Broadway in 1930 (with Ethel Waters and Buck and Bubbles), in 1933 (with Bill Robinson), and in 1939 (with Lena Horne), but none flew very high.
Columbia part OC.

THE NEW MOON

Music: Sigmund Romberg
Lyrics: Oscar Hammerstein II
Book: Oscar Hammerstein II, Frank Mandel, Laurence Schwab
Producers: Laurence Schwab & Frank Mandel
Director: (Edgar MacGregor uncredited)
Choreographer: Bobby Connolly
Cast: Evelyn Herbert, Robert Halliday, Gus Shy, Max Figman, William O'Neal
Songs: "Marianne"; "Softly, as in a Morning Sunrise"; "Stouthearted Men"; "One Kiss"; "Wanting You"; "Lover, Come Back to Me"
New York run: Imperial Theatre, September 19, 1928, 509 p.

The New Moon had to endure a tryout so disastrous that it was shut down completely while extensive alterations were made to the story, the score, and the cast. (Part of the problem was that both Sigmund Romberg and Oscar Hammerstein had to devote much of their time to other shows then in preparation: Romberg had *Rosalie* and Hammerstein had *Show Boat*.) After eight months the new *New Moon* reopened on the road with such musical pleasures as "Softly, as in a Morning Sunrise" and "Lover, Come Back to Me," and went on to win acclaim in New York.

What kept audiences happy was, in fact, deliberately designed as the successor to the same writers' *Desert Song,* with a similar improbably heroic tale loosely based on fact accompanied by a lush, pulse-pounding score. The story takes place in New Orleans in 1788, where Robert Misson (Robert Halliday), a French nobleman wanted for murder, serves as a bondsman and recruits stouthearted men in the cause of liberty. After his arrest, Robert is sent back to France on *The New Moon,* a vessel also carrying his beloved Marianne Beaunoir (Evelyn Herbert). Misson's followers, disguised as pirates, rescue their leader, who takes Marianne with him to establish a colony of free men on the Isle of Pines. *The New Moon* has something of a kinship with *Naughty Marietta* since they both dealt with a person of noble birth in disguise, and they were both set in New Orleans at roughly the same time. (They also shared the same historical error of making New Orleans a French colony when at the time it belonged to Spain.) Jeanette MacDonald and Nelson Eddy were in the 1940 movie version.
M-E London OC (1929); Capitol SC/ Chappell, London (1937)*/ TW.

Hold Everything! Frank Allworth, Bert Lahr, Victor Moore, Buddy Harak, and Harry Locke. (White)

HOLD EVERYTHING!

Music: Ray Henderson
Lyrics: B. G. DeSylva & Lew Brown
Book: B. G. DeSylva & John McGowan
Producers: Alex A. Aarons & Vinton Freedley
Director: (uncredited)
Choreographers: Sam Rose, Jack Haskell
Cast: Jack Whiting, Ona Munson, Bert Lahr, Betty Compton, Victor Moore, Nina Olivette, Frank Allworth, Gus Schilling
Songs: "Don't Hold Everything"; "You're the Cream in My Coffee"; "Too Good to Be True"; "To Know You Is to Love You"
New York run: Broadhurst Theatre, October 10, 1928; 413 p.

Bearing a title more applicable to a tale about wrestling, *Hold Everything!* was a saga of the manly art of boxing. In it, we are concerned with the ambitions of Sonny Jim Brooks (Jack Whiting), a welterweight challenger, and his girl, Sue Burke (Ona Munson), who is the cream in his coffee. Sonny Jim becomes temporarily distracted by socialite Norine Lloyd (Betty Compton) and for a while even considers her advice to try using boxing skills rather than slug it out with the champion. But when our hero finds out that the champ has insulted Sue, his killer instincts are aroused and he wins both the crown and his lady. The major attraction of the show turned out to be the uninhibited buffoon, Bert Lahr, as a punch-drunk pug. (When asked in one scene what book he was reading, Bert replied, "Da Woiks, by William Shakespeare.") During the run at the Broadhurst Theatre (on 44th Street west of Broadway), Whiting was succeeded by George Murphy. The film version was released in 1930 with Joe E. Brown and Winnie Lightner.

WHOOPEE

Music: Walter Donaldson
Lyrics: Gus Kahn
Book: William Anthony McGuire
Producer: Florenz Ziegfeld
Director: William Anthony McGuire
Choreographers: Seymour Felix, Tamara Geva
Cast: Eddie Cantor, Ruth Etting, Ethel Shutta, Paul Gregory, Frances Upton, Tamara Geva, Albert Hackett, George Olsen Orchestra, Buddy Ebsen
Songs: "I'm Bringing a Red Red Rose"; "Makin' Whoopee"; "Until You Get Somebody Else"; "Love Me or Leave Me"
New York run: New Amsterdam Theatre, December 4, 1928; 379 p.

Eddie Cantor was an eye-popping, bouncing comedian who had appeared in five *Ziegfeld Follies* before starring in this lavish Ziegfeld book musical. In the story, adapted from the 1923 play *The Nervous Wreck,* hypochondriac Henry Williams, in California for his health, becomes unwittingly involved with the daughter of a ranch owner whom he helps escape from marrying the local sheriff. After comic adventures that involve hiding out on an Indian reservation and Henry (in black-face) posing as a singing waiter, the girl is reunited with her true love, an Indian halfbreed who turns out to be white. The score, written by pop songwriters Walter Donaldson and Gus Kahn, produced two hits, "Love Me or Leave Me" and the Cantor specialty, "Makin' Whoopee." During the show's run, Paul Whiteman's Orchestra replaced George Olsen's for two months. A Broadway revival in 1979, originally presented at the Goodspeed Opera House in Connecticut, ran 204 performances. Eddie Cantor also starred in the 1930 film version. Smithsonian OC.

Whoopee. Eddie Cantor as Henry Williams.

FOLLOW THRU

Music: Ray Henderson
Lyrics: B. G. DeSylva & Lew Brown
Book: Laurence Schwab & B. G. DeSylva
Producers: Laurence Schwab & Frank Mandel
Director: Edgar MacGregor
Choreographer: Bobby Connolly
Cast: Jack Haley, Zelma O'Neal, Irene Delroy, Eleanor Powell, Madeline Cameron, John Barker
Songs: "My Lucky Star"; "Button Up Your Overcoat"; "You Wouldn't Fool Me, Would You?"; "I Want to Be Bad"
New York run: 46th Street Theatre, January 9, 1929; 403 p.

After collaborating on musical comedies about football (*Good News!*) and boxing (*Hold Everything!*), DeSylva, Brown and Henderson followed up with *Follow Thru*, which was about golf. Subtitled "A Musical Slice of Country Club Life," the show was an appropriately fleet-footed successor to the previous sporty musicals, with another catchy score (including "Button Up Your Overcoat"), some comic situations for Jack Haley (in his first major Broadway role), and a negligible plot about female rivalry for both the club championship and the golf pro. Most important, however, was the show's contagious high spirits. As Gilbert Gabriel reported in the *American,* "Wild-faced, free-legged kids shouted catch lines across the footlights that fairly roped and yanked the audience onto the stage." Jack Haley repeated his role in the 1930 movie version, which also featured Nancy Carroll and Buddy Rogers.
TW.

THE LITTLE SHOW

Music: Arthur Schwartz etc.
Lyrics: Howard Dietz, etc.
Sketches: Howard Dietz, George S. Kaufman, etc.
Producers: William A. Brady Jr. & Dwight Deere Wiman
Directors: Dwight Deere Wiman, Alexander Leftwich
Choreographer: Danny Dare
Cast: Clifton Webb, Fred Allen, Libby Holman, Romney Brent, Portland Hoffa, Bettina Hall, Jack McCauley, Peggy Conklin, Constance Cummings
Songs: "I've Made a Habit of You"; "Can't We Be Friends?" (Kay Swift-Paul James); "Hammacher-Schlemmer, I Love You"; "A Little Hut in Hoboken" (Herman Hupfeld); "I Guess I'll Have to Change My Plan"; "Moanin' Low" (music: Ralph Rainger)
New York run: Music Box, April 30, 1929; 321 p.

The Little Show was the first of 11 Broadway musicals to feature songs by the team of Arthur Schwartz and Howard Dietz. In its smartness, style, and intimacy (in 1929 a show with 29 in the cast qualified as little), the revue was something of an American counterpart to the British *Charlot Revues* and *This Year of Grace.* The most dramatic scene was the torrid dance Clifton Webb and Libby Holman performed after Miss Holman moaned "Moanin' Low" in a squalid Harlem tenement. The funniest sketch was George S. Kaufman's "The Still Alarm," about some nonchalant hotel guests, including Webb and Fred Allen, totally impervious to their being in the midst of a blazing fire. There were two subsequent *Little Shows*, neither one a success, though *The Third Little Show,* in 1931, co-starred Beatrice Lillie and Ernest Truex. Miss Lillie introduced Noël Coward's "Mad Dogs and Englishmen" in that one.

1929

SWEET ADELINE

Music: Jerome Kern
Lyrics & book: Oscar Hammerstein II
Producer: Arthur Hammerstein
Director: Reginald Hammerstein
Choreographer: Danny Dare
Cast: Helen Morgan, Charles Butterworth, Irene Franklin, Robert Chisholm, Violet Carlson, Max Hoffman Jr.
Songs: " 'Twas Not So Long Ago"; "Here Am I"; "Why Was I Born?"; "The Sun About to Rise"; "Some Girl Is on Your Mind"; "Don't Ever Leave Me"
New York run: Hammerstein's Theatre, September 3, 1929; 234 p.

Because of their admiration for Helen Morgan's performance in *Show Boat,* Jerome Kern and Oscar Hammerstein collaborated on a nostalgic musical designed as a vehicle to show off the singer's talents. Set in and around New York in 1898, the story concerns Addie Schmidt, the daughter of a Hoboken beergarden owner, and her three loves. After Tom Martin has gone to fight in the Spanish-American War, Addie — now known as Adeline Belmont — becomes a Broadway star and falls for wealthy socialite James Day. But his family disapproves and she happily ends up in the arms of composer Sid Barnett. Full of period charm, *Sweet Adeline* was something of a Hammerstein family affair, since it was produced by Oscar's uncle Arthur, directed by his brother Reginald, and played in Arthur's theatre (now a CBS television playhouse on Broadway between 53rd and 54th Streets). Irene Dunne starred in the 1935 movie.
TW.

BITTER SWEET

Music, lyrics & book: Noël Coward
Producers: Florenz Ziegfeld & Arch Selwyn
Director: Noël Coward
Choreographer: Tilly Losch
Cast: Evelyn Laye, Gerald Nodin, Max Kirby, Mireille, John Evelyn
Songs: "The Call of Life"; "If You Could Come With Me"; "I'll See You Again"; "Ladies of the Town"; "Dear Little Café"; "If Love Were All"; "Tokay"; "Ziguener"
New York run: Ziegfeld Theatre, November 5, 1929; 159 p.

Though celebrated for the brittle wit of his revue songs and sketches, as well as his plays, the multitalented Noël Coward was equally at home in the world of operetta. Indeed, no less than six of his eight book musicals were awash in oldfashioned sentiment, elegant period decor, and melodious, emotional ballads. The first of these, *Bitter Sweet,* was written simply because Coward felt that the time was right for a romantic renaissance in the theatre. After Gertrude Lawrence's vocal limitations ruled out her taking the leading role, the part went to the American actress, Peggy Wood, who starred in the London production, and the English actress, Evelyn Laye, who then starred in New York.

Living in Grosvenor Square, the widowed Marchioness of Shayne aids her niece in deciding whether to marry for love or position by recalling that day in 1875 when, as Sarah Millick, she joined music teacher Carl Linden in singing "I'll See You Again" — and promptly eloped with him to Vienna. Five years later, they were poor but happy café entertainers until Carl was killed in a duel. Sarah went on to become the renowned prima donna, Madame Sari Linden, then the wife of the wealthy Marquis of Shayne. Jeanette MacDonald and Nelson Eddy were in the second screen version, released in 1941.
Angel SC/ Heinemann, London (1934)/ TW.

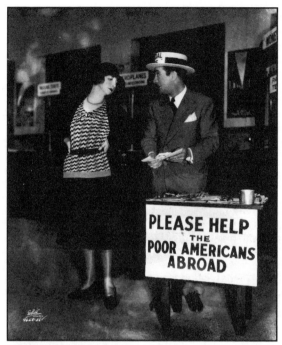

Fifty Million Frenchmen. Helen Broderick and William Gaxton. (White)

FIFTY MILLION FRENCHMEN

Music & lyrics: Cole Porter
Book: Herbert Fields
Producer: E. Ray Goetz
Director: Monty Woolley
Choreographer: Larry Ceballos
Cast: William Gaxton, Genevieve Tobin, Helen Broderick, Betty Compton, Evelyn Hoey, Jack Thompson, Thurston Hall
Songs: "You Do Something to Me"; "You've Got That Thing"; "Find Me a Primitive Man"; "The Tale of an Oyster"; "Paree, What Did You Do to Me?"; "You Don't Know Paree"
New York run: Lyric Theatre, November 27, 1929; 254 p.

Noted for his throbbing, minor-key melodies and his wordly, highly polished lyrics, Cole Porter was responsible for the scores of 23 Broadway musicals. His first hit — dubbed "A Musical Comedy Tour of Paris" — was a carefree tale concerning wealthy Peter Forbes (William Gaxton) who has a wager with a friend that he and Looloo Carroll (Genevieve Tobin) will be betrothed within a month. This gives Peter the excuse to become an impoverished tour guide so that, in pursuit of his beloved, he can determine if Looloo really loves him — and also so that they might enjoy such landmarks of the city as the Ritz Hotel Bar (where they mutually confess "You Do Something to Me"), the Café de la Paix, the Longchamps Racetrack, the Hotel Claridge, and Les Halles. The 1931 screen version retained the services of William Gaxton and Helen Broderick, but eliminated the songs. TW.

STRIKE UP THE BAND

Music: George Gershwin
Lyrics: Ira Gershwin
Book: Morrie Ryskind
Producer: Edgar Selwyn
Director: Alexander Leftwich
Choreographer: George Hale
Cast: Bobby Clark & Paul McCullough, Blanche Ring, Jerry Goff, Doris Carson, Dudley Clements, Red Nichols Orchestra
Songs: "I Mean to Say"; "Soon"; "Strike Up the Band"; "Mademoiselle in New Rochelle"; "I've Got a Crush on You"
New York run: Times Square Theatre, January 14, 1930; 191 p.

Strike Up the Band was first scheduled for a Broadway opening in 1927, but the original George S. Kaufman book was so uncompromisingly grim in its antiwar sentiment that the show closed on the road. Morrie Ryskind then rewrote the story, putting most of the action in a dream, and the leading roles were given to the zany team of Clark and McCullough. The revised script dealt with a war between the United States and Switzerland over the issue of tariffs on imported Swiss chocolate, with plenty of room for barbs aimed at jingoists, politicians, and White House advisers. Musical-comedy conventions, however, helped make it palatable to 1930 audiences. This was the first of a number of book shows and revues of the Thirties that, influenced by the Depression and the growing threat of another World War, were emboldened to make satirical observations on the problems then besetting the country and the world. Of interest to jazz buffs is that Red Nichols' pit band included such future luminaries as Benny Goodman, Gene Krupa, Glenn Miller, Jimmy Dorsey, and Jack Teagarden.

Flying High. Bert Lahr and Kate Smith. (Vandamm)

FLYING HIGH

Music: Ray Henderson
Lyrics: B. G. DeSylva & Lew Brown
Book: John McGowan, B. G. DeSylva & Lew Brown
Producer: George White
Directors: George White, Edward Clark Lilley
Choreographer: Bobby Connolly
Cast: Bert Lahr, Oscar Shaw, Kate Smith, Grace Brinkley, Russ Brown, Pearl Osgood
Songs: "I'll Know Him"; "Thank Your Father"; "Good for You — Bad for Me"; "Red Hot Chicago"; "Without Love"
New York run: Apollo Theatre, March 3, 1930; 357 p.

With athletic inspiration apparently exhausted, DeSylva, Brown and Henderson followed their musicals about football, boxing, and golf with one dealing with another current obsession, air travel. *Flying High*, however, was still something of a successor to *Hold Everything!* since it again put Bert Lahr in a role that enabled him to play a terrified cluck who must endure torturous preparations before he can triumph in a hazardous occupation. In this show, Lahr appeared as Rusty Krause, an airplane mechanic whose preparations for flight include a hilarious examining-room scene, and whose achievement is setting a record for the number of hours he is able to keep an airplane aloft—because he doesn't have the slightest idea how to get it down. Kate Smith played the comic role of Bert's mail-order fiancée. Lahr repeated his part in the 1931 film version, which also featured Pat O'Brien and Charlotte Greenwood.

FINE AND DANDY

Music: Kay Swift
Lyrics: Paul James
Book: Donald Ogden Stewart (Joe Cook uncredited)
Producers: Morris Green & Lewis Gensler
Directors: Morris Green, Frank McCoy
Choreographers: David Gould, Tom Nip
Cast: Joe Cook, Nell O'Day, Dave Chasen, Eleanor Powell, Alice Boulden, Joe Wagstaff
Songs: "Fine and Dandy"; "Can This Be Love?"; "Let's Go Eat Worms in the Garden"; "The Jig Hop"
New York run: Erlanger's Theatre, September 23, 1930; 255 p.

Comic Joe Cook was an innocent looking clown with a wide smile whose specialties were non sequitur stories (including his trademark routine about why he would not imitate four Hawaiians), Rube Goldberg-type inventions, and acrobatic and juggling skills. *Fine and Dandy*, a follow-up to his popular vehicle, *Rain or Shine*, not only included the Cook specialties but also featured a superior score (including the durable title song), the tapping of Eleanor Powell, and a tale that found Cook as Joe Squibb, the general manager of the Fordyce Drop Forge and Tool Factory, who ineptly copes with problems of labor and management. Erlanger's Theatre, now the St. James, stands on 44th Street west of Broadway.

GIRL CRAZY

Music: George Gershwin
Lyrics: Ira Gershwin
Book: Guy Bolton & John McGowan
Producers: Alex A. Aarons & Vinton Freedley
Director: Alexander Leftwich
Choreographer: George Hale
Cast: Willie Howard, Allen Kearns, Ginger Rogers, William Kent, Ethel Merman, Antonio & Renee DeMarco, Lew Parker, Roger Edens, Red Nichols Orchestra
Songs: "Bidin' My Time"; "Could You Use Me?"; "Embraceable You"; "I Got Rhythm"; "But Not for Me"; "Sam and Delilah"; "Treat Me Rough"
New York run: Alvin Theatre, October 14, 1930; 272 p.

Temporarily turning from the satiric world of their recent *Strike Up the Band*, the Gershwin brothers joined their former colleagues, librettist Guy Bolton and producers Aarons and Freedley, to escape to the more innocent world of conventional musical comedy. For *Girl Crazy*, however, they abandoned the East Coast haunts of high society that had been their customary locales in favor of the wide open spaces of Custerville, Arizona. There playboy Danny Churchill (Allen Kearns) has been sent by his wealthy father to manage a ranch in order to keep out of the clutches of predatory females. Arriving by taxi from New York, Danny soon turns the place into a dude ranch where Kate Fothergill (Ethel Merman in her first Broadway role) entertains guests with the undeniable assertion, "I Got Rhythm." Later our hero gets to croon "Embraceable You" with Molly Gray (Ginger Rogers in her second Broadway role), and helps taxi driver-turned-sheriff Gieber Goldfarb (Willie Howard in a part intended for Bert Lahr) apprehend the outlaw who has been threatening his life. Red Nichols' band included the same impressive personnel as in *Strike Up the Band*. Three film adaptations were made of *Girl Crazy*, with Judy Garland and Mickey Rooney co-starred in the 1943 version.
Columbia SC/ TW.

Three's a Crowd. Libby Holman singing "Something to Remember You By" as she bids farewell to matelot Fred MacMurray. (Apeda)

THREE'S A CROWD

Music: Arthur Schwartz, etc.
Lyrics: Howard Dietz, etc.
Sketches: Miscellaneous writers
Producer: Max Gordon
Director: Hassard Short
Choreographer: Albertina Rasch
Cast: Clifton Webb, Fred Allen, Libby Holman, Tamara Geva, Portland Hoffa, Earl Oxford, Fred MacMurray
Songs: "Something to Remember You By"; "Body and Soul" (Johnny Green-Edward Heyman, Robert Sour); "The Moment I Saw You"; "Forget All Your Books" (music: Burton Lane); "Right at the Start of It"
New York run: Selwyn Theatre, October 15, 1930; 272 p.

Once the sponsors of *The Second Little Show* decided that the stars of the first *Little Show* — Clifton Webb, Fred Allen, and Libby Holman — would not be in their new revue, fledgling producer Max Gordon persuaded the trio to appear in his own revue. He further assured that *Three's a Crowd* would be accepted in fact if not in name as the sequel to *The Little Show* by bringing along composer Arthur Schwartz and lyricist Howard Dietz (with Dietz additionally credited with having "conceived and compiled" the new show). The musical standouts of the evening were Miss Holman's masochistic "Body and Soul" and her "Something to Remember You By," a tearful ballad of farewell she sang to a matelot played by Fred MacMurray. Fred Allen won his biggest laughs as explorer Admiral Byrd, who has just returned from the Antarctic to announce his discovery of 500,000 square miles of brand new snow.

THE NEW YORKERS

Music & lyrics: Cole Porter
Book: Herbert Fields
Producer: E. Ray Goetz
Director: Monty Woolley
Choreographer: George Hale
Cast: Frances Williams, Charles King, Hope Williams, Ann Pennington, Richard Carle, Marie Cahill, Fred Waring Orchestra, Clayton, Jackson and Durante, Kathryn Crawford, Oscar Ragland
Songs: "Where Have You Been?"; "Love for Sale"; "Take Me Back to Manhattan"; "Let's Fly Away"; "I Happen to Like New York"
New York run: Broadway Theatre, December 8, 1930; 168 p.

The first stage production at the Broadway Theatre (on 53rd Street), *The New Yorkers* was something of a forerunner of *Pal Joey* in its amoral characters, cynical outlook, and flashy nightclub atmosphere. Just as Cole Porter and Herbert Fields' previous *Fifty Million Frenchmen* had offered a musical tour of Paris, so the new outing (with the same producer and director) offered a musical tour of high and low life in Manhattan, stopping off at a Park Avenue apartment, a speakeasy, a bootleg distillery, the Cotton Club in Harlem, and Reuben's Restaurant on Madison Avenue. The surrealistic satire concerns a socialite (Hope Williams) in love with a bootlegger (Charles King) because she is impressed with the way he bumps people off. Other characters include the lady's philandering parents and an irrepressible gangster henchman (Jimmy Durante), who brings the first act to a riotous close with his description of the varied products made from wood. Soon after the show's opening, Elisabeth Welch replaced Kathryn Crawford to sing the torchy invitation of a streetwalker, "Love for Sale."

THE BAND WAGON

Music: Arthur Schwartz
Lyrics: Howard Dietz
Sketches: George S. Kaufman, Howard Dietz
Producer: Max Gordon
Director: Hassard Short
Choreographer: Albertina Rasch
Cast: Fred & Adele Astaire, Frank Morgan, Helen Broderick, Tilly Losch, Philip Loeb, John Barker
Songs: "Sweet Music"; "High and Low"; "Hoops"; "Confession"; "New Sun in the Sky"; "I Love Louisa"; "Dancing in the Dark"; "White Heat"
New York run: New Amsterdam Theatre, June 3, 1931; 260 p.

Put together by the same creative team that had been responsible for *Three's a Crowd, The Band Wagon* may well have been the most sophisticated, imaginative, and musically distinguished revue ever mounted on Broadway. To assure that the production would have the same homogeneity of style as a book musical, there were no interpolations in the score and only two writers were credited for the sketches. Among the evening's pleasures: Fred and Adele Astaire (in their tenth and last Broadway appearance together) as two French children cavorting to "Hoops"; the principals riding on a Bavarian merry-go-round while singing "I Love Louisa"; Tilly Losch dancing to "Dancing in the Dark" on a slanted, mirrored stage; "The Pride of the Claghornes" sketch spoofing the Southern aristocracy's honor-of-the-family code. *The Band Wagon* was also the first New York production to use a double revolving stage for both its musical numbers and sketches. The 1953 Fred Astaire-Cyd Charisse film retained five songs, added others, and threw in a story line.
RCA OC.; Smithsonian part OC.

Cover designed by John Held, Jr.

The Band Wagon. Adele and Fred Astaire singing "Hoops." (Vandamm)

The Band Wagon. "The Pride of the Claghornes" sketch with Helen Broderick, Adele Astaire, Frank Morgan, and Fred Astaire. (Vandamm)

EARL CARROLL VANITIES

Music: Burton Lane, etc.
Lyrics: Harold Adamson, etc.
Sketches: Ralph Spence, Eddie Welch
Producer-director: Earl Carroll
Choreographers: George Hale, Gluck Sandor
Cast: Will Mahoney, Lillian Roth, William Demarest, Mitchell & Durant, Milton Watson
Songs: "Have a Heart"; "Heigh Ho, the Gang's All Here"; "Good Night, Sweetheart" (Ray Noble-Jimmy Campbell, Reg Connelly); "Tonight or Never" (Vincent Rose-Ray Klages, Jack Meskill)
New York run: Earl Carroll Theatre, August 27, 1931; 278 p.

A major rival to the *Ziegfeld Follies* and the *George White's Scandals* series was the *Earl Carroll Vanities,* which Carroll introduced in 1923. He staged 11 editions of a revue featuring girls even less modestly garbed and production numbers even more overblown than found in similar entertainments then being offered to keep the tired businessman awake. The 1931 edition was the first attraction at the newly built Earl Carroll Theatre at 50th Street and 7th Avenue, situated on the site of the previous theatre of the same name. No longer in existence, the playhouse was as much attraction as the show. Because of its 3,000-seat size, it enabled Carroll to sell orchestra seats at a top price of $3.30, for which theatregoers could enjoy such gaudy delights as a massive "Bolero" ballet accompanied by tom-toms and a "living curtain" of undraped showgirls posing as allegorical figures.

GEORGE WHITE'S SCANDALS

Music: Ray Henderson
Lyrics: Lew Brown
Sketches: Lew Brown, George White, Irving Caesar
Producer-director-choreographer: George White
Cast: Rudy Vallee, Ethel Merman, Willie & Eugene Howard, Everett Marshall, Ray Bolger, Ethel Barrymore Colt, Alice Faye
Songs: "Life Is Just a Bowl of Cherries"; "The Thrill Is Gone"; "This Is the Missus"; "Ladies and Gentlemen, That's Love"; "That's Why Darkies Were Born"; "My Song"
New York run: Apollo Theatre, September 14, 1931; 202 p.

The only challenger to the 1926 *Scandals* (see page 52) as the best of the series was the 11th Edition, which came along in 1931. Ray Henderson and Lew Brown (but minus B. G. DeSylva) were on hand for their fourth and last *Scandals* together with an impressive array of song hits introduced by pop crooner Rudy Vallee, powerhouse belter Ethel Merman (who had joined the cast during the tryout), and robust baritone Everett Marshall. Among the attractions were a celebration of the opening of the Empire State Building with Ray Bolger as a dancing Al Smith (with decor by former Ziegfeld designer Joseph Urban); a chins-up Depression anthem, "Life Is Just a Bowl of Cherries," trumpeted by Miss Merman; Willie and Eugene Howard in their classic comedy sketch "Pay the Two Dollars"; and a bold first-act finale, "That's Why Darkies Were Born," that took a compassionate view of Negro fortitude in the face of injustice.

The Cat and the Fiddle. Georges Metaxa, George Meader, and Bettina Hall. (White)

THE CAT AND THE FIDDLE

Music: Jerome Kern
Lyrics & book: Otto Harbach
Producer: Max Gordon
Director: José Ruben
Choreographer: Albertina Rasch
Cast: Georges Metaxa, Bettina Hall, Odette Myrtil, Eddie Foy Jr., José Ruben, Lawrence Grossmith, Doris Carson, George Meader
Songs: "The Night Was Made for Love"; "I Watch the Love Parade"; "Try to Forget"; "Poor Pierrot"; "She Didn't Say 'Yes' "; "A New Love Is Old"; "One Moment Alone"
New York run: Globe Theatre, October 15, 1931; 395 p.

The Cat and the Fiddle was a generally successful attempt to put the florid operetta form into a contemporary, intimate setting. In creating the work, Jerome Kern and Otto Harbach did without choruses, spectacles, and dragged-in comedy routines to keep the focus on the main story of what they called "A Musical Romance." Set in modern Brussels, it tells of the attraction between Victor Florescu (Georges Metaxa), a serious-minded Rumanian composer, and Shirley Sheridan (Bettina Hall), a vivacious American composer with a penchant for jazz. Though Victor is furious when a producer tries to lighten his rather heavy operetta, *The Passionate Pilgrim*, with some of Shirley's bright, uptempo numbers, true love eventually has hero and heroine singing in harmony. The true hero of the evening, however, was Jerome Kern whose score was an almost continuous flow of melodic pleasures, with songs well integrated into the story and with a highly advanced use of musical underscoring. In 1934, a film version was released starring Jeanette MacDonald and Ramon Novarro.
Epic (SC)/ TW.

OF THEE I SING

Music: George Gershwin
Lyrics: Ira Gershwin
Book: George S. Kaufman & Morrie Ryskind
Producer: Sam H. Harris
Director: George S. Kaufman
Choreographer: George Hale
Cast: William Gaxton, Victor Moore, Lois Moran, Grace Brinkley, June O'Dea, George Murphy, Dudley Clements, Edward H. Robins, Florenz Ames, Ralph Riggs, George E. Mack
Songs: "Wintergreen for President"; "Because, Because"; "Love Is Sweeping the Country"; "Of Thee I Sing, Baby"; "Here's a Kiss for Cinderella"; "Who Cares?"; "Hello, Good Morning"; "The Illegitimate Daughter"
New York run: Music Box, December 26, 1931; 441 p.

Constructed more in the style of a Gilbert and Sullivan comic opera than of a Broadway musical comedy, *Of Thee I Sing* was an extension of the satirical approach of the same writers' previous *Strike Up the Band*. Here, however, the technique was surer and the compromises to popular taste less apparent, with songs and story complementing each other and expressing a uniform point of view. Sharply and deftly skewered were such institutions as political conventions and campaigns, beauty pageants, marriage, the Vice Presidency, the Supreme Court, foreign affairs, and motherhood.

The fanciful tale covers the fortunes of the Presidential ticket of John P. Wintergreen and his running mate, Alexander Throttlebottom — abetted by Wintergreen's bride, Mary Turner (Lois Moran) — which, with its campaign song "Of Thee I Sing, Baby," sweeps the country on a platform of Love. Once in office, however, the President is threatened with impeachment because he jilted Diana Devereaux (Grace Brinkley), the Miss America contest winner he had promised to marry. She, it seems, is "the illegitimate daughter of the illegitimate son of an illegitimate nephew of Napoleon," and France is insulted because of this slight. After the First Lady somehow saves the day by giving birth to twins, France's honor is assuaged when Throttlebottom agrees to wed Diana because, according to the Constitution, "When the President of the United States is unable to fulfil his duties, his obligations are assumed by the Vice President."

Of Thee I Sing, the third longest running musical of the Thirties, became the first musical ever awarded the Pulitzer Prize for drama (though ironically George Gershwin was not included in the citation since his was a musical contribution and therefore not considered eligible for a literary award). It also established brash, sharp-featured William Gaxton and bumbling, dumpling-shaped Victor Moore, who played Wintergreen and Throttlebottom, as Broadway's leading musical-comedy team. After touring, the show returned to New York for a month-long engagement in May 1933. It then resumed its tour with a cast headed by Oscar Shaw, Donald Meek, and Ann Sothern.

In October 1933, a sequel, *Let 'Em Eat Cake,* written by the same writers and featuring the original leading players, opened on Broadway. Supposedly a satire on dictatorship, the show proved too acerbic and thematically confusing, and it remained only three months. The song "Mine," which was in this production, was added to *Of Thee I Sing* when the musical was revived in 1952. Jack Carson and Victor Moore were signed to play Wintergreen and Throttlebottom, but Moore decided against repeating his original role and the part went to Paul Hartman. George S. Kaufman again directed. In 1987, a concert version was performed with *Let 'Em Eat Cake* at the Brooklyn Academy of Music.
Capitol OC (1952); CBS OC (1987)/ Knopf (1932); Samuel French (1935)*; Chilton (1973)/ SF.

Of Thee I Sing. Victor Moore and William Gaxton, surrounded by political advisers, getting ready for the campaign. (Vandamm)

FACE THE MUSIC
Music & lyrics: Irving Berlin
Book: Moss Hart
Producer: Sam H. Harris
Directors: Hassard Short, George S. Kaufman
Choreographer: Albertina Rasch
Cast: Mary Boland, J. Harold Murray, Andrew Tombes, Hugh O'Connell, Katherine Carrington, David Burns
Songs: "Let's Have Another Cup o' Coffee"; "On a Roof in Manhattan"; "Soft Lights and Sweet Music"; "I Say It's Spinach"
New York run: New Amsterdam Theatre, February 17, 1932; 165 p.

The mood of cynicism created by the Depression continued to spawn a number of sharply satirical Broadway musicals. The Gershwin brothers, George S. Kaufman, and Morrie Ryskind had led the way with *Strike Up the Band* and *Of Thee I Sing,* and now it was the turn of Irving Berlin and Moss Hart (with Kaufman joining the project as director). In *Face the Music* the concern was with New York politicians and policemen with little tin boxes, the reduced financial circumstances of the city's elite (former wealthy socialites sing "Let's Have Another Cup o' Coffee" in the Automat), and the insane world of the theatre. In the leading role, Mary Boland played Mrs. Martin Van Buren Meshbesher, the wife of a police sergeant "lousy with money," who tries to lose some of it by backing a tasteless Broadway show, *The Rhinestone Girl,* that surprisingly becomes a hit. Despite the Seabury investigation into police corruption (which also figured in the 1959 musical, *Fiorello!*), the boys in blue manage to beat the rap when Mrs. Meshbesher contributes the profits from the show to the city's depleted treasury. Early in 1933 *Face the Music* returned to Broadway for a month-long run.

FLYING COLORS

Music: Arthur Schwartz
Lyrics & sketches: Howard Dietz
Producer: Max Gordon
Director: Howard Dietz
Choreographer: Albertina Rasch
Cast: Clifton Webb, Charles Butterworth, Tamara Geva, Patsy Kelly, Philip Loeb, Vilma & Buddy Ebsen, Larry Adler, Imogene Coca, Monette Moore
Songs: "Two-Faced Woman"; "A Rainy Day"; "A Shine on Your Shoes"; "Alone Together"; "Louisiana Hayride"; "Smokin' Reefers"
New York run: Imperial Theatre, September 15, 1932, 188 p.

Flying Colors flew in a direct line from *The Little Show, Three's a Crowd,* and *The Band Wagon.* Like all three, it had music by Arthur Schwartz and lyrics by Howard Dietz (though this time Dietz also received credit as sole sketch writer and director). Like the most recent two revues, it was produced by Max Gordon and was choreographed by Albertina Rasch, and it also featured two veterans of the series, Clifton Webb and Tamara Geva. Though too closely patterned after its illustrious predecessors (Brooks Atkinson headed his Sunday *Times* piece, "Flying the Band Wagon Colors"), the show was witty and attractive, and had its share of standout numbers: "A Shine on Your Shoes" presented Vilma and Buddy Ebsen dancing around a shoeshine stand accompanied by Larry Adler's harmonica; "Alone Together" offered Webb and Geva in a dramatic, sinuous dance; and "Louisiana Hayride" brought the first act to a jubilant close. Then there was Charles Butterworth's hilarious soapbox speech, "Harvey Woofter's Five Point Plan," on how to end the Depression. Times were tough for the show, too. After opening it at a $4.40 top, Gordon was soon forced to lower the ticket price to $2.20.

Flying Colors. Buddy Ebsen, Monette Moore, Vilma Ebsen, and Larry Adler performing "A Shine on Your Shoes." (White)

MUSIC IN THE AIR

Music: Jerome Kern
Lyrics & book: Oscar Hammerstein II
Producer: Peggy Fears (A. C. Blumenthal uncredited)
Directors: Jerome Kern & Oscar Hammerstein II
Cast: Reinald Werrenrath, Natalie Hall, Tullio Carminati, Katherine Carrington, Al Shean, Walter Slezak, Nicholas Joy, Marjorie Main
Songs: "I've Told Ev'ry Little Star"; "There's a Hill Beyond a Hill"; "And Love Was Born"; "I'm Alone"; "I Am So Eager"; "One More Dance"; "When the Spring Is in the Air"; "In Egern on the Tegern See"; "The Song Is You"; "We Belong Together"
New York run: Alvin Theatre, November 8, 1932; 342 p.

Hailed by Alexander Woollcott in *The New Yorker* as "that endearing refuge, that gracious shelter from a troubled world," the Jerome Kern-Oscar Hammerstein *Music in the Air* continued along the same path as the Jerome Kern-Otto Harbach *Cat and the Fiddle.* The setting was again modern Europe, the story again had to do with the preparations for an operetta, and the songs — among Kern's most memorable — and the underscoring again enhanced the characters and the situations. The plot of this "Musical Adventure" concerns Sieglinde and Karl (Katherine Carrington and Walter Slezak), two Bavarian naifs, who hike from Edendorf to Munich to help Sieglinde's father, Dr. Walther Lessing (Al Shean), interest a music publisher in his new composition, "I've Told Ev'ry Little Star." Soon they become involved with glamorous star Frieda Hatzfeld (Natalie Hall) and her lover, librettist Bruno Mahler (Tullio Carminati), during the rehearsals of Bruno's new work, *Tingle-Tangle.* When the temperamental diva walks out on the production, Sieglinde is given her big chance. Contrary to show-business legend, however, she proves totally inept, and when Frieda comes back Sieglinde sadly returns to her mountain village.

   Hammerstein brought *Music in the Air* back to Broadway in 1951, with a cast headed by Jane Pickens (Frieda), Dennis King (Bruno), and Charles Winninger (Lessing). Because of possible anti-German sentiment following World War II, he changed the locale from Munich to Zurich and made everybody Swiss. The show remained less than two months. The 1934 Hollywood version starred Gloria Swanson, John Boles, and Al Shean.
Capitol SC/ Chappell, London (1934)*/ TW.

Music in the Air. Katherine Carrington, Al Shean and Walter Slezak. (Vandamm)

TAKE A CHANCE

Music: Richard A. Whiting, Nacio Herb Brown, Vincent Youmans
Lyrics: B. G. DeSylva
Book: B. G. DeSylva, Laurence Schwab, Sid Silvers
Producers: Laurence Schwab & B. G. DeSylva
Director: Edgar MacGregor
Choreographer: Bobby Connolly
Cast: Jack Haley, Ethel Merman, Jack Whiting, Sid Silvers, June Knight, Mitzi Mayfair, Oscar Ragland, Robert Gleckler
Songs: "Should I Be Sweet?" (Youmans); "Turn Out the Lights" (Whiting, Brown); "Rise 'n' Shine" (Youmans); "You're an Old Smoothie" (Whiting, Brown); "Eadie Was a Lady" (Whiting; lyric with Roger Edens)
New York run: Apollo Theatre, November 26, 1932; 243 p.

In September 1932, a musical titled *Humpty Dumpty* began its tryout tour in Pittsburgh. It involved Lou Holtz, Ethel Merman, and Eddie Foy Jr. in what was basically a revue with songs and sketches dealing with incidents in American history. It was so poorly received that the show closed in five days. Within three weeks, however, the production was totally revised, partly recast (Holtz and Foy were replaced by Jack Whiting and Jack Haley), and had five new songs by Vincent Youmans. Retitled *Take a Chance* — to indicate something of the risks involved — the show was now an old-fashioned book musical concerned with a romance between the leading man and leading lady (Whiting and June Knight) who are appearing in a revue about American history called *Humpty Dumpty*. What turned it into a hit, though, were the comedy and specialty numbers, with Miss Merman given two show stoppers — "Rise 'n' Shine" and "Eadie Was a Lady" — that let her blast her way clear up to the second balcony. During the Broadway run, Haley and Sid Silvers were succeeded by the vaudeville team of Olsen and Johnson. The film version, released in 1933, featured June Knight and Lillian Roth.

GAY DIVORCE

Music & lyrics: Cole Porter
Book: Dwight Taylor
Producers: Dwight Deere Wiman & Tom Weatherly
Director: Howard Lindsay
Choreographers: Carl Randall, Barbara Newberry
Cast: Fred Astaire, Claire Luce, Luella Gear, Betty Starbuck, Erik Rhodes, Eric Blore, G. P. Huntley Jr.
Songs: "After You, Who?"; "Night and Day"; "How's Your Romance?"; "I've Got You on My Mind"; "Mister and Missus Fitch"
New York run: Ethel Barrymore Theatre, November 29, 1932; 248 p.

The first musical to play the Ethel Barrymore Theatre (on 47th Street west of Broadway), *Gay Divorce* was the only stage production in which Fred Astaire performed without sister Adele. In the story, adapted from an unproduced play, Astaire was seen as Guy Holden, a British novelist, who goes to a seaside resort to woo would-be divorcée Mimi Pratt (Claire Luce), primarily by convincing her — through song and dance — that night and day she is the one. Complications arise when Guy is mistaken for a professional corespondent (Erik Rhodes) who has been hired to ease Mimi's divorce. Though Astaire proved that he could carry both a weak plot and a new dancing partner, *Gay Divorce* (without the definite article, please) marked his final appearance on Broadway. The 1934 film version, retitled *The Gay Divorcee,* co-starred Fred with Ginger Rogers.

AS THOUSANDS CHEER

Music & lyrics: Irving Berlin
Sketches: Moss Hart
Producer: Sam H. Harris
Director: Hassard Short
Choreographer: Charles Weidman
Cast: Marilyn Miller, Clifton Webb, Helen Broderick, Ethel Waters, Hal Forde, Jerome Cowan, Harry Stockwell, José Limon, Letitia Ide, Thomas Hamilton, Leslie Adams
Songs: "How's Chances?"; "Heat Wave"; "Lonely Heart"; "Easter Parade"; "Supper Time"; "Harlem on My Mind"; "Not for All the Rice in China"
New York run: Music Box, September 30, 1933; 400 p.

Though it was a revue, the Irving Berlin-Moss Hart *As Thousands Cheer* was considered a successor to the Berlin-Hart book musical, *Face the Music,* since it also dealt satirically with topics of current interest. In fact, it was so concerned with topicality that the entire show was structured in the form of a newspaper, with various stories and features — each one preceded by a blowup of a headline — depicted in songs, dances and sketches. In addition to general news, there were sections devoted to comics, rotogravure (an opportunity to show the Easter Parade of half a century earlier), society, theatre, the weather report ("Heat Wave"), and advice to the lovelorn ("Lonely Heart"). As might be expected in a lighthearted entertainment, serious topics were avoided except for Ethel Waters' purposely jarring "Supper Time," introduced by the headline "UNKNOWN NEGRO LYNCHED BY FRENZIED MOB." Newsworthy individuals impersonated in the noteworthy show were Barbara Hutton and Joan Crawford (by Marilyn Miller in her 12th and final Broadway appearance); Douglas Fairbanks Jr., John D. Rockefeller, and Mahatma Gandhi (by Clifton Webb); Louise Hoover, Aimee Semple MacPherson, Queen Mary, and the Statue of Liberty (by Helen Broderick); and Josephine Baker (by Miss Waters).

As Thousands Cheer. King George V (Leslie Adams) and Queen Mary (Helen Broderick) are upset to read of the latest romantic escapade involving the Prince of Wales (Thomas Hamilton). (Vandamm)

ROBERTA

Music: Jerome Kern
Lyrics & book: Otto Harbach
Producer: Max Gordon
Director: (Hassard Short uncredited)
Choreographer: José Limon (John Lonergan uncredited)
Cast: Lyda Roberti, Bob Hope, Fay Templeton, Tamara, George Murphy, Sydney Greenstreet, Ray Middleton, Fred MacMurray
Songs: "Let's Begin"; "You're Devastating"; "Yesterdays"; "The Touch of Your Hand"; "I'll Be Hard to Handle" (lyric: Bernard Dougall); "Smoke Gets in Your Eyes"; "Something Had to Happen"
New York run: New Amsterdam Theatre, November 18, 1933; 295 p.

Based on Alice Duer Miller's popular novel, *Gowns by Roberta* (the original title was still used during the tryout), the production was expected to follow *The Cat and the Fiddle* and *Music in the Air* as another of Jerome Kern's well-integrated modern operettas set in present-day Europe. The work, however, turned out to be more of a formula musical comedy dependent upon sumptuously mounted production numbers (one was a fashion show), some comic interpolations, and a superior collection of songs — including "Smoke Gets in Your Eyes" and "Yesterdays" — that bore little relevance to the plot. Said plot had to do with a former All-American fullback, John Kent (Ray Middleton), who inherits a Paris dress salon owned by his Aunt Minnie (Fay Templeton). John also ends with Minnie's assistant, Russian Princess Stephanie (Tamara), as both business and marital partner. Bob Hope, in his first major Broadway role, played John's bandleader chum, Huckleberry Haines. Though *Roberta* was initially directed by Kern himself, the composer was replaced by the more experienced Hassard Short who refused program credit. In 1935, the first of two screen versions co-starred Irene Dunne, Fred Astaire, and Ginger Rogers.
Columbia SC/ TW.

Roberta. Bob Hope catches Lyda Roberti and Ray Middleton in an embarrassing situation. (Vandamm)

Ziegfeld Follies. Willie Howard and Fanny Brice in the sketch based on *Sailor, Beware!*

ZIEGFELD FOLLIES

Music: Vernon Duke, etc.
Lyrics: E. Y. Harburg, etc.
Sketches: Miscellaneous writers
Producer: Billie Burke Ziegfeld (Messrs. Shubert uncredited)
Directors: Bobby Connolly, Edward Clark Lilley, John Murray Anderson
Choreographers: Bobby Connolly, Robert Alton
Cast: Fanny Brice, Willie & Eugene Howard, Everett Marshall, Jane Froman, Vilma & Buddy Ebsen, Patricia Bowman, Cherry & June Preisser, Eve Arden, Robert Cummings, Ina Ray Hutton
Songs: "I Like the Likes of You"; "Suddenly"; "What Is There to Say?"; "The Last Round-Up" (Billy Hill); "Wagon Wheels" (Peter DeRose-Hill)
New York run: Winter Garden, January 4, 1934; 182 p.

In the mid-Thirties the Shubert brothers offered five revues at the Winter Garden that won general approval for their high level of comedy, inventive staging, attractive decor, and musical quality. The first of these, the 1934 *Ziegfeld Follies,* had begun its tryout tour so unpromisingly, however, that director John Murray Anderson and choreographer Robert Alton were rushed in to replace Bobby Connolly. They just barely whipped things into shape in time for the Broadway opening. To add authenticity to the show, the nominal sponsor was Ziegfeld's widow, Billie Burke, and the leading comic attracton was *Follies* veteran Fanny Brice. Miss Brice did takeoffs on evangelist Aimee Semple MacPherson and strip-tease dancers, impersonated a bratty child known as Baby Snooks, and appeared with another great clown, Willie Howard, in a frantic burlesque of the play *Sailor, Beware!* The durable "I Like the Likes of You" was sung in the show by Robert Cummings and danced to by Vilma and Buddy Ebsen.

NEW FACES

Music, lyrics & sketches: Miscellaneous writers
Producer: Charles Dillingham (Leonard Sillman uncredited)
Director-choreographer: Leonard Sillman
Cast: Leonard Sillman, Imogene Coca, Nancy Hamilton, Charles Walters, Henry Fonda, Teddy Lynch, James Shelton, Billie Heywood
Songs: "Lamplight" (James Shelton); "My Last Affair" (Haven Johnson); "The Gutter Song" (Shelton); "You're My Relaxation" (Charles Schwab-Robert Sour)
New York run: Fulton Theatre, March 15, 1934; 149 p.

Originally presented in Pasadena as *Low and Behold,* Leonard Sillman's *New Faces* had to give 137 auditions before the needed $15,000 was raised to open at the Fulton Theatre (then on 46th Street west of Broadway). Under the "supervision" of Elsie Janis, Sillman's dewy-eyed, intimate revue served much the same function as *The Garrick Gaieties* by providing a showcase for hitherto undiscovered talent — such as Henry Fonda, future film director Charles Walters, and chief comedienne Imogene Coca (though she had been around since 1925). Audiences particularly enjoyed Miss Coca's impish fan dance while bundled in an oversized polo coat, Nancy Hamilton's sketch in which "The Three Little Pigs" was presented in the manner of three recent dramas, and the song, "Lamplight," sung by its composer James Shelton. *New Faces* marked the 62nd and final Broadway musical credited to producer Charles Dillingham, who had merely lent the prestige of his name to the entertainment and who died five months after the opening. Sillman staged six subsequent editions of the tyro talent show, with the most successful offered in 1952 (see page 154.)

New Faces. Imogene Coca in her polo coat.

86

LIFE BEGINS AT 8:40

Music: Harold Arlen
Lyrics: Ira Gershwin & E. Y. Harburg
Sketches: Miscellaneous writers
Producers: Messrs. Shubert
Directors: John Murray Anderson, Philip Loeb
Choreographers: Robert Alton, Charles Weidman
Cast: Bert Lahr, Ray Bolger, Luella Gear, Frances Williams, Brian Donlevy, Dixie Dunbar, Earl Oxford
Songs: "You're a Builder-Upper"; "Fun to Be Fooled"; "What Can You Say in a Love Song?"; "Let's Take a Walk Around the Block"; "Things"
New York run: Winter Garden, August 27, 1934; 237 p.

The second of the Shubert-sponsored Winter Garden revues in the mid-Thirties, *Life Begins at 8:40* had something of the style of *The Band Wagon* and the topicality of *As Thousands Cheer*. With John Murray Anderson in overall charge, it was also the successor to the Anderson-directed *Ziegfeld Follies* that had opened the same year. (The show's title, which recalled Walter Pitkin's bestseller, *Life Begins at Forty,* referred to the time the curtain went up.) Again the accent was on comedy, with Bert Lahr winning praise for his newly acquired satirical skill, as revealed in his characterizations of a suicidally bent Frenchman, a stiff-upper-lip Englishman, and a pompous concert baritone sputtering about "the utter utter utter loveliness of things." Also well received were Ray Bolger's dance interpretation of the recent Max Baer-Primo Carnera championship fight and Luella Gear's takeoff on the peripatetic Eleanor Roosevelt breathlessly enumerating her day's activities.

THE GREAT WALTZ

Music: Johann Strauss Jr.
Lyrics: Desmond Carter
Book: Moss Hart
Producer: Max Gordon
Director: Hassard Short
Choreographer: Albertina Rasch
Cast: Marion Claire, Marie Burke, Guy Robertson, H. Reeves-Smith, Ernest Cossart, Alexandra Danilova
Songs: "You Are My Song"; "Love Will Find You"; "Like a Star in the Sky"; "With All My Heart"; "While You Love Me"; "Danube So Blue"
New York run: Center Theatre, September 22, 1934; 298 p.

One of the truly mammoth undertakings of the mid-Thirties, *The Great Waltz* opened at the 3,822-seat Center Theatre (then in Rockefeller Center one block south of the Radio City Music Hall) with 23 actors, 77 singers, 33 ballet dancers, 53 musicians, 90 backstage workers, and a wardrobe of over 500 costumes. The production cost, among the highest of any show to date, was $246,000. Based on an English version of a Viennese musical called *Waltzes from Vienna,* the operetta deals with the rivalry between Johann Strauss Sr. and Johann Strauss Jr., played by H. Reeves-Smith and Guy Robertson. After jealously thwarting his son's advancement, the old Waltz King — in the show's spectacular climax at Dommayer's Gardens — reluctantly abdicates his title when the younger man takes over the baton to conduct "The Blue Danube" (here titled "Danube So Blue"). Though critics were divided, *The Great Waltz* had a respectable run (at a $3.30 top), and reopened for an additional 49 performances in August 1935. AEI SC/ Capitol Los Angeles OC (1965)/ TW.

ANYTHING GOES

Music & lyrics: Cole Porter
Book: Guy Bolton & P. G. Wodehouse, Howard Lindsay & Russel Crouse
Producer: Vinton Freedley
Director: Howard Lindsay
Choreographer: Robert Alton
Cast: William Gaxton, Ethel Merman, Victor Moore, Bettina Hall, Vera Dunn, Leslie Barrie, Vivian Vance, Helen Raymond, George E. Mack, Houston Richards
Songs: "I Get a Kick Out of You"; "There'll Always Be a Lady Fair"; "All Through the Night"; "You're the Top"; "Anything Goes"; "Blow, Gabriel, Blow"; "Be Like the Bluebird"; "The Gypsy in Me"
New York run: Alvin Theatre, November 21, 1934; 420 p.

Following the debacle of a musical comedy called *Pardon My English* early in 1933, producer Vinton Freedley had to flee the country to avoid creditors. To help clear his mind and regain his health, Freedley spent most of his time in a fishing boat off the Pearl Island in the Gulf of Panama. While fishing he envisaged the perfect musical comedy with which he would launch his comeback: William Gaxton, Victor Moore, and Ethel Merman would play the leading roles, the score would be written by Cole Porter, and the libretto would be by the veteran team of Guy Bolton and P. G. Wodehouse who would tie everything together in a fun-filled story about a group of oddball characters on a ocean liner that is facing a bomb threat.

Once he returned to New York and paid off his debts, the producer rounded up his people for what was originally called *Bon Voyage,* then *Hard to Get.* With rehearsals about to begin, disaster struck when the *S.S. Morro Castle* went down in flames off the New Jersey coast with a loss of over 125 lives. Obviously, the script had to be changed. Since Bolton and Wodehouse were then in Europe, Freedley, in desperation, turned to his director, Howard Lindsay, who agreed to undertake the rewriting with a press agent and part-time librettist named Russel Crouse (Thereby launching the celebrated team that would be responsible for a total of seven musical-comedy librettos and eight plays).

Though still taking place on shipboard, the new story eliminated the bomb scare but retained the leading characters of the original plot: nightclub singer Reno Sweeney (Merman), her chum Billy Crocker (Gaxton) who stows away to be near Hope Harcourt (Bettina Hall), the debutante he loves, and Moon-Face Mooney (Moore). Public Enemy No. 13, who masquerades as a clergyman to avoid the long arm of the FBI. It may have been created out of tragedy, but *Anything Goes* (the title was chosen to indicate the desperation with which the show was put together) turned out to be the fourth longest running musical of the Thirties as well as one of the decade's most durable attractions. Porter's score, considered his best to date, included three Merman trademarks — "I Get a Kick Out of You," "You're the Top" (a duet with Gaxton), and "Blow, Gabriel, Blow." During the Broadway run, Miss Merman was succeeded by Benay Venuta.

Anything Goes was revived Off Broadway in 1962 with Hal Linden, Eileen Rodgers, and Mickey Deems, and a number of Porter interpolations. It ran 239 performances. In 1987, it was given a new production at Lincoln Center's Vivian Beaumount Theatre, which had the longest run of all. During the engagement, Patti LuPone was succeeded by Leslie Uggams, Howard McGillin by Gregg Edelman. (See page 277.) The 1936 film version offered Ethel Merman plus Bing Crosby and Charlie Ruggles; the 1956 film of the same name, also with Crosby, had nothing in common with the original except for 5 songs.
Smithsonian part OC; Epic OC (1962), RCA (1987)/TW.

Anything Goes. Ethel Merman leading the chorus in "Blow, Gabriel, Blow." (Vandamm)

AT HOME ABROAD

Music: Arthur Schwartz
Lyrics: Howard Dietz
Sketches: Miscellaneous writers
Producers: Messrs. Shubert
Directors: Vincente Minnelli, Thomas Mitchell
Choreographers: Gene Snyder, Harry Losee
Cast: Beatrice Lillie, Ethel Waters, Herb Williams, Eleanor Powell, Paul Haakon, Reginald Gardiner, Eddie Foy Jr., Vera Allen, John Payne
Songs: "Hottentot Potentate"; "Paree"; "Thief in the Night"; "Love Is a Dancing Thing"; "Loadin' Time"; "What a Wonderful World"; "Get Yourself a Geisha"; "Got a Bran' New Suit"
New York run: Winter Garden, September 19, 1935; 198 p.

Structured in the form of an around-the-world cruise — though carefully avoiding such countries as Germany, Italy, and Russia — *At Home Abroad* provided theatregoers with the chance to be abroad at home as they savored the pleasures of a variety of comic and colorful locales. These included a London department store for Beatrice Lillie's classic tongue-twisting sketch about ordering two dozen double damask dinner napkins; an African jungle where Ethel Waters proclaims herself the "Hottentot Potentate"; the Moulin Rouge in Paris to offer Miss Lillie's paean to the wonders of the city; a Balkan country where Eleanor Powell taps out spy messages; a West Indies dockside for Miss Waters' throbbing description "Loadin' Time"; and a Japanese garden where Miss Lillie joins a bevy of Nipponese maidens in extolling the advantages of getting one's self a geisha. The third Shubert-sponsored Winter Garden revue of the mid-Thirties, *At Home Abroad* marked the first complete stage production directed by Vincente Minnelli. In 1948, Arthur Schwartz and Howard Dietz conducted a more limited revue tour, *Inside U.S.A.*, which also starred Beatrice Lillie. Smithsonian OC.

Porgy and Bess. Ruby Elzy and J. Rosamond Johnson in the saucer burial scene. Anne Brown and Todd Duncan are to their left. (Vandamm)

Porgy and Bess. The setting of Catfish Row, designed by Sergei Soudeikine. (Vandamm)

PORGY AND BESS

Music: George Gershwin
Lyrics: DuBose Heyward, Ira Gershwin
Book: DuBose Heyward
Producer: Theatre Guild
Director: Rouben Mamoulian
Cast: Todd Duncan, Anne Brown, Warren Coleman, John W. Bubbles, Abbie Mitchell, Ruby Elzy, Georgette Harvey, Edward Matthews, Helen Dowdy, J. Rosamond Johnson
Songs: "Summertime" (Heyward); "A Woman Is a Sometime Thing" (Heyward); "My Man's Gone Now" (Heyward); "I Got Plenty o' Nuttin'" (Heyward, Gershwin); "Bess, You Is My Woman Now" (Heyward, Gershwin); "It Ain't Necessarily So" (Gershwin); "I Loves You, Porgy" (Heyward, Gershwin); "There's a Boat Dat's Leavin' Soon for New York" (Gershwin); "I'm on My Way" (Heyward)
New York run: Alvin Theatre, October 10, 1935; 124 p.

Universally accepted as the most popular opera written by an American composer, *Porgy and Bess* began life in 1925 as the novel *Porgy* by DuBose Heyward. Heyward's setting of Catfish Row in Charleston, South Carolina, and his dramatic story of the crippled beggar Porgy, the seductive Bess, the menacing Crown, and the slinky cocaine dealer Sportin' Life fired George Gershwin's imagination even before Heyward and his wife, Dorothy, adapted the book into a play two years later. After a number of delays, Gershwin began writing the opera late in 1933 with Heyward as librettist-lyricist and brother Ira Gershwin as co-lyricist. The composer's last Broadway score, the work was completed — including Gershwin's own orchestrations — in 20 months.

The initial production, with Todd Duncan and Anne Brown in the leads, was treated as such a major event that the larger dailies dispatched both their drama and music critics to cover the opening. It was not, however, a commercial success, though many of the solos and duets — "Summertime," "Bess, You Is My Woman Now," "I Got Plenty o' Nuttin'," "It Ain't Necessarily So" — soon caught on. Four revivals of *Porgy and Bess* have had extended Broadway runs. In 1942, again with Todd Duncan and Anne Brown but with Avon Long replacing John W. Bubbles as Sportin' Life, the musical ran successfully for 286 performances (at a $2.75 top ticket price) in a somewhat streamlined version with a smaller orchestra and no recitative. It was produced by Cheryl Crawford and directed by Robert Ross. The production then toured for 17 months, including a two-month return visit to New York. Ten years later, one of the most ambitious projects in theatre history was inaugurated with a four-year international tour directed by co-producer Robert Breen. Still more musical drama than opera, *Porgy and Bess* was performed in 23 cities in the United States and Canada, and — under the auspices of the State Department — in 28 countries throughout Europe (including well-publicized engagements in Leningrad and Moscow), the Middle East and Latin America. This company's 1953 stay in New York had the longest run the work has had to date. (See page 156.)

A mounting in 1976 by the Houston Grand Opera was staged at the Uris (now the Gershwin) Theatre on 51st Street west of Broadway. With an acclaimed performance by Clamma Dale as Bess and all the original musical portions restored, the production came closest to the composer's concept of the work as an opera. It was also the basis for the 1983 revival, the first adult, full-scale dramatic work ever staged at the 6,000-seat Radio City Music Hall. Two years later, on its 50th anniversary, *Porgy and Bess* entered the repertory of the Metropolitan Opera. In 1959, a screen adaptation was released with Sidney Poitier, Dorothy Dandridge, and Sammy Davis Jr.

MCA OC (1942); Columbia SC; RCA OC (1953); RCA OC (1976)/ Chilton (1973)/ TW.

JUBILEE

Music & lyrics: Cole Porter
Book: Moss Hart
Producers: Sam H. Harris & Max Gordon
Directors: Hassard Short, Monty Woolley
Choreographer: Albertina Rasch
Cast: Mary Boland, June Knight, Melville Cooper, Charles Walters, Derek Williams, Mark Plant, Montgomery Clift, May Boley, Margaret Adams
Songs: "Why Shouldn't I?"; "Begin the Beguine"; "A Picture of Me Without You"; "Me and Marie"; "Just One of Those Things"
New York run: Imperial Theatre, October 12, 1935; 169 p.

Seeking suitable inspiration for an elegant song-and-dance entertainment, Cole Porter and Moss Hart took off on a four-and-a-half month, 34,000-mile cruise around the world. Their hegira resulted in an airy concoction sparked by the recent Silver Jubilee of Britain's King George V and Queen Mary. The tale concerns itself with what might happen if members of a mythical royal family — thanks to a supposed uprising — were given the chance to do what they wanted while gadding about town incognito. King Melville Cooper spends his time perfecting sleight-of-hand tricks, Queen Mary Boland is thrilled to meet Mowgli the movie ape man, Prince Charles Walters learns how to begin the beguine from dancer June Knight, and Princess Margaret Adams answers her own question in "Why Shouldn't I?" by having just one of those crazy flings with a Noel Coward-type playwright. Then it's back to the pomp and circumstance of the royal jubilee. Though beloved by her theatre-going subjects, Miss Boland had to return to Hollywood after only four months; her successor Laura Hope Crews couldn't keep the celebration going a month.

Jubilee. Mary Boland and Melville Cooper singing "Me and Marie." (Vandamm)

JUMBO

Music: Richard Rodgers
Lyrics: Lorenz Hart
Book: Ben Hecht & Charles MacArthur
Producer: Billy Rose
Directors: John Murray Anderson, George Abbott
Choreographer: Allan K. Foster
Cast: Jimmy Durante, Paul Whiteman Orchestra, Donald Novis, Gloria Grafton, A. P. Kaye, A. Robins, Poodles Hanneford, Big Rosie, Tilda Getze
Songs: "Over and Over Again"; "The Circus Is on Parade"; "The Most Beautiful Girl in the World"; "My Romance"; "Little Girl Blue"
New York run: Hippodrome, November 16, 1935; 233 p.

The Hippodrome, once located on 43rd Street and 6th Avenue, was a huge barn of a theatre that had not been in use for five years when showman Billy Rose decided that it would be just the place to house the spectacular circus musical he named *Jumbo*. Designer Albert Johnson completely rebuilt the auditorium to make it resemble an actual circus, with a grandstand sloping up from a single circular revolving stage. The show marked the first of 34 musicals directed by George Abbott as well as the return to Broadway of Rodgers and Hart after almost three years in Hollywood. Plotted by Ben Hecht and Charles MacArthur to give plenty of opportunity for the specialty acts recruited from all over the world, the book had to do with a debt-ridden circus and what the well-meaning but inept publicity man Claudius B. Bowers (Jimmy Durante) does to help save the day. *Jumbo* cost an unprecedented $340,000 to open; it closed after rehearsing for six months and playing for five. The evening's highlight: the blue-tinted first-act finale, "Little Girl Blue," in which heroine Gloria Grafton (who had replaced Ella Logan before the premiere) dreams she is a child again being entertained by her favorite circus performers. Durante was also in the 1962 screen version, along with Doris Day and Martha Raye.

ZIEGFELD FOLLIES

Music: Vernon Duke
Lyrics: Ira Gershwin
Sketches: David Freedman
Producer: Billie Burke Ziegfeld (Messrs. Shubert uncredited)
Directors: John Murray Anderson, Edward Clark Lilley
Choreographers: Robert Alton, George Balanchine
Cast: Fanny Brice, Bob Hope, Gertrude Niesen, Josephine Baker, Hugh O'Connell, Harriet Hoctor, Eve Arden, Judy Canova, Cherry & June Preisser, Nicholas Brothers, John Hoysradt, Stan Kavanaugh
Songs: "Island in the West Indies"; "Words Without Music"; "That Moment of Moments"; "I Can't Get Started"
New York run: Winter Garden, January 30, 1936; 115 p.

Fanny Brice returned for her second Shubert-sponsored *Ziegfeld Follies* (it was her 15th and final Broadway show), along with a number of holdovers from the 1934 edition. They were joined by ballet choreographer George Balanchine making his Broadway debut. The revue was deemed superior to its predecessor, with Miss Brice up to her old shtick kidding modern dancing and playing Baby Snooks, and Bob Hope getting the chance to butter up Eve Arden in the classic "I Can't Get Started." Another highlight was the first-act finale spoofing the latest Hollywood extravaganza, "The Broadway Gold Melody Diggers of 42nd Street." The *Follies* reopened in the fall for 112 additional performances with Jane Pickens, Gypsy Rose Lee, and Cass Daley joining the cast.

ON YOUR TOES

Music: Richard Rodgers
Lyrics: Lorenz Hart
Book: Richard Rodgers, Lorenz Hart & George Abbott
Producer: Dwight Deere Wiman
Director: Worthington Miner (George Abbott uncredited)
Choreographer: George Balanchine
Cast: Ray Bolger, Luella Gear, Tamara Geva, Monty Woolley, Doris Carson, David Morris, Demetrios Vilan, George Church
Songs: "The Three B's"; "It's Got to Be Love"; "Too Good for the Average Man"; "There's a Small Hotel"; "The Heart Is Quicker Than the Eye"; "Quiet Night"; "Glad to Be Unhappy"; "On Your Toes"; "Slaughter on Tenth Avenue" (ballet)
New York run: Imperial Theatre, April 11, 1936; 315 p.

On Your Toes made a star of rubberlegged dancer Ray Bolger, and it also gave George Balanchine his first opportunity to create dances for a book musical. Most important, it signaled a major breakthrough in form by utilizing ballet as an integral part of the story. Junior Dolan (Bolger), an ex-vaudevillian now teaching music at Knickerbocker University, a WPA extension in New York, enlists the help of patroness Peggy Porterfield (Luella Gear) to persuade Sergei Alexandrovich (Monty Woolley), the director of the Russian Ballet, to stage a friend's jazzy "Slaughter on Tenth Avenue" ballet. While he may dream of sharing the pleasures of a small hotel with girlfriend Frankie Frayne (Doris Carson), Junior becomes involved with the company's prima ballerina, Vera Barnova (Tamara Geva), and even takes over the male lead in "Slaughter." This so enrages Vera's lover and regular dancing partner that he hires two thugs to kill Junior while he is performing on stage. To avoid being a target Junior keeps dancing even after the ballet is over, then — once the gunmen have been arrested — falls exhausted to the floor.

Richard Rodgers and Lorenz Hart had originally written the musical as a movie vehicle for Fred Astaire, but the dancer turned it down because he was afraid his public would not accept him without his trademark attire of top hat, white tie and tails. The team then rewrote the script as a stage musical and Lee Shubert took an option on it with Ray Bolger set for the male lead. When Shubert lost interest, the rights were picked up by Dwight Deere Wiman (it was the first of five Rodgers and Hart shows he would produce), with George Abbott joining the project as co-author and director. Production delays, however, prompted Abbott to withdraw as director, though he did return to restage the musical after its poorly-received Boston opening. Originally, Marilyn Miller and Gregory Ratoff were sought for the roles that went to Miss Geva and Mr. Woolley.

There have been two revivals of *On Your Toes* on Broadway. In 1954, Abbott and Balanchine put together a production starring Bobby Van, Vera Zorina (she had appeared in the role of the ballerina in London and in the movie version), and Elaine Stritch (who played Peggy and sang the interpolated "You Took Advantage of Me"). The general verdict was that the musical was hopelessly dated and it remained only two months. Twenty-nine years later, however, again staged by Abbott, it succeeded so well that it bested the original Broadway run. Natalia Makarova of the American Ballet Theatre made an impressive Main Stem debut in the show. She was replaced during the engagement by ballerinas Galina Panova and Valentina Kozlova, and Dina Merrill was replaced by Kitty Carlisle. (See page 264.) The 1939 movie, with Eddie Albert as Junior, used music only as background and for the ballets.
Columbia SC; MCA OC (1954); Polydor OC (1983)/ R&H.

On Your Toes. Luella Gear, Monty Woolley, Ray Bolger, and Demetrios Vilan. (White)

On Your Toes. Ray Bolger, George Church, and Tamara Geva in a dramatic moment from "Slaughter on Tenth Avenue." (White)

Red, Hot and Blue! Ethel Merman and Bob Hope. (Vandamm)

RED, HOT AND BLUE!

Music & lyrics: Cole Porter
Book: Howard Lindsay & Russel Crouse
Producer: Vinton Freedley
Director: Howard Lindsay
Choreographer: George Hale
Cast: Jimmy Durante, Ethel Merman, Bob Hope, Polly Walters, Paul & Grace Hartman, Vivian Vance, Lew Parker
Songs: "Ours"; "Down in the Depths (on the Ninetieth Floor)"; "You've Got Something"; "It's De-Lovely"; "Ridin' High"; "Red, Hot and Blue"
New York run: Alvin Theatre, October 29, 1936; 183 p.

Anxious to repeat the success of *Anything Goes,* producer Vinton Freedley signed its three stars and its three writers for his next musical, *Red, Hot and Blue!* But after overhearing Freedley promise Ethel Merman that hers would be the most prominent role, William Gaxton and Victor Moore bowed out and were replaced by Bob Hope and Jimmy Durante. The show, which seemed to be aiming for *Of Thee I Sing*-type political satire, offered Miss Merman as Nails O'Reilly Duquesne, a manicurist-turned-wealthy widow, Hope as Bob Hale, her lawyer and love interest, and Durante as Policy Pinkle, the captain of the polo team at Larks Nest Prison. Pinkle is released to help win a Congressional committee's approval for Nails and Bob's national lottery in which the first prize goes to the ticket holder who finds a girl who had sat on a hot waffle iron when she was four. The Supreme Court, however, declares the lottery unconstitutional on the grounds that it might benefit the American people. Though no red hot smash, the musical served to introduce three certifiable Cole Porter standards: "It's De-Lovely," "Down in the Depths," and "Ridin' High." It is also remembered for the battle of the billing, which was resolved by crossing the names of Jimmy Durante and Ethel Merman above the show's title.
AEI OC.

Note that Vincente Minnelli's name is misspelled twice.

THE SHOW IS ON

Music & lyrics: Miscellaneous writers
Sketches: David Freedman, Moss Hart
Producers: Messrs. Shubert
Directors: Vincente Minnelli, Edward Clark Lilley
Choreographer: Robert Alton, Harry Losee
Cast: Beatrice Lillie, Bert Lahr, Reginald Gardiner, Mitzi Mayfair, Paul Haakon, Gracie Barrie, Charles Walters, Vera Allen, Jack McCauley
Songs: "Now" (Vernon Duke-Ted Fetter); "Rhythm" (Richard Rodgers- Lorenz Hart); "Song of the Woodman" (Harold Arlen-E. Y. Harburg); "Long as You've Got Your Health" (Will Irwin-Harburg, Norman Zeno); "By Strauss" (George Gershwin-Ira Gershwin); "Little Old Lady" (Hoagy Carmichael-Stanley Adams)
New York run: Winter Garden, December 25, 1936; 237 p.

The fifth and final mid-Thirties revue presented by the Shuberts at the Winter Garden was one of the brightest, merriest, and most elegant of the decade's stage attractions. Featuring two superior clowns, Beatrice Lillie and Bert Lahr, *The Show Is On* was something of a successor to *At Home Abroad,* only this time the theme was around the world of show business. In songs, sketches, and production numbers, it looked in on a variety of phenomena and events — from excessively rhythmic pop singers to raffish burlesque shows, from John Gielgud's production of *Hamlet* (which is ruined by the outbursts of Miss Lillie's boorish socialite) to coquettish music-hall entertainers (Miss Lillie perched on a migratory half moon dispensing garters to favored gentlemen), and from he-man concert baritones (Lahr's classic "Song of the Woodman") to an old-fashioned tent show production of *Uncle Tom's Cabin. The Show Is On* returned briefly in the fall of 1937 with Rose King and Willie Howard.

BABES IN ARMS

Music: Richard Rodgers
Lyrics: Lorenz Hart
Book: Richard Rodgers & Lorenz Hart
Producer: Dwight Deere Wiman
Director: Robert Sinclair
Choreographer: George Balanchine
Cast: Mitzi Green, Wynn Murray, Ray Heatherton, Duke McHale, Alfred Drake, Ray McDonald, Grace McDonald, Nicholas Brothers, Dan Dailey
Songs: "Where or When"; "Babes in Arms"; "I Wish I Were in Love Again"; "My Funny Valentine"; "Johnny One Note"; "Imagine"; "All at Once"; "The Lady Is a Tramp"; "You Are So Fair"
New York run: Shubert Theatre, April 14, 1937; 289 p.

With such songs as "I Wish I Were in Love Again," "Johnny One Note," "The Lady Is a Tramp," "My Funny Valentine," and "Where or When," *Babes in Arms* could claim more hits than any other Rodgers and Hart musical. In the high-spirited, youthful show, a group of teenagers, whose parents are out-of-work vaudevillians, stage a revue to keep from being sent to a work farm. Unfortunately, the show is a bomb. Later, when a transatlantic French flyer lands nearby, they are able to attract enough publicity to put on a successful show and build their own youth center. Because the sets were modest and the cast boasted no stellar names, producer Dwight Deere Wiman priced his tickets at a $3.85 top. Among the show's Broadway debuts were those of Alfred Drake (he sang the title song) and Dan Dailey. The 1939 movie version featured Judy Garland and Mickey Rooney.
Columbia SC/ R&H.

I'D RATHER BE RIGHT

Music: Richard Rodgers
Lyrics: Lorenz Hart
Book: George S. Kaufman & Moss Hart
Producer: Sam H. Harris
Director: George S. Kaufman
Choreographers: Charles Weidman, Ned McGurn
Cast: George M. Cohan, Taylor Holmes, Joy Hodges, Austin Marshall, Marion Green, Mary Jane Walsh
Songs: "Have You Met Miss Jones?"; "Sweet Sixty-Five"; "We're Going to Balance the Budget"; "I'd Rather Be Right"; "Off the Record"
New York run: Alvin Theatre, November 2, 1937; 290 p.

I'd Rather Be Right was the most anxiously awaited theatrical event of the decade for two reasons: the central character was President Franklin D. Roosevelt and the part was being played by the legendary George M. Cohan, who was returning to the musical stage for the first time in ten years in the only song-and-dance show he ever appeared in that he did not write himself. The work, however, was considered not quite up to the satirical standards set by *Of Thee I Sing*, with which it was most frequently compared. The locale is New York's Central Park on the 4th of July. Peggy and Phil (Joy Hodges and Austin Marshall) hope to get married but Phil's boss won't give him a raise until Roosevelt balances the budget. Phil falls asleep and dreams that they meet FDR strolling through the park. After Phil explains the couple's dilemma, Roosevelt promises to help — which is only an excuse for some genial ribbing at the expense of Cabinet members, the Supreme Court, the PWA, fireside chats, Alf Landon, press conferences, and the President's decision to seek a third term.
Random House (1937)/ R&H.

I'd Rather Be Right. George M. Cohan as President Franklin D. Roosevelt giving a 4th of July speech. (Vandamm)

PINS AND NEEDLES

Music & lyrics: Harold Rome
Sketches: Miscellaneous writers
Producer: ILGWU
Director: Charles Friedman
Choreographer: Gluck Sandor
Cast: ILGWU members
Songs: "Sing Me a Song With Social Significance"; "Sunday in the Park"; "Nobody Makes a Pass at Me"; "Chain Store Daisy"; "One Big Union for Two"; "Four Little Angels of Peace"; "Doin' the Reactionary"
New York run: Labor Stage, November 27, 1937; 1,108 p.

Pins and Needles was initially presented for a limited engagement at the tiny Labor Stage (formerly the Princess Theatre) by and for members of the International Ladies Garment Workers Union, but it soon attracted audiences in such droves that it kept on running until it overtook *Irene* as the long-run record holder for musicals. Though reflecting a basically liberal, pro-union slant, the attitude was generally good-humored as it took aim at warmongers, bigots, reactionaries, Nazis, Fascists, Communists, and the DAR — and it even managed a few digs at the labor movement itself. Retitled *New Pins and Needles* in 1939, the show moved to the Windsor Theatre, then on 48th Street east of 7th Avenue, at a top ticket price of $1.65. Among those associated with the revue, songwriter Harold Rome, making his professional debut, was the one most responsible for its special flavor and appeal. In September 1938, Rome joined George S. Kaufman and Moss Hart in creating *Sing Out the News,* a more polished variation on *Pins and Needles,* which proved less successful.
Columbia SC.

HOORAY FOR WHAT!

Music: Harold Arlen
Lyrics: E. Y. Harburg
Book: Howard Lindsay & Russel Crouse
Producers: Messrs. Shubert
Directors: Vincente Minnelli, Howard Lindsay
Choreographers: Robert Alton, Agnes de Mille
Cast: Ed Wynn, Jack Whiting, Paul Haakon, June Clyde, Vivian Vance, Ruthanna Boris, Hugh Martin, Ralph Blane, Meg Mundy
Songs: "God's Country"; "I've Gone Romantic on You"; "Moanin' in the Mornin' "; "Down With Love"; "In the Shade of the New Apple Tree"
New York run: Winter Garden, December 1, 1937; 200 p.

Although it starred the clownish Ed Wynn, and even made room for his vaudeville specialties, *Hooray for What!* was primarily concerned with such weighty and timely matters as poison gas, munitions, diplomatic duplicity, espionage, and actual warfare. In the outlandish, satirical plot, Chuckles, a horticulturist, invents a gas to kill worms but then discovers that it can also kill humans. The invention sets off an arms race among the European powers who meet at a so-called Peace Conference in Geneva, where spies try to steal the formula from Chuckles' room at the Hotel de l'Espionage. When, using a mirror, a seductive spy copies the formula backwards, the gas turns out to be harmless and war is miraculously averted. *Hooray for What!* marked Agnes de Mille's first efforts as a Broadway choreographer, though most of her work was cut by the time the show reached New York.

THE CRADLE WILL ROCK

Music, lyrics & book: Marc Blitzstein
Producer: Sam H. Grisman
Director: Orson Welles
Cast: Howard DaSilva, Will Geer, Hiram Sherman, Olive Stanton, John Hoysradt, Marc Blitzstein
Songs: "The Freedom of the Press"; "Honolulu"; "Art for Art's Sake"; "Nickel Under the Foot"; "The Cradle Will Rock"; "Joe Worker"
New York run: Windsor Theatre, January 3, 1938; 108 p.

One of the most controversial stage productions of the decade, Marc Blitzstein's *The Cradle Will Rock* was initially a project of the WPA's Federal Theatre, with John Houseman as producer and Orson Welles as director. A grim parable dealing with the struggle for union recognition in a steel town, the work was scheduled to open June 16, 1937, at the Maxine Elliott Theatre, with a ticket scale of 25¢, 40¢, and 55¢. Because of political pressure, the Federal Theatre cancelled the production at the last minute, but Welles was determined to put on the show anywhere and anyway he could. That same night, he managed to secure the Venice Theatre (once known as Jolson's 59th Street Theatre), where the actors — who were forbidden from appearing on any stage by their own union — performed from their seats in various parts of the theatre, while Blitzstein provided piano accompaniment. The musical gave 19 performances in this fashion.

When producer Sam Grisman offered *The Cradle Will Rock* at his Windsor Theatre, the cast did perform on stage, though there was no scenery and the music was still played by the composer at the piano. The story of this "Play in Music" is little more than an animated left-wing political cartoon. In Steeltown, USA, the noble union organizer Larry Foreman (Howard DaSilva) does battle against the powerful and corrupt Mr. Mister (Will Geer), who owns everything and everyone in town, and eventually leads the workers to victory. In addition to the labor-management struggle, Blitzstein also turned his attention to the issue of prostitution, contrasting the character of a wistful street walker with the venality of journalists, artists, educators, religious leaders, and doctors. *The Cradle Will Rock* had brief revivals in 1947 with Alfred Drake as Larry Foreman, in 1964 with Jerry Orbach, and in 1983 (in a John Houseman production) with Randle Mell. American Legacy OC; Composer OC (1964)/ Random House (1938)/ TW.

The Cradle Will Rock. Marc Blitzstein at the piano.

I Married an Angel. Vera Zorina and Dennis King.

I MARRIED AN ANGEL

Music: Richard Rodgers
Lyrics: Lorenz Hart
Book: Richard Rodgers & Lorenz Hart
Producer: Dwight Deere Wiman
Director: Joshua Logan
Choreographer: George Balanchine
Cast: Dennis King, Vera Zorina, Vivienne Segal, Walter Slezak, Audrey Christie, Charles Walters
Songs: "Did You Ever Get Stung?"; "I Married an Angel"; "I'll Tell the Man in the Street"; "How to Win Friends and Influence People"; "Spring Is Here"; "A Twinkle in Your Eye"; "At the Roxy Music Hall"
New York run: Shubert Theatre, May 11, 1938; 338 p.

"Musical comedy has met its masters, and they have reared back and passed a 44th Street miracle," wrote Brooks Atkinson in the *Times* following the opening of *I Married an Angel.* That miracle had to do not only with the pleasures of the entertainment but also with the audience's total acceptance that the disillusioned hero's vow to marry only an angel actually comes true. The setting of this fantasy is Budapest where banker Willy Palaffi (Dennis King) finds that his celestial bride (Vera Zorina) causes all kinds of embarrassing problems with her heavenly honesty. Willy's sharp-tongued sister Peggy (Vivienne Segal) manages to save the marriage by dispensing such worldly advice to the angel as the proper use of a twinkle in her eye. The show's show stopper, unrelated to the proceedings or the locale, was the witty travesty of a typical Radio City Music Hall presentation. *I Married an Angel* was adapted by Rodgers and Hart from a Hungarian play on which they had previously based an unused movie script. The musical, the first of 14 staged by Joshua Logan, also marked the occasion of Zorina's Broadway debut. Jeanette MacDonald and Nelson Eddy were in the 1942 film. AEI part OC/ R&H.

HELLZAPOPPIN

Music: Sammy Fain, etc.
Lyrics: Charles Tobias, etc.
Sketches: Ole Olsen & Chic Johnson
Producers: Ole Olsen & Chic Johnson (Messrs. Shubert uncredited)
Director: Edward Duryea Dowling
Cast: Ole Olsen & Chic Johnson, Barto & Mann, Radio Rogues, Hal Sherman, Ray Kinney
Songs: "Fuddle Dee Duddle"; "Abe Lincoln" (Earl Robinson-Alfred Hayes); "It's Time to Say Aloha"; "Boomps-a-Daisy" (Annette Mills)
New York run: 46th Street Theatre, September 22, 1938; 1,404 p.

It was more of a raucous vaudeville show than a revue, it featured no performers whose names could attract Broadway theatregoers, and it received generally unfavorable notices. Yet when this legendary freak success closed up shop it had bested the long-run record for musicals recently established by *Pins and Needles*. *Hellzapoppin* was basically the same rowdy act that Olsen and Johnson had been performing all over the country for 14 years. But customers were attracted to its lowbrow high jinks, especially such audience-participation gimmicks as dancing in the aisles, and such running gags as the one of the little man walking through the audience with a plant for Mrs. Jones that grows and grows and grows. Within two months after its opening the show was transferred to the Winter Garden where it remained for the rest of its engagement. Olsen and Johnson, along with Martha Raye, were in the 1941 screen version.

Hellzapoppin. Behind Ole Olsen and Chic Johnson are the Radio Rogues (Sidney Chatton, Jimmy Hollywood, Eddie Bartel). The girls are Sally Bond and Margie Young. (DeMirjian)

Knickerbocker Holiday. Walter Huston, Jeanne Madden, and ladies of New Amsterdam. (Lucas)

KNICKERBOCKER HOLIDAY

Music: Kurt Weill
Lyrics & book: Maxwell Anderson
Producer: Playwrights' Company
Director: Joshua Logan
Choreographers: Carl Randall, Edwin Denby
Cast: Walter Huston, Ray Middleton, Jeanne Madden, Richard Kollmar, Robert Rounseville, Howard Freeman, Clarence Nordstrom
Songs: "There's Nowhere to Go but Up"; "It Never Was You"; "How Can You Tell an American?"; "September Song"; "The Scars"
New York run: Ethel Barrymore Theatre, October 19, 1938; 168 p.

A victim of Hitler's Germany, Kurt Weill settled in New York to become one of the Broadway theatre's most admired and influential composers. For *Knickerbocker Holiday,* the second of his eight American works, he was joined by playwright Maxwell Anderson to create what was probably the first musical to use an historical subject as the means through which views on contemporary matters could be expressed. Here the theme was totalitarianism versus democracy, as personified by Pieter Stuyvesant (Walter Huston), the autocratic governor of New Amsterdam in 1647, and Brom Broeck (Richard Kollmar), the freedom-loving "first American" who is opposed to any kind of government interference. The point became somewhat muddied when it appeared that Anderson's target was President Roosevelt rather than any of the peace-menacing dictators then in power. There was confusion of a more dramatic kind since Walter Huston, in his only Broadway musical, made Stuyvesant such a likable chap — especially when he sang of the anxieties of growing old in "September Song" — that audience sympathies tended to be with the wrong man. The 1944 screen version featured Nelson Eddy and Charles Coburn.
AEI OC/ Anderson House (1938)/ R&H.

Leave It to Me! Mary Martin.
(Vandamm)

LEAVE IT TO ME!

Music & lyrics: Cole Porter
Book: Bella & Samuel Spewack
Producer: Vinton Freedley
Director: Samuel Spewack
Choreographer: Robert Alton
Cast: William Gaxton, Victor Moore, Sophie Tucker, Tamara, Mary Martin, Edward H. Robins, Alexander Asro, George Tobias, Gene Kelly
Songs: "Get Out of Town"; "From Now On"; "Most Gentlemen Don't Like Love"; "My Heart Belongs to Daddy"; "I Want to Go Home"
New York run: Imperial Theatre, November 9, 1938; 291 p.

With a book distantly related to their own play, *Clear All Wires,* Bella and Samuel Spewack came up with a spoof of Communism and U.S. diplomacy that offered comedian Victor Moore one of his meatiest roles as mild-mannered Alonzo P. "Stinky" Goodhue. Goodhue is unwillingly named Ambassador to the Soviet Union because his ambitious wife (Sophie Tucker) has contributed generously to President Roosevelt's re-election campaign. Aided by foreign correspondent Buckley Joyce Thomas (William Gaxton), the Ambassador does everything he can to be recalled, but each blunder only succeeds in making him a bigger hero. Finally, he introduces a plan to ensure world peace — which, of course, no one wants — and Stinky is soon happily on his way back to Kansas. Mary Martin made a notable Broadway debut in *Leave It to Me!,* singing and coyly stripping to "My Heart Belongs to Daddy" while being stranded on a Siberian railroad station with a male quartet that included Gene Kelly. Two months after the musical closed it paid a two-week return visit to New York.
Chilton (1976)/ TW.

The Boys from Syracuse. Marcy Wescott, Wynn Murray, and Muriel Angelus singing "Sing for Your Supper." (Vandamm)

The Boys from Syracuse. Betty Bruce, Teddy Hart, and Eddie Albert. (Vandamm)

THE BOYS FROM SYRACUSE

Music: Richard Rodgers
Lyrics: Lorenz Hart
Book: George Abbott
Producer-director: George Abbott
Choreographer: George Balanchine
Cast: Jimmy Savo, Teddy Hart, Eddie Albert, Wynn Murray, Ronald Graham, Muriel Angelus, Marcy Wescott, Betty Bruce, Burl Ives
Songs: "Falling in Love With Love"; "The Shortest Day of the Year"; "This Can't Be Love"; "He and She"; "You Have Cast Your Shadow on the Sea"; "Sing for Your Supper"; "What Can You Do With a Man?"
New York run: Alvin Theatre, November 23, 1938; 235 p.

The genesis of *The Boys from Syracuse* began when Rodgers and Hart, while working on another show, were discussing the fact that no one had yet written a Broadway musical based on a play by Shakespeare. Their obvious choice was *The Comedy of Errors* (whose plot Shakespeare had borrowed from Plautus' *Menaechmi*), partly because Hart's brother, Teddy Hart, was always being confused with another comic actor, Jimmy Savo. The action takes place in Ephesus in ancient Asia Minor, and the mildly ribald tale concerns the efforts of two boys from Syracuse, Antipholus and his servant Dromio (Eddie Albert and Jimmy Savo), to find their long-lost twins who — for reasons of plot confusion — are also named Antipholus and Dromio (Ronald Graham and Teddy Hart). Complications arise when the wives of the Ephesians, Adriana (Muriel Angelus) and her servant Luce (Wynn Murray), mistake the two strangers for their husbands, though the couples eventually get sorted out after Adriana's sister Luciana (Marcy Wescott) and the Syracuse Antipholus admit their love while protesting "This Can't Be Love." In 1963, an Off-Broadway revival had a longer run than the original. Allan Jones, Joe Penner, and Martha Raye were in the 1940 film.

In 1981, *Oh, Brother!,* a second musical adaptation of the same basic tale, had a brief stay on Broadway. Other musicals inspired by Shakespeare have been *Swingin' the Dream* (1939) and *Babes in the Wood* (1964), both from *A Midsummer Night's Dream; Kiss Me, Kate* (1948), from *The Taming of the Shrew; West Side Story* (1957) and *Sensations* (1970), both from *Romeo and Juliet; Love and Let Love* (1968), *Your Own Thing* (1968), and *Music Is* (1976), all from *Twelfth Night; Two Gentlemen of Verona* (1971); and *Rockabye Hamlet* (1976). Columbia SC; Capitol OC (1963)/ R&H.

Too Many Girls. Eddie Bracken and Hal LeRoy help and inebriated Desi Arnaz confront Marcy Wescott. (Vandamm)

TOO MANY GIRLS

Music: Richard Rodgers
Lyrics: Lorenz Hart
Book: George Marion Jr.
Producer-director: George Abbott
Choreographer: Robert Alton
Cast: Marcy Wescott, Desi Arnaz, Hal LeRoy, Mary Jane Walsh, Diosa Costello, Richard Kollmar, Eddie Bracken, Leila Ernst, Van Johnson
Songs: "Love Never Went to College"; "Spic and Spanish"; "I Like to Recognize the Tune"; "I Didn't Know What Time It Was"; "She Could Shake the Maracas"; "Give It Back to the Indians"
New York run: Imperial Theatre, October 18, 1939; 249 p.

By 1939 — after such shows as *Leave It to Jane* and *Good News!* — a rah-rah college musical about football may not have been the most original idea along the Main Stem, but blessed with spirited songs by Rodgers and Hart, a youthful, talented cast, and fast-paced direction by George Abbott, *Too Many Girls* won high marks with both critics and public. Set in Pottawatomie College, Stop Gap, New Mexico (described as "one of those colleges that play football on Friday"), the musical featured an All-American backfield composed of Desi Arnaz, Hal LeRoy, Richard Kollmar (succeeded by Van Johnson for the tour), and Eddie Bracken, who also, unknown to her, act as bodyguards for wealthy coed Marcy Wescott. Soon boy students are pairing off with girl students, and Kollmar and Wescott get the chance to voice such sentiments as "Love Never Went to College" and "I Didn't Know What Time It Was." The 1940 movie version with Lucille Ball and Ann Miller also included members of the original cast.
Painted Smiles SC/ R&H.

DUBARRY WAS A LADY

Music & lyrics: Cole Porter
Book: Herbert Fields & B. G. DeSylva
Producer: B. G. DeSylva
Director: Edgar MacGregor
Choreographer: Robert Alton
Cast: Bert Lahr, Ethel Merman, Betty Grable, Benny Baker, Ronald Graham, Charles Walters, Kay Sutton
Songs: "When Love Beckoned (in Fifty-Second Street)"; "Well, Did You Evah?"; "But in the Morning, No"; "Do I Love You?"; "It Was Written in the Stars"; "Give Him the Oo-la-la"; "Katie Went to Haiti"; "Friendship"
New York run: 46th Street Theatre, December 6, 1939; 408 p.

Broadway's fifth longest-running musical of the Thirties, *DuBarry Was a Lady* was the first of three smash hits offered in succession by producer B.G. DeSylva. The show evolved through the merging of two ideas: Herbert Fields wanted to write a musical with Mae West as DuBarry and DeSylva wanted to write one about a washroom attendant in a swanky New York nightclub who is smitten by a Brenda Frazier-type debutante. Both concepts were combined by having the attendant, named Louis Blore, switch his affections to May Daly, the club's flashy singing star, and by having Louis — after taking a mickey finn — dream that he is King Louis XV and the singer his unaccommodating concubine. Ethel Merman and Bert Lahr, who stopped the show nightly with their raucous avowal of eternal friendship, were hailed as Broadway's royal couple, and Betty Grable won such favorable notice that she was soon whisked off to Hollywood stardom. During the Broadway run, Miss Merman was succeeded by Gypsy Rose Lee and Frances Williams. The show's movie version, in 1943, featured Lucille Ball, Gene Kelly, and Red Skelton.
TW.

DuBarry Was a Lady. Bert Lahr and Ethel Merman.

Louisiana Purchase. William Gaxton, Vera Zorina, Victor Moore, and Irene Bordoni at the Mardi Gras. (Lucas & Monroe)

LOUISIANA PURCHASE

Music & lyrics: Irving Berlin
Book: Morrie Ryskind & B. G. DeSylva
Producer: B. G. DeSylva (Irving Berlin uncredited)
Director: Edgar MacGregor
Choreographer: George Balanchine
Cast: William Gaxton, Vera Zorina, Victor Moore, Irene Bordoni, Carol Bruce, Nick Long Jr., Hugh Martin, Ralph Blane, Edward H. Robins
Songs: "Louisiana Purchase"; "It's a Lovely Day Tomorrow"; "Outside of That I Love You"; "You're Lonely and I'm Lonely"; "Latins Know How"; "What Chance Have I?"; "The Lord Done Fixed Up My Soul"; "Fools Fall in Love"; "You Can't Brush Me Off"
New York run: Imperial Theatre, May 28, 1940; 444 p.

After playing a Vice President in *Of Thee I Sing* and *Let 'Em Eat Cake* and an Ambassador in *Leave It to Me!,* Victor Moore endeared himself to audiences again by impersonating a United States Senator in *Louisiana Purchase.* In the libretto, prompted by recent revelations of corruption involving the late political leader Huey Long, the seemingly innocent Senator Oliver P. Loganberry goes to New Orleans to investigate the shady operations of the Louisiana Purchasing Company. Jim Taylor (William Gaxton), the company's president, tries to block the probe by involving the incorruptible Senator first with Marina Van Linden (Vera Zorina), a Viennese refugee, then with Mme. Yvonne Bordelaise (Irene Bordoni), a local restaurateuse. Loganberry manages to get out of the trap by marrying Yvonne, but he is ultimately defeated when, being a politician, he is unwilling to cross the picket line in front of the building in which his hearings are to take place. The second of producer B. G. DeSylva's three hits in a row, *Louisiana Purchase* marked Irving Berlin's return to Broadway after an absence of almost seven years. Moore, Zorina, and Bordoni were joined by Bob Hope for the 1941 movie.

CABIN IN THE SKY

Music: Vernon Duke
Lyrics: John Latouche
Book: Lynn Root
Producers: Albert Lewis & Vinton Freedley
Directors: George Balanchine, Albert Lewis
Choreographer: George Balanchine
Cast: Ethel Waters, Todd Duncan, Dooley Wilson, Katherine Dunham, Rex Ingram, J. Rosamond Johnson
Songs: "Taking a Chance on Love" (lyric with Ted Fetter); "Cabin in the Sky"; "Love Turned the Light Out"; "Honey in the Honeycomb"; "My Old Virginia Home (on the River Nile)"; "Do What You Wanna Do"
New York run: Martin Beck Theatre, October 25, 1940; 156 p.

The first major musical to play the Martin Beck Theatre (on 45th Street west of 8th Avenue), *Cabin in the Sky* was a parable of Southern Negro life with echoes of Ferenc Molnar's *Liliom* (which would be turned into the musical *Carousel*) and Marc Connelly's *The Green Pastures*. The fantasy deals with the struggle between the Lawd's General (Todd Duncan) and Lucifer Jr. (Rex Ingram) for the soul of shiftless Little Joe Jackson (Dooley Wilson), who has been fatally wounded in a street brawl. Because of the fervent prayers of Joe's devoted wife, Petunia (Ethel Waters), Joe is granted six months to make amends to allow him to get into Heaven. Lucifer Jr. offers temptation in the form of Georgia Brown (Katherine Dunham), but with Petunia's help Joe eventually manages to squeeze through the Pearly Gates. Miss Waters won resounding acclaim in this her only book musical, in which she sang the showstopper, "Taking a Chance on Love." In 1964, Rosetta LeNoire appeared in an adaptation which ran briefly Off Broadway. The 1943 film version gave Miss Waters the chance to repeat her role. Capitol OC (1964).

PANAMA HATTIE

Music & lyrics: Cole Porter
Book: Herbert Fields & B. G. DeSylva
Producer: B. G. DeSylva
Director: Edgar MacGregor
Choreographer: Robert Alton
Cast: Ethel Merman, Arthur Treacher, James Dunn, Rags Ragland, Pat Harrington, Frank Hyers, Phyllis Brooks, Betty Hutton, Joan Carroll, June Allyson, Lucille Bremer, Vera Ellen, Betsy Blair
Songs: "My Mother Would Love You"; "I've Still Got My Health"; "Fresh as a Daisy"; "Let's Be Buddies"; "Make It Another Old-Fashioned, Please"; "I'm Throwing a Ball Tonight"
New York run: 46th Street Theatre, October 30, 1940; 501 p.

According to Ethel Merman, Hattie Maloney in *Panama Hattie* was an expansion of the Katie who went to Haiti in *DuBarry Was a Lady*. The show was the first in which Miss Merman received solo star billing and it had the longest run of the five musicals in which she was spotlighted singing the songs of Cole Porter. Ethel's Hattie is a brassy, gold-hearted nightclub owner in Panama City who becomes engaged to divorcé Nick Bullitt (James Dunn), a Philadelphia Main Liner. In order for the couple to marry, however, Hattie must first win the approval of Nick's snotty eight-year-old daughter (Joan Carroll), which she accomplishes through the conciliatory "Let's Be Buddies." *Panama Hattie* was the last of the three-in-a-row hits produced by B. G. DeSylva. In 1942, a movie version co-starred Ann Sothern and Red Skelton.
TW.

PAL JOEY

Music: Richard Rodgers
Lyrics: Lorenz Hart
Book: John O'Hara (George Abbott uncredited)
Producer-director: George Abbott
Choreographer: Robert Alton
Cast: Vivienne Segal, Gene Kelly, June Havoc, Jack Durant, Leila Ernst, Jean Casto, Van Johnson, Stanley Donen, Tilda Getze
Songs: "You Mustn't Kick It Around"; "I Could Write a Book"; "That Terrific Rainbow"; "Happy Hunting Horn"; "Bewitched"; "The Flower Garden of My Heart"; "Zip"; "Den of Iniquity"; "Take Him"
New York run: Ethel Barrymore Theatre, December 25, 1940; 374 p.

With its heel for a hero, its smoky nightclub ambiance, and its true-to-life, untrue-to-anyone characters, *Pal Joey* was a major breakthrough in bringing about a more adult form of musical theatre. The idea originated with author John O'Hara who suggested to Rodgers and Hart that they collaborate on a musical treatment of O'Hara's series of *New Yorker* short stories about Joey Evans, a small-time Chicago entertainer. In the libretto (written with an uncredited assist from producer-director George Abbott), Joey gets a job at Mike's Club where he is attracted to Linda English (Leila Ernst) but drops her in favor of the rich, bewitched dowager, Vera Simpson (Vivienne Segal). Vera builds a glittering nightclub, the Chez Joey, for her paramour, but she soon tires of him, and at the end — after an encounter with blackmailers Ludlow Lowell (Jack Durant) and Gladys Bumps (June Havoc) — Joey is off in search of other conquests. *Pal Joey* marked the only Broadway musical in which Gene Kelly played a major role.

Though it was well received, the musical had to wait until a 1952 revival to be fully appreciated. Miss Segal repeated her original role and Harold Lang played Joey. During the run Helen Gallagher was succeeded by Nancy Walker as Gladys. (See page 153). In 1976, *Pal Joey* returned to Broadway for two months with Joan Copeland and Christopher Chadman. The 1957 screen version featured Frank Sinatra, Rita Hayworth, and Kim Novak.

CSP part OC (1952); Capitol part OC (1952)/ Random House (1952)/ R&H.

Pal Joey. Gene Kelly, June Havoc, and Jack Durant. (Fred Fehl)

LADY IN THE DARK

Music: Kurt Weill
Lyrics: Ira Gershwin
Book: Moss Hart
Producer: Sam H. Harris
Directors: Hassard Short, Moss Hart
Choreographer: Albertina Rasch
Cast: Gertrude Lawrence, Victor Mature, Danny Kaye, Macdonald Carey, Bert Lytell, Evelyn Wyckoff, Margaret Dale, Ron Field
Songs: "One Life to Live"; "Girl of the Moment"; "This Is New"; "The Princess of Pure Delight"; "My Ship"; "Jenny"; "Tschaikowsky"
New York run: Alvin Theatre, January 23, 1941; 467 p.

Though he originally conceived it as a vehicle for Katharine Cornell, Moss Hart turned *Lady in the Dark* into a vehicle for Gertrude Lawrence by enlisting the services of Kurt Weill and Ira Gershwin and changing it from a play to a musical. The work is concerned with *Allure* magazine editor Liza Elliott, whose inability to make up her mind has led her to seek psychiatric help. This feeling of insecurity contributes to her doubts about marrying her lover, publisher Kendall Nesbitt (Bert Lytell), and makes her think she is falling in love with movie star Randy Curtis (Victor Mature). In the end, however, she realizes that the man who can cure her neuroses is really Charley Johnson (Macdonald Carey), the magazine's cynical advertising manager. How does she know? Charley can complete the song "My Ship," which Liza had learned as a child but is now unable to finish. ("Ah! Sweet Mystery of Life" had served a similar function in *Naughty Marietta*.) All other musical pieces in *Lady in the Dark* — including the tongue-twisting "Tschaikowsky" for Danny Kaye and the raucous showstopper "Jenny" for Miss Lawrence, both part of the colorful circus scene — are performed within the dreams that Liza reveals to her doctor.

Lady in the Dark closed for vacation in June 1941, then reopened in September with Lytell replaced by Paul McGrath, Mature by Willard Parker, Carey by Walter Coy, and Kaye by Eric Brotherson. Following a tour, the musical returned to Broadway in February 1943 and remained for 83 performances. Ginger Rogers and Ray Milland were in the 1944 movie version.

RCA OC; AEI OC; Columbia SC/ Random House (1941)/ R&H.

Lady in the Dark. Margaret Dale, Danny Kaye, and Gertrude Lawrence. (Vandamm)

BEST FOOT FORWARD

Music & lyrics: Hugh Martin & Ralph Blane
Book: John Cecil Holm
Producer: George Abbott (Richard Rodgers uncredited)
Director: George Abbott
Choreographer: Gene Kelly
Cast: Rosemary Lane, Marty May, Gil Stratton Jr., Maureen Cannon, Nancy Walker, June Allyson, Kenny Bowers, Victoria Schools, Tommy Dix, Danny Daniels
Songs: "The Three B's"; "Buckle Down, Winsocki"; "Just a Little Joint With a Jukebox"; "What Do You Think I Am?"; "Ev'ry Time"; "Shady Lady Bird"
New York run: Ethel Barrymore Theatre, October 1, 1941; 326 p.

Taking place at Winsocki, a Pennsylvania prep school, *Best Foot Forward* is all about the complications that result from the arrival of Hollywood glamour girl Gale Joy (Rosemary Lane) who, as a publicity stunt, has accepted the invitation of Bud Hooper (Gil Stratton Jr.) to be his date at the annual prom. Not only does this provoke hurt feelings on the part of Bud's steady girl, Helen Schlessinger (Maureen Cannon), it also results in a near-riot when souvenir hungry prom-trotters strip the movie star down to her essentials. (John Cecil Holm's libretto was based on his own experience when, as a student at the Perkiomen School near Philadelphia, he had invited movie star Betty Compson to be his prom date. The story he wrote was his idea of what might have happened had she shown up.) The rousing "Buckle Down, Winsocki" became the best-known song in the show, which was the first to present Nancy Walker and June Allyson in major roles. In 1963, an Off-Broadway revival performed a similar function for 17-year-old Liza Minnelli and Christopher (then Ronald) Walken. The 1943 screen version featured Lucille Ball, and Misses Walker and Allyson.
Cadence OC (1963)/ TW.

Best Foot Forward. June Allyson, Victoria Schools, and Nancy Walker singing "The Three B's." (Vandamm)

Let's Face It! An awkward situation involving Houston Richards, Benny Baker, Mary Jane Walsh, Danny Kaye, and Jack Williams. (Vandamm)

LET'S FACE IT!

Music & lyrics: Cole Porter
Book: Herbert & Dorothy Fields
Producer: Vinton Freedley
Director: Edgar MacGregor
Choreographer: Charles Walters
Cast: Danny Kaye, Eve Arden, Benny Baker, Mary Jane Walsh, Edith Meiser, Vivian Vance, Nanette Fabray, Mary Parker & Billy Daniel, Jack Williams, Houston Richards
Songs: "Farming"; "Ev'rything I Love"; "Ace in the Hole"; "Let's Not Talk About Love"; "A Little Rumba Numba"; "I Hate You, Darling"; "Melody in 4-F" (Sylvia Fine - Max Liebman)
New York run: Imperial Theatre, October 29, 1941; 547 p.

Producer Vinton Freedley got the idea for *Let's Face It!* while reading a newspaper account about a number of patriotic women who were so anxious to help the morale of World War II soldiers that they wrote to army camps requesting permission to entertain servicemen in their homes. Using a 1925 Broadway hit, *The Cradle Snatchers,* as foundation, the script by Herbert and Dorothy Fields was about three Southampton matrons who, having grown suspicious of their husbands' frequent hunting trips, have enlisted the service of three rookies from a nearby army camp for an evening of fun and games. The inevitable embarrassments occur when the husbands and their girl friends — as well as the soldiers' girl friends — show up at the party. Danny Kaye (in his first starring role) scored a hit particularly with special material coauthored by his wife, Sylvia Fine. Kaye was succeeded during the Broadway run by José Ferrer. Bob Hope and Betty Hutton were in the 1943 movie version.
Smithsonian OC.

By Jupiter. Ray Bolger and Bertha Belmore singing "Life With Father." (Vandamm)

BY JUPITER

Music: Richard Rodgers
Lyrics: Lorenz Hart
Book: Richard Rodgers & Lorenz Hart
Producers: Dwight Deere Wiman & Richard Rodgers
Director: Joshua Logan
Choreographer: Robert Alton
Cast: Ray Bolger, Constance Moore, Benay Venuta, Ronald Graham, Bertha Belmore, Ralph Dumke, Vera Ellen, Margaret Bannerman
Songs: "Jupiter Forbid"; "Life With Father"; "Nobody's Heart"; "Ev'rything I've Got"; "Careless Rhapsody"; "Wait Till You See Her"
New York run: Shubert Theatre, June 3, 1942; 427 p.

Because of its ancient Greek characters and its Asia Minor setting, *By Jupiter* was something of a successor to the previous Rodgers and Hart hit, *The Boys from Syracuse.* The new work, which tried out in Boston under the title *All's Fair,* was based on the 1932 play, *The Warrior's Husband,* in which Katharine Hepburn had first attracted notice. The musical deals with the conflict between the Greeks and the legendary female warriors called Amazons, who live in a gynarchic land ruled by Queen Hippolyta (Benay Venuta). As one of his 12 labors, Hercules (Ralph Dumke) arrives with a Greek army led by Theseus (Ronald Graham) to steal the queen's magical girdle of Diana, the source of her strength. But when Hippolyta's sister Antiope (Constance Moore) takes one look at Theseus, she soon lays down her spear for love, a gesture her sister warriors only too willingly emulate. During the run, Miss Moore was succeeded by Nanette Fabray.

By Jupiter, which remained the longest on Broadway of any Rodgers and Hart musical during the team's partnership, was the last original show they wrote together. It could have stayed longer had not Ray Bolger (in his first starring role as Sapiens, the queen's husband) quit the cast to entertain American troops in the Far East. One curious aspect of the show's score is that "Wait Till You See Her," its best-known song, was dropped a month after the Broadway opening. In 1967, an Off-Broadway revival of *By Jupiter* ran for 118 performances. RCA OC (1967)/ R&H.

This Is the Army. Ezra Stone, Julie Oshins, and Philip Truex singing "The Army's Made a Man Out of Me." (Vandamm)

THIS IS THE ARMY

Music & lyrics: Irving Berlin
Sketches: (uncredited)
Producer: Uncle Sam
Directors: Ezra Stone, Joshua Logan
Choreographers: Robert Sidney, Nelson Barclift
Cast: Ezra Stone, Burl Ives, Gary Merrill, Julie Oshins, Robert Sidney, Alan Manson, Earl Oxford, Nelson Barclift, Stuart Churchill, Philip Truex, Irving Berlin
Songs: "This Is the Army, Mr. Jones"; "The Army's Made a Man Out of Me"; "I Left My Heart at the Stage Door Canteen"; "Mandy"; "I'm Getting Tired So I Can Sleep"; "Oh, How I Hate to Get Up in the Morning"; "American Eagles"; "This Time"
New York run: Broadway Theatre, July 4, 1942; 113 p.

Having already written songs for the all-soldier show, *Yip Yip Yaphank,* during World War I, Irving Berlin followed up with songs for the all-soldier show, *This Is the Army,* during World War II. The revue, put together as a benefit for the Army Emergency Relief Fund, both kidded and extolled the military life in a song-and-dance mixture of horseplay, nostalgia, and patriotism. Though most of the show reflected a draftee's view of the Army, there was also room for tributes to the Navy and the Air Force. Highlights included the opening "Military Minstrel Show"; the scene at the Stage Door Canteen with soldiers impersonating celebrities who worked and performed there; Berlin himself leading his World War I buddies in singing, "Oh, How I Hate to Get Up in the Morning"; and the finale with the cast members in full battle dress booming their determination to make certain that this time would be the last. *This Is the Army* played a limited 12-week engagement in New York, was filmed in 1943 with Ronald Reagan, then toured overseas until October 1945. In 1946, the Broadway revue *Call Me Mister* dealt with the adjustment of World War II servicemen to civilian life. CSP OC.

Oklahoma! Joan Roberts singing "Many a New Day."

Oklahoma! Celeste Holm and Lee Dixon.

Oklahoma! Howard Da Silva and Alfred Drake singing "Pore Jud." (Vandamm)

OKLAHOMA!

Music: Richard Rodgers
Lyrics & book: Oscar Hammerstein II
Producer: Theatre Guild
Director: Rouben Mamoulian
Choreographer: Agnes de Mille
Cast: Betty Garde, Alfred Drake, Joan Roberts, Joseph Buloff, Celeste Holm, Howard Da Silva, Lee Dixon, Joan McCracken, Bambi Linn, George S. Irving, George Church, Ralph Riggs, Marc Platt, Katharine Sergava
Songs: "Oh, What a Beautiful Mornin'"; "The Surrey With the Fringe on Top"; "Kansas City"; "I Cain't Say No"; "Many a New Day"; "People Will Say We're in Love"; "Pore Jud"; "Out of My Dreams"; "The Farmer and the Cowman"; "All er Nothin' "; "Oklahoma"
New York run: St. James Theatre, March 31, 1943; 2,212 p.

A recognized landmark in the evolution of the American musical theatre, *Oklahoma!* was the initial collaboration between Richard Rodgers and Oscar Hammerstein II (in all, they wrote nine Broadway shows together). Under the direction of Rouben Mamoulian and with choreography by Agnes de Mille (her first of 15 book musicals), the production not only fused story, songs, and dances, but introduced the dream ballet to reveal hidden fears and desires of the principal characters. In addition, the musical continued in the paths of *Show Boat* (written by Hammerstein) and *Porgy and Bess* (directed by Mamoulian) by further expanding Broadway's horizons in its depiction of the pioneering men and woman who had once tilled the land and tended the cattle of the American Southwest.

Based on Lynn Riggs' 1931 play *Green Grow the Lilacs, Oklahoma!* is set in Indian Territory soon after the turn of the century. The simple tale is mostly concerned with whether the decent Curly McLain (Alfred Drake) or the menacing Jud Fry (Howard Da Silva) will take Laurey Williams (Joan Roberts) to the box social. Though in a fit of pique, Laurey chooses Jud, she really loves Curly and they soon make plans to marry. At their wedding, there is a joyous celebration of Oklahoma's impending statehood, Jud is accidently killed in a fight with Curly, and the newlyweds prepare to ride off in their surrey with the fringe on top. A comic secondary plot has to do with a romantic triangle involving man-crazy Ado Annie Carnes (Celeste Holm), cowboy Will Parker (Lee Dixon), and peddler Ali Hakim (Joseph Buloff).

After trying out under the title *Away We Go!*, the show was renamed *Oklahoma!* for its Broadway engagement at the St. James Theatre (formerly Erlanger's). It remained there five years nine months, thereby setting a long-run record for musicals that it held until overtaken by *My Fair Lady* 15 years later. Among actors who replaced original-cast members were Howard Keel (Curly), Mary Hatcher (Laurey), and Shelley Winters (Ado Annie). A National Company toured for over a decade, including a return visit to New York that lasted 100 performances. The first road company was headed by Harry Stockwell (Curly), Evelyn Wyckoff (Laurey), Pamela Britton (Ado Annie), and David Burns (Ali Hakim). Those who subsequently toured included John Raitt (Curly), Florence Henderson (Laurey), and Barbara Cook (Ado Annie).

In 1969, the Music Theatre of Lincoln Center mounted a revival with Bruce Yarnell (Curly), Leigh Beery (Laurey), April Shawhan (Ado Annie), Margaret Hamilton (Aunt Eller), and Lee Roy Reams (Will). Ten years later, a new production directed by William Hammerstein (Oscar's son) returned to New York for eight months as part of a two-and-a-half year tour. (See page 255.) The 1955 movie version, the first film in Todd-AO, featured Gordon MacRae and Shirley Jones in the leading roles.

MCA OC; CSP part tour OC; RCA OC (1979)/ Random House (1943)/ R&H.

THE MERRY WIDOW
Music: Franz Lehár
Lyrics: Adrian Ross, Robert Gilbert
Book: Sidney Sheldon & Ben Roberts
Producer: Yolanda Mero-Irion for the New Opera Co.
Director: Felix Brentano
Choreographer: George Balanchine
Cast: Jan Kiepura, Marta Eggerth, Melville Cooper, Ruth Matteson, Robert Rounseville, David Wayne, Ralph Dumke, Gene Barry, Lubov Roudenko, Milada Mladova
Songs: Same as original production
New York run: Majestic Theatre, August 4, 1943; 322 p.

(See page 15.)

ONE TOUCH OF VENUS
Music: Kurt Weill
Lyrics: Ogden Nash
Book: S. J. Perelman & Ogden Nash
Producer: Cheryl Crawford
Director: Elia Kazan
Choreographer: Agnes de Mille
Cast: Mary Martin, Kenny Baker, John Boles, Paula Laurence, Teddy Hart, Ruth Bond, Sono Osato, Harry Clark, Allyn Ann McLerie, Helen Raymond, Lou Wills Jr., Pearl Lang
Songs: "One Touch of Venus"; "How Much I Love You"; "I'm a Stranger Here Myself"; "West Wind"; "Foolish Heart"; "The Trouble With Women"; "Speak Low"; "That's Him"; "Wooden Wedding"
New York run: Imperial Theatre, October 7, 1943; 567 p.

One Touch of Venus combined the music of composer Kurt Weill (it was his most lighthearted score) with the libretto of two celebrated humorists, poet Ogden Nash and short-story writer S.J. Perelman (it was their only Broadway book musical). In her first starring role, Mary Martin played a statue of Venus recently unveiled in a New York museum, the Whitelaw Savory Foundation of Modern Art, that comes to life after barber Rodney Hatch (Kenny Baker) places a ring on the statue's finger. There is much comic confusion when Savory (John Boles) falls in love with Venus and Venus falls in love with Rodney, but after dreaming of her humdrum life as a barber's wife in Ozone Heights, the goddess happily turns back to marble. Fortunately, Rodney meets a girl who looks just like the statue (Miss Martin, of course) who just loves living in Ozone Heights.

Though *One Touch of Venus* (whose hit song was the torchy "Speak Low") was a fantasy in the modern sophisticated vein of Rodgers and Hart's *I Married an Angel,* its origin was a short novel, *The Tinted Venus,* written in 1885 by the English author F. Anstey (né Thomas Anstey Guthrie) who had based his story on the Pygmalion myth. The musical's first draft, by Bella Spewack, suggested Marlene Dietrich for the role of Venus, but when the actress turned down the part the concept was changed from worldly exotic to youthfully innocent after Perelman and Nash replaced Spewack and Mary Martin replaced Dietrich. The movie version, released in 1948, starred Ava Gardner, Robert Walker, and Dick Haymes.
AEI OC/ Little, Brown (1943); Chilton (1973)/ TW.

One Touch of Venus. Barber Kenny Baker slipping the ring on statue Mary Martin's finger. (Vandamm)

CARMEN JONES

Music: Georges Bizet
Lyrics & book: Oscar Hammerstein II
Producer: Billy Rose
Directors: Hassard Short, Charles Friedman
Choreographer: Eugene Loring
Cast: Muriel Smith (or Inez Matthews), Luther Saxon, Carlotta Franzell, Glenn Bryant, June Hawkins, Cosy Cole
Songs: "Dat's Love"; "You Talk Just Like My Maw"; "Dere's a Café on de Corner"; "Beat Out dat Rhythm on a Drum"; "Stan' Up and Fight"; "Whizzin' Away Along de Track"; "Dis Flower"; "My Joe"
New York run: Broadway Theatre, December 2, 1943; 502 p.

Adapting his libretto from Meilhac and Halevy's for the 1875 premiere production of *Carmen,* and adhering as closely as possible to the original form, Oscar Hammerstein II set his idiomatic lyrics to Georges Bizet's music and updated the story to World War II. Now Carmen is a worker in a parachute factory in the South (rather than a cigarette factory in Seville), Joe (Don José) is an army corporal who falls in love with the temptress, Cindy Lou (Micaela) is the country girl who loves Joe, and Husky Miller is the boxer (replacing Escamillo the bull fighter) who wins Carmen away from Joe. As did the original, the work ends in tragedy as Joe stabs Carmen to death outside a sports stadium while the crowd can be heard cheering Husky. In addition to the staging, Hassard Short was also responsible for the striking color schemes used throughout the production. *Carmen Jones* returned twice to New York during its year-and-a-half nationwide tour. The 1954 film adaptation featured Dorothy Dandridge, Harry Belafonte, and Diahann Carroll. MCA OC/ Knopf (1945)/ R&H.

MEXICAN HAYRIDE

Music & lyrics: Cole Porter
Book: Herbert & Dorothy Fields
Producer: Michael Todd
Directors: Hassard Short, John Kennedy
Choreographer: Paul Haakon
Cast: Bobby Clark, June Havoc, George Givot, Wilbur Evans, Luba Malina, Corinna Mura, Paul Haakon, Edith Meiser, Bill Callahan, Candy Jones
Songs: "Sing to Me, Guitar"; "I Love You"; "There Must Be Someone for Me"; "Abracadabra"; "Carlotta"; "Girls"; "Count Your Blessings"
New York run: Winter Garden, January 28, 1944; 481 p.

One of Broadway's most lavish wartime attractions (it had a cast of 89), *Mexican Hayride* owed its success largely to its appealing Latin-flavored score by Cole Porter (including the hit ballad "I Love You"), its eye-dazzling decor, its rows of long-stemmed show girls, and — most of all — the buffooneries of prankish, leering Bobby Clark. Clark was seen as Joe Bascom, alias Humphrey Fish, a numbers racketeer on the lam in Mexico where, at a bull fight, he is mistakenly selected as the "Amigo Americano," or good-will ambassador. Alternately hailed by the populace and trailed by the police, Bascom bounds from Mexico City to Chepultepec, Xochimilco, and Taxco, assuming a number of disguises including that of a mariachi flute player and a tortilla-vending, cigar-chomping Indian squaw with a baby strapped to her back. Because of the sumptuousness of the production, the top ticket price was $5.50. Abbott and Costello (but no Porter songs) were in the 1948 Hollywood version. CSP OC.

Mexican Hayride. Bobby Clark (in his squaw disguise) and June Havoc cutting up during the "Count Your Blessings" number.

FOLLOW THE GIRLS

Music: Phil Charig
Lyrics: Dan Shaprio & Milton Pascal
Book: Guy Bolton, Eddie Davis & Fred Thompson
Producers: Dave Wolper & Albert Borde
Directors: Harry Delmar, Fred Thompson
Choreographer: Catherine Littlefield
Cast: Gertrude Niesen, Jackie Gleason, Buster West, Tim Herbert, Irina Baronova, Frank Parker, William Tabbert
Songs: "You're Perf"; "Twelve O'Clock and All Is Well"; "Follow the Girls"; "I Wanna Get Married"; "I'm Gonna Hang My Hat"
New York run: New Century Theatre, April 8, 1944; 882 p.

Though it was one of Broadway's most popular wartime attractions, *Follow the Girls* is all but forgotten today. The raucous and lively show did, however, make a star of Gertrude Niesen in her only book musical, and her rendition of "I Wanna Get Married" was an authentic musical-comedy showstopper. The disposable plot had something to do with a burlesque queen, Bubbles LaMarr, who becomes a favorite of sailors at the Spotlight Canteen in Great Neck, Long Island. The show, however, served to throw the spotlight not only on Miss Niesen as Bubbles, but also on the antics of Jackie Gleason as Goofy Gale and on the dancing of ballerina Irina Baronova. *Follow the Girls* was the first attraction to play the reopened and refurbished Jolson's 59th Street Theatre, renamed the New Century.

SONG OF NORWAY

Music & lyrics: Robert Wright & George Forrest based on Edvard Grieg
Book: Milton Lazarus
Producer: Edwin Lester
Directors: Edwin Lester, Charles K. Freeman
Choreographer: George Balanchine
Cast: Irra Petina, Lawrence Brooks, Robert Shafer, Helena Bliss, Sig Arno, Alexandra Danilova, Maria Tallchief, Ruthanna Boris
Songs: "The Legend"; "Hill of Dreams"; "Freddy and His Fiddle"; "Now!"; "Strange Music"; "Midsummer's Eve"; "Three Loves"; "I Love You"; "Piano Concerto in A Minor" (instrumental)
New York run: Imperial Theatre, August 21, 1944; 860 p.

Song of Norway had its premiere a continent away from Broadway in July 1944, when it was presented by Edwin Lester's Los Angeles and San Francisco Civic Light Opera Association. Following in the tradition of *Blossom Time,* it offered a score based on themes by a classical composer combined with a biographical plot unencumbered by too much fidelity to historical accuracy. Here we have a romanticized tale of the early years of Edvard Grieg (Lawrence Brooks) who, with his friend, poet Rikard Nordraak (Robert Shafer), is anxious to bring new artistic glory to their beloved Norway. Though temporarily distracted from this noble aim by a dalliance in Rome with a flirtatious (and fictitious) Italian prima donna (Irra Petina), Grieg is so affected by the news of Nordraak's death that he returns home to his indulgent wife (Helena Bliss). Suitably inspired after singing a reprise of their love duet, "Strange Music," the composer creates the A-Minor Piano Concerto. *Song of Norway* which was presented by the New York City Opera in 1981, was filmed in 1970 with Tauralv Maurstad and Florence Henderson. For other musicals with scores based on classical themes, see *Blossom Time,* page 38.
MCA OC; Columbia OC (1958)/ TW.

BLOOMER GIRL

Music: Harold Arlen
Lyrics: E. Y. Harburg
Book: Sig Herzig & Fred Saidy
Producers: John C. Wilson & Nat Goldstone
Directors: E. Y. Harburg, William Schorr
Choreographer: Agnes de Mille
Cast: Celeste Holm, David Brooks, Dooley Wilson, Joan McCracken, Richard Huey, Margaret Douglass, Mabel Taliaferro, Matt Briggs, Herbert Ross
Songs: "When the Boys Come Home"; "Evelina"; "It Was Good Enough for Grandma"; "The Eagle and Me"; "Right as the Rain"; "T'morra, T'morra"; "Sunday in Cicero Falls"; "I Got a Song"
New York run: Shubert Theatre, October 5, 1944; 654 p.

Continuing the Americana spirit of *Oklahoma!*, *Bloomer Girl* was not only concerned with the introduction of bloomers during the Civil War, it also covered various aspects of the women's reform movement and the struggle for civil rights. The action occurs in Cicero Falls, New York, in 1861, and covers the rebellion of Evelina Applegate (Celeste Holm) against her tyrannical father, a manufacturer of hoopskirts, who wants her to marry one of his salesmen. Evelina is so provoked that she joins her aunt, Amelia "Dolly" Bloomer (Margaret Douglass), in both her crusade for more practical clothing for women and in her abolitionist activities. Evelina's convictions, however, do not prevent her from singing the romantic duet, "Right as the Rain," with Jefferson Calhoun (David Brooks), a visiting Southern slaveholder, who is eventually won over to her cause. *Bloomer Girl* made a star of Celeste Holm (who was succeeded in her role by Nanette Fabray), and it was also noted for Agnes de Mille's "Civil War Ballet," depicting the anguish felt by women who must remain at home while their men are off fighting. The musical returned to New York for six weeks early in 1947.

Broadway has also seen the following Civil War musicals: *The Girl from Dixie* (1903), *Caroline* (1923), *My Maryland* (1927), *My Darlin' Aida* (1952), *Maggie Flynn* (1968), and *Shenandoah* (1975).
MCA OC/ TW.

Bloomer Girl. Joan McCracken showing off her bloomers to Margaret Douglass and Celeste Holm. (Vandamm)

ON THE TOWN

Music: Leonard Bernstein
Lyrics & book: Betty Comden & Adolph Green
Producers: Oliver Smith & Paul Feigay
Director: George Abbott
Choreographer: Jerome Robbins
Cast: Sono Osato, Nancy Walker, Betty Comden, Adolph Green, John Battles, Cris Alexander, Alice Pearce, Allyn Ann McLerie
Songs: "New York, New York"; "Come Up to My Place"; "I Get Carried Away"; "Lonely Town"; "Lucky to Be Me"; "Ya Got Me"; "Some Other Time"
New York run: Adelphi Theatre, December 28, 1944; 463 p.

On the Town heralded the Broadway arrival of four major talents — composer Leonard Bernstein, writing partners Betty Comden and Adolph Green, and choreographer Jerome Robbins. Based on the Robbins-Bernstein ballet, *Fancy Free,* the musical expanded the work into a carefree tour of New York City, where three sailors — played by John Battles, Adolph Green, and Cris Alexander — become involved with three girls — Sono Osato, Betty Comden, and Nancy Walker — on a 24-hour shore leave. One of the sailors (Battles) becomes so smitten by the current winner of the subway's "Miss Turnstiles" competition (Miss Osato) that he and his buddies pursue her through the Museum of Natural History, Central Park, Times Square, and Coney Island. The Adelphi Theatre was once located on 54th Street east of 7th Avenue.

There have been two New York revivals of *On the Town.* Joe Layton staged an Off-Broadway version in 1959, with Harold Lang, Wisa D'Orso, and Pat Carroll, and Ron Field staged a Broadway version in 1971 with Ron Husmann, Donna McKechnie, Bernadette Peters, and Phyllis Newman. The movie adaptation, released in 1949, co-starred Gene Kelly, Vera-Ellen, Frank Sinatra, and Betty Garrett. MCA part OC; Columbia OC/ TW.

UP IN CENTRAL PARK

Music: Sigmund Romberg
Lyrics: Dorothy Fields
Book: Herbert & Dorothy Fields
Producer: Michael Todd
Director: John Kennedy
Choreographer: Helen Tamiris
Cast: Wilbur Evans, Maureen Cannon, Betty Bruce, Noah Beery, Maurice Burke, Charles Irwin, Robert Rounseville
Songs: "Carousel in the Park"; "When You Walk in the Room"; "Close as Pages in a Book"; "The Big Back Yard"; "April Snow"
New York run: New Century Theatre, January 27, 1945; 504 p.

Celebrated for his lush scores for operettas in exotic locales (*The Desert Song, The New Moon*), Sigmund Romberg joined with lyricist Dorothy Fields to recapture the vintage Currier and Ives charms found up in New York's Central Park in the 1870s. The story, a combination of fact and fiction, deals with the efforts of John Matthews (Wilbur Evans), a *New York Times* reporter, to expose Tammany boss William Marcy Tweed (Noah Beery) and the other grafters who are lining their pockets with funds designated for the building of the park. Romance is supplied when John and Rosie Moore (Maureen Cannon), the daughter of a Tweed crony, vow love everlasting in their ardent duet, "Close as Pages in a Book." Deanna Durbin and Dick Haymes were in the 1948 movie version. MCA SC.

Carousel. The opening scene with John Raitt and Jan Clayton. (Vandamm)

CAROUSEL

Music: Richard Rodgers
Lyrics & book: Oscar Hammerstein II
Producer: Theatre Guild
Director: Rouben Mamoulian
Choreographer: Agnes de Mille
Cast: John Raitt, Jan Clayton, Murvyn Vye, Jean Darling, Christine Johnson, Eric Mattson, Bambi Linn, Peter Birch, Pearl Lang
Songs: "Carousel Waltz" (instrumental); "You're a Queer One, Julie Jordan"; "Mr. Snow"; "If I Loved You"; "Blow High, Blow Low"; "June Is Bustin' Out All Over"; "When the Children Are Asleep"; "Soliloquy"; "What's the Use of Wond'rin'?"; "You'll Never Walk Alone"; "The Highest Judge of All"
New York run: Majestic Theatre, April 19,1945; 890 p.

With *Carousel*, Rodgers and Hammerstein solidified their position as the dominant creators of musical theatre in the Forties. Reunited for the production with their *Oklahoma!* colleagues, the partners transported Ferenc Molnar's 1921 fantasy *Liliom* from Budapest to a New England fishing village between 1873 and 1888. Billy Bigelow (John Raitt), a swaggering carnival barker, meets Julie Jordan (Jan Clayton), a local factory worker, and — in the souring duet, "If I Loved You" — they are soon admitting their feelings for each other. After their marriage, Billy learns of his impending fatherhood — with his ambivalent emotions expressed in the "Soliloquy" — and, desperate for money, is killed in an attempted robbery. He is, however, allowed to return to earth to do one good deed. This is accomplished when, unseen by his daughter Louise (Bambi Linn), he shows up at her high school graduation to encourage the lonely girl to have confidence in herself by heeding the words to "You'll Never Walk Alone." For almost two years, *Carousel* at the Majestic Theatre (on 44th Street west of Broadway) played across the street from *Oklahoma!* at the St. James. During the Broadway run (the fifth longest of the decade), Raitt was replaced for a time by Howard Keel. The National Company traveled for one year nine months, ending its tour with a Broadway stand lasting 48 performances. Twenty years after the opening, John Raitt again played Billy Bigelow in a revival presented by the Music Theatre of Lincoln Center. A highly acclaimed new production opened in London in 1993 and New York in 1994. The 1956 film version starred Gordon MacRae and Shirley Jones.
MCA OC; RCA OC (1965); MCA SC (1987)/ Random House (1945)/ R&H.

THE RED MILL

Music: Victor Herbert
Lyrics: Henry Blossom, Forman Brown
Book: (uncredited)
Producers: Paula Stone & Hunt Stromberg Jr.
Director: Billy Gilbert
Choreographer: Aida Broadbent
Cast: Eddie Foy Jr., Michael O'Shea, Odette Myrtil, Dorothy Stone, Charles Collins, Ann Andre, Lorna Byron
Songs: Same as original production
New York run: Ziegfeld Theatre, October 16, 1945; 531 p.

(See page 13.)

SHOW BOAT

Music: Jerome Kern
Lyrics & book: Oscar Hammerstein II
Producers: Jerome Kern & Oscar Hammerstein II
Directors: Hassard Short, Oscar Hammerstein II
Choreographer: Helen Tamiris
Cast: Jan Clayton, Ralph Dumke, Carol Bruce, Charles Fredericks, Buddy Ebsen, Colette Lyons, Kenneth Spencer, Pearl Primus, Talley Beatty
Songs: Same as original production plus "Nobody Else but Me"
New York run: Ziegfeld Theatre, January 5, 1946; 418 p.

(See page 60.)

Show Boat. Buddy Ebsen and Colette Lyons strutting through "Goodbye, My Lady Love." (Eileen Darby)

ST. LOUIS WOMAN

Music: Harold Arlen
Lyrics: Johnny Mercer
Book: Arna Bontemps & Countee Cullen
Producer: Edward Gross
Director: Rouben Mamoulian
Choreographer: Charles Walters
Cast: Harold Nicholas, Fayard Nicholas, Pearl Bailey, Ruby Hill, Rex Ingram, June Hawkins, Juanita Hall, Lorenzo Fuller
Songs: "Cakewalk Your Lady"; "Come Rain or Come Shine"; "I Had Myself a True Love"; "Legalize My Name"; "Any Place I Hang My Hat Is Home"; "A Woman's Prerogative"; "Ridin' on the Moon"
New York run: Martin Beck Theatre, March 30, 1946; 113 p.

Though based on Arna Bontemps' novel, *God Sends Sunday, St. Louis Woman* seems also to have been a close relative of *Porgy and Bess.* Set in St. Louis in 1898, the musical tells of fickle Della Green (Ruby Hill in a part intended for Lena Horne), who is the woman of tough saloon owner Biglow Brown (Rex Ingram), but who falls for Li'l Augie (Harold Nicholas), a jockey with an incredible winning streak. Before Brown is killed by a discarded girlfriend, he puts a curse on Li'l Augie which ends both the winning streak and Della's affection. The two, however, are reunited for the final reprise of their ardent "Come Rain or Come Shine." In 1959, a revised version of *St. Louis Woman*, with other Harold Arlen songs added and now set in New Orleans, was performed in Amsterdam and Paris under the title *Free and Easy.*
Capitol OC/ N.A.L. (1973).

CALL ME MISTER

Music & lyrics: Harold Rome
Sketches: Arnold Auerbach, Arnold B. Horwitt
Producers: Melvyn Douglas & Herman Levin
Director: Robert H. Gordon
Choreographer: John Wray
Cast: Betty Garrett, Jules Munshin, Bill Callahan, Lawrence Winters, Paula Bane, Maria Karnilova, George S. Irving
Songs: "Goin' Home Train"; "Along With Me"; "The Red Ball Express"; "Military Life"; "The Face on the Dime"; "South America, Take It Away"; "Call Me Mister"
New York run: National Theatre, April 18, 1946; 734 p.

With its theme dealing with servicemen readjusting to civilian life, *Call Me Mister* was something of a follow-up to *This Is the Army.* The show's cast consisted of ex-GIs and ex-USO entertainers, and it took a somewhat satirical, yet basically good-humored and optimistic attitude toward military life and demobilization. Its most popular number was "South America, Take It Away," performed by Betty Garrett as a rumba-hating canteen hostess. Its funniest sketch found the Air Corps getting its lumps as the flyers were shown enjoying the glamorous life while periodically offering toasts "To the Blue Lady of the Clouds." In a serious moment, the revue faced up to post-war racial discrimination when Lawrence Winters, as a former driver with the supplies-carrying "Red Ball Express," is unable to get a job as a truck driver. *Call Me Mister* played the National Theatre (now the Nederlander) on 41st Street west of 7th Avenue. The 1951 movie version (with plot) co-starred Betty Grable and Dan Dailey.
CSP OC.

ANNIE GET YOUR GUN

Music & lyrics: Irving Berlin
Book: Herbert & Dorothy Fields
Producers: Richard Rodgers & Oscar Hammerstein II
Director: Joshua Logan
Choreographer: Helen Tamiris
Cast: Ethel Merman, Ray Middleton, Marty May, Kenny Bowers, Lea Penman, Betty Anne Nyman, William O'Neal, Lubov Roudenko, Daniel Nagrin, Harry Belaver, Ellen Hanley
Songs: "Doin' What Comes Natur'lly"; "The Girl That I Marry"; "You Can't Get a Man With a Gun"; "There's No Business Like Show Business"; "They Say It's Wonderful"; "Moonshine Lullaby"; "My Defenses Are Down"; "I'm an Indian Too"; "I Got Lost in His Arms"; "I Got the Sun in the Morning"; "Anything You Can Do"
New York run: Imperial Theatre, May 16, 1946; 1,147 p.

Annie Get Your Gun was the first of two shows Irving Berlin wrote for Ethel Merman (the other was *Call Me Madam*). The third longest running musical of the Forties, it was also the biggest Broadway hit of their respective careers. Originally, however, composer Jerome Kern was to have written the songs with lyricist Dorothy Fields (also the co-librettist), but Kern's death as he was about to begin the assignment brought Berlin into the project for both music and lyrics. The idea for the show, the only Rodgers and Hammerstein musical production without a Rodgers and Hammerstein score, is credited to Miss Fields who felt that Ethel Merman as Annie Oakley would be surefire casting.

Though unspecified, the period of the story is the mid-1880s. Annie Oakley, an illiterate hillbilly living near Cincinnati, demonstrates her remarkable marksmanship, and is persuaded — through the convincing claim "There's No Business Like Show Business" — to join Col. Buffalo Bill's travelling Wild West Show. Annie, who needs only one look to fall hopelessly in love with Frank Butler (Ray Middleton), the show's featured shooting ace, soon eclipses Butler as the main attraction, which doesn't help the cause of romance. She exhibits her skills at such locales as the Minneapolis Fair Grounds (where she hits the targets while riding on a motorcycle) and at Governor's Island, New York, where, in a shooting contest with Frank, she realizes that the only way to win the man is to let him win the match. The National Company's tour, which began in October 1947, lasted for one year seven months with Mary Martin heading the original touring cast. In 1966, Miss Merman recreated the role of Annie Oakley for a production sponsored by the Music Theatre of Lincoln Center. This revival, which also had Bruce Yarnell and Jerry Orbach in the cast, included a new Berlin song, "An Old-Fashioned Wedding." After a brief tour, the show played two months at the Broadway Theatre. Betty Hutton and Howard Keel were in the 1950 screen adaptation.

Following *Annie Get Your Gun,* other show business musical biographies have been written about Gypsy Rose Lee (Sandra Church in *Gypsy,* 1959); Edmund Kean (Alfred Drake in *Kean,* 1961); Sophie Tucker (Libi Staiger in *Sophie,* 1963); Laurette Taylor (Mary Martin in *Jennie,* 1963); Fanny Brice (Barbra Streisand in *Funny Girl,* 1964); George M. Cohan (Joel Grey in *George M!,* 1968); the Marx Brothers (Lewis J. Stadlen, Daniel Fortus, Irwin Pearl, and Alvin Kupperman in *Minnie's Boys,* 1970); Mack Sennett and Mabel Normand (Robert Preston and Bernadette Peters in *Mack & Mabel,* 1974); Phineas T. Barnum (Jim Dale in *Barnum,* 1980); Federico Fellini (Raul Julia in *Nine,* 1982); Tallulah Bankhead (Helen Gallagher in *Tallulah,* 1983); Marilyn Monroe (Alyson Reed in *Marilyn,* 1983); Ned Harrigan and Tony Hart (Harry Groener and Mark Hamill in *Harrigan 'n Hart,* 1985); and Ellie Greenfield (Dinah Manoff in *Leader of the Pack,* 1985).

MCA OC; RCA OC (1966)/ R&H.

Cover designed by Lucinda
Ballard.

Annie Get Your Gun. "There's No Business Like Show Business" sing William
O'Neal, Marty May, Ethel Merman, and Ray Middleton. (Vandamm)

STREET SCENE

Music: Kurt Weill
Lyrics: Langston Hughes
Book: Elmer Rice
Producers: Dwight Deere Wiman & The Playwrights' Co.
Director: Charles Friedman
Choreographer: Anna Sokolow
Cast: Norman Cordon, Anne Jeffreys, Polyna Stoska, Brian Sullivan, Hope Emerson, Sheila Bond, Danny Daniels, Don Saxon, Juanita Hall
Songs: "Somehow I Never Could Believe"; "Ice Cream"; "Wrapped in a Ribbon and Tied in a Bow"; "Wouldn't You Like to Be on Broadway?"; "What Good Would the Moon Be?"; "Moon-Faced, Starry-Eyed"; "Remember That I Care"; "We'll Go Away Together"
New York run: Adelphi Theatre, January 9, 1947; 148 p.

Adapted by Elmer Rice from his 1929 play, *Street Scene* was the most operatic of all the Broadway productions with music by Kurt Weill. Something of a white Northern counterpart to *Porgy and Bess,* the work takes a melodramatic look at the inhabitants of a New York City tenement during an oppressively hot summer day. Among those inhabitants are the members of the Maurrant family — Anna (Polyna Stoska) whose loveless marriage (as revealed through the impassioned aria "Somehow I Never Could Believe") drives her to an affair that ends in tragedy; Anna's bullying, drunken husband Frank (Norman Cordon); and their frustrated daughter Rose (Anne Jeffreys) who cannot give herself either to the smooth-talking sharpie Harry Easter (Don Saxon) or to the earnest neighbor Sam Kaplan (Brian Sullivan). In 1959, *Street Scene* entered the repertory of the New York City Opera.
Columbia OC/ R&H.

Street Scene. Anne Jeffreys and Don Saxon. (Vandamm)

Finian's Rainbow. Albert Sharpe, David Wayne, and Anita Alvarez in a tense moment.

FINIAN'S RAINBOW

Music: Burton Lane
Lyrics: E. Y. Harburg
Book: E. Y. Harburg & Fred Saidy
Producers: Lee Sabinson & William Katzell
Director: Bretaigne Windust
Choreographer: Michael Kidd
Cast: Ella Logan, Albert Sharpe, Donald Richards, David Wayne, Anita Alvarez, Robert Pitkin
Songs: "How Are Things in Glocca Morra?"; "If This Isn't Love"; "Look to the Rainbow"; "Old Devil Moon"; "Something Sort of Grandish"; "Necessity"; "When the Idle Poor Become the Idle Rich"; "When I'm Not Near the Girl I Love"; "That Great Come-and-Get-It Day"
New York run: 46th Street Theatre, January 10, 1947; 725 p.

E. Y. Harburg got the idea for *Finian's Rainbow* because he wanted to satirize an economic system that requires gold reserves to be buried at Fort Knox. He then began thinking of leprechauns and their legendary crock of gold that could grant three wishes. In the story that Harburg and Fred Saidy devised, Finian McLonergan (Albert Sharpe), an Irish immigrant, is in Rainbow Valley, Missitucky, to bury a crock of gold which, he is sure, will grow and make him rich. Also part of the fantasy are Og (David Wayne), the leprechaun whose crock has been stolen, Finian's daughter Sharon (Ella Logan), who dreams wistfully of Glocca Morra, Woody Mahoney (Donald Richards), a labor organizer who blames "That Old Devil Moon" for the way he feels about Sharon, and a bigoted Southern Senator, Billboard Rawkins (Robert Pitkin), who — as one of the three wishes — turns black. At the end, everyone comes to understand that riches are found not in gold but in people trusting one another. A 1960 revival had a brief Broadway run. The 1968 movie version starred Fred Astaire, Petula Clark, and Tommy Steele.
Columbia OC; RCA OC (1960)/ Berkley Books (1968)/ TW.

SWEETHEARTS

Music: Victor Herbert
Lyrics: Robert B. Smith
Book: John Cecil Holm
Producers: Paula Stone & Michael Sloane
Director: John Kennedy
Choreographers: Catherine Littlefield, Theodore Adolphus
Cast:　Bobby Clark, Marjorie Gateson, Gloria Story, Mark Dawson, Robert Shackleton, June Knight, Cornell MacNeil
Songs: 6 cut from original production; "To the Land of My Own Romance" (lyric: Harry B. Smith) and "I Might Be Your Once-in-a-While" added.
New York run: Shubert Theatre, January 21, 1947; 288 p.

(See page 19.)

BRIGADOON

Music: Frederick Loewe
Lyrics & book: Alan Jay Lerner
Producer: Cheryl Crawford
Director: Robert Lewis
Choreographer: Agnes de Mille
Cast:　David Brooks, Marion Bell, Pamela Britton, Lee Sullivan, George Keane, James Mitchell, William Hansen, Elliott Sullivan, Helen Gallagher, Hayes Gordon, Lidija Franklin
Songs: "Brigadoon"; "Down on MacConnachy Square"; "Waiting for My Dearie"; "I'll Go Home With Bonnie Jean"; "The Heather on the Hill"; "Come to Me, Bend to Me"; "Almost Like Being in Love"; "There but for You Go I"; "My Mother's Wedding Day"; "From This Day On"
New York run: Ziegfeld Theatre, March 13, 1947; 581 p.

By dealing with themes of substance, by their adherence to the concept of the integrated musical, and by their ability to make the past come vividly alive to modern audiences, Lerner and Loewe established their special niche in the musical theatre while still laying claim to being the stylistic heirs of Rodgers and Hammerstein. *Brigadoon,* their third Broadway musical and first hit, was motivated partly by Lerner's fondness for the works of James M. Barrie and partly by a German story, *Germelshausen,* by Friedrich Gerstäcker.

The fantasy is about two American tourists, Tommy Albright and Jeff Douglas (David Brooks and George Keane), who stumble upon a mist-clouded Scottish town that, they eventually discover, reawakens only one day every hundred years. Tommy, who enjoys wandering through the heather on the hill with a local lass, Fiona MacLaren (Marion Bell), returns to New York after learning of the curse that has caused the town's excessively somnolent condition. True love, however, pulls him back to the highlands. The tale was made believable not only through its evocative score but also through Agnes de Mille's ballets, especially the emotion-charged "Sword Dance" performed by James Mitchell during a wedding ceremony and the anguished "Funeral Dance" performed by Lidija Franklin.

A Broadway revival of *Brigadoon* in 1980 did not remain awake very long, but a 1986 production by the New York City Opera was well received. Hollywood's 1954 version co-starred Gene Kelly, Cyd Charisse, and Van Johnson. RCA OC/ Coward-McCann (1947); Chilton (1973)/ TW.

Brigadoon. George Keane, David Brooks, and William Hansen. (Vandamm)

HIGH BUTTON SHOES

Music: Jule Styne
Lyrics: Sammy Cahn
Book: Stephen Longstreet (George Abbott, Phil Silvers uncredited)
Producers: Monte Proser & Joseph Kipness
Director: George Abbott
Choreographer: Jerome Robbins
Cast: Phil Silvers, Nanette Fabray, Jack McCauley, Mark Dawson, Joey Faye, Lois Lee, Sondra Lee, Helen Gallagher, Nathaniel Frey, Johnny Stewart, Paul Godkin
Songs: "Can't You Just See Yourself?"; "You're My Girl"; "Papa, Won't You Dance With Me?"; "On a Sunday by the Sea"; "I Still Get Jealous"
New York run: New Century Theatre, October 9, 1947; 727 p.

High Button Shoes, Jule Styne's initial Broadway assignment, offered Phil Silvers his first starring opportunity in the typical role of a brash, bumbling con artist. Though Stephen Longstreet was credited with adapting the story from his own semi-autobiographical novel, *The Sisters Liked Them Handsome,* the musical was completely rewritten by director George Abbott, with an assist from Silvers. In the plot, set in New Brunswick, New Jersey, in 1913, Harrison Floy (Silvers) hoodwinks the Longstreet family into letting him sell some of the valueless property they own. After running off with the profits to Atlantic City (where Jerome Robbins' classic "Keystone Kops" ballet is staged), Floy loses and recovers the money — then loses it forever by betting on the wrong college football team. The musical's showstopper was an old-fashioned song-and-dance polka, "Papa, Won't You Dance With Me?," performed by Nanette Fabray and Jack McCauley.
RCA OC/ TW.

ALLEGRO

Music: Richard Rodgers
Lyrics & book: Oscar Hammerstein II
Producer: Theatre Guild
Director: Agnes de Mille (Oscar Hammerstein II uncredited)
Choreographer: Agnes de Mille
Cast: John Battles, Annamary Dickey, William Ching, John Conte, Muriel O'Malley, Lisa Kirk, Roberta Jonay
Songs: "A Fellow Needs a Girl"; "You Are Never Away"; "So Far"; "Money Isn't Ev'rything"; "The Gentleman Is a Dope"; "Allegro"
New York run: Majestic Theatre, October 10, 1947; 315 p.

The third Rodgers and Hammerstein Broadway musical, *Allegro* was their first with a story that had not been based on a previous source. It was a particularly ambitious undertaking, with a theme dealing with the corrupting effect of big institutions on the young and idealistic. The saga is told through the life of a doctor, Joseph Taylor Jr. (John Battles), from his birth in a small midwest American town to his 35th year. We follow Joe's progress as he grows up, goes to school, marries a local belle (Roberta Jonay), joins the staff of a large Chicago hospital that panders to wealthy hypochondriacs, discovers that his wife is unfaithful, and, in the end, returns to his home town with his adoring nurse (Lisa Kirk) to rededicate his life to healing the sick and helping the needy. The show's innovations included a Greek chorus to comment on the action both to the actors and the audience, and the use of multi-level performing areas with nonrepresentational sets.
RCA OC/ Random House (1947)/ R&H.

MAKE MINE MANHATTAN

Music: Richard Lewine
Lyrics & sketches: Arnold B. Horwitt
Producer: Joseph Hyman
Directors: Hassard Short, Max Liebman
Choreographer: Lee Sherman
Cast: Sid Caesar, David Burns, Sheila Bond, Joshua Shelley, Kyle McDonnell, Danny Daniels, Nelle Fisher, Ray Harrison, Jack Kilty, Larry Carr
Songs: "Phil the Fiddler"; "Saturday Night in Central Park"; "I Fell in Love With You"; "My Brudder and Me"; "Gentleman Friend"
New York run: Broadhurst Theatre, January 15, 1948; 429 p.

Partly because of the increasing importance of books in book musicals and partly because of the increasing influence of television, 1948 was the last year in which traditional revues found large and receptive audiences. Adhering to its titular request, *Make Mine Manhattan* took a mostly satirical but always light-hearted look at the city's most prominent borough as it covered such matters as the forthcoming establishment of the United Nations' permanent home, the pretentions of Rodgers and Hammerstein's *Allegro*, the distinctive menu at the Schrafft's restaurant chain, the continuous cacophony of street noises, and — recognizing the existence of two other boroughs — the problems of a Bronx boy who must use an intricate series of subway trains to travel to see his girl at the far end of Brooklyn. Sid Caesar, who did imitations, including one of a penny gum machine, was succeeded for the tour by Bert Lahr.
Painted Smiles SC.

INSIDE U.S.A.

Music: Arthur Schwartz
Lyrics: Howard Dietz
Sketches: Arnold Auerbach, Arnold B. Horwitt, Moss Hart
Producer: Arthur Schwartz
Director: Robert H. Gordon
Choreographer: Helen Tamiris
Cast: Beatrice Lillie, Jack Haley, John Tyers, Herb Shriner, Valerie Bettis, Lewis Nye, Carl Reiner, Thelma Carpenter, Estelle Loring, Eric Victor, Talley Beatty, Jack Cassidy
Songs: "Inside U.S.A."; "Blue Grass"; "Rhode Island Is Famous for You"; "Haunted Heart"; "At the Mardi Gras"; "My Gal Is Mine Once More"; "First Prize at the Fair"
New York run: New Century Theatre, April 30, 1948; 399 p.

Expanding the geographical area of the recently opened *Make Mine Manhattan*, and contracting it from their 1935 revue *At Home Abroad*, Arthur Schwartz and Howard Dietz put together an All-American revue, *Inside U.S.A.*, which borrowed nothing more than the title from John Gunther's sociological survey. With Beatrice Lillie and Jack Haley as comical cicerones, the itinerary included visits to Pittsburgh (where a choral society takes on industrial pollution), the Kentucky Derby (for a lament of one whose lover has been lost betting the ponies), a San Francisco waterfront (the scene of the ballad "Haunted Heart"), the Wisconsin State Fair, the New Orleans Mardi Gras (Bea Lillie is queen), a Wyoming rodeo, and Alberquerque (where two Indians, Miss Lillie and Haley, resolutely refuse to take the country back). *Inside U.S.A.* was the last of seven revues written by Schwartz and Dietz.

LOVE LIFE

Music: Kurt Weill
Lyrics & book: Alan Jay Lerner
Producer: Cheryl Crawford
Director: Elia Kazan
Choreographer: Michael Kidd
Cast: Nanette Fabray, Ray Middleton, Johnny Stewart, Cheryl Archer, Jay Marshall
Songs: "Here I'll Stay"; "Progress"; "I Remember It Well"; "Green-Up Time"; "Economics"; "Mr. Right"
New York run: 46th Street Theatre, October 7, 1948; 252 p.

The only collaboration between Kurt Weill and Alan Jay Lerner, *Love Life* was a highly unconventional work. Billed as "A Vaudeville," it related the story of a non-aging couple (Nanette Fabray and Ray Middleton) and their two children from 1791 to the present, with the theme being the gradual changes in the relationship between people as life in America becomes more complex. The musical pieces were incorporated into the show mostly as commentaries on the characters and situations, in much the same way that Weill had used songs in his early German works. As for the musical's structure, there was no linear plot — with beginning, middle and end — but rather a series of separate but connecting scenes interspersed with vaudeville acts through which the authors conveyed their views. Not quite the format for a long-running smash, perhaps, but the show's innovations did turn up in later productions such as *Company* and *A Chorus Line* (non-linear stories), *Hallelujah, Baby!* (characters did not age over a long period of time), and *Chicago* (conceived as "A Musical Vaudeville").

WHERE'S CHARLEY?

Music & lyrics: Frank Loesser
Book: George Abbott
Producers: Cy Feuer & Ernest Martin
Director: George Abbott
Choreographer: George Balanchine
Cast: Ray Bolger, Allyn Ann McLerie, Byron Palmer, Doretta Morrow, Horace Cooper, Jane Lawrence, Paul England, Cornell MacNeil
Songs: "The New Ashmoleon Marching Society and Students' Conservatory Band"; "My Darling, My Darling"; "Make a Miracle"; "Lovelier Than Ever"; "Once in Love With Amy"; "At the Red Rose Cotillion"
New York run: St. James Theatre, October 11, 1948; 792 p.

Where's Charley? was based on Brandon Thomas's durable 1892 London farce, *Charley's Aunt*. The first Broadway book musical with a score by Frank Loesser (he wrote five shows in all), the musical is concerned with the madcap doings that result when Oxford undergraduates Charley Wykeham (Ray Bolger) and Jack Chesney (Byron Palmer) entertain their proper lady friends, Amy Spettigue (Allyn Ann McLerie) and Kitty Verdun (Doretta Morrow), in their rooms. To do so, Charley must also play chaperon by disguising himself as his own rich aunt "from Brazil where the nuts come from." Transvestite misunderstanding results in complications when the "aunt" must flee the amorous advances of the girls' money-hungry guardian, and when the real aunt makes an unexpected appearance. The show gave Ray Bolger his biggest hit, plus the nightly opportunity to lead the audience in joining him in singing "Once in Love With Amy." Bolger brought the touring company back to Broadway in 1951 for 48 performances, and repeated his part in the 1952 movie version.
M-E London OC (1958)/ MTI.

AS THE GIRLS GO

Music: Jimmy McHugh
Lyrics: Harold Adamson
Book: William Roos
Producer: Michael Todd
Director: Howard Bay
Choreographer: Hermes Pan
Cast: Bobby Clark, Irene Rich, Bill Callahan, Kathryn Lee, Betty Jane Watson, Hobart Cavanaugh, Betty Lou Barto, Dick Dana, Gregg Sherwood, Jo Sullivan, Buddy Schwab
Songs: "As the Girls Go"; "You Say the Nicest Things, Baby"; "There's No Getting Away from You"; "Lucky in the Rain"; "Father's Day"
New York run: Winter Garden, November 13, 1948; 420 p.

A throwback to the days when a great personality could carry a musical to success without any help from the book, *As the Girls Go* was a gaudy, rowdy, fast-paced song-and-dance show totally dependent on the antics of one of the theatre's outstanding clowns, Bobby Clark, here making his final Broadway appearance. Clark played Waldo Wellington, the husband of the first woman President of the United States (Irene Rich), and initially the production was planned as a political satire in the tradition of *Of Thee I Sing.* After a disastrous tryout in Boston, however, the plot was largely discarded as Clark leered, pranced, chased Amazonian show girls, blew soap bubbles out of a trumpet, masqueraded as a female barber, and, without looking, tossed his hat clear across the stage and onto a hatrack. During the run, Fran Warren replaced Betty Jane Watson in the romantic lead. *As the Girls Go* was the first Broadway attraction to charge $7.20 for orchestra seats.

LEND AN EAR

Music, lyrics & sketches: Charles Gaynor
Producers: William Katzell, Franklin Gilbert, William Eythe
Directors: Gower Champion, Hal Gerson
Choreographer: Gower Champion
Cast: William Eythe, Carol Channing, Yvonne Adair, Gene Nelson, Jennie Lou Law, Gloria Hamilton, Bob Scheerer
Songs: "Give Your Heart a Chance to Sing"; "Doin' the Old Yahoo Step"; "Molly O'Reilly"; "Who Hit Me?"
New York run: National Theatre, December 16, 1948; 460 p.

Billed as "An Intimate Musical Revue" (there were 21 in the cast), *Lend an Ear* was the first of 14 musicals to be directed and choreographed by Gower Champion. It also revealed the triple talents of writer Charles Gaynor, and it marked the Broadway debut of a squeaky-voiced, saucer-eyed blonde named Carol Channing. Initially presented seven years earlier in Pittsburgh, the youthful show came to New York after a successful engagement in Los Angeles. Among its satirical topics: psychoanalists; the influence of gossip columnists; a tourist-eye view of Santo Domingo; a third-rate opera company that must speak its lines because it cannot afford orchestral accompaniment; queens of the silent screen; and "The Gladiola Girl," an encapsulated typical musical comedy of the mid-Twenties about flappers and lounge lizards on a Long Island estate where everyone dances "The Old Yahoo Step."
Samuel French (1971)*/ SF.

Kiss Me, Kate. Alfred Drake taming his shrew Patricia Morison. (Eileen Darby)

KISS ME, KATE

Music & lyrics: Cole Porter
Book: Samuel & Bella Spewack
Producers: Saint Subber & Lemuel Ayers
Director: John C. Wilson
Choreographer: Hanya Holm
Cast: Alfred Drake, Patricia Morison, Harold Lang, Lisa Kirk, Harry Clark, Jack Diamond, Annabelle Hill, Lorenzo Fuller, Marc Breaux
Songs: "Another Op'nin', Another Show"; "Why Can't You Behave?"; "Wunderbar"; "So in Love"; "We Open in Venice"; "Tom, Dick or Harry"; "I've Come to Wive It Wealthily in Padua"; "I Hate Men"; "Were Thine That Special Face"; "Too Darn Hot"; "Where Is the Life That Late I Led?"; "Always True to You in My Fashion"; "Bianca"; "Brush Up Your Shakespeare"; "I Am Ashamed That Women Are So Simple" (lyric: Shakespeare)
New York run: New Century Theatre, December 30, 1948; 1,070 p.

After having collaborated ten years earlier on *Leave It to Me!,* Cole Porter and the husband-wife team of Samuel and Bella Spewack were reunited for *Kiss Me, Kate,* the composer's biggest hit and the fourth longest running musical of the Forties. The idea for the show began germinating in 1935 when producer Saint Subber, then a stagehand for the Theatre Guild's production of *The Taming of the Shrew,* became aware that its stars, Alfred Lunt and Lynn Fontanne, quarrelled in private almost as much as did the charaters they were portraying in the play. *Kiss Me, Kate* takes place backstage and onstage at Ford's Theatre in Baltimore, from five p.m. to midnight during one day of a tryout of a musical version of *The Taming of the Shrew.* In the plot, egotistical actor-producer Fred Graham (Alfred Drake) and his temperamental co-star and ex-wife, Lili Vanessi (Patricia Morison) fight and make up and eventually demonstrate their enduring affection for each other — just like Shakespeare's Petruchio and Kate. A subplot involves actress Lois Lane (Lisa Kirk) whose romance with actor Bill Calhoun (Harold Lang) is complicated by Bill's weakness for gambling.

Because of the musical's construction, it is possible to follow the story of *The Taming of the Shrew* even though the play-within-the-play is offered only in excerpts. For his lyrics in the musical numbers sung during *The Shrew's* performance, Porter made use of such Shakespearean lines as "I come to wive it wealthily in Padua," "Were thine that special face," "Where is the life that late I led?," and Kate's finale speech beginning "I am ashamed that women are so simple." The more modern sentiments — "Why Can't You Behave?," "So in Love," "Too Darn Hot," and "Always True to You in My Fashion" — were restricted to the theatre's backstage area.

Kiss Me, Kate (the title is from Petruchio's last command in *The Taming of the Shrew)* marked Alfred Drake's first starring part on Broadway and the only major musical in which Patricia Morison originated a leading role. (She won it after it had been rejected by Jarmila Novotna, Mary Martin, Lily Pons, and Jeanette MacDonald.) During the run, Drake was succeeded by Keith Andes and Ted Scott, Miss Morison by Anne Jeffreys, Lisa Kirk by Betty Ann Grove, and Harold Lang by Danny Daniels. The National Company, which toured for one year 11 months, started out with a cast headed by Andes, Jeffreys, Julie Wilson, and Marc Platt, with the first three eventually succeeded by Bob Wright, Frances McCann, and Betty George. In 1953, the Hollywood version put Howard Keel, Kathryn Grayson, Ann Miller, and Tommy Rall in the leads. For other musicals based on Shakespeare, see *The Boys from Syracuse,* page 107.
Columbia OC; Capitol OC/ Knopf (1953); Chilton (1973)/ TW.

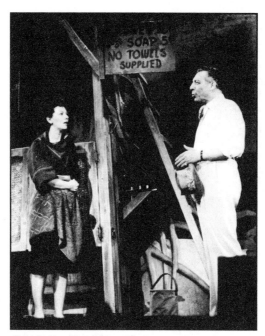

South Pacific. Mary Martin and Ezio Pinza.

South Pacific. William Tabbert singing "Younger Than Spring-time" to Betta St. John.

SOUTH PACIFIC

Music: Richard Rodgers
Lyrics: Oscar Hammerstein II
Book: Oscar Hammerstein II & Joshua Logan
Producers: Richard Rodgers & Oscar Hammerstein II, Leland Hayward & Joshua Logan
Director: Joshua Logan
Cast: Mary Martin, Ezio Pinza, Myron McCormick, Juanita Hall, William Tabbert, Betta St. John, Martin Wolfson, Harvey Stephens, Richard Eastham, Henry Slate, Fred Sadoff, Archie Savage
Songs: "A Cockeyed Optimist"; "Some Enchanted Evening"; "Bloody Mary"; "There Is Nothin' Like a Dame"; "Bali Ha'i"; "I'm Gonna Wash That Man Right Outa My Hair"; "A Wonderful Guy"; "Younger Than Springtime"; "Happy Talk"; "Honey Bun"; "You've Got to Be Carefully Taught"; "This Nearly Was Mine"
New York run: Majestic Theatre, April 7, 1949; 1,925 p.

The catalyst for the musical was director Joshua Logan who, early in 1948, strongly urged Rodgers and Hammerstein to adapt a short story in James Michener's wartime collection *Tales of the South Pacific* as their next Broadway production. "Fo' Dolla," the story Logan recommended, was about Lt. Joe Cable's tender and tragic romance with a Polynesian girl, but it struck the partners as too close to *Madama Butterfly* to sustain interest throughout an entire evening. Their solution was to make this a secondary plot while using another Michener tale, "Our Heroine," as the main story. That one had to do with the unlikely attraction between Nellie Forbush, a naive Navy nurse from Little Rock, and Emile de Becque, a worldly French planter living on a Pacific island, who fall in love on an enchanted evening. Both stories were combined by having Cable and de Becque go on a dangerous mission together behind Japanese lines, from which only de Becque returns. One of the musical's major themes — expressed through the song "You've Got to Be Carefully Taught" — is the folly of the racial prejudice, an issue that comes up when Emile tells Nellie that he had lived with a native woman who bore him two children.

South Pacific was the first of two musicals (the other was *The Sound of Music*) in which Mary Martin, who played Nellie, was seen as a Rodgers and Hammerstein heroine, and it marked the Broadway debut of Metropolitan Opera basso Ezio Pinza, who played de Becque. It was the second longest running musical of the decade as well as the second musical to be awarded the Pulitzer Prize for drama. Among actors who appeared in the production during its Broadway tenure were Martha Wright and Cloris Leachman (both played Nellie), Ray Middleton (de Becque), Shirley Jones (one of the nurses), Gene Saks (Professor), and Jack Weston (Stewpot).

The touring company, which was seen in 118 cities over a period of five years, had a cast originally headed by Janet Blair (Nellie), Richard Eastham (de Becque), Diosa Costello (Bloody Mary), Ray Walston (Luther), Julia Migenes (de Becque's daughter), and Alan Baxter (Comdr. Harbison). Cast replacements on the road included Connie Russell (Nellie), Irene Bordoni (Bloody Mary), and David Burns and Benny Baker (Luther). In 1967, *South Pacific* was revived by the Music Theatre of Lincoln Center with Florence Henderson and Giorgio Tozzi in the leads; 20 years later it was staged by the New York City Opera. The 1958 screen version co-starred Mitzi Gaynor and Rosanno Brazzi (with Tozzi's voice). Columbia OC; Columbia OC (1967); CBS SC (1986)/ Random House (1949)/ R&H.

MISS LIBERTY

Music & lyrics: Irving Berlin
Book: Robert E. Sherwood
Producers: Irving Berlin, Robert E. Sherwood & Moss Hart
Director: Moss Hart
Choreographer: Jerome Robbins
Cast: Eddie Albert, Allyn Ann McLerie, Mary McCarty, Charles Dingle, Philip Bourneuf, Ethel Griffies, Herbert Berghof, Tommy Rall, Janice Rule, Maria Karnilova, Dody Goodman
Songs: "Little Fish in a Big Pond"; "Let's Take an Old-Fashioned Walk"; "Homework"; "Paris Wakes Up and Smiles"; "Only for Americans"; "Just One Way to Say I Love You"; "You Can Have Him"; "Give Me Your Tired, Your Poor" (poem: Emma Lazarus)
New York run: Imperial Theatre, July 15, 1949; 308 p.

Miss Liberty boasted impressive credentials: songs by Irving Berlin, book by Robert E. Sherwood (his only musical), and direction by Moss Hart. If the results fell somewhat short of expectations, the show was still very much in the Americana mold of *Oklahoma!* and *Bloomer Girl* that offered a comforting view of the past to make audiences feel confident about the future. Here the story — set in New York and Paris in 1885 — deals with the rivalry between two newspapers, the *Herald* and the *World*, and the search for the model who posed for the Statue of Liberty. When the wrong model is brought to New York amid much hoopla, there is the inevitable consternation when the error is discovered. A happy ending is devised, however, just in time for the statue's dedication when all join in singing "Give Me Your Tired, Your Poor."
Columbia OC/ Samuel French (1986)*/ SF.

LOST IN THE STARS

Music: Kurt Weill
Lyrics & book: Maxwell Anderson
Producer: Playwrights' Company
Director: Rouben Mamoulian
Cast: Todd Duncan, Leslie Banks, Warren Coleman, Inez Matthews, Julian Mayfield, Frank Roane, Sheila Guyse, Herbert Coleman
Songs: "The Hills of Ixipo"; "Thousands of Miles"; "Train to Johannesburg"; "The Little Grey House"; "Trouble Man"; "Lost in the Stars"; "Stay Well"; "Cry, the Beloved Country"; "Big Mole"; "A Bird of Passage"
New York run: Music Box, October 30, 1949; 273 p.

Regarding the musical adaptation of Alan Paton's novel of South Africa, *Cry, the Beloved Country,* Kurt Weill once explained, "We wanted to treat the race problem as part of the human problem. The tragedy through which we are living is the tragedy of all men, white or black, rich or poor, young or old." After Absalom Kumalo (Julian Mayfield), the son of black minister Stephen Kumalo (Todd Duncan), accidentally kills a white man in an attempted robbery in Johannesburg, he is courageous enough to admit his guilt and face hanging, even though his companions, protesting their innocence, go free. As Absalom is about to die, Stephen is visited by the father of the slain man. Though James Jarvis (Leslie Banks) is a firm believer in apartheid, he admires the minister for his courage and honesty, and the play ends with each man saying, "I have a friend." *Lost in the Stars* was Kurt Weill's last Broadway production. In 1958, the work became part of the repertory of the New York City Opera, and in 1972 it was presented on Broadway with Brock Peters as Stephen Kumalo. Peters and Melba Moore were in the 1974 film version.
MCA OC/ Chilton (1976)/ R&H.

Miss Liberty. Allyn Ann McLerie, Eddie Albert, Mary McCarty, Charles Dingle, Maria Karnilova, and Tommy Rall lead the cast in singing "Give Me Your Tired, Your Poor."

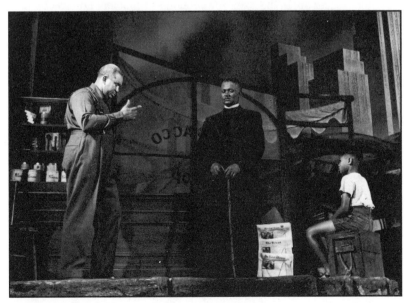

Lost in the Stars. Warren Coleman, Todd Duncan, and Herbert Coleman. (Karger-Pix)

GENTLEMEN PREFER BLONDES

Music: Jule Styne
Lyrics: Leo Robin
Book: Joseph Stein & Anita Loos
Producers: Herman Levin & Oliver Smith
Director: John C. Wilson
Choreographer: Agnes de Mille
Cast: Carol Channing, Yvonne Adair, Jack McCauley, Eric Brotherson, Alice Pearce, Rex Evans, Anita Alvarez, George S. Irving, Mort Marshall, Howard Morris, Charles "Honi" Coles, Cholly Atkins
Songs: "Bye, Bye, Baby"; "A Little Girl from Little Rock"; "Just a Kiss Apart"; "It's Delightful Down in Chile"; "Diamonds Are a Girl's Best Friend"
New York run: Ziegfeld Theatre, December 8, 1949; 740 p.

Based on Anita Loos' popular 1926 novel and play of the same name, *Gentlemen Prefer Blondes* took a satirical look at the wild and wacky Twenties, though there was no attempt at parodying the songs and styles as in the manner of Sandy Wilson's *The Boy Friend.* Carol Channing, in her first major role, scored such a success as the gold-digging little girl from Little Rock that she was elevated to stardom during the show's run. The scenes occur mostly aboard the *Ile de France,* which is taking Lorelei Lee and her chum Dorothy Shaw (Yvonne Adair) to Paris, courtesy of Lorelei's generous friend, button tycoon Gus Esmond (Jack McCauley). En route, the girls meet a number of accommodating gentlemen, including Sir Francis Beekman (Rex Evans) who loses a diamond tiara to Lorelei (who thereby wins a best friend) and Henry Spofford (Eric Brotherson), a Philadelphia Main Liner who loses his heart to Dorothy. The 1953 movie version offered Marilyn Monroe and Jane Russell, plus a hybrid score.

In 1973, a new stage version, called *Lorelei,* retained ten songs from the original score and added five new ones by Jule Styne, Betty Comden and Adolph Green. Carol Channing again headed the cast which included Tamara Long (Dorothy), Peter Palmer (Gus), Lee Roy Reams (Henry), and Jack Fletcher (Sir Francis). The book, now credited to Kenny Solms and Gail Parent, retained the same basic story, except for a modern-day prologue and epilogue that found Lorelei reminiscing about the past. After touring 11 months, *Lorelei* opened on Broadway in January 1974, and gave 320 performances.
Columbia OC; MGM OC (1973, 1974).

Gentlemen Prefer Blondes. Carol Channing singing "Diamonds Are a Girl's Best Friend." (Fred Fehl)

Call Me Madam. Ethel Merman as Sally Adams. (Vandamm)

CALL ME MADAM

Music & lyrics: Irving Berlin
Book: Howard Lindsay & Russel Crouse
Producer: Leland Hayward
Director: George Abbott
Choreographer: Jerome Robbins
Cast: Ethel Merman, Paul Lukas, Russell Nype, Galina Talva, Pat Harrington, Alan Hewitt, Tommy Rall, Nathaniel Frey
Songs: "The Hostess With the Mostes' on the Ball"; "Can You Use Any Money Today?"; "Marrying for Love"; "It's a Lovely Day Today"; "They Like Ike"; "The Best Thing for You"; "You're Just in Love"
New York run: Imperial Theatre, October 12, 1950; 644 p.

Once President Harry S. Truman named Washington party-giver Perle Mesta Ambassador to Luxembourg, the foundation was laid for a musical-comedy satire that would kid politics, foreign affairs, and the familiar sight of the comically gauche American abroad. Once Ethel Merman and Irving Berlin joined Howard Lindsay and Russel Crouse in the enterprise, the foundation was laid for a solid Broadway hit. The story, according to the program, takes place "in two mythical countries, one is Lichtenburg, the other the United States of America." When Sally Adams, the hostess with the mostes' on the ball, becomes Ambassador to the tiny duchy, she surprises and charms the local gentry, especially Foreign Minister Cosmo Constantine (Paul Lukas), with her no-nonsense, undiplomatic manner. In a subplot, Sally's young aide Kenneth Gibson (Russell Nype) finds himself falling for Lichtenburg's Princess Marie (Galina Talva), a condition that prompts the ambassador to itemize the symptoms in the classic contrapuntal duet, "You're Just in Love." In a running gag, Sally periodically chats with President Truman on the telephone, thereby justifying the nightly gimmick of Truman look-alike Irving Fisher taking a bow during the curtain calls. The film version, also starring Ethel Merman, was released in 1953. Three years later, Miss Merman appeared in *Happy Hunting*, another Lindsay-Crouse stage musical contrasting American brashness with European courtliness that was also sparked by a topical event, the wedding of Grace Kelly and Prince Rainier of Monaco. RCA OC (minus Merman); MCA OC (only Merman)/ Irving Berlin Ltd., London (1956)*/ MTI.

GUYS AND DOLLS

Music & lyrics: Frank Loesser
Book: Abe Burrows
Producers: Cy Feuer & Ernest Martin
Director: George S. Kaufman
Choreographer: Michael Kidd
Cast: Robert Alda, Vivian Blaine, Sam Levene, Isabel Bigley, Pat Rooney Sr., B. S. Pully, Stubby Kaye, Tom Pedi, Johnny Silver, Peter Gennaro, Onna White, Buddy Schwab
Songs: "Fugue for Tinhorns"; "Follow the Fold"; "The Oldest Established"; "I'll Know"; "A Bushel and a Peck"; "Adelaide's Lament"; "Guys and Dolls"; "If I Were a Bell"; "My Time of Day"; "I've Never Been in Love Before"; "Take Back Your Mink"; "More I Cannot Wish You"; "Luck Be a Lady"; "Sue Me"; "Sit Down, You're Rockin' the Boat"; "Marry the Man Today"
New York run: 46th Street Theatre, November 24, 1950; 1,200 p.

Though it turned out to be one of Broadway's most hilarious musical comedies — as well as an acknowledged classic in the field — *Guys and Dolls* was originally planned as a serious romantic story. Much impressed by the success of *South Pacific,* producers Cy Feuer and Ernest Martin felt that if such a compelling musical play could be written about the unlikely romance between naive Nellie Forbush and sophisticated Emile de Becque, an equally affecting story could be created out of the unlikely romance between a pure-at-heart Salvation Army-type reformer and a slick Broadway gambler, the two leading characters in Damon Runyon's short story "The Idyll of Miss Sarah Brown." For the score, the producers enlisted Frank Loesser (with whom they had been associated on *Where's Charley?*), then tried some 11 librettists though none came up with an acceptable script. The last of these writers, Jo Swerling, had a contract giving him primary credit as author no matter how many subsequent changes might be made, which is the reason his name always appears on programs as co-librettist. After so many script rejections, Feuer and Martin changed their minds and now decided that *Guys and Dolls* could only work if it were played for laughs. This led them to Abe Burrows, a radio and television comedy writer without theatrical experience, who wrote an entirely new book that he fitted to Loesser's already existing score.

In this so-called "Musical Fable of Broadway," the high-minded lowlifes and spunky do-gooders of Damon Runyon's world come colorfully alive in such characters as Sky Masterson (Robert Alda), the bet-on-anything gambler; Nathan Detroit (Sam Levene), the perpetually harried organizer of the oldest established permanent floating crap game in New York, who bets Sky that he can't make the next girl he sees fall in love with him; Miss Sarah Brown (Isabel Bigley) of the Save-a-Soul Mission on Times Square, who *is* the next girl Sky sees and who does succumb; and Miss Adelaide (Vivian Blaine), the main attraction at the Hot Box nightclub, whose psychosomatic perpetual cold stems from her being engaged to Nathan for 14 years. One of the show's memorable scenes occurs in the mission where Nicely-Nicely Johnson (Stubby Kaye) confesses his sins in the rousing "Sit Down, You're Rockin' the Boat." *Guys and Dolls* was the fifth longest-running Broadway musical of the Fifties. Its touring company traveled for two years four months with a cast originally headed by Allan Jones (Sky), Pamela Britton (Adelaide), Julie Oshins (Nathan), and Jan Clayton (Sarah).

A Broadway revival of *Guys and Dolls* with an all-black cast was mounted in 1976. In it were James Randolph (Sky), Norma Donaldson (Adelaide), Robert Guillaume (Nathan), Ernestine Jackson (Sarah), and Ken Page (Nicely-Nicely). The run lasted 239 performances. The film version, released in 1955, starred Marlon Brando, Vivian Blaine, Frank Sinatra, and Jean Simmons.
MCA OC; Motown OC (1976)/ Doubleday Anchor (1956)/ MTI.

Guys and Dolls. Sam Levene and Vivian Blaine singing "Sue Me." (Eileen Darby)

Guys and Dolls. Robert Alda throws the dice as Stubby Kaye, B. S. Pully, Johnny Silver, and Sam Levene watch. (Eileen Darby)

The King and I. Anna and son (Gertrude Lawrence and Sandy Kennedy) arrive in Bangkok. (Vandamm)

The King and I. "Shall We Dance?" Anna (Gertrude Lawrence) asks the King (Yul Brynner). (Vandamm)

THE KING AND I

Music: Richard Rodgers
Lyrics & book: Oscar Hammerstein II
Producers: Richard Rodgers & Oscar Hammerstein II
Director: John van Druten
Choreographer: Jerome Robbins
Cast: Gertrude Lawrence, Yul Brynner, Dorothy Sarnoff, Doretta Morrow, Larry Douglas, Johnny Stewart, Sandy Kennedy, Lee Becker Theodore, Gemze de Lappe, Yuriko, Baayork Lee
Songs: "I Whistle a Happy Tune"; "My Lord and Master"; "Hello, Young Lovers"; "March of the Siamese Children" (instrumental); "A Puzzlement"; "Getting to Know You"; "We Kiss in a Shadow"; "Shall I Tell You What I Think of You?"; "Something Wonderful"; "I Have Dreamed"; "Shall We Dance?"
New York run: St. James Theatre, March 29,1951; 1,246 p.

Upon reading Margaret Landon's novel, *Anna and the King of Siam*, and seeing the film version, Gertrude Lawrence became convinced that this would be the ideal vehicle for her return to the musical stage. She first sounded out Cole Porter about the project, then turned to Rodgers and Hammerstein who, though aware of her vocal limitations, readily agreed to write and produce it. Based on the diaries of an adventurous Englishwoman, Anna Leonowens, the story of *The King and I* (a title Miss Lawrence never liked) is set in Bangkok in the early 1860s. Anna, the new governess and teacher to King Mongkut's many children, has frequent clashes with the autocratic, semi-barbaric ruler, but eventually—and discretely—comes to love him. She exerts great influence in helping to democratize the country, and after the King's death remains as adviser to his successor, Crown Prince Chulalongkorn (Johnny Stewart). A tragic secondary plot concerns the furtive romance between Tuptim (Doretta Morrow), one of Mongkut's wives, and her lover Lun Tha (Larry Douglas). Of dramatic importance in the plot was Jerme Robbins' narrative ballet, "The Small House of Uncle Thomas," based on *Uncle Tom's Cabin*.

Cast as the King was Yul Brynner, a virtually unknown actor who won the role after attempts had been made to interest Rex Harrison, Noël Coward, and Alfred Drake (Drake did replace Brynner briefly during the run). Following Miss Lawrence's death in September 1952, Anna was played successively by Constance Carpenter, Annamary Dickey, and Patricia Morison. *The King and I's* Broadway run was the fourth longest of the decade, and the musical toured for over a year and a half with Miss Morison and Brynner.

Though in 1964 Darren McGavin played the Siamese monarch opposite Risë Stevens' Anna in the premiere production of the Music Theatre of Lincoln Center, and others have played it throughout the country, the role of King Mongkut became the virtual personal property of Yul Brynner. By the sheer force of his personality and without any change in the script, he managed to switch the dramatic spotlight from Anna to the King. In 1956, Brynner co-starred in the film version with Deborah Kerr. Twenty years later, now solo starred, he began touring in a new stage production (with Constance Towers as Anna) that played New York in 1977 (see page 248), and London 1979. Brynner resumed touring in 1981 and returned to New York in December 1984, with Mary Beth Peil as Anna. By the end of this engagement, King Yul had had a reign lasting 4,625 performances. A major Broadway revival, with Lou Diamond Phillips as the King, opened in 1996.

MCA OC; RCA OC (1964); RCA OC (1977)/ Random House (1951)/ R&H.

A TREE GROWS IN BROOKLYN

Music: Arthur Schwartz
Lyrics: Dorothy Fields
Book: George Abbott & Betty Smith
Producers: George Abbott & Robert Fryer
Director: George Abbott
Choreographer: Herbert Ross
Cast: Shirley Booth, Johnny Johnston, Marcia Van Dyke, Nomi Mitty, Nathaniel Frey, Harland Dixon, Lou Wills Jr.
Songs: "Make the Man Love Me"; "I'm Like a New Broom"; "Look Who's Dancing"; "Love Is the Reason"; "I'll Buy You a Star"; "He Had Refinement"; "Growing Pains"
New York run: Alvin Theatre, April 19, 1951; 270 p.

Far removed from the sophisticated revues and book musicals Arthur Schwartz and Dorothy Fields were usually associated with was this sentimental, nostalgic view of a Brooklyn working-class family at the turn of the century. Betty Smith, who had originally written her autobiographical novel as a play, shared adaptation credit with director-producer George Abbott for a work that was initially supposed to have a score by Irving Berlin. The story relates the saga of the Nolan clan: the charming but weak Johnny (Johnny Johnston), who finds relief in the bottle; his hard-working, devoted wife Katie (Marcia Van Dyke); their daughter Francie (Nomi Mitty), who idolizes her father; and Katie's sister, the amiable, available Cissy (Shirley Booth), whose affairs with a string of unwed husbands help lighten the basically tragic story. Miss Booth, who scored an impressive hit, was seen two years later in *By the Beautiful Sea,* another Arthur Schwartz-Dorothy Fields musical that was also set in turn-of-the-century Brooklyn. Columbia OC/ Harper (1951).

PAINT YOUR WAGON

Music: Frederick Loewe
Lyrics & book: Alan Jay Lerner
Producer: Cheryl Crawford
Director: Daniel Mann
Choreographer: Agnes de Mille
Cast: James Barton, Olga San Juan, Tony Bavaar, James Mitchell, Kay Medford, Gemze de Lappe, Marijane Maricle
Songs: "I Talk to the Trees"; "What's Goin' on Here?"; "They Call the Wind Maria"; "I Still See Elisa"; "Another Autumn"; "Wand'rin' Star"
New York run: Shubert Theatre, November 12, 1951; 289 p.

Filling their musical play with authentic incidents and backgrounds, Lerner and Loewe struck it rich both musically and dramatically with a work that captured the flavor of the roistering, robust California gold fields of 1853. James Barton, returning to the musical stage for the first time in 20 years, took the part of Ben Rumson, a grizzled prospector whose daughter Jennifer (Olga San Juan) discovers gold near their camp. Word of the strike quickly spreads and before long there are over 4,000 inhabitants of the new town of Rumson. Jennifer, who has fallen in love with Julio (Tony Bavaar), a Mexican prospector, goes East to school but returns to Julio when the gold strike peters out. Rumson is now virtually a ghost town, and Ben is left with nothing but his hopes and dreams. During the Broadway run, Barton was succeeded by Burl Ives and Eddie Dowling. The 1969 film version, with Clint Eastwood, Lee Marvin and Jean Seberg told a different story.
RCA OC/ Coward-McCann (1952)/ TW.

PAL JOEY

Music: Richard Rodgers
Lyrics: Lorenz Hart
Book: John O'Hara (George Abbott uncredited)
Producers: Jule Styne & Leonard Key
Directors: Robert Alton, David Alexander
Choreographer: Robert Alton
Cast: Vivienne Segal, Harold Lang, Helen Gallagher, Lionel Stander, Patricia Northrop, Elaine Stritch, Helen Wood, Barbara Nichols, Jack Waldron, Robert Fortier
Songs: Same as original production
New York run: Broadhurst Theatre, January 3, 1952; 540 p.

(See page 112.)

Pal Joey. Harold Lang (as Joey) is distracted by Patricia Northrop much to the irritation of patroness Vivienne Segal. (Eileen Darby)

NEW FACES OF 1952

Music, lyrics & sketches: Miscellaneous writers
Producer: Leonard Sillman
Directors: John Murray Anderson, John Beal
Choreographer: Richard Barstow
Cast: Ronny Graham, Eartha Kitt, Robert Clary, June Carroll, Virginia de Luce, Alice Ghostley, Carol Lawrence, Paul Lynde
Songs: "Lucky Pierre" (Ronny Graham); "Guess Who I Saw Today" (Murray Grand-Elisse Boyd); "Love Is a Simple Thing" (Arthur Siegel-June Carroll); "Boston Beguine" (Sheldon Harnick); "Lizzie Bordon" (Michael Brown); "I'm in Love with Miss Logan" (Graham); "Penny Candy" (Siegel-Carroll); "Monotonous" (Siegel-Carroll)
New York run: Royale Theatre, May 16, 1952; 365 p.

Of the seven *New Faces* revues assembled by Leonard Sillman, the 1952 edition was the most admired, both for the talent of the performers and the cleverness of the writing. Among the numbers were "Boston Beguine," Alice Ghostley's revelation of improper behavior in a proper surrounding; "Lizzie Borden," a sprightly hoedown celebrating an unsightly deed; "Guess Who I Saw Today," a rueful ballad of infidelity sung by June Carroll; "Monotonous," in which Eartha Kitt purred about her boring life; Ronny Graham's sendup of Truman Capote called "Oedipus Goes South"; Mel Brooks' burlesque of *Death of a Salesman,* in which a pickpocket feels betrayed by a son who shuns the family business; and Paul Lynde's speech, while swathed in bandages, about his misadventures on an African safari. The Royale Theatre is on 45th Street west of Broadway. In 1954, the film version was released with the original performers.
RCA OC.

WISH YOU WERE HERE

Music & lyrics: Harold Rome
Book: Arthur Kober & Joshua Logan
Producers: Leland Hayward & Joshua Logan
Director: Joshua Logan
Choreographer: Joshua Logan (Jerome Robbins uncredited)
Cast: Sheila Bond, Jack Cassidy, Patricia Marand, Sidney Armus, Paul Valentine, Harry Clark, Florence Henderson, Tom Tryon, Larry Blyden, Phyllis Newman, Reid Shelton
Songs: "Social Director"; "Goodbye Love"; "Could Be"; "Tripping the Light Fantastic"; "Where Did the Night Go?"; "Summer Afternoon"; "Don José of Far Rockaway"; "Wish You Were Here"; "Flattery"
New York run: Imperial Theatre, June 25, 1952; 598 p.

It was known as the musical with the swimming pool, but *Wish You Were Here* had other things going for it, including a cast of ingratiating actors, a warm and witty score by Harold Rome, and a director, Joshua Logan, who wouldn't stop making improvements even after the Broadway opening (among them were new dances choreographed by Jerome Robbins). The musical, which Arthur Kober and Logan adapted from Kober's 1937 play, *Having Wonderful Time,* is set in Camp Karefree, an adult summer camp "where friendships are formed to last a whole lifetime through," and is concerned with middle-class New Yorkers trying to make the most of a two-week vacation in the Catskills. Mainly it's about Teddy Stern (Patricia Marand), a secretary from Brooklyn, who finds true love — after a series of misunderstandings — with Chick Miller (Jack Cassidy), a law student working as a waiter by day and a dancing partner by night.
RCA OC/ MTI.

WONDERFUL TOWN

Music: Leonard Bernstein
Lyrics: Betty Comden & Adolph Green
Book: Joseph Fields & Jerome Chodorov
Producer: Robert Fryer
Director: George Abbott (Jerome Robbins uncredited)
Choreographer: Donald Saddler
Cast: Rosalind Russell, George Gaynes, Edie Adams, Henry Lascoe, Dort Clark, Dody Goodman, Nathaniel Frey, Joe Layton
Songs: "Christopher Street"; "Ohio"; "One Hundred Easy Ways"; "What a Waste"; "A Little Bit in Love"; "A Quiet Girl"; "Conga!"; "Swing!"; "It's Love"; "Wrong Note Rag"
New York run: Winter Garden, February 25, 1953; 559 p.

Because it again showed New York as just about the liveliest, friendliest place on earth, and because it again had a score by Leonard Bernstein, Betty Comden and Adolph Green and direction by George Abbott, *Wonderful Town* is generally accepted as the successor to *On The Town*. The songwriters, in fact, became involved in the project only five weeks before rehearsals when they took over the assignment from Leroy Anderson and Arnold Horwitt, who had bowed out over a disagreement with librettists Joseph Fields (brother of Herbert and Dorothy) and Jerome Chodorov. The musical was based on Ruth McKinney's *New Yorker* short stories — which Fields and Chodorov had already turned into the 1940 Broadway hit *My Sister Eileen* — and concerns the adventures of Miss McKinney and her sister in Greenwich Village after arriving from Ohio seeking careers. Ruth has problems getting her stories accepted by *The Manhatter* magazine and Eileen (Edie Adams) has problems warding off admirers. On a freelance newspaper assignment, Ruth gets to interview seven over-amorous, Conga-dancing Brazilian naval cadets, who cause a near-riot. Though this lands Ruth in jail, she also manages to land a handsome magazine editor (George Gaynes). Rosalind Russell, as Ruth, scored resoundingly in her only major musical-comedy role, and was succeeded during the run by Carol Channing.
MCA OC/ Random House (1953); Chilton (1976)/ TW.

Wonderful Town. Edie Adams and Rosalind Russell singing "Ohio." (Vandamm)

PORGY AND BESS

Music: George Gershwin
Lyrics: DuBose Heyward, Ira Gershwin
Book: DuBose Heyward
Producers: Blevins Davis & Robert Breen
Director: Robert Breen
Cast: LeVern Hutcherson (or Leslie Scott, Irving Barnes), Leontyne Price (or Urylee Leonardos), Cab Calloway, John McCurry, Helen Colbert, Helen Thigpen, Georgia Burke, Helen Dowdy
Songs: Same as original production
New York run: Ziegfeld Theatre, March 10, 1953; 305 p.

(See page 91.)

CAN-CAN

Music & lyrics: Cole Porter
Book: Abe Burrows
Producers: Cy Feuer & Ernest Martin
Director: Abe Burrows
Choreographer: Michael Kidd
Cast: Lilo, Peter Cookson, Hans Conried, Gwen Verdon, Erik Rhodes, Dania Krupska, Phil Leeds, DeeDee Wood
Songs: "Never Give Anything Away"; "C'est Magnifique"; "Come Along With Me"; "Live and Let Live"; "I Am in Love"; "Montmart' "; "Allez-vous-en"; "Never Never Be an Artist"; "It's All Right With Me"; "I Love Paris"; "Can-Can"
New York run: Shubert Theatre, May 7, 1953; 892 p.

To make sure that his script for *Can-Can* would be historically authentic, Abe Burrows traveled to Paris where he researched the records of the courts, the police, and the Chamber of Deputies. To his surprise, Burrows discovered that there were then a number of blue-nose organizations devoted to the suppression of such immoral exhibitions as the high-kicking, derriere-baring dance. This gave him the outline for his plot. Set in 1893, it tells of La Mome Pistache who is so distressed about the investigation of her Bal du Paradis — where the chief attraction is the Can-Can — that she tries to vamp the highly moral investigating judge, Aristide Forestier. Eventually, the two fall in love and when the case comes to trial, Forestier himself takes over the defense and wins acquittal. Though originally intended for Carol Channing, the role of Pistache went to the French actress Lilo (who introduced "I Love Paris"), but most of the kudos were for Gwen Verdon (who stopped the show with an Apache dance and the sexy "Garden of Eden" ballet) in her first major Broadway role.

In 1981, *Can-Can* again kicked up its heels — albeit briefly — in a revival starring Zizi Jeanmaire and Ron Husmann that was directed by Burrows. The altered Hollywood version, released in 1960, featured Frank Sinatra, Shirley MacLaine, and Maurice Chevalier.
Capitol OC/ TW.

Me and Juliet. Isabel Bigley singing "I'm Your Girl" to Bill Hayes. (Eileen Darby)

ME AND JULIET

Music: Richard Rodgers
Lyrics & book: Oscar Hammerstein II
Producers: Richard Rodgers & Oscar Hammerstein II
Director: George Abbott
Choreographer: Robert Alton
Cast: Isabel Bigley, Bill Hayes, Joan McCracken, Ray Walston, Mark Dawson, George S. Irving, Barbara Carroll, Shirley MacLaine
Songs: "A Very Special Day"; "Marriage-Type Love"; "Keep It Gay"; "The Big Black Giant"; "No Other Love"; "It's Me"; "I'm Your Girl"
New York run: Majestic Theatre, May 28, 1953; 358 p.

Writing in the lighter form of musical comedy rather than in their more accustomed "serious" form of musical play, Rodgers and Hammerstein created *Me and Juliet* as their Valentine to show business. The action — in *Kiss Me, Kate* fashion — takes place both backstage and onstage of a theatre during the performance of a play. Here the tale concerns a romance between a singer in the chorus (Isabel Bigley) and the assistant stage manager (Bill Hayes) whose newfound bliss is temporarily threatened by the jealous, heavy-drinking electrician (Mark Dawson). The melody of the show's best-known song, "No Other Love," had been previously used as background for the "Beneath the Southern Cross" episode in the NBC-TV series, *Victory at Sea. Me and Juliet* was the 29th and penultimate Broadway musical choreographed by Robert Alton.
RCA OC/ Random House (1953)/ R&H.

KISMET

Music & lyrics: Robert Wright & George Forrest based on Alexander Borodin
Book: Charles Lederer & Luther Davis
Producers: Charles Lederer, Edwin Lester
Director: Albert Marre
Choreographer: Jack Cole
Cast: Alfred Drake, Doretta Morrow, Joan Diener, Henry Calvin, Richard Kiley, Steve Reeves, Beatrice Kraft
Songs: "Sands of Time"; "Rhymes Have I"; "Not Since Nineveh"; "Baubles, Bangles and Beads"; "Stranger in Paradise"; "Night of My Nights"; "And This Is My Beloved"; "The Olive Tree"
New York run: Ziegfeld Theatre, December 3, 1953; 583 p.

The story of *Kismet* was adapted from a 1911 play by Edward Knoblock that was closely identified with Otis Skinner. The music of *Kismet* was adapted from themes Alexander Borodin composed for such works as the "Polovtsian Dances" ("Stranger in Paradise") and the D-Major String Quartet ("And This Is My Beloved," "Baubles, Bangles and Beads"). In this "Musical Arabian Night," the action occurs within a 24-hour period from dawn to dawn in ancient Baghdad, where a roguish public poet (Alfred Drake) assumes the identity of Hajj the beggar and has a series of unlikely adventures. By the time they have ended, he has drowned the wicked Wazir (Henry Calvin), has seen his daughter Marsinah (Doretta Morrow) wedded to the handsome Caliph (Richard Kiley), has been appointed Emir of Baghdad, and has gone off into the desert with the Wazir's luscious wife Lalume (Joan Diener). Before coming to New York, *Kismet* had first been presented in the summer of 1953 by Edwin Lester's Los Angeles and San Francisco Civic Light Opera Association. The film version, with Howard Keel and Ann Blyth, was released in 1955.

In 1965 the musical was revived by the Music Theatre of Lincoln Center with Alfred Drake again giving a bravura performance, and in 1985 it was added to the repertory of the New York City Opera. An all-black variation, *Timbuktu,* arrived on Broadway in 1978 and remained for 221 performances. It kept the music but switched the locale to the ancient African kingdom of Mali, and its cast was headed by Eartha Kitt, Ira Hawkins, Melba Moore, and Gilbert Price. For other musicals with scores based on classical themes, see *Blossom Time* page 38. Columbia OC; RCA OC (1965)/ Random House (1954)/ MTI.

The Threepenny Opera. Lotte Lenya as Jenny.

THE THREEPENNY OPERA

Music: Kurt Weill
Lyrics & book: Marc Blitzstein
Producers: Carmen Capalbo & Stanley Chase
Director: Carmen Capalbo
Cast: Lotte Lenya, Scott Merrill, Leon Lishner, Jo Sullivan, Charlotte Rae, Beatrice Arthur, Gerald Price, John Astin, Joseph Beruh, Gerrianne Raphael
Songs: "The Ballad of Mack the Knife"; "Army Song"; "Love Song"; "Pirate Jenny"; "Tango-Ballad"; "Ballad of the Easy Life"; "Barbara Song"; "Useless Song"; "Solomon Song"
New York run: Theatre de Lys, March 10, 1954; 95 p. Reopened: September 20, 1955; 2,611 p.

The reason for the two engagements noted above is that the initial showing of Marc Blitzstein's English-language version of the Kurt Weill-Bertold Brecht *Die Dreigroschenoper* at the Theatre de Lys (now the Lucille Lortel) had to be terminated because of a prior booking. Led by critic Brooks Atkinson, public demand brought it back 15 months after the closing, with cast replacements including Frederic Downs for Leon Lishner, Jane Connell for Charlotte Rae, Tige Andrews for Gerald Price, Eddie Lawrence for Joseph Beruh, and Chris Chase for Gerrianne Raphael. At this writing, the return engagement is the second longest running production ever mounted Off Broadway. In its original form, the work was presented in Berlin in 1928 on the 200th anniverasy of *The Beggar's Opera* — credited as the first ballad opera, or musical comedy — on which it was based. The play's bitter, raffish view of contemporary morality, combined with its jingly, beer-hall tunes, quickly made it a favorite throughout Europe, and in 1933 the first American adaptation had a brief run on Broadway.

Set in Victorian London, *The Threepenny Opera* spins the tale of Macheath (Scott Merrill), an outlaw known as Mack the Knife. Mack marries Polly Peachum (Jo Sullivan), the daughter of the leader of Soho's underworld, but he is betrayed by his in-laws and is sent to Newgate Prison. After being freed by Lucy Brown (Beatrice Arthur), the police chief's daughter, Mack is again betrayed — this time by Jenny the whore (Lotte Lenya, Weill's widow, who had originated the role in Berlin). Sentenced to be hanged, Mack receives a last-minute reprieve from the queen, thus providing the play with a mock-heroic ending. Among the more than 200 actors who played the 22 parts during the show's run were Carole Cook, Valerie Bettis, and Dolly Haas (Jenny); James Mitchell and Jerry Orbach (Mack); Pert Kelton and Nancy Andrews (Mrs. Peachum); Georgia Brown (Lucy); Edward Asner (Peachum); and Estelle Parsons (Mrs. Coaxer). The 1964 film version featured Hildegarde Neff and Kurt Jurgens.

In 1976, Joseph Papp's New York Shakespeare Festival at Lincoln Center offered an even more abrasive version of *The Threepenny Opera* in an adaptation by Ralph Manheim and John Willett. With a cast headed by Raul Julia (Mack) and Ellen Greene (Jenny), the show also played Broadway for a total run of 307 performances.

The Beggar's Opera, the 18th Century English musical that had inspired the German version, was first presented in America in 1750. Its most recent production was in 1972 when the Chelsea Theatre of Brooklyn staged a revival that was also shown at an Off Broadway theatre in Manhattan. It ran 253 performances. Another variation, *Beggar's Holiday,* updating the scene to modern America, opened on Broadway in 1946. The music was by Duke Ellington, the lyrics and libretto by John Latouche, and the cast included Alfred Drake, Zero Mostel, and Bernice Parks.

Polydor OC; Columbia OC (1976)/ R&H.

The Golden Apple. Salesman Jonathan Lucas displays his wares for Kaye Ballard, Priscilla Gillette, and Stephen Douglass. (Vandamm)

THE GOLDEN APPLE

Music: Jerome Moross
Lyrics & book: John Latouche
Producers: T. Edward Hambleton & Norris Houghton
Director: Norman Lloyd
Choreographer: Hanya Holm
Cast: Priscilla Gillette, Stephen Douglass, Kaye Ballard, Jack Whiting, Bibi Osterwald, Jonathan Lucas, Portia Nelson, Jerry Stiller, Dean Michener, Shannon Bolin
Songs: "My Love Is on the Way"; "It's the Going Home Together"; "Helen Is Always Willing"; "Lazy Afternoon"; "Windflowers"
New York run: Phoenix Theatre, March 11, 1954; 173 p.

Using Homer's *Odyssey* and *Iliad* as models, Jerome Moross and John Latouche updated the epics to the period between 1900 and 1910 and relocated the action in the state of Washington. With spoken dialogue cut to a minimum, the story is told through a steady stream of musical numbers (including the popular hit, "Lazy Afternoon") and relates the consternation caused in the town of Angel's Roost (near Mt. Olympus) when a salesman named Paris (Jonathan Lucas) flies in in a balloon and abducts old Menelaus' always-willing wife, Helen (Kaye Ballard). The stalwart Ulysses (Stephen Douglass), who has just returned from the Spanish-American War, feels so duty-bound to retrieve the errant Helen that he leaves his wife Penelope (Priscilla Gillette) to go in search of the pair. Ulysses stays away ten years, during which time he resists various temptations, whips Paris in a bareknuckles fight, and is finally reunited with his incredibly patient spouse. Following its well-received opening at the downtown Phoenix Theatre, *The Golden Apple* moved uptown to the Alvin where it had a disappointingly short run.
Elektra OC/ Random House (1954)/ TW.

THE PAJAMA GAME

Music & lyrics: Richard Adler & Jerry Ross
Book: George Abbott & Richard Bissell
Producers: Frederick Brisson, Robert Griffith & Harold Prince
Directors: George Abbott & Jerome Robbins
Choreographer: Bob Fosse
Cast: John Raitt, Janis Paige, Eddie Foy Jr., Carol Haney, Reta Shaw, Ralph
    Dunn, Stanley Prager, Peter Gennaro, Shirley MacLaine
Songs: "I'm Not at All in Love"; "I'll Never Be Jealous Again"; "Hey, There";
    "Once a Year Day"; "Small Talk"; "There Once Was a Man"; "Steam
    Heat"; "Hernando's Hideaway"
New York run: St. James Theatre, May 13, 1954; 1,063 p.

When Frank Loesser was approached to write the score for the musical adaptation of Richard Bissell's novel, *7½ Cents,* he had to turn it down, but he did recommend a young team, Richard Adler and Jerry Ross, who had never before written songs for a book musical. Their work — including such hits as "Hey, There" and "Hernando's Hideaway" — was impressive and so was the show, which Bissell, another Broadway newcomer, adapted in collaboration with veteran director George Abbott. (Other neophytes involved were co-director Jerome Robbins, choreographer Bob Fosse, and the trio of producers.)

The Pajama Game is concerned with the activities at the Sleep-Tite Pajama Factory in Cedar Rapids, Iowa, where Sid Sorokin (John Raitt), the new plant superintendent, has taken a shine to Babe Williams (Janis Paige), a union activist. Their romance suffers a setback when the workers go on strike for a seven-and-a-half cents hourly raise, but eventually management and labor are again singing in tune. During the run, chorus dancer Shirley MacLaine attracted notice when she substituted for Carol Haney in the "Steam Heat" number and was soon off to Hollywood. The musical toured for two years with Larry Douglas and Fran Warren. In 1973, the show was revived briefly on Broadway with a cast headed by Hal Linden, Barbara McNair, and Cab Calloway. John Raitt and Eddie Foy, Jr. repeated their original roles in the 1957 movie, which also starred Doris Day.

In 1958, Richard Bissell's novel, *Say, Darling,* which the author had based on his experience with *The Pajama Game,* was itself turned into a musical by Bissell, his wife Marian, and Abe Burrows. Burrows also directed, and Jule Styne, Betty Comden and Adolph Green supplied nine songs. The show ran 10 months. Columbia OC/ Random House (1954)/ MTI.

The Pajama Game. The picnic scene with Shirley MacLaine, John Raitt, and Janis Paige. (Talbot)

THE BOY FRIEND

Music, lyrics & book: Sandy Wilson
Producers: Cy Feuer & Ernest Martin
Director: Vida Hope (Cy Feuer uncredited)
Choreographer: John Heawood
Cast: Julie Andrews, John Hewer, Eric Berry, Ruth Altman, Bob Scheerer, Ann Wakefield, Millicent Martin, Dilys Lay, Stella Claire, Buddy Schwab
Songs: "The Boy Friend"; "Won't You Charleston With Me?"; "I Could Be Happy With You"; "Sur La Plage"; "A Room in Bloomsbury"; "The Riviera"; "It's Never Too Late to Fall in Love"; "Poor Little Pierrette"
New York run: Royale Theatre, September 30 ,1954; 485 p.

Though he was the first British writer of musicals since Noël Coward to win success in New York, composer-lyricist-librettist Sandy Wilson has, to date, seen only one of his works performed on Broadway. *The Boy Friend,* which had opened in London (where it would achieve a run of 2,048 performances), was in the tradition of Charles Gaynor's "Gladiola Girl" in *Lend an Ear* in that it offered an affectionate sendup of musical comedies of the Twenties, with the songs not only recalling the styles of that era but also establishing their own musical individuality. The tale is set in 1926 on the Riviera where Polly Browne, an English heiress attending Mme. Dubonnet's finishing school, meets Tony who, though of noble lineage, is posing as a delivery boy. They fall in love to such sweet sentiments as "I Could Be Happy With You" ("If you could be happy with me"), and though they have the expected misunderstanding, are happily reunited when, costumed as Pierrette and Pierrot, they both show up at the Carnival Ball. The musical also served to introduce Broadway to the charms of Julie Andrews who played Polly.

    The Boy Friend enjoyed an even longer run in a 1958 Off Broadway production that lasted 763 performances. Ellen McCown played Polly, Gerrianne Raphael her friend Maisie, and Bill Mullikin was Tony. The musical was again revived, this time on Broadway, in 1970, with Judy Carne (Polly), Sandy Duncan (Maisie), and Ronald Young (Tony). This version remained for four months. The cast of the 1972 film treatment included Twiggy and Tommy Tune.
RCA OC; MCA OC (1970)/ Dutton (1955)/ MTI.

The Boy Friend. Julie Andrews with Millicent Martin, Dilys Lay, Ann Wakefield, and Stella Claire. (Eileen Darby)

Peter Pan. "I'm Flying" sings Mary Martin as Peter Pan. (John Engstead)

PETER PAN

Music: Mark Charlap*; Jule Styne**
Lyrics: Carolyn Leigh*; Betty Comden & Adolph Green**
Play: James M. Barrie
Producers: Richard Halliday, Edwin Lester
Director-choreographer: Jerome Robbins
Cast: Mary Martin, Cyril Ritchard, Kathy Nolan, Margalo Gillmore, Joe E. Marks, Sondra Lee, Joseph Stafford, Robert Harrington
Songs: "Tender Shepherd"*; "I've Got to Crow"*; "Neverland"**; "I'm Flying"*; "Wendy"**; "I Won't Grow Up"*; "Mysterious Lady"**; "Captain Hook's Waltz"**
New York run: Winter Garden, October 20, 1954; 152 p.

When Jerome Robbins decided that the time was ripe to stage a new version of *Peter Pan,* with Mary Martin as the boy who wouldn't grow up and Cyril Ritchard as Captain Hook, he initially planned to use only a few incidental songs by newcomers Mark Charlap and Carolyn Leigh. After the play began evolving into a full-fledged musical, however, he went to the more experienced team of Jule Styne, Betty Comden and Adolph Green for the additional numbers. Following its unveiling as part of Edwin Lester's Los Angeles and San Francisco Civic Light Opera series, the show came to New York offering such pleasures as Miss Martin singing and flying at the same time and Ritchard playing the villainous Hook as a giggling, mincing Restoration dandy.

Peter Pan was first presented in New York in 1905 with Maude Adams as Peter, a role she virtually made her own for eight years. It was revived in 1924 with Marilyn Miller singing two songs by Jerome Kern, and in 1950 with Jean Arthur, Boris Karloff plus five songs by Leonard Bernstein. That version lasted nine months. A 1979 revival, starring Sandy Duncan in a production based on the 1954 musical, turned out to be the longest running — or flying — *Peter Pan* ever performed in New York. (See page 254.)
RCA OC/ SF.

Fanny. Ezio Pinza and Walter Slezak.
(Zinn Arthur)

FANNY

Music & lyrics: Harold Rome
Book: S. N. Behrman & Joshua Logan
Producers: David Merrick & Joshua Logan
Director: Joshua Logan
Choreographer: Helen Tamiris
Cast: Ezio Pinza, Walter Slezak, Florence Henderson, William Tabbert, Nejla Ates, Gerald Price, Alan Carney
Songs: "Restless Heart"; "Never Too Late for Love"; "Why Be Afraid to Dance?"; "Welcome Home"; "I Like You"; "Fanny"; "To My Wife"; "Love Is a Very Light Thing"; "Be Kind to Your Parents"
New York run: Majestic Theatre, November 4, 1954; 888 p.

Fanny takes us to the colorful, bustling port of Marseilles "not so long ago" for a musical version of Marcel Pagnol's French film trilogy, *Marius, Fanny,* and *César.* Compressed into one story, the heavily plotted tale — with its intensely emotional score — concerns Marius (William Tabbert), who yearns to go to sea; his father, César (Ezio Pinza), the local café owner; Panisse (Walter Slezak), a well-to-do middle-aged sail maker; and Fanny Cabanis (Florence Henderson), the girl beloved by both Marius and Panisse. Though Fanny conceives a child with Marius just before he ships off, Panisse marries her and brings up the boy as his own. When Marius returns demanding both Fanny and their son, César convinces him that Panisse has the more rightful claim. Years later, however, the dying Panisse dictates a letter to Marius offering him Fanny's hand in marriage.

Although Rodgers and Hammerstein had been sought to write it, *Fanny* became a collaboration between Harold Rome and Joshua Logan, who had worked together on *Wish You Were Here,* plus playwright S.N. Behrman. It also marked the first of 27 Broadway musicals produced by David Merrick. During the Broadway run, Pinza was succeeded by another former Metropolitan Opera star, Lawrence Tibbett, and Slezak by Billy Gilbert. No songs were retained for the 1960 movie version with Leslie Caron, Maurice Chevalier, and Charles Boyer. RCA OC/ Random House (1955)/ TW.

House of Flowers. Pearl Bailey as Mme. Fleur. (Zinn Arthur)

HOUSE OF FLOWERS

Music: Harold Arlen
Lyrics: Truman Capote & Harold Arlen
Book: Truman Capote
Producer: Saint Subber
Director: Peter Brook
Choreographer: Herbert Ross
Cast: Pearl Bailey, Diahann Carroll, Juanita Hall, Ray Walston, Dino DiLuca, Geoffrey Holder, Rawn Spearman, Frederick O'Neal, Carmen De Lavallade, Alvin Ailey, Arthur Mitchell
Songs: "A Sleepin' Bee"; "Smellin' of Vanilla"; "House of Flowers"; "Two Ladies in de Shade of de Banana Tree"; "I'm Gonna Leave Off Wearin' My Shoes"; "I Never Has Seen Snow"
New York run: Alvin Theatre, December 30, 1954; 165 p.

The genesis of *House of Flowers* occurred in 1948 when Truman Capote was visiting Port-au-Prince, Haiti, where he enjoyed frequenting the lively local bordellos. He first wrote a short story about one such establishment, then turned it into the libretto for a Broadway musical. Producer Saint Subber brought in Harold Arlen who also shared lyric-writing chores with Capote. In the plot, Madame Fleur (Pearl Bailey) is the protective, domineering horticulturist of the House of Flowers, which is in competition with a similar enterprise run by Madame Tango (Juanita Hall). Fleur is delighted to discover a new floral attraction named Ottilie (Diahann Carroll), but the innocent girl gives up all possibilities of professional advancement in favor of keeping herself for the equally innocent Royal (Rawn Spearman). *House of Flowers,* the first musical directed by Peter Brook, is particularly remembered for its colorful Oliver Messel sets and its atmospheric Harold Arlen music. In 1968, a somewhat revised version was offered Off Broadway with Josephine Premice as Madame Fleur.
Columbia OC; UA OC (1968)/ Random House (1968).

PLAIN AND FANCY

Music: Albert Hague
Lyrics: Arnold B. Horwitt
Book: Joseph Stein & Will Glickman
Producers: Richard Kollmar & James Gardiner
Director: Morton Da Costa
Choreographer: Helen Tamiris
Cast: Richard Derr, Barbara Cook, David Daniels, Shirl Conway, Stefan Schna-
bel, Gloria Marlowe, Nancy Andrews
Songs: "It Wonders Me"; "Plenty of Pennsylvania"; "Young and Foolish"; "This
Is All Very New to Me"; "Follow Your Heart"; "I'll Show Him"
New York run: Mark Hellinger Theatre, January 27, 1955; 461 p.

Like *Brigadoon, Plain and Fancy* used the visit of two sophisticated New Yorkers
to a strange rural community so that audiences might become acquainted with
its special customs and traditions. Here visitors Don King and Ruth Winters
(Richard Derr and Shirl Conway) have come to Bird-in-Hand, Pennsylvania, to
sell a farm Don owns to Amish farmer Jacob Yoder (Stefan Schnabel), a member
of a fundamentalist religious sect that gets along without telephones, automo-
biles, indoor plumbing, or even buttons. Yoder has arranged an unwanted marriage for his daughter, Katie (Gloria Marlowe), though her young and foolish
heart still belongs to her childhood sweetheart Peter Reber (David Daniels).
When Yoder's barn is struck by lightning and burns down, Peter is blamed for
putting a hex on it and he is shunned by members of the community. By rescuing
his brother from a carnival brawl, however, he proves himself worthy of their —
and Katie's — esteem. The Mark Hellinger Theatre, originally a movie house
named the Hollywood, stands at 51st Street and Broadway.
Capitol OC/ Random House (1955)/ SF.

SILK STOCKINGS

Music & lyrics: Cole Porter
Book: George S. Kaufman, Leueen McGrath & Abe Burrows
Producers: Cy Feuer & Ernest Martin
Director: Cy Feuer
Choreographer: Eugene Loring
Cast: Hildegarde Neff, Don Ameche, Gretchen Wyler, George Tobias, Leon Be-
lasco, Henry Lascoe, David Opatoshu, Julie Newmar, Onna White
Songs: "Paris Loves Lovers"; "It's a Chemical Reaction, That's All"; "All of
You"; "Too Bad"; "Satin and Silk"; "Without Love"; "Silk Stockings";
"The Red Blues"
New York run: Imperial Theatre, February 24, 1955; 478 p.

Cole Porter's last Broadway musical — and his sixth with a French setting —
was based on the popular 1939 film, *Ninotchka,* in which Greta Garbo was seen
as a dour Russian official who succumbs to the charms of both Paris and a
French count played by Melvyn Douglas. In the musical, Ninotchka (Hildegarde
Neff) is again doubly seduced, though this time the man is the fast-talking American talent agent Steve Canfield (Don Ameche), involved in convincing a Soviet
composer to write the score for a gaudy movie version of *War and Peace.* During
the Philadelphia tryout, prospects for the show looked so bleak that co-producer
Cy Feuer took over as director from George S. Kaufman, and Abe Burrows was
summoned to take over as librettist from Kaufman and Leueen McGrath (then
Mrs. Kaufman). The movie version was released in 1957 with Fred Astaire and
Cyd Charisse in the leads.
RCA OC/ TW.

DAMN YANKEES

Music & lyrics: Richard Adler & Jerry Ross
Book: George Abbott & Douglass Wallop (Richard Bissell uncredited)
Producers: Frederick Brisson, Robert Griffith & Harold Prince
Director: George Abbott
Choreographer: Bob Fosse
Cast: Gwen Verdon, Stephen Douglass, Ray Walston, Russ Brown, Shannon Bolin, Rae Allen, Jean Stapleton, Nathaniel Frey, Robert Shafer
Songs: "Heart"; "Shoeless Joe from Hannibal, Mo."; "A Little Brains — a Little Talent"; "Whatever Lola Wants"; "Near to You"; "Two Lost Souls"
New York run: 46th Street Theatre, May 5, 1955; 1,019 p.

Damn Yankees was something of a stylistic follow-up to *The Pajama Game* since it was put together by the same songwriters, librettist-director, choreographer, producers, music director (Harold Hastings), and orchestrator (Don Walker). With the author as collaborator, they adapted the work from Douglass Wallop's novel, *The Year the Yankees Lost the Pennant,* and managed to turn it into such a clean hit that it broke the longheld jinx against shows dealing with baseball. In this variation on the *Faust* legend (which had been used in musical theatre as far back as *The Black Crook* in 1866), a middle-aged Washington Senators fan (Robert Shafer) is so devoted that he sells his soul to the devil (Ray Walston as "Mr. Applegate") just for a chance to play on his favorite team. Suddenly transformed into a young man, now named Joe Hardy (Stephen Douglass), the fan not only joins the team but becomes its ace pitcher and hitter. Fortunately for him, there is a contractural escape clause, and Applegate — even aided by the seductive Lola (Gwen Verdon) who usually gets what she wants — cannot prevent Joe from returning home to his wife at the end of a year. (Miss Verdon, who also appeared in the 1958 screen version, was elevated to stardom during the show's run.) The touring company, led by Sherry O'Neil and Bobby Clark (in his last stage role as Applegate), traveled for one year four months.
RCA OC/ Random House (1956)/ MTI.

Damn Yankees. Gwen Verdon and Ray Walston. (Talbot)

MY FAIR LADY

Music: Frederick Loewe
Lyrics & book: Alan Jay Lerner
Producer: Herman Levin
Director: Moss Hart
Choreographer: Hanya Holm
Cast: Rex Harrison, Julie Andrews, Stanley Holloway, Cathleen Nesbitt, Robert Coote, John Michael King, Christopher Hewett, Reid Shelton
Songs: "Why Can't the English?"; "Wouldn't It Be Loverly?"; "With a Little Bit of Luck"; "I'm an Ordinary Man"; "The Rain in Spain"; "I Could Have Danced All Night"; "On the Street Where You Live"; "Show Me"; "Get Me to the Church on Time"; "A Hymn to Him"; "Without You"; "I've Grown Accustomed to Her Face"
New York run: Mark Hellinger Theatre, March 15, 1956; 2,717 p.

The most influential musical of the Fifties and one of the most distinguished productions of all time came about as a result of the efforts of Hungarian film producer Gabriel Pascal, who devoted the last two years of his life to a quest for writers to adapt George Bernard Shaw's 1914 play *Pygmalion* into a stage musical. After being rejected by the likes of Rodgers and Hammerstein and Noël Coward, Pascal won the committment of Alan Jay Lerner and Frederick Loewe once they decided to use most of Shaw's original dialogue and to expand the action to include scenes at Tottenham Court Road, the Ascot races, and the Embassy Ball. They were also scrupulous to maintain the Shavian flavor in the songs, most apparent in such pieces as "Why Can't the English?," "Show Me," "Get Me to the Church on Time," and "Without You."

Shaw's concern with class distinction and his belief that barriers would fall if all Englishmen would learn to speak their language properly was conveyed through a story about Eliza Doolittle, a scruffy cockney flower seller in Covent Garden, who takes lessons from phonetician Henry Higgins to help her qualify for a job in a florist shop. Eliza succeeds so well that she outgrows her social station and, in a development added by librettist Lerner, even gets the misogynous speech professor to fall in love with her — or at least grow accustomed to her face. Rex Harrison (who played Higgins), Julie Andrews (who won the part of Eliza after Mary Martin had turned it down), and Stanley Holloway (as Eliza's roistering father, Alfred P. Doolittle) all became forever identified with their roles in *My Fair Lady* which, for over nine years, was the longest running musical in Broadway history. The touring company, originally headed by Brian Aherne and Anne Rogers, traveled for six years nine months.

Two major revivals were staged in New York. In 1976, the musical ran for 377 performances with Ian Richardson, Christine Andreas, and George Rose. In 1981, it lasted 119 with Rex Harrison, Nancy Ringham, and Milo O'Shea. Harrison and Holloway repeated their roles in the 1964 movie version, also starring Audrey Hepburn.

A previous musical based on a Shaw play was the 1909 *Chocolate Soldier* (from *Arms and the Man*); a subsequent musical was the 1968 *Her First Roman* (from *Caesar and Cleopatra*). The notable success of *My Fair Lady* prompted a number of adaptations — offered on Broadway and off — of classics of British literature: Jane Austen's *Pride and Prejudice* (*First Impressions*, 1959); William Wycherley's *The Country Wife* (*She Shall Have Music*, 1959); Oscar Wilde's *The Importance of Being Earnest* (*Ernest in Love*, 1960); Sheridan's *The Rivals* (*All in Love*, 1961); Goldsmith's *She Stoops to Conquer* (*O, Marry Me!*, 1961); Dickens' *Oliver Twist* (*Oliver!*, 1963); H.G. Wells' *Kipps* (*Half a Sixpence*, 1965); Dickens' *Pickwick Papers* (*Pickwick*, 1965); and Arnold Bennett's *Buried Alive* (*Darling of the Day*, 1968).

Columbia OC; Columbia OC (1976); London SC (1987)/ Coward-McCann (1956)/ TW.

My Fair Lady. Stanley Holloway, with cronies Gordon Dilworth and Rod McLennon, singing "With A Little Bit of Luck." (Friedman-Abeles)

My Fair Lady. Robert Coote, Julie Andrews, and Rex Harrison in "The Rain in Spain" number. (Friedman-Abeles)

THE MOST HAPPY FELLA

Music, lyrics & book: Frank Loesser
Producers: Kermit Bloomgarden & Lynn Loesser
Director: Joseph Anthony
Choreographer: Dania Krupska
Cast: Robert Weede, Jo Sullivan, Art Lund, Susan Johnson, Shorty Long, Mona Paulee
Songs: "Somebody Somewhere"; "The Most Happy Fella"; "Standing on the Corner"; "Joey, Joey, Joey"; "Rosabella"; "Abbondanza"; "Sposalizio"; "Happy to Make Your Acquaintance"; "Big 'D'"; "My Heart Is So Full of You"; "Warm All Over"
New York run: Imperial Theatre, May 3,1956; 676 p.

Serving as his own librettist, composer-lyricist Frank Loesser adapted Sidney Howard's 1924 play, *They Knew What They Wanted*, into a cohesive, ambitious work, with more than 30 separate musical numbers including arias, duets, trios, quartets, and choral pieces, plus recitatives. Robust, emotional expressions ("Joey, Joey, Joey," "My Heart Is So Full of You") were interspersed with more traditional Broadway specialties ("Big 'D'," "Standing on the Corner"), though in the manner of an opera the program credits did not list individual selections.

Set in California's Napa Valley, *The Most Happy Fella* is about Tony Esposito (Robert Weede), an aging Italian vineyard owner, who proposed by mail to Rosabella (Jo Sullivan), a San Francisco waitress, and she accepts, partly because Tony has sent her a photograph of Joe (Art Lund), his handsome ranch foreman. Rosabella is so upset at finding Tony physically unattractive that on her wedding night she gives herself to Joe. Tony is distraught over his wife's pregnancy, but there is a reconciliation, and the vintner (somewhat similar to the situation in *Fanny*) offers to raise the child as his own. In 1979, *The Most Happy Fella* was revived on Broadway with Giorgio Tozzi as Tony. A much more successful revival played on Broadway in 1992.
Columbia OC; RCA OC (1992)/MTI.

The Most Happy Fella. Robert Weede and neighbors singing the title song. (Arthur Cantor)

LI'L ABNER

Music: Gene de Paul
Lyrics: Johnny Mercer
Book: Norman Panama & Melvin Frank
Producers: Norman Panama, Melvin Frank & Michael Kidd
Director-choreographer: Michael Kidd
Cast: Edie Adams, Peter Palmer, Howard St. John, Stubby Kaye, Charlotte Rae, Tina Louise, Joe E. Marks, Julie Newmar, Grover Dale
Songs: "If I Had My Druthers"; "Jubilation T. Cornpone"; "Namely You"; "The Country's in the Very Best of Hands"; "Oh, Happy Day"
New York run: St. James Theatre, November 15, 1956; 693 p.

Following the lead of *Finian's Rainbow*, *Li'l Abner* was a musical fantasy set in a rural Southern community that aimed satirical darts at existing social conditions. Here the main targets are the government's propensity for bull-dozing areas for atom-bomb tests, right-wing militarists, inefficient politicians, and conformity. Based on the comic strip by Al Capp (who, ironically, would later adopt some of the views the show derided), *Li'l Abner* takes place in Dogpatch, U.S.A., where mini-skirted Daisy Mae (Edie Adams) is forever trying to get dimwitted Abner Yokum (Peter Palmer) to marry her, where Marryin' Sam (Stubby Kaye) exuberantly leads the townspeople in singing the praises of the South's most incompetent general, Jubilation T. Cornpone, and where the annual big event (as well as the musical's big production number) is the frenetic man-chasing race on Sadie Hawkins' Day. The 1959 movie again featured Peter Palmer as Abner.

Comic strips also supplied the bases for such other Broadway musicals as *Buster Brown* (1905), *Little Nemo* (1908), *Bringing Up Father* (1925), *It's a Bird It's a Plane It's Superman* (1966), *You're a Good Man, Charlie Brown* (1967), *Annie* (1977), *Snoopy* (1982), and *Doonesbury* (1983). Columbia OC/ TW.

BELLS ARE RINGING

Music: Jule Styne
Lyrics & book: Betty Comden & Adolph Green
Producer: Theatre Guild
Director: Jerome Robbins
Choreographers: Jerome Robbins, Bob Fosse
Cast: Judy Holliday, Sydney Chaplin, Jean Stapleton, Eddie Lawrence, Dort Clark, George S. Irving, Peter Gennaro, Bernie West
Songs: "It's a Perfect Relationship"; "Hello, Hello There!"; "Is It a Crime?"; "I Met a Girl"; "Long Before I Knew You"; "Just in Time"; "Drop That Name"; "The Party's Over"; "I'm Going Back"
New York run: Shubert Theatre, November 29, 1956; 924 p.

Ever since appearing with Judy Holliday in a nightclub revue, Betty Comden and Adolph Green had wanted to write a musical for her. The story they eventually hit upon was one in which Miss Holliday played Ella Peterson, a chatty telephone operator at the Susanswerphone service (run by Jean Stapleton) who gets so involved with one client, playwright Jeff Moss (Sydney Chaplin), that — without revealing her identity — she arranges to meet him and help him overcome his writer's block. They also sing and dance in the subway, entertain fellow New Yorkers in Central Park, and fall in love. With Miss Holliday's winning performance and a score containing three enduring songs ("Long Before I Knew You," "Just in Time," and "The Party's Over"), *Bells Are Ringing* had the longest run of the eight musicals written together by Styne, Comden and Green. Miss Holliday repeated her role in the 1960 movie version, which also starred Dean Martin. Columbia OC/ Random House (1957)/ TW.

Candide. Max Adrian, Louis Edmonds, Barbara Cook, and Robert Rounseville. (Friedman-Abeles)

CANDIDE

Music: Leonard Bernstein
Lyrics: Richard Wilbur, etc.
Book: Lillian Hellman
Producer: Ethel Linder Reiner
Director: Tyrone Guthrie
Cast: Max Adrian, Robert Rounseville, Barbara Cook, Irra Petina, William Olvis, Louis Edmonds, Conrad Bain
Songs: "The Best of All Possible Worlds"; "Oh, Happy We"; "It Must Be So"; "Glitter and Be Gay"; "I Am Easily Assimilated" (lyric: Bernstein); "Eldorado" (lyric: Hellman); "Bon Voyage"; "What's the Use?"; "Make Our Garden Grow"
New York run: Martin Beck Theatre, December 1, 1956; 73 p.

Based on Voltaire's classic satire on mindless optimism, *Candide* covers the travels and travails of the eponymous hero (Robert Rounseville) who journeys from his home in Westphalia searching for his beloved Cunegonde (Barbara Cook) in Lisbon (during the Spanish Inquisition), Paris, Buenos Aires, Venice, and back to Westphalia. Throughout the tale the gullible young man remains firm in his belief — as espoused by his philosophy professor, Dr. Pangloss (Max Adrian) — that "this is the best of all possible worlds." In the end, at last reunited with Cunegonde, Candide (like the hero of the later musical, *Pippin*) comes to realize that perfection can never be attained and that one must accept life's realities and try to do one's best. Despite the musical's highly praised score (Leonard Bernstein's original lyricist, John Latouche, had died early in the preparation) and attractive production, the show's initial run lasted less than three months.

In 1973, a revised version was staged by the Chelsea Theatre Center of Brooklyn. Hugh Wheeler contributed a new libretto, Stephen Sondheim some new lyrics, and Harold Prince a total-theatre concept. Following its limited run, the musical was successfully remounted at the Broadway Theatre. The auditorium was completely remodeled, with musicians playing from various parts of the house, and the audience seated on stools surrounded by ten different acting areas linked by ramps, bridges, platforms, and trap doors. (See page 239.) In 1982, *Candide* was added to the repertory of the New York City Opera.
Columbia OC; Columbia OC (1973); New World OC (1982)/ Random House (1957)/ MTI.

NEW GIRL IN TOWN

Music & lyrics: Bob Merrill
Book: George Abbott
Producers: Frederick Brisson, Robert Griffith & Harold Prince
Director: George Abbott
Choreographer: Bob Fosse
Cast: Gwen Verdon, Thelma Ritter, George Wallace, Cameron Prud'homme, Mark Dawson
Songs: "Sunshine Girl"; "Flings"; "It's Good to Be Alive"; "Look at 'Er"; "At the Check Apron Ball"; "If That Was Love"
New York run: 46th Street Theatre, May 14, 1957; 431 p.

Composer-lyricist Bob Merrill had first conceived of the idea of a musical version of Eugene O'Neill's 1921 play *Anna Christie* as a movie under the title of *A Saint She Ain't.* When that was abandoned he found director George Abbott highly receptive to its possibilities as a stage musical, particularly as a vehicle for Gwen Verdon. In the story, set near New York's waterfront at the turn of the century, barge captain Chris Christopherson (Cameron Prud'homme) is excited at the news that his daughter Anna will be returning from St. Paul. When she does appear, she is quickly sized up by Chris' slattern friend Marthy (Thelma Ritter) as a street walker. After Anna joins her father on his barge, she meets sailor Matt Burke (George Wallace), and they fall in love. When she tells her story to the two men they get smashed, but fortunately there is a reconciliation. In 1959, Merrill wrote the songs for *Take Me Along,* based on another O'Neill play *Ah, Wilderness!*
RCA OC/ Random House (1958)/ MTI.

New Girl in Town. Harvey Hohnecker, Gwen Verdon, and Harvey Jung dancing "At the Check Apron Ball." (Friedman-Abeles)

Carol Lawrence and Larry Kert.

West Side Story. The Jets performing the "Gee, Officer Krupke" number. (Eileen Darby)

WEST SIDE STORY

Music: Leonard Bernstein
Lyrics: Stephen Sondheim
Conception: Jerome Robbins
Book: Arthur Laurents
Producers: Robert Griffith & Harold Prince
Director: Jerome Robbins
Choreographers: Jerome Robbins & Peter Gennaro
Cast: Carol Lawrence, Larry Kert, Chita Rivera, Art Smith, Mickey Calin, Ken LeRoy, Lee Becker Theodore, David Winter, Tony Mordente, Eddie Roll, Martin Charnin
Songs: "Something's Coming"; "Maria"; "Tonight"; "America"; "Cool"; "One Hand, One Heart"; "I Feel Pretty"; "Somewhere"; "Gee, Officer Krupke"; "A Boy Like That"; "I Have a Love"
New York run: Winter Garden, September 26, 1957; 732 p.

In 1949, Jerome Robbins brought together composer Leonard Bernstein and playwright Arthur Laurents (his first experience as a librettist) to work on a modern musical version of *Romeo and Juliet*. Called *East Side Story,* it was about a Jewish boy's star-crossed romance with an Italian Catholic girl set against the clashing street gangs on New York's lower East Side. Heavy schedules, however forced the trio to suspend the project for six years and by the time they got together again the conflict seemed dated. Far more timely, they now felt, would be the love story of a native-born boy of Polish descent and a newly arrived Puerto Rican girl set against the clashing street gangs on the city's West Side. At this time Bernstein decided against writing his own lyrics and he turned the task over to Stephen Sondheim, a 27-year-old Broadway neophyte.

In *West Side Story,* Tony (Larry Kert), once the leader of the Jets street gang, now tries to keep his distance from his former group and the rival Puerto Rican Sharks. He becomes particularly committed to peaceful coexistence once he meets a girl named Maria (Carol Lawrence) at a high school dance, and — with Maria's fire escape as a balcony — they express their mutual devotion to the soaring sentiments of "Tonight." But after Tony kills Maria's brother Bernardo (Ken LeRoy) while trying to break up a rumble, warfare erupts anew, and even Maria's best friend, Anita (Chita Rivera), urges her to stay away from Tony. In the end, Tony is killed by one of the Sharks and Maria is left grieving over his body.

With its galvanic choreography, compelling music and lyrics, and unflinching look at contemporary street life, *West Side Story* was a jolting work, not alone for its theme but for its advanced use of dance within the framework of a musical play. After cutting short its initial Broadway run to go on tour, the company returned to New York ten weeks later for an additional 249 performances.

Since then there have been two major revivals. In 1968, the Music Theatre of Lincoln Center sponsored a production that ran for 89 performances. Tony was played by Kurt Peterson, Maria by Victoria Mallory, and Anita by Barbara Luna. In 1980, the musical was mounted at the Minskoff Theatre under Robbins' direction, and had a 333-performance run. The cast was headed by Ken Marshall, Jossie de Guzman, and Debbie Allen. The film version, with Richard Beymer, Natalie Wood, George Chakiris, and Rita Moreno, was released in 1961. For other Broadway musicals based on Shakespeare, see *The Boys from Syracuse,* page 107.

Columbia OC; DGG SC (1985)/ Random House (1958); Chilton (1973)/ MTI.

JAMAICA

Music: Harold Arlen
Lyrics: E.Y. Harburg
Book: E.Y. Harburg & Fred Saidy (Joseph Stein uncredited)
Producer: David Merrick
Driector: Robert Lewis
Choreographer: Jack Cole
Cast: Lena Horne, Ricardo Montalban, Josephine Premice, Adelaide Hall, Ossie Davis, Erik Rhodes, Joe Adams, Alvin Ailey, Billy Wilson
Songs: "Pretty to Walk With"; "Push the Button"; "Little Biscuit"; "Cocoanut Sweet"; "Pity the Sunset"; "Take It Slow, Joe"; "Ain't It the Truth?"; "I Don't Think I'll End It All Today"
New York run: Imperial Theatre, October 31, 1957; 558 p.

Aided by evocative music, provocative lyrics, lush decor, and the sparkling presence of Lena Horne, *Jamaica* overcame a weak book to become one of the hits of the season. Something of a Caribbean companion to Harold Arlen's most recent musical *House of Flowers,* the new work dealt with a fisherman named Koli (Ricardo Montalban), who enjoys the simple life on mythical Pigeon Island near Jamaica, and Savannah (Miss Horne) , his inamorata who yearns for the glittering, mechanized life on another mythical island called Manhattan. After being tempted by a slick pearl dealer, Savannah — to no one's surprise — is content to remain with Koli in their tropical paradise. Originally, Harry Belafonte was to have been starred in the show but illness forced his replacement by the equally stellar Lena Horne, thereby altering the story's emphasis.
RCA OC/ TW.

Jamaica. Ricardo Montalban and Lena Horne. (Friedman-Abeles)

THE MUSIC MAN

Music, lyrics & book: Meredith Willson
Producer: Kermit Bloomgarden
Director: Morton Da Costa
Choreographer: Onna White
Cast: Robert Preston, Barbara Cook, David Burns, Pert Kelton, Iggie Wolfington, The Buffalo Bills, Eddie Hodges, Helen Raymond
Songs: "Rock Island"; "Trouble"; "Goodnight My Someone"; "Seventy-Six Trombones"; "Sincere"; "The Sadder-but-Wiser Girl"; "Marian the Librarian"; "My White Knight"; "Wells Fargo Wagon"; "Shipoopi"; "Lida Rose"; "Gary, Indiana"; "Till There Was You"
New York run: Majestic Theatre, December 19, 1957; 1,375 p.

It took eight years to write — including over 30 drafts and 40 songs — but by the time it was produced on Broadway, *The Music Man* had clearly established newcomer Meredith Willson among the most impressive talents of the musical theatre. The idea for the show had first been suggested by Willson's friend, Frank Loesser, who enjoyed listening to the composer's tales of growing up in a small Iowa town. Though the plot was credited in part to Frank Lacey, the musical emerged as a very personal expression through which Willson captured all the innocent charm of a bygone America. The story begins on the Fourth of July, 1912, in River City, Iowa. Enter "Professor" Harold Hill, who has arrived to hornswoggle the citizens into believing he can teach the local youngsters how to play in a marching band that would rival the once-mammoth parade featuring "Seventy-Six Trombones." But instead of skipping town before the instruments arrive, Hill is persuaded to remain by the town's librarian, Marian Paroo (Barbara Cook). The musical ends with the children being hailed by their parents, even though they can barely produce any recognizable sound from their instruments.

The role of Professor Harold Hill was rejected by a number of actors, including Danny Kaye, Dan Dailey, Phil Harris, and Gene Kelly, before it went to Robert Preston who gave a memorably dynamic performance in his first appearance on the musical stage. Preston also repeated the part in the 1962 movie version. During the show's Broadway run, the third longest of the decade's musicals, Preston was succeeded by Eddie Albert and Bert Parks. For the road tour, which lasted three years seven months, Forrest Tucker played the professor and Joan Weldon was Marian. *The Music Man* returned briefly to New York in 1980, with a cast headed by Dick Van Dyke and Meg Bussert.
Capitol OC/ Putnam (1958)/ MTI.

The Music Man. Barbara Cook and Robert Preston singing "Till There Was You." (Friedman-Abeles)

Flower Drum Song. Miyoshi Umeki singing "A Hundred Million Miracles," accompanied by Juanita Hall and Keye Luke. (Friedman-Abeles)

FLOWER DRUM SONG

Music: Richard Rodgers
Lyrics: Oscar Hammerstein II
Book: Oscar Hammerstein II & Joseph Fields
Producers: Richard Rodgers, Oscar Hammerstein II & Joseph Fields
Director: Gene Kelly
Choreographer: Carol Haney
Cast: Miyoshi Umeki, Larry Blyden, Pat Suzuki, Juanita Hall, Ed Kenney, Keye Luke, Arabella Hong, Jack Soo, Anita Ellis
Songs: "You Are Beautiful"; "A Hundred Million Miracles"; "I Enjoy Being a Girl"; "I Am Going to Like It Here"; "Don't Marry Me"; "Grant Avenue"; "Love, Look Away"; "Sunday"
New York run: St. James Theatre, December 1, 1958; 600 p.

Upon reading Chin Y. Lee's novel, *The Flower Drum Song,* librettist Joseph Fields bought the dramatic rights and then took the idea to Rodgers and Hammerstein. The resulting production — the only Broadway musical ever directed by Gene Kelly — dealt in a lighthearted way with the conflict between San Francisco's traditionalist older Chinese-Americans and their Americanized children who are anxious to break away. Mei Li (Miyoshi Umeki), a timid "picture bride" from China, has arrived to fulfill her contract to marry Sammy Fong (Larry Blyden), a local nightclub owner, but Sammy prefers Linda Low (Pat Suzuki), who quite obviously enjoys being a girl. The problem is resolved when Sammy's friend Wang Ta (Ed Kenney) conveniently falls in love with Mei Li. Miyoshi Umeki appeared in the 1961 film version, along with Nancy Kwan and James Shigeta. Columbia OC/ Farrar, Straus (1959)/ R&H.

REDHEAD

Music: Albert Hague
Lyrics: Dorothy Fields
Book: Herbert & Dorothy Fields, Sidney Sheldon, David Shaw
Producers: Robert Fryer & Lawrence Carr
Director-choreographer: Bob Fosse
Cast: Gwen Verdon, Richard Kiley, Leonard Stone, Doris Rich, Cynthia Latham
Songs: "The Right Finger of My Left Hand"; "Just for Once"; "Merely Marvelous"; "The Uncle Sam Rag"; "Erbie Fitch's Twitch"; "My Girl Is Just Enough Woman for Me"; "Look Who's In Love"
New York run: 46th Street Theatre, February 5, 1959; 452 p.

One of the theatre's rare musical whodunits, *Redhead* had been in the works — it was first called *The Works* — ever since 1950 when Herbert and Dorothy Fields began writing it with Beatrice Lillie in mind for the starring role. Six years later, with Sidney Sheldon joining them, they rewrote it for Gewn Verdon, but there were further complications caused by Miss Verdon's contract with Robert Fryer and Lawrence Carr to star in a musical being written by David Shaw. The problem was solved when the producers decided to switch their activities to *Redhead* and Shaw was added to the roster of writers. The show, which was the first to charge $9.20 for orchestra seats, also marked Bob Fosse's initial effort as a director as well as choreographer. The story takes place in London in the early 1900s. At the Simpson Sisters' Waxworks, where all the wax images are made by Essie Whimple, a model of a recently murdered young woman offends her brother, Tom Baxter (Richard Kiley). Essie and Tom join forces to solve the murder which, after Essie gets the chance to perform "Erbie Fitch's Twitch" at the Odeon Music Hall, they do.
RCA OC/ MTI.

Redhead. Richard Kiley and Gwen Verdon in a tense situation. (Friedman-Abeles)

DESTRY RIDES AGAIN

Music & lyrics: Harold Rome
Book: Leonard Gershe
Producer: David Merrick
Director-choreographer: Michael Kidd
Cast: Andy Griffith, Dolores Gray, Scott Brady, Jack Prince, Swen Swenson, Marc Breaux, George Reeder
Songs: "Ballad of the Gun"; "I Know Your Kind"; "Anyone Would Love You"; "Once Knew a Fella"; "That Ring on the Finger"; "I Say Hello"
New York run: Imperial Theatre, April 23, 1959; 473 p.

Hollywood's classic Western had been filmed three times before David Merrick decided to turn the durable sagebrush saga into a Broadway musical. A whoopin', shootin', hollerin' show, it starred Andy Griffith (in his only musical) as Thomas Jefferson Destry Jr., the violence-hating sheriff, and Dolores Gray as the peppery saloon entertainer known as Frenchy. The story, set in the brawling frontier town of Bottleneck just before the turn of the century, involves the traditional confrontation between good guys and bad guys in scenes set in such equally traditional locales as the Last Chance Saloon and Rose Lovejoy's establishment in Paradise Alley. Contrary to the movie industry's morals code that never permitted a happy ending for a woman of easy virtue, Frenchy is not killed protecting Destry but ends up in his arms. The show's choreographic highlight: the crackling, whipcracking dance performed by outlaws Swen Swenson, Marc Breaux, and George Reeder.
MCA OC/ TW.

Destry Rides Again. An embarrassing moment when Destry accidentally tears off part of Frenchy's dress. Andy Griffith, Scott Brady, and Dolores Gray. (Friedman-Abeles)

Once Upon a Mattress. Carol Burnett explaining that she's really so "Shy." (Friedman-Abeles)

ONCE UPON A MATTRESS

Music: Mary Rodgers
Lyrics: Marshall Barer
Book: Jay Thompson, Dean Fuller & Marshall Barer
Producers: T. Edward Hambleton, Norris Houghton, William & Jean Eckart
Director: George Abbott
Choreographer: Joe Layton
Cast: Joseph Bova, Carol Burnett, Allen Case, Jack Gilford, Anne Jones, Matt Mattox, Harry Snow, Jane White
Songs: "Many Moons Ago"; "In a Little While"; "Shy"; "Sensitivity"; "Happily Ever After"; "Very Soft Shoes"
New York run: Phoenix Theater, May 11, 1959; 460 p.

Once Upon a Mattress was first created as a one-act musical by Mary Rodgers (daughter of Richard Rodgers) and Marshall Barer at an adult summer camp. With Jay Thompson and Dean Fuller, they expanded the work, based on the fairy tale *The Princess and the Pea,* into a full evening's entertainment. Carol Burnett made a notable stage debut in the show as Princess Winnifred who arrives dripping wet in the throne room of an ancient kingdom because, as she explains, "I swam the moat." She is there as a contender for the hand of Prince Dauntless the Drab (Joseph Bova), whose domineering mother, Queen Agravain (Jane White), has decreed that he will wed only a true princess of royal blood. Winnifred passes the test being unable to sleep on a pile of mattresses with a pea on the bottom — though, as the finale reveals — her sleeplessness was really caused by a helpful Minstrel (Harry Snow) who had filled her bed with all sorts of uncomfortable objects. After opening at the downtown Phoenix Theatre, *Once Upon A Mattress* then played the Alvin, the Winter Garden, the Cort, and the St. James. MCA   OC/ R&H.

GYPSY

Music: Jule Styne
Lyrics: Stephen Sondheim
Book: Arthur Laurents
Producers: David Merrick & Leland Hayward
Director-choreographer: Jerome Robbins
Cast: Ethel Merman, Jack Klugman, Sandra Church, Lane Bradbury, Maria Karnilova, Paul Wallace, Jacqueline Mayro, Karen Moore, Joe Silver
Songs: "Let Me Entertain You"; "Some People"; "Small World"; "Little Lamb"; "You'll Never Get Away from Me"; "If Momma Was Married"; "All I Need Is the Girl"; "Everything's Coming Up Roses"; "Together"; "You Gotta Have a Gimmick"; "Rose's Turn"
New York run: Broadway Theatre, May 21, 1959; 702 p.

With Ethel Merman giving the performance of her life a Gypsy Rose Lee's ruthless mother and with an exceptionally strong score and story, *Gypsy* was one of the musical theatre's most distinguished achievements. The germination of the show began with producer David Merrick, who needed to read but one chapter of Miss Lee's autobiography to convince him of its stage potential. Stephen Sondheim, joining *West Side Story* colleagues Arthur Laurents and Jerome Robbins, was originally to have supplied the music as well as the lyrics, but Miss Merman wanted a more experienced composer and Jule Styne was brought is. The Styne-Sondheim team created such overwhelming expressions of raw ambition as "Some People" and "Everything's Coming Up Roses" that they seen took their place among Miss Merman's most closely identified songs.

In the story, Mama Rose is determined to escape from a life of playing bingo and paying rent by pushing the vaudeville career of her younger daughter Jun (Lane Bradbury); after June elopes with a hoofer, she focuses all her attention on her older, less talented daughter, Louise (Sandra Church). Eventually, Louise becomes burlesque stripper Gypsy Rose Lee, and Rose suffers a breakdown — expressed through the shattering "Rose's Turn" — when she realizes that she is no longer needed in her daughter's career. Mama Rose was the last stage role Ethel Merman created and the first in which she toured. In 1974, a new production of *Gypsy* opened in New York after playing in London. Angela Lansbury starred, Arthur Laurents directed, and it ran 120 performances. The film version, in 1962, starred Rosalind Russell and Natalie Wood. A celebrated revival of the musical opened on Broadway in 1989, starring Tyne Daley. For other show-business musical biographies, see *Annie Get Your Gun,* page 130. Columbia OC; RCA OC (1974)/Random House (1960); Chilton (1973)/TW.

Gypsy. Sandra Church, Ethel Merman, and Jack Klugman. (Friedman-Abeles)

Gypsy. Ethel Merman doing her climactic "Rose's Turn." (Friedman-Abeles)

TAKE ME ALONG

Music & lyrics: Bob Merrill
Book: Joseph Stein & Robert Russell
Producer: David Merrick
Director: Peter Glenville
Choreographer: Onna White
Cast: Jackie Gleason, Walter Pidgeon, Eileen Herlie, Robert Morse, Una Merkel, Peter Conlow, Susan Luckey, Valerie Harper
Songs: "I Would Die"; "Sid Ol' Kid"; "Staying Young"; "I Get Embarrassed"; "We're Home"; "Take Me Along"; "Promise Me a Rose"; "Nine O'Clock"; "But Yours"
New York run: Shubert Theatre, October 22, 1959; 448 p.

Having written a score for a musical version of Eugene O'Neill's somber *Anna Christie,* Bob Merrill followed it up with a score for a musical version of O'Neill's 1933 sentimental comedy, *Ah, Wilderness!* Though casting the exuberant Jackie Gleason as the bibulous Sid Davis tended to divert the focus from the main story, *Take Me Along* was a faithful rendering of the playwright's view of an adolescent's growing pains.

The action takes place in the cozy environs of Centerville, Connecticut, during July 1910. Young Richard Miller (Robert Morse), the son of newspaper publisher Nat Miller (Walter Pidgeon), ardently woos Muriel Macomber (Susan Luckey) by quoting literary morsels that her father finds so objectionable he withdraws his advertisements from Nat's paper. With Muriel forbidden to see him, Richard goes on a binge; once they are reconciled he gets ready to go to Yale. A secondary plot concerns Sid's repeated efforts to quit drinking, get a steady job, and marry Nat's spinster sister Lily (Eileen Herlie). During the Broadway run, Pidgeon was succeeded by Sidney Blackmer and Gleason by William Bendix. The musical's Broadway revival in 1985 gave only one performance.
RCA OC/ TW.

THE SOUND OF MUSIC

Music: Richard Rodgers
Lyrics: Oscar Hammerstein II
Book: Howard Lindsay & Russel Crouse
Producers: Leland Hayward, Richard Halliday, Richard Rodgers & Oscar
  Hammerstein II
Director: Vincent J. Donehue
Choreographer: Joe Layton
Cast: Mary Martin,Theodore Bikel, Patricia Neway, Kurt Kasznar, Marion Mar-
  lowe, Lauri Peters, Brian Davies, John Randolph, Nan McFarland, Joey
  Heatherton
Songs: "The Sound of Music"; "Maria"; "My Favorite Things"; "Do-Re-Mi";
  "Sixteen Going on Seventeen"; "The Lonely Goatherd"; "How Can
  Love Survive?"; "So Long, Farewell"; "Climb Ev'ry Mountain"; "An Or-
  dinary Couple"; "Edelweiss"
New York run: Lunt-Fontanne Theatre, November 16, 1959; 1,443 p.

The second longest running Broadway musical of the Fifties, *The Sound of Music* also marked the 35th and final work of Oscar Hammerstein II, who died nine months after the opening (his last lyric was for "Edelweiss"). Primarily at the urging of director Vincent J. Donehue, the story was adapted as a star vehicle for Mary Martin from Maria Von Trapp's autobiography *The Trapp Family Singers* and also the German film version. Miss Martin's husband, Richard Halliday, and Leland Hayward became partners in sponsoring the project and Howard Lindsay and Russel Crouse were engaged to write the book. Initially, they planned to use only authentic music sung by the Trapps in their concerts plus an additional song to be supplied by Rodgers and Hammerstein. When the songwriters balked at this arrangement, they were asked to contribute the entire score and they also joined Halliday and Hayward as producers.

The musical, set in 1938, takes place in Salzburg in the Austrian Tyrol. Maria Rainer, a free-spirited postulant at Nonnberg Abbey, has been giving her superiors concern because of her fondness for taking off to the mountains listening to the sound of music. At the request of the Mother Abbess (Patricia Neway), — and as something of a variation on *The King and I* — Maria is hired as governess to the seven children of the wealthy, autocratic Capt. Georg Von Trapp (Theodore Bikel). Maria soon wins the affection of her charges — in part by teaching them such songs as "Do-Re-Mi," "The Lonely Goatherd," and "So Long, Farewell." Though Von Trapp is engaged to the socially prominent Elsa Schraeder (Marion Marlowe), he and Maria fall in love and marry. Their happiness, however, is almost immediately shattered by the German invasion of Austria. The Von Trapp family, which has become celebrated for its amateur concerts, gives a final performance before heeding the message of "Climb Ev'ry Mountain" and fleeing over the Alps to the safety of Switzerland. A subplot in *The Sound of Music* concerns the teenage romance between Von Trapp's daughter Liesl (Lauri Peters) and Rolf Gruber, an incipient Nazi (Brian Davies).

During the Broadway run (the Lunt-Fontanne Theatre, where the show opened, was once the Globe), Miss Martin was succeeded by Martha Wright, Jeannie Carson, and Nancy Dussault. In 1961, Jon Voight took over the part of Rolf. Florence Henderson and John Myhers originally headed the touring company which traveled two years nine months. The popular movie version, which came out in 1965, co-starred Julie Andrews and Christopher Plummer.
Columbia OC/ Random House (1960)/ R&H.

The Sound of Music. Theodore Bikel, Marion Marlowe, and Kurt Kasznar. (Friedman-Abeles)

The Sound of Music. Brian Davies and Lauri Peters. (Toni Frissell)

The Sound of Music. Mary Martin and Theodore Bikel lead the Trapp Family in "Edelweiss." (Friedman-Abeles)

LITTLE MARY SUNSHINE

Music, lyrics & book: Rick Besoyan
Producers: Howard Barker, Cynthia Baer, Robert Chambers
Directors: Ray Harrison, Rick Besoyan
Choreographer: Ray Harrison
Cast: Eileen Brennan, William Graham, John McMartin, Elmarie Wendel
Songs: "Look for a Sky of Blue"; "Tell a Handsome Stranger"; "Once in a Blue Moon"; "Colorado Love Call"; "Every Little Nothing"; "Do You Ever Dream of Vienna?"; "Naughty, Naughty Nancy"
New York run: Orpheum Theatre, November 18, 1959; 1,143 p.

Little Mary Sunshine was a witty, melodious takeoff on the *Rose-Marie* school of robust heroics and excessively ardent love songs. Its engagement at the Orpheum Theatre on lower 2nd Avenue is currently the seventh longest of any Off-Broadway musical. Set in the Colorado Rockies early in the century, the tale is primarily concerned with Mary Potts (Eileen Brennan), proprietress of the Colorado Inn, and valorous Capt. "Big Jim" Warrington of the Forest Rangers (William Graham), who gets to rescue his beloved from the clutches of the lecherous Indian Yellow Feather just in time for their echoing "Colorado Love Call" duet. The production marked the impressive New York theatre debuts of both Eileen Brennan and composer-lyricist-librettist Rick Besoyan. Besoyan (who died in 1970 at the age of 45) followed up in 1963 with *The Student Gypsy,* a less successful spoof of European mythical-kingdom operettas, which also featured Miss Brennan. The earliest operetta burlesque on Broadway was Rodgers and Hart's "Rose of Arizona" in the 1926 *Garrick Gaieties.*
Capitol OC/Samuel French, London(1960)*/ SF

FIORELLO!

Music: Jerry Bock
Lyrics: Sheldon Harnick
Book: Jerome Weidman & George Abbott
Producers: Robert Griffith & Harold Prince
Director: George Abbott
Choreographer: Peter Gennaro
Cast: Tom Bosley, Patricia Wilson, Ellen Hanley, Howard Da Silva, Mark Dawson, Nathaniel Frey, Pat Stanley, Eileen Rodgers, Ron Husmann
Songs: "Politics and Poker"; "The Name's LaGuardia"; "I Love a Cop"; "Till Tomorrow"; "When Did I Fall in Love?"; "Little Tin Box"
New York run: Broadhurst Theatre, November 23, 1959; 795 p.

New York's favorite mayor, Fiorello LaGuardia, was a peppery, pugnacious reformer whose exuberant personality readily lent itself to depiction on the musical stage. With Tom Bosley making an auspicious Broadway bow in the title role, *Fiorello!* encompassed the ten-year period in LaGuardia's life before he became mayor. Beginning with his surprise election to Congress prior to World War I, it includes such events as his enlistment in the Air Force, his first race for mayor against the unbeatable James J. Walker (who was himself the subject of a 1969 musical *Jimmy,* with Frank Gorshin in the title part), the death of LaGuardia's first wife, the revelation of Walker's cronies with their hands caught in little tin boxes, and the preparations for the victorious LaGuardia campaign of 1933 which he won as a Fusion candidate. *Fiorello!* had the distinction of being the third musical to be awarded the Pulitzer Prize for drama. A year after the show's opening, its composer, lyricist, librettists, director, producers, music director (Harold Hastings), and orchestrator (Irwin Kostal) were reunited for *Tenderloin,* which was about another New York reformer just before the turn of the century.
Capitol OC/ Random House (1960); Chilton (1976)/ TW.

Fiorello! Tom Bosley, Patricia Wilson, Nathaniel Frey, and Ellen Hanley singing "Till Tomorrow." (Eileen Darby)

GREENWILLOW

Music & lyrics: Frank Loesser
Book: Lesser Samuels & Frank Loesser
Producer: Robert Willey
Director: George Roy Hill
Choreographer: Joe Layton
Cast: Anthony Perkins, Cecil Kelloway, Pert Kelton, Ellen McCown, William Chapman, Grover Dale
Songs: "A Day Borrowed from Heaven"; "The Music of Home"; "Gideon Briggs, I Love You"; "Summertime Love"; "Walking Away Whistling"; "Never Will I Marry"; "Faraway Boy"
New York run: Alvin Theatre, March 8, 1960; 95 p.

B.J. Chute's novel was turned into a homespun fantasy that had to do with quaint superstitions and folklore of a mythical village located on the Meander River — or somewhere down the road from Brigadoon and Glocca Morra. The whimsical tale takes up the conflict of young Gideon Briggs (Anthony Perkins) who would like nothing better than to remain at home and marry his summertime love, Dorrie (Ellen McCown), but who fears that the curse of his family's "call to wander solitary" will someday make him run off to sail distant seas. Though tarrying on Broadway only three months, *Greenwillow* has long been admired for the airy, otherworldly charms of Frank Loesser's atypical score. The production also marked Anthony Perkins' first — and so far only — Broadway musical. Columbia OC.

BYE BYE BIRDIE

Music: Charles Strouse
Lyrics: Lee Adams
Book: Michael Stewart
Producer: Edward Padula
Director-choreographer: Gower Champion
Cast: Chita Rivera, Dick Van Dyke, Kay Medford, Paul Lynde, Dick Gautier, Michael J. Pollard, Susan Watson, Charles Nelson Reilly
Songs: "An English Teacher"; "The Telephone Hour"; "How Lovely to Be a Woman"; "Put on a Happy Face"; "One Boy"; "One Last Kiss"; "A Lot of Livin' to Do"; "Kids"; "Baby, Talk to Me"; "Rosie"
New York run: Martin Beck Theatre, April 14, 1960; 607 p.

Bye Bye Birdie provided the launching pad for the Broadway careers of songwriters Charles Strouse and Lee Adams, librettist Michael Stewart, and director-choreographer Gower Champion (his first of nine book musicals). It was also the earliest musical about the rock and roll phenomenon and the effect of its idols on impressionable teenagers. The attitude, however, was generally sympathetic toward adolescent emotions, offering something of a fresh-air antidote to the picture of modern youth conveyed by *West Side Story.* The singing idol in this case is Conrad Birdie (suggesting Elvis Presley), and the young people he is shown affecting are the clean-cut kids of Sweet Apple, Ohio. Birdie is managed by Albert Peterson (Dick Van Dyke) who, with his secretary Rose Grant (Chita Rivera), contrives a publicity stunt involving Kim McAfee (Susan Watson) kissing Birdie on Ed Sullivan's television show just before he is drafted into the Army. Complications involve Kim's jealous boyfriend (Michael J. Pollard) and her exasperated father (Paul Lynde), as well as Albert's querulous mother (Kay Medford) and his relationship with Rose, who wants him to get out of the music business and become an English teacher. During the run, Dick Van Dyke was succeeded by Gene Rayburn, Chita Rivera by Gretchen Wyler. Van Dyke repeated his role in the 1963 film version (also starring Ann-Margret), and Miss Rivera repeated her role in the short-lived 1981 sequel, *Bring Back Birdie* (also with Donald O'Connor). Columbia OC/ DBS Publications (1962)/ TW.

The Fantasticks. Jerry Orbach, Rita Gardner, and Kenneth Nelson. (Friedman-Abeles))

THE FANTASTICKS

Music: Harvey Schmidt
Lyrics & book: Tom Jones
Producer: Lore Noto
Director: Word Baker
Cast: Jerry Orbach, Rita Gardner, Kenneth Nelson, William Larson, Hugh Thomas, Tom Jones, George Curley, Richard Stauffer
Songs: "Try to Remember"; "Much More"; "It Depends on What You Pay"; "Soon   It's Gonna Rain"; "I Can See It"; "Plant a Radish"; "Round and Round"; "They Were You"
New York run: Sullivan Street Playhouse, May 3, 1960; 17,162 p.

The statistics alone are, well, fantastic. No other New York stage production has ever played so many performances, and there is still no end in sight. Moreover, by the time of the show's 33rd year at the 150-seat Greenwich Village Theatre, there had been over 10,000 productions throughout the World, of which some 500 were performed in more than 66 foreign countries. There have also been 15 national touring companies. As for profits, the original backers have so far received a return of over 10,000% on their initial investment of $16,500. Curiously, the original critical reception was not encouraging and producer Lore Noto seriously considered closing the show after its first week. But an Off- Broadway award, the popularity of the song "Try to Remember," and, most important, word of mouth, all helped turn the musical's fortunes around.

The whimsical fantasy is concerned with the theme of seasonal rebirth—or the paradox of "why Spring is born out of Winter's laboring pains." The tale, freely adapted from Edmond Rostand's 1894 play, *Les Romanesques*, is told with a cast of eight and performed on a platform with a minimum of props. The neighboring fathers (Hugh Thomas and William Larsen) of Luisa and Matt (Rita Gardner and Kenneth Nelson), though good friends, feel they must appear as enemies to make sure that their progenies fall in love. Having thought up this bit of logic they next find a way to reverse themselves by hiring El Gallo (Jerry Orbach), aided by The Old Actor (Tom Jones) and The Indian (George Curley), to perform a mock rape by moonlight so that Matt might prove his valor, thus paving the way for a reconciliation. But daylight reveals the parental deception, the lovers quarrel, and the young man goes off to see the world. After a number of degrading experiences, he returns home to Luisa's waiting arms firm in the knowledge that "without a hurt the heart is hollow."

To date, the New York company has had over 35 El Gallos (including Bert Convy, David Cryer, and Keith Charles), over 35 Luisas (including Eileen Fulton, Betsy Joslyn, Kathryn Morath, and Judy Blazer), and 30 Matts (including Craig Carnelia and Bruce Cryer). F. Murray Abraham played The Old Actor in 1967, and producer Lore Noto played the Boy's Father from 1970 to 1986.

Harvey Schmidt and Tom Jones had originally written the musical under the title *Joy Comes to Dead Horse*, in which the characters were Mexican and Anglo families living on adjoining ranches in the American Southwest. Dissatisfied with the overblown concept, they cut the story down to one act, reduced the number of characters, and retitled the show *The Fantasticks*. It was staged in this fashion at Barnard College in the summer of 1959. Lore Noto saw it there, and at his urging Schmidt and Jones rewrote it once again, this time as an intimate two-act musical.

Ploydor OC/Drama Book Publishers (1964)/MTI.

IRMA LA DOUCE

Music: Marguerite Monnot
Lyrics & book: Julian More, David Heneker & Monty Norman
Producer: David Merrick
Director: Peter Brook
Choreographer: Onna White
Cast: Elizabeth Seal, Keith Michell, Clive Revill, George S. Irving, Stuart Damon, Fred Gwynne, Elliott Gould
Songs: "The Bridge of Caulaincourt"; "Our Language of Love"; "Dis-Donc"; "Irma la Douce"; "There Is Only One Paris for That"
New York run: Plymouth Theatre, September 29, 1960; 524 p.

Broadway's first hit with music by a French composer, *Irma la Douce* originated in Paris in 1956 with book and lyrics by Alexandre Breffort and ran for four years. The English-language adaptation opened two years later in London and gave 1,512 performances. With Elizabeth Seal, Keith Michell, and Clive Revill recreating their roles in New York — Miss Seal was the only female member of the cast — the production at the Plymouth Theatre (on 45th Street west of Broadway) was a virtual carbon of the West End original. In the story, Irma is a pure-at-heart Parisian prostitute and Nestor (Mr. Michell) is a poor student who is anxious to have Irma all for his own. The student gets the idea to disguise himself as an aged benefactor named Oscar who supposedly has enough money to be the lady's only patron. Nestor, however, grows jealous of Irma's affection for Oscar and "kills" him. He is sent to Devil's Island, but manages to escape, prove his innocence, and return to his beloved. All the songs — including the chief ballad, "Our Language of Love" — were cut from the 1963 film version starring Shirley MacLaine and Jack Lemmon.
Columbia OC/ TW.

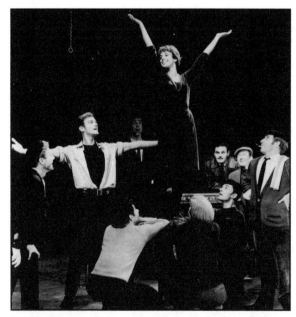

Irma la Douce. The main performers in the scene are Keith Michell, Elizabeth Seal, and Clive Revill. (Friedman-Abeles)

THE UNSINKABLE MOLLY BROWN

Music & lyrics: Meredith Willson
Book: Richard Morris
Producers: Theatre Guild & Dore Schary
Director: Dore Schary
Choreographer: Peter Gennaro
Cast: Tammy Grimes, Harve Presnell, Cameron Prud'homme, Mony Dalmes, Edith Meiser, Mitchell Gregg, Christopher Hewett
Songs: "I Ain't Down Yet"; "Belly Up to the Bar, Boys"; "Colorado, My Home"; "I'll Never Say No to You"; "My Own Brass Bed"; "Are You Sure?"; "Dolce Far Niente"
New York run: Winter Garden, November 3, 1960; 532 p.

Providing Tammy Grimes with her most rewarding role in a musical, *The Unsinkable Molly Brown* retold the saga of a near-legendary figure of the Colorado silver mines who rose from a poverty-stricken background in Hannibal, Missouri, through her spunky determination to be "up where the people are," and by having the good fortune to marry a lucky prospector, "Leadville Johnny" Brown (Harve Presnell). After failing to crash Denver society, Molly drags Johnny off to Europe where despite her gaucheries, or because of them, she becomes a social leader in Monte Carlo. Molly almost loses Johnny, but following her heroism displayed during the sinking of the *Titanic,* she wins back her husband and wins over the elite of Denver. The score Meredith Willson turned out was much in the same Americana vein as *The Music Man,* complete with breezy marches, rugged male choruses, back country dance numbers, and revivalistic exhortations. The movie version came out in 1964 with Debbie Reynolds as Molly and Presnell again as Johnny.
Capitol OC/ Putnam (1961)/ MTI.

The Unsinkable Molly Brown. Tammy Grimes and Harve Presnell. (Friedman-Abeles)

Camelot. Julie Andrews and Richard Burton. (Friedman-Abeles)

Camelot. Julie Andrews leading the courtiers in "The Lusty Month of May." (Friedman-Abeles)

CAMELOT

Music: Frederick Loewe
Lyrics & book: Alan Jay Lerner
Producers: Alan Jay Lerner, Frederick Loewe & Moss Hart
Director: Moss Hart (Alan Jay Lerner uncredited)
Choreographer: Hanya Holm
Cast: Richard Burton, Julie Andrews, Roddy McDowall, Robert Coote, Robert Goulet, M'el Dowd, John Cullum, Bruce Yarnell, David Hurst, Michael Kermoyan
Songs: "I Wonder What the King Is Doing Tonight"; "The Simple Joys of Maidenhood"; "Camelot"; "Follow Me"; "C'est Moi"; "The Lusty Month of May"; "Then You May Take Me to the Fair"; "How to Handle a Woman"; "Before I Gaze at You Again"; "If Ever I Would Leave You"; "What Do the Simple Folk Do?"; "Fie on Goodness!"; "I Loved You Once in Silence"; "Guenevere"
New York run: Majestic Theatre, December 3, 1960; 873 p.

Lerner and Loewe's first Broadway undertaking following their spectacular success, *My Fair Lady,* was based on T.H. White's retelling of the Arthurian legend, *The Once and Future King.* Originally titled *Jenny Kissed Me, Camelot* reunited the composer and lyricist with director Moss Hart (who joined Lerner and Loewe as co-producer), fair lady Julie Andrews, Col. Blimpish actor Robert Coote, choreographer Hanya Holm, scene designer Oliver Smith, music director Franz Allers, and orchestrators Robert Russell Bennett and Philip J. Lang. During the tryout, Moss Hart (who died a year later) was hospitalized with a heart attack and Lerner temporarily took over as director. The show had the biggest advance sale in Broadway history up to that time.

The opulently mounted production was a somewhat somber affair that dealt with the chivalrous Knights of the Round Table and the tragic romantic triangle involving noble King Arthur (Richard Burton), his errant Queen Guenevere (Julie Andrews), and Arthur's trusted Sir Lancelot du Lac (Robert Goulet). At the end, with his kingdom in ruins and his wife with another man, the King can still urge a young boy to tell everyone the story "that once there was a fleeting wisp of glory call Camelot." The touring company, which traveled for a year and a half, had a cast headed by William Squire (Arthur), Kathryn Grayson (Guenevere), Robert Peterson (Lancelot), Jan Moody (Morgan Le Fay), and Arthur Treacher (King Pellinore).

In 1980, Richard Burton recreated his original role in a touring revival that played a limited New York engagement in July. Christine Ebersole played Guenevere and Richard Muenz was Lancelot. Because of ill health, Burton was succeeded on the road by Richard Harris who also came back briefly to New York — in November 1981 — with Meg Bussert now playing the queen. In all, this company toured for almost three years. Harris had previously played King Arthur in the 1967 film version, which also starred Vanessa Redgrave (Guenevere) and Franco Nero (Lancelot).

A previous — and far more lighthearted — view of King Arthur's court was found in Rodgers and Hart's 1927 hit, *A Connecticut Yankee.*
Columbia OC/ Random House (1961); Chilton (1976)/ TW.

DO RE MI

Music: Jule Styne
Lyrics: Betty Comden & Adolph Green
Book: Garson Kanin
Producer: David Merrick
Director: Garson Kanin
Choreographers: Marc Breaux & DeeDee Wood
Cast: Phil Silvers, Nancy Walker, John Reardon, David Burns, George Mathews, George Givot, Nancy Dussault
Songs: "It's Legitimate"; "I Know About Love"; "Cry Like the Wind"; "Fireworks"; "What's New at the Zoo?"; "The Late Late Show"; "Adventure"; "Make Someone Happy"
New York run: St. James Theatre, December 26, 1960; 400 p.

A raucous satire on the music business — with special emphasis on the jukebox industry — *Do Re Mi* was full of characters reminiscent of the raffish denizens of *Guys and Dolls*. It was particularly blessed by offering two outstanding clowns in Phil Silvers as the pushiest of patsies and Nancy Walker as his long-suffering spouse. The story, which Garson Kanin adapted from his own novel, concerns Hubie Cram, a would-be bigshot, who induces three retired slot-machine mobsters (David Burns, George Mathews, and George Givot) to muscle in on the jukebox racket. Though this does not make him the fawned-upon tycoon he has always dreamed of becoming, Hubie does succeed in turning a waitress (Nancy Dussault) into a singing star. He also shows his musical knowledge by instructing a group of studio musicians on how each one is to play his instrument. His modest comment: "You hang around, you learn."
RCA OC/ TW.

Do Re Mi. "It's Legitimate" sing Phil Silvers, George Mathews, George Givot, and David Burns. (Friedman-Abeles)

CARNIVAL

Music & lyrics: Bob Merrill
Book: Michael Stewart
Producer: David Merrick
Director-choreographer: Gower Champion
Cast: Anna Maria Alberghetti, James Mitchell, Kaye Ballard, Pierre Olaf, Jerry Orbach, Henry Lascoe, Anita Gillette
Songs: "Direct from Vienna"; "Mira"; "Yes, My Heart"; "Love Makes the World Go Round"; "Beautiful Candy"; "Grand Imperial Cirque de Paris"; "Always Always You"; "She's My Love"
New York run: Imperial Theatre, April 13, 1961; 719 p.

Though the 1953 movie *Lili* had but one song, it did have two extended dance sequences which qualified it as the first screen musical to be adapted as a stage musical. Since the single song was "Hi Lili, Hi Lo," it presented a challenge for Bob Merrill to come up with a "theme" for *Carnival* with the same flavor but sufficiently distinctive on its own. He met the challenge with "Love Makes the World Go Round," whose melody from a wheezing concertina opens the show on a bare, pre-dawn setting as the weary members of a seedy French carnival set up the tents. With this strikingly effective opening (there is no overture), director Gower Champion reaffirmed his reputation for imaginative stagecraft, which was later bolstered by a joyously self-deluding dance number as the company proudly imagines itself as the "Grand Imperial Cirque de Paris." In the story, Anna Maria Alberghetti appeared as the waif who comes from the town of Mira to join the carnival where she falls for the egotistical magician Marco the Magnificent (James Mitchell), befriends the show's puppets, and ends in the arms of the disillusioned crippled puppeteer (Jerry Orbach). During the Broadway run, Miss Alberghetti was succeeded by Susan Watson and sister Carla Alberghetti. Polydor OC/ DBS Publications (1968)/ TW.

MILK AND HONEY

Music & lyrics: Jerry Herman
Book: Don Appell
Producer: Gerald Oestreicher
Director: Albert Marre
Choreographer: Donald Saddler
Cast: Robert Weede, Mimi Benzell, Molly Picon, Tommy Rall, Lanna Saunders, Juki Arkin
Songs: "Shalom"; "Milk and Honey"; "There's No Reason in the World"; "That Was Yesterday"; "Let's Not Waste A Moment"; "Like A Young Man"; "As Simple As That"
New York run: Martin Beck Theatre, October 10, 1961, 543 p.

For his initial Broadway assignment, composer-lyricist Jerry Herman joined playwright Don Appell to create the first musical with an Israeli setting. After spending some weeks in Israel, the writers agreed on a story concerning American tourists so that the score would not have to be written entirely in a minor key. *Milk and Honey* (originally titled *Shalom*) was primarily about a romance that blooms in a desert *moshav* between a middle-aged man separated from his wife (Robert Weede) and an almost middle-aged widow (Mimi Benzell). Though Phil would like Ruth to remain with him, she is unhappy about an extended non-matrimonial relationship, and — when last seen — Phil is on his way to make one final appeal for a divorce. Comic relief was provided by Molly Picon (a star of the Yiddish theatre in her only Broadway musical) as a husband-hunting widow. RCA OC/ TW.

How to Succeed in Business Without Really Trying. Robert Morse and Bonnie Scott. (Friedman-Abeles)

HOW TO SUCCEED IN BUSINESS WITHOUT REALLY TRYING

Music & lyrics: Frank Loesser
Book: Abe Burrows
Producers: Cy Feuer & Ernest Martin
Director: Abe Burrows
Choreographers: Bob Fosse, Hugh Lambert
Cast: Robert Morse, Rudy Vallee, Bonnie Scott, Virginia Martin, Charles Nelson Reilly, Ruth Kobart, Sammy Smith, Donna McKechnie
Songs: "Coffee Break"; "The Company Way"; "A Secretary Is Not a Toy"; "Grand Old Ivy"; "Paris Original"; "Rosemary"; "I Believe in You"; "Brotherhood of Man"
New York run: 46th Street Theatre, October 14, 1961; 1,417 p.

The program credit for *How to Succeed in Business Without Really Trying* indicates that the musical was based on Shepherd Mead's tongue-in-cheek manual, but since the book had no plot Abe Burrows' script was actually based on an unproduced play by Jack Weinstock and Willie Gilbert (whose program credit, also incorrect, indicates that they were co-librettists). That play had been sent to producers Cy Feuer and Ernest Martin who then enlisted Burrows and Frank Loesser, their *Guys and Dolls* team, to turn it into a musical comedy. Bob Fosse was brought in during rehearsals to take charge of the musical staging.

In the sassy sendup of the Horatio Alger myth, our disarmingly boyish hero J. Pierpont Finch (Robert Morse) owes his advancement — from window washer to Chairman of the Board of the World Wide Wicket Company — not to hard work but to his ability to make others work hard for him. As it traces Finch's step-by-step back-stabbing way up the corporate ladder, the show skewers such aspects of Big Business as nepotism, old-school ties, the coffee break, the office party, the sycophantic yes-men, the executive washroom (where Finch serenades his image in the mirror with the worshipful "I Believe in You"), and the boardroom presentation. The musical became the fourth to win the Pulitzer Prize for drama. Robert Morse and Rudy Vallee, who played J.B. Biggley, the stuffy president of the company, were also in the 1967 movie.
RCA OC/ Frank Music, London (1963)*/ MTI.

NO STRINGS

Music & lyrics: Richard Rodgers
Book: Samuel Taylor
Producer: Richard Rodgers
Director-choreographer: Joe Layton
Cast: Richard Kiley, Diahann Carroll, Polly Rowles, Noelle Adam, Bernice Massi, Don Chastain, Alvin Epstein, Mitchell Gregg
Songs: "The Sweetest Sounds"; "Loads of Love"; "La La La"; "Nobody Told Me"; "Look No Further"; "Maine"; "No Strings"
New York run: 54th Street Theatre, March 15, 1962; 580 p.

One appearance on the Jack Paar television show was all it took for Diahann Carroll to convince Richard Rodgers that she should be starred on Broadway in a Richard Rodgers musical. *No Strings,* the musical that resulted, was Rodgers' first production after the death of his partner, Oscar Hammerstein II, and the only one for which the composer also supplied his own lyrics. The work proved to be highly innovative in a number of ways: it placed the orchestra backstage, it put musicians onstage to accompany singers, it had the principals and chorus move scenery and props in full view of the audience, and — conforming to the show's title — it removed the string section from the orchestra. In addition, it was concerned with an interracial love affair, though the matter of race was never discussed. The leading characters were Barbara Woodruff (Miss Carroll), a high fashion model living in Paris, and David Jordan (Richard Kiley), a former Pulitzer Prize-winning novelist now a sponging "Europe bum." After meeting they enjoy hearing the sweetest sounds in such romantic surroundings as Monte Carlo, Honfleur, Deauville, and St. Tropez. The story ends, with no strings attached, as the writer returns home alone to Maine to try to resume his career. During the run, Kiley and Miss Carroll were succeeded by Howard Keel and Barbara McNair, who then toured. The 54th Street Theatre, formerly the Adelphi, was renamed the George Abbott before it was demolished.
Capitol OC/ Random House (1962)/ R&H.

No Strings. Diahann Carroll and Richard Kiley.
(Friedman-Abeles)

A FUNNY THING HAPPENED ON THE WAY TO THE FORUM

Music & lyrics: Stephen Sondheim
Book: Burt Shevelove & Larry Gelbart
Producer: Harold Prince
Director: George Abbott (Jerome Robbins uncredited)
Choreographer: Jack Cole
Cast: Zero Mostel, John Carradine, Raymond Walburn, Jack Gilford, David Burns, Ruth Kobart, Brian Davies, Preshy Marker, Ronald Holgate, Eddie Phillips
Songs: "Comedy Tonight"; "Love I Hear"; "Free"; "Lovely"; "Pretty Little Picture"; "Everybody Ought to Have a Maid"; "I'm Calm"; "Impossible"; "Bring Me My Bride"; "That'll Show Him"
New York run: Alvin Theatre, May 8, 1962; 964 p.

Having already written a musical at Yale inspired by the farcical plays of Titus Maccius Plautus (254 BC-184 BC), Burt Shevelove got together with Larry Gelbart and Stephen Sondheim to give Broadway a taste of what once convulsed Roman audiences. To come up with a suitable script — which would also adhere to the classic unities of time, place and action — the writers researched all 21 of the playwright's surviving comedies, then put together an original story incorporating such typical, laugh-catching Plautus characters as the conniving slave, the callow hero (named Hero), the doddering old man, the seductive courtesan, the lustful husband and his shrewish wife, and the macho warrior. One situation in the musical — regarding the doddering old man who is kept from entering his house because he thinks it is haunted — was discovered in a play with the curiously prophetic title of *Mostellaria*.

Originally intended as a vehicle for Phil Silvers, then for Milton Berle, *A Funny Thing Happened on the Way to the Forum* opened with Zero Mostel as Pseudolus, a slave who is forced to go through a series of outlandish adventures before being allowed his freedom. Though Broadway audiences immediately took to George Abbott's frantically paced show, the outlook had not looked promising during the pre-New York tryout and director Jerome Robbins was called in. His most important change: beginning the musical with the song "Comedy Tonight," which set just the right mood for the madcap doings that followed. In addition to being Harold Prince's first solo producing effort, the show was the first Broadway offering with music as well as lyrics by Stephen Sondheim. During the run, Mostel was succeeded by Dick Shawn, David Burns by Frank McHugh (as Senex, a lascivious slave owner), Jack Gilford by Lee Goodman (as Hysterium, a nervous slave) and John Carradine by Erik Rhodes (as Marcus Lycus, a dealer in courtesans). The touring cast included Jerry Lester (Pseudolus), Paul Hartman (Senex), Arnold Stang (Hysterium), Erik Rhodes (Marcus Lycus), Edward Everett Horton (Erronius, the doddering old man), and Donna McKechnie (Philia, a slave).

In 1972, Phil Silvers got his chance to play Pseudolus in a well-received revival whose run was cut short by the star's illness. Larry Blyden, who was also co-producer, appeared as Hysterium, and others in the cast were Mort Marshall (Senex), Carl Ballantine (Lycus), and Reginald Owen (Erronius). Burt Shevelove was the director. Both Mostel (as Pseudolus) and Silvers (as Lycus) were in the 1966 screen version along with Jack Gilford.
Capitol OC/ Dodd, Mead (1963)/ MTI.

A Funny Thing Happened on the Way to the Forum. John Carradine and Zero Mostel. (Friedman-Abeles)

STOP THE WORLD — I WANT TO GET OFF

Music, lyrics & book: Leslie Bricusse & Anthony Newley
Producer: David Merrick
Director: Anthony Newley
Choreographers: Virginia Mason, John Broome
Cast: Anthony Newley, Anna Quayle, Jennifer Baker, Susan Baker
Songs: "Typically English"; "Gonna Build a Mountain"; "Once in a Lifetime"; "Someone Nice Like You"; "What Kind Of Fool Am I?"
New York run: Shubert Theatre, October 3, 1962; 555 p.

A hit in London a year before it was presented in New York, *Stop the World — I Want to Get Off* unveiled the multiple talents of the British team of Leslie Bricusse and Anthony Newley. Newley starred in the musical, in which he played Littlechap, and the allegorical tale had much to say about man's drive for fame and power and the disillusionment that sets in once these goals are attained. (Rodgers and Hammerstein had previously dealt with the same general theme in *Allegro*.) In a setting designed by Sean Kenny to resemble a circus tent, Littlechap — wearing white-face clown makeup — rises in the world of business and politics after marrying the boss's daughter (Anna Quayle). Not above a little philandering with Russian, German, and American girls (all played by Miss Quayle), Littlechap ends his days ruminating — in "What Kind of Fool Am I?" — about his misspent life. Newley was succeeded during the run by Joel Grey, and his part in the 1966 movie was played by Tony Tanner. A revised adaptation came back to Broadway in 1978 with Sammy Davis Jr. Davis also did a film version of this verison under the modest rubric *Sammy Stops the World*. Polydor OC/ TW.

LITTLE ME

Music: Cy Coleman
Lyrics: Carolyn Leigh
Book: Neil Simon
Producers: Cy Feuer & Ernest Martin
Directors: Cy Feuer & Bob Fosse
Choreographer: Bob Fosse
Cast: Sid Caesar, Virginia Martin, Nancy Andrews, Mort Marshall, Joey Faye, Swen Swenson, Peter Turgeon, Mickey Deems, Gretchen Cryer
Songs: "The Other Side of the Tracks"; "I Love You"; "Be a Performer"; "Boom-Boom"; "I've Got Your Number"; "Real Live Girl"; "Poor Little Hollywood Star"; "Here's to Us"
New York run: Lunt-Fontanne Theatre, November 17, 1962; 257 p.

Although Neil Simon's wickedly funny, outlandishly plotted libretto for *Little Me* was based on Patrick Dennis' novel about the rise of a voluptuous beauty from Drifters' Row, Venezuela, Illinois, to a Southampton estate, it was written primarily to show off the protean comic gifts of Sid Caesar playing all seven of the men who figured prominently in our heroine's life. Chief among the Caesar characterizations was Noble Eggleston, the over-achieving snob who loves poor Belle Schlumpfert as much as he is able ("considering you're riffraff and I am well-to-do"), studies medicine and law at Harvard and Yale, becomes a flying ace in World War I, wins election as governor of both North and South Dakota, and, eventually, is the man with whom Belle literally walks into the sunset. The actor was also seen as Amos Pinchley, an 88-year-old miserly banker; Val du Val, a flashy French entertainer; Fred Poitrine, the hick soldier who marries Belle and quickly expires; Otto Schnitzler, a dictatorial Hollywood director; Prince Cherney, the lachrymose impoverished ruler of the duchy of Rosenzweig; and Noble Jr., an over-achieving chip who studies both at Juilliard and Georgia Tech to become a musical engineer. Highlights of the score were the wistful "Real Live Girl," sung by World War I doughboys, and the sassy, seductive "I've Got Your Number," sung and danced by Swen Swenson, as Belle's faithful admirer.

In 1982, a revised version of *Little Me* — with James Coco, Victor Garber and Mary Gordon Murray — had a disappointingly short run on Broadway. RCA OC/ Random House (1977)/ TW.

Little Me. Sid Caesar (as Amos Pinchley) and Virginia Martin. (Friedman-Abeles)

OLIVER!

Music, lyrics & book: Lionel Bart
Producers: David Merrick & Donald Albery
Director: Peter Cole
Cast: Clive Revill, Georgia Brown, Bruce Prochnik, Willoughby Goddard, Hope Jackman, Danny Sewell, David Jones, Geoffrey Lumb
Songs: "Food Glorious Food"; "Where Is Love?"; "Consider Yourself"; "You've Got to Pick a Pocket or Two"; "It's a Fine Life"; "Oom-Pah-Pah"; "I'd Do Anything"; "As Long as He Needs Me"; "Who Will Buy?"; "Reviewing the Situation"
New York run: Imperial Theatre, January 6, 1963; 774 p.

Lionel Bart's *Oliver!,* which opened in London in 1960, held the West End long-run record for a musical until overtaken by *Jesus Christ Superstar,* and its Broadway facsimile—also directed by Peter Cole and designed by Sean Kenny—was the longest running musical import until overtaken by *Evita.* Adapted from Charles Dickens' *Oliver Twist,* the stage version offered a somewhat jollied up view of the ordeal of an orphan (played by Bruce Prochnik) who dares to ask for more food at the workhouse, is sent out into the cruel world, fall in with a band of juvenile pickpockets under the benign control of Fagin (Clive Revill), and is eventually rescued from a life of fraternal crime by kindly, wealthy Mr. Brownlow (Geoffrey Lumb), who turns out to be Oliver's grandfather. Kenny's ingenious, atmospheric settings were much admired as were the tuneful. rousing score. The work, however, did not last long in a 1984 revival with Ron Moody (the London and 1968 film version Fagin) and Patti LuPone.

Five other Dickens novels were seen on Broadway in musical adaptations: *Barnaby Rudge (Dolly Varden,* 1902); *The Posthumous Papers of the Pickwick Club (Mr Pickwick,* 1903; *Pickwick,* 1965); *A Christmas Carol (Comin' Uptown,* 1979); *David Copperfield (Copperfield,* 1981); *The Mystery of Edwin Drood* 1985). For other musicals based on British literary classics, see *My Fair Lady,* page 168.
RCA OC.TW.

Oliver! Georgia Brown, David Jones, Bruce Prochnik, and Clive Revill in the "I'd Do Anything" number. (Friedman-Abeles)

She Loves Me. Daniel Massey and Barbara Cook. (Eileen Darby)

SHE LOVES ME

Music: Jerry Bock
Lyrics: Sheldon Harnick
Book: Joe Masteroff
Producer-director: Harold Prince
Choreographer: Carol Haney
Cast: Barbara Cook, Daniel Massey, Barbara Baxley, Jack Cassidy, Ludwig Donath, Nathaniel Frey, Ralph Williams
Songs: "Days Gone By"; "Tonight at Eight"; "Will He Like Me?"; "Dear Friend"; "Ice Cream"; "She Loves Me"; "A Trip to the Library"; "Grand Knowing You"; "Twelve Days to Christmas"
New York run: Eugene O'Neill Theatre, April 23, 1963; 301 p.

With its beguiling European setting, attractive characters, tender love story, and, most important, closely integrated, melody drenched score, *She Loves Me* recalled the atmosphere and charm of the Kern-Harbach *The Cat and the Fiddle* and the Kern-Hammerstein *Music in the Air.* The new musical, the first to be directed as well as produced by Harold Prince, was based on a Hungarian play, *Parfumerie,* by Miklos Laszlo, that had already been used as the basis for two films, *The Shop Around the Corner* and *In the Good Old Summertime.* Set in the 1930s in "A City in Europe" — which could only be Budapest — the tale is concerned with the people who work in Maraczek's Parfumerie, principally the constantly squabbling sales clerk Amalia Balash (Barbara Cook) and the manager Georg Nowack (Daniel Massey). It is soon revealed that they are anonymous pen pals who agree to meet one night at the Café Imperiale, though neither knows the other's identity. Georg realizes who Amalia is when he sees her waiting for him in the restaurant, but he doesn't let on and the unhappy Amalia pours out her heart in a longing plea to her unknown "Dear Friend." After she calls in sick, their relationship blossoms into love when Georg brings her ice cream; eventually, he is emboldened to reveal his identity by quoting from one of Amalia's letters.

She Loves Me would have starred Julie Andrews had she not been tied up with a film. A successful revival of the musical opened on Broadway in June of 1993.

Polydor OC/Dodd, Mead (1963)/TW.

110 IN THE SHADE

Music: Harvey Schmidt
Lyrics: Tom Jones
Book: N. Richard Nash
Producer: David Merrick
Director: Joseph Anthony
Choreographer: Agnes de Mille
Cast: Robert Horton, Inga Swenson, Stephen Douglass, Will Geer, Steve Roland, Anthony Teague, Lesley Ann Warren, Gretchen Cryer
Songs: "Love, Don't Turn Away"; "Rain Song"; "You're Not Foolin' Me"; "Old Maid"; "Everything Beautiful Happens at Night"; "Melisande"; "Simple Little Things"; "Little Red Hat"; "Is It Really Me?"
New York run: Broadhurst Theatre, October 24, 1963; 330 p.

Harvey Schmidt and Tom Jones followed their runaway Off-Broadway hit, *The Fantasticks,* with an equally wistful and appealing score for *110 in the Shade,* which N. Richard Nash adapted from his own 1954 play, *The Rainmaker.* The action of the story takes place in a drought-stricken Western town on a hot summer day from dawn to midnight. The sudden appearance of a brash rainmaker, Bill Starbuck (Robert Horton in a part first announced for Hal Holbrook), lifts the spirits of all but plain Lizzie Curry (Inga Swenson) who calls him a fake. Lizzie, whose life is as parched as the weather, is attracted to the flamboyant con man and they make love while the town is enjoying its annual picnic. Starbuck wants Lizzie to run away with him, but since her dreams are really only of simple little things, she is happy to remain with the more dependable suitor, Sheriff File (Stephen Douglass). Then darned if a miracle doesn't happen and the rains come. RCA OC/ TW.

110 in the Shade. Robert Horton and Inga Swenson. (Friedman-Abeles)

HELLO, DOLLY!

Music & lyrics: Jerry Herman
Book: Michael Stewart
Producer: David Merrick
Director-choreographer: Gower Champion
Cast: Carol Channing, David Burns, Eileen Brennan, Sondra Lee, Charles Nelson Reilly, Jerry Dodge, Gordon Connell, Igors Gavon, Alice Playten, David Hartman
Songs: "It Takes a Woman"; "Put on Your Sunday Clothes"; "Ribbons Down My Back"; "Dancing"; "Before the Parade Passes By"; "Hello, Dolly!"; "It Only Takes a Moment"; "So Long, Dearie"
New York run: St. James Theatre, January 16,1964; 2,844 p.

For over ten months — until it was overtaken by *Fiddler on the Roof* — *Hello, Dolly!* held the record as Broadway's longest running musical. Its tryout tour, however, was hardly a harbinger of even a moderate success. New writers had to be called in, three songs were dropped and three added (including the first-act finale, "Before the Parade Passes By"), and Jerry Dodge replaced one of the two leading juveniles. But director Gower Champion made it all work and the musical won a rousing Broadway reception.

The turn-of-the-century tale centers around Dolly Gallagher Levi, a New York matchmaker, engaged to help a pompous Yonkers merchant, Horace Vandergelder (David Burns), in his pursuit of a mate. But the matchmaker sets her cap for Vandergelder herself, and eventually he acknowledges that it fits. Along the way, the exuberant Dolly helps two of Vandergelder's clerks, Barnaby Tucker and Cornelius Hackl (Jerry Dodge and Charles Nelson Reilly) enjoy a night at the Harmonia Gardens restaurant with dressmaker Irene Malloy and her assistant Minnie Fay (Eileen Brennan and Sondra Lee). After her grand entrance into the restaurant, Dolly sets off a rousing, high-kicking reception by the waiters welcoming her back to a once favored haunt.

Hello, Dolly! had an unusually lengthy history. Its first version, in 1835, was a London play, *A Day Well Spent*, by John Oxenford. Seven years later, *Einen Jux Will er Sich Machen (He Wants to Have a Lark)*, a Viennese variation by Johann Nestroy, was produced. In 1938, Thornton Wilder turned the Nestroy play into *The Merchant of Yonkers,* and 17 years after that he rewrote it as *The Matchmaker*. Both Wilder plays had Broadway runs. Another forerunner of *Hello, Dolly!* was the 1891 musical, *A Trip to Chinatown.*

Once Ethel Merman had turned down the chance to be the first song-and-dance Dolly, Carol Channing seized the opportunity to make it one of her two most closely identified roles. During the Broadway run she was succeeded by Ginger Rogers, Martha Raye, Betty Grable, Bibi Osterwald, Pearl Bailey (who starred in an all-black company and was frequently spelled by Thelma Carpenter), Phyllis Diller, and — at last — Ethel Merman. David Burns was replaced by Max Showalter, and Cab Calloway had the Vandergelder part opposite Miss Bailey. During Miss Merman's tenure, Russell Nype played Cornelius. The show returned to New York in 1974 with Miss Bailey and Billy Daniels leading an all-black cast, and in 1978 it came back with Miss Channing and Eddie Bracken as part of a year-and-a-half tour. A new production began touring in 1994, once again with Carol Channing as Dolly Levi. It ran for a few months on Broadway in 1995. The show's film version, released in 1969, co-starred Barbra Streisand and Walter Matthau.

RCA OC (Channing); RCA OC (Bailey); RCA OC (Martin); Varese (30th Anniversary recording-Channing)/ DBS (1966)/ TW.

Carol Channing

Ginger Rogers

Martha Raye

Betty Grable

Pearl Bailey

WHAT MAKES SAMMY RUN?

Music & lyrics: Ervin Drake
Book: Budd & Stuart Schulberg
Producer: Joseph Cates
Director: Abe Burrows
Choreographer: Matt Mattox
Cast: Steve Lawrence, Sally Ann Howes, Robert Alda, Bernice Massi, Barry Newman, Walter Klavun
Songs: "A Tender Spot"; "My Home Town"; "A Room Without Windows"; "Something to Live For"; "The Friendliest Thing"
New York run: 54th Street Theatre, February 27, 1964; 540 p.

Unscrupulous Sammy Glick was first immortalized in Budd Schulberg's novel about the double dealing world of Hollywood. In the musical version, adapted by Schulberg and his brother Stuart, he was something of a relative to *How to Succeed's* J. Pierpont Finch, as the story covers Sammy's rise from his days as a newspaper copy boy, through his job as a script writer at World Wide Pictures and his affair with fellow-writer Kit Sargent (Sally Ann Howes), to his elevation as studio chief and his marriage to his boss's nymphomaniac daughter (Bernice Massi). At the play's end, left without friends and with an unfaithful wife, Sammy is still running. Playing the role of Sammy was nightclub and recording star Steve Lawrence, who helped turn a vision of romantic isolation, "A Room Without Windows," into a popular song hit.
Columbia OC/ Random House (1965)/ TW.

Funny Girl. Barbra Streisand singing "I'm the Greatest Star" as Danny Meehan watches. (Henry Grossman)

FUNNY GIRL

Music: Jule Styne
Lyrics: Bob Merrill
Book: Isobel Lennart
Producer: Ray Stark
Directors: Jerome Robbins, Garson Kanin
Choreographer: Carol Haney
Cast: Barbra Streisand, Sydney Chaplin, Kay Medford, Danny Meehan, Jean Stapleton, Roger DeKoven, Joseph Macaulay, Lainie Kazan, Buzz Miller, George Reeder, Larry Fuller
Songs: "I'm the Greatest Star"; "Cornet Man"; I Want to Be Seen With You Tonight"; "People"; "You Are Woman"; "Don't Rain on My Parade"; "Sadie, Sadie"; "Who Are You Now?"; "The Music That Makes Me Dance"
New York run: Winter Garden, March 26, 1964; 1,348 p.

The funny girl of the title refers to Fanny Brice, and the story, told mostly in flashback, covers the major events in the life of the celebrated comedienne — her discovery by impresario Florenz Ziegfeld, her triumphs in the *Ziegfeld Follies,* her infatuation with and stormy marriage to smooth-talking con man Nick Arnstein, and the breakup of that marriage after Nick has served time for masterminding the theft of Wall Street securities. Film producer Ray Stark, Miss Brice's son-in-law, had long wanted to make a movie based on the Fanny Brice story, but he became convinced that it should first be done on the stage. Mary Martin, Anne Bancroft, and Carol Burnett had all turned down the leading part before it was won by Barbra Streisand, whose only other Broadway experience had been in a supporting role in *I Can Get It for You Wholesale.* Miss Streisand succeeded so well — her recording of "People" was a hit before *Funny Girl* opened — that she became even more renowned than the woman she portrayed.

At first there was hope that the *Gypsy* team of Jule Styne and Stephen Sondheim would be reunited to write the score, but Sondheim wasn't interested and Styne contacted Bob Merrill. Some of their songs, however, virtually replaced those used in comparable situations in *Gypsy* — "I'm the Greatest Star" for "Some People," "Don't Rain on My Parade" for "Everything's Coming Up Roses," and "The Music That Makes Me Dance" (which suggested Fanny Brice's closely identified theme song, "My Man") for "Rose's Turn." When Jerome Robbins, the original director, walked out in a dispute with the author, he was succeeded by Bob Fosse, who didn't stay long, then by Garson Kanin, who quit after Robbins was lured back.

The musical was variously announced under such titles as *A Very Special Person, My Man,* and *The Luckiest People* before David Merrick (who was to have been the show's co-producer) suggested *Funny Girl.* Numerous script alterations — including 40 rewrites of the final scene alone — and five opening-night postponements were required before the show was considered ready for its official premiere. During the Broadway run, Miss Streisand was followed by Mimi Hines, and Sydney Chaplin, who played Nick Arnstein, by Johnny Desmond. The road company, which toured for 13 months was headed by Marilyn Michaels (Fanny), Anthony George (Nick), and Lillian Roth (Fanny's mother). Miss Streisand also starred in the 1968 film version and its 1975 sequel, *Funny Lady.* For other show-business musical biographies, see *Annie Get Your Gun,* page 130.

Capitol OC/ Random House (1964)/ TW.

HIGH SPIRITS

Music, lyrics & book: Hugh Martin & Timothy Gray
Producers: Lester Osterman, Robert Fletcher & Richard Horner
Director: Noël Coward (Gower Champion uncredited)
Choreographer: Danny Daniels
Cast: Beatrice Lillie, Tammy Grimes, Edward Woodward, Louise Troy
Songs: "Was She Prettier Than I?"; "The Bicycle Song"; "Forever and a Day";
   "I Know Your Heart"; "Faster Than Sound"; "If I Gave You"; "Home
   Sweet Heaven"; "Something Is Coming to Tea"
New York run: Alvin Theatre, April 7, 1964; 375 p.

Hugh Martin and Timothy Gray had wanted to adapt Noël Coward's 1941 play
Blithe Spirit as early as 1953, but permission was not granted until seven years
later. In their musical version — initially titled *Faster Than Sound* — Beatrice
Lillie (in her 13th and final Broadway appearance) portrayed the antic spiritualist
Mme. Arcati who disrupts the second marriage of writer Charles Condomine
(Edward Woodward) by bringing the shade of his first wife, Elvira (Tammy
Grimes), back from the dead. In an attempt to take her former husband with her
to the spirit world, Elvira accidentally causes the death of Ruth (Louise Troy), the
second wife, who takes revenge by playing some ghostly tricks of her own. As
director, Noël Coward made sure that *High Spirits* was in the proper blithe spirit
of his play, but friction during the Philadelphia tryout between him and Miss Lillie
prompted Mr. Coward's replacement by Gower Champion.
ABC Paramount OC/ TW.

Fiddler on the Roof. Tevye (Zero Mostel) is none too happy that daughter
Tzeitel (Joanna Merlin) is marrying a poor tailor (Austin Pendleton).
(Friedman-Abeles)

FIDDLER ON THE ROOF

Music; Jerry Bock
Lyrics: Sheldon Harnick
Book: Joseph Stein
Producer: Harold Prince
Director-choreographer: Jerome Robbins
Cast: Zero Mostel, Maria Karnilova, Beatrice Arthur, Joanna Merlin, Austin Pendleton, Bert Convy, Julia Migenes, Michael Granger, Tanya Everett, Leonard Frey, Maurice Edwards
Songs: "Tradition"; "Matchmaker, Matchmaker"; "If I Were a Rich Man"; "Sabbath Prayer"; "To Life"; "Miracle of Miracles"; "Sunrise, Sunset"; "Now I Have Everything"; "Do You Love Me?"; "Far from the Home I Love"; "Anatevka"
New York run: Imperial Theatre, September 22, 1964; 3,242 p.

One of Broadway's classic musicals, *Fiddler on the Roof* defied the accepted rules of commercial success by dealing with persecution, poverty, and the problems of holding on to traditions in the midst of a hostile world. But despite a story and setting that many thought had limited appeal, the theme struck such a universal response that the fiddler was perched precariously on his roof for seven years nine months, thus becoming the longest running production — musical or nonmusical — in Broadway history. (The record, however, was broken by *Grease* in December 1979.)

The plot is set in the Jewish village of Anatevka, Russia, in 1905, and deals mainly with the efforts of Tevye (Zero Mostel), a dairyman, his wife Golde (Maria Karnilova), and their five daughters to cope with their harsh existence. Tzeitel (Joanna Merlin), the oldest daughter, marries a poor tailor (Austin Pendleton), after Tevye had promised her to a well-to-do middle-aged butcher (Michael Granger). Hodel (Julia Migenes), the second daughter, marries a revolutionary (Bert Convy) and follows him to Siberia. Chava (Tanya Everett), the third daughter, marries out of her religion. When, at the end, the Czar's Cossacks destroy Anatevka, Tevye, still holding on to his faith and his traditions, bravely prepares to take what's left of his family to America. Though Zero Mostel became closely identified with the role of Tevye he proved not to be indispensable, since the musical had no trouble continuing with his successors Luther Adler, Herschel Bernardi, Harry Goz, Jerry Jarrett, Paul Lipson, and Jan Peerce. Six actresses replaced Maria Karnilova as Golde, including Martha Schlamme, Dolores Wilson, and Peg Murray. During the Broadway engagement, Pia Zadora took over as Bielke, the youngest daughter, and Bette Midler was seen for a time as Tzeitel. In 1976, *Fiddler on the Roof* came back to New York with Mostel and Thelma Lee in the leading roles; in 1981, it returned — at Lincoln Center's New York State Theatre — with Herschel Bernardi and Maria Karnilova. The national tour, originally featuring Luther Adler and Dolores Wilson, was on the road for two years three months. Topol, who played Tevye in London, was seen in the 1971 screen version which also featured Norma Crane and Molly Picon.

The idea for *Fiddler on the Roof* was planted when Jerry Bock, Sheldon Harnick, and Joseph Stein decided to make a musical out of Sholom Aleichem's short story, "Tevye and His Daughters." They took the first draft to producer Harold Prince who advised them that no other director but Jerome Robbins could possibly give the material the universal quality that it required. The first choice for Tevye was Danny Kaye; among others considered at various times were Howard Da Silva, Tom Bosley, and Danny Thomas.

RCA OC/ Crown (1964); Chilton (1973)/ MTI.

GOLDEN BOY

Music: Charles Strouse
Lyrics: Lee Adams
Book: Clifford Odets, William Gibson
Producer: Hillard Elkins
Director: Arthur Penn
Choreographer: Donald McKayle
Cast: Sammy Davis Jr., Billy Daniels, Paula Wayne, Kenneth Tobey, Ted Beniades, Louis Gossett, Jaime Rogers, Lola Falana
Songs: "Night Song"; "Don't Forget 127th Street"; "Lorna's Here"; "This Is the Life"; "While the City Sleeps"; "I Want to Be With You"
New York run: Majestic Theatre, October 20, 1964; 569 p.

For his first offering as a Broadway producer, Hillard Elkins hit upon the idea that by changing the leading character in Clifford Odets' 1937 drama *Golden Boy* from an Italian-American boxer named Joe Bonaparte to a Negro American boxer named Joe Wellington, the result would be a musical play of substance and significance. Odets himself agreed to write the libretto but his death during the show's early stages created major problems that remained unsolved until playwright William Gibson took over the adaptation and Arthur Penn replaced the original director during the tryout. With Sammy Davis Jr. giving a sensitive performance as the young man who breaks out of his Harlem surroundings by becoming a professional fighter, and with such effectively choreographed scenes as the opening gym workout and the climactic prizefight, *Golden Boy* won a favorable Broadway decision and remained almost a year and a half.
Capitol OC/ Atheneum (1965)/ SF.

DO I HEAR A WALTZ?

Music: Richard Rodgers
Lyrics: Stephen Sondheim
Book: Arthur Laurents
Producer: Richard Rodgers
Director: John Dexter
Choreographer: Herbert Ross
Cast: Elizabeth Allen, Sergio Franchi, Carol Bruce, Madeline Sherwood, Julienne Marie, Stuart Damon, Fleury D'Antonakis, Jack Manning
Songs: "Someone Woke Up"; "This Week Americans"; "What Do We Do? We Fly!"; "Someone Like You"; "Here We Are Again"; "Take the Moment"; "Moon in My Window"; "We're Gonna Be All Right"; "Do I Hear a Waltz?"; "Stay"; "Thank You So Much"
New York run: 46th Street Theatre, March 18, 1965; 220 p.

Since Stephen Sondheim was something of a protégé of Oscar Hammerstein II, it was almost inevitable that Richard Rodgers would team up with him after Hammerstein's death. Their single joint effort resulted in *Do I Hear a Waltz?*, which Arthur Laurents adapted from his own play, *The Time of the Cuckoo,* first produced in 1952. Taking place in Venice, the tale concerns Leona Samish (Elizabeth Allen), who has an intense but foredoomed affair with Renato Di Rossi (Sergio Franchi), a married shopkeeper. Though initially, there was to have been no dancing in the musical, the authors felt during the Boston tryout that the rueful story needed more movement and choreographer Herbert Ross was called in. His contribution was most apparent in the scene in which Leona — who has always been sure she will know true love if she hears an imaginary waltz — hears it, sings about it, and dances to it.
Columbia OC/ Random House (1966)/ R&H.

HALF A SIXPENCE

Music & lyrics: David Heneker
Book: Beverly Cross
Producers: Allen-Hodgdon, Stevens Productions, Harold Fielding
Director: Gene Saks
Choreographer: Onna White
Cast: Tommy Steele, Ann Shoemaker, James Grout, Carrie Nye, Polly James, Grover Dale, Will Mackenzie, John Cleese
Songs: "Half a Sixpence"; "Money to Burn"; "She's Too Far Above Me"; "If the Rain's Got to Fall"; "Long Ago"; "Flash Bang Wallop"
New York run: Broadhurst Theatre, April 25, 1965; 512 p.

H.G. Wells' novel, *Kipps,* supplied the basis for this period musical in which Tommy Steele (for whom it was written) starred in London in 1963, in New York in 1965, and on film in 1967. *Half a Sixpence* is about Arthur Kipps, an orphan who becomes a draper's apprentice in Folkestone, England, at the turn of the century. Arthur inherits a fortune, becomes engaged to highborn Helen Walsingham (Carrie Nye), breaks off the engagement to marry Ann Pornick (Polly James), a working class girl, loses his money to Helen's brother (John Cleese) in a phony business scheme, and ends up contentedly as the owner of a book shop. There were some changes in the score for the New York engagement, which was enlivened by Onna White's rousing dances, especially the high-kicking, banjo-plucking "Money to Burn." During the run, Steele was succeeded by Tony Tanner, Joel Grey, and Dick Kalman. For other Broadway musicals based on British literary classics, see *My Fair Lady,* page 168.
RCA OC/ Dramatic Publ. Co. (1967)*/ DPC.

Half a Sixpence. Tommy Steele playing the banjo for his pub cronies in the "Money to Burn" number. (Friedman-Abeles)

The Roar of the Greasepaint — The Smell of the Crowd. Cyril Ritchard and Anthony Newley. (Henry Grossman)

THE ROAR OF THE GREASEPAINT — THE SMELL OF THE CROWD

Music, lyrics & book: Leslie Bricusse & Anthony Newley
Producer: David Merrick
Director: Anthony Newley
Choreographer: Gillian Lynne
Cast: Anthony Newley, Cyril Ritchard, Sally Smith, Gilbert Price, Joyce Jillson
Songs: "A Wonderful Day Like Today"; "Where Would You Be Without Me?"; "My First Love Song"; "Look at That Face"; "The Joker"; "Who Can I Turn To?"; "Feeling Good"; "Nothing Can Stop Me Now!"; "My Way"; "Sweet Beginning"
New York run: Shubert Theatre, May 16, 1965; 232 p.

The Roar of the Greasepaint — The Smell of the Crowd was another allegorical musical in the same style as the previous Anthony Newley-Leslie Bricusse *Stop the World — I Want to Get Off.* Again Newley starred and directed, Sean Kenny designed the symbolic set (this one resembling a huge gaming table), and David Merrick was the producer. Here the writers are concerned with the weighty theme of Playing the Game, which covers such universal topics as religion (the supplicating ballad, "Who Can I Turn To?," is addressed to God), hunger, work, love, success, death, and rebellion. Leading the cast were Cyril Ritchard as Sir, representing ruling class authority, and Anthony Newley as Cocky, representing the masses who submissively play the game according to the existing rules — no matter how unfair they are. In the end, emboldened by a character called The Negro (Gilbert Price), Cocky challenges Sir's dominance, and they both realize that power must be shared between them. Though the musical folded in England without opening in London, Merrick secured the American rights and sent the production on a 13½-week tryout tour, thus allowing the infectious music-hall type songs to win favor before the show reached Broadway.
RCA OC/ TW.

ON A CLEAR DAY YOU CAN SEE FOREVER

Music: Burton Lane
Lyrics & book: Alan Jay Lerner
Producer: Alan Jay Lerner
Director: Robert Lewis
Choreographer: Herbert Ross
Cast: Barbara Harris, John Cullum, Titos Vandis, William Daniels, Clifford David, Rae Allen
Songs: "Hurry! It's Lovely Up Here"; "On a Clear Day"; "On the S.S. Bernard Cohn"; "She Wasn't You"; "Melinda"; "What Did I Have That I Don't Have?"; "Wait Till We're Sixty-Five"; "Come Back to Me"
New York run: Mark Hellinger Theatre, October 17, 1965; 280 p.

Alan Jay Lerner's fascination with the phenomenon of extrasensory perception (ESP) led to his teaming with composer Richard Rodgers in 1962 to write a musical called *I Picked a Daisy*. When that partnership failed to work out, Lerner turned to Burton Lane, and the show was retitled *On a Clear Day You Can See Forever*. Though Barbara Harris was the only actress ever considered for the female lead, at least six actors were announced for the male lead until it went to Louis Jordan — and *he* was replaced by John Cullum during the Boston tryout. The musical (the first with a top ticket price of $11.90) is concerned with Daisy Gamble who can predict the future and, when hypnotized by Dr. Mark Bruckner, can also recall her life as Melinda Wells in 18th Century London. When Mark's infatuation with Melinda makes her something of a rival to the real-life alter ego, Daisy runs away. In the end, however, his stirring plea "Come Back to Me" is so persuasive that the couple is reunited. The 1970 film version starred Barbra Streisand and Yves Montand.
RCA OC/ Random House (1966)/ TW.

On a Clear Day You Can See Forever. John Cullum and Barbara Harris. (Bert Andrews)

Man of La Mancha. Richard Kiley as Don Quixote. (Bob Golby)

MAN OF LA MANCHA

Music: Mitch Leigh
Lyrics: Joe Darion
Book: Dale Wasserman
Producers: Albert Selden & Hal James
Director: Albert Marre
Choreographer: Jack Cole
Cast: Richard Kiley, Joan Diener, Irving Jacobson, Ray Middleton, Robert Rounseville, Jon Cypher, Gerrianne Raphael
Songs: "Man of La Mancha"; "Dulcinea"; "I Really Like Him"; "Little Bird, Little Bird"; "To Each His Dulcinea"; "The Impossible Dream"; "Knight of the Woeful Countenance"
New York run: ANTA Washington Square Theater, November 22, 1965; 2,328 p.

When, in *Man of La Mancha,* the dauntless, demented Don Quixote proclaims his quest to dream the impossible dream, the words not only expressed the theme of the musical but they could also have applied to the production itself. Though it won acclaim off Broadway (the theatre in which it opened, on West 4th Street, is no longer standing) and on Broadway (when it was transferred to the Martin Beck in March 1968), the idea of a windmill-tilting old gaffer as hero of a musical hardly seemed a formula for a successful run. Nor was there any encouraging track record for the show's composer, lyricist, or librettist. In fact, after the musical first tried out at the Goodspeed Opera House in Connecticut, it was considered so special that it was deliberately unveiled in New York far from the theatre district. Yet after its run of five years seven months, *Man of La Mancha* went into the record books as the third longest running musical of the Sixties.

The idea of transforming Dale Wasserman's television play, *I, Don Quixote,* into a musical first occurred to director Albert Marre. Orignially, the score was to have been a collaboration between composer Mitch Leigh and co-lyricists W.H. Auden and Chester Kallman, and Michael Redgrave was announced for the role of the Don. The plot of *Man of La Mancha* unfolds as a story that novelist Miguel de Cervantes y Saavedra, imprisoned for debts during the Spanish Inquisition, tells to his fellow prisoners. In addition to Don Quixote, the major characters are the Don's faithful servant Sancho (Irving Jacobson) and the serving wench Aldonza (Joan Diener), whom the Don worships as the virginal Dulcinea and for whom he does battle to be worthy of knighthood. Though she scorns him for his foolishness, Aldonza is eventually won over — as the Don lays dying — to believing in his dream.

Richard Kiley gave his most celebrated performance as the Man of La Mancha, a role he relinquished during the run to José Ferrer, John Cullum, David Atkinson, Hal Holbrook, Bob Wright, Claudio Brook (from Mexico), Keith Michell (from England), Somegoro Ichikawa (from Japan), Charles West (from Australia), and Gideon Singer (from Israel). James Coco took over the small part of the Barber in 1966, and Joey Faye replaced Irving Jacobson as Sancho in 1968. The National Company toured for three years six months, with José Ferrer playing the original lead. In 1972, Kiley, Diener, and Jacobson were reunited when *Man of La Mancha* gave 140 performances at Lincoln Center's Vivian Beaumont Theatre. Kiley also played the Don in New York in 1977, heading a cast that included Emily Yancy and Tony Martinez, and remained for 124 performances. The 1972 screen version starred Peter O'Toole, Sophia Loren, and James Coco (as Sancho). Historic note: In 1889, Reginald De Koven and Harry B. Smith collaborated on an operetta based on the same story. Called *Don Quixote,* it was tried out in Chicago but never reached New York.

MCA OC/ Random House (1966); Chilton (1976)/ TW.

Sweet Charity. Gwen Verdon singing "If My Friends Could See Me Now." (Friedman-Abeles)

SWEET CHARITY

Music: Cy Coleman
Lyrics: Dorothy Fields
Book: Neil Simon
Producers: Robert Fryer, Lawrence Carr, Sylvia & Joseph Harris
Director-choreographer: Bob Fosse
Cast: Gwen Verdon, John McMartin, Helen Gallagher, Thelma Oliver, James Luisi, Ruth Buzzi, Barbara Sharma
Songs: "Big Spender"; "If My Friends Could See Me Now"; "There's Gotta Be Something Better Than This"; "The Rhythm of Life"; "Baby Dream Your Dreams"; "Sweet Charity"; "Where Am I Going?"; "I'm a Brass Band"
New York run: Palace Theatre, January 29, 1966; 608 p.

Charity Hope Valentine — with her heart not only on her sleeve but tattooed on her arm — is a New York taxi dancer who knows there's gotta be something better to do than work at the Fan-Dango Ballroom. She gets innocently involved with an Italian movie star (James Luisi), then seriously involved with straight-laced Oscar Lindquist (John McMartin) after they meet in a stuck elevator at the 92nd Street "Y." Though Oscar eventually asks Charity to be his wife, the revelation of her employment makes the union impossible, and when last seen Charity is still a girl who lives "hopefully ever after."

The play's heroine was brought touchingly to life by Gwen Verdon after Bob Fosse, her husband at the time, decided to adapt as well as direct a musical treatment of Federico Fellini's film *Nights of Cabiria.* Originally intended as the first half of a double bill of one-act musicals, *Sweet Charity* was fleshed out to two acts when Neil Simon took over the writing. The musical was also the first legitimate show to play the Palace, the legendary vaudeville mecca on Broadway at 47th Street. A revival was mounted in 1986 (see page 272), with Debbie Allen (succeeded by Ann Reinking) as Charity, and a 1969 screen version starred Shirley MacLaine. The 1973 musical *Seesaw,* also with songs by Coleman and Fields and a book (though uncredited) by Neil Simon, was another New York tale of an ill-matched too-trusting kook and a too-square guy.
Columbia OC; EMI OC (1986)/ Random House (1966)/ TW.

MAME

Music & lyrics: Jerry Herman
Book: Jerome Lawrence & Robert E. Lee
Producers: Robert Fryer, Lawrence Carr, Sylvia & Joseph Harris
Director: Gene Saks
Choreographer: Onna White
Cast: Angela Lansbury, Beatrice Arthur, Jane Connell, Willard Waterman, Frankie Michaels, Charles Braswell, Jerry Lanning
Songs: "It's Today"; "Open a New Window"; "My Best Girl"; "We Need a Little Christmas"; "Mame"; "Bosom Buddies"; "That's How Young I Feel"; "If He Walked Into My Life"
New York run: Winter Garden, May 24, 1966; 1,508 p.

Once Mary Martin had turned down the title role in *Mame,* some 40 other actresses had to be eliminated before the part went to Angela Lansbury — who quickly established herself as one of the reigning queens of Broadway. Her vehicle, the fifth longest running musical of the Sixties, was an adaptation of Patrick Dennis' novel, *Auntie Mame,* which had also been the basis of the 1954 play. The show's musical-comedy lineage, however, could be traced to *Hello, Dolly!,* since it again spotlighted an antic, middle-aged matchmaking widow, and it again had a bubbling score by Jerry Herman including another strutting title song.

Set mostly in and around Mame's home at 3 Beekman Place, New York, the tale covers the period from 1928 to 1946. Firmly dedicated to the credo that "Life is a banquet and most poor sons-of-bitches are starving to death," Mame Dennis brings up her orphaned nephew Patrick (Frankie Michaels) in an aggressively permissive atmosphere as she urges him to live life to the fullest by opening a new window every day. After being wiped out by the stock market crash, Mame lands a part in — and manages to ruin — a musical comedy starring her bosom buddy Vera Charles (Beatrice Arthur), then recoups her fortunes by marrying Southern aristocrat Beauregard Jackson Pickett Burnside (Charles Braswell). Even Beau's death climbing an Alp cannot deter the indomitable Mame, whose final triumph is steering Patrick out of the clutches of a birdbrained snob and into the arms of a more appropriate mate. During the Broadway run, Miss Lansbury was followed by Celeste Holm, Janis Paige, Jane Morgan, and Ann Miller. Heading the four road companies were, respectively, Miss Holm, Miss Lansbury, Susan Hayward, and Janet Blair. Miss Lansbury also starred in a 1983 Broadway revival which had a brief run. The 1974 Hollywood version found Miss Arthur repeating her original role in a cast headed by Lucille Ball and Robert Preston. Columbia OC/ Random House (1967)/ TW.

Mame. Bosom buddies Angela Lansbury and Beatrice Arthur. (Friedman-Abeles)

THE APPLE TREE

Music: Jerry Bock
Lyrics: Sheldon Harnick
Book: Jerry Bock & Sheldon Harnick, with Jerome Coopersmith
Producer: Stuart Ostrow
Director: Mike Nichols
Choreographers: Herbert Ross, Lee Theodore
Cast: Barbara Harris, Larry Blyden, Alan Alda, Carmen Alvarez, Robert Klein
Songs: "Here in Eden"; "Eve"; "Beautiful, Beautiful World"; "Go to Sleep, Whatever You Are"; "It's a Fish"; "What Makes Me Love Him"; "Oh, to Be a Movie Star"; "Gorgeous"
New York run: Shubert Theatre, October 18, 1966; 463 p.

While they were initially to have been linked by the unifying theme of man, woman, and the devil, the three one-act musicals that comprised *The Apple Tree* had nothing in common except for some subtle interrelated musical themes and a whimsical reference to the color brown. In Broadway's first — and so far only — musical triple bill, Act I was based on Mark Twain's "The Diary of Adam and Eve" and dealt with the dawn of humanity and innocence; Act II was based on Frank R. Stockton's short story "The Lady or the Tiger?," in which a warrior's fate, unresolved in the plot, was determined by the choice of door he enters; and Act III was based on Jules Feiffer's fantasy, "Passionella," about a poor chimney sweep who yearned to become — and did become — a moooooooooovie star. Though originally to have been directed by Gower Champion, *The Apple Tree* marked Mike Nichols' first association with a musical. Historic note: A full-length musical version of "The Lady or the Tiger?" was presented on Broadway in 1888 with DeWolf Hopper in the lead.
Columbia OC/ Random House (1967)/ MTI.

Cabaret. Lotte Lenya and Jack Gilford singing "It Couldn't Please Me More." (Friedman-Abeles)

Cabaret. "Willkommen, bienvenue, welcome," sings Joel Grey. (Friedman-Abeles)

CABARET

Music: John Kander
Lyrics: Fred Ebb
Book: Joe Masteroff
Producer-director: Harold Prince
Choreographer: Ron Field
Cast: Jill Haworth, Jack Gilford, Bert Convy, Lotte Lenya, Joel Grey, Peg Murray, Edward Winter
Songs: "Willkommen"; "Don't Tell Mama"; "Perfectly Marvelous"; "Two Ladies"; "It Couldn't Please Me More"; "Tomorrow Belongs to Me"; "The Money Song"; "Married"; "If You Could See Her"; "Cabaret"
New York run: Broadhurst Theatre, November 20, 1966; 1,165 p.

Claiming derivation from both Christopher Isherwood's *Berlin Stories* and John van Druten's 1951 dramatization, *I Am a Camera, Cabaret* turned a sleazy Berlin nightclub into a metaphor for the decadent world of pre-Hitler Germany, with the floorshow numbers used as commentaries on situations in the plot. At the Kit Kat Klub, where the epicene Master of Ceremonies (Joel Grey) bids one and all "Willkommen, bienvenue, welcome," the star attraction is the hedonistic British expatriate Sally Bowles (Jill Haworth), who also beckons customers with her own siren song to "Come to the cabaret, old chum." The main stories revolve around Sally's brief liaison with Clifford Bradshaw (Bert Convy), an American writer, and the more tragic romance between Fraulein Schneider (Lotte Lenya), a pragmatic landlady, and her Jewish suitor Herr Schultz (Jack Gilford). Helping to recreate the mood of a world in decay was the fluid direction of Harold Prince (it was his idea to add the Master of Ceremonies as a unifying symbol), a John Kander-Fred Ebb score that purposely evoked Kurt Weill, and the settings of Boris Aronson that recalled the paintings of George Grosz.

During the Broadway run, Miss Haworth was succeeded by Anita Gillette, Melissa Hart, and Tandy Cronyn. For the tour, which lasted one year seven months, the leads were taken by Miss Hart, Leo Fuchs (Schultz), Gene Rupert (Clifford), Signe Hasso (Fraulein), and Robert Salvio (MC). The 1972 film version retained Joel Grey (who also starred in the 1987 Broadway revival), but added Liza Minnelli, Michael York, Marisa Berenson, and a new story line.
Columbia OC/ Random House (1967); Chilton (1976)/ TW.

I Do! I Do! Robert Preston and Mary Martin.
(Friedman-Abeles)

I DO! I DO!

Music: Harvey Schmidt
Lyrics & book: Tom Jones
Producer: David Merrick
Director: Gower Champion
Cast: Mary Martin, Robert Preston
Songs: "I Love My Wife"; "My Cup Runneth Over"; "Love Isn't Everything"; "Nobody's Perfect"; "The Honeymoon Is Over"; "Where Are the Snows?"; "When the Kids Get Married"; "Someone Needs Me"; "Roll Up the Ribbons"
New York run: 46th Street Theatre, December 5, 1966; 560 p.

I Do! I Do! may have been the first Broadway musical ever to have a cast consisting entirely of two people, but since those people were Mary Martin and Robert Preston, no one could possibly have felt the need for anyone else on stage. In all other ways, however, the musical —which was adapted from Jan de Hartog's 1951 play, *The Fourposter* — was an ambitious undertaking, covering 50 years in the life of a married couple, Agnes and Michael, from their wedding day to the day they move out of their house. In between, they bring up a family, quarrel, threaten to break up, have a reconciliation, plan for a life without children in the house, and reveal in song exactly what they mean to each other. Apart from its stars, who were followed on Broadway by Carol Lawrence and Gordon MacRae, the production was especially noted for Gower Champion's inventive direction. A later musical with only two characters — but each with three alter egos — was the 1979 hit, *They're Playing Our Song.*
RCA OC/ MTI.

YOU'RE A GOOD MAN, CHARLIE BROWN

Music, lyrics & book: Clark Gesner
Producers: Arthur Whitelaw & Gene Persson
Director: Joseph Hardy
Choreographer: Patricia Birch
Cast: Bill Hinnant, Reva Rose, Karen Johnson, Bob Balaban, Skip Hinnant, Gary Burghoff
Songs: "You're a Good Man, Charlie Brown"; "My Blanket and Me"; "The Kite"; "Book Report"; "T.E.A.M. (The Baseball Game)"; "Little Known Facts"; "Suppertime"; "Happiness"
New York run: Theatre 80 St. Marks, March 7, 1967; 1,597 p.

With Charles Schultz's appealing comic strip "Peanuts" as general inspiration, Clark Gesner created a musical out of events in "a day made up of little moments picked from all the days of Charlie Brown, from Valentine's Day to the baseball season, from wild optimism to utter despair, all mixed with the lives of his friends (both human and non-human) and strung together on the string of a single day, from bright uncertain morning to hopeful starlit evening." The human characters, none supposedly older than six, include crabby, authoritarian Lucy (Reva Rose), music-loving Schroeder (Skip Hinnant), sweet and innocent Patty (Karen Johnson), blanket-hugging Linus (Bob Balaban), and perplexed, uncertain and eternally put-upon Charlie Brown himself (Gary Burghoff). The non-human character, of course, is Charlie Brown's highly imaginative pet dog Snoopy (Bill Hinnant), who likes to pretend that he's a World War I flying ace forever in search of the infamous Red Baron.

Gesner at first had no plans for his "Peanuts" songs other than as a recording, and initially MGM issued the album as part of its kiddie line. Producer Arthur Whitelaw, however, persuaded the writer to put together a theatrical concept, and he presented it at a tiny East Village theatre where it remained four years. Between 1967 and 1971, six road companies were performing throughout the United States. A second musical based on the "Peanuts" characters was *Snoopy,* written by Larry Grossman and Hal Hackaday. It opened Off Broadway in 1982 and ran for 152 performances. For other musicals taken from American comic strips, see *Li'l Abner*, page 171.
Polydor OC/ Random House (1967)/ TW.

You're a Good Man, Charlie Brown. Karen Johnson, Bob Balaban, Skip Hinnant, Reva Rose, Bill Hinnant, and Gary Burghoff. (Lawrence Belling)

YOUR OWN THING

Music & lyrics: Hal Hester & Danny Apolinar
Book: Donald Driver
Producers: Zev Bufman & Dorothy Love
Director: Donald Driver
Cast: Leland Palmer, Marian Mercer, Rusty Thacker, Tom Ligon, Danny Apolinar, Michael Valenti, John Kuhner
Songs: "The Flowers"; "I'm Me!"; "Come Away Death" (lyric: Shakespeare); "I'm on My Way to the Top"; "The Now Generation"; "The Middle Years"
New York run: Orpheum Theatre, January 13, 1968; 933 p.

An Off-Broadway musical of the Now, Me-Too and Let-It-All-Hang-Out Generation, *Your Own Thing* retold in contemporary style (accompanied by film and slide projections) the story of Shakespeare's *Twelfth Night* as it might apply to a twin brother and sister singing team (Tom Ligon and Leland Palmer) who are shipwrecked on Manhattan Island. Once the siblings split up, much confusion is caused when sister Viola disguises herself in male attire to join The Four Apocalypse, a rock group at a discotheque owned by Olivia (Marian Mercer). Thinking Viola a man, Olivia is attracted to her, but matters eventually get sorted out — Olivia happily settles for twin brother Sebastian and Viola wins Orson (Rusty Thacker), the group's manager. Coincidentally, shortly before *Your Own Thing* opened, another musical based on *Twelfth Night,* called *Love and Let Love,* began a brief Off-Broadway run. After it closed, Marcia Rodd, who played Olivia, took over the same part in *Your Own Thing.* Additional cast replacements were Raul Julia (Orson) and Sandy Duncan (Viola). For other musicals based on Shakespeare, see *The Boys from Syracuse,* page 107.
RCA OC/ Dell (1970)/ TW.

THE HAPPY TIME

Music: John Kander
Lyrics: Fred Ebb
Book: N. Richard Nash
Producer: David Merrick
Director-choreographer: Gower Champion
Cast: Robert Goulet, David Wayne, Mike Rupert, Julie Gregg, George S. Irving, Charles Durning
Songs: "The Happy Time"; "Tomorrow Morning"; "Please Stay"; "I Don't Remember You"; "The Life of the Party"; "Seeing Things"; "A Certain Girl"
New York run: Broadway Theatre, January 18, 1968; 286 p.

A gentle, nostalgic look at a French-Canadian family, *The Happy Time* was adapted from the novel by Robert Fontaine and the play by Samuel Taylor. The story is primarily concerned with the coming of age of Bibi Bonnard (Mike Rupert) and his desire to see the world with his Uncle Jacques (Robert Goulet), a footloose magazine photographer who has returned to his family for a brief visit. But Bibi's plans to run off with Jacques are opposed by the usually permissive Grandpère Bonnard (David Wayne) who manages — with Jacques' help — to convince Bibi to remain at home. The use of blow-up photographs to establish the mood for the various scenes was one of director Gower Champion's most effective touches. *The Happy Time* bore a certain resemblance to *110 in the Shade,* a previous musical by N. Richard Nash that had also been presented by David Merrick. That one also offered a smooth-talking visitor to a small town who excites the people's imagination, and leaves them with renewed appreciation of their own values.
RCA OC/ Dramatic Publ. Co. (1969)*/ DPC.

GEORGE M!

Music & lyrics: George M. Cohan
Book: Michael Stewart, John & Fran Pascal
Producers: David Black, Konrad Matthaei, Lorin Price
Director-choreographer: Joe Layton
Cast: Joel Grey, Betty Ann Grove, Jerry Dodge, Jill O'Hara, Bernadette Peters, Jamie Donnelly, Jacqueline Alloway, Loni Ackerman
Songs: "Musical Comedy Man"; "All Aboard for Broadway"; "My Town"; "Billie"; "Ring to the Name of Rose"; "Give My Regards to Broadway"; "Forty-Five Minutes from Broadway"; "So Long, Mary"; "Mary's a Grand Old Name"; "Yankee Doodle Dandy"; "Nellie Kelly, I Love You"; "Harrigan"; "Over There"; "You're a Grand Old Flag"
New York run: Palace Theatre, April 10, 1968; 427 p.

In this biographical musical celebrating the achievements of composer-lyricist-librettist-playwright-director-producer-actor-singer-dancer George M. Cohan, the story takes us from his birth in Providence, Rhode Island, in 1878, through his successes and failures and ends with his final Broadway triumph in 1937 playing President Roosevelt in *I'd Rather Be Right,* the only musical in which he appeared that he did not write himself. With Joel Grey as the pushy, not entirely sympathetic flag-waving hero, the show devoted its first-act finale to the reconstruction of the scene — familiar to anyone who has seen James Cagney in the movie *Yankee Doodle Dandy* — in which Cohan introduced "Give My Regards to Broadway" on the Southampton pier in *Little Johnny Jones.* For other show-business biographies see *Annie Get Your Gun*, page 130.
Columbia OC/ TW.

George M! Joel Grey strutting through "Give My Regards to Broadway." (Friedman-Abeles)

HAIR

Music: Galt MacDermot
Lyrics & book: Gerome Ragni & James Rado
Producer: Michael Butler
Director: Tom O'Horgan
Choreographer: Julie Arenal
Cast: Steve Curry, Ronald Dyson, Sally Eaton, Leata Galloway, Paul Jabara, Diane Keaton, Lynn Kellogg, Melba Moore, Shelley Plimpton, James Rado, Gerome Ragni, Lamont Washington
Songs: "Aquarius"; "Manchester England"; "Ain't Got No"; "I Got Life"; "Hair"; "Frank Mills"; "Hare Krishna"; "Where Do I Go?"; "Easy to Be Hard"; "Good Morning Starshine"; "Let the Sunshine In"
New York run: Biltmore Theatre, April 29, 1968; 1,750 p.

As much a product of its time as *Pins and Needles* and *This Is the Army* were of theirs, *Hair* grew out of the emotional turmoil of the Vietnam War years with its concomitant anti-establishment movement that produced a generation of drug-influenced, sex-obsessed social dropouts. With barely a discernable story line, this loosely structured musical celebrated the untethered lifestyle of hippies and flower children who welcomed the dawning of the Age of Aquarius by opposing the draft, the work ethic, and accepted standards of behavior and dress.

The "American Tribal Love-Rock Musical" (as it was billed) was first presented on October 29, 1967 under the direction of Gerald Freedman at Joseph Papp's New York Shakespeare Festival Public Theatre near Astor Place. At a $2.50 ticket price, it remained for about a month and a half, then moved to a Broadway nightclub called Cheetah. At that point, Michael Butler, a fledgling producer, took over the show for a Broadway run at the Biltmore Theatre (on 47th Street west of Broadway). Butler had it restaged by Tom O'Horgan, rechoreographed, redesigned, recostumed, relighted, and reorchestrated, and there were cast changes such as Lynn Kellogg for Jill O'Hara, Melba Moore for Jonelle Allen, and coauthor James Rado for Walker Daniels in the role of a draftee who spends his last civilian hours with a tribe of hippies. During its run — the fourth longest of a musical during the Sixties — *Hair* achieved something of a Broadway breakthrough by ending the first act in semi-darkness with the entire cast totally starkers. At one time, seven road companies were touring the United States. In 1977, Butler revived the musical but this time it ran only a month. The 1979 film version had a cast headed by John Savage, Treat Williams, and Beverly D'Angelo.

RCA OC (1967); RCA OC (1968)/ Pocket Books (1969); Stein & Day (1979)/ TW.

Hair. James Rado and Gerome Ragni. (Dagmar)

Zorba. Maria Karnilova and Herschel Bernardi in the "Y'assou" number. (Friedman-Abeles)

ZORBA

Music: John Kander
Lyrics: Fred Ebb
Book: Joseph Stein
Producer-director: Harold Prince
Choreographer: Ron Field
Cast: Herschel Bernardi, Maria Karnilova, John Cunningham, Carmen Alvarez, Lorraine Serabian, James Luisi
Songs: "Life Is"; "The First Time"; "The Top of the Hill"; "No Boom Boom"; "The Butterfly"; "Only Love"; "Y'assou"; "Happy Birthday"; "I Am Free"
New York run: Imperial Theatre, November 17, 1968; 305 p.

Although it reunited the *Cabaret* team of composer John Kander, lyricist Fred Ebb, and producer-director Harold Prince, *Zorba* was more of an Aegean counterpart to *Fiddler on the Roof,* with its larger-than-life aging hero and its stageful of earthy, ethnic types. It also had the same producer, librettist, set designer (Boris Aronson), and costume designer (Patricia Zipprodt), and its leading roles were played by two *Fiddler* alumni, Herschel Bernardi and Maria Karnilova. The story, however, was far grimmer, and the people of Crete a colder, more menacing lot than the colorful villagers of Anatevka. The tale involves the ebulient Zorba (Bernardi) with a studious young man named Nikos (John Cunningham) who has inherited an abandoned mine on the island of Crete. This sets off a series of tragic events, including the suicide of a Cretan youth out of unrequited love for a young Widow (Carmen Alvarez), the vengeful murder of the Widow by the youth's family, the discovery that the mine is inoperable, and the death of Hortense (Maria Karnilova), a coquettish French cocotte in love with Zorba. Nothing, however, can dampen Zorba's lust for life and his determination to live it to the fullest.

The production, the first to charge $15 for Saturday night orchestra seats, was based on Nikos Kazantzakis's novel *Zorba the Greek,* which became a 1964 movie with Anthony Quinn and Lila Kedrova, directed by Michael Cacoyannis. Cacoyannis also directed Quinn and Kedrova in a new production of the musical in 1983. It began its cross-country tour early in the year, had a longer Broadway run than the original, then toured again through July 1986. (See page 268.) Capitol OC; RCA OC (1983)/ Random House (1969)/ SF.

PROMISES, PROMISES

Music: Burt Bacharach
Lyrics: Hal David
Book: Neil Simon
Producer: David Merrick
Director: Robert Moore
Choreographer: Michael Bennett
Cast: Jerry Orbach, Jill O'Hara, Edward Winter, Norman Shelly, A. Larry Haines, Marian Mercer, Ken Howard, Donna McKechnie
Songs: "You'll Think of Someone"; "She Likes Basketball"; "Knowing When to Leave"; "Wanting Things"; "Whoever You Are"; "A Young Pretty Girl Like You"; "I'll Never Fall in Love Again"; "Promises, Promises"
New York run: Shubert Theatre, December 1, 1968; 1,281 p.

Two of the most successful pop song writers of the mid-Sixties, Burt Bacharach and Hal David, made a worthy — and so far only — contribution to the Broadway theatre with their score for *Promises, Promises*. Adapted from the 1960 movie, *The Apartment*, the musical followed such other recent offerings as *How to Succeed in Business Without Really Trying, I Can Get It for You Wholesale,* and *What Makes Sammy Run?* by revealing yet another method of getting ahead in the business world. Chuck Baxter (Jerry Orbach), the faceless hero of *Promises, Promises,* does it simply by lending his apartment to various executives of Consolidated Life for their extramarital dalliances. Among them is J.D. Sheldrake (Edward Winter) whose paramour, Fran Kubelik (Jill O'Hara), just happens to be the girl beloved by Chuck. Fran eventually reciprocates his feeling when he rescues her from a suicide attempt after J.D. decides to go back to his wife.

During the Broadway run, Orbach was succeeded by Tony Roberts, Miss O'Hara by Jenny O'Hara (her sister) and Lorna Luft. Roberts and Melissa Hart headed the road company which toured for 14 months.
United Artists OC/ Random House (1969)/ TW.

DAMES AT SEA

Music: Jim Wise
Lyrics & book: George Haimsohn & Robin Miller
Producers: Jordan Hott & Jack Millstein
Director-choreographer: Neal Kenyon
Cast: Bernadette Peters, David Christmas, Steve Elmore, Tamara Long
Songs: "It's You"; "That Mister Man of Mine"; "Choo-Choo Honeymoon"; "The Sailor of My Dreams"; "Good Times Are Here to Stay"; "Dames at Sea"; "Raining in My Heart"; "Singapore Sue"; "Star Tar"
New York run: Bouwerie Lane Theatre, December 20, 1968; 575 p.

Dames at Sea, an affectionate spoof of early Hollywood musicals, was inspired in part by the same 1933 backstage movie on which the more elaborate *42nd Street* was later based. In this imaginative six-character show, Ruby (Bernadette Peters), a sweet young thing fresh from Centerville, Utah, lands a job in the chorus of a Broadway-bound musical, *Dames at Sea,* meets sailor-songwriter Dick (David Christmas), and . . . well, you know what happens. One switch, though, is that because the musical in preparation loses its theatre and must be performed on the deck of a battleship, Ruby gets her big break when the star (Tamara Long) can't go on because she's seasick. During the run, Miss Peters was succeeded by Pia Zadora, Bonnie Franklin, Barbara Sharma, and Loni Ackerman. The musical, which returned for an additional 170 performances at the Plaza 9 Music Hall in the Plaza Hotel, was revived Off Broadway in 1985.
Columbia OC/ Samuel French (1969)*/ SF.

1776

Music & lyrics: Sherman Edwards
Book: Peter Stone
Producer: Stuart Ostrow
Director: Peter Hunt
Choreographer: Onna White
Cast: William Daniels, Howard Da Silva, Paul Hecht, Clifford David, Ken Howard, Virginia Vestoff, Ronald Holgate, Betty Buckley
Songs: "Sit Down, John"; "The Lees of Old Virginia"; "But Mr. Adams"; "He Plays the Violin"; "Cool, Cool, Considerate Men"; "Momma Look Sharp"; "The Egg"; "Molasses to Rum"; "Is Anybody There?"
New York run: 46th Street Theatre, March 16, 1969; 1,217 p.

After researching the project for seven years, Sherman Edwards took two-and-a-half years to write the songs and the libretto for a musical history lesson about the signing of the Declaration of Independence. During preparations, however, the more experienced librettist Peter Stone was brought in. Sticking to the actual events with as much fidelity as possible, Edwards and Stone concentrated their musical on the debates, intrigues, and compromises involving the delegates to the second Continental Congress that met for three stifling summer months in Philadelphia to produce the historic document. Major figures in the production were such advocates of independence as John Adams of Massachusetts (William Daniels), Benjamin Franklin of Pennsylvania (Howard Da Silva), Thomas Jefferson (Ken Howard) and Richard Henry Lee (Ronald Holgate) both of Virginia, and such opponents as John Dickinson of Pennsylvania (Paul Hecht) and Edward Rutledge of South Carolina (Clifford David). Although the writers based their work on historical fact, they did take such liberties as having the debate on the wording of the Declaration occur before, not after, the actual vote for independence. Also altered was the signing of the document, which actually took many months to complete but which — for dramatic effectiveness — was made to take place on the 4th of July, the day the Declaration was proclaimed.

1776 was the only musical by Sherman Edwards, who died in 1981. During the Broadway engagement, Daniels was succeeded by John Cunningham, Da Silva by Jay Garner, and David by John Cullum. The touring company, which traveled for two years two months, included Patrick Bedford (Adams), Rex Everhart (Franklin), George Hearn (Dickinson), and Jon Cypher (Jefferson). Daniels, Da Silva, Howard, and Holgate were also in the 1972 screen version. For other musicals about the American Revolution, see *Dearest Enemy,* page 48.
Columbia OC/ Viking (1969); Chilton (1973)/ MTI.

1776. William Daniels, Howard Da Silva, Betty Buckley, and Ken Howard. (Martha Swope)

PURLIE

Music: Gary Geld
Lyrics: Peter Udell
Book: Ossie Davis, Philip Rose, Peter Udell
Producer-director: Philip Rose
Choreographer: Louis Johnson
Cast: Cleavon Little, Melba Moore, John Heffernan, Sherman Hemsley, Novella Nelson, George Faison
Songs: "Walk Him Up the Stairs"; "New Fangled Preacher Man"; "Purlie"; "Skinnin' a Cat"; "I Got Love"; "First Thing Monday Mornin' "
New York run: Broadway Theatre, March 15, 1970: 688 p.

With little ballyhoo, *Purlie* opened on Broadway to generally favorable notices and enthusiastic audiences, and became the sleeper hit of the season. The musical was adapted from the 1961 play *Purlie Victorious,* a folkish satire on racial stereotypes written by co-librettist Ossie Davis, and is concerned with the efforts of a self-styled new-fangled preacher man (Cleavon Little) to buy the Big Bethel Church in a rural Georgia town. This puts Purlie in confrontation with the bigoted plantation owner, Cap'n Cotchipee (John Heffernan), who also wants the church. Eventually, of course, the Cap'n is outsmarted and Purlie emerges victorious with both his church and his new wife Lutiebelle (Melba Moore). Robert Guillaume, who succeeded Cleavon Little during the Broadway run, toured in the musical which returned briefly to New York at the end of 1972.
Ampex OC/ Samuel French (1971)*/ SF.

APPLAUSE

Music: Charles Strouse
Lyrics: Lee Adams
Book: Betty Comden & Adolph Green
Producers: Joseph Kipness & Lawrence Kasha
Director-choreographer: Ron Field
Cast: Lauren Bacall, Len Cariou, Robert Mandan, Ann Williams, Brandon Maggart, Penny Fuller, Lee Roy Reams, Bonnie Franklin
Songs: "Think How It's Gonna Be"; "But Alive"; "Who's That Girl?"; "Applause"; "Fasten Your Seat Belts"; "Welcome to the Theatre"; "One of a Kind"; "Something Greater"
New York run: Palace Theatre, March 30, 1970; 896 p.

It took only one Broadway musical for Lauren Bacall to join the roster of powerhouse female stars who have won distinction in the theatre. And she did it by appearing as another powerhouse female star, Margo Channing, in a musical version of the 1950 movie, *All About Eve.* The genesis of *Applause* took place in 1966 when Charles Strouse and Lee Adams were signed to create the score. Miss Bacall agreed to be in the show two years later, but it was not until early 1969 that the original librettist was replaced by Betty Comden and Adolph Green. The ambitions, tensions, insecurities, loyalties, and disloyalties of the theatre were exposed in a somewhat farfetched tale in which theatre doyenne Margo Channing befriends an adoring fan, Eve Harrington (Penny Fuller), who promptly schemes to take over her part, her man, and anything else needed to help Eve's career. Though Margo is not a musical-comedy star, thereby eliminating show-within-a-show numbers, Ron Field found opportunities for dance routines in such hangouts as a Greenwich Village gay bar and Joe Allen's restaurant. During the Broadway run, the leading role was assumed by Anne Baxter (Eve in the movie) and Arlene Dahl.
MCA OC/ Random House (1971); Chilton (1976)/ TW.

COMPANY

Music & lyrics: Stephen Sondheim
Book: George Furth
Producer-director: Harold Prince
Choreographer: Michael Bennett
Cast: Dean Jones, Elaine Stritch, Barbara Barrie, John Cunningham, Charles Kimbrough, Donna McKechnie, Charles Braswell, Susan Browning, Steve Elmore, Beth Howland, Pamela Myers, Merle Louise
Songs: "Company"; "The Little Things You Do Together"; "Sorry-Grateful"; "You Could Drive a Person Crazy"; "Someone Is Waiting"; "Another Hundred People"; "Getting Married Today"; "What Would We Do Without You?"; "Barcelona"; "The Ladies who Lunch"; "Being Alive"
New York run: Alvin Theatre, April 26, 1970: 706 p.

Company was the first of six Broadway musicals created by the most influential and daring team of the Seventies, composer-lyricist Stephen Sondheim and director Harold Prince. In putting this work together they avoided the conventional dramatic structure of the linear story by using five separate stories dealing with marriage that were held together by a single character who influences and is influenced by his "good and crazy" married friends. Moreover, it was a bold example of the concept musical — in which the style of telling is as important as what is being told — with songs used as commentaries on the situations and characters, and the actors performing in a cage-like skeletal setting (by Boris Aronson) that made use of stairways, an elevator, and projections.

Initially, *Company* was a collection of 11 one-act plays by George Furth. Prince, however, saw it as a musical reflecting how life in a big city influences various couples, and Furth then revised three of the plays and added two others. The character of the bachelor Robert was brought in to connect the episodes, with the occasion of his 35th birthday party used as a framework. While the couples are less than idyllically happy — they fight, make plans to divorce, smoke pot, drink too much — the general philosophy, summed up in Robert's closing solo "Being Alive," is that it's better to be married than single.

Because of illness, Dean Jones, the original Robert, was replaced by Larry Kert within a month after the Broadway opening. During the run, Elaine Stritch, as a middle-aged guzzler who has the sardonic show-stopper "The Ladies who Lunch," was succeeded by Jane Russell and Vivian Blaine. The show's year-long tour had a cast headed by George Chakiris and Miss Stritch.
Columbia OC/ Random House (1970); Chilton (1973)/ MTI.

Company. Susan Browning, Donna McKechnie, and Pamela Myers. (Martha Swope)

229

The Rothschilds. Hal Linden as Mayer Rothschild. (Martha Swope)

THE ROTHSCHILDS

Music: Jerry Bock
Lyrics: Sheldon Harnick
Book: Sherman Yellen
Producers: Lester Osterman & Hillard Elkins
Director-choreographer: Michael Kidd
Cast: Hal Linden, Paul Hecht, Leila Martin, Keene Curtis, Jill Clayburgh, Chris Sarandon
Songs: ''One Room''; ''He Tossed a Coin''; ''Sons''; ''Rothschild and Sons'';
''I'm in Love! I'm in Love!''; ''In My Own Lifetime''
New York run: Lunt-Fontanne Theatre, October 19, 1970; 507 p.

Adapted from Frederic Morton's best-selling account of the rise of the international banking family, *The Rothschilds* had several points of similarity with *Fiddler on the Roof.* Its songs were written by the same team, Jerry Bock and Sheldon Harnick (it was their seventh and last work together), the subject matter also concerned the struggle of European Jews to live in an oppressive world, and it even substituted a family of five sons for a family of five daughters. But unlike their poor Anatevka relatives, the Rothschilds did manage to escape the bonds of the Frankfort ghetto and, led by Mayer Rothschild (Hal Linden), work their way up to a position of wealth and affluence all over Europe. Actually, Bock and Harnick had been offered the story while they were still working on *Fiddler,* and it wasn't until some time later, when the musical had a new libretto by Sherman Yellen, that they felt it was sufficiently strong enough to withstand inevitable comparisons.
Columbia OC/ SF.

NO, NO, NANETTE

Music: Vincent Youmans
Lyrics: Irving Caesar
Book: Burt Shevelove
Producer: Pyxidium Ltd. (Cyma Rubin)
Director: Burt Shevelove
Choreographer: Donald Saddler
Cast: Ruby Keeler, Jack Gilford, Bobby Van, Helen Gallagher, Patsy Kelly, Susan Watson, Roger Rathburn, Loni Ackerman
Songs: Same as original production, plus "I've Confessed to the Breeze" (lyric: Otto Harbach); "Take a Little One-Step" (lyric: Zelda Sears)
New York run: 46th Street Theatre, January 19, 1971; 861 p.

(See page 47.)

No, No, Nanette. Helen Gallagher and Bobby Van dancing to "You Can Dance With Any Girl at All." (Friedman-Abeles)

Follies. Alexis Smith singing "Could I Leave You?" (Martha Swope)

FOLLIES

Music & lyrics: Stephen Sondheim
Book: James Goldman
Producer: Harold Prince
Directors: Harold Prince & Michael Bennett
Choreographer: Michael Bennett
Cast: Alexis Smith, Gene Nelson, Dorothy Collins, John McMartin, Yvonne DeCarlo, Fifi D'Orsay, Mary McCarty, Ethel Shutta, Arnold Moss, Ethel Barrymore Colt, Michael Bartlett, Sheila Smith, Justine Johnston, Virginia Sandifur, Kurt Peterson, Victoria Mallory, Marti Rolph
Songs: "Waiting for the Girls Upstairs"; "Ah, Paris!"; "Broadway Baby"; "The Road You Didn't Take"; "In Buddy's Eyes"; "Who's That Woman?"; "I'm Still Here"; "Too Many Mornings"; "The Right Girl"; "Could I Leave You?"; "Losing My Mind"; "The Story of Lucy and Jessie"
New York run: Winter Garden, April 4, 1971; 522 p.

Taking place at a reunion of performers who had appeared in various editions of the *Weismann Follies* (a fictitious counterpart of the Ziegfeld revue), the musical dealt with the reality of life as contrasted with the unreality of the theatre, a theme it explored principally through the lives of two couples, the upper-class, unhappy Phyllis and Ben Stone (Alexis Smith and John McMartin) and the middle-class, unhappy Sally and Buddy Plummer (Dorothy Collins and Gene Nelson). The second of the Stephen Sondheim-Harold Prince musicals, *Follies* also depicted these couples as they were in their youth, a flashback device that prompted the composer to come up with songs purposely reminiscent of the styles of some of the theatre's great songwriters of the past. In 1985, a highly acclaimed all-star concert version was staged at Avery Fisher Hall. The musical bore a certain kinship with *Company,* which also was about jaded, ambivalent characters, took a disenchanted view of marriage, and used the structural device of a party to bring a group of people together.

Capitol OC; RCA OC (1985)/Random House (1971)/ MTI.

GODSPELL

Music & lyrics: Stephen Schwartz
Book: John-Michael Tebelak
Producers: Edgar Lansbury, Stuart Duncan, Joseph Beruh
Director: John-Michael Tebelak
Cast: Lamar Alford, David Haskell, Johanne Jonas, Robin Lamont, Sonia Manzano, Jeffrey Mylett, Stephen Nathan
Songs: "Prepare Ye the Way of the Lord"; "Save the People"; "Day by Day"; "All for the Best"; "All Good Gifts"; "Light of the World"; "Turn Back, O Man"; "We Beseech Thee"; "On the Willows"
New York run: Cherry Lane Theatre, May 17, 1971; 2,651 p.

The Seventies brought the Bible to the New York musical stage. Genesis supplied the source of both *Two by Two* (Noah and the Ark) in 1970 and *Joseph and the Amazing Technicolor Dreamcoat* in 1976 (performed at the Brooklyn Academy of Music); the Gospel According to St. Matthew was the origin of *Godspell* in 1971, *Jesus Christ Superstar* also in 1971, and *Your Arms Too Short to Box With God* in 1976. *Godspell* was a whimsical retelling of the last seven days of Christ, with Jesus in clownlike makeup sporting a superman "S" on his shirt; his disciples dressed like flower children; and the parables enacted in a frolicsome, contemporary manner. The work was first shown in nonmusical form as a workshop production at Café La Mama. When it was decided to turn *Godspell* into a musical, songs were then added by Stephen Schwartz. The show was presented in a Greenwich Village theatre for three months, then moved to the Promenade (on Broadway and 76th Street) for a total run of 2,124 performances, making it currently the fourth longest running Off-Broadway musical. The show's official "on" Broadway opening took place June 22, 1976, at the Broadhurst, where it ran for 527 performances. At one time there were seven road companies touring the United States. *Godspell* was revived in 1988 and gave 248 Off-Broadway performances. The film version, released in 1973, featured Victor Garber and David Haskell.
Arista OC/ TM.

JESUS CHRIST SUPERSTAR

Music: Andrew Lloyd Webber
Lyrics: Tim Rice
Conception: Tom O'Horgan
Producer: Robert Stigwood
Director: Tom O'Horgan
Cast: Jeff Fenholt, Yvonne Elliman, Ben Vereen, Barry Dennen, Anita Morris
Songs: "Heaven on Their Minds"; "What's the Buzz?"; "Everything's Alright"; "I Don't Know How to Love Him"; "King Herod's Song"; "Could We Start Again, Please?"; "Superstar"
New York run: Mark Hellinger Theatre, October 12, 1971; 720 p.

Even though conceived as a theatre work, *Jesus Christ Superstar* appeared as a record before being presented on the stage because composer Andrew Lloyd Webber and lyricist Tim Rice were unable to find a producer willing to take a chance on so daring a production. Once it became a Gold Record album, however, the path was smoothed for its Broadway premiere. The self-described "rock opera" retold the last seven days of Christ in such a flamboyant, campy, and mind-blowing fashion that despite a mixed press and the opposition from various religious groups the show became a media hype and a boxoffice hit. The movie version was released in 1973 with Ted Neeley and Carl Anderson.
MCA OC/ Stein & Day (1979)/ MTI.

TWO GENTLEMEN OF VERONA

Music: Galt MacDermot
Lyrics: John Guare
Book: John Guare & Mel Shapiro
Producer: Joseph Papp for the New York Shakespeare Festival
Director: Mel Shapiro
Choreographer: Jean Erdman
Cast: Jonelle Allen, Diana Davila, Clifton Davis, Raul Julia, Norman Matlock, Alix Elias, John Bottoms, Stockard Channing
Songs: "Follow the Rainbow"; "Bring All the Boys Back Home"; "Night Letter"; "Who Is Silvia?" (lyric: Shakespeare); "Calla Lily Lady"
New York run: St. James Theatre, December 1, 1971; 627 p.

Two Gentlemen of Verona was originally scheduled to be presented without songs as part of the New York Shakespeare Festival's series of free productions in Central Park. At the recommendation of director Mel Shapiro, a rock score was added to help give the modern adaptation of the play the proper contemporary flavor. The show proved so popular in its open-air presentation in the Summer of 1971 that it was transferred to Broadway, where its blend of anachronistic colloquialisms, ethnic references, and the Bard's own words (the song "Who Is Silvia?" uses the original text) won a receptive audience. The story spins the tale of two Veronese friends, the noble Valentine (Clifton Davis) and the ignoble Proteus (Raul Julia), whose adventures in Milan are complicated by Julia (Diana Davila), who loves Proteus, and Silvia (Jonelle Allen), who Loves Valentine. For other musicals based on Shakespeare, see *The Boys from Syracuse,* page 107. ABC OC/ Holt, Rinehart (1971); Stein & Day (1979)/ TW.

GREASE

Music, lyrics & book: Jim Jacobs & Warren Casey
Producers: Kenneth Waissman & Maxine Fox
Director: Tom Moore
Choreographer: Patricia Birch
Cast: Adrienne Barbeau, Barry Bostwick, Carole Demas, Timothy Meyers
Songs: "Summer Nights"; "Freddy, My Love"; "Greased Lightnin' "; "Mooning"; "Look at Me, I'm Sandra Dee"; "We Go Together"; "It's Raining on Prom Night"; "Beauty School Dropout"; "Alone at a Drive-In Movie"; "There Are Worse Things I Could Do"
New York run: Eden Theatre, February 14, 1972; 3,388 p.

A surprise runaway hit, *Grease* opened at the Off-Broadway Eden Theatre (formerly the Phoenix), then moved on Broadway to the Broadhurst and then the Royale. And there it remained until April 13, 1980, for a record run that was not overtaken until *A Chorus Line* danced past the mark. The show, which began life as a five-hour amateur production in a Chicago trolley barn, took a satirically on-target view of the dress, manners, morals, and music of teenagers at the beginning of the rock and roll era. Set in the fictitious Rydell High School in Chicago, it is chiefly concerned with the attraction between greaser Danny Zuko (Barry Bostwick) and prim and proper Sandy Dumbrowski (Carole Demas), who eventually learns that there is little virtue in virtue. Mocking individuality and championing conformity, the musical hit a responsive chord in youthful audiences that could identify with teenagers having little on their minds except hanging out and making out. On Broadway, Danny was played by nine actors including Treat Williams. John Travolta, who was Danny in the 1978 movie opposite Olivia Newton-John, played Doody in the first of three touring companies.
Polydor OC/ Pocket Books (1972); Stein & Day (1979)/ SF.

SUGAR

Music: Jule Styne
Lyrics: Bob Merrill
Book: Peter Stone
Producer: David Merrick
Director-choreographer: Gower Champion
Cast: Robert Morse, Tony Roberts, Cyril Ritchard, Elaine Joyce, Sheila Smith, Steve Condos, Pamela Blair
Songs: "Sun on My Face"; "Sugar"; "What Do You Give to a Man Who's Had Everything?"; "When You Meet a Man in Chicago"
New York run: Majestic Theatre, April 9, 1972; 505 p.

Given the creative talents involved and the fact that it was based on the popular 1959 movie *Some Like It Hot, Sugar* might have been expected to be a more distinguised offering than it was. But there was so much dissention during the show's preparations (at one point the composer, lyricist and librettist were all threatened with replacement) that it was something of a miracle that the musical did turn out to be both entertaining and profitable. In the farcical story, set in 1931, Robert Morse and Tony Roberts played two dance-band musicians who witness the St. Valentine's Day gangland massacre in Chicago. They manage to escape from Spats Palazzo's thugs by disguising themselves as members of an all-girl orchestra, Sweet Sue and Her Society Syncopaters, which takes them to Miami for a series of romantic complications resulting when boys are mistaken for girls. Elaine Joyce appeared as Sugar Kane, the part immortalized on the screen by Marilyn Monroe.
United Artists OC/ TW.

DON'T BOTHER ME, I CAN'T COPE

Music & lyrics: Micki Grant
Conception: Vinnette Carroll
Producers: Edward Padula & Arch Lustberg
Director: Vinnette Carroll
Choreographer: George Faison
Cast: Alex Bradford, Hope Clarke, Micki Grant, Bobby Hill, Arnold Wilkerson
Songs: "Don't Bother Me, I Can't Cope"; "Fighting for Pharaoh"; "Good Vibrations"; "It Takes a Whole Lot of Human Feeling"; "Thank Heaven for You"
New York run: Playhouse Theatre, April 19, 1972; 1,065 p.

A generally good-humored look at the social problems faced by black people today, *Don't Bother Me, I Can't Cope* was essentially a procession of musical numbers, both sung and danced, based on gospel, rock, calypso, and folk music. The show originated as a workshop project of Vinnette Carroll's Urban Arts Corps Theatre, after which it made appearances in Washington, Philadelphia, and Detroit before opening in New York at the Playhouse Theatre (on 48th Street east of 7th Avenue). Though stressing black pride and dignity, this "Musical Entertainment" still found room for some tongue-in-cheek self kidding which helped give it a broad enough appeal to keep it running on Broadway for two and one-half years.
Polydor OC/ Samuel French (1972)*/ SF.

Pippin. Ben Vereen, flanked by Ann Reinking and Candy Brown, in the "Magic to Do" number. (Martha Swope)

PIPPIN

Music & lyrics: Stephen Schwartz
Book: Roger O. Hirson (Bob Fosse uncredited)
Producer: Stuart Ostrow
Director-choreographer: Bob Fosse
Cast: Eric Berry, Jill Clayburgh, Leland Palmer, Irene Ryan, Ben Vereen, John Rubinstein, Ann Reinking
Songs: "Magic to Do"; "Corner of the Sky"; "Simple Joys"; "No Time at All"; "Morning Glow"; "On the Right Track"; "Kind of Woman"; "Extraordinary"; "Love Song"
New York run: Imperial Theatre, October 23, 1972; 1,944 p.

Stephen Schwartz collaborated on the original version of *Pippin* — called *Pippin Pippin* — when he was still a student at Carnegie Tech, but it was not until the success of *Godspell* that a producer was willing to take a chance on him or his work. As insurance, however, Stuart Ostrow brought in playwright Roger O. Hirson to rewrite the book and, most signifcantly, Bob Fosse to serve as director-choreographer. Fosse, also the uncredited co-librettist, put his conceptual stamp on the musical by expanding it into a razzle-dazzle magic show within the framework of a *commedia dell'arte* performance. Helping to give the production a unifying concept was another Fosse touch, the half-God half-Devil Leading Player (Ben Vereen), a character developed from the Master of Ceremonies in *Cabaret*.

In the tale, Pippin (John Rubinstein), the son of Charlemagne (Eric Berry), is a Candide-like figure seeking glory first in war, then as a lover, and finally as a leader of social causes. After failing at all three, he is happy to compromise by settling down to middle-class domesticity with a widow named Catherine (Jill Clayburgh). During the Broadway run — the fourth longest of the decade — Betty Buckley succeeded Miss Clayburgh, and Dorothy Stickney took over as the fifth actress to play Berthe, Pippin's grandmother, whose showstopper was the vaudeville sing-along, "No Time at All." Two road companies toured in *Pippin,* the second of which traveled a full year.

Motown OC/ Drama Book Specialists (1975)/ MTI.

A LITTLE NIGHT MUSIC

Music & lyrics: Stephen Sondheim
Book: Hugh Wheeler
Producer-director: Harold Prince
Choreographer: Patricia Birch
Cast: Glynis Johns, Len Cariou, Hermione Gingold, Victoria Mallory, Laurence Guittard, Patricia Elliott, Mark Lambert, D. Jamin-Bartlett, George Lee Andrews
Songs: "Night Waltz"; "The Glamorous Life"; "Remember?"; "You Must Meet My Wife"; "Liaisons"; "In Praise of Women"; "Every Day a Little Death"; "A Weekend in the Country"; "It Would Have Been Wonderful"; "Send in the Clowns"; "The Miller's Son"
New York run: Shubert Theatre, February 25, 1973; 600 p.

Not Mozart's K. 525 but Ingmar Bergmen's 1955 film *Sommarnattens Leende (Smiles of a Summer Night)* was the inspiration for *A Little Night Music,* which offered a wry, witty view of a group of men and women from the standpoints of age and social position. The work claimed two musical innovations: the entire Stephen Sondheim score was composed in 3/4 time (or multiples thereof) and it had an overture sung by a quintet (whose members reappeared throughout the evening in the manner of a Greek chorus). Is also contained, in "Send in the Clowns," the best known song the composer has written to date.

Taking place in Sweden at the turn of the century, the story deals with the complicated romantic world of a middle-aged lawyer, Fredrik Egerman (Len Cariou); his virginal child-bride Anne (Victoria Mallory); his con Henrik (Mark Lambert), who is in love with Anne; his former mistress,.the actress Desirée Armfeldt (Glynis Johns); Desirée's current lover, the vain, aristocratic Count Carl-Magnus Malcolm (Laurence Guittard); and the count's suicidal wife, Charlotte (Patricia Elliott). The proper partners are paired off at a weekend at the country house of Desirée's mother (Hermoine Gingoid), a former concubine of assorted members of the nobility. The musical toured for a year with Jean Simmons, Margaret Hamilton, and George Lee Andrews. It was added to the repertory of the New York City Opera in 1990. A film version, released in 1978, co-starred Elizabeth Taylor, Len Cariou, Diana Rigg, and Hermione Gingold.
Columbia OC/Dodd, Mead (1973); Chilton (1976)/MTI.

A Little Night Music. Len Cariou and Glynis Johns. (Martha Swope)

Irene. Debbie Reynolds and Patsy Kelly singing "Mother, Angel, Darling." (Friedman-Abeles)

IRENE

Music: Harry Tierney, etc.
Lyrics: Joseph McCarthy, etc.
Book: Joseph Stein, Hugh Wheeler, Harry Rigby
Producers: Harry Rigby, Albert Selden, Jerome Minskoff
Director: Gower Champion
Choreographer: Peter Gennaro
Cast: Debbie Reynolds, Patsy Kelly, George S. Irving, Monte Markham, Ruth Warrick, Janie Sell, Carmen Alvarez
Songs: "Alice Blue Gown"; "They Go Wild, Simply Wild Over Me" (music: Fred Fisher); "Mother, Angel, Darling" (Charles Gaynor); "The Last Part of Ev'ry Party"; "Irene"; "You Made Me Love You" (music: James Monaco); "I'm Always Chasing Rainbows"(music: Harry Carroll) (added)
New York run: Minskoff Theatre, March 13, 1973; 604 p.

(See page 32.)

RAISIN

Music: Judd Woldin
Lyrics: Robert Brittan
Book: Robert Nemiroff & Charlotte Zaltzberg (Joseph Stein uncredited)
Producer: Robert Nemiroff
Director-choreographer: Donald McKayle
Cast: Virginia Capers, Joe Morton, Ernestine Jackson, Ralph Carter, Debbie Allen, Robert Jackson, Ted Ross
Songs: "Whose Little Angry Man"; "A Whole Lotta Sunlight"; "Sweet Time"; "You Done Right"; "He Come Down This Morning"; "Sidewalk Tree"; "Not Anymore"; "Measure the Valleys"
New York run: 46th Street Theatre, October 18, 1973; 847 p.

Faithfully adapted from Lorraine Hansberry's 1959 play, *A Raisin in the Sun, Raisin* offered a warm, touching picture of a black family living in Chicago's Southside ghetto in the 1950s. Matriarch Lena Younger (Virginia Capers) wants to use her late husband's insurance money to buy a house in the white neighborhood of Clybourne Park, while her son, Walter Lee (Joe Morton), wants to use it to buy a liquor store. Lena gives Walter Lee part of the money for the store, but one of his partners absconds with it, and Walter Lee is faced with the temptation of buckling under and selling the house back to the Clybourne Park Association. At the end, with pride intact, the Youngers prepare to move into their new home. Miss Capers, who won high praise for her performance, headed the touring company for a year and a half. The play's title was taken from a poem by Langston Hughes — "What happens to a dream deferred?/ Does it dry up/ Like a raisin in the sun?"
Columbia OC/ Samuel French (1978)*/ SF.

CANDIDE

Music: Leonard Bernstein
Lyrics: Richard Wilbur, etc.
Book: Hugh Wheeler
Producer: Chelsea Theatre Center of Brooklyn
Director: Harold Prince
Choreographer: Patricia Birch
Cast: Lewis J. Stadlen, Mark Baker, Maureen Brennan, Sam Freed, June Gable, Deborah St. Darr
Songs: "Life Is Happiness Indeed" (lyric: Stephen Sondheim); "The Best of All Possible Worlds"; "Oh, Happy We"; "It Must Be So"; "Glitter and Be Gay"; "Auto Da Fé" ("What a Day") (lyric: Sondheim); "This World" (lyric: Sondheim); "I Am Easily Assimilated" (lyric: Bernstein); "Bon Voyage"; "Make Our Garden Grow"
New York run: Broadway Theatre, March 10, 1974; 740 p.

(See page 172.)

THE MAGIC SHOW

Music & lyrics: Stephen Schwartz
Book: Bob Randall
Producers: Edgar Lansbury, Joseph Beruh, Ivan Reitman
Director-choreographer: Grover Dale
Cast: Doug Henning, Dale Soules, David Ogden Stiers, Anita Morris
Songs: "Up to His Old Tricks"; "Lion Tamer"; "Style"; "The Goldfarb Variations"; "West End Avenue"
New York run: Cort Theatre, May 28, 1974; 1,920 p.

The fact that the program credit, "MAGIC BY DOUG HENNING," was on the same line and in the same size letters as that of the songwriter and the librettist indicates the importance of Henning's contribution. For *The Magic Show* was little more than a sleight-of-hand show accompanied by a slight-of-substance plot — something about an ambitious young magician at a seedy Passaic, New Jersey, nightclub who triumphs over a jealous old-timer — plus a collection of ten songs. While Henning won praise as an illusionist, his bag of tricks was not his exclusive property since Joe Adalbo took over the part during half the show's run at the Cort Theatre (on 48th Street east of 7th Avenue). The fifth longest running Broadway musical of the 1970s, *The Magic Show* was Stephen Schwartz's third in a row — the others were *Godspell* and *Pippin* — to play over 1,900 performances.
Bell OC.

The Magic Show. Doug Henning manages to separate Anita Morris. (Kenn Duncan)

The Wiz. Andre De Shields and Tiger Haynes. (Martha Swope)

THE WIZ

Music & Lyrics: Charlie Smalls
Book: William F. Brown
Producer: Ken Harper
Director: Geoffrey Holder (Gilbert Moses uncredited)
Choreographer: George Faison
Cast: Tiger Haynes, Ted Ross, Hinton Battle, Stephanie Mills, Clarice Taylor, Mabel King, Andre De Shields, Tasha Thomas, DeeDee Bridgewater
Songs: "He's the Wizard"; "Ease on Down the Road"; "Slide Some Oil to Me"; "Be a Lion"; "Don't Nobody Bring Me No Bad News"; "If You Believe"
New York run: Majestic Theatre, January 5, 1975; 1,672 p.

Though following such illustrious *Wizard of Oz* predecessors as the stage version of 1903 and the screen version of 1939, *The Wiz* was an original concept with an all-black cast, a new rock score, and dialogue that made the fairytale relevant to modern audiences. It still, however, told the same basic story about Dorothy (Stephanie Mills), the little girl from Kansas who is blown by a tornado into Munchkinland in the Land of Oz, meets the Scarecrow (Hinton Battle), the Tinman (Tiger Haynes), and the Lion (Ted Ross) on the Yellow Brick Road, defeats the evil witch (Mabel King), and has an audience with the supposedly all-powerful Wizard (Andre De Shields). Though the Wiz is a phony, he does convince Dorothy that she can do anything she wants if she just believes in herself.

The idea for *The Wiz* originated with producer Ken Harper who had to surmount myriad problems in guiding the show to Broadway. After almost shutting down the musical in Baltimore, he replaced director Gilbert Moses with Geoffrey Holder (also the costume designer) in Detroit, and posted the closing notice on opening night in New York. But a concerted publicity and advertising campaign —plus favorable audience reaction — helped produce a real miracle, and *The Wiz* went on to a four-year run. It also spawned two touring companies that traveled for three years. The 1978 movie version featured Diana Ross, Michael Jackson, Nipsey Russell, Ted Ross, Lena Horne, and Richard Pryor. Atlantic OC/ Stein & Day (1979)/ SF.

SHENANDOAH

Music: Gary Geld
Lyrics: Peter Udell
Book: James Lee Barrett, with Philip Rose, Peter Udell
Producers: Philip Rose, Gloria & Louis Sher
Director: Philip Rose
Choreographer: Robert Tucker
Cast: John Cullum, Donna Theodore, Penelope Milford, Joel Higgins, Ted Agress, Gordon Halliday, Chip Ford
Songs: "I've Heard It All Before"; "Next to Lovin' I Like Fightin' "; "The Pickers Are Comin' "; "Meditation"; "We Make a Beautiful Pair"; "Violets and Silverbells"; "Freedom"; "The Only Home I Know"
New York run: Alvin Theatre, January 7, 1975; 1,050 p.

Of all the movies that have been turned into Broadway musicals, the 1965 release, *Shenandoah,* would seem to have been the most unsuitable. A strongly anti-war polemic, the story is set in the Shenandoah Valley of Virginia during the Civil War. Charlie Anderson (John Cullum), the widowed patriarch of a family of farmers, is determined that the only cause in which any of his six sons will take up arms is in defense of their land. When his youngest son is kidnapped by Northern soldiers, however, Charlie and most of his family go off to find him. While they are away, the eldest son, his wife and baby are all killed, and there is further suffering before what is left of the Anderson family have an emotional reunion in church. First tried out at the Goodspeed Opera House in Connecticut, *Shenandoah* had an appealing Rodgers and Hammerstein flavor and it enjoyed an unexpected long run. It was revived briefly in 1989 with John Cullum. For other musicals about the Civil War, see *Bloomer Girl,* page 125.
RCA OC/ Samuel French (1975)*/ SF.

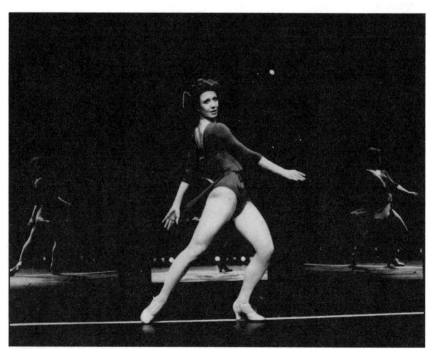

A Chorus Line. Donna McKechnie performing "The Music and the Mirror."
(© Martha Swope)

A CHORUS LINE

Music: Marvin Hamlisch
Lyrics: Edward Kleban
Conception: Michael Bennett
Book: James Kirkwood & Nicholas Dante
Producer: Joseph Papp for the New York Shakespeare Festival
Director: Michael Bennett
Choreographers: Michael Bennett & Bob Avian
Cast: Kelly Bishop, Pamela Blair, Wayne Cilento, Kay Cole, Patricia Garland, Baayork Lee, Priscilla Lopez, Robert LuPone, Donna McKechnie, Michel Stuart, Thommie Walsh, Sammy Williams
Songs: "I Hope I Get It"; "At the Ballet"; "Nothing"; "The Music and the Mirror"; "One"; "What I Did for Love"
New York run: Public Theatre, April 15, 1975; 6,137 p.

Although it dealt with the hopes, fears, frustrations, and insecurities of a specific group of dancers auditioning for a chorus line, the musical skillfully conveyed the universal experience of anyone who has ever stood in line in an effort to present his or her qualifications for a job. Since that means just about all of us. *A Chorus Line* managed to create such a strong empathetical bond with its audiences that it became far and away the longest running production — musical or dramatic — ever staged on Broadway.

Director-choreographer Michael Bennett — who also receives program credit for having "conceived" the show — had long wanted to stage a work that would be a celebration of chorus dancers, known as "gypsies," who contribute so much and receive so little glory. Early in 1974, Bennett rented a studio where he invited 24 dancers to talk about themselves and their careers. Out of these rap sessions came some 30 hours of taped revelations, which gave the director the idea of creating his musical in the form of an audition. After he and Nicholas Dante, one of his dancers, had edited the tapes, producer Joseph Papp offered to sponsor the project as a workshop production at his Hew York Shakespeare Festival Public Theatre. Marvin Hamlisch and Edward Klaban were engaged to write the score, and playwright James Kirkwood was brought in to work with Dante on the book. The show opened at the Newman Theatre (part of the Public Theatre's complex) in mid April 1975, at a $10 top ticket price. Word of mouth made it a hit even before the critics were invited to view it on May 21, and it remained at the downtown playhouse for 101 performances. On July 25, 1975, *A Chorus Line* moved to the Shubert Theatre. It won the Pulitzer Prize for drama for the 1975-76 season.

Avoiding a linear plot structure, the musical is basically a series of vignettes as 18 applicants vie for places in an eight-member chorus line. Goaded by a largely unseen — and rather sadistic — director named Zach (Robert LuPone), each applicant in turn reveals truths that, supposedly, will help the director make his final choices. Among those auditioning are Cassie (Donna McKechnie), a former featured dancer now down on her luck who was once romantically involved with Zach; the street-smart but vulnerable Sheila (Kelly Bishop) who recalls how she had been attracted to dancing because "everything was beautiful at the ballet"; the still-hopeful Diana (Priscilla Lopez), who had once failed a method acting class; the voluptuous Val (Pamela Blair) who uses silicone to enlarge her talent; and the pathetic Paul (Sammy Williams) who relates his humiliating experience as a drag queen.

There have been two touring companies of *A Chorus Line,* the first traveling for seven years, the second for five years eight months. The film version was released in 1985.
Columbia OC/TW.

Chicago. Lawyer Jerry Orbach coaches murderess Gwen Verdon how to appear demure in the courtroom. (Martha Swope)

CHICAGO

Music: John Kander
Lyrics: Fred Ebb
Book: Fred Ebb & Bob Fosse
Producers: Robert Fryer & James Cresson
Director-choreographer: Bob Fosse
Cast: Gwen Verdon, Chita Rivera, Jerry Orbach, Barney Martin, Mary McCarty, M. O'Haughey, Graciela Daniele
Songs: "All That Jazz"; "All I Care About"; "Roxie"; "My Own Best Friend"; "Mr. Cellophane"; "Razzle Dazzle"; "Class"; "Nowadays"
New York run: 46th Street Theatre, June 3, 1975; 898 p.

Bob Fosse first planned a musical production of Maurine Dallas Watkins' 1926 play as early as the mid-Fifties, with Gwen Verdon as the star and Robert Fryer as the producer. It took some 13 years, however, for him to clear the rights to the story of Roxie Hart, a married chorus girl who kills her faithless lover, avoids prison through the histrionic efforts of razzle-dazzle lawyer Billy Flynn (Jerry Orbach), and ends up as a vaudeville headliner with another "scintillating sinner," Velma Kelly (Chita Rivera). Though the show was a scathing indictment of American huckstering, vulgarity, and decadence, its atmosphere strongly recalled the Berlin of *Cabaret,* which also had songs by John Kander and Fred Ebb and whose film version was directed by Bob Fosse.

In Fosse's conceptual treatment, which had much in common with his *commedia dell'arte* approach in *Pippin, Chicago* was created as "A Musical Vaudeville" with a Master of Ceremonies introducing each number as if it were a variety act. (A previous effort to combine vaudeville within a musical play was the Kurt Weill-Alan Jay Lerner *Love Life.*) Soon after *Chicago's* Broadway opening, Miss Verdon was temporarily replaced by Liza Minnelli because of illness; during the run she was succeeded by Ann Reinking.
Arista OC/ Samuel French (1976)*/ SF.

PACIFIC OVERTURES
Music & lyrics: Stephen Sondheim
Book: John Weidman
Producer-director: Harold Prince
Choreographer: Patricia Birch
Cast: Mako, Soon-Teck Oh, Yuki Shimoda, Sab Shimono, Isao Sato
Songs: "There Is No Other Way"; "Four Black Dragons"; "Chrysanthemum Tea"; "Welcome to Kanagawa"; "Someone in a Tree"; "Please Hello"; "A Bowler Hat"; "Pretty Lady"; "Next"
New York run: Winter Garden, January 11, 1976; 193 p.

Few Broadway musicals have ever dared so much on so many levels as *Pacific Overtures*. In recounting the history of the emergence of Japan from a serenely isolated country to its present position in the forefront of international commerce, the musical covers a 120-year period, beginning with Comm. Matthew Perry's threateningly persuasive visit to the Floating Kingdom in 1853, and taking us through changes in social order, customs and dress that were the price Japan paid for its present-day affluence. To present such an ambitiously didactic work, the musical's creators chose to relate the saga not only from the Japanese point of view but also through an approximation of the ancient form of Japanese theatre known as Kabuki. Moreover, Stephen Sondheim's score, while accessible to Occidental ears, was a far more faithful recreation of Oriental music and poetic expression than had ever before been attempted on Broadway. Also adding to the show's dramatic impact were director Harold Prince's lavish conceptual approach and the stunning visual effects created by designer Boris Aronson. In 1984, a revival of *Pacific Overtures* was offered in a scaled-down, Off-Broadway production.
RCA OC/ Dodd, Mead (1977)/ MTI.

I LOVE MY WIFE
Music: Cy Coleman
Lyrics & book: Michael Stewart
Producers: Terry Allen Kramer & Harry Rigby
Director: Gene Saks
Choreographer: Onna White
Cast: Ilene Graff, Lenny Baker, Joanna Gleason, James Naughton
Songs: "Love Revolution"; "Someone Wonderful I Missed"; "Sexually Free"; "Hey There, Good Times"; "Lovers on Christmas Eve"; "Everybody Today Is Turning On"; "I Love My Wife"
New York run: Ethel Barrymore Theatre, April 17, 1977; 872 p.

The sexual revolution of the 1960s hit Broadway a bit late with a musical about mate-swapping in the sinful citadel of Trenton, New Jersey. At the urging of the husbands, two happily married, well-adjusted couples agree to catch up with the amoral freedom they've been hearing and reading about by having themselves a *ménage à quatre*. Of course, since they are such basically decent, clean-living people, they abandon the idea at the last minute because — as the men agree in song — "I love my wife." The idea for the musical began when Michael Stewart saw a French farce in which songs were introduced by lip-synching actors without any attempt to fit them into the story line. *I Love My Wife* followed this general concept by using the musical numbers — sung by both the four actors and an instrumental quartet that turns up throughout the show — to make observations on the morals and mores of the time. During the run, Tom and Dick Smothers were among those who succeeded Lenny Baker and James Naughton.
Atlantic OC/ Samuel French (1980)*/ SF.

Annie. Annie (Andrea McArdle), Daddy Warbucks (Reid Shelton), and Sandy. (Martha Swope)

Annie. Orphans Diana Barrows, Robyn Finn, Donna Graham, Danielle Brisebois, Shelley Bruce, and Janine Ruane singing "You're Never Fully Dressed Without a Smile." (Martha Swope)

ANNIE

Music: Charles Strouse
Lyrics: Martin Charnin
Book: Thomas Meehan
Producer: Mike Nichols
Director: Martin Charnin
Choreographer: Peter Gennaro
Cast: Andrea McArdle, Reid Shelton, Dorothy Loudon, Sandy Faison, Robert Fitch, Barbara Erwin, Raymond Thorne, Laurie Beechman, Danielle Brisebois, Shelley Bruce
Songs: "Maybe"; "It's the Hard-Knock Life"; "Tomorrow"; "Little Girls"; "I Think I'm Gonna Like It Here"; "N.Y.C."; "Easy Street"; "You're Never Fully Dressed Without a Smile"; "Something Was Missing"; "I Don't Need Anything but You"; "Annie"; "A New Deal for Christmas"
New York run: Alvin Theatre, April 21, 1977; 2,377 p.

The idea of turning Harold Gray's "Little Orphan Annie" comic strip into a musical was the inspiration of lyricist-director Martin Charnin, who then contacted playwright Thomas Meehan and composer Charles Strouse to join him in the project. Though their initial reaction was an unqualified "Ughhh," Meehan and Strouse were soon won over by Charnin's approach, which was to use only the three continuing characters in the strip — Annie, Daddy Warbucks, and Annie's mutt Sandy — and fit them into an original story. Because Meehan saw Annie as "a metaphorical figure standing for innate decency, courage and optimism in the face of hard times, pessimism and despair," he decided to set his fable in New York City in the midst of the Depression. Annie (Andrea McArdle), an 11-year-old foundling at the Municipal Orphanage, yearns for her parents to rescue her from the clutches of mean-spirited, bibulous Agatha Hannigan (Dorothy Loudon), the orphanage's matron. Presently, a miraculous parent-figure does show up in the person of billionaire Oliver Warbucks (Reid Shelton) whose secretary, Grace Farrell (Sandy Faison), has invited Annie to spend Christmas with him. Warbucks, in fact, becomes so fond of the child that he plans to adopt her, a situation that is temporarily blocked by the machinations of Miss Hannigan. But the industrialist enlists the aid of his friend President Roosevelt (Raymond Thorne), and everyone — at least everyone who believes that tomorrow is only a day away — looks forward to having a New Deal for Christmas. (It should be noted that Lionel Bart's musical *Oliver!* is also about a young orphan who escapes a life of deprivation by being adopted by a wealthy gentleman.)

When tried out at the Goodspeed Opera House in Connecticut (where Miss McArdle replaced another girl shortly before the opening and Miss Loudon was not yet in the cast), *Annie* won the approval of Mike Nichols who offered to produce it on Broadway. The show was quickly adopted by theatregoers who made it the third longest running musical of the 1970s. During the run, Warbucks was also played by Keene Curtis, John Schuck, Harve Presnell, and Rhodes Reason; Annie by Shelley Bruce, Sarah Jessica Parker, Allison Smith, and Alyson Kirk; and Miss Hannigan by Alice Ghostley, Dolores Wilson, Betty Hutton, Marcia Lewis, Ruth Kobart, and June Havoc. There were four road companies of *Annie,* with the first traveling three and a half years. In 1982, the movie version was released with Albert Finney, Aileen Quinn, Ann Reinking, and Carol Burnett.

For other musicals taken from comic strips, see *Li'l Abner,* page 171.
Columbia OC/ MTI.

THE KING AND I

Music: Richard Rodgers
Lyrics & book: Oscar Hammerstein II
Producers: Lee Guber & Shelly Gross
Director: Yuriko
Choreographer: Jerome Robbins (dances recreated by Yuriko)
Cast: Yul Brynner, Constance Towers, Michael Kermoyan, Hye-Young Choi, Martin Vidnovic, June Angela, Susan Kikuchi, John Michael King, Gene Profanato, Marianne Tatum
Songs: Same as original production
New York run: Uris Theatre, May 2, 1977; 696 p.

See page 151.

The King and I. King Yul Brynner giving a royal command to governess Constance Towers. (Ernst Haas)

On the Twentieth Century.
Kevin Kline, John Cullum, and
Judy Kaye. (Martha Swope)

ON THE TWENTIETH CENTURY

Music: Cy Coleman
Lyrics & book: Betty Comden & Adolph Green
Producers: Robert Fryer, Mary Lea Johnson, James Cresson, etc.
Director: Harold Prince
Choreographer: Larry Fuller
Cast: John Cullum, Madeline Kahn, Imogene Coca, George Coe, Dean Dittman, Kevin Kline, Judy Kaye, George Lee Andrews
Songs: "On the Twentieth Century"; "I Rise Again"; "Veronique"; "Never"; "Our Private World"; "Repent"; "We've Got It All"
New York run: St. James Theatre, February 19, 1978; 449 p.

Ben Hecht and Charles MacArthur's 1932 show-business farce, *Twentieth Century* (which they had based on a play by Bruce Millholland) was turned into a musical that was not so much backstage as on track, since most of the action takes place aboard the Twentieth Century Limited (in a stunning art-deco set by Robin Wagner) as it speeds from Chicago to New York. Producer-director Oscar Jaffee (John Cullum), the flamboyant High Priest of Broadway now in desperate straights, makes a last-ditch effort to rise again by signing tempestuous movie star Lily Garland (Madeline Kahn), to act in his next epic, *The Passion of Mary Magdalene*. Oscar, who had once been Lily's mentor and lover — and had changed her name from Mildred Plotka — must now also contend with Lily's latest love, actor Bruce Granit (Kevin Kline), and a rival producer, Max Jacobs (George Lee Andrews). But we know that the two are meant for each other when Lily, tricked into signing Oscar's contract, affixes the name Peter Rabbit.

Though the character of Oscar Jaffee had been originally modeled after David Belasco and Jed Harris, Cullum played him as John Barrymore, with the love-hate relationship of Oscar and Lily also recalling Fred and Lili in *Kiss Me, Kate*. Two months after the opening, Miss Kahn was replaced by Judy Kaye. Columbia OC/ Drama Book Specialists (1981)/ SF.

1978

DANCIN'

Music & lyrics: Miscellaneous writers
Producers: Jules Fisher, Shubert Organization, Columbia Pictures
Director-choreographer: Bob Fosse
Cast: Sandahl Bergman, Rene Ceballos, Christopher Chadman, Wayne
         Cilento, Vicki Frederick, Edward Love, Ann Reinking, Charles Ward
Songs: 23 musical pieces from Bach to Jerry Jeff Walker
New York run: Broadhurst Theatre, March 27, 1978; 1,774 p.

An extension of Bob Fosse's previous work in *Pippin* and *Chicago* — plus Michael Bennett's in *A Chorus Line* — *Dancin'* represented the final triumph of the Broadway choreographer by doing away with practically everything else but. In essence, it was Fosse's attempt to create a popular-dance version of a ballet program performed on Broadway for a commercial run, and it succeeded so well in attracting an audience — especially foreign visitors who might have difficulty in following a book musical — that it remained in New York for four years three months, and toured for over a year. The precision, grace and sheer vitality of the dancers (particularly Ann Reinking) merited high praise in such numbers as the easy-going, high-strutting "I Wanna Be a Dancin' Man," performed by the entire company; the dithyrambic recreation of Benny Goodman's "Sing, Sing, Sing"; and the finale, "America," a collage of ten routines by turn comic, ironic, and rousing.

THE BEST LITTLE WHOREHOUSE IN TEXAS

Music & lyrics: Carol Hall
Book: Larry L. King & Peter Masterson
Producer: Universal Pictures (Stevie Phillips)
Directors: Peter Masterson & Tommy Tune
Choreographer: Tommy Tune
Cast: Carlin Glynn, Henderson Forsythe, Delores Hall, Pamela Blair, Jay Garner, Clint Allmon
Songs: "A Li'l Ole Bitty Pissant Country Place"; "Girl, You're a Woman";
         "Twenty-Four Hours of Lovin' "; "Texas Has a Whorehouse in It"; "Bus
         from Amarillo"; "Good Old Girl"; "Hard Candy Christmas"
New York run: Entermedia Theatre, April 17, 1978; 1,703 p.

The legendary Texas brothel known as the Chicken Ranch (so-called because in the Depression customers were allowed to pay with poultry) was in existence from the 1840s to 1973, when it was shut down through the efforts of a crusading, oilier-than-thou Houston radio commentator and his vigilante Watch Dogs. The story of the brothel and its last days became the subject of a raunchy, romping musical that was tried out at the Actor's Studio, opened at the Off-Broadway Entermedia Theatre (formerly the Eden), where it played 64 performances, then moved to the 46th Street Theatre on June 19. The show was put together entirely by four transplanted Texans who wanted to collaborate on a musical about the Lone Star State that would be, in the words of songwriter Carol Hall, "funny and nostalgic and tender." Carlin Glynn played Miss Mona Stangley, the whorehouse proprietor, and Henderson Forsythe the blunt-talking local sheriff, Ed Earl Dodd, who had once been Mona's lover. Alexis Smith was seen as Miss Mona in the second of three road companies that toured for three and a half years. The film version, released in 1982, co-starred Dolly Parton and Burt Reynolds.
MCA OC/ Samuel French (1983)*/ SF.

AIN'T MISBEHAVIN'

Music: Fats Waller
Lyrics: Miscellaneous writers
Conception: Murray Horwitz & Richard Maltby Jr.
Producers: Emanuel Azenberg, Dasha Epstein, Shubert Organization, Jane
      Gaynor, Ron Dante
Director: Richard Maltby Jr.
Choreographer: Arthur Faria
Cast: Nell Carter, Andre De Shields, Armelia McQueen, Ken Page, Charlaine
      Woodard
Songs: 30 written or recorded by Fats Waller
New York run: Longacre Theatre, May 9, 1978; 1,604 p.

While it was not the first entertainment presented on or off Broadway to feature the songs of a particular composer or lyricist, *Ain't Misbehavin'*, "The New Fats Waller Musical Show," was such a popular attraction that it opened the way for two subsequent "catalogue" musicals, *Eubie!*, spotlighting the work of Eubie Blake, and *Sophisticated Ladies*, which did the same for Duke Ellington. *Ain't Misbehavin'* began as a limited-run cabaret entertainment at the Manhattan Theatre Club on February 8, 1978. Its enthusiastic reception prompted its transfer to Broadway at the Longacre Theatre, where Charlaine Woodard replaced Irene Cara. Among the numbers performed were 18 written by Waller either as songs or instrumental pieces (some with new lyrics by Richard Maltby Jr. and Murray Horwitz) and 12 others that Waller recorded. Through costuming, decor, and arrangements, the show evoked the flavor of a Harlem nightclub in theThirties, with the playful spirit of Waller himself coming through in the performances and the staging. During the Broadway run, Miss Woodard was succeeded by Debbie Allen. The musical's touring company traveled for two years seven months. In 1988 the show had a brief Broadway revival.
RCA OC/ MTI.

Ain't Misbehavin'. Armelia McQueen, Ken Page, Charlaine Woodard, Andre De Shields, and Nell Carter. (Martha Swope)

I'M GETTING MY ACT TOGETHER AND TAKING IT ON THE ROAD

Music: Nancy Ford
Lyrics & book: Gretchen Cryer
Producer: Joseph Papp for the New York Shakespeare Festival
Director: Word Baker
Cast: Gretchen Cryer, Joel Fabiani, Betty Aberlin, Don Scardino
Songs: "Natural High"; "Miss America"; "Dear Tom"; "Old Friend"; "Strong Woman Number"; "Happy Birthday"
New York run: Public Theatre, June 14, 1978; 1,165 p.

In all their works to date, composer Nancy Ford and lyricist-librettist Gretchen Cryer have been preeminently identified as feminist writers. *I'm Getting My Act Together and Taking It on the Road,* by far their most personal expression, even had the central role, that of a divorced 39-year-old pop singer attempting a comeback, played by Miss Cryer herself. The story finds her auditioning a new act for her dubious manager (Joel Fabiani), in which she presents herself as honestly as she can, without makeup or fancy gowns or any kind of audience-pandering. Through her songs, the singer gradually becomes the embodiment of the outspoken, totally liberated woman who knows exactly who she is and where she is going. After six months at the New York Shakespeare Festival Public Theatre, the musical was transferred to the Circle in the Square in Greenwich Village. During the run, Miss Cryer was succeeded by Virginia Vestoff, Betty Aberlin, Carol Hall, Betty Buckley, Anne Kaye, Nancy Ford, and Phyllis Newman.
CSP OC/ Samuel French (1980)*/ SF.

THEY'RE PLAYING OUR SONG

Music: Marvin Hamlisch
Lyrics: Carole Bayer Sager
Book: Neil Simon
Producer: Emanuel Azenberg
Director: Robert Moore
Choreographer: Patricia Birch
Cast: Lucie Arnaz, Robert Klein
Songs: "Fallin'"; "If He Really Knew Me"; "They're Playing Our Song"; "Just for Tonight"; "When You're in My Arms"; "Right"
New York run: Imperial Theatre, February 11, 1979; 1,082 p.

They're Playing Our Song was based in part on composer Marvin Hamlisch's own frequently stormy affair with his then lyricist-in-residence, Carole Bayer Sager. In this musical *drame à clef,* Vernon Gersch, a wise-cracking, neurotic songwriter who likes to spend his time telling his troubles to a tape recorder, and Sonia Walsk, a wise-cracking, neurotic lyric writer whose wardrobe is made up of used theatre costumes, try to have both a professional and a personal relationship despite constant interruptions caused by telephone calls from Sonia's former lover for whom she still feels great affection. To tell their story, the authors hit upon the notion — as in *I Do! I Do!* — of using only two characters, though in this case each one has three singing alter egos. Four actors succeeded Robert Klein during the Broadway run (including Tony Roberts and Victor Garber), and five succeeded Lucie Arnaz (including Stockard Channing and Anita Gillette). The show's first road company (with Garber and Ellen Greene) toured for two years; the second (with John Hammil and Lorna Luft) for one year three months.
Casablanca OC/ Random House (1980)/ SF.

Sweeney Todd. Angela Lansbury and Len Cariou.
(Martha Swope)

SWEENEY TODD

Music & lyrics: Stephen Sondheim
Book: Hugh Wheeler
Producers: Richard Barr, Charles Woodward, Robert Fryer, etc.
Director: Harold Prince
Choreographer: Larry Fuller
Cast: Angela Lansbury, Len Cariou, Vistor Garber, Ken Jennings, Merle
  Louise, Edmund Lyndeck, Sarah Rice, Cris Groenendaal
Songs: "The Ballad of Sweeney Todd"; "The Worst Pies in London";
  "Johanna"; "Pretty Women"; "Epiphany"; "A Little Priest"; "By the
  Sea"; "Not While I'm Around"
New York run: Uris Theatre, March 1, 1979; 557 p.

Easily the most grisly musical ever presented for a commercial Broadway run,
the near-operatic *Sweeney Todd* was a bold, even audience-intimidating attack
on the cannibalizing effects of the Industrial Revolution on a Brechtian, vermin-
infested London. The indictment was conveyed through the tale of a half-mad
barber (Len Cariou) who returns home after escaping from an unjust imprison-
ment to take vengeance on the judge who sentenced him, then ravished his wife,
and now plans to marry his daughter. But Sweeney doesn't limit himself to one
victim; he turns his indiscriminate rage against everyone in London by systemati-
cally slitting the throats of his customers, whose corpses are then made into
meat pies by Todd's enterprising accomplice, Mrs. Lovett (Angela Lansbury). At
the end, of course, all the bad ones are properly and gruesomely punished.

First shown on the London stage in 1847 as *A String of Pearls, or The Fiend
of Fleet Street,* by George Dibdin Pitt, the Grand Guignol story has been presented in many versions since then, most recently Christopher Bond's 1973 London play, *Sweeney Todd,* on which Hugh Wheeler based his libretto. The fifth and
most uncompromising collaboration between composer-lyricist Stephen
Sondheim and director Harold Prince, the production was also noted for its tow-
ering setting (by Eugene and Franne Lee) made from an iron foundry. During the
run at the Uris Theatre (now the Gershwin, on 51st west of Broadway), Miss
Lansbury was succeeded by Dorothy Loudon, Mr. Cariou by George Hearn. In
1984, the musical entered the repertory of the New York City Opera; in 1989, it
was revived Off-Broadway with Bob Gunton and Beth Fowler.
RCA OC/ Dodd, Mead (1979)/ MTI.

PETER PAN

Music: Mark Charlap; Jule Styne
Lyrics: Carolyn Leigh; Betty Comden & Adolph Green
Play: James M. Barrie
Producers: Zev Bufman & James Nederlander
Director-choreographer: Rob Iscove (Ron Field, uncredited)
Cast: Sandy Duncan, George Rose, Beth Fowler, Arnold Soboloff, Marsha Kramer
Songs: Same as original production
New York run: Lunt-Fontanne Theatre, September 6, 1979; 551 p.

(See page 163.)

EVITA

Music: Andrew Lloyd Webber
Lyrics: Tim Rice
Producer: Robert Stigwood
Director: Harold Prince
Choreographer: Larry Fuller
Cast: Patti LuPone, Mandy Patinkin, Bob Gunton, Mark Syers, Jane Ohringer
Songs: "On This Night of a Thousand Stars"; "Buenos Aires"; "I'd Be Surprisingly Good for You"; "Another Suitcase in Another Hall"; "A New Argentina"; "Don't Cry for Me, Argentina"; "High Flying Adored"; "Rainbow Tour"; "The Actress Hasn't Learned"; "And the Money Kept Rolling In"; "Dice Are Rolling"
New York run: Broadway Theatre, September 25, 1979; 1,567 p.

Because of its huge success in London (where it opened in 1978 and ran 2,900 performances), *Evita* was such a pre-sold hit in New York that it was able to surmount a mixed critical reception and remain on Broadway for three years nine months. Based on events in the life of Argentina's notorious Eva Peron, the musical —with Patti LuPone as Eva — begins in 1934 when Eva Duarte is 15, takes her from her hometown to Buenos Aires where she becomes a model, film actress, and the wife of Gen. Juan Peron (Bob Gunton). When Peron is elected president, Eva becomes the most powerful woman in South America, and though she does little to improve the conditions of her people, is regarded as a saint when she dies of cancer at the age of 33. Another character in the musical, the slightly misplaced Che Guevera (Mandy Patinkin), serves as narrator, observer, and conscience.

Though the plot is told entirely through song and dance (there is no credit for librettist) and the work had originated as a record project, the highly theatrical concept devised by authors Andrew Lloyd Webber and Tim Rice and director Harold Prince — as well as the popularity of "Don't Cry for Me, Argentina" — helped turn *Evita* into an internationally acclaimed musical. During the Broadway run, six actresses took over the title role from Miss LuPone: Terri Klausner, Nancy Opel, and Pamela Blake (matinees), and Derin Altay, Loni Ackerman, and Florence Lacey (evenings). The show's three touring companies traveled a total of three and one-half years.
MCA OC/ MTI.

SUGAR BABIES

Music: Jimmy McHugh, etc.
Lyrics: Dorothy Fields, etc.
Conception: Ralph G. Allen & Harry Rigby
Sketches: Ralph G. Allen
Producers: Terry Allen Kramer & Harry Rigby
Directors: Ernest Flatt, Rudy Tronto
Choreographer: Ernest Flatt
Cast: Mickey Rooney, Ann Miller, Sid Stone, Jack Fletcher, Ann Jillian, Bob Williams, Scot Stewart
Songs: "A Good Old Burlesque Show" (lyric: Arthur Malvin); "I Feel a Song Comin' On"; "Don't Blame Me"; "Mr. Banjo Man" (music & lyric: Malvin); "I'm Keeping Myself Available for You" (lyric: Malvin); "Warm and Willing" (lyric: Jay Livingston & Ray Evans); "Exactly Like You"; "I Can't Give You Anything but Love"; "I'm Shooting High" (lyric: Ted Koehler); "On the Sunny Side of the Street"; "You Can't Blame Your Uncle Sammy" (lyric: Al Dubin & Irwin Dash).
New York run: Mark Hellinger Theatre, October 8, 1979; 1,208 p.

Like *Star and Garter, Wine, Women and Song,* and *Michael Todd's Peep Show* of an earlier era, *Sugar Babies* was an idealized version of a burlesque show. According to sketch writer Ralph G. Allen, who conceived the entertainment with co-producer Harry Rigby, the show was a celebration of American variety entertainment from 1905 to 1930 and the aim was to recreate as authentically as possible some of the classic low-comedy sketches and routines of that period. Making his Broadway debut top banana Mickey Rooney appeared in such traditional roles as the lascivious judge in a manic courtroom scene, as the naughty little boy in "The Little Red Schoolhouse," and as Countess Francine, complete with cotton-candy wig and exaggerated bosoms, leading her troupe of female minstrels. Also memorable, if hardly authentic, was the session at the grand piano with Mickey and Ann Miller going through Jimmy McHugh standards. Rooney was followed on Broadway by Joey Bishop, Rip Taylor, and Eddie Bracken, then headed the touring company with the leg-flashing Miss Miller. The show was on the road for almost three and a half years.
B'way Entertainment OC/ Samuel French (1983)*/ SF.

OKLAHOMA!

Music: Richard Rodgers
Lyrics & book: Oscar Hammerstein II
Producers: Zev Bufman & James Nederlander
Director: William Hammerstein
Choreographer: Agnes de Mille (dances recreated by Gemze de Lappe)
Cast: Laurence Guittard, Christine Andreas, Mary Wickes, Christine Ebersole, Martin Vidnovic, Harry Groener, Bruce Adler
Songs: Same as original production
New York run: Palace Theatre, December 13, 1979; 293 p.

(See page 119.)

BARNUM

Music: Cy Coleman
Lyrics: Michael Stewart
Book: Mark Bramble
Producers: Judy Gordon, Cy Coleman, Maurice & Lois Rosenfield
Director-choreographer: Joe Layton
Cast: Jim Dale, Glenn Close, Marianne Tatum, Terri White, Leonard John Crofoot, William C. Witter
Songs: "There Is a Sucker Born Ev'ry Minute"; "The Colors of My Life"; "One Brick at a Time"; "Bigger Isn't Better"; "Come Follow the Band"; "Black and White"; "The Prince of Humbug"; "Join the Circus"
New York run: St. James Theatre, April 30, 1980; 854 p.

The story of America's "Prince of Humbug," Phineas Taylor Barnum, had long attracted producers and writers as a fitting subject for a musical, but it was not until Cy Coleman, Michael Stewart, and Mark Bramble got together with director-choreographer Joe Layton that a way was found to depict the colorful impresario's life on stage. Their solution: don't bother too much with character-ization or biographical detail, simply offer the show as a total circus concept with the entire cast constantly in motion tumbling, clowning, marching, twirling, and flying through the air. Best of all, give the title role to Jim Dale, an actor who can dance, juggle, leap off a trampoline, and sing and walk a tightrope at the same time.

The musical offers a guided tour of the highlights of Barnum's career from 1835 to 1880, when the showman joins James A. Bailey (William C. Witter) in cre-ating "The Greatest Show on Earth." Along the way, we are treated to such leg-endary sucker-bait attractions as Joice Heth (Terri White), George Washington's alleged 160-year-old nurse, the midget Tom Thumb (Leonard John Crofoot), Jumbo the elephant, the Swedish Nightingale Jenny Lind (Marianne Tatum), and — finally — the three-ring circus. What conflict there is is supplied by the unful-filled desire of Barnum's wife Chairy (Glenn Close) to settle down to a more pro-saic life. During the run, Dale was succeeded by Tony Orlando and Mike Burstyn. For other show-business biographies, see *Annie Get Your Gun,* page 130. Columbia OC/ Doubleday (1980)/ TW.

Barnum. Jim Dale and Glenn Close. (Martha Swope)

42nd Street. Jerry Orbach and
Wanda Richert. (Martha Swope)

42nd STREET

Music: Harry Warren
Lyrics: Al Dubin
Book: Michael Stewart & Mark Bramble
Producer: David Merrick
Director-choreographer: Gower Champion
Cast: Jerry Orbach, Tammy Grimes, Wanda Richert, Lee Roy Reams, Joseph Bova, Carole Cook
Songs: "Young and Healthy"; "Shadow Waltz"; "Go Into Your Dance"; "You're Getting to Be a Habit With Me"; "Dames"; "We're in the Money"; "Lullaby of Broadway"; "About a Quarter to Nine"; "Shuffle Off to Buffalo"; "Forty-Second Street"
New York run: Winter Garden, August 25, 1980; 3,486 p.

Re-creating the classic 1933 backstage movie musical of the same name, *42nd Street* followed its cliché-riddled model with a minimum of camp but with a maximum of high-powered, ingenious choreography devised by Gower Champion (who died the day the musical opened on Broadway). Once again the simple-minded saga relates the tale of stage-struck chorus girl Peggy Sawyer (Wanda Richert) from Allentown, Pennsylvania, who gets her big chance when Dorothy Brock (Tammy Grimes), the star of *Pretty Lady*, breaks her ankle during the show's tryout, and Peggy goes on to triumph on "naughty, bawdy, gaudy, sporty 42nd Street." Among changes from the movie: the ending now indicated a possible romance between Peggy and the hard driving director Julian Marsh (Jerry Orbach) rather than juvenile lead Billy Lawlor (Lee Roy Reams), and nine more Harry Worred songs (seven of which also written with Al Dubin) were added to the four Warren-Dublin numbers that were retained.

The musical, which opened with a new top ticket price of $30, had two Broadway antecedents. A sketch in the *Ziegfeld Follies of 1939* offered Fanny Brice and Bob Hope in a takeoff on the film, which was also spoofed in the 1968 Off-Broadway hit *Dames at Sea*. During the run, the part of Dorothy was also played by Millicent Martin, Elizabeth Allen, Anne Rodgers, and Dolores Gray; Julian by Barry Nelson and Jamie Ross. The first touring company was originally headed by Nelson and Miss Gray, the second by Jon Cypher and Miss Martin. RCA OC/ TW.

The Pirates of Penzance. Kevin Kline, Rex Smith, and pirates (© Martha Swope)

THE PIRATES OF PENZANCE

Music: Arthur Sullivan
Lyrics & book: William S. Gilbert
Producer: Joseph Papp for the New York Shakespeare Festival
Director: Wilford Leach
Choreographer: Graciela Daniele
Cast: Kevin Kline, Estelle Parsons, Linda Ronstadt, George Rose, Rex Smith, Tony Azito
Songs: "Oh, Better Far to Live and Die"; "Oh, Is There Not One Maiden Breast?"; "Poor Wandering One"; "I Am the Very Model of a Modern Major-General"; "When the Foeman Bares His Steel"; "When a Felon's Not Engaged in His Employment"; "With Cat-Like Tread"
New York run: Uris Theatre, January 8, 1981; 772 p.

When, on December 31, 1879, *The Pirates of Penzance* opened in New York at the 5th Avenue Theatre, it marked the only occasion that a Gilbert and Sullivan comic opera had its première in a city other than London. When, 101 years later, it opened in New York at the Uris Theatre, it marked the only occasion — so far — that a Gilbert and Sullivan comic opera had a commercial Broadway run. With its modern orchestrations, bravura performances, and slightly campy approach, this version had been acclaimed when it was presented the previous summer in Central Park, where it played 42 free performances as part of Joseph Papp's New York Shakespeare Festival. (When moved to Broadway, the only major cast change was Estelle Parsons for Patricia Routledge as Ruth.) The operetta's ardent arias and duets and sprightly patter songs are mated to a charmingly inane tale of poor Frederic (Rex Smith), who after accidentally being apprenticed to a pirate (Kevin Kline), falls in love with Mabel (Linda Ronstadt), one of the eight daughters of a very model of a modern Major- General (George Rose).

Among those who appeared in the Broadway production after the original cast were Treat Williams (Pirate King); Kaye Ballard (Ruth); Maureen McGovern, Kathryn Morath, and Pam Dawber (Mabel); George S. Irving (Major-General); and Robby Benson, Patrick Cassidy, and Peter Noone (Frederic). The road company was initially headed by Barry Bostwick, Jo Anne Worley, Pam Dawber, Clive Revill, and Andy Gibb. The original Broadway cast — except for the substitution of Angela Lansbury for Miss Parsons — appeared in the 1983 film version. Elektra OC/ MTI.

Sophisticated Ladies. The "Caravan" number led by Gregg Burge. (Kenn Duncan)

SOPHISTICATED LADIES

Music: Duke Ellington
Lyrics: Miscellaneous writers
Conception: Donald McKayle
Producers: Roger Berlind, Manheim Fox, Sondra Gilman, Burton Litwin, Louise Westergaard
Director: Michael Smuin
Choreographers: Donald McKayle, Michael Smuin, Henry LeTang
Cast: Gregory Hines, Judith Jamison, Phyllis Hyman, P. J. Benjamin, Hinton Battle, Terri Klausner, Gregg Burge, Mercedes Ellington, Priscilla Baskerville
Songs: 36 from the Duke Ellington catalogue
New York run: Lunt-Fontanne Theatre, March 1, 1981; 767 p.

Though different in concept, *Sophisticated Ladies* followed the lead of *Ain't Misbehavin'* and *Eubie!* by being an entertainment built around the catalogue of a single composer. Here the celebration of the music of Duke Ellington was far more of an elaborate, brassy nightclub floor show than its predecessors, with a 21-piece on-stage orchestra (led by Ellington's son Mercer Ellington) and a castful of such highpowered steppers as Gregory Hines, Judith Jamison, Hinton Battle, and Gregg Burge. The show's Broadway success was totally unexpected. Its opening-night tryout in Washington had gone so badly that director Donald McKayle, who had conceived the production, was replaced by ballet choreographer Michael Smuin. Despite his inexperience in the world of Broadway, Smuin turned things around by adding nine songs, rearranging the sequence of the 36 numbers, introducing new dance routines, and dropping all existing dialogue.

During the Broadway run, Gregory Hines was succeeded by his brother, Maurice Hines, and P. J. Benjamin by Don Correia. The first of two road companies was headed by Harold Nicholas, Paula Kelly, and Freda Payne. RCA OC/ R&H.

WOMAN OF THE YEAR

Music: John Kander
Lyrics: Fred Ebb
Book: Peter Stone
Producers: Lawrence Kasha, David Landay, James Nederlander, etc.
Director: Robert Moore
Choreographer: Tony Charmoli
Cast: Lauren Bacall, Harry Guardino, Roderick Cook, Marilyn Cooper, Eivind Harum, Grace Keagy, Rex Everhart, Jamie Ross
Songs: "Woman of the Year"; "One of the Boys"; "The Grass Is Always Greener"; "We're Gonna Work It Out"
New York run: Palace Theatre, March 29, 1981; 770 p.

Updating the 1942 movie, *Woman of the Year* told a battle-of-the-sexes story with Lauren Bacall as Tess Harding, a Barbara Walters-type television personality, and Harry Guardino as Sam Craig, a satirical cartoonish suggesting Garry Trudeau. Angered by some television comments made by Tess about "funnies," Sam retaliates by putting her in his strip as a character named "Tessie Cat." The two meet, explode, marry, continue to explode, and eventually decide to try to work things out. *Woman of the Year* had certain points of similarity with Miss Bacall's previous musical, *Applause.* Both shows were told in flashback, and both involved a strong-willed public personality trying to solve the problem of juggling a career and marriage. During the musical's run, Miss Bacall was succeeded by Raquel Welch, Debbie Reynolds, and Louise Troy.
Arista OC/ Samuel French (1984)*/ SF.

JOSEPH AND THE AMAZING TECHNICOLOR DREAMCOAT

Music: Andrew Lloyd Webber
Lyrics: Tim Rice
Producers: Zev Bufman & Susan Rose
Director-choreographer: Tony Tanner
Cast: Bill Hutton, Laurie Beechman, David Ardeo, Tom Carder
Songs: "Joseph's Coat"; "One More Angel in Heaven"; "Go, Go, Go Joseph"; "Pharaoh's Story"; "Those Canaan Days"; "Benjamin Calypso"; "Any Dream Will Do"
New York run: Entermedia Theatre, November 18, 1981; 824 p.

Joseph and the Amazing Technicolor Dreamcoat, the first collaboration of Andrew Lloyd Webber and Tim Rice, lasted all of 15 minutes when it was initially presented in a London school in 1968. Five years later, by now expanded to 40 minutes, the work was offered on the West End and then expanded again to almost 90 minutes. In 1976, *Joseph* had its first New York showing at the Brooklyn Academy of Music. The 1981 production, which ran 77 performances in an East Village theatre, moved to the Royale on January 27, 1982, where it remained for 747 performances. Told entirely in song, this biblical cantata — actually an eclectic grabbag of rock, country, vaudeville song-and-dance, French ballad, and calypso — relates the Old Testament tale of Joseph (Bill Hutton), Jacob's favorite of 12 sons, to whom papa gives a resplendent coat of many colors. Joseph's jealous brothers thereupon sell him into slavery and he is taken to Egypt where he interprets the dream of an Elvis Presley-type Pharaoh (Tom Carder). His wise prophecy so impresses the Pharaoh that he becomes Egypt's Number Two man and saves the country from famine. During the Broadway run, Andy Gibb and David Cassidy were two of the four actors who succeeded Bill Hutton.
Chrysalis OC/ Holt, Rinehart (1982)/ MTI.

DREAMGIRLS

Music: Henry Krieger
Lyrics & book: Tom Eyen
Producers: Michael Bennett, Bob Avian, Geffen Records
Director: Michael Bennett
Choreographers: Michael Bennett, Michael Peters
Cast: Obba Babatunde, Cleavant Derricks, Loretta Devine, Ben Harney, Jennifer Holliday, Sheryl Lee Ralph, Deborah Burrell
Songs: "Fake Your Way to the Top"; "Cadillac Car"; "Steppin' to the Bad Side"; "Dreamgirls"; "And I Am Telling You I'm Not Going"; "I Am Changing"; "When I First Saw You"; "Hard to Say Goodbye, My Love"
New York run: Imperial Theatre, December 20, 1981; 1,522 p.

With *Dreamgirls,* Michael Bennett returned to the heartbreak world of show business that he had explored in *A Chorus Line* to create another high-voltage concept musical. Tom Eyen's tough-tender book about the corruption of innocence was primarily based on the story of the Supremes. The success of the black vocal trio of the 1960s was maneuvered by Motown Records chief Berry Gordy at the price of dropping lead singer Florence Ballard in favor of Diana Ross because Ballard didn't present the right image (she drifted into obscurity and died at the age of 32). In the musical, it is Effie Melody White (Jennifer Holliday), the heavyset lead singer of a rhythm and blues trio (the other two: Sheryl Lee Ralph and Loretta Devine), who is sacrificed because a slick manager (Ben Harney) feels that the singers — whom he names the Dreams — must offer a more glamorous appearance to enable them to cross over to the more lucrative pop mainstream. Unlike Florence Ballard, however Effie surmounts a difficult period and goes on to win fame on her own.

To keep his glitzy, glittery show in constant fluid motion through some 20 scenes — beginning in 1962 on the stage of the Harlem Apollo and ending ten years later in Hollywood — Bennett was aided by set designer Robin Wagner, costume designer Theoni V. Aldredge, and lighting designer Tharon Musser (all of whom had worked on *A Chorus Line*). Also contributing to the production's close weave was Henry Krieger's Motown-influenced score with over 30 musical numbers used both for specialties and as dramatic dialogue. Impressive newcomer Jennifer Holliday repeated her role in the touring company. A new touring production of *Dreamgirls* returned to Broadway in 1987.
Geffen OC.

Dreamgirls. Loretta Devine, Jennifer Holliday, Sheryl Lee Ralph, and Cleavant Derricks. (Martha Swope)

NINE

Music & lyrics: Maury Yeston
Book: Arthur Kopit, Mario Fratti
Producers: Michel Stuart, Harvey Klaris, Roger Berlind, etc.
Director: Tommy Tune
Choreographers: Tommy Tune, Thommie Walsh
Cast: Raul Julia, Karen Akers, Shelly Burch, Taina Elg, Lilianne Montevecchi, Anita Morris, Kathi Moss
Songs: "My Husband Makes Movies"; "A Call from the Vatican"; "Only With You"; "Folies Bergères"; "Nine"; "Be Italian"; "Unusual Way"; "The Grand Canal"; "Simple"; "Be on Your Own"
New York run: 46th Street Theatre, May 9, 1982; 732 p.

The influence of the director-choreographer was emphasized again with Tommy Tune's highly stylized, visually striking production of *Nine*. The musical evolved from composer-lyricist Maury Yeston's fascination with Federico Fellini's semi-autobiographical 1963 film *8½,* and — appropriately — it took nine years for it to make it to Broadway. During the show's creation, disagreements arose over the libretto by Mario Fratti, prompting his replacement by Arthur Kopit, and Tune's decision to have a cast of 21 women and only one adult male. The story spotlights Guido Contini (Raul Julia), a celebrated but tormented director who has come to a Venetian spa for a rest, and his relationships with his wife (Karen Akers), his mistress (Anita Morris), his protégé (Shelly Burch), his producer (Lilianne Montevecchi), and his mother (Taina Elg). The production, which flashes back to Guido's youth and also takes place in his imagination, offers such inventive touches as an "overture" in which Guido conducts his women as if they were instruments, and an impressionistic version of the Folies Bergères. During the Broadway run, Julia was succeeded by Bert Convy and Sergio Franchi. CBS OC/ Doubleday (1983)/ SF.

LITTLE SHOP OF HORRORS

Music: Alan Menken
Lyrics & book: Howard Ashman
Producers: WPA Theatre, David Geffen, Cameron Mackintosh
Director: Howard Ashman
Choreographer: Edie Cowan
Cast: Ellen Greene, Lee Wilkof, Hy Anzell, Franc Luz, Leilani Jones
Songs: "Little Shop of Horrors"; "Skid Row"; "Grow for Me"; "Somewhere That's Green"; "Suddenly Seymour"
New York run: Orpheum Theatre, July 27, 1982; 2,209 p.

A campy musical about a man-eating Venus's-flytrap with all the principals dead by the end of the show would seem far riskier than the usual theatrical enterprise, but *Little Shop of Horrors* won over a majority of the critics to its offbeat humor, and remained for over 2,000 performances at its Lower East Side theatre. Based on the low-budget 1960 Roger Corman movie, the musical is set in a flower shop inconveniently located on Skid Row where meek Seymour Krelbourn (Lee Wilkof) breeds a tiny plant that he names Audrey II out of love for salesgirl Audrey (Ellen Greene). Since the mysterious plant needs blood to live, Seymour, in a Faustian pact, agrees to feed it in return for a guarantee that it will attract publicity to make him rich and famous. Soon this unlikely Sweeney Todd has found a way to do in anyone he wants, and when last seen the monstrous mutant is about to devour the audience. A film version was released in 1986. Geffen OC/ Doubleday (1982)/ SF.

CATS

Music: Andrew Lloyd Webber
Lyrics: Based on T.S. Eliot
Producers: Cameron Mackintosh, Really Useful Co., Ltd., David Geffen
Directors: Trevor Nunn, Gillian Lynne
Choreographer: Gillian Lynne
Cast: Betty Buckley, Rene Clemente, Harry Groener, Stephen Hanan, Reed Jones, Christine Langner, Terrence V. Mann, Anna McNeely, Ken Page, Timothy Scott
Songs: "Jellicle Songs for Jellicle Cats"; "The Old Gumbie Cat"; "The Rum Tum Tugger"; "Old Deuteronomy"; "The Jellicle Ball"; "Grizabella"; "Macavity"; "Mr. Mistoffelees"; "Memory"
New York run: Winter Garden, October 7, 1982; 7,485 p.

At this writing, *Cats* is still running in London (where it opened May 11, 1981) and in New York. Charged with incredible energy flare, and imagination, the feline fantasy has been staged in its Broadway version as even more of an environmental experience than it was in its West End original. With the entire Winter Garden auditorium transformed into an enormous junkyard, a theatergoer is confronted by such sights as outsized garbagy object spiling into the audience, a stage area without a proscenium arch, and a ceiling that has been lowered and turned into a twinkling canopy suggesting both cats' eyes and stars.

Composer Andrew Lloyd Webber began setting music to T.S. Eliot's poems in *Old Possum's Book of Practical Cats* in 1977. Later, he arranged the music for concerts, and still later—now in collaboration with director Trevor Nunn—he reworked the concept into a dramatic structure. In the song-and-dance spectacle, which has only the barest thread of a story line and no spoken dialogue, are such whimsically named characters as Jennyanddots; the Old Gumbie Cat who sits all day and becomes active only at night; the never satisfied Rum Tum Rugger; Bustopher Jones the well-fed, elegant cat about town; Mungojerrie and Rumpleteazer, those two knockabout clowns and cat burglers; the patriarchal Old Deuteronomy; Skimpleshanks the Railway Cat; and the mysterious Mr. Mistoffelees. The musical's song hit, "Memory," is sung by Grizabella (Betty Buckley), the faded Glamour Cat who, at the evening's end, ascends to the cats' heaven known as the Heaviside Layer. *Cats* surpassed the all-time longevity record for Broadway musicals, concluding its run on September 10, 2000 after nearly 18 years and over 7,400 performances.
Geffen OC/Faber & Faber, London (1981)

Cats. Betty Buckley as Grizabella. (Photofest)

ON YOUR TOES

Music: Richard Rodgers
Lyrics: Lorenz Hart
Book: Richard Rodgers, Lorenz Hart & George Abbott
Producers: Alfred de Liagre Jr., Roger L. Stevens, John Mauceri, Donald Seawell, Andre Pastoria
Director: George Abbott
Choreographers: George Balanchine, Donald Saddler, Peter Martins
Cast: Natalia Makarova, George S. Irving, Dina Merrill, George de la Peña, Christine Andreas, Lara Teeter, Betty Ann Grove, Peter Slutsker, Michael Vita
Songs: Same as original production
New York run: Virginia Theatre, March 6, 1983; 505 p.

(See page 94.)

MY ONE AND ONLY

Music: George Gershwin
Lyrics: Ira Gershwin
Book: Peter Stone, Timothy S. Meyer
Producers: Paramount Theatres (Dan Sherkow), Lester Allen, Francine LeFrak, Kenneth Greenblatt, Mark Schwartz
Director-choreographers: Thommie Walsh & Tommy Tune (Mike Nichols, Michael Bennett uncredited)
Cast: Twiggy, Tommy Tune, Charles "Honi" Coles, Bruce McGill, Denny Dillon, Roscoe Lee Browne
Songs: "I Can't Be Bothered Now"; "Blah, Blah, Blah"; "Boy Wanted"; "Soon"; "High Hat"; "Sweet and Low-Down"; "He Loves and She Loves"; " 'S Wonderful"; "Strike Up the Band"; "Nice Work If You Can Get It"; "My One and Only"; "Funny Face"; "Kickin' the Clouds Away" (lyric with B.G. DeSylva); "How Long Has This Been Going On?"
New York run: St. James Theatre, May 1, 1983; 767 p.

Within a week after the Broadway première of *Nine,* which he had directed, Tommy Tune was in rehearsal with Twiggy for what was originally announced as a revival of the Gershwins' 1927 musical *Funny Face.* By the time the show opened in New York, however, it had a completely new story, at least four directors, a score with only six of the original 12 songs (augmented by 11 other Gershwin standards), and it was now called *My One and Only.* Initially, the director and librettist were to have been Peter Sellars and Timothy Meyer, but after disagreements Sellars was replaced first by Mike Nichols then by Tune and Thommie Walsh, and Meyer by Peter Stone. The resulting book, still set in 1927, was an often anachronistic framework for the imaginatively staged song-and-dance numbers which found Tune playing a barnstorming aviator and Twiggy a champion swimmer who incongruously get involved with a bootlegging Harlem minister (Roscoe Lee Browne), an enigmatical tap-dancing philosopher (Charles "Honi" Coles), and a blackmailing Russian spy (Bruce McGill). Twiggy and Tune were succeeded on Broadway by Sandy Duncan and Don Correia. For the tour, Tune was co-starred with Miss Duncan.
Atlantic OC.

On Your Toes. George de la Peña and Natalia Makarova in the "Princess Zenobia" ballet. (Martha Swope)

My One and Only. Tommy Tune and Charles "Honi" Coles dancing to the title song. (Kenn Duncan)

LA CAGE AUX FOLLES

Music & lyrics: Jerry Herman
Book: Harvey Fierstein
Producer: Allan Carr
Director: Arthur Laurents
Choreographer: Scott Salmon
Cast: George Hearn, Gene Barry, Jay Garner, John Weiner, Elizabeth Parrish, Leslie Stevens, William Thomas Jr., Merle Louise
Songs: "A Little More Mascara"; "With You on My Arm"; "Song on the Sand"; "La Cage aux Folles"; "I Am What I Am"; "Masculinity"; "The Best of Times"
New York run: Palace Theatre, August 21, 1983, 1,761 p.

French author Jean Poiret's successful play and film about the relationship between the owner of a St. Tropez drag-queen nightclub and his star attraction provided Broadway with its first homosexual musical. In the story, the flamboyant Albin (George Hearn) — known on the stage as Zaza — and the more conservative Georges (Gene Barry) are middle-aged lovers who have been together for over 20 years. Their domestic peace is shattered, however, when Jean-Michel (John Weiner), Georges' son as a result of a youthful indiscretion, advises his father that he plans to wed the daughter of Edouard Dindon (Jay Garner), a local morals crusader. In order that Georges appear to his future in-laws as an upstanding citizen, he agrees that Albin must somehow be put back into the closet. Though hurt and defiant ("I Am What I Am"), Albin swallows his pride and aids the deception by dressing up as Georges' wife. After inadvertently revealing that he is what he is, Albin is not above a little blackmail to force Dindon to permit the marriage to take place.

Except for the homosexual angle, *La Cage aux Folles* (the name of Georges' nightclub) was in the tradition of the big, splashy Broadway book musical, complete with a glamorous chorus line (which even has two female dancers among the Cagelles). And though it was originally to have been put together by a different team of collaborators (when it was known as *The Queen of Basin Street*), the musical was a predestined smash by the time of its Boston tryout. The show marked Jerry Herman's tenth score (as well as his first hit since *Mame*) and playwright Harvey Fierstein's first experience as a librettist. George Hearn, who scored a notable hit as Albin, was succeeded by Walter Charles and Keene Curtis; Gene Barry was followed by Jamie Ross, Keith Michell, Van Johnson, Steeve Arlen, and Peter Marshall. The show's two road companies were headed by, respectively, Michell (replaced by Barry) and Charles, and by Marshall and Curtis. *La Cage aux Folles* was the first musical to charge $47.50 for orchestra seats.

Male actors appearing in drag have long been part of the Broadway musical scene. In the late 19th Century, Tony Hart made a specialty of performing women's roles in Harrigan and Hart shows, and other early female impersonators were Julian Eltinge (the most celebrated of all) and Bert Savoy (of the team of Savoy and Brennan). Later actors who donned feminine attire — usually as a transvestite sight gag — included Ole Olsen in *Hellzapoppin*, Bobby Clark in *Mexican Hayride, Sweethearts*, and *As the Girls Go*, Ray Bolger in *Where's Charley?*, Myron McCormick in *South Pacific*, Bert Lahr (as Queen Victoria) in *Two on the Aisle*, Jack Gilford in *A Funny Thing Happened on the Way to the Forum*, Robert Morse and Tony Roberts in *Sugar*, Mickey Rooney in *Sugar Babies*, and James Coco in the revival of *Little Me*. Actual homosexual — or at least effeminate — characters have been portrayed by Bobbie Watson in *Irene*, Danny Kaye in *Lady in the Dark*, Ray Bolger in *By Jupiter*, Joel Grey in *Cabaret*, Rene Auberjonois in *Coco*, Lee Roy Reams in *Applause*, Tommy Tune in *Seesaw*, and Michel Stuart and Sammy Williams in *A Chorus Line*.
RCA OC/ Samuel French (1987)*/ SF.

La Cage aux Folles. Les Cagelles. (Martha Swope)

La Cage aux Folles. The "Masculinity" number with Gene Barry and George Hearn. (Martha Swope)

Zorba. Anthony Quinn in the title role. (Martha Swope)

ZORBA

Music: John Kander
Lyrics: Fred Ebb
Book: Joseph Stein
Producers: Barry & Fran Weissler, Kenneth Greenblatt & John Pomerantz
Director: Michael Cacoyannis
Choreographer: Graciela Daniele
Cast: Anthony Quinn, Lila Kedrova, Robert Westenberg, Debbie Shapiro
Songs: Same as original production, plus "Mine Song" and "Woman"
New York run: Broadway Theatre, October 16, 1983; 362 p.

(See page 225.)

THE TAP DANCE KID

Music: Henry Krieger
Lyrics: Robert Lorick
Book: Charles Blackwell
Producers: Stanley White, Evelyn Barron, Harvey Klaris, Michel Stuart
Director: Vivian Matalon
Choreographer: Danny Daniels
Cast: Hinton Battle, Samuel E. Wright, Hattie Winston, Alfonso Ribeiro, Alan Weeks, Martine Allard, Jackie Lowe
Songs: "Dancing Is Everything"; "Fabulous Feet"; "Class Act"; "I Remember How It Was"; "Dance If It Makes You Happy"
New York run: Broadhurst Theatre, December 21, 1983; 669 p.

The methods by which ambitious young blacks have been able to box or sing their way out of the ghetto have been documented in such musicals as *Golden Boy* and *Dreamgirls,* but *The Tap Dance Kid* offered the unaccustomed situation of an upper middle-class family in which a successful lawyer (Samuel E. Wright) tries to stifle the dreams of his ten-year-old son Willie (Alfonso Ribeiro) to follow the profession of his Uncle Dipsey (Hinton Battle) and become a dancer. Featuring Battle's exciting footwork, the show surmounted a divided press to chalk up a surprisingly long Broadway run. The musical's origin was a television play (in which librettist Charles Blackwell played the father) that had been based on a novel, *Nobody's Family Is Going to Change,* by Louise Fitzhugh.
Polydor OC/ Samuel French (1988)*/ SF.

SUNDAY IN THE PARK WITH GEORGE

Music & lyrics: Stephen Sondheim
Book: James Lapine
Producers: Shubert Organization & Emanuel Azenberg
Director: James Lapine
Cast: Mandy Patinkin, Bernadette Peters, Charles Kimbrough, Barbara Bryne, Dana Ivey, William Parry, Robert Westenberg
Songs: "Sunday in the Park With George"; "Finishing the Hat"; "We Do Not Belong Together"; "Beautiful"; "Sunday"; "Children and Art"; "Move On"
New York run: Booth Theatre, May 2, 1984; 604 p.

After six productions in a row with director Harold Prince, Stephen Sondheim joined with director-librettist James Lapine for an especially challenging and personal work. *Sunday in the Park With George* reveals what the authors feel about art, the creative process, the artist's sacrifice of human emotions, and the need to avoid being influenced by what is currently trendy and faddish. To express these feelings, Sondheim and Lapine concentrated on the creation of one painting, Georges Seurat's "A Sunday Afternoon on the Island of La Grande Jatte."

In the first act, which takes place on the island in 1884, George (Mandy Patinkin) is busily painting the Parisians who are enjoying a day off strolling through a park on the Seine. We get to know the people and their relationships with one another, and in particular we get to know George and his relationship with Dot (Bernadette Peters), his model and mistress. The artist's preoccupation with his work, however, makes theirs a doomed romance, and the model, who is pregnant, accepts a baker's offer of marriage. The second act jumps to the present in New York, where the painter's great-grandson, a multi-media sculptor also named George, is at a creative impasse after completing his seventh "Chromolume." His confidence is restored, however, when he visits La Grande Jatte and is urged by the ghost of his great-grandmother to stop worrying about where he is going and what others think and "just keep moving on."

Sunday in the Park With George, which was first staged as a Playwrights Horizons workshop production in July 1983, was awarded the 1985 Pulitzer Prize for drama. During its run, Patinkin was spelled by Robert Westenberg and Harry Groener, and Miss Peters was succeeded by Betsy Joslyn and Maryann Plunkett.
RCA OC/ Dodd, Mead (1986).

Sunday in the Park With George. Mandy Patinkin and Bernadette Peters. (Martha Swope)

BIG RIVER

Music & lyrics: Roger Miller
Book: William Hauptman
Producers: Rocco Landesman, Heidi Landesman, Rick Steiner, M. Anthony
 Fisher, Dodger Productions
Director: Des McAnuff
Choreographer: Janet Watson
Cast: Rene Auberjonois, Reathal Bean, Susan Browning, Patti Cohenour, Gor-
 don Connell, Bob Gunton, Daniel H. Jenkins, Ron Richardson
Songs: "Guv'ment"; "Muddy Water"; "River in the Rain"; "Waiting for the Light
 to Shine"; "Worlds Apart"; "You Ought to Be Here With Me"; "Leaving's
 Not the Only Way to Go"
New York run: Eugene O'Neill Theatre, April 25, 1985; 1,005 p.

Producers Rocco and Heidi Landesman came up with the idea of a musical version of Mark Twain's *Adventures of Huckleberry Finn* primarily because they
were anxious to find the right property that would best introduce Broadway to the
talents of country music songwriter Roger Miller. *Big River* was tried out at the
American Repertory Theatre (ART) in Cambridge, Massachusetts, early in 1984,
and then at the La Jolla Playhouse in California before those connected with the
show felt that it was ready for New York. Set in 1849, with the action taking place
both on the Mississippi River and in various locations along its banks (thanks to
Heidi Landesman's atmospheric settings), the imaginative and faithfully conceived adaptation of the picaresque novel is concerned primarily with the relationship between Huck Finn and the runaway slave Jim (Daniel H. Jenkins and
Ron Richardson) as they enjoy the untethered life traveling on a raft down the
Mississippi from Hannibal, Missouri, to Hillsboro, Arkansas. In 1957, a previous
musical based on Mark Twain's Mississippi River stories was offered Off Broadway under the title *Livin' the Life.*
MCA OC/ Grove Press (1986)/ R&H.

Big River. Ron Richardson and Daniel
H. Jenkins. (Martha Swope)

SONG AND DANCE

Music: Andrew Lloyd Webber
Lyrics: Don Black, Richard Maltby Jr.
Adaptation: Richard Maltby Jr.
Producers: Cameron Mackintosh, Shubert Organization, FWM Producing Group
Director: Richard Maltby Jr.
Choreographer: Peter Martins
Cast: Bernadette Peters, Christopher d'Amboise, Gregg Burge, Charlotte d'Amboise, Cynthia Onrubia, Scott Wise
Songs: "Capped Teeth and Caesar Salad"; "So Much to Do in New York"; "Unexpected Song"; "Come Back With the Same Look in Your Eyes"; "Tell Me on a Sunday"
New York run: Royale Theatre, September 18, 1985; 474 p.

The "Dance" of the title originated in 1979 when Andrew Lloyd Webber composed a set of variations on Paganini's A-Minor Caprice that seemed perfect for a ballet; the "Song" originated a year later with a one-woman television show, *Tell Me on a Sunday,* consisting entirely of musical pieces. Two years after that both works were presented together in London as a full evening's entertainment. In New York, this unconventional package won praise for Bernadette Peters, whose task in Act I was to create, without dialogue, the character of a free-spirited English girl who has dalliances in America with four men. The second act offered a choreographic self-examination of one of the men (Christopher d'Amboise) and the two halves were joined when girl and boy were reunited. After a year on Broadway, Miss Peters was succeeded by Betty Buckley. RCA OC/ R&H.

THE MYSTERY OF EDWIN DROOD

Music, lyrics & book: Rupert Holmes
Producer: Joseph Papp for the New York Shakespeare Festival
Director: Wilford Leach
Choreographer: Graciela Daniele
Cast: George Rose, Cleo Laine, Betty Buckley, Howard McGillin, Patti Cohenour, Jana Schneider, John Herrera, Jerome Dempsey
Songs: "Moonfall"; "The Wages Of Sin"; "No Good Can Come from Bad"; "Ceylon"; "Perfect Strangers"; "Both Sides of the Coin"; "Off to the Races"; "Don't Quit While You're Ahead"
New York run: Imperial Theatre, December 2, 1985; 608 p.

The Mystery of Edwin Drood came to Broadway after being initially presented the previous summer in a series of free performances sponsored by the New York Shakespeare Festival at the Delacorte Theatre in Central Park. It was the first stage work of composer-lyricist-librettist Rupert Holmes, whose lifelong fascination with Charles Dickens' unfinished novel had been the catalyst for the project. Since there were no clues as to Drood's murderer or even if a murder had been committed, Holmes decided to let the audience provide the show's ending by voting how it turns out. The writer's second major decision was to offer the musical as if it were being performed by an acting company at London's Music Hall Royale in 1873, complete with such conventions as a Chairman (George Rose) to comment on the action and a woman (Betty Buckley) to play the part of Edwin Drood. During the run, Miss Buckley was replaced by Donna Murphy, and Cleo Laine (as the mysterious Princess Puffer) by Loretta Swit and Karen Morrow. On November 13, 1986, in an attempt to attract more theatre-goers, the musical's title was officially changed to *Drood.* Polydor OC/ Doubleday (1986)/ TW.

SWEET CHARITY

Music: Cy Coleman
Lyrics: Dorothy Fields
Book: Neil Simon
Producers: Jerome Minskoff, James Nederlander, Arthur Rubin, Joseph Harris
Director-choreographer: Bob Fosse
Cast: Debbie Allen, Michael Rupert, Bebe Neuwirth, Allison Williams, Lee
        Wilkof, Mark Jacoby, Irving Allen Lee
Songs: Same as original production
New York run: Minskoff Theatre, April 27, 1986; 368 p.

(See page 216.)

Me and My Girl. Robert Lindsay and Maryann Plunkett dancing to the title song.
(Alan Berliner)

ME AND MY GIRL

Music: Noel Gay
Lyrics: Douglas Furber, etc.
Book: L. Arthur Rose & Douglas Furber; revised by Stephen Fry
Producers: Richard Armitage, Terry Allen Kramer, James Nederlander, Stage Promotions Ltd.
Director: Mike Ockrent
Choreographer: Gillian Gregory
Cast: Robert Lindsay, Maryann Plunkett, George S. Irving, Jane Connell, Jane Summerhays, Nick Ullett, Timothy Jerome, Thomas Toner, Justine Johnston, Elizabeth Larner
Songs: "Thinking of No-One But Me"; "The Family Solicitor"; "Me and My Girl"; "Hold My Hand" (music with Maurice Elwin; lyric: Harry Graham); "Once You Lose Your Heart" (lyric: Noel Gay); "The Lambeth Walk"; "The Sun Has Got His Hat On" (lyric: Frank Butler); "Take It on the Chin"; "Love Makes the World Go Round" (lyric: Gay); "Leaning on a Lamppost" (lyric: Gay)
New York run: Marquis Theatre, August 10, 1986; 1,412 p.

One of the most unlikely Broadway hits of 1986 was an almost fifty-year-old London musical comedy that, despite its near record-breaking run of 1,646 performances, had always been deemed too "English" to be considered for a New York showing before. Yet, followed by a successful West End reincarnation in 1985, *Me and My Girl* became an instant smash upon being offered as the premiere attraction at the newly built Marquis Theatre (located in the Marriott Marquis Hotel on Broadway between 45th and 46th Streets). Part of the reason had to do with the imaginative staging, Noel Gay's simple, catchy melodies, and the show's general spirit of eager-to-please innocent merriment. But most of the show's popularity surely was due to the protean talents of Robert Lindsay, the original star of the London revival who made his Broadway debut in the musical. (Lindsay was subsequently succeeded by Jim Dale and James Brennan.) The road company, which began touring in 1987, was initially headed by Tim Curry.

It was producer Richard Armitage, the son of the composer (Gay's real name was Reginald Armitage), who first saw the potential in bringing back *Me and My Girl.* The younger Armitage devoted years to tracking down the original score and script, then signed playwright Stephen Fry to do the text revisions with an assist from director Mike Ockrent. The book was still about a pugnacious Cockney, Bill Snibson (Lindsay), who turns up as the long-lost heir to the Earldom of Hareford. Complications arise over Bill's devotion to his Lambeth sweetie, Sally Smith (Maryann Plunkett), and the efforts of the Hareford clan (led by George S. Irving and Jane Connell) to send her back where she belongs. But the bluebloods—who even join in the high-strutting, thumb-cocking dance known as "The Lambeth Walk"—eventually give their consent and Bill ends up with both his inheritance and his girl (who has been miraculously transformed, *Pygmalion* fashion, into an elegant lady).

The character of Bill Snibson was originated in 1935 by the diminutive clown Lupino Lane in *Twenty to One,* a race-track yarn in which Bill tilts with the stuffy killjoys of the Anti-Gambling League. Lane became so attached to the part that two years later he had the show's librettists fashion a new musical for him about Bill's tilting with the stuffy members of the aristocracy. *Me and My Girl* was such a personal triumph that Lane toured in it extensively and brought it back to London in 1941, 1945, and 1949.
MCA OC/ Samuel French, London (1954)*/ SF.

Les Misérables. Colm Wilkinson, Michael Maguire and David Bryant manning the barricade. (Michael Le Poer Trench/Bob Marshak)

LES MISÉRABLES

Music: Claude-Michel Schönberg
Lyrics: Herbert Kretzmer
Conception: Alain Boublil & Claude-Michel Schönberg
Original French Text: Alain Boublil & Jean-Marc Natel
Adaptation: Trevor Nunn & John Caird
Producer: Cameron Mackintosh
Directors: Trevor Nunn & John Caird
Choreographer: Kate Flatt
Cast: Colm Wilkinson, Terrence Mann, Randy Graff, Michael Maguire, Leo Burmester, Frances Ruffelle, David Bryant, Judy Kuhn, Jennifer Butt, Braden Danner
Songs: "I Dreamed a Dream"; "Who Am I?"; "Castle on a Cloud"; "Master of the House"; "Red and Black"; "Do You Hear the People Sing?"; "In My Life"; "On My Own" (Lyric with Trevor Nunn & John Caird); "A Little Fall of Rain", Rain"; "Drink With Me"; "Bring Him Home"; "Empty Chairs at Empty Tables"
New York run: Broadway Theatre, March 12,1987; 6,680 p.

Something of a follow-up to the Royal Shakespeare Company's highly acclaimed non-musical dramatization of Charles Dickens' *Life and Adventures of Nicholas Nickleby, Les Misérables* was again directed by Trevor Nunn and John Caird, designed by John Napier, and lighted by David Hersey. (This time, however, it was produced by Cameron Mackintosh in partnership with the RSC.) Once more those responsible put together an epic saga dealing with the theme of social injustice and the plight of the downtrodden that had inspired the earlier massive 19th-century literary classic.

Originally conceived in 1979 by the French team of composer Claude-Michel Schönberg and lyricist Alain Boublil (with the collaboration of poet Jean-Marc Natel), the pop opera gives dramatic life to Victor Hugo's sprawling 1,200 page novel of suffering and salvation during a tumultuous period in French history. The story takes the valiant hero Jean Valjean from 1815 (after he has been paroled following 19 years on a chain gang for stealing a loaf of bread) to the illfated 1832 student uprising in Paris, when Valjean saves the life of Marius (David Bryant), the beloved of his adopted daughter Cosette (Judy Kuhn). Throughout the saga, Valjean is relentlessly hounded by the fanatic police inspector Javert (Terrence Mann) for breaking his parole, a pursuit that ends only when Javert, after chasing his quarry through the sewers of Paris, drowns himself in the Seine because he has violated his obsessive code of justice by letting Valjean escape.

With Herbert Kretzmer writing the English lyrics (and James Fenton credited for "additional material"), *Les Misérables* was successfully launched in London in 1985 at the RSC's Barbican Theatre, then brought to New York two years later by Mackintosh with the original lead, Colm Wilkinson, repeating his impressive performance as Valjean. (Wilkinson was subsequently replaced by Gary Morris, Timothy Shew, and William Solo.) Equally vital to the musical's appeal were Nunn and Caird's inventive, fluid staging and Napier's atmospheric sets—including an immense barricade for the uprising—that moved on a mammoth turntable. *Les Misérables* was the first musical in Broadway history to open at a top ticket price of $50. Prior to this production, the most successful musical of French origin (which also crossed the Atlantic via London) had been *Irma la Douce*. Besides the original Broadway cast album, many other recordings of the show are available. Geffen OC.

STARLIGHT EXPRESS

Music: Andrew Lloyd Webber
Lyricist: Richard Stilgoe
Producers: Martin Starger & Lord Grade
Director: Trevor Nunn
Choreographer: Arlene Phillips
Cast: Ken Ard, Jamie Beth Chandler, Steve Fowler, Jane Krakowski, Andrea McArdle, Greg Mowry, Reva Rice, Robert Torti
Songs: "Rolling Stock"; "Engine of Love"; "Pumping Iron"; "Make Up My Heart"; "Starlight Express"; "I Am the Starlight"; "Only You"; "One Rock and Roll Too Many"; "Light at the End of the Tunnel"
New York run: Gershwin Theatre, March 15, 1987; 761 p.

At a cost of well over $8 million—the highest in Broadway history—*Starlight Express* solidified the British invasion by joining *Cats, Me and My Girl,* and *Les Misérables* as one of the four biggest Main Stem attractions during the first half of 1987. Dubbed *Cats* on wheels, this hi-tech spectacle offered not only humanized railroad trains but put them on roller skates zooming on multilevel tracks around a glow-in-the-dark Erector-set panorama of the United States (created by John Napier), dominated by a gigantic steel suspension bridge that could turn, spin, dip and rise. The original idea for the fantasy began in 1973 when Andrew Lloyd Webber was asked to write a rock score for an animated television series based on the British equivalent of *The Little Engine That Could.* That never worked out but it started the composer thinking about a vaguely Cinderella-ish fable in which a battered steam engine named Rusty, encouraged by his father named Poppa, wins a race against a flashy diesel locomotive named Greaseball and a slick electric locomotive named Electra. First opening in London in 1984, the show itself became a flashy, slick hit (the original version offered skaters on ramps that encircled the theatre), then was reconceived for the American production requiring the renovation of the Gershwin Theatre (formerly the Uris) that alone cost $2.5 million.
MCA SC.

Starlight Express. The "Engine of Love" number with Greg Mowry, Reva Rice, Jane Krakowski, Lola Knox (understudy for Jamie Beth Chandler), and Andrea McArdle. (©Martha Swope)

ANYTHING GOES

Music & lyrics: Cole Porter
Book: Timothy Crouse & John Weidman based on original by P. G. Wodehouse & Guy Bolton, Howard Lindsay & Russel Crouse
Producer: Lincoln Center Theatre (Gregory Mosher, Bernard Gersten)
Director: Jerry Zaks
Choreographer: Michael Smuin
Cast: Patti LuPone, Howard McGillin, Bill McCutcheon, Rex Everhart, Anne Francine, Linda Hart, Anthony Heald, Kathleen Mahony-Bennett
Songs: Same as original production plus "No Cure Like Travel"; "Easy to Love"; "I Want to Row on the Crew"; "Friendship"; "It's De-Lovely"; "Goodbye, Little Dream, Goodbye"
New York run: Vivian Beaumont Theatre, October 13, 1987; 804 p.

(See page 88.)

INTO THE WOODS

Music & lyrics: Stephen Sondheim
Book: James Lapine
Producers: Heidi Landesman, Rocco Landesman, Rick Steiner, M. Anthony Fisher, Frederic Mayerson, Jujamcyn Theatres
Director: James Lapine
Cast: Bernadette Peters, Joanna Gleason, Chip Zien, Tom Aldredge, Robert Westenberg, Barbara Bryne, Kim Crosby, Danielle Ferland, Merle Louise, Ben Wright, Joy Franz, Edmund Lyndeck, Kay McClelland, Lauren Mitchell
Songs: "Into the Woods"; "Hello, Little Girl"; "I Know Things Now"; "Giants in the Sky"; "Agony"; "It Takes Two"; "Stay With Me"; "Any Moment"; "Last Midnight"; "No More"; "No One Is Alone"; "Children Will Listen"
New York run: Martin Beck Theatre, November 5, 1987; 764 p.

First tried out at the Old Globe Theatre in San Diego in December 1986, *Into the Woods* took a look at the darker—or grimmer—side of fairy tales in dealing with the themes of communal responsibility, the importance of showing consideration to others, and the values we pass on to our children. The story brings together such familiar characters as Cinderella and her Prince, Jack the Giant Killer, Little Red Ridinghood and the Wolf, Rapunzel, Snow White, and Sleeping Beauty, plus two original characters, a Baker and his wife, and puts them in a plotty tale that gets somewhat burdened down by the allegorical references. This was Stephen Sondheim's second musical with librettist-director James Lapine, the first being *Sunday in the Park With George.* It also involved the same costar (Bernadette Peters), set designer (Tony Straiges), costume designer (Patricia Zipprodt), lighting designer (Richard Nelson), and music director (Paul Gemignani). During the run, Miss Peters was followed by Phylicia Rashad, Betsy Joslyn, Nancy Dussault, and Ellen Foley. In the summer of 1988, Dick Cavett took over the part of the Narrator for two months. The road company, which toured for 10 months, was headed by Cleo Laine (Witch), Mary Gordon Murray (Cinderella), and Charlotte Rae (Jack's Mother).
RCA OC/ Theatre Comm. Group (1987)/ TW.

THE PHANTOM OF THE OPERA

Music: Andrew Lloyd Webber
Lyrics: Charles Hart, Richard Stilgoe
Book: Richard Stilgoe & Andrew Lloyd Webber
Producer: Cameron Mackintosh & The Really Useful Theatre Co.
Director: Harold Prince
Choreographer: Gillian Lynne
Cast: Michael Crawford, Sarah Brightman, Steve Barton, Judy Kaye, Cris Groenendaal, Nicholas Wyman, Leila Martin, David Romano, Elisa Heinsohn, George Lee Andrews
Song: "Think of Me"; "Angel of Music"; "The Phantom of the Opera"; "The Music of the Night"; "Prima Donna"; "All I Ask of You"; "Masquerade"; "Wishing You Were Somehow Here Again"; "The Point of No Return"
New York run: Majestic Theatre, January 26,1988; (still running 6/08)

Turn-of-the-century French novelist Gaston Leroux wrote *Le Fantôme de l'Opéra* after visiting the subterranean depths of the Paris Opera House—including its man-made lake. Though not a success when published in 1911, the ghoulish tale of the mad, disfigured Phantom who lives in the bowels of the theatre and does away with those who would thwart the operatic career of his beloved Christine, became internationally celebrated in 1925 when it served as a movie vehicle for Lon Chaney. (Subsequent film versions were made in 1943 with Claude Rains, in 1962 with Herbert Lom, in 1989 with Robert Englund, and—for television—in 1982 with Maximilian Schell.)

In 1984 a stage adaptation, using excerpts from public-domain operas by Verdi, Gounod, and Offenbach, was written and directed by Ken Hill and produced by Joan Littlewood at an East London fringe theatre. Andrew Lloyd Webber thought it might be developed into a campy West End musical— something along the lines of *The Rocky Horror Show*—that he would co-produce with Cameron Mackintosh. After reading the Leroux novel, however, Lloyd Webber realized that far from being a penny dreadful, Leroux's work was a genuinely romantic and moving tale, and he decided to write the score himself. His lyricist and co-adapter was Richard Stilgoe and his director was Harold Prince. After a tryout of the first act at a summer festival at his home in Sydmonton (with Colm Wilkinson as the Phantom and Lloyd Webber's wife Sarah Brightman as Christine), the composer felt that there was need for a more romantic approach in the lyrics and, after first trying to enlist Alan Jay Lerner and then Tim Rice, he settled on the relatively inexperienced Charles Hart to augment Stilgoe's work.

The Phantom of the Opera opened in London in 1986 with Michael Crawford and Miss Brightman. It won a resoundingly affirmative reception for its cast, staging, and scenic effects, including a chandelier that descends from the auditorium ceiling and crashes on stage. At this writing, the musical is still running at Her Majesty's Theatre. Basically the same production was transferred to Broadway, with Crawford, Miss Brightman, and Steve Barton (as The Phantom's romantic rival) repeating their roles. A presold hit with an $18 million advance, the show made Andrew Lloyd Webber the first composer to have three musicals running simultaneously in London and New York. (The other two: *Cats* and *Starlight Express*.)

The Phantom of the Opera is the most financially successful musical to date. At this writing there are 13 companies playing the show around the world, including productions in Toronto, San Francisco, Hamburg, Sydney, and two American touring companies.

Polydor OC/ Henry Holt (1987).

The Phantom of the Opera. Michael Crawford and Sarah Brightman. (Clive Barda)

CHESS

Music: Benny Andersson and Bjorn Ulvaeus
Lyrics: Tim Rice
Book: Richard Nelson; based on an idea by Tim Rice
Producer: Shubert Organization; 3 Knights Ltd.; Robert Fox Ltd.
Director: Trevor Nunn
Choreographer: Lynne Taylor-Corbett
Cast: Judy Kuhn, David Carroll, Philip Casnoff, Dennnis Parlato, Marcia Mitzman, Paul Harman, Harry Goz, Ann Crumb
Songs: "The Story of Chess"; "Quartet"; "Nobody's Side"; "Terrace Duet"; "Pity the Child"; "Heaven Help My Heart"; "Anthem"; "One Night in Bangkok"; "You and I"; "I Know Him So Well"; "Someone Else's Story"; "Endgame"
New York run: Imperial Theatre, April 28, 1988; 68 p.

There have been musicals about the cold war (e.g. *Leave It to Me!, Silk Stockings*), but *Chess* was the first to treat the conflict seriously, using an international chess match as a metaphor. Tim Rice first tried to interest his former partner, Andrew Lloyd Webber, in the project. Like the Lloyd Webber-Rice shows *Jesus Christ Superstar* and *Evita, Chess* originated as a successful record album before it became a stage production. The story concerns itself with a romantic triangle involving a Bobby Fischer type American chess champion, his Russian opponent who defects to the West, and the Hungarian born American "second" who transfers her affections from the American to the Russian without bringing happiness to anyone. As staged in London, the show was an elaborate high tech spectacle with minimal dialogue. Though a sellout for most of its three year run, it never quite made back its initial investment there. A revised version, in a more conventional dramatic form (and the added song "Someone Else's Story"), opened in New York, where the show lost $6 million. RCA OC

JEROME ROBBINS' BROADWAY

Music and lyrics: Miscellaneous writers
Producers: The Shubert Organization, Roger Berlind, Suntory Intl. Corp., Byron
Goldman, Emanuel Azenberg
Director and Choreographer: Jerome Robbins
Cast: Jason Alexander, Charlotte d'Amboise, Susann Fletcher, Susan
Kikuchi, Michael Kubala, Robert LaFosse, Jane Lanier, Joey McKneely,
Luis Perez, Faith Prince, Debbie Shapiro, Scott Wise
Songs: "New York, New York" (Leonard Bernstein-Betty Comden, Adolph
Green); "Charleston" (Morton Gould); "Comedy Tonight" (Stephen
Sondheim); "West Side Story" dances (Berstein); "The Small House of
Uncle Thomas" (Richard Rodgers-Oscar Hammerstein II); "You Gotta
Have a Gimmick" (Styne-Sondheim); "I'm Flying" (Mark Charlap-
Carolyn Leigh); "On a Sunday by the Sea" ballat (Styne); "Mr Monotony"
(Irving Berlin); "Fiddler on the Roof" scenes (Jerry Bock-Sheldon
Harnick)
New York run: Imperial Theatre, February 26, 1989; 633 p.

The stage equivalent of MGM's *That's Entertainment* series, *Jerome Robbins'
Broadway* is a sampling of highlights from Robbins' 21-year career—from *On the
Town* in 1944 to *Fiddler on the Roof* in 1964. Featured in this well-organized
déjà vu revue (which cost $8.8 million and utilizes a cast of 62) are sequences
from nine of the 15 productions for which Robbins' served as choreographer or
director-choreographer, plus one number, "Comedy Tonight" from *A Funny
Thing Happened on the Way to the Forum,* which he had been called in to stage
during the show's tryour and for which he received no program credit. Another
piece, Irving Berlin's "Mr. Monotony," makes its Broadway debut in this
production since it had been cut out of both *Miss Liberty* and *Call Me Madam.*
The show established a new top ticket price of $55, subsequenlty raised to $60.
So far during the run, Jason Alexander has been succeeded by Terrence Mann,
and Debbie Shapiro by Karen Mason.
RCA OC.

Grand Hotel. David Carroll and Liliane Montevecchi (Martha Swope)

GRAND HOTEL

Music and lyrics: Robert Wright and George Forrest; *Music and lyrics by Maury Yeston; **Lyrics revised by Maury Yeston

Book: Luther Davis; based on Vicki Baum's Grand Hotel

Producers: Martin Richards, Mary Lee Johnson, Sam Crothers, Sander Jacobs, Kenneth D. Greenblatt, Paramount Pictures, Jujamcyn Theatres, in association with Marvin A. Krauss

Director and Choreographer: Tommy Tune

Cast: John Wylie, Yvonne Marceau and Pierre Dulaline, Timothy Jerome, Jane Krakowski, Michael Jeter, Karen Akers, Liliane Montevecchi, David Carroll

Songs: "The Grand Parade"*; "As It Should Be"**; "Some Have, Some Have Not"**; "At the Grand Hotel"*; "Who Couldn't Dance With You"; "The Boston Merger"**; "Love Can't Happen"*; "I Waltz Alone"**; "Roses at the Station"**

New York run: Martin Beck Theatre; November 12, 1989; 1,018 p.

Instead of a linear story, Tommy Tune interwove the stories of the staff and guests of the Grand Hotel with a choreographer's vision and swirled them about for almost two intermissionless hours. The stories of the penniless Baron (David Carroll) turned cat burglar who fell in love with the aging ballerina (Liliane Montevecchi) instead of stealing her jewels as he had planned; the devoted dogsbody (Karen Akers) who loves the ballerina; the industrial magnate (Timothy Jerome) who wrestles with his conscience before surrendering to the big lie; the young out of work typist (Jane Krakowski) who dreams of becoming a success in Hollywood but has to sell herself first; and the accountant (Michael Jeter) who wants to live before his unnamed fatal illness carries him off were all fluidly unfolded through crosscutting scenes and dance, dance, dance on a dazzling Tony Walton set that placed the orchestra on a level above the hotel lobby.

During the run, the production moved to the Gershwin Theatre. David Carroll was replaced by John Schneider and later by Rex Smith; Liliane Montevecchi by Zina Bethune and later by Cyd Charisse (making her Broadway debut); Michael Jeter by Austin Pendelton; Jane Krakowski by Lynette Perry; Karen Akers by Valerie Cutko.

Vicki Baum's novel had been a play in Berlin, had had a successful run on Broadway (459 performances during the 1930-31 season) and had been a 1932 megastarred Hollywood film, with a cast headed by Greta Garbo, John and Lionel Barrymore, and Joan Crawford. In 1958 the team of Wright and Forrest, book writer Luther Davis and director Albert Marre presented *At the Grand* in California. (It opened in Los Angeles and closed in San Francisco.) "We'll Take a Glass Together" was from that earlier version. The cast was headed by Paul Muni and Joan Diener and lasted eight weeks.

RCA/OC

GYPSY

Music: Jule Styne
Lyrics: Stephen Sondheim
Book: Arthur Laurents
Producers: Barry and Fran Weissler
Director: Arthur Laurents
Choreography: Original production directed and choreographed by Jerome Robbins; Mr. Robbins' choreography reproduced by Bonnie Walker
Cast: Tyne Daley, Crista Moore, Tracy Venner, Robert Lambert, Jonathan Hadary, John Remme
Songs: Same as original production
New York run: St. James Theatre, November 16, 1989; 477 p.

(See page 182.)

CITY OF ANGELS

Music: Cy Coleman
Lyrics: David Zippel
Book: Larry Gelbart
Producers: Nick Vanoff, Roger Berlind, Jujamcyn Theaters, Suntory International Corp., The Shubert Organization
Director: Michael Blakemore
Choreographer: musical numbers staged by Walter Painter
Cast: James Naughton, Gregg Edelman, Randy Graff, Dee Hoty, Kay McClelland, Rene Auberjonois
Songs: "Double Talk"; "What You Don't Know About Women"; "The Buddy System"; "With Every Breath I Take"; "Ev'rybody's Gotta Be Somewhere"; "All Ya Have to Do Is Wait"; "You're Nothing Without Me"; "It Needs Work"; "You Can Always Count on Me"
New York run: Virginia Theatre, December 11, 1989; 878 p.

In *City of Angels*, a spoof of the hard boiled private eye movies of the '40s, Larry Gelbart (*A Funny Thing Happened on the Way to the Forum*) chronicled the troubles of Stein (Greg Edelman), a writer of detective fiction who is in Hollywood working to adapt his own novel about the detective Stone (James Naughton) into a screenplay. The story begins with Stone in hospital with a bullet wound in his shoulder commenting on how it happened. Shortly thereafter, the scene shifts as a man sitting at a typewriter appears on stage. The man is Stein and the story Stone is telling is the film Stein is writing. As he rewrites, the film is rewound and the actors move backwards and speak backwards. The film sequences are in black, white and gray, and the writer is in living color. Two casts are listed in the program, the Hollywood cast and the film cast. Each Hollywood actor has a counterpart in the film cast on stage, and the action shifts between the film and the real people of the story. Stein's personal life falls apart as his wife accuses him of selling out and she returns to New York. Eventually he realizes he *has* sold out, and he reclaims his values. Michael Blakemore's direction, aided by the Angel City 4, a scat singing Greek chorus, Robin Wagner's sets (grayish for the film sequences and creamy for the "live" scenes) and Florence Klotz's costumes (black, whtie and gray for the film and color for the "real" people) sorted everything out.

Mr. Coleman had been represented on Broadway in April 1989 by *Welcome to the Club* (book by A. E. Hochner and lyrics by A.E. Hochner and Cy Coleman). It lasted 12 performances.
CBS Records Inc./OC

ASPECTS OF LOVE

Music: Andrew Lloyd Webber
Lyrics: Don Black and Charles Hart
Book: Andrew Lloyd Webber; based on the novel by David Garnett
Producer: The Really Useful Theatre Company Inc.
Director: Trevor Nunn
Choreographer: Gillian Lynne
Cast: Ann Crumb, Michael Ball, Kevin Colson, Walter Charles, Kathleen Rowe McAllen, Deanna DuClos, Danielle DuClos
Songs: "Love Changes Everything"; "Seeing Is Believing"; "A Memory of Happy Moments"; "She'd Be Far Better Off With You"; "Other Pleasures"; "The First Man You Remember"; "Anything But Lonely"
New York run: Broadhurst Theatre, April 8, 1990; 377 p.

Andrew Lloyd Webber first mounted a "cabaret" production of *Aspects of Love* in 1983 at the annual music festival on his Sydmonton estate. The musical again involved him with his *The Phantom of the Opera* colleagues Charles Hart, Gillian Lynne, Maria Bjornson, and Andrew Bridges, and reunited him with director Trevor Nunn for the first time since *Starlight Express.*

Based on the novelized autobiography of David Garnett, a minor Bloomsbury figure and a nephew of Virginia Woolf, the prologue of this through-composed soap opera of musical beds covers a seventeen year period. It begins in 1964 with Alex recounting the story of his life ("Love Changes Everything"). Flashback to 1947 when, at 17, he fell in love with 25 year old Rose Vibert, the star of a touring acting company. He persuaded her to spend her forthcoming two week layoff period lying in with him at his Uncle George's unoccupied estate. George unexpectedly arrived (from an assignation in Paris with mistress Giulietta, who lives in Rome) and fell in love with Rose. In La Ronde fashion, Alex returns to the army, George continues his relationship with Giulietta, but eventually marries Rose (she also has a bit of a fling with Giulietta). George and Rose produce a daughter (who may or may not be the daughter of Alex), Jenny, who falls madly in love with Alex when he gets back to George and Rose some twelve years later. George dies, Alex falls in love with Giulietta. Perhaps to continue this madness.
Polydor/London OC

Aspects of Love. Ann Crumb and Michael Ball (Clive Barda)

ONCE ON THIS ISLAND

Music: Stephen Flaherty
Lyrics and book: Lynn Ahrens (based on *My Love, My Love* by Rosa Guy)
Producers: Shubert Organization, Capital Cities/ABC, Suntory International and James Walsh in association with Playwrights Horizons
Director and choreographer: Graciela Daniele
Cast: Jerry Dixon, Andrea Frierson, Sheila Gibbs, La Chanze, Kecia Lewis-Evans, Afi McClendon, Gerry McIntyre, Milton Craig Nealey, Nikki Rene, Eric Riley, Ellis E. Williams
Songs: "We Dance"; "One Small Girl"; "And the Gods Heard Her Prayer"; "Pray"; "Forever Yours"; "The Sad Tale of Beauxhommes"; "Mama Will Provide"; "Some Girls"; "Why We Tell the Story"
New York run: Booth Theater, October 18, 1990; 469 p.

Set in the French Antilles, the story of *Once on This Island* is a fable told to calm a young girl during a storm. It tells of the journey of Ti Moune (La Chanze), plucked from just such a storm by the gods and sheltered in a tree. She grows into a beautiful peasant girl who rescues Daniel (Jerry Dixon), the mulatto son of a wealthy landowner after he has been hurt in an automobile accident. Ti Moune makes a pact with the gods—her life for Daniel's— for she is convinced that the power of her love is so strong it can conquer death. Eventually he is healed, and even though he is grateful for her help, he rejects her love. The gods give her eternal life by turning her into a tree. The musical was first produced at Playwrights Horizons for 3 weeks in May 1990, then transferred in tact to the Booth Theatre in October.
RCA/OC.

Miss Saigon. Lea Salonga and Rian R. Baldomero. (Trench/Marcus)

MISS SAIGON

Music: Claude-Michel Schönberg
Lyrics: Richard Maltby, Jr. and Alain Boublil; adapted from original French lyrics by Alain Boublil; additional material by Richard Maltby, Jr.
Producer: Cameron Mackintosh
Director: Nicholas Hytner
Musical Staging: Bob Avian
Cast: Jonathan Pryce, Lea Salonga, Hinton Battle, Willy Falk, Barry K. Bernal, Liz Callaway, Kam Cheng
Songs: "The Heat Is On in Saigon"; "The Movie in My Mind"; "Why God, Why?"; "Sun and Moon"; "The Last Night of the World"; "The Morning of the Dragon"; "I'd Give My Life for You"; "What a Waste"; "The American Dream"
New York run: Broadway Theatre, April 11,1991; 4,092 p.

First there was difficulty finding a suitable Broadway house. *Les Misérables* moved to the Imperial to make the Broadway available, and while the Broadway is one of New York's larger houses, it is much smaller than London's Drury Lane (a significant fact when the production includes sets such as a life-size helicopter), where *Miss Saigon* opened September 20, 1989. Then in August 1990 Actors Equity ruled that Asian actors must have acting opportunities racism has denied them in the past, and that Jonathan Pryce (who had created the role in London) could not play the Eurasian pimp. Cameron Mackintosh threatened to cancel the production and to return the $25 million in advance ticket sales. (The advance later grew to about $37 million.) After petitioning by its members, Actors Equity reversed its decision saying it "had applied an honest and moral principle in an inappropriate manner." Later Equity challenged the casting of Lea Salonga in the title role, but lost in arbitration. Then the helicopter landed.

Claude-Michel Schönberg and Alain Boublil *(Les Misérables)* updated Belasco/Puccini's *Madama Butterfly* to a through-sung musical (only some of the songs are listed in the program). In a 1989 interview Mr. Schönberg and Mr. Boublil explained that seeing a news photograph of a Vietnamese woman giving up her child to an American G.I. during the fall of Saigon gave them the idea for a modern operatic story showing the clash of two cultures. There the similarity to Puccini ends. The tale begins with the fall of Saigon in 1975, then crosses time and place between 1975 and 1978 in Saigon, Bangkok, and the United States. Kim (Lea Salonga and at some performances Kam Cheng), a young Vietnamese woman from the country is forced to become a bar girl in Saigon. On her first meeting with Chris (Willy Falk), a Marine guard at the U.S. Embassy, they fall in love. Not knowing she is pregnant, Chris, evacuated by that famous helicopter, returns home and marries. A few years later he and his American wife come back to find Kim, who wants Chris to take their son back to the U.S. To make sure he does, she kills herself. Superimposed on this innocence is the Engineer (Jonathan Pryce), the pimp, the fixer, the sleazy epitome of naked greed who can survive under any circumstances.

During the run, Jonathan Pryce was replaced by Francis Ruivivar, then Herman Sebek. Lea Salonga was replaced by Leila Florentino.

With the opening of *Miss Saigon,* Cameron Mackintosh had four productions in New York — *Cats, Les Misérables* and *The Phantom of the Opera* being the other three. *Miss Saigon* was the first musical production to charge $100 for the mezzanine seats.

Geffen OC (London).

THE SECRET GARDEN

Music: Lucy Simon
Book and lyrics: Marsha Norman; based on the novel by Frances Hodgson Burnett
Producers: Heidi Landesman, Rick Steiner, Frederick H. Mayerson, Elizabeth Williams, Jujamcyn Theatres and Dodger Productions
Director: Susan H. Schulman
Choreographer: Michael Lichtefeld
Cast: John Babcock, Daisy Eagan, Alison Fraser, Rebecca Luker, John Cameron Mitchell, Mandy Patinkin, Barbara Rosenblat, Tom Toner, Robert Westenberg
Songs: "There's a Girl"; "The House Upon the Hill"; " I Heard Someone Crying"; "A Fine White Horse"; "Show Me the Key"; "Lily's Eyes"; "Round Shouldered Man"; "The Girl I Mean to Be"; "Come Spirit, Come Charm"; "How Could I Ever Know?"
New York run: St. James Theater, April 25, 1991; 706 p.

Inspired by the sentimental Frances Hodgson Burnett novel, *The Secret Garden* tells the story of a spoiled, lonely Mary Lennox (Daisy Eagan, but Kimberly Mahon on Tuesday evenings and Wednesday matinees), who, orphaned by a cholera epidemic in India, is sent to live at Misselthwaite Manor in Yorkshire with her uncle Archibald (Mandy Patinkin). Still in mourning for his wife, Lily (Rebecca Luker), who died 10 years earlier in childbirth, and grief stricken for his bedridden 10 year old son, Archibald suffuses the manor with gloom and mystery. Mary discovers a secret garden, formerly Lily's, and in revitalizing it she restores life to her sick cousin and her miserable uncle. Marsha Norman who had previously won the Pulitzer Prize for her play *'night Mother,* won a Tony for Best Book of a Musical. Daisy Eagan became the youngest actress ever to win a Tony.
Columbia OC.

The Secret Garden. Daisy Eagan, Rebecca Luker, Mandy Patinkin. (Bob Marshak)

The Will Rogers Follies. Keith Carradine and the ensemble.

THE WILL ROGERS FOLLIES

Music: Cy Coleman
Lyrics: Betty Comden and Adolph Green
Book: Peter Stone
Producers: Pierre Cossette, Martin Richards, Sam Crothers, James M. Nederlander, Stewart F. Lane, Max Weitzenhoffer in association with Japan Satellite Broadcasting, Inc.
Director and choreographer: Tommy Tune
Cast: Keith Carradine, Dee Hoty, Dick Latessa, Cady Huffman, Vince Bruce, Paul Ukena Jr., and the voice of Gregory Peck
Songs: "Will-a-Manina"; "Give a Man Enough Rope"; "My Unknown Someone"; "No Man Left for Me"; "Once in a While"; "Without You"; "Just a Couple Indian Boys"; "Never Met a Man I Didn't Like"
New York run: The Palace Theatre, May 1, 1991; 983 p.

Ziegfeld's *Follies* were revues with innumerable dancing girls on stairways they could ascend and descend, assorted acts, and headliners. *The Will Rogers Follies* has lots of dancing girls ascending and descending the stairway, the disembodied voice of Florenz Ziegfeld coming from the rafters, and a dog act. Rogers was one of the headliners of the *Follies,* but in Peter Stone's book Rogers (Keith Carradine) seems to have been the only one. Designed as a "this is my life" production, Rogers returns from heaven to put on—with Ziegfeld's guidance (the voice of Gregory Peck)—one more Follies. Periodically Ziegfeld's Favorite (Cady Huffman) traipses across the stage holding up cards to identify the scene. Tommy Tune's exhuberantly inventive dances recalled some of the flavor of the Ziegfeld productions. During the run Keith Carradine was succeeded by Mac Davis and Larry Gatlin, Dee Hoty by Nancy Ringham, and Cady Huffman by Marla Maples.
Columbia OC.

CRAZY FOR YOU

Music: George Gershwin
Lyrics: Ira Gershwin
Book: Ken Ludwig; co-conceived by Ken Ludwig and Mike Ockrent; inspired by material by Guy Bolton and John McGowan
Producer: Roger Horchow and Elizabeth Williams
Director: Mike Ockrent
Choreographer: Susan Stroman
Cast: Harry Groener, Jodi Benson, Beth Leavel, Bruce Adler, Jane Connell, John Hillner, Irene Pawk, Stephen Temperley, Amelia White, The Manhattan Rhythm Kings
Songs: "K-ra-zy for You"; "I Can't Be Bothered Now"; "Bidin' My Time"; "Things Are Looking Up"; "Could You Use Me"; "Shall We Dance?"; "Someone to Watch Over Me"; "Slap That Bass" (orchestration by Sid Ramin); "Embraceable You"; "Tonight's the Night" (lyric by Ira Gershwin and Gus Kahn); "I Got Rhythm"; "The Real American Folk Song (Is a Rag)"; "What Causes That?"; "Naughty Baby" (lyric by Ira Gershwin and Desmond Carter); "Stiff Upper Lip"; "They Can't Take That Away from Me"; "But Not for Me"; "Nice Work If You Can Get It"
New York run: Shubert Theatre, February 19, 1992; 1,622 p.

For *Crazy for You,* Ken Ludwig (author of *Lend Me a Tenor*) and Mike Ockrent (director of *Me and My Girl*) used five numbers and part of a sixth ("Bidin' My Time," "Could You Use Me?," "Embraceable You," "I Got Rhythm," "But Not For Me," and part of "Bronco Busters") from the 1930 score of *Girl Crazy,* and added a dozen more songs, of which two ("Tonight's the Night" and "What Causes That?") were rediscovered in a warehouse in Seacaucus, New Jersey in 1982. In their version of boy-meets-girl, banker Bobby Child (Harry Groener), who would rather be in show business, is sent by his overbearing mother (Jane Connell) to foreclose a mortgage on a property in Deadrock, Arkansas. (Bobby also has an overbearing fiancee.) The property turns out to be a theatre. Bobby falls for the postmistress (Jodi Benson) who just happens to be the daughter of the man with the mortgage. Then boy loses girl, and for a while there are mistaken identities a la Marx Brothers. At the end they "put on a show" to save the theatre, and boy gets girl back.
Broadway Angel OC.

Crazy For You. Harry Groener and ensemble (Joan Marcus)

FIVE GUYS NAMED MOE

Music and lyrics: Miscellaneous writers
Book: Clarke Peters
Producer: Cameron Mackintosh
Director-Choreographer: Charles Augins
Cast: Jerry Dixon, Doug Eskew, Milton Craig Nealy, Kevin Ramsey, Jeffrey D. Sams, Glen Turner
Songs: "Early in the Morning" (Louis Jordan/Leo Hickman/Dallas Bartley); "Beware, Brother, Beware" (Morry Lasco/Dick Adams/Fleecie Moore); "I LIke 'em Fat Like That" (Claude Demetriou/Louis Jordan); "Push Ka Pi Shi Pie" (Joe Willoughby/Louis Jordan/Walt Merrick); "Ain't Nobody Here But Us Chickens" (Joan Whitney/Alex Kramer); "Choo, Choo, Ch'boogie" (Vaughn Horton/Denver Darling/Milton Gabler); "Is You Is or Is You Ain't My Baby?" (S. Austin/Louis Jordan)
New York run: Eugene O'Neill Theatre, April 8, 1992; 445 p.

Some of the songs associated with Louis Jordan (alto sax player, band singer, composer, and lyricist) are presented in a perfectly innocuous story of five guys named Moe who leap out of a jukebox to reveal to a sixth named Nomax how to repair his relationship with his friend Lorraine. Clarke Peters and Charles Augins also involve the audience in lending a helping hand, first by showering them (hundreds of leaflets are thrown from the stage and from the balcony) with the printed lyrics of "Push Ka Pi Shi Pie," so that everyone can teach Nomax the song, and later by having the actors lead a conga line out to the bar to buy refreshments after all that hard work. The story line gets lost in Act II, but the energy, charm and talent of all six guys appeals to audiences in what is a watered down version of a British Music Hall production.
Columbia OC.

Five Guys Named Moe. Jeffrey Sams, Kevin Ramsey, Doug Eskew, Milton Craig Nealy, Glenn Turner, Jerry Dixon (seated) (Joan Marcus)

GUYS AND DOLLS

Music and lyrics: Frank Loesser
Book: Jo Swerling and Abe Burrows
Producers: Dodger Productions, Roger Berlind, Jujamcyn Theaters/TV ASAHI, Kardana Productions and The John F. Kennedy Center for the Performing Arts
Director: Jerry Zaks
Choreographer: Christopher Chadman
Cast: Peter Gallagher, Nathan Lane, Josie de Guzman, Faith Prince, Walter Bobbie, John Carpenter, Steve Ryan, Ernie Sabella, J.K. Simmons, Herschel Sparber, Gary Chryst, Scott Wise
Songs: Same as the original production
New York run: Martin Beck Theatre, April 14, 1992; 1,143 p.

(See page 148.)
RCA OC.

Guys and Dolls. Peter Gallagher and Josie de Guzman (Martha Swope)

Guys and Dolls. Faith Prince and Nathan Lane as Miss Adelaide and Nathan Detroit (Martha Swope)

Guys and Dolls. "Sit Down You're Rockin' the Boat" (Martha Swope)

JELLY'S LAST JAM

Music: Jelly Roll Morton, musical adaptation and additional music composed by Luther Henderson
Lyrics: Susan Birkenhead
Book: George C. Wolfe
Producers: Margo Lion and Pamela Koslow in association with PolyGram Diversified Entertainment, 126 Second Avenue Corp./Hal Luftig, Roger Hess, Jujamcyn Theaters/TV Ashahi and Herb Alpert
Director: George C. Wolfe
Choreographer: Hope Clarke
Tap Choreography: Gregory Hines and Ted L. Levy
Cast: Gregory Hines, Keith David, Savion Glover, Stanley Wayne Mathis, Tonya Pinkins, Mary Bond Davis, Ann Duquesnay, Mamie Duncan-Gibbs, Stephanie Pope, Ruben Santiago-Hudson, Allison Williams
Songs: "Jelly's Jam"; "In My Day"; "The Creole Way" (music by Luther Henderson); "The Whole World's Waiting' to Sing Your Song"; "Lonely Boy Blues" (traditional); "Michigan Water"; "Something More"; "That's How You Jazz"; "The Chicago Stomp"; "Play the Music for Me"; "Lovin' Is a Lowdown Blues"; "Dr. Jazz" (music by King Oliver and Walter Melrose); "Good Ole New York"; "Too Late Daddy"; "That's the Way We Do Things in New Yawk"; "The Last Rites" (music by Henderson/Morton)
New York run: Virginia Theatre, April 26, 1992; 569 p.

Unlike other "and then he wrote" biographies of composers, *Jelly's Last Jam* not only explores the music, but also explores the man. In the opening scene Jelly Roll Morton (Gregory Hines) is at death facing the Chimney Man (Keith David), the "concierge of your soul," who accuses Morton of having denied his African heritage and of believing that he invented jazz. He forces Morton to re-examine his life and to possibly save his soul. In a series of flashbacks led by the Hunnies (Mamie Duncan-Gibbs, Stephanie Pope and Allison M. Williams), Jelly's life and sins are revealed. Gregory Hines' brilliant and likable performance softened some of the bragadoccio and cruelty of the man.

George C. Wolfe has said "we are all mutts here. We reinvent ourselves striving for some sort of purity." Ferdinand Joseph Le Menthe Morton, a middle class, light skinned Creole of color who disdained darker skinned blacks, reinvented himself to deny his race ("ain't no coon stock in this Creole"), but he absorbed all the culture and street sounds of New Orleans and expressed them in his own music. Keith David was replaced by Ben Vereen during the run, Gregory Hines by Brian Mitchell.
Mercury OC

Jelly's Last Jam. Keith David and Gregory Hines (Martha Swope)

FALSETTOS

Music and lyrics: William Finn
Book: William Finn and James Lapine
Producer: Barry and Fran Weissler
Director: James Lapine
Cast: Michael Rupert, Stephen Bogardus, Chip Zien, Barbara Walsh, Heather MacRae, Carrolee Carmello, Jonathan Kaplan, Andrew Harrison Leeds
Songs: "Four Jews in a Room Bitching"; "A Tight Knit Family"; "Love Is Blind"; "Thrill of First Love"; "I'm Breaking Down"; "March of the Falsettos"; "Making a Home"; "I Never Wanted to Love You"; "Everyone Hates His Parents"; "Unlikely Lovers"; "What Would I Do"
New York run: John Golden Theatre, April 29,1992; 486 p.

William Finn's *Falsettos* was originally three separately produced one-act musicals—*In Troussers* (1987), *The March of the Falsettos* (1981), and *Falsettoland* (1990). In 1991 the Hartford Stage combined the last two into one production .

Falsettos takes place from 1979 to 1981 and is a story of neurotic, bisexual Marvin (Michael Rupert), who leaves his wife Trina (Barbara Walsh) and son Jason (Jonathan Kaplan) to have a life with his friend Wizzer (Stephen Bogardus). Later, Trina marries Marvin's psychiatrist (Chip Zien). Wizzer leaves Marvin, then they reconcile. As Wizzer is dying of AIDS, Jason holds his bar mitzvah in Wizzer's hospital room. This basically simple tale of friends, lovers and family values is told with warmth, love, compassion, and without camp. Michael Rupert, Stephen Bogardus and Chip Zien created their roles in *The March of the Falsettos* and continued them in *Falsettoland*. Mandy Patinkin took over the role of Marvin during the run.

DRG Records recorded *March of the Falsettos* (with Alison Fraser as Trina) and *Falsettoland* (with Faith Prince as Trina). These two recordings are now combined into one package. With the exception of the addition of "I'm Breaking Down," the score is the same.
DRG.

THE MOST HAPPY FELLA

Music, lyrics & book: Frank Loesser
Producers: The Goodspeed Opera House, Center Theatre Group/Ahmanson Theatre,   Lincoln Center Theatre, The Shubert Organization & Japan Satellite Broadcasting/Stagevision
Director: Gerald Gutierrez
Choreographer: Liza Gennaro
Cast: Spiro Malas, Sophie Hayden, Claudia Catania, Buddy Crutchfield, Tad Ingram, Liz Larsen, Mark Lotito, Bill Nabel, Charles Pistone, Scott Waara
Songs: Same as original production
New York run: Booth Theatre, February 13, 1992; 229 p.

(See page 170.)
RCA Victor 1992 OC.

TOMMY

Music and lyrics: Pete Townshend
Book: Pete Townshend and Des McAnuff
Producer: PACE Theatrical Group and Dodger Productions with Kardana
     Productions, Inc.
Director: Des McAnuff
Choreographer: Wayne Cilento
Cast: Marcia Mitzman, Jonathan Dokuchitz, Paul Kandel, Carly Jane
     Steinborn, Crysta Macalush, Michael Cerveris, Buddy Smith, Cheryl
     Freeman, Anthony Barrile, Michael McElroy, Lee Morgan, Sherie Scott
Songs: "Overture"; "Captain Walker"; "It's a Boy"; "We've Won"; "Twenty-One";
     "Amazing Journey"; "Christmas"; "See Me, Feel Me"; "Do You Think It's
     Alright"; "Fiddle About"; "Eyesight to the Blind"; "Acid Queen"; "Pinball
     Wizard"; "I'm Free"; "We're Not Going to Take It"
New York run: St. James Theatre, April 22, 1993; 899 p.

Written in 1969 as a rock opera by Peter Townshend and recorded by the British
rock group The Who, *Tommy* was performed by the group in a concert version
around the world; at the Metropolitan Opera House in 1970 and made into a Ken
Russell film in 1975.

   Peter Townshend and director Des McAnuff have softened the story of the
young boy who loses all his senses when, at the age of four, he witnesses his
father killing his mother's lover. Unable to communicate, abused by his family and
the town louts, he somehow becomes a pinball wizard; eventually recovers his
senses and develops into a messianic superstar. At curtain's drop he returns to
the bosom of his family. The plot was clarified by dazzling sets and spectacular
video projections.

   Rock purists have complained that this new version has removed all the fire
and rage of the original which was written at the time of Woodstock, the Vietnam
War, and other assorted ills of society which so inflamed the generation that its
only solution seemed to be to drop out.
RCA Victor OC.

Tommy. Buddy Smith (Tommy) and Paul Kandel. (Marcus/Bryan-Brown)

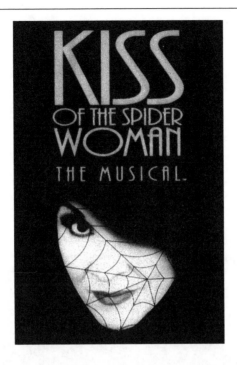

KISS OF THE SPIDER WOMAN–THE MUSICAL

Music: John Kander
Lyrics: Fred Ebb
Book: Terrence McNally; based on the novel by Manuel Puig
Producer: Livent (U.S.) Inc.
Director: Harold Prince
Choreographer: Vincent Paterson
Cast: Chita Rivera, Brent Carver, Anthony Crivello, Merle Louise, Herndon Lackey, Kristi Carnahan
Songs: "Her Name Is Aurora"; "Over the Wall"; "Where You Are"; "Morphine Tango"; "You Could Never Shame Me"; "Gimme Love"; "Mama, It's Me"; "The Day After That"; "Anything for Him"
New York run: Broadhurst Theatre, May 3, 1993; 906 p.

Kiss of the Spider Woman (originally a novel by Manuel Puig; a film version was released in 1984) was originally presented in 1990 as a work in progress at the Performing Arts Center of the State University of New York in Purchase, New York, and was eventually revised and presented first in Toronto and then in London.

The grim story of life in a prison cell in a South American police state unfolds the changing relationship between Molina (Brent Carver) a gay window dresser jailed on a morals charge and his heterosexual cellmate Valentin (Anthony Crivello), a revolutionary. The warden enlists Molina to get Valentin to reveal his fellow revolutionaries. To survive the brutality of prison life, Molina dreams of Aurora, the Spider Woman (Chita Rivera), a grade-B movie star and relates her adventures to Valentin.

During the run Chita Rivera was replaced by Vanessa Williams and later by Maria Concita Alonso. Jeff Hyslop and later Howard McGillian, replaced Brent Carver, and Anthony Crivello was replaced by Brian Mitchell.
RCA/Victor OC.

SHE LOVES ME

Music: Jerry Bock
Lyrics: Sheldon Harnick
Book: Joe Masteroff
Producer: James M. Nederlander and Elliot Martin with Herbert Wasserman Freddy Bienstock, Roger L. Stevens present The Roundabout Theatre Company (Todd Haimes, Producing Director) production
Director: Scott Ellis
Musical Staging: Rob Marshall
Cast: Boyd Gaines, Diane Fratantoni, Sally Mayes, Jonathan Freeman, Brad Kane, Lee Wilkof, Louis Zorich, Howard McGillin
Songs: Same as original production
New York run: Brooks Atkinson Theatre, October 7, 1993; 294 p. (61 p. previously at the Roundabout Theatre)

(See page 202.)
Varese Sarabande OC.

Carousel. Michael Hayden and Sally Murphy in "If I Loved You." (Marcus/Bryan-Brown)

CAROUSEL

Music: Richard Rodgers
Lyrics & book: Oscar Hammerstein II; based on the play *Liliom* by Ferenc Molnar as adapted by Benjamin F. Glazer
Producer: Lincoln Center Theatre under the direction of Andre Bishop and Bernard Gersten, by arrangement with The Royal National Theatre, Cameron Mackintosh and the Rodgers and Hammerstein Organization
Director: Nicholas Hytner
Choreographer: Sir Kenneth MacMillan
Cast: Robert Breuler, Sandra Brown, Kate Buddeke, Michael Hayden, Eddie Korbich, Audra Ann McDonald, Sally Murphy, Jon Marshall Sharp, Fisher Stevens, Shirley Verrett, Jeff Weiss
Songs: Same as original production
New York run: Vivian Beaumont Theatre, March 24, 1994; 322 p.

(See page 127.)
Broadway Angel OC.

Beauty and the Beast. Susan Egan and Terrence Mann. (Joan Marcus)

BEAUTY AND THE BEAST

Music: Alan Menken
Lyrics: Howard Ashman and Tim Rice (asterisk designates lyrics by Rice)
Book: Linda Wolverton
Producer: Walt Disney Productions
Director: Robert Jess Roth
Choreographer: Matt West
Cast: Susan Egan, Terrence Mann, Burke Moses, Gary Beach, Beth Fowler, Tom Bosley, Heath Lamberts, Eleanor Glockner, Stacey Logan, Brian Press, Kenny Raskin
Songs: "Belle"; "No Matter What"*; "Me"*; "Home"*; "How Long Must This Go On?"*; "If I Can't Love Her"*; "Beauty and the Beast"; "The Mob Song"; "The Battle"; "Transformation"*
New York run: Palace Theatre, April 18, 1994; 5,461 p.

The story of the wicked witch turning a prince into a beast (and his staff into household objects) who can only be returned to his princely state by learning to love and be loved has been with us since the eighteenth century. *Beauty and the Beast* is the stage version of the Walt Disney animated film with five new songs by Menken and Tim Rice. Howard Ashman (*Little Shop of Horrors*), who had written the lyrics for the film score, died in 1991.

If it is at all possible for humans to resemble cartoon characters, the actors resemble their cartoon versions with some degree of success. Terrence Mann as the Beast, Susan Egan as Belle, Tom Bosley as her father, Beth Fowler as the teapot, Burke Moses as Gaston (who wants to win Belle), and Gary Beach as the candelabra all struggle through the padding and claws and other assorted effects gamely. During the run, Jeff McCarthy succeeded Terrence Mann; Marc Kudisch replaced Burke Moses; Lee Roy Reems succeeded Gary Beach; Sara Uriarte replaced Susan Egan; and Cass Morgan replaced Beth Fowler. Disney OC.

PASSION

Music and lyrics: Stephen Sondheim
Book: James Lapine; based on the film *Passione d'Amore* directed by Ettore Scola
Producer: The Shubert Organization, Capital Cities/ABC, Roger Berlind, Scott Rudin by arrangement with Lincoln Center Theatre
Director: James Lapine
Cast: Donna Murphy, Jere Shea, Gregg Edelman, Marin Mazzie, Tom Aldredge, Francis Ruivivar
Songs: No songs are listed in the program
New York run: Plymouth Theatre, May 9, 1994; 280 p.

Based on the satiric film *Passione d'Amore (*which was based on Igino Tarchetti's novel *Fosca), Passion* is a nearly two-hour chamber opera on the theme of love. The production opens in Milan with Giorgio (Jere Shea) as an army officer in bed with his mistress Clara (Marin Mazzie), a beautiful married woman singing of their perfect love. Later he is transferred to an army outpost and they promise to write to each other to "make love with our words." At the outpost, Giorgio meets Fosca (Donna Murphy), his captain's sickly unattractive cousin, who rentlessly pursues him and offers "love without reason." Terrified by this naked emotion, Giorgio asks Clara to marry him, but she refuses to leave her child, which frees him to surrender to Fosca's obsessive love. In an interview in *The New York Times*, Mr. Sondheim states, "*Passion* is about how the force of somebody's feelings for you can crack you open and how it is the life force in a deadened world."
Angel Records OC.

GREASE

Music, lyrics and book: Jim Jacobs and Warren Casey
Director and Choreographer: Jeff Calhoun
Producers: The Tommy Tune production presented by Barry and Fran Weissler and Jujamcyn Theaters, in association with Pace Theatrical Group, the Broadway Fund and TV Asahi
Cast: Rosie O'Donnell, Ricky Paull Goldin, Susan Wood, Sam Harris, Marcia Lewis, Billy Porter, Michelle Blakely, Brian Bradley, Paul Castree, Hunter Foster, Carlos Lopez, Megan Mullally, Jason Opsahl, Sandra Purpuro, Heather Stokes, Jessica Stone
Songs: Same as original
New York run: Eugene O'Neill Theatre, May 11, 1994; 1,505 p.

(See page 234.)
RCA Victor (1994) OC.

SHOW BOAT

Music: Jerome Kern
Lyrics & book: Oscar Hammerstein II; Based on the novel *Show Boat* by Edna Ferber
Producer: Livent (U.S.) Inc.
Director: Harold Prince
Choreographer: Susan Stroman
Cast: John McMartin, Elaine Stritch, Rebecca Luker, Mark Jacoby, Lonette McKee, Joel Blum, Dorothy Stanley, Gretha Boston, Doug LaBrecque, Michael Bell
Songs: "Cotton Blossom"; "Where's the Mate For Me"; "Make Believe"; "Ol' Man River"; "Can't Help Lovin' Dat Man"; "Till Good Luck Comes My Way"; "Mis'ry's Comin' Aroun'"; "I Have the Room Above Her"; "You Are Love"; "Life Upon the Wicked Stage"; "Why Do I Love You?"; "Bill" (lyrics by P.G. Wodehouse, revised by Oscar Hammerstein II); "Dance Away the Night"; "After the Ball" (music and lyrics by Charles K. Harris)
New York run: Gershwin Theatre, October 2, 1994; (947p.)

(See pages 60 and 128.)
RCA OC (Toronto Cast); Capitol (Broadway Cast).

Show Boat. Rebecca Luker (Magnolia) and Mark Jacoby (Gaylord). (Catherine Ashmore/Martha Swope)

SUNSET BOULEVARD

Music: Andrew Lloyd Webber
Book & lyrics: Don Black & Christopher Hampton; Based on the Billy Wilder film
Producer: The Really Useful Company
Director: Trevor Nunn
Musical Staging: Bob Avian
Cast: Glenn Close, Alan Campbell, George Hearn, Alice Ripley, Alan Oppenheimer, Vincent Tumeo
Songs: "Surrender"; "With One Look"; "The Greatest Star of All"; "New Ways to Dream"; "This Time Next Year"; "Sunset Boulevard"; "As If We Never Said Goodbye"; "Too Much in Love to Care"
New York run: Minskoff Theatre, November 17, 1994; (977p.)

Sunset Boulevard, based on the 1950 Billy Wilder film, opened in London in July, 1993 with Patti LuPone as Norma Desmond, the former silent screen star desperate for a come back. Ms. LuPone's contract stipulated that she would star in the Broadway production, when it opened. British reviewers were cool to the production, but not to Ms. Lupone and she seemed to be Broadway bound. The Los Angeles production opened in December of that year with unanimous raves for Glenn Close. In keeping with the established British theatrical custom of a great deal of hype about the progress of a production, there was much to-do about whether Ms. LuPone's contract would be honored. Patti LuPone was bought out, Faye Dunaway was announced for Los Angeles, and Glenn Close for New York. Shortly after rehearsals with Ms. Dunaway began, Really Useful (Lloyd Webber's production company) decided the really useful thing to do–rather than have Ms. Dunaway play the role–was to sell the Los Angeles sets to the Toronto company and go on to New York.

Designer John Napier, who created the tire for *Cats*, the barricade for *Les Misérables* and the helicopter for *Miss Saigon,* opens *Sunset Boulevard* with Joe's corpse floating at the top of Norma Desmond's pool as if it were seen from the bottom (and later introduces Norma Desmond's mansion, which rises into the air to reveal a party at another apartment). As in the film, Joe (Alan Campbell) then narrates the story of the aging actress (Glenn Close), her young lover Joe and her attempt to return to the screen as Salome in a script written by the two of them. During the run, Glenn Close was replaced by Betty Buckley, who had replaced Patti LuPone in London.

Really Useful/Polydor OC (London);
Really Useful/Polydor L.A. OC (Los Angeles).

Sunset Boulevard. Glenn Close as Norma Desmond. (Joan Marcus)

Sunset Boulevard. Norma and her beauty experts. (Joan Marcus)

HOW TO SUCCEED IN BUSINESS WITHOUT REALLY TRYING

Music & lyrics: Frank Loesser
Book: Abe Burrows, Jack Weinstock and Willie Gilbert
Producer: Dodger Productions and Kardana Productions, Inc., The John F. Kennedy Center for the Performing Arts, The Nederlander Organization
Director: Des McAnuff
Choreographer: Wayne Cilento
Cast: Matthew Broderick, Megan Mullally, Jeff Blumenkrantz, Jonathan Freemen, Victoria Clark, Luba Mason, Gerry Vichi, Lillias White, Ronn Carroll
Songs: Same as original production
New York run: Richard Rodgers Theatre, March 23, 1995; 548 p.

(See page 196.)
RCA Victor OC/1995.

How to Succeed in Business Without Really Trying. Matthew Broderick and Sarah Jessica Parker. (Joan Marcus)

VICTOR/VICTORIA

Music: Henry Mancini; additional musical material Frank Wildhorn (asterisk denotes Wildhorn)
Lyrics: Leslie Bricusse
Book: Blake Edwards
Producer: Blake Edwards, Tony Adams, John Scher; Endemol Theatre Productions, Inc.; PolyGram Ventures, Inc.
Director: Blake Edwards
Choreographer: Rob Marshall
Cast: Julie Andrews, Tony Roberts, Michael Nouri, Rachel York, Robert B. Shull, Adam Heller, Michael Cripe, Gregory Jbara
Songs: "Paris by Night"; "If I Were a Man"; "Trust Me"*; "Le Jazz Hot"; "The Tango"; "Paris Makes Me Horny"; "Crazy World"; "Louis Says"*; "King's Dilemma"; "Almost a Love Song"; "Living in the Shadows"*; "Victor/Victoria"
New York run: Marquis Theatre, October 25, 1995; (734p.)

Based on the 1982 Blake Edwards' film which starred Julie Andrews, Robert Preston and James Garner, *Victor/Victoria* is the story of a woman (Julie Andrews) who plays a man playing a woman in Paris in the 1930s. Tony Roberts is Toddy the aging self-called "drag queen" whose idea it is to transform Victoria into Victor, a Polish count and female impersonator who finds fame and eventually love. Michael Nouri was the Chicago gangster who could not understand why as he explains in "King's Dilemma," "the girl I love is a guy." The show was "in development" for over ten years. Following Henry Mancini's death, Frank Wildhorn was brought in to add music on the pre-Broadway tour.

Ms. Andrews was nominated for a Tony for her performance, but rejected the nomination because, as she explained in a curtain speech, "However, flattered as I am, and honored to be also nominated, I have to say how deeply sad I am to be the only nominee in this extraordinarily gifted company."
Philips OC.

THE KING AND I

Music: Richard Rodgers
Lyrics and book: Oscar Hammerstein II
Producer: Dodger Productions; James M. Nederlander, Perseus Productions with John Frost and the Adelaide Festival Centre in association with The Rodgers and Hammerstein Organization
Director: Christopher Renshaw
Choreographer: Jerome Robbins
Cast: Donna Murphy, Lou Diamond Phillips, Randall Duk Kim, Taewon Kim, Joohee Choi, Jose Llana, John Curless, Guy Paul, Ryan Hopkins, John Chang
New York run: Neil Simon Theatre, April 11, 1996; 780 p.

(See pages 151 and 248.)

The King and I. Lou Diamond Phillips and Donna Murphy. (Joan Marcus)

A FUNNY THING
HAPPENED ON THE WAY TO THE FORUM

Music: Stephen Sondheim
Book: Burt Shevelove and Larry Gelbart
Producer: Jujamcyn Theaters, Scott Rudin/Paramount Pictures, The Viertel-Baruch-
    Frankel Group, Roger Berlind and Dodger Productions
Director: Jerry Zaks
Choreographer: Rob Marshall
Cast: Nathan Lane, Mark Linn-Baker, Lewis J. Stadlen, Ernie Sabella, William
    Duell, Mary Testa, Jessica Boevers, Cris Groenendaal, Jim Stanek, Leigh
    Zimmerman
Songs: Same as original production
New York run: St. James Theatre; April 18, 1996; 715 p.

(See page 198.)
Angel OC.

A Funny Thing Happened on the Way to the Forum. Leigh
Zimmerman and Nathan Lane. (Joan Marcus)

RENT

Music, lyrics & book: Jonathan Larson
Producer: Jeffrey Seller, Kevin McCollum, Allan S. Gordon and New York Theatre Workshop
Director: Michael Greif
Choreographer: Marlies Yearby
Cast: Gilles Chaisson, Taye Diggs, Wilson Jermaine Heredia, Rodney Hicks, Kristen Lee Kelly, Jesse L. Martin, Idina Menzel, Aiko Nakasone, Timothy Britten Parker, Adam Pascal, Anthony Rapp, Daphne Rubin-Vega, Gwen Stewart, Byron Utley, Fredi Walker
Songs: "Rent"; "One Song Glory"; "Light My Candle"; "I Should Tell You"; "Tango: Maureen"; "I'll Cover You"; "Over the Moon"; "Seasons of Love"; "Without You"; "Your Eyes"
New York run: Nederlander Theatre, April 29, 1996; 5,124 p.

Hailed as the first rock musical since *Hair* to deal with concerns of generation, *Rent* opened February 13, 1996 at the 150-seat New York Theatre Workshop for a six-week run, but was immediately sold out. By the time *Rent* came to Broadway at the end of April it had had rave reviews, four pages in the Sunday edition of the *New York Times*, and had won the Pulitzer Prize for Drama. In May it was selected as Best New Musical of the season by the New York Drama Critics Circle and in June won Tony awards for Best Musical, Best Book of a Musical and Best Original Score. The only tragedy of the production was that Jonathan Larson had died of an aortic aneurysm in January on the night of the final dress rehearsal.

Rent is set in the lower east side of Manhattan (sometimes referred to as Alphabet City because the Avenues are named A, B and C) which has become home to artists, squatters, drug dealers, the homeless and the poor. Based loosely on *La bohème*, the characters now are Mark (Anthony Rapp), a filmmaker and the narrator; Roger (Adam Pascal), an HIV positive musician who wants to make a contribution before he dies; Mimi (Daphne Rubin-Vega), a drug addicted dancer working in an S&M club; Angel (Wilson Jermaine Heredia), a drag queen; and his lover Tom (Jesse L. Martin). All of them are concerned with making their downtown world understandable to the uptown world without selling out. Their love for one another is what makes their lives bearable.
Dreamworks (Geffen) OC.

BRING IN 'DA NOISE, BRING IN 'DA FUNK

Music: Daryl Waters, Zane Mark, Anne Duquesnay
Lyrics: Reg E. Gaines, George C. Wolfe, Anne Duquesnay
Book: Reg E. Gaines (conceived by George C. Wolfe and based on an idea by George C. Wolfe and Savion Glover)
Producers: The Joseph Papp Public Theater/ New York Shakespeare Festival (George C. Wolfe: Producer; Rosemarie Tichler: Artistic Producer; Laurie Beckelman: Executive Director; Joey Parnes: Executive Producer); NYSF Associate Producer Wally Hausum
Director: George C. Wolfe
Choreographer: Savion Glover
Cast: Savion Glover, Vincent Bingham, Jared Crawford, Ann Duquesnay, Dule Hill, Raymond King, Jimmy Tate, Baakari Wilder, Jeffrey Wright
Songs: "Bring in 'Da Noise Bring in 'Da Funk"; "The Door to Isle Goree"; "Slave Ships"; "Som'thin' From Nuthin'/ The Circle Stomp"; "The Pan Handlers"; "The Lynching Blues"; "Chicago Bound"; "Shifting Sounds"; "Industrialization"; "The Chicago Riot Rag"; "I Got the Beat/ Dark Tower"; "The Whirligig Stomp"; "Now That's Tap"; "The Uncle Huck-a-Buck Song"; "Kid Go!"; "The Lost Beat Swing"; "Them Conkheads"; "Hot Fun"; "Blackout"; "Gospel/ Hip Hop Rant"; "Drummin'"; "Taxi"; "Conversations"
New York run: Ambassador Theatre, April 25, 1996; 1,135 p.

After becoming artistic director of the New York Shakespeare Festival/ Public Theater in 1993 (until 2004), George C. Wolfe created *Bring In 'Da Noise, Bring In 'Da Funk*, a musical spectacle that visualized the African-American experience in the United States from slavery to the present. Previously Wolfe had distinguished himself as writer/ director of the play *The Colored Museum,* the director of the original Broadway production of *Angels in America,* and the director/ writer *of Jelly's Last Jam.*

Opening at the Public and then transferring to Broadway, it was a strong rival to *Rent* as the musical event of 1996. For *Bring In 'Da Noise, Bring In 'Da Funk* Wolfe harnessed the talents of several emerging composers and lyricists, including Anne Duquesnay, who appeared in the show as da Singer, the chorus/ narrator. Savion Glover made his Broadway debut in *The Tap Dance Kid. In Bring in 'Da Noise,* at the age of 22, he starred as 'da Beat and Lil 'Dahlin' as well as being the choreographer.
RCA OC

Bring in 'Da Noise, Bring in 'Da Funk. Savion Glover.
(Michal Daniel)

CHICAGO

Music: John Kander
Lyrics: Fred Ebb
Book: Fred Ebb & Bob Fosse
Producers: Barry & Fran Weissler in association with Kardana/ Hart Sharp Entertainment
Director: Walter Bobbie
Choreographer: Ann Reinking in the style of Bob Fosse
Cast: Ann Reinking, Bebe Neuwirth, James Naughton, Joel Grey, Marcia Lewis, J. Loeffelholz, D. Sabella
Songs: Same as in the original production
New York run: Richard Rodgers Theatre, November 14, 1996 (still running 6/11)

(See page 244.)
RCA Victor OC

TITANIC

Music & lyrics: Maury Yeston
Book & story: Peter Stone
Producers: Dodger Endemol Theatricals, Richard S. Pechter, the John F. Kennedy Center for the Performing Arts
Director: Richard Jones
Choreographer: Lynne Taylor-Corbett
Cast: Bill Buell, Judith Blazer, Victoria Clark, Alma Cuervo, John Cunningham, Michael Cerveris, David Garrison, Brian d'Arcy James, Larry Keith, Martin Moran, Jennifer Piech, Theresa McCarthy, Don Stephenson
Songs: "In Every Age"; "How Did They Build Titanic?" "There She Is"; "I Must Get on That Ship"; "Godspeed Titanic"; "Barrett's Song"; "Lady's Maid"; "What a Remarkable Age This Is"; "No Moon"; "The Proposal/ The Night Was Alive"; "The Blame"; "We'll Meet Tomorrow"; "Still"
New York run: Lunt-Fontanne Theatre, April 23, 1997; 804 p.

In the prologue, "In Every Age," Thomas Andrews (Michael Cerveris), shipbuilder and designer of *Titanic,* explains how each generation's dreams are grander than those of the past. His dream has been to create a floating city. (*Titanic* had three libraries, a gymnasium, a Turkish bath, a putting course and a 33-foot indoor swimming pool.)

The scene shifts to the dock at Southampton, showing the soaring gangplank where everyone is readying for the maiden voyage of *Titanic.* A stoker (Brian d'Arcy James) wonders "How Did They Build *Titanic*?"; then other crewmen greet her with "There She Is." After the final loading of the passengers, the stevedores and those left onshore wish bon voyage with "God Speed *Titanic.*"

While the first four days crossing the Atlantic were uneventful for the passengers, the manager of the White Star Line, J. Bruce Ismay (David Garrison), spent most of his time urging Captain E. J. Smith (John Cunningham) to increase speed. Disaster struck on the night of April 14, when the lookout spotted an iceberg ("No Moon") and the ship reacted too slowly to it.

The passengers were awakened ("Dressed in Your Pajamas in the Grand Salon"). On the boat deck, families were separated, and women and children in first and second classes were instructed in life belt use and then lowered into the 20 available lifeboats ("We'll Meet Tomorrow"). To ensure the safety of all passengers, there should have been 54 lifeboats, but that many would have taken away too much deck space from first class. The third-class passengers had the stairways barred to them and could not get to the boat deck. *Titanic* sank in about two and a half hours. Of the 2,228 passengers and crew, only 711 survived. The orchestra did not play "Nearer My God to Thee." It was "Autumn."
RCAVictor OC

JEKYLL AND HYDE

Music: Frank Wildhorn
Book & lyrics: Leslie Bricusse
Producers: Pace Theatrical Group & Fox Theatricals in association with Jerry Frankel, Magicworks Entertainment, & Landmark Entertainment Group
Director: Robin Phillips
Choreographer: Joey Pizzi
Cast: Robert Cuccioli, Linda Eder, Christine Noll, George Meritt, Robert Evan, Barrie Ingham
Songs: "Lost In the Darkness"; "Façade"; "Take Me as I Am"; "Letting Go"; "No One Knows Who I Am; "Good 'N'Evil"; "This Is The Moment"; "Alive"; "Someone Like You"; "Once Upon a Dream"; "In His Eyes"; "Dangerous Game"; "The Way Back"; "A New Life"; "Confrontation"
New York run: Plymouth Theatre, April 28, 1997; 1,543 p.

In this version of Robert Louis Stevenson's novella *The Strange Case of Dr. Jekyll and Mr. Hyde,* Dr. Jekyll (Robert Cuccioli) is concerned with developing a serum that will separate the good from the evil in each person, and which will also cure mental illness. Because his father is a patient in a mental hospital, Jekyll petitions the Board of Governors for permission to use the serum on his father. The board denies his request because the members feel the patients should not be used as guinea pigs. Thereupon, Jekyll tests the formula on himself and becomes Hyde. In his Hyde personality, he sets about killing off the board members and anyone else who displeases him.

During the run, Robert Cuccioli was replaced by Jack Wagner, Sebastian Bach, and finally David Hasselhoff.

Before the production arrived on Broadway, it had a 36-week national tour and two recordings — one a concept album with Colm Wilkenson and Linda Eder and the other a double CD released by Atlantic Theatre.

Wildhorn's next two productions were *The Scarlet Pimpernel* and *The Civil War.* He wrote the music for *The Civil War and the book and lyrics were credited to Wildhorn, Gregory Boyd, and Jack Murphy. It opened on April 22, 1999 but lasted only 61 performances.*

THE SCARLET PIMPERNEL

Music: Frank Wildhorn
Lyrics & book: Nan Knighton
Producers: Pierre Cossette, Bill Haber, Hallmark Entertainment, Ted Forstmann, Kathleen Raitt
Director: Peter Hunt
Choreographer: Adam Pelty
Cast: Douglas Sills, Christine Andreas, Marine Jahan, Tim Shew, Philip Hoffman, James Judy, Terrence Mann, Sandy Rosenberg, Pamela Burrell, Giles Chaisson, Ed Dixon, Allen Fitzpatrick, Bill Bowers, Adam Pelty, Ron Sharpe, William Thomas Evans, Dave Clemmons, R.F. Daley, David Cromwell, Ken Labey, Eric Bennyhoff, Jeff Garner, James Dybas
Songs: "Madame Guillotine"; "Believe"; "Vivez!"; "Prayer"; "Into the Fire"; "Falcon in the Dive"; "When I Look at You"; "The Scarlet Pimpernel"; "Where's the Girl?"; The Creation of Man"; "The Riddle"; "They Seek Him Here"; "Only Love"; "She Was There"; "Storybook"; "Lullaby"; "You Are My Home"
New York run: Minskoff Theater, November 9, 1997; 772 p.

Baroness Orczy wrote *The Scarlet Pimpernel* as a novel but had difficulty getting it published. At the suggestion of a publisher, she and her husband, Montague Barstow, turned it into a play, which opened in London on January 5, 1905, starring Julia Neilson and Fred Terry. After the success of the theatrical venture, the novel was published. Since then the novel has been the basis for films (most notably, the 1934 film starring Leslie Howard and Merle Oberon) and, more recently, two television productions.

    The Scarlet Pimpernel opened at the Minskoff Theater on November 9, 1997; shut down October 1, 1998; had an eight-day layoff; then reworked, restaged, recast, and reopened November 4, 1998; closed in April 1999; toured for the summer and opened again September 9, 1999; and finally closed January 2, 2000. The initial reviews were not exactly welcoming, and the audience did not come. During the summer of 1998, Radio City Entertainment and Ted Forstmann acquired the rights to the production. Robert Longbottom became director and choreographer, Rachel York replaced Christine Andreas, and Rex Smith replaced Terrence Mann.

    Six years before the initial production, there had been a *Scarlet Pimpernel* concept album. After the 1997 opening, Atlantic Theatre issued an original cast album and subsequently issued an "encore" album with the November 1998 cast.
Atlantic Theatre OC
Atlantic Theatre Encore

THE LION KING

Music & lyrics: Elton John & Tim Rice, with additional music & lyrics by Lebo M, Mark Mancina, Jay Rifkin, Julie Taymor, Hans Zimmer

Book: Roger Allers & Irene Mecchi, adapted from the screenplay by Irene Mecchi, Jonathan Roberts, Linda Woolverton

Producer: Disney

Director: Julie Taymor

Choreographer: Garth Fagan

Cast: John Vickery, Samuel E. Wright, Geoff Hoyle, Tsidii Le Loka, Tom Alan Robbins, Gina Breedlove, Jason Raize, Heather Headley, Stanley Wayne Mathis, Tracy Nicole Chapman, Kevin Cahoon, Scott Irby-Ranniar, Kajuana Shuford, Max Casella

Songs: "Circle of Life"; "The Morning Report"; "I Just Can't Wait to Be King"; "Chow Down"; "They Live in You"; "Be Prepared"; "Hakuna Matata"; "One By One"; "The Madness of King Scar"; "Shadowland"; "Endless Night"; "Can't You Feel the Love Tonight"; "He Lives in You"; "King of Pride Rock"

New York run: New Amsterdam Theater, November 13, 1997 (still running 6/11)

Disney's first Broadway production, *Beauty and the Beast*, faithfully recreated a film into a three-dimensional theater piece. *The Lion King* roared onto the stage with such imaginative use of masks, puppetry, modern dance, music, and color, from the opening African chant song — which segues into "Circle of Life," with a parade of animals in both aisles of the theater — to the reprise of "Circle of Life" finale, that Julie Taymor's *The Lion King* is truly theatrical.

The slightly expanded story follows the screenplay. Mufasa (Samuel E. Wright) and his wife Sarabi (Gina Breedlove) present their new heir to the people. Scar (John Vickery), Mufasa's evil brother, covets the throne for himself. After Mufasa is murdered, Scar banishes young Simba (Scott Irby-Ranniar). Eventually, after battling his uncle and his own personal fears, the grown-up Simba (Jason Raize) and Nala (Heather Headley) return to take over the pride. During the run, Mary Randle replaced Heather Headley, David "Dakota" Sanchez replaced Scott Irby-Ranniar, and Imani Parks replaced Kajuama Shuford.

Walt Disney Records OC

The Lion King. (Joan Marcus)

RAGTIME

Music: Stephen Flaherty
Lyrics: Lynn Ahrens
Book: Terrence McNally
Producer: Livent (US) Inc.
Director: Frank Galati
Musical staging: Graciela Daniele
Cast: Brian Stokes Mitchell, Peter Friedman, Marin Mazzie, Audra McDonald, Marc Jacoby, Jim Corti, Tommy Hollis, Lynette Perry, Steven Sutcliffe, Judy Kaye
Songs: "Ragtime"; "Goodbye, My Love"; "The Crime of the Century"; "What Kind of Woman"; "A Shtetl Iz Amereke"; "Success"; "Gettin' Ready Rag"; "Henry Ford"; "Nothing Like the City"; " Your Daddy's Son"; "New Music"; "Wheels of a Dream"; "The Night That Goldman Spoke at Union Square"; "Lawrence, Massachusetts"; "Gliding"; "Justice"; "President"; "Till We Reach That Day"; "Harry Houdini, Master Escapist"; "Coalhouse's Soliloquy"; "Coalhouse Demands"; "What a Game"; "Atlantic City"; "Buffalo Nickel Photoplay, Inc."; "Our Children"; "Sarah Brown Eyes"; "He Wanted to Say"; "Back to Before"; "Look What You've Done"; "Make Them Hear You"
New York run: Ford Center for the Performing Arts, January 18, 1998; 861 p.

Terrence McNally's adaptation of E. L. Doctorow's complex novel about American Society from the turn of the century to World War I interweaves the stories of a WASP family, a Jewish immigrant and his daughter, and Coalhouse Walker, Jr., a black musician, with such historical figures as Henry Ford, Evelyn Nesbit, Emma Goldman, J. P. Morgan, Harry Houdini, and Booker T. Washington. It deals with the transition of the United States from a WASP-dominated society to a multiethnic society.

In the opening scene, Mother (Marin Mazzie) is saying goodbye to Father (Mark Jacoby) as he is about to depart with Admiral Peary for an expedition to the North Pole. At the same time, Tateh (Peter Friedman) is arriving with his daughter from Europe full of hope for a better life. The third group in this pageant is Coalhouse Walker, Jr. (Brian Stokes Mitchell) and people of Harlem. The interaction among these groups begins when Mother finds Sara's baby buried in the garden and saves both baby and Mother ("What Kind of Woman").

During the run, Alton-Fitzgerald White replaced Brian Stokes Mitchell, Donna Bullock replaced Marin Mazzie, And LaChanze replaced Audra McDonald.

Ragtime had opened in Toronto in December 1996, and a Los Angeles company opened in May 1997. Garth Drabinsky developed The Ford Center especially for *Ragtime* by combining the Lyric and Apollo Theatres. The Ford Motor Company donated a "significant amount" of money over a period of years and had naming rights. In 1999 Livent (US) Inc. went bankrupt and closed the production in January 2000. SFX Entertainment bought the touring company. RCA OC

CABARET

Music: John Kander
Lyrics: Fred Ebb
Book: Joe Masteroff
Producer: Roundabout Theatre Company; Todd Haimes, Artistic Director
Director: Sam Mendes
Choreographer & co-director: Rob Marshall
Cast: Natasha Richardson, Alan Cumming, Ron Rifkin, John Benjamin Hickey, Denis O'Hare, Michele Pawk, Mary Louise Wilson
Songs: Same as in original production, except "Main Herr" and "Maybe This Time" added from 1972 film
New York run: The Henry Miller Theatre, March 19, 1998; 2,377 p.

In July 1998 the production shut down for four weeks because a scaffold collapsed a few doors away. In November 1998 the production moved to a much larger and newly renovated Studio 54.
(See page 219.)
RCA Victor OC

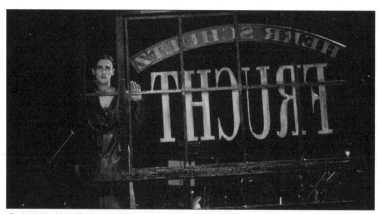

Cabaret. Alan Cumming. (Joan Marcus)

Cabaret. Natasha Richardson. (Joan Marcus)

FOOTLOOSE

Music: Tim Snow (except *Kenny Loggins, **Sammy Hagar, +Jim Steinman, ++Eric Carmen)
Lyrics: Dean Pitchford (except "Footloose" lyric with Kenny Loggins)
Book: Dean Pitchford & Walter Bobbie, from the original screenplay by Dean Pitchford
Producer: Dodger Endemol Theatricals
Director: Walter Bobbie
Choreographer: A.C.Ciulla
Cast: Jeremy Kushnier, Jennifer Laura Thompson, Catherine Cox, Stephen Lee Anderson, Dee Hoty, Catherine Campbell, Adam Lefevre, Donna Lee Marshall, John Hillner, Stacy Francis, Kathy Deitch, Rosalind Brown, Billy Hartung, Jim Ambler, Bryant Carroll, Nick Sullivan, Robin Baxter, Tom Plotkin, John Deyle, Artie Harris, Hunter Foster, Paul Castree
Songs: "Footloose"*; "On Any Sunday"; "The Girl Gets Around"**; "I Can't Stand Still"; "Somebody's Eyes"; "Learning to Be Silent"; Holding Out for a Hero"+; "I'm Free*/ Heaven Help Me"; "Let's Make Believe We're in Love"; "Let's Hear It for the Boy"; "Can You Find It in Your Heart"; "Mama Says"; "Almost Paradise"++; "Dancing Is Not a Crime"; "I Confess"
New York run: Richard Rodgers Theatre, October 22, 1998; 708 p.

Based on the screenplay for the 1984 film of the same name, *Footloose* is the story of Ren (Jeremy Kushnier) and his mother Ethel (Catherine Cox) who move from Chicago to a small Midwestern town when the parents divorce. Here, dancing within the city limits is forbidden by an ordinance instigated by Rev. Shaw Moore (Stephen Lee Anderson) because years earlier four teenagers were killed in a car crash coming home from a dance (among them was Rev. Moore's son). Rev. Moore's high-spirited daughter Ariel (Jennifer Laura Thompson) becomes enchanted with Ren. He, buoyed up by this enchantment, challenges the Reverend and the City Council on the law. After much soul searching, Rev. Moore sees the light and agrees with the students that "Dancing Is Not a Crime."

Prior to its New York opening, *Footloose* had had a run of bad luck. The Washington critics panned the production, and when it moved to New York, the set did not fit into the theatre. Despite its generally poor reviews, it ran for a year and a half.

Walter Bobbie had previously directed the revival of *Chicago* (which he also directed for City Center's Encore series). Dean Pitchford wrote the musical *Carrie*. Q Records OC

FOSSE

Music & lyrics: Miscellaneous writers
Conceived by: Richard Maltby, Chet Walker, Ann Reinking
Producer: Livent (US) Inc.
Director: Richard Maltby, Jr.
Choreography: Bob Fosse, recreated by Chet Walker
Co-director & co-choreographer: Ann Reinking
Cast: Valarie Pettiford, Jane Lanier, Eugene Fleming, Desmond Richardson,
Sergio Trujillo, Kim Morgan Greene, Mary Ann Lamb, Dane Moore,
Elizabeth Parkinson, Scott Wise, Andy Blankenbuehler, Shannon Lewis
Songs: "Life Is Just a Bowl of Cherries" (Lew Brown and Ray Henderson);
"Calypso" (G. Harrell)/ "Snake In the Grass" (Frederick Loewe); "Bye Bye
Blackbird" (Ray Henderson and Mort Dixon); "From the Edge" (G. Harrell);
"Percussion 4" (G. Harnell); "Big Spender" (Cy Coleman and Dorothy
Fields); "Crunchy Granola Suite" (Neil Diamond); "Hooray for Hollywood"
(Richard Whiting and Johnny Mercer); "From This Moment On" (Cole
Porter); "Alley Dance" (Jule Styne and Leo Robin); "Walking the Cat"
(Patrick S. Brady); "I Wanna Be a Dancin' Man" (Harry Warren and Johnny
Mercer); "Shoeless Joe From Hannibal, Mo" (Richard Adler and Jerry
Ross); "Dancing in the Dark" (Arthur Schwartz and Howard Dietz); "I Love
a Piano" (Irving Berlin); "Steam Heat" (Richard Adler and Jerry Ross);
"Rich Man's Frug" (Cy Coleman); "Silky Thoughts" (Patrick S. Brady);
"Cool Hand Luke" (Lalo Schifrin); "Big Noise From Winnetka" (music: Ray
Bauduc/ Bob Haggart; lyrics: Bob Crosby/ Gil Rodin); "Nowadays"; "The
Hot Honey Rag" (John Kander and Fred Ebb); "Glory"; "Manson Trio"
(Stephen Schwartz); "Mein Herr" (John Kander and Fred Ebb); "Take
Off with Us — Three Pas De Deux" (Stanley R. Lebowsky and Fred
K. Tobias); "Razzle Dazzle" (John Kander and Fred Ebb); "Who's Sorry
Now?" (music: Harry Ruby; lyrics: Ted Snyder & Bert Kalmar); "There'll
Be Some Changes Made" (W. Benton Overstreet & Billy Higgins); "Mr.
Bojangles" (Jerry Jeff Walker); "Sing, Sing, Sing" (Louis Prima)
New York run: Broadhurst Theatre, January 14, 1999; 1,093 p.

With the arrival of *Fosse*, three simultaneous productions on Broadway were
devoted to the work of Bob Fosse; the other two were the revivals of *Chicago*
and *Cabaret*. *Fosse* is a compilation of the dances created by Bob Fosse, from
his days as a nightclub performer through the 1986 production *Big Deal*. Chet
Walker and Ann Reinking recreated the dances. Six of the pieces were from the
1978 production *Dancin'*. There is no chronology or narrative — merely all the
Fosse hallmarks: the snapping fingers, the bent knees and elbows, the turned-
out leg, and the gloves and hats. The casts of *Chicago* and *Fosse* are almost
interchangeable, with Ann Reinking and Bebe Neuwirth seeming to have moved
from show to show with ease.
RCAVictor OC

ANNIE GET YOUR GUN

Music & lyrics: Irving Berlin
Book: Herbert & Dorothy Fields, revised by Peter Stone
Producers: Barry & Fran Weissler with Kardana, Michael Watt, Irving Welzer, Hal
        Luftig
Director: Graciele Daniele
Choreographer: Graciele Daniele & Jeff Calhoun
Cast: Bernadette Peters, Tom Wopat, Ron Holgate, Valerie Wright, Andrew
        Palermo, Kevin Bailey, Ronn Carroll, Gregory Zaragoza, Cassidy Ladden,
        Mia Walker, Trevor McQueen Eaton, Carlos Lopez, Brad Bradley, Patrick
        Wetzel, Marvin Laird, Julia Fowler, Jenny-Lynn Suckling
Songs: Same as in original production, except "I'm an Indian Too" was cut
New York run: Marquis Theatre, March 4, 1999; 1,046 p.

(See page 130.)
    Bernadette Peters won a Tony in 1999 for her performance. After Ms. Peters left the cast, Susan Lucci, Cheryl Ladd, and then Reba McIntyre — making her Broadway debut — replaced her. (Ms. Lucci had been a vacation replacement for Ms. Peters). Ms. McEntire, the country singer, with her inspired performance, seems to have laid to rest the ghost of Ethel Merman, to whom everyone undertaking the role has been compared. Later Brent Barrett replaced Tom Wopat. Ms. McIntyre's replacement was Crystal Bernard, and Tom Wopat returned to the cast.
Angel OC with Bernadette Peters and Tom Wopat

KISS ME, KATE

Music & lyrics: Cole Porter
Book: Sam & Bella Spewack
Producers: Roger Berlind & Roger Horchow
Director: Michael Blakemore
Choreographer: Kathleen Marshall
Cast: Brian Stokes Mitchell, Marin Mazzie, Amy Spanger, Michael Berresse,
        John Horton, Merwin Foard, Adriane Lenox, Stanley Wayne Mathis,
        Michael Mulheren, Lee Wilkof, Ron Holgate
Songs: Same as in original production, except "From This Moment On" was added
New York run: Martin Beck Theater, November 18, 1999; 881 p.

(See page 141.)
DRG OC

AIDA

Music: Elton John
Lyrics: Tim Rice
Book: Linda Wolverton, Robert Falls, & David Henry Hwang, "suggested by the opera"
Producers: Hyperion Theatricals under the direction of Peter Schneider & Thomas Schumacher
Director: Robert Falls
Choreographer: Wayne Cilento
Cast: Heather Headley, Adam Pascal, Sherie Rene Scott, John Hickok, Damian Perkins, Tyrees Allen, Daniel Oreskes
Songs: "Every Story Is a Love Story"; "Fortune Favors the Brave"; "The Past Is Another Land"; "Another Pyramid"; "How I Know You"; "My Strongest Suit"; "Enchantment Passing Through"; "The Dance of the Robe"; "Not Me"; "Elaborate Lives"; "The Gods Love Nubia"; "A Step Too Far"; "Easy As Life"; "Like Father, Like Son"; "Written in the Stars"; "I Know the Truth"
New York run: Palace Theatre, March 23, 2000; 1,852 p.

In the Egyptian wing of a modern museum where a young man and woman take notice of each other, the statue of Amneris (Sherie Rene Scott) comes to life to explain to the museum goers that "Every Story Is a Love Story." She tells the story of Radames (Adam Pascal, formerly of *Rent*) and Aida (Heather Headly, formerly of *The Lion King*). In ancient Egypt, Radames battled the Nubians and captured a group of prisoners, among whom was the Nubian King and the Princess Aida. Not knowing of her royal birth, and wanting to spare her from working in the copper mines, Radames gave her as a slave to Amneris, to whom he had been engaged for nine years.

At a banquet, Radames' father announces that Amneris and Radames are to marry in a week. Later Radames finds a little time to tell Aida of his growing interest in her. Taken to the Nubian camp, she is persuaded by the Nubians to lead them back to Nubia. She begs Radames to help the Nubians and admits her love for him. Radames plans to call off his wedding and to help Aida and her father escape. Pharaoh brands Radames as a traitor and sentences the couple to be buried alive. Amneris convinces her father to bury them in the same grave. As they slowly die, Radames promises Aida he will spend eternity looking for her. In an epilogue, the present-day Aida and Radames find each other and true love in the Egyptian Wing.

When it opened in Atlanta, it was called *Elaborate Lives: the Legend of Aida*. It previewed in Chicago before it came to Broadway, and there had been a concept album.
Buena Vista Records OC

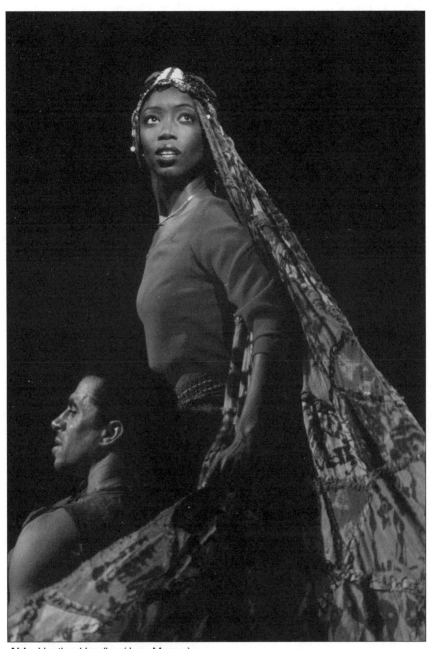

Aida. Heather Headley. (Joan Marcus)

CONTACT

Music & lyrics: Miscellaneous writers
Book: John Weidman; conceived by Susan Stroman & John Weidman
Producers: Lincoln Center Theatre at the Vivian Beaumont
Director & choreographer: Susan Stroman
Cast: Jason Antoon, Holly Cruikshank, Boyd Gaines, Sean Martin Hingston, David MacGillivray, Stephanie Michels, Scott Taylor, Deborah Yates, Karen Ziemba
Music: "My Heart Stood Still" (Richard Rodgers & Lorenz Hart, performed by Stephane Grappelli); "Anitra's Dance" from *Peer Gynt* Suite No. 1, Edvard Greig, "Waltz Eugene" from *Eugene Onegin,* Op. 24, and "La Farandole" from "L'Arlesienne Suite No. 2" (all performed by the New York Philharmonic, Leonard Bernstein, conductor); "O Mio Babbino Caro" (Giacomo Puccini, performed by Andre Kostelanetz and his orchestra); "You're Nobody til Somebody Loves You" (Russ Morgan, Larry Stock, and James Cavanaugh, performed by Dean Martin); "Powerful Stuff" (Wally Wilson, Michael Henderson, and Robert S. Field, performed by The Fabulous Thunderbirds); "Put a Lid on It" (Tom Maxwell, performed by Squirrel Nut Zippers); "Sweet Lorraine" (Clifford Burwell/Maxwell Parish, performed by Stephane Grappelli); "Runaround Sue" (Ernest Maresca/Dion DiMucci, performed by Dion); "Beyond the Sea" (Charles Trenet/Jack Lawrence, performed by Royal Crown Revue, Arte Butler, conductor); "See What I Mean?" (J. Chapman, performed by Al Cooper and his Savoy Sultans); "Simply Irresistible" (written and performed by Robert Palmer); "Do You Wanna Dance?" (Bobby Freeman, performed by The Beach Boys); "Topsy" (William Edgar Batt/ Eddie Durham, performed by The Royal Crown Revue); "Sing, Sing, Sing" (Louis Prima, performed by Benny Goodman); "Christopher Columbus" (Andy Razaf); "Moondance" (written and performed by Van Morrison)
New York run: Vivian Beaumont Theater, March 30, 2000; 1,010 p.

In 1998, Andre Bishop, Artistic Director of Lincoln Center Theatre, asked Susan Stroman, whose previous work he had admired, to develop a project for his theatre. Ms. Stroman then involved her friend John Weidman (*Pacific Overtures* and *Anything Goes*). Based on an incident Ms. Stroman had seen in a swing club, the pair created *Contact* and mounted it as a workshop presentation for Mr. Bishop — and guests, who were so enthusiastic about it that the creators were asked to expand the piece because it ran only an hour. Rather than do that, Ms. Stroman and Mr. Weidman decided to add two shorter pieces to complete the evening.

Contact opened for a limited run in October 1999 at the Newhouse Theater in Lincoln Center, an Off-Broadway-sized house; it received rave reviews and within the week had sold out its entire run. In March 2000, the production moved upstairs to the Vivian Beaumont Theatre, a Broadway-sized house.

Described as a dance play in three short stories, and performed with no original score or orchestra (all the music is taped), *Contact* caused a furor (mostly by the Musicians Union) when the Tony Administrative Committee deemed it a new musical and eligible for Tony nomination.

All three plays deal with the contacts people have with each other. In the first, Jean-Honore Fragonard's painting *The Swing* inspired "Swinging." The cast is a servant, an aristocrat, and a girl on a swing, all being ribald and vastly amusing. "Did You Move," the second piece, features Karen Ziemba dining in a Queens restaurant in 1954 with her abusive husband. The only way she can escape this relationship is through her fantasies. The third, "Contact," tells the story of an advertising copywriter who fails in his attempt at suicide. He wanders into a swing club where he sees a young woman in a yellow dress who gives him hope. After much angst, she turns out to be the girl in the downstairs apartment.
RCAVictor OC

THE MUSIC MAN

Music, lyrics & book: Meredith Willson
Story: Meredith Willson & Franklin Lacey
Producers: Dodger Theatricals, The John F. Kennedy Center for the Performing Arts, Elizabeth Williams/ Anita Waxman, Kardana-Swinsky Productions, Lorie Cowen Levy/ Dede Harris
Director & choreographer: Susan Stroman
Cast: Craig Bierko, Rebecca Luker, Ralph Byers, Michael-Leon Wooley, Jordan Puryear, Martha Hawley, Jack Doyle, Paul Benedict, Leslie Hendrix, Tracy Nicole Chapman, John Sloman, Blake Hammond, Max Casella, Katherine McGrath, Michael Phelan, Ruth Williamson, Kate Levering, Ann Brown
Songs: Same as in the original production
New York run: Neil Simon Theatre, April 27, 2000; 699 p.

(See page 177.)
Atlantic Records OC

THE FULL MONTY

Music & lyrics: David Yazbek
Book: Terrence McNally
Producers: Fox Searchlight Pictures, Lindsay Law, Thomas Hall
Director: Jack O'Brien
Choreographer: Jerry Mitchell
Cast: John Ellison Conlee, Nicholas Cutro, Jason Danieley, Lisa Datz, Andre De Shields, Thomas Michael Fiss, Kathleen Freeman, Romain Fruge, Annie Golden, Marcus Neville, Emily Skinner, Patrick Wilson
Songs: "Scrap"; "It's a Woman's World"; "Man"; "Big-Ass Rock"; "Big Black Man"; "You Rule My World"; "Michael Jordan's Ball"; "Breeze off the River"; "You Walk With Me"; "Let It Go"
New York run: Eugene O'Neill Theatre, October 26, 2000; 769 p.

In *The Full Monty*, Terrence McNally (*Ragtime, Kiss of the Spider Woman*) moved the story from the film's Sheffield, England, to Buffalo, New York. The universal contemporary problems — unemployment, single parenthood, and loneliness — lost nothing in the transfer. He added three characters who were not in the film: Georgie Bukatinsky (Jerry's wife), Keno (the male dancer), and Jeanette Burnmeister (the men's accompanist).

After learning that some of the wives are attending a "Girls Night Out" at a Chippendale-type club (where admission is $50) and hearing their delighted screams at the entertainment, Jerry Bukatinsky (Patrick Wilson) wonders why "real men" couldn't strip and help solve some of their financial problems ("Man"). He convinces five of his friends to join him in the venture. After weeks of rehearsals for the production and learning about themselves, the big night arrives. Yes, they go "the full Monty," at least for a few seconds.
RCA Victor OC

The Full Monty. The cast in their most famous number. (Carol Rosegg)

FOLLIES

Music & lyrics: Stephen Sondheim
Book: James Goldman
Producer: The Roundabout Theatre Company
Director: Matthew Warchus
Choreographer: Kathleen Marshall
Cast: Blythe Danner, Gregory Harrison, Judith Ivey, Treat Williams, Polly Bergen, Marge Champion, Betty Garrett, Joan Roberts, Donald Saddler, Jane White, Carol Woods, Louis Zorich, Roxane Barlow, Carol Bentley, Erin Dilly, Kelli O'Hara
Songs: Same as in the original production
New York run: Belasco Theatre, April 5, 2001; 117 p.

(See page 232.)

THE PRODUCERS

Music & lyrics: Mel Brooks
Book: Mel Brooks & Thomas Meehan
Producers: Rocco Landesman, Clear Channel Entertainment, The Frankel F.X. Baruch-Viertel-Routh Group, Bob and Harvey Weinstein, Rick Steiner, Robert Silerman, Mel Brooks, in association with James D. Stern/ Douglas Meyer
Director & choreographer: Susan Stroman
Cast: Nathan Lane, Matthew Broderick, Roger Bart, Gary Beach, Cady Huffman, Brad Oscar, Madeline Doherty, Kathy Fitzgerald, Eric Gunhus, Peter Marinos, Jennifer Smith, Ray Wills
Songs: "Opening Night"; "The King of Broadway"; "We Can Do It"; "I Wanna Be a Producer"; "In Old Bavaria"; "Der Guten Tag Hop Clop"; "Keep It Gay"; "When You Got It, Flaunt It"; "Along Came Bialy"; "That Face"; "Haben Sie Gehoert Das Deutsche Band?"; "You Never Say 'Good Luck' on Opening Night"; "Springtime for Hitler"; "Where Did We Go Right?"; "Betrayed"; " 'Til Him"; "Prisoners of Love"; "Goodbye!"
New York run: St. James Theatre, April 19, 2001; 2,502 p.

Thirty-three years after the film *The Producers*, Mel Brooks and Tom Meehan (*Annie*) recreated an even zanier musical of it, and so successfully that the day after the production opened, the top ticket price was raised from $90 to $100.

Broadway producer Max Bialystock (Nathan Lane) and his nerdy accountant Leo Bloom (Matthew Broderick) decide that the only way to make money as Broadway producers is to stage a production that is sure to flop, staff it with a production team that has not had any success, sell off more than 100% of the shares, and then take the money and run with it to Rio when it closes after the first night, because no one worries about the money when a show flops. They find *Springtime for Hitler,* a valentine to Hitler written by Franz Liebkind (Brad Oscar), a Nazi playwright and pigeon breeder (even the pigeons sport swastikas on their wings) living in Greenwich Village. Max cons his harem of white-haired ladies who back his plays out of $2 million. He has them make out their checks to "cash," suggesting that is the name of the play. Unfortunately for the team, the production is a great success ("Where Did We Go Right?") Leo runs off to Rio with the money — and Ulla (Cady Huffman), the Swedish sexpot who is their secretary and a member of the *Springtime* cast. Max is arrested, and Leo, conscience stricken, returns to New York to defend Max and accept his own share of the blame. Both are jailed but are soon freed. They return to Broadway where their production *Prisoners of Love* is as successful as Mel Brooks's *The Producers*.

Director-choreographer Susan Stroman has added to the hilarity with her staging of the old ladies tap dancing with their walking frames, the dancing Nazis (reflected in a mirror as in a Busby Berkley number) forming a swastika, and the Hitler character (Gary Beach) sitting at the edge of the stage singing "Springtime for Hitler" in a Judy Garland moment. With the opening of *The Producers*, Stroman had three shows on Broadway. The other two were *The Music Man* and *Contact*.

British actor Henry Goodman replaced Nathan Lane, and Steven Weber replaced Matthew Broderick. Goodman had previously appeared on Broadway in *Art* and had been in the London productions of *Chicago* and *Guys and Dolls*. Mr. Goodman lasted 30 performances and was replaced by Brad Oscar. Weber, well known for his television work, made his Broadway debut. Subsequently Louis J. Stadlen and Don Stephenson were Bialystock and Bloom. *The Producers* garnered 15 Tony nominations and won 12 awards.

The Producers. In the foreground from left to right, Matthew Broderick, Nathan Lane, and Gary Beach. (Paul Kolnik)

42nd STREET

Music: Harry Warren
Lyrics: Al Dubin
Book: Michael Stewart & Mark Bramble (based on the novel by Bradford Ropes)
Producers: Dodger Management Group
Director: Mark Bramble
Musical staging & new choreography: Randy Skinner
Original direction & choreography: Gower Champion
Cast: Michael Cumpsty, Christine Ebersole, Kate Levering, Michael Arnold, Mary Testa. Jonathan Freeman, Allen Fitzpatrick, Mylinda Hull, David Elser, Billy Stritch, Michael McCarty, Richard Muenz
Songs: Same as in the original production
New York run: Ford Center for the Performing Arts, May 3, 2001; 1,524 p.

(See page 257.)
Atlantic 2001 OC

URINETOWN

Music & lyrics: Mark Hollmann
Book & lyrics: Greg Kotis
Producer: The Araca Group & Dodger Theatricals in association with TheaterDreams, Inc. & Lauren Mitchell
Director: John Rando
Musical Staging: John Carrafa
Cast: David Beach, Rachel Coloff, Rick Crom, John Cullum, John Deyle, Hunter Foster, Victor W. Hawks, Erin Hill, Ken Jennings, Spencer Kayden, Daniel Marcus, Jeff McCarthy, Nancy Opel, Peter Reardon, Don Richard, Lawrence E. Street, Jennifer Laura Thompson, Kay Walbye
Songs: "Too Much Exposition"; "Urinetown"; "It's a Privilege to Pee"; "Look at the Sky"; "Don't Be the Bunny"; "Snuff That Girl"; "Run Freedom, Run!"; "We're Not Sorry"; "I See a River"
New York run: The Henry Miller Theatre, September 20, 2001; 965 p.

Unable to afford the price of admission to a public toilet while in Paris, Greg Kotis conceived the idea of a corporation owning the rights to a city's water supply and allowing the citizens to use public facilities for a fee. He thought it would have to be a musical "because it is so absurd." As it developed, it became a satiric commentary on the role of government, the responsibilities of citizens, and old-fashioned musicals.

After having been a success in the 1999 Fringe Festival, Urinetown was presented Off-Broadway in May 2001 and moved in September to Broadway. RCA OC

Urinetown. Jeff McCarthy, left, and Spencer Kayden. (Joan Marcus)

MAMMA MIA !

Music & Lyrics: Benny Andersson & Bjorn Ulvaeus
Book: Catherine Johnson
Producers: Judy Craymer, Richard East, Bjorn Ulvaeus for Littlestar presentation,
      in association with Universal
Director: Phyllida Lloyd
Choreographer: Anthony Van Laast
Cast: Louise Pitre, Judy Kaye, Tina Madigan, Ken Marks, Karen Mason, Joe
      Machota, Dean Nolen
Songs: "Honey Honey"; "Money, Money, Money"; "Mamma Mia"; "Chiquitita";
      "Dancing Queen"; "Lay All Your Love on Me"; "Gimme! Gimme! Gimme!";
      "The Name of the Game"; "Knowing Me Knowing You"; "Slipping Through
      My Fingers"; "Take a Chance on Me"
New York run: Winter Garden Theatre, October 18, 2001 (still running 6/11)

Catherine Johnson has woven twenty of ABBA's songs into the book of *Mamma Mia!* The story tells of twenty-year-old Sophie Sheridan (Tina Madigan) and her single mother Donna (Louise Pitre) who live on a Greek island where Donna runs a taverna. Sophie is about to marry and, having discovered her mother's diary, learns that she has three possible fathers. She invites all three men to the wedding without telling her mother.

Donna was once part of a rock trio called Donna and the Dynamos with Tanya (Karen Mason) and Rosie (Judy Kaye), now a cookbook writer. Later, when all twenty songs have been presented, the wedding happens, but no one ever is told who Sophie's father is.

Mamma Mia! opened in London, where it was still playing when the North American production opened. It played in Toronto and Chicago before coming to Broadway.
Decca Broadway OC

Mamma Mia! Louise Pitre. (Joan Marcus)

OKLAHOMA!

Music: Richard Rodgers
Lyrics & book: Oscar Hammerstein II
Producer: Cameron Mackintosh, produced in arrangement with the Rodgers and Hammerstein Organization
Director: Trevor Nunn
Choreographer: Susan Stroman
Cast: Patrick Wilson, Josefina Gabrielle, Jessica Boevers, Justin Bohon, Ronn Carroll, Shuler Hensley, Aasif Mandavi, Andrea Martin
Songs: Same as in original production
New York run: Gershwin Theatre, March 21, 2002; 388 p.

(See page 119.)

THOROUGHLY MODERN MILLIE

New Music: Jeanine Tesori
New Lyrics: Dick Scanlan
Book: Richard Morris & Dick Scanlan; original story & screenplay by Richard Morris for Universal Pictures Film
Producer: Michael Leavitt, Fox Theatricals, Hal Luftig, Stewart F. Lane, James L. Nederlander, Independent Presenters Network, L.Mages/ M. Glick, Bernstein/ Manocherian/ Dramatic Forces, John York Nobel, Whoopi Goldberg
Director: Michael Mayer
Choreographer: Rob Ashford
Cast: Sutton Foster, Sheryl Lee Ralph, Harriet Harris, Marc Kudisch, Gavin Creel, Angela Christian, Ken Leung, Francis Jue, Anne L. Nathan
Songs: "Not for the Life of Me"; "Only in New York"; "Forget About the Boy"; "I'm Falling in Love with Someone"; "Long as I'm Here with You"; "Gimme Gimme"
New York run: Marquis Theatre, April 18, 2002; 904 p.

Millie Dillmount (Sutton Foster) arrives in New York from Kansas ("Not for the Life of Me"). Her plan is to work for a rich man and eventually to marry him. She checks into the Hotel Priscilla; here she meets Miss Dorothy with whom she becomes very friendly ("How the Other Half Lives"). The owner of the hotel, Ms. Meers (Harriet Harris), plans to kidnap Miss Dorothy for her white slavery ring because Miss Dorothy seems to have no family who would notice if she were to disappear.

Millie finds a job with a handsome boss, Mr. Graydon (Marc Kudisch), whom she plans to marry. In the meantime, Millie, Miss Dorothy, Jimmy Smith, and even Muzzy Von Hossmere (Sheryl Lee Ralph) get to know New York ("Only in New York"). Millie introduces Miss Dorothy to Mr. Graydon, and they fall in love. Miss Dorothy is kidnapped by Mrs. Meers. She is rescued, and everyone lives happily ever after when it is revealed that Muzzy is the stepmother of Jimmy and Miss Dorothy, and Jimmy is the richest bachelor in the world.

The production originated at the La Jolla Playhouse in La Jolla, California. Sutton Foster stepped into the role of Millie just a week before previews began at La Jolla.

The Broadway production was based on the 1967 film that starred Julie Andrews, Carol Channing, Bea Lillie, and Mary Tyler Moore.
RCA OC

INTO THE WOODS

Music & lyrics: Stephen Sondheim
Book: James Lapine
Producers: Dodger Theatricals, TheatreDreams Inc., associate producer: Lauren Mitchell
Director: James Lapine
Choreographer: John Carrafa
Cast: Vanessa Williams, John McMartin, Laura Benati, Marylouise Burke, Stephen deRosa, Gregg Edelman, Molly Ephraim, Kerry O'Malley, Christopher Sieber, Adam Wylie, Melissa Dye, Dennis Kelly, Pamela Myers, Trent Armand Kendall, Chad Kimball, Amanda Naughton, Jennifer Malneke, the recorded voice of Judi Dench as the Giant
Songs: Same as in the original production
New York run: Broadhurst Theatre, April 30, 2002; 279 p.

(See page 277.)

HAIRSPRAY

Music: Marc Shaiman
Lyrics: Scott Wittman & Marc Shaiman
Book: Mark O'Donnell & Thomas Meehan, based upon the New Line Cinema film written & directed by John Waters
Producers: Margo Lion, Adam Epstein, The Baruch-Viertel-Routh-Frankel Group, James D. Stern/ Douglas L. Meyer, Rick Steiner/ Frederic H. Mayerson, SEL & GFO, New Line Cinema in association with Clear Channel Entertainment, A. Gordon/ E. McAllister, D. Harris/ M. Swinsky, J&B Osher
Choreographer: Jerry Mitchell
Director: Jack O'Brien
Cast: Marissa Jaret Winokur, Harvey Fierstein, Laura Bell Bundy, Mary Bond Davis, Kerry Butler, Linda Hart, Jackie Hoffman, Matthew Morrison, Corey Reynolds, Clarke Thorell, Joel Vig, Danelle Eugenia Wilson, Dick Latessa
Songs: "Good Morning Baltimore"; "The Nicest Kids in Town"; "Mama, I'm a Big Girl Now"; "I Can Hear the Bells"; "Run and Tell That"; "I Know Where I've Been"; "Big, Blonde and Beautiful"; "Timeless to Me"
New York run: Neil Simon Theatre, August 15, 2002; 2,642 p.

Hairspray is based on John Waters's 1988 film, which is set in 1962 Baltimore. "Good Morning Baltimore," sings chunky Tracy Turnblat (Marissa Jaret Winokur) as she goes off to school, because she is so happy with everything. After school she races home with her friend Penny (Kerry Butler) to see "The Corny Collins Show" (Baltimore's answer to *American Bandstand*), where they learn all the new dances and Tracy drools for Link Larkin (Matthew Morrison), a performer on the show. The Ultra Clutch Hairspray Company is about to sponsor a competition for Miss Teenage Hairspray. Tracy, Penny, and friends all vie for the title. "The Corny Collins Show" is segregated, except for one day a month when there is a "Negro Day." Tracy decides that the show should be integrated and sets about to see that this is done. With the help of her school friends and Motormouth Maybelle (Mary Bond Davis), Tracy gets the title, integrates Baltimore, and gets Link.

Harvey Fierstein (Edna Turnblat), as Tracy's mother who takes in laundry to help meet the bills, returned to Broadway for the first time since *Torch Song Trilogy*. Dressed in a fat suit, he gives an endearing performance. With Dick Lasessa (Wilbur Turnblat, Tracy's father) he stops the show ("Timeless to Me"). Sony OC

Hairspray. Clarke Thorell as Corny Collins with cast. (Paul Kolnik)

FLOWER DRUM SONG

Music: Richard Rodgers
Lyrics: Oscar Hammerstein II
Book: David Henry Hwang, based on the original book by Oscar Hammerstein II
Producers: Benjamin Mordecai, Michael A. Jenkins, Waxman/ Williams Entertainment, Center Theatre Group/ Mark Taper Forum (Gordon Davidson, Artistic Director; Charles Dillingham, Managing Director), Robert G. Bartner, Robert Dragotta, Temple Gill, Marcia Roberts, Kelpie Arts, Stephanie McClelland, Judith Resnick, and Dramatic Forces (Dori Berinstein, Jennifer Manocherian, Barrie Loeks, Jim Loeks); produced by arrangement with the Rodgers and Hammerstein Organization; Associate Producer: Dallas Summer Musicals, Inc., Brian Brolly, Alice Chebba Walsh, and Ernest De Leon Escaler; produced in association with Lexington Entertainment Group and the Singapore Repertory Theatre
Director & choreographer: Robert Longbottom
Cast: Lea Salonga, Alvin Ing, Sandra Allen, Jose Llana, Jodi Long, Randall Duk Kim, Hoon Lee, Allen Liu, David Chase
Songs: Same as in the original production
New York run: Virginia Theatre, October 17, 2002; 169 p.

(See page 178.)
DRG OC

MOVIN' OUT

Music & lyrics: Billy Joel
Conceived by: Twyla Tharp
Producers: James L. Nederlander, Hal Luftig, Scott E. Nederlander, Terry Allen
        Kramer, Clear Channel Entertainment, Emanuel Azenberg
Director & choreographer: Twyla Tharp
Cast: John Selya, Elizabeth Parkinson, Benjamin G. Bowman, Keith Roberts,
        Ashley Tuttle, Scott Wise, lead vocalist Matt Cavanaugh
Songs: "It's Still Rock and Roll to Me"; "Scenes from an Italian Restaurant";
        "Movin' Out (Anthony's Song)"; "Reverie (Villa D'este/ Just The Way
        You Are")"; "This Night"; "Summer, Highland Falls"; "We Didn't Start The
        Fire"; "She's Got a Way"; "The Stranger"; "Elegy (The Great Peconic)";
        "Invention in C Minor"; "Angry Young Man"; "Big Shot"; "Big Man on
        Mulberry Street"; "Captain Jack"; "Innocent Man"; "Pressure"; "Goodnight
        Saigon"; "Air (Dublinesque)"; "Shameless"; "James"; "River of Dreams/
        Keeping The Faith/ Only The Good Die Young"; "I've Loved These Days"
New York run: Richard Rodgers Theatre, October 24, 2002; 1303 p.

Twyla Tharp choreographed, directed, and shaped a collection of Billy Joel songs into a "rock ballet." While the nonsinging dancers danced her significant athletic steps, a rock band played above/ behind them with pianist Matt Cavanaugh doing the vocals of those familiar tunes that Joel orchestrated.

Brenda and Eddie, and James and Judy, are teenage couples growing up on Long Island in the 1960s and have to confront the Vietnam war and all the other social changes of the time. The characters were drawn from Joel's songs while Tharp crafted the thin compelling plot. It ran over three years, toured the US, and had a brief London run.

Movin' Out had continued the projectile of Tharp's career in modern dance, film, television, and now a Broadway hit. Her 2006 follow up, *The Times They Are A-Changin'*, based on the songs of Bob Dylan, did not repeat the Joel show's success. It ran only 28 performances on Broadway.
Sony OC

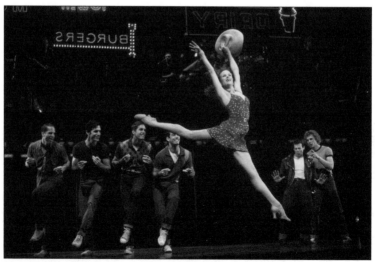

Movin' Out. Elizabeth Parkinson and company. (Joan Marcus)

MAN OF LA MANCHA

Music: Mitch Leigh
Lyrics: Joe Darion
Book: Dale Wasserman (based on the novel *Don Quixote* by Miguel Cervantes)
Producers: David Stone, Jon B. Platt, Susan Quint Gallin, Sandy Gallin, Seth M. Siegel, & USA OSTAR Theatricals; produced in association with Mary Lu Roffe
Director: Jonathan Kent
Choreographer: Luis Perez
Cast: Brian Stokes Mitchell, Mary Elizabeth Mastrantonio, Ernie Sabella, Stephen Bogardus, Mark Jacoby, Natascia Diaz, Don Mayo, Olga Merediz, Frederick B. Owens, Jaime Torocellini
Songs: Same as in the original production
New York run: Martin Beck (now Al Hirschfeld) Theatre, December 5, 2002; 304 p.

(See page 215.)
RCA Victor OC

NINE

Music & lyrics: Maury Yeston
Book: Arthur Kopit, adapted from the Italian by Mario Fratti
Producer: The Roundabout Theatre Company
Director: David Leveaux
Choreographer: Jonathan Butterell
Cast: Antonio Banderas, Laura Benati, Jane Krakowski, Mary Stuart Masterson, Chita Rivera, Nell Campbell, Mary Beth Peil, Deidre Goodwin
Songs: Same as in the original
New York run: Eugene O'Neil Theatre, April 10, 2003; 283 p.

(See page 262.)
PS Classics OC

GYPSY

Music: Jule Styne
Lyrics: Stephen Sondheim
Book: Arthur Laurents
Producers: Robert Fox, Ron Kastner, Roger Marino, Michael Watt, Harvey Weinstein, WWLC
Director: Sam Mendes
Choreographer: Jerome Robbins; Additional Choreography by Jerry Mitchell
Cast: Bernadette Peters, Tammy Blanchard, John Dossett, Brooks Ashmanskas, Julie Halston, Heather Lee, William Parry, MacIntyre Dixon, Kate Buddeke, David Burtka, Michael McCormick, Kate Reinders
Songs: Same as in the original
New York run: Shubert Theatre, May 1, 2003; 451 p.

(See page 182.)
Angel Records OC

AVENUE Q

Music: Robert Lopez & Jeff Marx
Lyrics: Robert Lopez & Jeff Marx
Book: Jeff Whitty, based on a concept by Robert Lopez & Jeff Marx
Producers: Kevin McCollum, Robyn Goodman, Jeffrey Seller, Vineyard Theatre (Artistic Director: Douglas Aibel; Managing Director: Bardo Ramirez) & the New Group (Artistic Director: Scott Elliott; Executive Director: Geoff Rich)
Associate Producers: Sonny Everett, Walter Grossman, Morton Swinsky
Director: Jason Moore
Choreographer: Ken Roberson
Songs: "The Avenue Q Theme"; "What Do You Do with a B.A. in English?"; "It Sucks to Be Me"; "If You Were Gay"; "Purpose"; "Everyone's a Little Bit Racist"; "The Internet Is for Porn"; "Mix Tape"; "I'm Not Wearing Underwear Today"; "Special"; "You Can Be as Loud as the Hell You Want (When You're Makin' Love)"; "Fantasies Come True"; "My Girlfriend, Who Lives in Canada"; "There's a Fine, Fine Line"; "There Is Life Outside Your Apartment"; "The More You Ruv Someone"; "Schadenfreude"; "I Wish I Could Go Back to College"; "The Money Song"; "School for Monsters"; "For Now"
Cast: John Tartaglia, Stephanie D'Abruzzo, Rick Lyon, Natalie Venetia Belcon, Jordan Gelber, Ann Harada, Jennifer Barnhart
New York run: John Golden Theatre, July 31, 2003; 2,534 p.

Avenue Q opened in 2002 at Off-Broadway's Vineyard Theatre, quickly sold out, and then moved to Broadway, overcoming doubts as to whether this subversive "puppet show" was "too small" for Broadway.

The show is set in an a very far-off NYC borough that is the only place its disaffected, poorly employed denizens can afford to live because Manhattan is so forbiddingly expensive. The East Village goes up to Avenue D, and so the fictional Avenue Q is a lengthy extension. We meet a recent college graduate and his neighbors that include a kindergarten teacher, child star Gary Coleman who is now a building superintendent, an unemployed comedian and his uncredentialed therapist wife, and a male couple who may be gay. Together they commiserate and share their lives and problems.

Besides the show's comic and poignant score, its big appeal was designer and original cast member Rick Lyon's awesome puppets. These are held by actors in plain sight, but the other characters react only to the puppets. Lyon worked on the classic PBS children's series *Sesame Street,* and his creations have a jarring similarity, but here themes of racism, homosexuality, and pornography are addressed.

Avenue Q repeated its previous success on Broadway and even managed to win the Tony Award for Best Musical. It has also been produced in London and Las Vegas.
BMG OC

Avenue Q. Kate Monster, left, and Stephanie D'Abruzzo. (Carol Rosegg)

Wicked. Kristin Chenoweth, left, and Idina Menzel. (Joan Marcus)

WICKED

Music & lyrics: Stephen Schwartz
Book: Winnie Holzman, based on the novel by Gregory Maguire
Producers: Marc Platt, Universal Pictures, the Araca Group, Jon B. Platt, David Stone
Director: Joe Mantello
Choreographer: Wayne Cilento
Cast: Kristin Chenoweth, Idina Menzel, Joel Grey, Carole Shelley, Norbert Leo Butz, Michelle Federer, Christopher Fitzgerald, William Youmans, Sean McCourt, Cristy Candler
Songs: "No One Mourns the Wicked"; "Dear Old Shiz"; "The Wizard and I"; "What Is This Feeling?"; "Something Bad"; "Dancing Through Life"; "Popular "; "I'm Not That Girl"; "One Short Day"; "A Sentimental Man"; "Defying Gravity"; "Thank Goodness"; "The Wicked Witch of the East"; "Wonderful"; "As Long as You're Mine"; "No Good Deed"; "March of the Witch Hunters"; "For Good"
New York run: Gershwin Theatre, October 30, 2003 (still running 6/11)

Wicked is loosely based on novelist Gregory MaGuire's inventive exploration of *The Wizard of Oz,* which is told from the perspective of the witches. Stephen Schwartz was so enthusiastic after reading it he sought and obtained the theatrical rights and adapted it in collaboration with book writer Winnie Holtzman.

The Shiz University, presided over by headmistress Madame Morrible, is where student witches the noble green Elphaba (Idina Menzel), "The Wicked Witch of the East," and the ambitious Glinda (Kristin Chenoweth), "The Good Witch of the North," meet and eventually clash. The origins of Toto, the munchkins, the Tin Man, the Cowardly Lion, the Scarecrow, the Yellow Brick Road, and the Wizard are all explained.

Decca Broadway OC

WONDERFUL TOWN

Music: Leonard Bersnstein
Lyrics: Betty Comden & Adolph Green
Book: Joseph Fields & Jerome Chodorov, based on their play *My Sister Eileen,* based on short stories by Ruth McKenney
Producers: Roger Berlind & Barry & Fran Weissler, produced in association with Edwin W. Schloss, Allen Spivak, Clear Channel Entertainment, & Harvey Weinstein; Associate Producer: Daniel M. Posener
Director & choreographer: Kathleen Marshall
Cast: Donna Murphy, Jennifer Westfeldt, Peter Benson, Gregg Edelman, David Margulies, Raymond Jaramillo McLeod, Nancy Anderson, Ken Barnett, Linda Mugleston
Songs: Same as in the original production
New York run: Al Hirschfeld Theatre, November 23, 2003; 497 p.

(See page 155.)
DRG OC (there was a later second release with tracks recorded by Brooke Shields who replaced Donna Murphy as Ruth.)

FIDDLER ON THE ROOF

Music: Jerry Bock
Lyrics: Sheldon Harnick
Book: Joseph Stein
Producers: James L. Nederlander, Stewart F. Lane, Bonnie Comley, Harbor Entertainment, Terry Allen Kramer, Bob Boyett, Lawrence Horowitz, Clear Channel Entertainment
Director: David Leveaux
Musical staging: Jonathan Butterell
Choreographer: Jerome Robbins
Cast: Alfred Molina, Randy Graff, Nancy Opel, Stephen Lee Anderson, David Ayers, John Cariani, Nick Danielson, Phillip Hoffman, Sally Murphy, Tricia Paoluccio ,Robert Petkoff, David Wohl
Songs: Same as in the original production, plus "Topsy-Turvy"
New York run: Minskoff Theatre, February 26, 2004; 781 p.

(See page 209.)
PS Classics OC

PACIFIC OVERTURES

Music & lyrics: Stephen Sondheim
Book: John Weidman; additional material by Hugh Wheeler
Producer: The Roundabout Theatre Company, in association with Gorgeous Entertainment
Director & choreographer: Amon Miyamoto
Cast: B.D. Wong, Evan D'Angeles, Joseph Anthony Foronda, Yoko Fumoto, Alvin Y. F. Ing, Francis Jue, Darren Lee, Hoon Lee, Michael K. Lee, Ming Lee, Telly Leung, Paolo Montalban, Alan Muraoka, Mayumi Omagari, Daniel Jay Park, Hazel Anne Raymundo, Sab Shimono, Yuka Takara, Scott Watanabe
Songs: Same as in the original production
New York run: Studio 54, December 2, 2004; 69 p.

(See page 245.)
PS Classics OC

LA CAGE AUX FOLLES

Music & lyrics: Jerry Herman
Book: Harvey Fierstein
Producers: James L. Nederlander, Clear Channel Entertainment, Kenneth D. Greenblatt, Terry Allen Kramer & Martin Richards
Associate Producers: TGA Entertainment, Ltd., Leni Sender, Bob Cuillo, Kathi Glist
Director: Jerry Zaks
Choreographer: Jerry Mitchell
Cast: Gary Beach, Daniel Davis, Linda Balgord, Gavin Creel, Angela Gaylor, Michael Mulheren, John Shuman, Michael Benjamin Washington, Ruth Williamson, Merwin Foard
Songs: Same as in the original production
New York run: Marquis Theatre, December 9, 2004; 229 p.

(See page 266.)

DIRTY ROTTEN SCOUNDRELS

Music & lyrics: David Yazbek
Book: Jeffrey Lane
Producers: Marty Bell, David Brown, Aldo Scrofani, Roy Furman, Dede Harris, Amanda Lipitz, Greg Smith, Ruth Hendel, Chase Mishkin, Barry Tatelman, Susan Tatelman, Debra Black, Sharon Karmazin, Joyce Schweickert, Bernie Abrams, Michael Speyer, Barbara Whitman, Weissberger Theater Group (Jay Harris, Producer), Cheryl Wiesenfeld, Jean Cheever, Clear Channel Entertainment & Harvey Weinstein; produced in association with MGM On Stage
Director: Jack O'Brien
Choreographer: Jerry Mitchell
Cast: Norbert Leo Butz, John Lithgow, Sherie René Scott, Sara Gettelfinger, Joanna Gleason, Gregory Jbara
Songs: "Give Them What They Want"; "What Was a Woman to Do?"; "Great Big Stuff"; "Chimp in a Suit"; "Oklahoma?"; "All About Ruprecht"; "Here I Am"; "Nothing Is Too Wonderful to Be True"; "The Miracle"; "Rüffhousin' mit Shüffhausen"; "Like Zis/ Like Zat"; "The More We Dance"; "Love Is My Legs"; "Love Sneaks In"; "Son of Great Big Stuff"; "The Reckoning"; "Dirty Rotten Number"
New York run: Imperial Theatre, March 3, 2005; 627 p.

Much of *The Full Monty's* creative team reunited for *Dirty Rotten Scoundrels*, about con men preying on wealthy women on The French Rivera. Previously this story was filmed with Steve Martin and Michael Caine, and before that with Marlon Brando and David Niven.

Both John Lithgow as the old-time crook and Norbert Leo Butz as the upstart criminal had their grand moments, but Butz got the Tony award for Best Actor in a Musical.

Replacements included Jonathan Pryce and Keith Carradine for Lithgow, Rachel York for Sherie Rene Scott, Lucie Arnaz for Joanna Gleason, Richard Kind for Gregory Jbara, and Brian d'Arcy James for Butz.
Ghostlight OC

Dirty Rotten Scoundrels. From left to right, Norbert Leo Butz, John Lithgow, and Sherie René Scott. (Carol Rosegg)

MONTY PYTHON'S SPAMALOT

Music: John Du Prez & Eric Idle
Lyrics: Eric Idle
Book: Eric Idle, based on the screenplay *Monty Python and The Holy Grail* by Eric Idle, John Cleese, Terry Gilliam, Terry Jones, Michael Palin, Graham Chapman
Producers: Boyett Ostar Productions, The Shubert Organization (Gerald Schoenfeld: Chairman; Philip J. Smith: President; Robert E. Wankel: Executive Vice President), Arielle Tepper, Stephanie McClelland, Lawrence Horowitz, Élan V. McAllister, Allan S. Gordon, Independent Presenters Network, Roy Furman, GRS Associates, Jam Theatricals, TGA Entertainment, Ltd. and Clear Channel Entertainment; Associate Producer: Randi Grossman and Tisch/ Avnet Financial
Director: Mike Nichols
Choreographer: Casey Nicholaw
Cast: Hank Azaria, Tim Curry, David Hyde Pierce, Christian Borle, Michael McGrath, Sara Ramirez, Christoher Sieber, John Cleese as the recorded voice of God
Songs: "Fisch Schlapping Song"; "King Arthur's Song"; "I Am Not Dead Yet"; "Come with Me"; "The Song That Goes Like This"; "All for One"; "Knights of the Round Table"; "Find Your Grail"; "Run Away"; "Always Look on the Bright Side of Life"; "Brave Sir Robin"; "You Won't Succeed on Broadway"; " The Diva's Lament"; "Where Are You?"; "Here Are You"; "His Name Is Lancelot"; "I'm All Alone"; "The Holy Grail"
New York run: Shubert Theatre, March 17, 2005; 1,575 p.

Member of the celebrated British comedy troupe Monty Python's Flying Circus Eric Idle's vision of translating their 1975 film *Monty Python and The Holy Grail* into a Broadway production was realized in this production.

Spamalot, under Mike Nichols's direction, had a cast of comic talents including Hank Azaria, Tim Curry, David Hyde-Pierce, Christopher Seiber, and newcomer Sara Ramirez as "The Lady of The Lake," cavorting around Medieval England.

A limbless, blood-gushing knight, a giant killer rabbit, the knights riding on hobbyhorses with coconuts being thumped for sound effects in full view were among the visual bits. The score included songs from the movie and originals that mocked many popular culture references. A member of the audience had a specific seat involved in the zany proceedings.

The show headed to Broadway from a tryout in Chicago with the buzz that it was "the next *Producers*." There was a subsequent North American tour and productions in Las Vegas, London, and Australia.
Decca Broadway OC

Monty Python's Spamalot. (Joan Marcus)

THE 25th ANNUAL PUTNAM COUNTY SPELLING BEE

Music & lyrics: William Finn
Book: Rachel Sheinkin, conceived by Rebecca Feldman, with additional material by Jay Reiss
Producers: David Stone, James L. Nederlander, Barbara Whitman, Patrick Catullo, Barrington Stage Company, Second Stage Theatre
Director: James Lapine
Choreographer: Dan Knechtges
Cast: Derrick Baskin, Deborah S. Craig, Jesse Tyler Ferguson, Dan Fogler, Lisa Howard, Celia Keenan-Bogler, Jose Llana, Jay Reiss, Sarah Saltzberg
Songs: "The 25th Annual Putnam County Spelling Bee"; "The Spelling Bee Rules/ My Favorite Moment of the Bee"; "My Friend, the Dictionary"; "The First Goodbye"; "Pandemonium"; "I'm Not That Smart"; "The Second Goodbye"; "Magic Foot"; "Prayer of the Comfort Counselor"; "My Unfortunate Erection"; "Woe Is Me"; "I Speak Six Languages"; "The I Love You Song"; "The Last Goodbye"
New York run: Circle in the Square Theatre, April 15, 2005; 1,136 p.

With young-looking adults playing the high-school aged contestants at *The 25th Annual Putnam County Spelling Bee*, it was a take on the universal theme of adolescence. Acclaimed playwright Wendy Wasserstein brought friend composer/ lyricist William Finn to see her nanny Sarah Salzberg perform in the original one-act play version performed by an improv comedy group. Finn was impressed by the show and got book writer Rachel Sheinkin involved to rework it into a full-length production.

After a workshop at The Barrington Stage Company in 2004, it opened in New York at Off-Broadway's Second Stage Theatre in January of 2005. Then it transferred to Broadway's Circle in the Square with its three-sided seating design, which added to the authenticity of the experience, as audiences had the sense of being at a high-school gymnasium to watch a real spelling bee.

Another factor of its success and enjoyment was that several audience members got to go onstage to be in the spelling bee with the six high school characters, which was presided over by adult actors portraying a judge, a guidance counselor, and a moderator. There were also specially announced "over 16," adults-only performances with risqué words being asked and the cast engaging in profane ad-libs. Ghostlight OC

THE LIGHT IN THE PIAZZA

Music & lyrics: Adam Guettel
Book: Craig Lucas
Producers: Lincoln Center Theater (André Bishop: Artistic Director; Bernard Gersten: Executive Producer); LCT Musical Theater Associate Producer: Ira Weitzman; produced by arrangement with Turner Entertainment Co.
Director: Bartlett Sher
Musical staging: Jonathan Butterell
Cast: Victoria Clark, Kelli O'Hara, Matthew Morrison, Mark Harelik, Sarah Uriarte Berry, Michael Berresse, Beau Gravitte, Joseph Siravo, Patti Cohenour
Songs: "Statues and Stories"; "The Beauty Is"; "Il Mondo Era Vuoto"; "Passeggiata"; "The Joy You Feel"; "Dividing Day"; "Hysteria"; "Say It Somehow"; "Aiutami"; "The Light in the Piazza"; "Octet"; "Tirade"; "Let's Walk"; "Love to Me"; "Fable"
New York run: Vivian Beaumont Theatre, April 18, 2005; 504 p.

Grandson of Richard Rodgers and son of Mary Rogers, Adam Guettel had begun to make his mark in musical theater with his praised score for Off-Broadway's *Floyd Collins* in 1996. *The Light in the Piazza* fulfilled that early promise and kept a noted theatrical dynasty current.

Based on a novella by Elizabeth Spencer, which was filmed in 1962 with Olivia de Havilland, *The Light in the Piazza* is set in Florence and Rome in 1953. Tourist Margaret Johnson, a middle-aged, upper-middle-class American is in Florence with her young daughter Clara. Clara falls in love and begins a romance with local boy, Fabrizio Naccarelli. To the audience and his family everything is wonderful, until it is revealed that as the result of a childhood injury, Clara has the mentality of a child. After much soul searching and arguing with her husband, Margaret conceals this from the Naccarelli family, allowing the wedding to take place and leaving Clara to have as normal a life as possible.

Guettel's complex score was orchestrated for piano, harp, guitar, and strings and a small section of wind and percussionists. The achievements of Michael Yeargan's sets, Catherine Zuber's costumes, and Christopher Akerlind's lighting all contributed greatly to the show's visual aesthetics. Originally developed in Seattle and Chicago, *The Light in the Pizza's* limited run at Lincoln Center was extended several times due to its popularity. The show was broadcast on PBS's *Live from Lincoln Center* shortly before its over 500-performance run ended.
Nonesuch OC

SWEENEY TODD

Music & lyrics: Stephen Sondheim
Book: Hugh Wheeler, from an adaptation by Christopher Bond
Producers: Thomas Viertel, Steven Baruch, Marc Routh, Richard Frankel, the Ambassador Theatre Group, Adam Kenwright, Tulchin/ Bartner/ Bagert
Director: John Doyle
Cast: Patti LuPone, Michael Cerveris, Benjamin Magnuson, Mark Jacoby, Lauren Molina, John Arbo, Donna Lynne Champlin, Manoel Felciano, Alexander Gemignani, Diana DiMarzio
Songs: Same as in the original production
New York run: Eugene O'Neil Theatre, November 3, 2005; 349 p.

Nonesuch OC

JERSEY BOYS

Music: Bob Gaudio
Lyrics: Bob Crewe
Book: Marshall Brickman & Rick Elice
Producers: Dodger Theatricals, Joseph J. Grano, Pelican Group, Tamara Kinsella; produced in association with Latitude Link, Rick Steiner, & Osher/ Staton/ Bell/ Mayerson Group
Director: Des McAnuff
Choreographer: Sergio Trujillo
Cast: John Lloyd Young, Christian Hoff, Daniel Reichard, J. Robert Spencer, Tituss Burgess, Steve Gouveia, Peter Gregus, Donnie Kehr, Michael Longoria, Mark Lotito, Jennifer Naimo, Erica Piccininni, Sara Schmidt
Songs: "Oh What a Night"; "Silhouettes"; "You're the Apple of My Eye"; "I Can't Give You Anything but Love"; "Earth Angel"; "Sunday Kind of Love"; "My Mother's Eyes"; "I Go Ape"; "Short Shorts"; "I'm in the Mood for Love/ Moody's Mood for Love"; "Cry for Me"; "An Angel Cried"; "I Still Care"; "Trance"; "Sherry"; "Big Girls Don't Cry"; "Walk Like a Man"; "Oh What a Night"; "My Boyfriend's Back"; "My Eyes Adored You"; "Dawn"; "Big Man in Town"; "Beggin'"; "Stay"; "Let's Hang On"; "Opus 17"; "Bye Bye Baby"; "C'mon Marianne"; "Can't Take My Eyes Off of You"; "Working My Way Back to You"; "Fallen Angel"; "Rag Doll"; "Who Loves You";
New York run: August Wilson Theatre (formerly The Virginia), November 6, 2005; (still running 6/11)

Jersey Boys premiered in La Jolla, California in October 2004. With the large catalogue of popular 60s pop group the Four Season songs as its foundation, *Jersey Boys* was a jukebox musical. Marshall Brickman and Rick Elice's book crafted a take on the behind-the-scenes and origins of a band. Talented young men playing weddings and lounges and getting mixed up with the Mob, persevering through the wilderness and then a big break, and then more clashes and conflicts were all played out to the sounds "Sherry," "Walk Like a Man," "Rag Doll," and other familiar tunes.

Once again Des McAnuf's directorial command was all over the stage keeping this show-business documentary saga moving across decades and also providing concert-style performance interludes. John Lloyd Young as Frankie Valli and Christian Hoff and Daniel Reichard as other band mates were all greatly talented and appealing. While still on Broadway, a national US tour was sent out, and it opened in London in 2008.
Rhino/WEA OC

Jersey Boys. From left to right, J. Robert Spencer, John Lloyd Young, Daniel Reichard, and Christian Hoff. (Joan Marcus)

THE COLOR PURPLE

Music & lyrics: Brenda Russell, Allee Willis, Stephen Bray
Book: Marsha Norman, based on the novel by Alice Walker
Producers: Oprah Winfrey , Scott Sanders, Roy Furman, Quincy Jones, Creative Battery, Anna Fantaci, Cheryl Lachowicz, Independent Presenters Network, David Lowy, Stephanie McClelland, Gary Winnick, Jan Kallish, Nederlander Presentations, Inc., Bob Weinstein, Harvey Weinstein, Andrew Asnes, Adam Zotovich, Todd Johnson
Director: Gary Griffin
Choreographer: Donald Byrd
Cast: LaChanze, Brandon Victor Dixon, Felicia P. Fields, Reneé Elise Goldsberry, Kingsley Leggs, Krisha Marcano, Elisabeth Withers-Mendes, James Brown III
Songs: "Huckleberry Pie"; "Mysterious Ways"; "Somebody Gonna Love You"; "Our Prayer"; "Big Dog"; "Hell No!"; "Brown Betty"; "Shug Avery Comin' to Town"; "Too Beautiful for Words"; "Push da Button"; "Uh-Oh!"; "What About Love?"; "African Homeland"; "The Color Purple"; "Mister's Song"; "Miss Celie's Pants"; "Any Little Thing"; "I'm Here"
New York run: Broadway Theatre, December 1, 2005; 910 p.

As the 1985 film *The Color Purple* brought her an Oscar nomination for best supporting actress as Sofia, television talk-show titan Oprah Winfrey had a special affinity for the material and became the lead producer for the Broadway musical version.

Adapted from Alice Walker's 1982 Pulitzer Prize winning novel set in rural Georgia in 1909, it depicts the difficult lives of mostly African-American women. Her father has abused 14-year-old Celie, and he has given her second child by him away. A few years later he gives her away into marriage along with a cow to the equally odious Mister. She is now separated from her beloved younger sister Nettie, who later goes to Africa to be with a missionary family, which has also adopted Celie's babies. They have a long correspondence, though Mister steals her letters. She befriends Mister's son's strong-willed wife Sofia. Mister's longtime mistress, the worldly nightclub singer Shug Avery comes to stay, and the two form a close a friendship. By 1949 all of these often-sad conflicts are resolved.

The score by a team of newcomers was accomplished, artfully blending the tragic and sometimes comic aspects of the plot. The production itself was faithful to the modern classic novel. During the run, LaChanze as Celie was replaced by American Idol star Fantasia and pop/ R&B star Chaka Khan came into the show as Shug Avery.
Angel Records OC

The Color Purple. From left to right, Reneé Elise Goldsberry and LaChanze. (Paul Kolnik)

THE PAJAMA GAME

Music & lyrics: Richard Adler & Jerry Ross
Book: George Abbott & Richard Bissell, based on Richard Bissell's novel *7 ½ Cents*; revisions for this production by Peter Ackerman
Producer: The Roundabout Theatre Company & by special arrangement with Jeffrey Richards, James Fuld, Jr., Scott Landis
Director & choreographer: Kathleen Marshall
Cast: Harry Connick, Jr., Kelli O'Hara, Michael McKean, Peter Benson, Bridget Berger, Stephen Berger, Kate Chapman, Paula Leggett Chase, Joyce Chittick, Jennifer Cody, David Eggers, Michael Halling, Megan Lawrence, Bianca Marroquin, Michael McCormick
Songs: Same as in the original production
New York run: American Airlines Theatre, February 23, 2006; 129 p.

(See page 161.)

THE DROWSY CHAPERONE
by special arrangement with Paul Mack

Music & lyrics: Lisa Lambert & Greg Morrison
Book: Bob Martin & Don McKellar
Producers: Kevin McCollum, Roy Miller, Boyett Ostar Productions, Stephanie McClelland, Barbara Freitag, Jill Furman
Associate Producers: Sonny Everett & Mariano Tolentino Jr.
Director & choreographer: Casey Nicholaw
Cast: Bob Martin, Sutton Foster, Beth Leavel, Danny Burstein, Georgia Engel, Edward Hibbert, Troy Britton Johnson, Eddie Korbich, Garth Kravits, Jason Kravits, Kecia Lewis-Evans, Jennifer Smith, Lenny Wolpe
Songs: "Fancy Dress"; "Cold Feets"; "Show Off"; "As We Stumble Along"; "I Am Aldolpho"; "Accident Waiting to Happen"; "Toledo Surprise"; "Message from a Nightingale"; "Bride's Lament"; "Love Is Always Lovely"; "I Do, I Do in the Sky"
New York run: Marquis Theatre, May 1, 2006; 674 p.

The curmudgeonly antisocial "Man in Chair"(Bob Martin) addresses the audience from his dreary apartment and holds forth about his consuming passion, original cast recordings of show tunes. He goes on to discuss his favorite musical, one from the 1920s, *The Drowsy Chaperone*. As he continues, his apartment is invaded by characters from the show (some coming out of the refrigerator) and it transforms into various sets from the production. The action of the show is often halted as Man in Chair comments.

The Drowsy Chaperone began in 1999 as a private gag send-up of old musicals by its creators at parties. For The Toronto Fringe Festival, the character of Man in Chair was added for performer Bob Martin. Then it was produced at the nonprofit Theatre Passe Muraille in Toronto and, after much acclaim, moved to the 1,000 seat Winter Garden there. After it ended its Toronto run in 2001 it was produced in Los Angeles in 2005, and later that year it finally reached Broadway.

The score was a send-up of period musicals, and it was staged and choreographed by Casey Nicholaw. Wistfully droll Bob Martin was Man in Chair in its many incarnations, and for Broadway, Sutton Foster went against sweet-young-thing type and played an acrobatic show girl. Replacing Martin was John Glover, and near the end of the run, comedian Bob Saget.
Ghostlight OC
Nonesuch OC

The Drowsy Chaperone. Sutton Foster kicking high with the cast. (Joan Marcus)

THE FANTASTICKS

Music: Harvey Schmidt
Lyrics & Book: Tom Jones
Producers: Steven Baruch, Richard Frankel, Marc Routh, Thomas Viertel
Director: Tom Jones
Musical staging: Janet Watson
Cast: Thomas Bruce, Leo Burmester, Santino Fontana, Sara Jean Ford, Burke Moses, Robert Oliver, Martin Vidnovic
Songs: Same as in the original production
New York run: Snapple Theater Center/ Jerry Orbach Theater, August 16, 2006; 678 p.

The Fantasticks closed on January 13, 2002 after 17,162 performances at Greenwich Village's Sullivan Street Playhouse. Four years later, a revival, directed by co-creator Tom Jones, opened. The good feelings it inspired were magnified by having it play at the 2007 renamed "Jerry Orbach Theater," near Times Square. He was the original El Gallo who died in 2004 at the age of 69. The corner of 53rd Street and 8th Avenue is named for him as well.
(See page 189.)

A CHORUS LINE

Music: Marvin Hamlisch
Lyrics: Edward Kleban
Book: James Kirkwood & Nicholas Dante; conceived by Michael Bennett
Producer: Vienna Waits Productions
Director: Bob Avian
Choreographer: Michael Bennett; recreated by Baayork Lee
Cast: Charlotte d'Amboise, Deidre Goodwin, Michael Berresse, Ken Alan, Brad Anderson, Michelle Aravena, David Baum, Mike Cannon, E. Clayton Cornelious, Natalie Cortez, Mara Davi, Jessica Lee Goldyn, Tyler Hanes, Nadine Isenegger, James T. Lane, Lorin Latarro, Paul McGill, Heather Parcells, Michael Paternostro, Alisan Porter, Jeffrey Howard Schecter, Yuka Takara, Jason Tam, Grant Turner, Chryssie Whitehead, Tony Yazbeck
Songs: Same as in the original production
New York run: Gerald Schoenfeld (formerly Plymouth) Theatre, October 5, 2006; 759 p.

(See page 243.)
Sony OC

MARY POPPINS

Music & lyrics: Richard M. Sherman & Robert B. Sherman (new songs and additional music and lyrics by George Stiles and Anthony Drewe*)
Book: Julian Fellowes
Producers: Disney Theatrical Productions & Cameron Mackintosh
Director: Richard Eyre; Co-Director: Matthew Bourne
Choreographer: Matthew Bourne
Cast: Ashley Brown, Gavin Lee, Rebecca Luker, Jane Carr, Ruth Gottschall, Michael McCarty, Cass Morgan, Nick Corley, James Hindman, Sean McCourt, Katherine Doherty, Kathryn Faughnan, Matthew Gumley, Henry Hodges
Songs: "Chim Chim Cher-ee"; "Cherry Tree Lane";* "The Perfect Nanny"; "Practically Perfect";* "Jolly Holiday"; "Being Mrs. Banks";* "A Spoonful of Sugar";* "Precision and Order";* "Feed the Birds"; "Supercalifragilisticexpialidocious"; "Brimstone and Treacle";* "Step in Time"; "Anything Can Happen"*
New York run: New Amsterdam Theatre, November 16, 2006 (still running 6/11)

Cameron Mackintosh and Disney joined forces to produce a stage production of the classic musical film *Mary Poppins*. This fusion of the 1964 film, P.L. Travers's original stories, and new material opened in London in 2004 to a great reception and closed there three years later. With some changes, it opened on Broadway in 2006. Ashley Brown was Mary Poppins, who flew into Bob Crowley's designed Banks household on her parrot-headed umbrella to be Jane and Michael's new nanny. Acrobatic Gavin Lee from the London cast was the chimney sweep Bert who accompanied them on their adventures.

Matthew Bourne, who co-directed and choreographed, created his usual quirky touches, most visible during a scene in the park where the statues came to life.

New songs by George Stiles and Anthony Drewe supplemented the ones from the film.

Disney OC London

COMPANY

Music & lyrics: Stephen Sondheim
Book: George Furth
Producers: Marc Routh, Richard Frankel, Thomas Viertel, Steven Baruch, the Ambassador Theatre Group, Tulchin/Bartner Productions, Darren Bagert, Cincinnati Playhouse in the Park
Director & musical staging: John Doyle
Cast: Raúl Esparza, Barbara Walsh, Keith Buterbaugh, Matt Castle, Robert Cunningham, Angel Desai, Kelly Jeanne Grant, Kristin Huffman, Amy Justman, Heather Laws, Leenya Rideout, Fred Rose, Bruce Sabath, Elizabeth Stanley
Songs: Same as in the original, with "Marry Me a Little" replacing "Tick Tock"
New York run: Ethel Barrymore Theatre, November 29, 2006; 246 p.

(See page 229.)
Nonesuch OC

SPRING AWAKENING

Music: Duncan Sheik
Lyrics & book: Steven Sater; based on the play by Franz Wedekind
Producers: Ira Pittelman, Tom Hulce, Jeffrey Richards, Jerry Frankel, Atlantic Theater Company, Jeffrey Sine, Freddy DeMann, Max Cooper, Mort Swinsky, Cindy Gutterman, Jay Gutterman, Joe McGinnis, Judith Ann Abrams, ZenDog Productions, CarJac Productions, Aron Bergson Productions, Jennifer Manocherian, Ted Snowdon, Harold Thau, Terry E. Schnuck, Cold Spring Productions, Amanda Dubois, Elizabeth Eynon Wetherell, Jennifer Maloney , Tamara Tunie, Joe Cilibrasi and StyleFour Productions; Associate Producer: Joan Cullman Productions, Patricia Flicker Addiss
Director: Michael Mayer
Choreographer: Bill T. Jones
Cast: Jonathan Groff, Lea Michele, John Gallagher Jr., Skylar Astin, Lilli Cooper, Brian Charles Johnson, Lauren Pritchard, Phoebe Strole, Jonathan B. Wright, Remy Zaken, Stephen Spinella, Christine Estabrook
Songs: "Mama Who Bore Me"; "All That's Known"; "The Bitch of Living"; "My Junk"; "Touch Me"; "The Word of Your Body"; "The Dark I Know Well"; "And Then There Were None"; "The Mirror-Blue Night"; "I Believe"; "The Guilty Ones"; "Don't Do Sadness"; "Blue Wind"; "Left Behind"; "Totally Fucked"; "Whispering"; "Those You've Known"; "The Song of Purple Summer"
New York run: Eugene O'Neil Theatre, December 10, 2006; 859 p.

Based on playwright Franz Wedekind's 1891 play set in a German provincial town, this rock adaptation utilized the time period and characters but with a modern sensibility. Teenage Wendela's mother can't bring herself to explain the facts of life to her daughter. This causes disastrous consequences after Wendela falls in love with the dashing student Melchior. In addition to burgeoning adolescent sexuality, the musical also explores homosexuality, peer pressure, teen suicide, abortion, masturbation, and adult hypocrisy.

Modern dance figure Bill T. Jones (choreographing on Broadway for the first time) brought a contemporary feeling that was jolting to the material, notably when the schoolboys were jumping up and down on their desks.

Director Michael Mayer shepherded *Spring Awakening* throughout a seven-year trail of workshops, concerts, and rewrites before the show opened at Off-Broadway's Atlantic Theatre Company in May of 2006. The show then repeated its success when it moved to Broadway that fall.
Decca Broadway OC

Spring Awakening. The cast rocks out. (Joan Marcus)

THE WEDDING SINGER

Music: Matthew Sklar
Lyrics: Chad Bequelin
Book: Tim Herlihy & Chad Bequelin
Producers: Margo Lion, New Line Cinema, the Araca Group, Roy Furman, Douglas L. Meyer, James D. Stern Productions, Rick Steiner, Osher/ Staton/ Bell/ Mayerson Group, and Jam Theatricals; produced in association with Jay Furman, Michael Gill, Lawrence Horowitz, Rhoda Mayerson, Marisa Sechrest, Gary Winnick, Dancap Productions, Inc., Élan V. McAllister, Allan S. Gordon, and Adam Epstein; in association with Jujamcyn Theaters (Rocco Landesman: President; Paul Libin: Producing Director; Jack Viertel: Creative Director).
Director: John Rando
Choreographer: Rob Ashford
Cast: Stephen Lynch, Laura Benanti, Richard H. Blake, Kevin Cahoon, Felicia Finley, Matthew Saldivar, Amy Spanger, Rita Gardner, Adinah Alexander
Songs: "It's Your Wedding Day"; "Someday"; "A Note from Linda"; "Pop"; "Somebody Kill Me" (Tim Herlihy & Adam Sandler); "A Note from Grandma"; "Casualty of Love"; "Come Out of the Dumpster"; "Today You Are a Man"; "George's Prayer"; "Not That Kind of Thing"; "Saturday Night in the City"; "All About the Green"; "Right in Front of Your Eyes"; "Single"; "If I Told You"; "Let Me Come Home"; "Move That Thing"; "Grow Old with You" (Tim Herlily & Adam Sandler)
New York Run: Al Hirschfeld Theatre, April 27, 2006; 285 p.

The Wedding Singer was based on the 1998 film of the same name that starred Adam Sandler and Drew Barrymore (Sandler co-wrote two of the show's songs with Tim Herlily). Stephen Lynch portrays Robbie, the title character, who aspires to be a rock star but has never gotten further than performing as a cheesy emcee/ entertainer at weddings, and not doing a very good job of it. The premise of the plot is simple: boy meets girl, but both are engaged to creeps. Somehow, they manage to avoid falling in love until the inevitable final scene. Laura Benanti played Julia, with Felicia Finley as Robbie's fiancée Linda (who dumps him at the altar) and Richard H. Blake as Julia's cretinous boyfriend Glen. The gimmick of the show is that it takes place in 1985, with the writers strip-mining '80s popular culture and sprinkling references throughout the story. Then new technology that is now commonplace is the source of much of the humor, as are period songs and political issues of the day. The final scene takes place at a Las Vegas quickie wedding chapel, with impersonators of such '80s icons as Billy Idol, Tina Turner, Cyndi Lauper, and Mr. T. assisting the proceedings. Even Ronald and Nancy Reagan make a cameo, munching on jelly beans.

The '80s weren't kitschy enough for theatergoers, however, and although the production was easily digestible, like cotton candy, it wasn't very filling. *The Wedding Singer* received five Tony and eight Drama Desk nominations, but won none.
Sony OC

TARZAN

Music & Lyrics: Phil Collins
Book: David Henry Hwang
Producers: Disney Theatrical Productions (under the direction of Thomas Schumacher)
Director: Bob Crowley
Choreographer: Leonora Stapleton
Cast: Josh Strickland, Merle Dandridge, Jenn Gambatese, Chester Gregory II, Shuler Hensley, Timothy Jerome, Donnie R. Keshawarz, Daniel Manche, Alex Rutherford
Songs: "Two Worlds"; "You'll Be in My Heart"; "Jungle Funk"; "Who Better Than Me?"; "No Other Way"; "I Need to Know"; "Son of Man"; "Sure As Sun Turns to Moon"; "Waiting for This Moment"; "Trashin' the Camp"; "Like No Man I've Ever Seen"; "Strangers Like Me"; "For the First Time"; "Everything That I Am"
New York run: Richard Rodgers Theatre, May 10, 2006; 486 p.

With the triumph of *Beauty and the Beast* and *The Lion King*, Disney Theatrical Productions attempted a third success on Broadway with a stage adaptation of Disney's 1999 animated film *Tarzan*. The bloated production was described in the *New York Times* as "a giant writhing green blob with music" and "a super deluxe daycare center." Although *Tarzan* played for a year on Broadway, its success didn't come close to matching those of its vaunted predecessors and closed after a year of poor reviews and limpid ticket sales.

Like those of *The Lion King*, the songs, written by pop star Phil Collins, had an exotic African flavor and included the hit "You'll Be in My Heart." Collins augmented the five songs he penned for the film with nine more. The plot of the musical closely matched the film (both drawn from the original story by Edgar Rice Burroughs), with former *American Idol* contestant Josh Strickland making his stage debut as the free-swinging king of the jungle. This wasn't the first time the loin-clothed yodeler had hit Broadway. A stage play, *Tarzan of the Apes*, starring Ronald Adair, swung into the Broadhurst Theater in 1921, but was also a failure. Walt Disney Records OC

DR. SEUSS' HOW THE GRINCH STOLE CHRISTMAS

Music: Mel Marvin
Lyrics: Timothy Mason
Book: Timothy Mason
Producers: Running Subway, EMI Music Publishing, Michael Speyer, Bernie Abrams, Allen Spivak, Janet Pailet, Spark Productions, Maximum Entertainment, and Jonathan Reinis; presented by Target Stores
Director: Matt August
Choreographer: John DeLuca
Cast: Patrick Page, John Cullum, Rusty Ross, Kaitlin Hopkins, Michael McCormick, Jan Neuberger, Price Waldman, Nicole Bocchi, Caroline London
Songs: "Who Likes Christmas?"; "I Hate Christmas Eve"; "Whatchama Who"; "Welcome, Christmas" (music: Albert Hague; lyric: Dr. Seuss); "Once in a Year"; "One of a Kind"; "Now's the Time"; "You're a Mean One, Mr. Grinch" (music: Albert Hague; lyric: Dr. Seuss)
New York run: Hilton Theatre, November 8, 2006; 107 p.; St. James Theatre, November 9, 2007; 96 p.

With the blessings of the estate of the late children's author Theodore Geisel (a.k.a. "Dr. Seuss"), a musical based on Geisel's book *How the Grinch Stole Christmas* was first staged in Minneapolis in 1994. The book had previously been dramatized as a 30-minute animated television special, narrated by Boris Karloff and featuring songs composed by Albert Hague with lyrics provided by Dr. Seuss himself. Two of the songs were included in the Broadway version.

Grinch proved extremely popular and was brought back for seasonal revivals, with an annual production running in San Diego beginning in 1998. In 2006, it was produced for Broadway by Maximum Entertainment producer Avram C. Freedberg. With 12 performances a week, the most of any Broadway show up to that time, *Grinch* soon topped *Wicked*'s streak of 100 consecutive weeks as the top-grossing weekly musical.

One year later, the show was brought back for a return engagement, but striking stagehands halted production on its second day. Nearly two weeks later, with Broadway's labor problems settled, the show resumed its run. In its second season, Ed Dixon replaced John Cullum as Old Max and Athena Ripka replaced Nicole Bocchi as one of the rotating Cindy Lou Whos.

LES MISÉRABLES

Music: Claude-Michel Schönberg
Lyrics: Herbert Kretzmer
Conception: Alain Boublil & Claude-Michel Schönberg
Original French Text: Alain Boublil & Jean-Marc Natel
Adaptation: Trevor Nunn & John Caird
Producer: Cameron Mackintosh
Directors: Trevor Nunn & John Caird
Choreographer: Kate Flatt
Cast: Gary Beach, Alexander Gemignani, Norm Lewis, Daphne Rubin-Vega, Ali Ewoldt, Jenny Galloway, Adam Jacobs, Celia Keenan-Bolger, Aaron Lazar
Songs: Same as original production
New York run: Broadhurst Theatre, November 9, 2006; 463 p.

The first revival of this long-running favorite borrowed its resources from the third American touring company. There were minor changes in the lighting design, and some cuts that had been previously made to the original Broadway production were restored. Actors coming on board midway through the run included Lea Salonga (Fantine), Ben Davis (Javert), Drew Sarich (Jean Valjean), and Max Von Essen (Enjolras). Salonga was eventually replaced by Judy Kuhn, who originated the role of Cosette in the show's initial Broadway run.

(See page 275.)

Les Misérables. The Company of Les Misérables. (Joan Marcus)

CURTAINS

Music: John Kander
Lyrics: Fred Ebb; additional lyrics by John Kander & Rupert Holmes
Book: Rupert Holmes; original book & concept by Peter Stone
Producers: Roger Berlind, Roger Horchow, Daryl Roth, Jane Bergère, Ted Hartley & Center Theatre Group
Director: Scott Ellis
Choreographer: Rob Ashford
Cast: David Hyde Pierce, Debra Monk, Karen Ziemba, Jason Danieley, Jill Paice, Edward Hibbert, John Bolton, Michael X. Martin, Michael McCormick, Noah Racey, Ernie Sabella, Megan Sikora, Nili Bassman
Songs: "Wide Open Spaces"; "What Kind of Man?"; "Thinking of Him"; "The Woman's Dead"; "Show People"; "Coffee Shop Nights"; "In the Same Boat"; "I Miss the Music"; "Thataway!"; "He Did It"; "It's a Business"; "Kansasland"; "A Tough Act to Follow";
New York run: Al Hirschfeld Theatre, March 22, 2007); 511 p.

Peter Stone (d. 2003) and Fred Ebb (d. 2004) left behind *Curtains*, a backstage murder mystery. Set in Boston in 1959, the unlamented leading lady of the trying-out musical, *Robbin' Hood of the Old West*, is murdered during her opening night curtain call. Musical theater fan Lt. Frank Cioffi arrives to investigate and solve the case. *Frasier* and *Spamalot* star David Hyde-Pierce won the Tony Award for Best Actor in a Musical for his performance as the detective.
Manhattan Records OC

Legally Blonde. Orfeh, left, and Laura Bell Bundy. (Paul Kolnik)

LEGALLY BLONDE

Music & Lyrics: Laurence O'Keefe & Nell Benjamin
Book: Heather Hach
Producers: Hal Luftig, Fox Theatricals, Dori Berinstein, James L. Nederlander, Independent Presenters Network, Roy Furman, Amanda Lipitz, Broadway Asia, Barbara Whitman, FWPM Group, Ruth Hendel, Cheryl Wiesenfeld, Hal Goldberg, David Binder, James D. Stern, Douglas L. Meyer, Stewart F. Lane, Bonnie Comley, Robert G. Bartner, Michael A. Jenkins, Albert Nocciolino & Warren Trepp; produced in association with MGM Onstage, Darcie Denkert and Dean Stolber; Associate Producer: PMC Productions, Yasuhiro Kawana, Andrew Asnes & Adam Zotovich; produced for Fox Theatricals by Kristin Caskey & Mike Isaacson
Director & choreographer: Jerry Mitchell
Cast: Laura Bell Bundy, Richard H. Blake, Christian Borle, Orfeh, Michael Rupert, Kate Shindle, Leslie Kritzer, Nikki Snelson, Annaleigh Ashford, April Berry, DeQuina Moore, Andy Karl
Songs: "Omigod You Guys"; "Serious"; "Daughter of Delta Nu"; "What You Want"; "The Harvard Variations"; "Blood in the Water"; "Positive"; "Ireland"; "Chip on My Shoulder"; "So Much Better"; "Whipped into Shape"; "Take It Like a Man"; " "Bend and Snap"; "There! Right There!"; "Legally Blonde"; "Legally Blonde Remix"; "Find My Way/ Finale"
New York run: Palace Theatre, April 29, 2007; 595 p.

Based on the novel by Amanda Brown and the film starring Reese Witherspoon, *Legally Blonde* tried out in San Francisco in February of 2007 before arriving in New York. Blonde UCLA sorority president Elle Woods is devastated that her fiance Warner Huntington has broken up with her in search of seriousness. After recovering from the shock, she resolves to change her ways and follows him to Harvard, which he is attending.

Clashing with snobby classmates and appalled professors, she eventually saves the day as a legal intern working on a scandalous murder case and finds true love with fellow intern Emmett Forrest.

Choreographer Jerry Mitchell made his Broadway directorial debut with *Legally Blonde*. As Elle, Laura Bell Bundy was acclaimed by critics and audiences alike for her musical comedy talents and immense charm.

Several special MTV televised broadcasts of the entire show increased its popularity. In another synergistic sign of the times, a television reality program was being developed to find a replacement for Laura Bell Bundy. A future US tour and London production was also soon announced.
Ghostlight Records OC

110 IN THE SHADE

Music: Harvey Schmidt
Lyrics: Tom Jones
Book: N. Richard Nash, based on his play, *The Rainmaker*
Producer: Roundabout Theatre Company
Director: Lonny Price
Choreographer: Dan Knechtges
Cast: Audra McDonald, John Cullum, Steve Kazee, Christopher Innvar, Devin Richards, Michael Scott, Chris Butler, Carla Duren, Bobby Steggert, Will Swenson, Darius Nichols, Elisa Van Duyne, Betsy Wolfe, Valisia Lekae Little, Colleen Fitzpatrick
Songs: Same as in the original production
New York run: Studio 54, May 9, 2007; 94 p.

(See page 203.)
PS Classics OC

XANADU

Music & lyrics: Jeff Lynne & John Farrar
Book: Douglas Carter Beane
Producers: Rob Ahrens, Dan Vickery, Sara Murchison, Dale Smith, Tara Smith, B. Swibel
Director: Christopher Ashley
Choreographer: Dan Knechtges
Cast: Kerry Butler, Cheyenne Jackson, Tony Roberts, Jackie Hoffman, Mary Testa, Curtis Holbrook, Anika Larsen, Kenita R. Miller, Marty Thomas, Andre Ward
Songs: "I'm Alive"; "Magic"; "Evil Woman"; "Whenever You're Away from Me"; "Dancin'"; "Don't Walk Away"; "Fool"; "Suspended in Time"; "The Fall"; "Have You Never Been Mellow?"; "Xanadu"
New York run: Helen Hayes Theatre, July 10, 2007; 512 p.

The 1980 Olivia Newton-John/ Gene Kelley cult classic *Xanadu* turned out to be perfect Broadway musical material. Douglas Cater Beane's book not only borrows from the movie (which itself was based on a 1947 Rita Hayworth film *Down to Earth*) but also from the mythology classic *Clash of the Titans*. Greek muse Clio, disguised as Australian Kira, descends from Mt. Olympus in 1980 to Venice Beach, California. Her mission is to inspire Sonny, a struggling artist, to realize his dream of opening a roller disco. They fall in love, which causes complications.

During a year of workshops and readings, a score comprised of songs from the movie, others by the songwriters, and two ELO songs was decided on. While in previews on Broadway, leading man James Carpinello injured his foot during one of the many roller skating sequences and had to permanently leave the show. After understudies and cast members covered the part, *All Shook Up's* Elvis, Cheyenne Jackson took over. Kerry Butler was the muse, Broadway veteran Tony Roberts was the Gene Kelly sage part, and Jackie Hoffman and Mary Testa were the muse's evil sisters. Xanadu opened in the summer of 2007 to very positive reviews and became a hit with the public.
MCA OC

YOUNG FRANKENSTEIN

Music & lyrics: Mel Brooks
Book: Mel Brooks & Thomas Meehan, based on the story & screenplay by Gene Wilder & Mel Brooks
Producers: Robert F.X. Sillerman & Mel Brooks, produced in association with the R/ F/ B/ V Group
Director and choreographer: Susan Stroman
Cast: Roger Bart, Sutton Foster, Shuler Hensley, Andrea Martin, Megan Mullally, Christopher Fitzgerald, Fred Applegate, Linda Mugleston, Jim Borstelmann, Paul Castree
Songs: "The Happiest Town"; "The Brain"; "Together Again"; "Roll in the Hay"; "Join the Family Business"; "He Vas My Boyfriend"; "The Law"; "Life, Life"; "Welcome to Transylvania"; "The Transylvania Mania"; "He's Loose"; "Listen to Your Heart"; "Surprise"; "Please Send Me Someone"; "Man About Town"; "Putting on the Ritz (Irving Berlin)"; "Deep Love"; "Frederick's Soliloquy"; "Finale Ultimo"
New York run: Hilton Theatre, November 8, 2007; 485 p.

Mel Brooks followed up the success of *The Producers* with a musical version of his film comedy classic *Young Frankenstein*. Much of same *Producers* creative team reunited, and a cast of accomplished musical comedy performers were gathered up to translate Brooks's 1974 black and white parody of 1930's Universal horror films to the Broadway stage. Castles, laboratories, lightening bolts, rampaging torch carrying villagers, and even a hayride were recreated. The monster was suitably green, visibly stitched together, and did the famous "Putting On The Ritz" number in tie and tails.

After trying out for four weeks of August 2007 in Seattle, Washington, Young Frankenstein opened on Broadway in November of 2007. Audiences in the mood to laugh at Mel Brooks's humor flocked to see it.
Decca Broadway OC

Young Frankenstein. Megan Mullally (Elizabeth) revels in the spotlight while Andrea Martin (Frau Blücher) and Christopher Fitzgerald (Igor) appear indifferent. (Joan Marcus)

GREASE

Music, lyrics, & book: Jim Jacobs & Warren Casey
Producers: Paul Nicholas, David Ian, Nederlander Presentations, Inc., and Terry Allen Kramer
Director: Kathleen Marshall
Choreographer: Kathleen Marshall
Cast: Max Crumm, Laura Osnes, Ryan Patrick Binder, Susan Blommaert, Jeb Brown, Stephen R. Buntrock, Daniel Everidge, Allison Fischer, Natalie Hill, Jenny Powers, Matthew Saldivar, Kirsten Wyatt
Songs: Same as original production, with the addition of four songs from the film adaptation: "Hopelessly Devoted to You" (John Farrar), "Sandy" (Scott Simon & Louis St. Louis) "You're the One That I Want" (John Farrar), and "Grease" (Barry Gibb)
New York run: Brooks Atkinson Theatre, August 19, 2007; 554 p.

Max Crumm and Laura Osnes were chosen to portray Danny and Sandy by viewers of an NBC reality show titled *Grease: You're the One That I Want!*, produced specifically to cast the leads of the Broadway revival.

(See page 234.)

Grease. Max Crumm is Danny and Laura Osnes is Sandy in this scene from the revival of Grease. (Joan Marcus)

THE LITTLE MERMAID

Music: Alan Menken
Lyrics: Howard Ashman & Glenn Slater
Book: Doug Wright
Producers: Disney Theatrical Productions (under the direction of Thomas Schumacher)
Director: Francesca Zambello
Choreographer: Stephen Mear
Cast: Sierra Boggess, Derrick Baskin, Trevor Braun, Tituss Burgess, Brian D'Addario, Jonathan Freeman, Cody Hanford, Eddie Korbich, Norm Lewis, Tyler Maynard, Sean Palmer, Sherie Rene Scott
Songs: "Fathoms Below"; "Daughters of Triton" (lyric: Howard Ashman); "The World Above"; "Human Stuff"; "I Want the Good Times Back"; "Part of Your World" (lyric: Howard Ashman); "She's in Love"; "Her Voice"; "Under the Sea" (lyric: Howard Ashman); "Sweet Child"; "Poor Unfortunate Souls" (lyric: Howard Ashman); "Positoovity"; "Beyond My Wildest Dreams"; "Les Poissons" (lyric: Howard Ashman); "One Step Closer"; "Kiss the Girl" (lyric: Howard Ashman); "If Only"; "The Contest"; "Finale Ultimo"
New York run: Lunt-Fontanne Theatre, January 10, 2008; 685 p.

Having been unable to meet expectations for *Tarzan*, Disney Theatrical Productions tried again with a stage version of the 1989 Disney animated feature *The Little Mermaid*. The production had its premiere at the Lunt-Fontanne Theatre, which had been hosting Disney's breakthrough musical, the long-running and hugely successful *Beauty and the Beast*, since 1999. Disney Theatrical shut down *Beauty* voluntarily, not wishing to split the potential audience for *Mermaid*.

Due to the 2007 Broadway stagehands strike, the show's debut was delayed by a month, but it finally opened on January 10, 2008, with the film's voiceover stars, Jodi Benson and Pat Carroll, in attendance. The score utilized the songs from the film, written by Alan Menken and Howard Ashman, but because Ashman had died in 1991, Glenn Slater provided lyrics for the additional numbers.

To achieve the story's unique underwater effect, the actors wore "heelies," sneakers with embedded wheels in the heels, to simulate the gliding of the characters under the sea. The plot followed that of its animated predecessor closely, although some critics observed that the charm had been removed from the show. Characters' personalities were fleshed out (especially those of Prince Eric and Ursula the sea witch) and a new, more dramatic ending was written. Critical response was mixed, but ticket sales were brisk and the show became a splash hit, running until the following summer, when Thomas Schumacher decided to shut it down, explaining, "It would be fiscally irresponsible to our shareholders to risk operating losses with such a big show in the historically challenging fall months. We are closing the Broadway production to concentrate on the long future life of this title."
Walt Disney Records OC

SUNDAY IN THE PARK WITH GEORGE

Music & lyrics: Stephen Sondheim
Book: James Lapine
Producers: Roundabout Theatre Company (Todd Haimes: Artistic Director; Harold Wolpert: Managing Director; Julia C. Levy: Executive Director; Gene Feist: Founding Director); produced in association with Boy Boyett, Debra Black, Jam Theatricals, Stephanie McClelland, Stewart F. Lane, Bonnie Comley, Barbara Manocherian, Jennifer Manocherian, Ostar Productions, Caro Newling, Neal Street Productions, and Mark Rubinstein; originally produced by the Menier Chocolate Factory (David Babani: Artistic Director)
Director: Sam Buntrock
Cast: Michael Cumpsty, Daniel Evans, Alexander Gemignani, Jessica Molaskey, Jenna Russell, Mary Beth Peil, Santino Fontana
Songs: Same as original production
New York run: Studio 54, June 29, 2008; 149 p.

This limited engagement revival of Sondheim's 1984 classic was praised for its innovative set design, including a 3-D animation of the famous painting by Georges Seurat. Evans and Russell received Tony nominations for their performances as George and Dot.

(See page 269.)

Sunday in the Park with George. Daniel Evans (as artist Georges Seurat) sketches while Jenna Russell (Dot) admires his work. (Joan Marcus)

IN THE HEIGHTS

Music & lyrics: Lin-Manuel Miranda
Book: Quiara Alegría Hudes
Producers: Kevin McCollum, Jeffrey Seller, Jill Furman, Sander Jacobs, Robyn Goodman, Walt Grossman, Peter Fine, Sonny Everett, Mike Skipper
Director: Thomas Kail
Choreographer: Andy Blankenbuehler
Cast: Lin-Manuel Miranda, Andréa Burns, Janet Dacal, Robin De Jesús, Carlos Gomez, Mandy Gonzalez, Christopher Jackson, Priscilla Lopez, Olga Merediz
Songs: "In the Heights"; "Breathe"; "Benny's Dispatch"; "It Won't Be Long Now"; "Inutil"; "No Me Diga"; "96,000"; "Paciencia y Fe (Patience and Faith)"; "When You're Home"; "Piragua"; "Siempre (Always)"; "The Club/ Fireworks"; "Sunrise"; "Hundreds of Stories"; "Enough"; "Carnaval del Barrio"; "Atención"; "Alabanza"; "Everything I Know"; "Champagne"; "When the Sun Goes Down"
New York run: Richard Rodgers Theatre, March 9, 2008; 1,184 p.

The winner of five Tony Awards, including Best Musical, *In the Heights* is a slice of urban life that tells the stories of various inhabitants of a barrio in Washington Heights, in the northern region of Manhattan. The community is populated by Dominican Americans and Nuyoricans who are all struggling to maintain their businesses and decide which traditions to maintain and which to leave behind.

The action centers on a bodega owned by Usnavi, a son of immigrants, who was named for the first sight his parents saw upon arriving in New York harbor: a U.S. Navy ship. The story focuses on several characters. Usnavi wishes to sell his bodega and return to his homeland, Stanford student Nina tries to reconcile the fact that she has lost her scholarship; she then falls in love with Benny, who works for her father's automobile dispatch service. Abuela Claudia, the beloved neighborhood matriarch, dreams of winning the lottery and buys what turns out to be a winning ticket at Usnavi's bodega. The relationships are thinly drawn and somewhat predictable, but the mundane story (described by one reviewer as "Spanish schmaltz") was overwhelmed by the exhilarating music and dance sequences.

In the Heights was created in 1999 by Lin-Manuel Miranda when he was a college student at Wesleyan University. Two Wesleyan seniors, John Buffalo Mailer (son of novelist and playwright Norman Mailer) and Thomas Kail, helped him adapt the show for Broadway, with Kail serving as director and Miranda playing the central role of Usnavi.

Miranda's music and Andy Blankenbuehler's choreography more than made up for the book's deficiencies. The score, an invigorating blend of hip-hop, salsa, meringue, and soul, was vibrant and spirited. Using rap as a form of recitative was an ingenious development that helped make *In the Heights* popular with younger audiences. Similarly, the zesty dance routines kept things hopping throughout the production. The *New York Times* described the opening song as "among the most galvanizing opening numbers in recent Broadway memory." Miranda played Usnavi throughout the show's long run, but half of the key roles changed hands before the show finally closed after more than 1,100 performances.

Ghostlight OC

SOUTH PACIFIC

Music: Richard Rodgers
Lyrics: Oscar Hammerstein II
Book: Oscar Hammerstein II & Joshua Logan
Producers: Lincoln Center Theatre (André Bishop: Artistic Director; Bernard Gersten: Executive Producer; produced in association with Bob Boyett)
Director: Bartlett Sher
Cast: Kelli O'Hara, Paulo Szot, Loretta Ables Sayre, Danny Burstein, Sean Cullen, Li Jun Li, Matthew Morrison, Victor W. Hawks, Luka Kain
Songs: Same as original production, with the additions of "My Girl Back Home," sung by Lt. Cable, which was cut from the original production, and "Now Is the Time," sung by Emile, which was also cut, to be replaced by a reprise of "Some Enchanted Evening."
New York run: Vivian Beaumont Theatre, April 3, 2008; 996 p.

Nearly 60 years after its initial run, *South Pacific* finally served another hitch on Broadway. The revival was received almost as enthusiastically as the original, with universally rave reviews and seven Tonys, including Best Revival. Critics gushed over James A. Michener's timeless story of men and women serving on a Pacific island during World War II. The message of racial tolerance communicated in the story was much more daring stuff in 1949, but the concept was just as relevant to 21st-century audiences and did not appear dated at all. The sumptuous score, beautifully played by a full orchestra, was complemented by a ravishing and colorful set, along with winning performances by O'Hara and Broadway newcomer Szot, a Polish-Brazilian baritone who became the first from his country to win a Tony (Best Leading Actor).

(See page 143.)

South Pacific. Loretta Ables Sayre leads the SeaBees in "Bloody Mary." (Joan Marcus)

GYPSY

Music: Jule Styne
Lyrics: Stephen Sondheim
Book: Arthur Laurents
Producers: Roger Berlind, the R/ F/ B/ V Group, Roy Furman, Debra Black, Ted Hartley, Roger Horchow, David Ian, Scott Rudin, and Jack Viertel
Director: Arthur Laurents
Choreographer: Jerome Robbins, reproduced by Bonnie Walker
Cast: Patti LuPone, Laura Benanti, Boyd Gaines, Leigh Ann Larkin, Tony Yazbeck, Marilyn Caskey, Alison Fraser, Lenora Nemetz, Bill Bateman, Jim Bracchitta, Sami Gayle, Bill Raymond, Brian Reddy, Emma Rowley
Songs: Same as original production
New York run: St. James Theatre, March 27, 2008, 332 p.

In 2008, at age 91, Arthur Laurents returned to Broadway to direct the revival of *Gypsy*, for which he had written the original book in 1959. He had directed the first revival of the show in 1974 in a production originating in London's West End that starred Angela Lansbury, who won a Tony for her performance. Two other revivals had taken place in the interim: one in 1989 starring Tyne Daly and another in 2003 with Bernadette Peters.

LuPone was an inspired choice to play the never-say-die Mama Rose, and the Broadway community was thrilled at the prospect of her belting out the classic Styne/ Sondheim songs. LuPone, Boyd Gaines, and Laura Benanti all won Tonys and Drama Desk Awards for their performances. Like the 2003 revival, however, the production closed at a loss. The night before the show's final staging, LuPone shocked the audience by chastising a patron for taking photographs during her performance of "Rose's Turn."

(See page 182.)

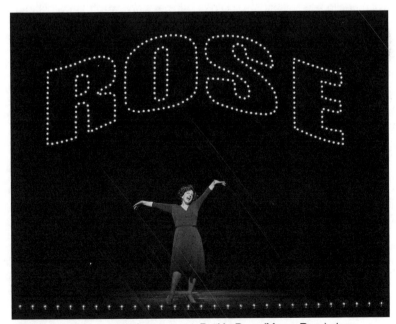

Gypsy. In this show-stopping moment, Patti LuPone (Mama Rose) sings "Rose's Turn." (Joan Marcus)

A TALE OF TWO CITIES

Music & lyrics: Jill Santoriello
Book: Jill Santoriello
Producers: Barbra Russell, Ron Sharpe, Bernard Brogan, Sharon A. Fordham, Theater Associates-David Sonnenberg/ Rami Evar, the Monagle Group, Joseph J. Grano, Fanok Entertainment, Mary Laminack, Nancy Audet, Paul Audet, Jim Barry, Gasperino Entertainment, Vincent Russell, William Broderick, and Alex Santoriello; produced in association with David Bryant, Spencer S. Brody, and Harry Casey
Director: Warren Carlyle
Choreographer: Warren Carlyle
Cast: James Barbour, Craig Bennett, Brandi Burkhardt, Kevin Earley, Gregg Edelman, Aaron Lazar, Katherine McGrath, Les Minski, Natalie Toro, Nick Wyman, Catherine Missal, Michael Hayward-Jones
Songs: "The Way It Ought to Be"; "You'll Never Be Alone"; "No Honest Way"; "Round and Round"; "Reflection"; "The Promise"; "I Can't Recall"; "Resurrection Man"; "If Dreams Came True"; "Out of Sight, Out of Mind"; "I Always Knew"; "Little One"; "Until Tomorrow"; "Everything Stays the Same"; "Without a Word"; "Let Her Be a Child"
New York run: Al Hirschfeld Theatre, September 18, 2008; 60 p.

With their colorful characters and compelling storylines, Charles Dickens's novels have been popular subjects for adaptation for Broadway musicals. Six had been attempted, but only *Oliver!* (1963) and *The Mystery of Edwin Drood* (1985) had seen any success. Jill Santoriello began working on a musical version of *A Tale of Two Cities* in the late 1980s. After many years of readings, workshops, and invitation-only events, the show finally succeeded in landing a pre-Broadway tryout in 2007 at the Asolo Repertory Theatre in Sarasota, Florida. When the show sold out its entire run and garnered Best Musical honors from *Sarasota* magazine, it finally made its debut on Broadway.

Santoriello was faithful to Dickens's original story, which takes place before and during the French Revolution. It depicts the brutal battle between French peasants and the aristocracy, focusing on Sydney Carton (James Barbour), a self-pitying yet brilliant British barrister, and Charles Darnay (Aaron Lazar), a virtuous aristocrat who is the nephew of the despised Marquis St. Evrémonde (Les Minski). Darnay has been targeted for treason by British spies and is eventually sentenced to the guillotine. The show traces the transformation of Carton from soused cynic to heroic martyr. James Barbour was hailed by audiences and nominated for a Drama Desk Award for his charismatic portrayal of Carton, despite the *New York Times*' dismissing his acting as a "high camp, hair-tossing performance."

The success of the pre-Broadway engagement, however, failed to translate to New York and scathingly negative reviews punctured Santoriello's balloon, with her personal musical revolution ending less than two months after its debut. Critics likened the show to a poor copy of *Les Misérables*, but part of the blame for the reduced audiences can be placed at the gates of Wall Street. Three days before the show opened, the stock market fell precipitously and, as the recession deepened, theatergoers stayed home in droves. *Tale*'s box office didn't suffer as much as other shows did, but the downturn in the economy plus the snarky notices decapitated the show as effectively as its ever-present guillotine.

Since the end of its run, *Tale* has shown promise in regional productions, with a successful concert performance produced in London that was broadcast on PBS.

Tale Productions (SC)

BILLY ELLIOT: THE MUSICAL

Music: Elton John
Lyrics: Lee Hall
Book: Lee Hall
Producers: Universal Pictures, Working Title, the Old Vic Company, Tim Bevan, Eric Fellner, Jon Finn, and Sally Greene; produced in association with the Weinstein Company
Director: Stephen Daldry
Choreographer: Peter Darling
Cast: David Alvarez, Trent Kowalik, Kiril Kulish, Santino Fontana, Haydn Gwynne, Gregory Jbara, Carole Shelley, David Bologna, Frank Dolce
Songs: "The Stars Look Down"; "Shine"; "Grandma's Song"; "Solidarity"; "Expressing Yourself"; "The Letter"; "Born to Boogie"; "Angry Dance"; "Merry Christmas Maggie Thatcher"; "Deep Into the Ground"; "He Could Be a Star"; "Electricity"; "Once We Were Kings"
New York run: Imperial Theatre, November 13, 2008 (still running 6/11)

Billy Elliot focuses on two crises that come head to head in a working-class community in County Durham in northeast England. One involves the debilitating 1984–85 coal miners' strike that threatened the well-being of many families whose members struggled to survive while not being able to work. The other centers around 11-year-old Billy Elliot, the son and brother of two of the striking miners, who eschews boxing lessons in favor of learning ballet. His father is initially embarrassed by his son's less-than-manly aspirations, but eventually recognizes Billy's talent and sacrifices his own status among his co-workers by helping Billy realize his dream to attend the prestigious Royal Ballet School in London.

The musical was based on the 2000 motion picture, with a score provided by Elton John and lyricist/ librettist Lee Hall. It made its initial premiere in London's West End before transferring to Broadway, where it became a substantial hit, earning a record-tying 15 Tony Award nominations while winning 10, including Best Musical. Three actors, David Alvarez, Trent Kowalik, and Kiril Kulish, rotated in the title role, each exhibiting dancing skills that drew critical descriptions of "breathtaking" and "exhilarating." (The trio shared the Tony for Leading Actor in a Musical.) Superlatives have gushed ever since like an oil geyser from just about every quarter.
Decca Broadway (OC)

IRVING BERLIN'S WHITE CHRISTMAS

Music & lyrics: Irving Berlin
Book: David Ives & Paul Blake
Producers: Kevin McCollum, John Gore, Tom McGrath, Paul Blake, the Producing Office, Dan Markley, Sonny Everett, and Broadway Across America (John Gore: CEO; Thomas B. McGrath: Chairman; Beth Williams: COO & Head of Production); produced in association with Paramount Pictures Corporation
Director: Walter Bobbie
Choreographer: Randy Skinner
Cast: Stephen Bogardus, Jeffry Denman, Kerry O'Malley, Meredith Patterson, Charles Dean, Melody Hollis, Susan Mansur
Songs: "Happy Holiday"; "White Christmas"; "Let Yourself Go"; "Love and the Weather"; "Sisters"; "The Best Things Happen When You're Dancing"; "Snow"; "What Can You Do with a General?"; "Let Me Sing and I'm Happy"; "Count Your Blessings Instead of Sheep"; "Blue Skies"; "I Love a Piano"; "Falling Out of Love Can Be Fun"; "Love You Didn't Do Right By Me"/ "How Deep Is the Ocean"; "We'll Follow the Old Man"; "I've Got My Love to Keep Me Warm"
New York run: Marquis Theatre, November 23, 2008; 53 p.; November 22, 2009; 51 p.

Following the lead of *Dr. Seuss' How the Grinch Stole Christmas*, this musical, based on the popular 1954 film version of *White Christmas*, returned for an encore run a year after it made its Broadway debut. The original film, which starred Bing Crosby, Danny Kaye, and Rosemary Clooney, had grown in stature in recent years, prompting the production of a stage version, which was presented on the increasingly family-oriented Broadway scene.

The musical version closely follows the plot of the film, with minor variances. After World War II, a general retires to run a winter inn in Vermont. When the lack of snow threatens the inn's holiday season, two of the general's former enlisted men, both of whom have become top entertainers, come to their superior's rescue by bringing their musical revue to the inn. Most of the songs in the movie were retained, including the iconic title number, with other Berlin favorites added to the score, such as "I've Got My Love to Keep Me Warm" and "How Deep Is the Ocean." The show had two successful limited runs during consecutive seasons at the Marquis Theatre. In the show's second run, the leads were portrayed by James Clow, Tony Yazbeck, Mara Davi, Melissa Errico, David Ogden Stiers, and Ruth Williamson. Although critics were mainly impressed with Randy Skinner's scintillating choreography, the *New York Times* acidly described the production as "fresh and appealing as a roll of Necco wafers found in a mothballed Christmas stocking."
Ghostlight OC

SHREK: THE MUSICAL

Music: Jeanine Tesori
Lyrics: David Lindsay-Abaire
Book: David Lindsay-Abaire
Producers: DreamWorks Theatricals and Neal Street Productions
Director: Jason Moore
Choreographer: Josh Prince
Cast: Sutton Foster, Brian d'Arcy James, Christopher Sieber, Daniel Breaker, John Tartaglia, Haven Burton, Jennifer Cody, Bobby Daye, Ryan Duncan
Songs: "Big Bright Beautiful World"; "Story of My Life"; "The Goodbye Song"; "Don't Let Me Go"; "I Know It's Today"; "What's Up, Duloc?"; "Travel Song"; "Donkey Pot Pie"; "This Is How a Dream Comes True"; "Who I'd Be"; "Morning Person"; "I Think I Got You Beat"; "The Ballad of Farquaad"; "Make a Move"; "When Words Fail"; "Build a Wall"; "Freak Flag"
New York run: Broadway Theatre, December 14, 2008; 441 p.

Critics complained that most motion pictures that were transferred to the musical stage lacked "heart," but many were pleased with this adaptation of DreamWorks' 2001 animated version of William Steig's book. The show ran for a respectable 441 performances, attracting families, tourists, and younger theatergoers who might never otherwise have set foot in a Broadway theater.

The story parallels that of *Beauty and the Beast*, except that in *Shrek*, both romantic leads are grotesque ogres with hearts of gold, although Princess Fiona is under a spell that renders her beautiful during the day and ugly after dark. In Act I, Shrek and his faithful companion, Donkey, rescue Princess Fiona from a remote castle, and in Act II, they battle the diminutive despot, Lord Farquaad, who is determined to marry Fiona and become king.

The original out-of-town tryout took place in Seattle, with many of the cast principals (James, Foster, and Sieber) making the transition to the Broadway production. The voice that gives admonitions to the audience to silence their cell phones belonged to Julie Andrews. Beginning on October 2, 2009, the ensemble sang "I'm a Believer" for the finale, in tribute to the popular recording by Smash Mouth (originally a hit for the Monkees) that played over the closing credits of the film.
Decca OC

WEST SIDE STORY

Music: Leonard Bernstein
Lyrics: Stephen Sondheim
Conception: Jerome Robbins
Book: Arthur Laurents
Producers: Kevin McCollum, James L. Nederlander, Jeffrey Seller, Terry Allen Kramer, Sander Jacobs, Roy Furman/ Jill Furman Willis, Freddy DeMann, Robyn Goodman/ Walt Grossman, Hal Luftig, Roy Miller, the Weinstein Company, and Broadway Across America (John Gore: CEO; Thomas B. McGrath: Chairman; Beth Williams: COO & Head of Production)
Director: Arthur Laurents
Choreography: Jerome Robbins, reproduced by Joey McKneely
Cast: George Akram, Matt Cavenaugh, Cody Green, Karen Olivo, Josefina Scaglione, Kyle Coffman, Joey Haro, Curtis Holbrook, Lee Sellars, Tro Shaw, Ryan Steele, Greg Vinkler
Songs: Same as original production
New York run: Palace Theatre, March 19, 2009; 748 p.

Director Arthur Laurents was not happy with the last revival of *West Side Story* (1980), so for this edition, he decided to make the musical more contemporary by incorporating Spanish lyrics and dialogue into the English libretto. The translations were effected by Lin-Manuel Miranda, composer of *In the Heights*. Two of the translated songs, "Un Hombre Así" ("A Boy Like That") and "Me Siento Hermosa" ("I Feel Pretty") were later returned to their original English versions.

West Side Story. Josefina Scaglione (Maria) sings "I Feel Pretty," unaware that her boyfriend Tony, played by Matt Cavenaugh, has just killed her brother Bernardo in a knife fight. (Joan Marcus)

HAIR

Music: Galt MacDermot
Lyrics & book: Gerome Ragni & James Rado
Producers: The Joseph Papp Public Theater/ New York Shakespeare Festival (Oskar Eustis: Artistic Director; Andrew D. Hamingson: Executive Director), Jeffrey Richards, Jerry Frankel, Gary Goddard Entertainment, Kathleen K. Johnson, Nederlander Productions, Fran Kirmser Productions/ Jed Bernstein, Marc Frankel, Broadway Across America (John Gore: CEO; Thomas B. McGrath: Chairman; Beth Williams: COO & Head of Production), Barbara Manocherian/ Wencarlar Productions, JK Productions/ Terry Schnuck, Andy Sandberg, Jam Theatricals, the Weinstein Company/ Norton Herrick, and Jujamcyn Theaters (Rocco Landesman: President; Paul Libin: Producing Director; Jack Viertel: Creative Director; Jordan Roth: Vice President); produced by arrangement with Elizabeth Ireland McCann
Director: Diane Paulus
Choreographer: Karole Armitage
Cast: Gavin Creel, Will Swenson, Sasha Allen, Allison Case, Caissie Levy, Darius Nichols, Bryce Ryness, Kacie Sheik, Megan Lawrence, Andrew Kober
Songs: Same as original production, with the addition of "Oh Great God of Power," "Yes, I's Finished on Y'all's Farmlands," and "Give Up All Desires."
New York run: Al Hirschfeld Theatre, March 31, 2009; 519 p.

This hugely successful revival was bolstered by a top-to-bottom scrubbing of the score, with original composer Galt MacDermot and surviving lyricist James Rado supervising. A key member of the onstage band, drummer Bernard "Pretty" Purdie, played on the original Off-Broadway recording of the show in 1967. Cast members broke down the fourth wall by invading the audience, scattering flowers, braiding audience members' hair, and standing on seats. Reviewers were ecstatic over the joyous exuberance of the cast, the music with a groove that wouldn't quit, and the colorful junkyard set. *Hair*'s popularity waned when the original Broadway cast departed to perform the show in London's West End.

ROCK OF AGES

Music & lyrics: Various (see song listings for individual writers)
Book: Chris D'Arienzo
Producers: Matthew Weaver, Carl Levin, Jeff Davis, Barry Habib, Scott Prisand, Relativity Media, and Corner Store Fund; produced in association with Janet Billig Rich, Hillary Weaver, Toni Habib, Paula Davis, Simon and Stefany Bergson/ Jennifer Maloney, Charles Rolecek, Susanne Brook, Israel Wolfson, Sara Katz/Jayson Raitt, Max Gottlieb/ John Butler, David Kaufman/ Jay Franks, Michael Wittlin, Prospect Pictures, Laura Smith/ Bill Bodnar, Happy Walters, Michele Caro, and the Araca Group
Director: Kristin Hanggi
Choreographer: Kelly Devine
Cast: Constantine Maroulis, Amy Spanger, James Carpinello, Adam Dannheisser, Mitchell Jarvis, Michele Mais, Lauren Molina, Paul Schoeffler, Wesley Taylor
Songs: "Cum On Feel the Noize" (Neville Holder and James Lea); "Just Like Paradise" (David Lee Roth and Brett Tuggle); "Nothin' But a Good Time" (Bobby Dall, Bruce Anthony Johannessen, Bret Michael, and Rikki Rocket); "Sister Christian" (Kelly Keagy); "We Built This City" (Dennis Lambert, Martin George Page, Bernie Taupin, and Peter Wolf); "Too Much on My Hands" (Tommy Shaw); "I Wanna Rock" (Dee Snider); "We're Not Gonna Take It" (Dee Snider); "More Than Words" (Nuno Bettencourt and Gary F. Cherone); "Heaven" (Jerry Dixon, Jani Lane, Erik Turner, and Joey Allen); "To Be with You" (David Grahame and Eric Martin); "Waiting for a Girl Like You" (Michael Leslie Jones); "Wanted Dead or Alive" (Jon Bon Jovi and Richard S. Sambora); "Renegade" (Tommy Shaw); "I Want to Know What Love Is" (Michael Leslie Jones); "Harden My Heart" (Marvin Webster Ross); "Shadows of the Night" (D. L. Byron); "Here I Go Again" (David Coverdale and Bernard Marsden); "The Final Countdown" (Joey Tempest); "Any Way You Want It" (Steve Perry and Neal Schon); "High Enough" (Jack Blades, Ted Nugent, and Tommy Shaw); "Beaver Hunt" (David Gibbs and Chris Hardwick); "Kiss Me Deadly" (Mick Smiley); "I Hate Myself for Loving You" (Desmond Child); "Heat of the Moment" (Geoffrey Downs and John K. Wetton); "Hit Me with Your Best Shot" (E. Schwartz); "I Can't Fight This Feeling" (Kevin Cronin); "Ever Rose Has Its Thorn" (Bobby Dall, Bruce Anthony Johannessen, Bret Michael, and Rikki Rocket); "Keep on Loving You" (Kevin Cronin); "Oh, Sherrie" (Steve Perry, Randy Goodrum, Bill Cuomo, and Craig Krampf); "The Search Is Over" (Frank Sullivan and Jim Peterik); "Don't Stop Believing" (Jonathan Cain, Neal J. Schon, and Steve Perry)
New York run: Brooks Atkinson Theatre, April 7, 2009 (still running 6/11)

This jukebox musical was a tribute to glam rock and heavy metal groups of the 1980s, with a book written by Chris D'Arienzo. The story takes place in 1987 on Hollywood's Sunset Strip. The tossed tresses displayed in this show made the production of *Hair*, showing just down the street, seem like it needed a treatment of Rogaine.

Fortunately, however, *Rock of Ages* didn't take itself too seriously, and the wit and self-mocking of the '80s rock scene made for tremendously good fun. In the story, would-be actresses and guitar gods dream of fame while they hone their acts, which was pretty much what the '80s were all about. The plot is no different than those of old Mickey Rooney/ Judy Garland musicals such as *Babes in Arms*: let's save our nightclub from being shut down by the greedy German real estate developer. But because of the tongue-in-cheek, let's-chuckle-at-what-we-thought-was-cool nostalgia of the show, it worked, whether or not you were familiar with black leather-and-denim groups such as Poison, Journey, Bon Jovi, and Twisted Sister. Production closed temporarily on January 9, 2011, to facilitate a move to the Helen Hayes Theatre, where it resumed performances on March 24, 2011. Watertower Music OC

Rock of Ages. Constantine Maroulis (as Drew Boley) wants to rock. (Joan Marcus)

NEXT TO NORMAL

Music: Tom Kitt
Lyrics: Brian Yorkey
Book: Brian Yorkey
Producers: David Stone, James L. Nederlander, Barbara Whitman, Patrick Catullo, and Second State Theatre (Carole Rothman: Artistic Director; Ellen Richard: Executive Director)
Director: Michael Greif
Cast: Alice Ripley, J. Robert Spencer, Adam Chanler-Berat, Jennifer Damiano, Louis Hobson, Aaron Tveit
Songs: "Just Another Day"; "Everything Else"; "Who's Crazy/ My Psychopharmacologist and I"; "Perfect for You"; "I Miss the Mountains"; "It's Gonna Be Good"; "He's Not Here"; "You Don't Know"; "I Am the One"; "Superboy and the Invisible Girl"; "I'm Alive"; "Make Up Your Mind/ Catch Me I'm Falling"; "I Dreamed a Dance"; "There's a World"; "I've Been"; "Didn't I See This Movie?"; "A Light in the Dark"; "Wish I Were Here"; "Song of Forgetting"; "Better Than Before"; "How Could I Ever Forget?"; "Maybe"; "So Anyway"; "Light"
New York run: Booth Theatre, April 15, 2009; 733 p.

The electroshock therapy that Alice Ripley receives in *Next to Normal* is exactly what the innovative musical brought to Broadway in 2009: a new and electrically charged concept that became a brilliant beacon in a season saturated with revivals, touristy stage adaptations of popular films, and little else. With no choreography to speak of, only six cast members, and a set that looked like it was left over from *The Hollywood Squares* game show, just about everything was different about this musical. *Next to Normal*'s plot is simple: a family falls apart while dealing with the mother's battle with bipolar disorder. Central character Diana Goodman (Alice Ripley) goes through an emotional roller coaster during the show, which reflected the rising and falling moods of the story, as moments of humor are balanced with scenes of unspeakable pain, both physical and emotional. The result was the season's biggest hit. The *New York Times* called it "something much more than a feel-good musical: it is a feel-everything musical."

Next to Normal was nominated for 11 Tony Awards, winning three, for Best Score, Best Orchestration, and Best Actress for Alice Ripley's incandescent performance as the afflicted Diana. Although Tom Kitt's music was scored for a small rock combo, the tasteful inclusion of acoustic guitar, violin, and cello helped attenuate the softer, sadder, more sensitive sequences in the script. The show won the Pulitzer Prize for Drama for 2010. Notable replacements during the show's run included Marin Mazzie and Brian d'Arcy James.
Ghostlight OC

MEMPHIS

Music: David Bryan
Lyrics: Joe DiPietro & David Bryan
Book: Joe DiPietro
Producers: Junkyard Dog Productions, Barbara and Buddy Freitag, Marleen and Kenny Alhadeff, Latitude Link, Jim and Susan Blair, Demos Bizar Entertainment, Land Line Productions, Apples and Oranges Productions, Dave Copley, Dancap Productions, Inc., Alex and Katya Lukianov, Tony Ponturo, 2 Guys Productions, and Richard Winkler; produced in association with Lauren Doll, Eric and Marsi Gardiner, Linda and Bill Potter, Broadway Across America (John Gore: CEO; Thomas B. McGrath: Chairman; Beth Williams: COO & Head of Production), Jocko Productions, Patty Baker, Dan Frishwasser, Bob Bartner/ Scott and Kaylin Union, Loraine Boyle/ Chase Mishkin, Remmel T. Dickinson/ Memphis Orpheum Group and ShadowCatcher Entertainment/ Vijay and Sita Vashee
Director: Christopher Ashley
Choreographer: Sergio Trujillo
Cast: Chad Kimball, Montego Glover, Derrick Bastin, J. Bernard Calloway, James Monroe Iglehart, Cass Morgan, John Eric Parker
Songs: "Underground"; "The Music of My Soul"; "Scratch My Itch"; "Ain't Nothin' But a Kiss"; "Hello, My Name Is Huey"; "Everybody Wants to Be Black on Saturday Night"; "Make Me Stronger"; "Colored Woman"; "Someday"; "She's My Sister"; "Radio"; "Say a Prayer"; "Crazy Little Huey"; "Big Love"; "Love Will Stand When All Else Fails"; "Stand Up"; "Change Don't Come Easy"; "Tear the House Down"; "Memphis Lives in Me"; "Steal Your Rock 'n' Roll"
New York run: Shubert Theatre, October 19, 2009 (still running 6/11)

In mid-'50s Memphis, Huey Calhoun is just a good ol' boy who happens to like black music. He doesn't care that white people aren't welcome in black bars, much less his dating African-American women, but he ruffles a lot of feathers by doing just that, romancing Felicia, the sister of Delray, owner of a popular black nightclub in town, and acting as manager for her career as a singer. Eventually, Huey lands a job as a disc jockey on a local radio station and becomes a local sensation, attracting white teenaged listeners to black rhythm and blues. His interracial relationship with Felicia, however, lands him in hot water when he auditions for a national television program and his career takes a nosedive. Felicia eventually becomes a bigger star than Huey (à la *A Star Is Born*) and in the penultimate scene, invites him up onstage on the eve of a national tour for one last song together.

The story was loosely based on the life of WHBQ disc jockey Dewey Phillips, host of Memphis's popular *Red, Hot and Blue* radio program. The similarity, however, ends there. The music Huey Calhoun champions in *Memphis* is more similar to '60s Motown and gospel than it is the raw R&B recorded by such '50s artists as Junior Parker, Rufus Thomas, and Howlin' Wolf. This had little consequence to the acceptance of *Memphis*, however, which overcame the inaccuracies of the music through its brightly lit and colorful sets, exuberant choreography, and spirited performances by the cast. Chad Kimball played Huey as if he were George W. Bush during his partying days, utilizing an innocent Texas drawl and aw-shucks personality. In a season that was light on nonderivative material, *Memphis* won four Tony Awards, including Best Musical and Best Score for its writers, Joe DiPietro and Bon Jovi keyboardist David Bryan.
Rhino OC

FINIAN'S RAINBOW

Music: Burton Lane
Lyrics: E. Y. Harburg
Book: E. Y. Harburg & Fred Saidy
Producers: David Richenthal, Jack Viertel, Alan D. Marks, Michael Speyer, Bernard Abrams, David M. Milch, Stephen Moore, Debbie Bisno/ Myla Lerner, and Jujamcyn Theaters (Jordan Roth: President; Paul Libin: Producing Director; Jack Viertel: Creative Director); produced in association with Melly Garcia, Jamie deRoy, Jon Bierman, Richard Driehaus, Kevin Spirtas, Jay Binder, and StageVentures 2009 Limited Partnership
Director: Warren Carlyle
Choreographer: Warren Carlyle
Cast: Kate Baldwin, Jim Norton, Alina Faye, Cheyenne Jackson, David Schramm, Guy Davis, Christopher Fitzgerald, Chuck Cooper
Songs: Same as original production
New York run: St. James Theatre, October 29, 2009; 92 p.

E. Y. Harburg and Fred Saidy's sharply disguised satire of racial prejudice, Southern politics, and economic unrest struck a relevant chord when this revival (the show's first in a half century) made its debut at the onset of a severe American recession. But despite garnering glowing reviews, the producers closed the show after less than 100 performances.

(See page 133.)

Finian's Rainbow. Cheyenne Jackson (as idealistic Woody Mahoney) announces Shears and Robust's granting of unlimited credit to Kate Baldwin (Sharon), Jim Norton (Finian), and the sharecroppers of fictional Missitucky. (Joan Marcus)

RAGTIME

Music: Stephen Flaherty
Lyrics: Lynn Ahrens
Book: Terrence McNally
Producers: Kevin McCollum, Roy Furman, Scott Delman, Roger Berlind, Max Cooper, Tom Kirdahy/ Devlin Elliott, Jeffrey Sine, Stephanie McClelland, Roy Miller, LAMS Productions, Inc., Jana Robbins, Sharon Karmazin, Morris Berchard/ Eric Falkenstein, RialtoGals Productions, Independent Presenters Network, Held-Haffner Productions, HRH Foundation, and Emanuel Azenberg; produced in association with the John F. Kennedy Center for the Performing Arts
Director: Marcia Milgrom Dodge
Choreographer: Marcia Milgrom Dodge
Cast: Christiane Noll, Ron Bohmer, Christopher Cox, Quentin Earl Darrington, Robert Petkoff, Bobby Steggert, Stephanie Umoh, Jonathan Hammond, Donna Migliaccio, Savannah Wise, Eric Jordan Young
Songs: Same as original production
New York run: Neil Simon Theatre, November 15, 2009; 65 p.

The restaging of *Ragtime* was the first revival of any musical from the 1990s. Produced anew for the John F. Kennedy Center for the Performing Arts in Washington, D.C., the revised version employed a stripped-down staging consisting of multitiered skeletal scaffolding, with minimal sets and props. This created a stark contrast to the sumptuous costumes and Ahrens and Flaherty's rich score. The show received critical acclaim, but the large cast and orchestra required substantial profits to function and the show closed after less than two months.

(See page 311.)

Ragtime. The famous opening "Prologue," featuring Quentin Earl Darrington as Coalhouse Walker Jr. (bottom center). (Joan Marcus)

FELA!

Music: Fela Anikulapo-Kuti
Lyrics: Fela Anikulapo-Kuti
Book: Jim Lewis & Bill T. Jones
Producers: Shawn "Jay-Z" Carter, Will & Jada Pinkett Smith, Ruth and Stephen Hendel, Roy Gabay, Sony Pictures Entertainment, Edward Tyler Nahem, Slava Smolokowski, Ken Greiner and Chip Meyrelles, Douglas G. Smith, Steve Semlitz/ Cathy Glaser, Daryl Roth/ True Love Productions, Susan Dietz/ Mort Swinsky, and Knitting Factory Entertainment
Director: Bill T. Jones
Choreographer: Bill T. Jones
Cast: Sahr Ngaujah, Kevin Mambo, Saycon Sengbloh, Lillias White, Ismael Kouyaté, Gelan Lambert
Songs: "Everything Scatter"; "Iba Orisa" (traditional Yoruba chant); Medzi Medzi (music: E. T. Mensah); "Mr. Syms" (music: John Coltrane); "Manteca" (music: Chano Pozo); "I Got the Feeling" (music and lyric: James Brown); "Originality/ Yellow Fever"; "Trouble Sleep"; "Teacher Don't Teach Me Nonsense"; "Lover" (lyric: Jim Lewis); "Upside Down"; "Expensive Shit"; "Pipeline" (lyric: Jim Lewis); "I.T.T. (International Thief Thief)"; "Water No Get Enemy"; "Egbe Mio"; "Zombie"; "Na Poi"; "Sorrow Tears and Blood"; "Iba Orisa/ Shakara"; "Rain" (music: Aaron Johnson and Jordan McLean; lyric: Bill T. Jones and Jim Lewis); "Coffin for Head of State"
New York run: Eugene O'Neill Theatre, November 23, 2009; 463 p.

This musical celebrates the life of Fela Anikulapo-Kuti, a Nigerian composer, musician, political activist, and pioneer of Afrobeat music. Formulating Afrobeat in the early 1960s, Fela took his music to the United States, where he became influenced by the American Black Power movement. After returning to Nigeria, he formed his own communal compound called the Kalakuta Republic and declared its independence from Nigeria. His music now focused on attacking Nigeria's corrupt and oppressive military government, which inspired an attack on Fela and his family, during which Fela's mother, a political activist herself, was killed.

Although the show deals with events surrounding the 1977 invasion of the Kalakuta Republic, *Fela!* is dominated not by story, but by the pulsing music and irresistible rhythms of Afrobeat and Bill T. Jones's scintillating choreography, which won a Tony Award. The character of Fela is onstage continuously, with the magnetic Sahr Ngaujah, who originated the role, playing five shows a week and alternate Kevin Mambo the other three. *Fela!* was the most original, refreshing, and different production to hit Broadway during the 2009–10 season, a show that the *New York Times* said "melts walls."
Knitting Factory OC

A LITTLE NIGHT MUSIC

Music and lyrics: Stephen Sondheim
Book: Hugh Wheeler
Producers: Thomas Viertel, Steven Baruch, Marc Routh, Richard Frankel, the Menier Chocolate Factory (David Babani: Artistic Director), Roger Berlind, David Babani, Sonia Friedman Productions, Andrew Fell, Daryl Roth/ Jane Bergère, Harvey Weinstein/ Raise the Roof 3, Beverly Bartner/ Dancap Productions, Nica Burns/ Max Weitzenhoffer, Eric Falkenstein/ Anna Czekaj, Jerry Frankel/ Ronald Frankel, and James D. Stern/ Douglas L. Meyer
Director: Trevor Nunn
Choreography: Lynn Page
Cast: Angela Lansbury, Catherine Zeta-Jones, Alexander Hanson, Erin Davie, Hunter Ryan Herdlicka, Leigh Ann Larkin, Aaron Lazar, Ramona Mallory, Bradley Dean
Songs: Same as original production
New York run: Walter Kerr Theatre, December 13, 2009; 425 p.

The first revival of this redoubtable classic enjoyed a run almost as long as the original. Two notable cast replacements occurred on July 13, 2010 (after a month hiatus), when Angela Lansbury and Catherine Zeta-Jones were replaced by, respectively, Bernadette Peters and Elaine Stritch. Zeta-Jones, in her Broadway debut, won a Tony for her performance as Desirée Armfeldt.

(See page 237.)

A Little Night Music. Alexander Hanson (Fredrik) and Catherine Zeta-Jones (Desirée) share a quiet moment. (Joan Marcus)

THE ADDAMS FAMILY

Music & lyrics: Andrew Lippa
Book: Marshall Brickman and Rick Elice
Producers: Stuart Oken, Roy Furman, Michael Leavitt, Five Cent Productions, Stephen Schuler, Decca Theatricals, Scott M. Delman, Stuart Ditsky, Terry Allen Kramer, Stephanie P. McClelland, James L. Nederlander, Eva Price, Jam Theatricals/ Mary Lu Roffe, Pittsburgh CLO/ Gutterman-Swinsky, Vivek Tiwary/ Gary Kaplan, the Weinstein Company/ Clarence, LLC, and Adam Zotovich/ Tribe Theatricals; produced by special arrangement with Elephant Eye Theatrical
Director: Phelim McDermott and Julian Crouch
Choreographer: Sergio Trujillo
Cast: Nathan Lane, Bebe Neuwirth, Kevin Chamberlin, Jackie Hoffman, Zachary James, Adam Riegler, Krysta Rodriguez, Terrence Mann, Carolee Carmello, Wesley Taylor
Songs: "The Addams Family Theme" (Vic Mizzy); "When You're an Addams"; "Pulled"; "Where Did We Go Wrong"; "One Normal Night"; "Morticia"; "What If?"; "Full Disclosure"; "Waiting"; "Just Around the Corner"; "The Moon and Me"; "Happy/ Sad"; "Crazier Than You"; "Let's Not Talk About Anything Else but Love"; "In the Arms"; "Live Before We Die"; "Tango de Amor"; "Move Toward the Darkness"; "Not Today"
New York run: Lunt-Fontanne Theatre, April 8, 2010; (still running 6/11)

The creators of *The Addams Family* initially sought to focus on Charles Addams's surreal *New Yorker* drawings for inspiration rather than the more accessible 1960s television sitcom. When the script was finally completed, however, it was the sitcom that won out, with the Broadway show including Vic Mizzy's infectious finger-snapping theme song. Like the TV show, the Broadway version is a ghoulash of morbid jokes and unabashed sentimentality concerning the members of the eccentric family. Matriarch Morticia is afraid of growing old, teenaged Wednesday is concerned that her new, normal boyfriend Lucas is too different from her (a perverse Montague/ Capulet coupling), and bullet-headed Uncle Fester has fallen in love with the moon. By show's end, everything is wrapped up in nice, tidy packages: Gomez and Morticia are tangoing again, Wednesday and Lucas are getting married, and Fester launches himself skyward with a rocket strapped to his back.

Adding such Broadway scene stealers as Nathan Lane and Bebe Neuwirth made *The Addams Family* a surefire hit, despite a book that was described by the *New Yorker* itself as "an endless illustration of the family's evident pathological characteristics."

The story was nothing new, harkening back to nearly every episode of the television version, which often depicted an encounter between the members of the Addams clan and citizens of "normal" society. An undistinguished score by Andrew Lippa seemed to be the nail in the coffin for this production, but somehow, the show was a success, playing to sold-out audiences well into its second year. This was due in part to the presence of Lane, nostalgia for the show and its characters, a script that played well to children as well as adults, and an effective marketing campaign. Beginning March 22, 2011, Roger Rees replaced Nathan Lane as Gomez Addams.

Decca Broadway OC

MILLION DOLLAR QUARTET

Music & lyrics: Arranged by Chuck Mead
Book: Colin Escott and Floyd Mutrux
Producers: Relevant Theatricals, John Cossette Productions, American Pop Anthology, Broadway Across America (John Gore: CEO; Thomas B. McGrath: Chairman; Beth Williams: COO & Head of Production), and James L. Nederlander
Director: Eric Schaeffer
Cast: Eddie Clendening, Lance Guest, Levi Kreis, Rob Lyons, Hunter Foster, and Elizabeth Stanley
Songs: "Blue Suede Shoes" (Carl Perkins); "Real Wild Child" (John O'Keefe, John Greenan, and Dave Owens); "Matchbox" (Carl Perkins); "Who Do You Love?" (Ellas McDaniel); "Folsom Prison Blues" (Johnny Cash); "Fever" (Eddie Cooley and John Davenport); "Memories Are Made of This" (Terry Gilkyson, Richard Dehr, and Frank Miller); "That's All Right" (Arthur Crudup); "Brown Eyed Handsome Man" (Chuck Berry); "Down by the Riverside" (traditional); "Sixteen Tons" (Merle Travis); "My Babe" (Willie Dixon); "Long Tall Sally" (Robert Blackwell, Enotris Johnson, and Richard Penniman); "Peace in the Valley" (Thomas A. Dorsey); "I Walk the Line" (Johnny Cash); "I Hear You Knockin'" (Dave Bartholomew and Pearl King); "Party" (Jessie Mae Robinson); "Great Balls of Fire" (Otis Blackwell and Jack Hammer); "Hound Dog" (Jerry Leiber and Mike Stoller); "Ghost Riders in the Sky" (Stan Jones); "See You Later Alligator" (Robert Guidry); "Whole Lotta Shakin' Going' On" (Curly Williams)
New York run: Nederlander Theatre, April 11, 2010; 489 p.

On December 4, 1956, at the legendary Sun Recording Studios in Memphis, Tennessee, Sun artists Johnny Cash, Jerry Lee Lewis, and Carl Perkins received an old friend, former Sun recording star Elvis Presley, who was now with RCA Victor records and already a worldwide sensation. The four enjoyed an impromptu jam session, consisting mostly of gospel numbers and spirituals. The session wasn't discovered until years later, but when it was, it was dubbed "The Million Dollar Quartet," despite the fact that Cash had departed the studio before producer Sam Phillips could roll tape.

Music historian Colin Escott and writing partner Floyd Mutrux expanded this scenario to include more secular rockabilly and rhythm and blues hits from the mid-1950s (only "Down by the Riverside" and "Peace in the Valley" were actually recorded that day). The show dramatizes the event by turning it into a jukebox musical, with astoundingly authentic performances by the actors (who played their own instruments) as the members of the quartet. Levi Kreis won a Tony for his riveting portrayal of the self-professed "wild child," Jerry Lee Lewis. Lewis himself joined the cast during the encore on the evening of September 10, 2010.
MDQ Merchandising LLC OC

LA CAGE AUX FOLLES

Music & lyrics: Jerry Herman
Book: Harvey Fierstein
Producers: Sonia Friedman Productions, David Babani, Barry and Fran Weissler, Edwin W. Schloss, Robert G Bartner/ Norman Tulchin, Broadway Across America (John Gore: CEO; Thomas B. McGrath: Chairman; Beth Williams: COO and Head of Production), Matthew Mitchell, Raise the Roof 4, Richard Winkler/ Bensinger Taylor/ Laudenslager Bergère, Arlene Scanlan/ John O'Boyle, Independent Presenters Network, Olympus Theatricals, Allen Spivak, Jerry Frankel/ Bat-Barry Productions, Nederlander Presentations, Inc., and INC/ Harvey Weinstein
Director: Terry Johnson
Choreographer: Lynne Page
Cast: Kelsey Grammer, Douglas Hodge, Fred Applegate, Veanne Cox, Chris Hoch, Elena Shaddow, A. J. Shively, Nick Adams, Christine Andreas, Sean A. Carmon, Nicholas Cunningham, Robin De Jesús, Sean Patrick Doyle
Songs: Same as original production
New York run: Longacre Theatre, April 18, 2010; 433 p.

This revival was well received by critics and the public, receiving 11 Tony Award nominations and winning three, including Best Musical Revival and Best Actor for Russell Hodge, who also played Albin in the 2008 London revival. Notable cast replacements during its run include Jeffrey Tambor (who withdrew nine days after his debut), librettist Harvey Fierstein (replacing Hodge), and Allyce Beasley.

(See page 266.)

La Cage Aux Follies. Douglas Hodge (as drag queen Albin) and Kelsey Grammer (as his long-suffering partner Georges). (Joan Marcus)

AMERICAN IDIOT

Music: Green Day
Lyrics: Billie Joe Armstrong
Book: Billie Joe Armstrong and Michael Mayer
Producer: Tom Hulce, Ira Pittelman, Ruth and Stephen Hendel, Vivek Tiwary/ Gary Kaplan, Aged In Wood and Burnt Umber, Scott M. Delman, Latitude Link, Hop Theatricals, Jeffrey Finn, Larry Welk, Bensinger Filerman and Moellenberg Taylor, Allan S. Gordon/ Élan McAllister, and Berkeley Repertory Theatre; produced in association with Awaken Entertainment, John Pinckard, and John Domo
Director: Michael Mayer
Choreographer: Stephen Hoggett
Cast: John Gallagher Jr., Michael Esper, Mary Faber, Rebecca Naomi Jones, Christina Sajous, Stark Sands, Tony Vincent
Songs: "American Idiot"; "Jesus of Suburbia"; "City of the Damned"; "I Don't Care"; "Dearly Beloved"; "Tales of Another Broken Home"; "Holiday"; "Boulevard of Broken Dreams"; "Favorite Son"; "Are We the Waiting"; "St. Jimmy"; "Give Me Novocaine"; "Last of the American Girls/ She's a Rebel"; "Last Night on Earth"; "Too Much Too Soon"; "Before the Lobotomy"; "Extraordinary Girl"; "When It's Time"; "Know Your Enemy"; "21 Guns"; "Letterbomb"; "Wake Me Up When September Ends"; "The Death of St. Jimmy"; "East 12th Street"; "Nobody Likes You"; "Rock and Roll Girlfriend"; "We're Coming Home Again"; "Whatsername"; "Good Riddance (Time of Your Life)"
New York run: St. James Theatre, April 20, 2010; 422 p.

Punk rock favorites Green Day produced *American Idiot* around their 2004 concept album of the same name, expanding it by adding tunes from another album, *21st Century Breakdown*, various singles, and one unreleased song ("When It's Time"). At the outset, Green Day leader Billie Joe Armstrong designed the album with a story in mind that linked the songs together; for this, he drew inspiration from Broadway shows like Britain's *Rocky Horror Show* and America's *West Side Story*.

The story is nothing new in Broadway or in film. Three friends, Johnny, Will, and Tunny, are unhappy with their stifling and mundane life in suburbia, and each decides on a different route to find himself. Johnny and Tunny escape to the big city, while Will stays home with his pregnant girlfriend. Finding nothing exciting about urban life, Tunny enlists in the army. Each friend's experiences incorporate the proverbial trio of sex, drugs, and rock and roll. The characters represent not just the rage that typifies the punk rock scene, but a grander concept: disaffected teenagers yearning for identity in a conformist world. It's really *Rebel Without a Cause* for the 21st century.

The *New York Times* found the show "thrilling" and "charged with urgency." Orchestrator Tom Kitt (*Next to Normal*) ensured that the music ran the gamut of emotions, reflecting sullen hopelessness, brash bombast, and lush tenderness. Billie Joe Armstrong himself played the role of St. Jimmy for one week, from September 28 to October 3, 2010. He would return in the role sporadically in the early months of 2011, but interest waned when Armstrong wasn't in the show, and at this writing, it was scheduled to close on April 24, 2011, after 421 performances, with Armstrong returning to the cast for the final three weeks.
Reprise OC

PROMISES, PROMISES

Music: Burt Bacharach
Lyrics: Hal David
Book: Neil Simon
Producers: Broadway Across America (John Gore: CEO; Thomas B. McGrath: Chairman; Beth Williams: COO & Head of Production), Craig Zadan, Neil Meron, the Weinstein Company, Terry Allen Kramer, Candy Spelling, Pat Addiss, Bernie Abrams/ Michael Speyer, and Takonkiet Viravan/ Scenario Thailand
Director & Choreographer: Rob Ashford
Cast: Kristin Chenoweth, Sean Hayes, Tony Goldwyn, Brooks Ashmanskas, Peter Benson, Katie Finneran, Seán Martin Hingston, Ken Land, Dick Latessa, Helen Anker, Mayumi Miguel
Songs: Same as original production, with the additions of "I Say a Little Prayer" and "A House Is Not a Home"
New York run: Broadway Theatre, April 25, 2010; 289 p.

(See page 226.)

The first revival of this adaptation of the 1960 movie *The Apartment* was also one of the first so-called jukebox musicals, consisting solely of material written by a popular songwriting team, the hugely popular Burt Bacharach and Hal David. The production earned four Tony nominations, but came away empty.

Promises, Promises. Kristin Chenowith (Fran) sings "I Say a Little Prayer."
(Joan Marcus)

RAIN—A Tribute to the Beatles on Broadway

Music & lyrics: John Lennon & Paul McCartney (except where indicated)
Producers: Annerin Productions, Magic Arts & Entertainment/ Tix Productions,
Nederlander Presentations, Inc., and RAIN
Scenic design: Scott Christensen & Todd Skinner
Cast: Joe Bithorn, Ralph Castelli, Joey Curatolo, Steve Landes, Mark Beyer
Songs: "I Want to Hold Your Hand"; "All My Loving"; "This Boy"; "I Saw Her
Standing There"; "A Hard Day's Night"; "I'm Happy Just to Dance with
You"; "Yesterday"; "I Feel Fine"; "Day Tripper"; " Twist and Shout" (Bert
Berns & Phil Medley); "Sgt. Pepper's Lonely Hearts Club Band"; "With a
Little Help from My Friends"; "Eleanor Rigby"; "Strawberry Fields Forever";
"When I'm 64"; "A Day in the Life"; "Hello Goodbye"; "I Am the Walrus";
"Girl"; "We Can Work It Out"; "Blackbird"; "I've Just Seen a Face"; "While
My Guitar Gently Weeps" (George Harrison); "Come Together"; "Get
Back"; "Revolution"; "The End"; "Give Peace a Chance"; "Let It Be"; "Hey
Jude"
New York run: Neil Simon Theatre, October 26, 2010; Brooks Atkinson Theatre,
February 8, 2011 (still running 6/11)

Not since *Beatlemania* (1977–79) have the Beatles been on Broadway, but with
Rain, the music of the most influential rock group of all time has been enhanced
by a theatrical production worthy of the genius of the Beatles' music. Many jukebox
musicals (*Mamma Mia!*, *Rock of Ages*, *Jersey Boys*) attempt to incorporate a
group of songs into a storyline fit for Broadway, but what *Rain* does instead is
visually encapsulate the mood of the Beatles' music through a multimedia concert,
highlighted by a whirling circus of graphics, psychedelic lighting, sound effects,
and projections.

The four musicians who portray John Lennon, Paul McCartney, George
Harrison, and Ringo Starr perform the Beatles' songs live with note-for-note
precision. Their expertise shows a keen familiarity with the original recordings,
as fans of the group would be most attentive to every minor detail employed.
The result is an emotional roller-coaster ride through the Beatles' career: from
their vaunted first appearance on *The Ed Sullivan Show* in 1964, through their
psychedelic "Sgt. Pepper" years, to their final meltdown, which concluded with
their famed rooftop performance in London in 1969.

The show took a brief hiatus on January 15, 2011, to facilitate a move to the
Brooks Atkinson Theatre, where it resumed performances on February 8.

INDEXES

Show Index

Addams Family, The (2010), 374
Aida (2000), 316
Ain't Misbehavin' (1978), 251
Allegro (1947), 136
American Idiot (2010), 377
Andre Charlot's Revue of 1924 (1924), 42
Annie (1977), 247
Annie Get Your Gun (1946), 130
Annie Get Your Gun (1999), 315
Anything Goes (1934), 88
Anything Goes (1987), 277
Applause (1970), 228
Apple Tree, The (1966), 218
As the Girls Go (1948), 139
As Thousands Cheer (1933), 83
Aspects of Love (1990), 283
At Home Abroad (1935), 89
Avenue Q (2003), 330

Babes in Arms (1937), 98
Babes in Toyland (1903), 8
Band Wagon, The (1931), 74
Barnum (1980), 256
Beauty and the Beast (1994), 297
Bells Are Ringing (1956), 171
Best Foot Forward (1941), 114
Best Little Whorehouse in Texas, The (1978), 250
Big River (1985), 270
Billy Elliot: The Musical (2008), 361
Bitter Sweet (1929), 68
Black Crook, The (1866), 3
Blackbirds of 1928 (1928), 63
Bloomer Girl (1944), 125
Blossom Time (1921), 38
Blue Paradise, The (1915), 21
Boy Friend, The (1954), 162
Boys from Syracuse, The (1938), 107
Brigadoon (1947), 134
Bring In 'Da Noise, Bring In 'Da Funk (1996), 306
By Jupiter (1942), 116
Bye Bye Birdie (1960), 188

Cabaret (1966), 219
Cabaret (1998), 312
Cabin in the Sky (1940), 111
Call Me Madam (1950), 147
Call Me Mister (1946), 129
Camelot (1960), 193
Can-Can (1953), 156
Candide (1956), 172
Candide (1974), 239
Carmen Jones (1943), 122
Carnival (1961), 195
Carousel (1945), 127
Carousel (1994), 296
Cat and the Fiddle, The (1931), 77
Cats (1982), 263
Chess (1988), 279

Chicago (1975), 244,
Chicago (1996), 307
Chocolate Soldier, The (1909), 16
Chorus Line, A (1975), 243
Chorus Line, A (2006), 343
City of Angels (1989), 282
Cocoanuts, The (1925), 51
Color Purple, The (2005) 340
Company (1970), 229
Company (2006), 344
Contact (2000), 318
Connecticut Yankee, A (1927), 58
Countess Maritza (1926), 53
Cradle Will Rock, The (1938), 101
Crazy for You (1992), 288
Curtains (2007), 350

Dames at Sea (1968), 226
Damn Yankees (1955), 167
Dancin' (1978), 250
Dearest Enemy (1925), 48
Desert Song, The (1926), 54
Destry Rides Again (1959), 180
Dirty Rotten Scoundrels (2005), 334
Do I Hear a Waltz? (1965), 210
Do Re Mi (1960), 194
Don't Bother Me, I Can't Cope (1972), 235
Dr. Seuss' How the Grinch Stole Christmas (2006), 348
Dreamgirls (1981), 261
Drowsy Chaperone, The (2006), 342
DuBarry Was a Lady (1939), 109

Earl Carroll Vanities (1931), 76
Evangeline (1874), 4
Evita (1979), 254

Face the Music (1932), 79
Falsettos (1992), 293
Fanny (1954), 164
Fantasticks, The (1960), 189
Fantasticks, The (2006), 343
Fela! (2009), 372
Fiddler on the Roof (1964), 209
Fiddler on the Roof (2004), 333
Fifty Million Frenchmen (1929), 69
Fine and Dandy (1930), 72
Finian's Rainbow (1947), 133
Finian's Rainbow (2009), 370
Fiorello! (1959), 186
Firefly, The (1912), 18
Five Guys Named Moe (1992), 289
Florodora (1900), 6
Flower Drum Song (1958), 178
Flower Drum Song (2002), 327
Flying Colors (1932), 80
Flying High (1930), 71
Follies (1971), 232

Follies (2001), 320
Follies of 1907 (1907), 14
Follow the Girls (1944), 124
Follow Thru (1929), 67
Footloose (1998), 313
Fosse (1999), 314
Fortune Teller, The (1898), 6
Forty-five Minutes from Broadway (1906), 13
42nd Street (1980), 257
42nd Street (2001), 322
Full Monty, The (2000), 319
Funny Face (1927), 59
Funny Girl (1964), 207
Funny Thing Happened on the Way to the Forum,
    A (1962), 198
Funny Thing Happened on the Way to the Forum,
    A (1996), 304

Garrick Gaieties, The (1925), 46
Gay Divorce (1932), 82
Gentlemen Prefer Blondes (1949),146
George M! (1968), 223
George White's Scandals (1922), 40
George White's Scandals (1926), 52
George White's Scandals (1931), 76
Girl Crazy (1930), 72
Girl from Utah, The (1914), 19
Godspell (1971), 233
Golden Apple, The (1954), 160
Golden Boy (1964), 210
Good News! (1927), 56
Grand Hotel (1989), 281
Grease (1972), 234
Grease (1994), 298
Grease (2007), 354
Great Waltz, The (1934), 87
Greenwich Village Follies (1919), 31
Greenwillow (1960), 187
Guys and Dolls (1950), 148
Guys and Dolls (1992), 290
Gypsy (1959), 182
Gypsy (1989), 282
Gypsy (2003), 329
Gypsy (2008), 359

Hair (1968), 224
Hair (2009), 365
Hairspray (2002), 326
Half a Sixpence (1965), 211
Happy Time, The (1968), 222
Hello, Dolly! (1964), 204
Hellzapoppin (1938), 103
High Button Shoes (1947), 136
High Spirits (1964), 208
Hit the Deck! (1927), 56
Hold Everything! (1928), 65
Hooray for What! (1937), 100
House of Flowers (1954), 165
How to Succeed in Business Without Really
    Trying (1961), 196
How to Succeed in Business Without Really
    Trying (1995), 302

I Do! I Do! (1966), 220
I Love My Wife (1977), 245
I Married an Angel (1938), 102

I'd Rather Be Right (1937), 98
I'm Getting My Act Together and Taking It on the
    Road (1978), 252
In the Heights (2008), 357
Inside U.S.A. (1948), 137
Into the Woods (1987), 277
Into the Woods (2002), 326
Irene (1919), 32
Irene (1973), 238
Irma la Douce (1960), 190
Irving Berlin's White Christmas (2008), 362

Jamaica (1957), 176
Jekyll and Hyde (1997), 308
Jelly's Last Jam (1992), 292
Jerome Robbins' Broadway (1989), 279
Jersey Boys (2005), 339
Jesus Christ Superstar (1971), 233
Joseph and the Amazing Technicolor
    Dreamcoat (1981), 260
Jubilee (1935), 92
Jumbo (1935), 93

King and I, The (1951), 151
King and I, The (1977), 248
King and I, The (1996), 303
Kismet (1953), 158
Kiss Me, Kate (1948), 141
Kiss Me, Kate (1999), 315
Kiss of the Spider Woman—The Musical (1993),
    295
Knickerbocker Holiday (1938), 104

La Cage aux Folles (1983), 266
La Cage aux Folles (2004), 333
La Cage aux Folles (2010), 376
Lady, Be Good! (1924), 44
Lady in the Dark (1941), 113
Leave It to Jane (1917), 26
Leave It to Me! (1938), 105
Legally Blonde (2007), 351
Lend an Ear (1948), 139
Les Misérables (1987), 275
Les Misérables (2006), 349
Let's Face It! (1941), 115
Life Begins at 8:40 (1934), 87
Light in the Piazza, The (2005), 338
Li'l Abner (1956), 171
Lion King, The (1997), 310
Little Johnny Jones (1904), 10
Little Mary Sunshine (1959), 186
Little Me (1962), 200
Little Mermaid, The (2008), 355
Little Night Music, A (1973), 237
Little Night Music, A (2009), 373
Little Shop of Horrors (1982), 262
Little Show, The (1929), 67
Lost in the Stars (1949), 144
Louisiana Purchase (1940), 110
Love Life (1948), 138

Madame Sherry (1910), 17
Mamma Mia!, (2001), 324
Mlle. Modiste (1905), 10
Magic Show, The (1974), 240
Make Mine Manhattan (1948), 137

Show Index

Mame (1966), 217
Man of La Mancha (1965), 215
Man of La Mancha (2002), 329
Mary Poppins (2006), 344
Maytime (1917), 24
Me and Juliet (1953), 157
Me and My Girl (1986), 273
Memphis (2009), 369
Merry Widow, The (1907), 15
Merry Widow, The (1943), 120
Mexican Hayride (1944), 122
Milk and Honey (1961), 195
Million Dollar Quartet (2010), 375
Miss Liberty (1949), 144
Miss Saigon (1991), 285
Monty Python's Spamalot (2005) 336
Most Happy Fella, The (1956), 170
Most Happy Fella, The (1992), 293
Movin' Out (2002), 328
Mulligan Guard Ball, The (1879), 4
Music Box Revue (1921), 37
Music in the Air (1932), 81
Music Man, The (1957), 177
Music Man, The (2000), 319
My Fair Lady (1956), 168
My One and Only (1983), 264
Mystery of Edwin Drood, The (1985), 271
Naughty Marietta (1910), 17
New Faces (1934), 86
New Faces of 1952 (1952), 154
New Girl in Town (1957), 173
New Moon, The (1928), 64
New Yorkers, The (1930), 74
Next to Normal (2009), 368
Nine (1982), 262
Nine (2003), 329
No, No, Nanette (1925), 47
No, No, Nanette (1971), 231
No Strings (1962), 197

Of Thee I Sing (1931), 78
Oh, Boy! (1917), 24
Oh, Kay! (1926), 53
Oh, Lady! Lady!! (1918), 26
Oklahoma! (1943), 119
Oklahoma! (1979), 255
Oklahoma! (2002), 325
Oliver! (1963), 201
On a Clear Day You Can See
Forever (1965), 213
On the Town (1944), 126
On the Twentieth Century (1978), 249
On Your Toes (1936), 94
On Your Toes (1983), 264
Once on This Island (1990), 284
Once Upon a Mattress (1959), 181
110 in the Shade (1963), 203
110 in the Shade (2007), 352
One Touch of Venus (1943), 120

Pacific Overtures (1976), 245
Pacific Overtures (2004), 333
Paint Your Wagon (1951), 152
Pajama Game, The (1954), 161
Pajama Game, The (2006), 341
Pal Joey (1940), 112

Pal Joey (1952), 153
Panama Hattie (1940), 111
Passion (1994), 298
Peggy-Ann (1926), 54
Peter Pan (1954), 163
Peter Pan (1979), 254
Phantom of the Opera, The (1988), 278
Pink Lady, The (1911), 18
Pins and Needles (1937), 100
Pippin (1972), 236
Pirates of Penzance, The (1981), 258
Plain and Fancy (1955), 166
Poppy (1923), 40
Porgy and Bess (1935), 91
Porgy and Bess (1953), 156
Producers, The (2001), 321
Promises, Promises (1968), 226
Promises, Promises (2010), 378
Purlie (1970), 228

Ragtime (1998), 311
Ragtime (2009), 371
Rain—A Tribute to the Beatles on Broadway
(2010), 379
Raisin (1973), 239
Red, Hot and Blue! (1936), 96
Red Mill, The (1906), 13
Red Mill, The (1945), 128
Redhead (1959), 179
Rent (1996), 305
Rio Rita (1927), 55
Roar of the Greasepaint—The Smell of the
Crowd, The (1965), 212
Roberta (1933), 84
Robin Hood (1891), 5
Rock of Ages (2009), 366
Rosalie (1928), 62
Rose-Marie (1924), 43
Rothschilds, The (1970), 230

St. Louis Woman (1946), 129
Sally (1920), 33
Scarlet Pimpernel (1997), 309
Secret Garden, The (1991), 286
1776 (1969), 227
She Loves Me (1963), 202
She Loves Me (1993), 296
Shenandoah (1975), 242
Show Boat (1927), 60
Show Boat (1946), 128
Show Boat (1994), 299
Show Is On, The (1936), 97
Shrek: The Musical (2008), 363
Shuffle Along (1921), 34
Silk Stockings (1955), 166
Sinbad (1918), 29
Song and Dance (1985), 271
Song of Norway (1944), 124
Sophisticated Ladies (1981), 259
Sound of Music, The (1959), 184
South Pacific (1949), 143
South Pacific (2008), 358
Spring Awakening (2006), 345
Starlight Express (1987), 276
Stop the World—I Want to Get Off (1962), 199
Street Scene (1947), 132
Strike Up the Band (1930), 70

Student Prince in Heidelberg, The (1924), 45
Sugar (1972), 235
Sugar Babies (1979), 255
Sunday in the Park With George (1984), 269
Sunday in the Park With George (2008), 356
Sunny (1925), 50
Sunset Boulevard (1994), 300
Sweeney Todd (1979), 253
Sweeney Todd (2005), 338
Sweet Adeline (1929), 68
Sweet Charity (1966), 216
Sweet Charity (1986), 272
Sweethearts (1913), 19
Sweethearts (1947), 134

Take a Chance (1932), 82
Take Me Along (1959), 183
Tale of Two Cities, A (2008), 360
Tap Dance Kid, The (1983), 268
Tarzan (2006), 347
They're Playing Our Song (1979), 252
This Is the Army (1942), 117
Thoroughly Modern Millie (2002), 325
Three Musketeers, The (1928), 63
Threepenny Opera, The (1954), 159
Three's a Crowd (1930), 73
Tip-Toes (1925), 52
Titanic (1997) 307
Tommy (1993), 294
Too Many Girls (1939), 108
Tree Grows in Brooklyn, A (1951), 152
Trip to Chinatown, A (1891), 5
25th Annual Putnam County Spelling Bee, The
    (2005), 337
Two Gentlemen of Verona (1971), 234

Unsinkable Molly Brown, The (1960), 191
Up in Central Park (1945), 126

Urinetown (2001), 323

Vagabond King, The (1925), 48
Very Good Eddie (1915), 23
Victor/Victoria (1995), 303

Watch Your Step (1914), 20
Wedding Singer, The (2006), 346
West Side Story (1957), 175
West Side Story (2009), 364
What Makes Sammy Run? (1964), 206
Where's Charley? (1948), 138
Whoopee (1928), 66
Wicked (2003), 332
Will Rogers Follies, The (1991), 287
Wish You Were Here (1952),154
Wiz, The (1975), 241
Wizard of Oz, The (1903), 8
Woman of The Year (1981), 260
Wonderful Town (1953), 155
Wonderful Town (2003), 332

Xanadu (2007), 352

Young Frankenstein (2007), 353
You're a Good Man, Charlie Brown (1967), 221
Your Own Thing (1968), 222

Ziegfeld Follies (1907), 14
Ziegfeld Follies (1915), 20
Ziegfeld Follies (1918), 29
Ziegfeld Follies (1919), 31
Ziegfeld Follies (1921), 34
Ziegfeld Follies (1922), 38
Ziegfeld Follies (1934), 85
Ziegfeld Follies (1936), 93
Zorba (1968), 225
Zorba (1983), 268

Composer/Lyricist Index

Adams, Lee
Applause, 228
Bye Bye Birdie, 188
Golden Boy, 210

Adamson, Harold
As the Girls Go, 139
Earl Carroll Vanities, 76

Adler, Richard
Damn Yankees, 167
Pajama Game, The, 161, 341

Ahrens, Lynn
Once on This Island, 284
Ragtime, 311, 371

Anderson, Maxwell
Knickerbocker Holiday, 104
Lost in the Stars, 144

Andersson, Benny
Chess, 279
Mamma Mia!, 324

Anikulapo-Kuti, Fela
Fela!, 372

Apolinar, Danny
Your Own Thing, 222

Arlen, Harold
Bloomer Girl, 125
Hooray for What!, 100
House of Flowers, 165
Jamaica, 176
Life Begins at 8:40, 87
St. Louis Woman, 129

Armstrong, Billie Joe
American Idiot, 377

Ashman, Howard
Beauty and the Beast, 297
Little Mermaid, The, 355
Little Shop of Horrors, 262

Atteridge, Harold
Sinbad, 29

Bacharach, Burt
Promises, Promises, 226, 378

Barer, Marshall
Once Upon a Mattress, 181

Bart, Lionel
Oliver!, 201

Baum, L. Frank
Wizard of Oz, The, 8

Benjamin, Neil
Legally Blonde, 351

Bequelin, Chad
Wedding Singer, The, 346

Berlin, Irving
Annie Get Your Gun, 130, 315
As Thousands Cheer, 83
Call Me Madam, 147
Cocoanuts, The, 51
Face the Music, 79
Irving Berlin's White Christmas, 362
Louisiana Purchase, 110
Miss Liberty, 144
Music Box Revue, 37
This Is the Army, 117
Watch Your Step, 20
Ziegfeld Follies, 31

Bernstein, Leonard
Candide, 172 & 239
On the Town, 126
West Side Story, 175, 364
Wonderful Town, 155, 332

Besoyan, Rick
Little Mary Sunshine, 186

Bizet, Georges
Carmen Jones, 122

Black, Don
Aspects of Love, 283
Song and Dance, 271
Sunset Boulevard, 300

Blake, Eubie
Shuffle Along, 34

Blane, Ralph
Best Foot Forward, 114

Blitzstein, Marc
Cradle Will Rock, The, 101
Threepenny Opera, The, 159

Blossom, Henry
Mlle. Modiste, 10
Red Mill, The, 13, 128

Bock, Jerry
Apple Tree, The, 218
Fiddler on the Roof, 209, 333
Fiorello!, 186

Rothschilds, The, 230
She Loves Me, 202, 296

Braham, David
Mulligan Guard Ball, The, 4

Boublil, Alain
Miss Saigon, 285

Bray, Stephen
Color Purple, The, 340

Bricusse, Leslie
Jekyll and Hyde, 308
Roar of the Greasepaint—The Smell of the
Crowd, The, 212
Stop the World—I Want to Get Off, 199
Victor/Victoria, 303

Brittan, Robert
Raisin, 239

Brooks, Mel
Producers, The, 321
Young Frankenstein, 353

Brown, Forman
Red Mill, The, 128

Brown, Lew
Flying High, 71
Follow Thru, 67
George White's Scandals, 52, 76
Good News!, 56
Hold Everything!, 65

Brown, Nacio Herb
Take a Chance, 82

Bryan, David
Memphis, 369

Buck, Gene
Ziegfeld Follies, 20, 38

Caesar, Irving
No, No, Nanette, 47, 231

Cahn, Sammy
High Button Shoes, 136

Capote, Truman
House of Flowers, 165

Carter, Desmond
Great Waltz, The, 87

Caryll, Ivan
Pink Lady, The, 18

Casey, Warren
Grease, 234, 298, 354

Charig, Phil
Follow the Girls, 124

Charlap, Mark
Peter Pan, 163, 254

Charnin, Martin
Annie, 247

Clement, Frank
Florodora, 6

Cohan, George M.
Forty-five Minutes from
Broadway, 13
George M!, 223
Little Johnny Jones, 10

Coleman, Cy
Barnum, 256
City of Angels, 282
I Love My Wife, 245
Little Me, 200
On the Twentieth Century, 249
Sweet Charity, 216, 272
Will Rogers Follies, The, 287

Collins, Phil
Tarzan, 347

Comden, Betty
Bells Are Ringing, 171
Do Re Mi, 194
On the Town, 126
On the Twentieth Century, 249
Peter Pan, 163, 254
Will Rogers Follies, The, 287
Wonderful Town, 155, 332

Coward, Noel
Bitter Sweet, 68

Crewe, Bob
Jersey Boys, 339

Cryer, Gretchen
I'm Getting My Act Together and Taking It on the
Road, 252

Darion, Joe
Man of La Mancha, 215, 329

David, Hal
Promises, Promises, 226, 378

DeKoven, Reginald
Robin Hood, 5

de Paul, Gene
Li'l Abner, 171

DeSylva, B. G.
Flying High, 71
Follow Thru, 67
George White's Scandals, 40, 52
Good News!, 56
Hold Everything!, 65
Take a Chance, 82

Dietz, Howard
At Home Abroad, 89
Band Wagon, The, 74
Flying Colors, 80
Inside U.S.A., 137
Little Show, The, 67
Three's a Crowd, 73

DiPietro, Joe
Memphis, 369

Donaldson, Walter
Whoopee, 66

Donnelly, Dorothy
Blossom Time, 38
Poppy, 40
Student Prince in Heidelberg, The, 45

Drake, Ervin
What Makes Sammy Run?, 206

Drewe, Anthony
Mary Poppins, 344

Dubin, Al
42nd Street, 257, 322

Duke, Vernon
Cabin in the Sky, 111
Ziegfeld Follies, 85, 93

Du Prez, John
Monty Python's Spamalot, 336

Duquesnay, Anne
Bring In 'Da Noise, Bring In 'Da Funk, 306

Ebb, Fred
Cabaret, 219, 312
Chicago, 244, 307
Curtains, 350
Happy Time, The, 222
Kiss of the Spider Woman—The Musical, 295
Woman of the Year, 260
Zorba, 225, 268

Edwards, Sherman
1776, 227

Eliot, T. S.
Cats, 263

Ellington, Duke
Sophisticated Ladies, 259

Eyen, Tom
Dreamgirls, 261

Eysler, Edmund
Blue Paradise, The, 21

Fain, Sammy
Hellzapoppin, 103

Falls, Robert
Aida, 316

Farrar, John
Xanadu, 352

Fields, Dorothy
Blackbirds of 1928, 63
Redhead, 179
Sugar Babies, 255
Sweet Charity, 216, 272
Tree Grows in Brooklyn, A, 152
Up in Central Park, 126

Finn, William
Falsettos, 293
25th Annual Putnam County Spelling Bee,
The, 337

Flaherty, Stephen
Once on This Island, 284
Ragtime, 311, 371

Ford, Nancy
I'm Getting My Act Together and
Taking It on the Road, 252

Forrest, George
Kismet, 158
Song of Norway, 124

Friml, Rudolf
Firefly, The, 18
Rose-Marie, 43
Three Musketeers, The, 63
Vagabond King, The, 48

Furber, Douglas
Me and My Girl, 273

Gaines, Reg E.
Bring In 'Da Noise, Bring In 'Da Funk, 306

Gaudio, Bob
Jersey Boys, 339

Gaunt, Percy
Trip to Chinatown, A, 5

Gay, Noel
Me and My Girl, 273

Gaynor, Charles
Lend an Ear, 139

Geld, Gary
Purlie, 228
Shenandoah, 242

Gershwin, George
Crazy for You, 288
Funny Face, 59
George White's Scandals, 40
Girl Crazy, 72
Lady, Be Good!, 44
My One and Only, 264
Of Thee I Sing, 78
Oh, Kay!, 53
Porgy and Bess, 91, 156
Rosalie, 62

Strike Up the Band, 70
Tip-Toes, 52

Gershwin, Ira
Crazy for You, 288
Funny Face, 59
Girl Crazy, 72
Lady, Be Good!, 44
Lady in the Dark, 113
Life Begins at 8:40, 87
My One and Only, 264
Of Thee I Sing, 78
Oh, Kay!, 53
Porgy and Bess, 91, 156
Rosalie, 62
Strike Up the Band, 70
Tip-Toes, 52
Ziegfeld Follies, 93

Gesner, Clark
You're a Good Man, Charlie Brown, 221

Gilbert, Robert
Merry Widow, The, 120

Gilbert, William S.
Pirates of Penzance, The, 258

Goodwin, J. Cheever
Evangeline, 4

Grant, Micki
Don't Bother Me, I Can't Cope, 235

Gray, Timothy
High Spirits, 208

Green, Adolph
Bells Are Ringing, 171
Do Re Mi, 194
On the Town, 126
On the Twentieth Century, 249
Peter Pan, 163, 254
Will Rogers Follies, The, 287
Wonderful Town, 155, 332

Green Day
American Idiot, 377

Greene, Schuyler
Very Good Eddie, 23

Grey, Clifford
Hit the Deck!, 56
Sally, 33
Three Musketeers, The, 63

Guare, John
Two Gentlemen of Verona, 234

Guettel, Adam
Light in the Piazza, The, 338

Hague, Albert
Plain and Fancy, 166
Redhead, 179

Haimsohn, George
Dames at Sea, 226

Hall, Carol
Best Little Whorehouse in Texas, The, 250

Hall, Lee
Billy Elliot: The Musical, 361

Hamlisch, Marvin
Chorus Line, A, 243, 343
They're Playing Our Song, 252

Hammerstein II, Oscar
Allegro, 136
Carmen Jones, 122
Carousel, 127, 296
Desert Song, The, 54
Flower Drum Song, 178 & 327
King and I, The, 151, 248, 303
Me and Juliet, 157
Music in the Air, 81
New Moon, The, 64
Oklahoma!, 119, 255, 325
Rose-Marie, 43
Show Boat, 60, 128, 299
Sound of Music, The, 184
South Pacific, 143, 358
Sunny, 50
Sweet Adeline, 68

Hampton, Christopher
Sunset Boulevard, 300

Harbach, Otto
Cat and the Fiddle, The, 77
Desert Song, The, 54
Firefly, The, 18
Madame Sherry, 17
Roberta, 84
Rose-Marie, 43
Sunny, 50

Harburg, E. Y.
Bloomer Girl, 125
Finian's Rainbow, 133, 370
Hooray for What!, 100
Jamaica, 176
Life Begins at 8:40, 87
Ziegfeld Follies, 85

Harnick, Sheldon
Apple Tree, The, 218
Fiddler on the Roof, 209, 333
Fiorello!, 186
Rothschilds, The, 230
She Loves Me, 202, 296

Harrigan, Edward
Mulligan Guard Ball, The, 4

Hart, Charles
Aspects of Love, 283
Phantom of the Opera, The, 278

Hart, Lorenz
Babes in Arms, 98
Boys from Syracuse, The, 107
By Jupiter, 116
Connecticut Yankee, A, 58
Dearest Enemy, 48
Garrick Gaieties, The, 46
I Married an Angel, 102
I'd Rather Be Right, 98
Jumbo, 93
On Your Toes, 94, 264
Pal Joey, 112, 153
Peggy-Ann, 54
Too Many Girls, 108

Henderson, Ray
Flying High, 71
Follow Thru, 67
George White's Scandals, 52, 76
Good News!, 56
Hold Everything!, 65

Henderson, Luther
Jelly's Last Jam, 292

Heneker, David
Half a Sixpence, 211
Irma la Douce, 190

Herbert, Victor
Babes in Toyland, 8
Fortune Teller, The, 6
Mlle. Modiste, 10
Naughty Marietta, 17
Red Mill, The, 13, 128
Sweethearts, 19, 134

Herman, Jerry
Hello, Dolly!, 204
La Cage aux Folles, 266, 333, 376
Mame, 217
Milk and Honey, 195

Hester, Hal
Your Own Thing, 222

Heyward, DuBose
Porgy and Bess, 91 & 156

Hirsch, Louis A.
Ziegfeld Follies, 20, 38

Hollman, Mark
Urinetown, 323

Holmes, Rupert
Curtains, 346
Mystery of Edwin Drood, The, 271

Hooker, Brian
Vagabond King, The, 48

Horwitt, Arnold B.
Make Mine Manhattan, 137
Plain and Fancy, 166

Hoschna, Karl
Madame Sherry, 17

Hoyt, Charles H.
Trip to Chinatown, A, 5

Hughes, Langston
Street Scene, 132

Hwang, David Henry
Aida, 316

Idle, Eric
Monty Python's Spamalot, 336

Jacobs, Jim
Grease, 234, 298, 354

James, Paul
Fine and Dandy, 72

Jones, Stephen
Poppy, 40

Joel, Billy
Movin' Out, 328

John, Elton
Aida, 316
Billy Elliot: The Musical, 361
Lion King, The, 310

Jones, Tom
Fantasticks, The, 189, 343
I Do! I Do!, 220
110 in the Shade, 203, 352

Kahn, Gus
Whoopee, 66

Kalman, Emmerich
Countess Maritza, 53

Kander, John
Cabaret, 219, 312
Chicago, 244, 307
Curtains, 350
Happy Time, The, 222
Kiss of the Spider Woman—The Musical, 295
Woman of the Year, 260
Zorba, 225, 268

Kern, Jerome
Cat and the Fiddle, The, 77
Girl from Utah, The, 19
Leave It to Jane, 26
Music in the Air, 81
Oh, Boy!, 24
Oh, Lady! Lady!!, 26
Roberta, 84
Sally, 33
Show Boat, 60, 128, 299
Sunny, 50
Sweet Adeline, 68
Very Good Eddie, 23

Kitt, Tom
Next to Normal, 368

Kleban, Edward
Chorus Line, A, 243, 343

Knighton, Nan
Scarlet Pimpernel, The, 309

Kotis, Greg
Urinetown, 323

Kretzmer, Herbert
Les Misérables, 275, 349

Krieger, Henry
Dreamgirls, 261
Tap Dance Kid, The, 268

Lambert, Lisa
Drowsy Chaperone, The, 342

Lane, Burton
Earl Carroll Vanities, 76
Finian's Rainbow, 133, 370
On a Clear Day You Can See Forever, 213

Larson, Jonathan
Rent, 305

Latouche, John
Cabin in the Sky, 111
Golden Apple, The, 160

Lehar, Franz
Merry Widow, The, 15, 120

Leigh, Carolyn
Little Me, 200
Peter Pan, 163, 254

Leigh, Mitch
Man of La Mancha, 215, 329

Lennon, John
Rain—A Tribute to the Beatles on Broadway, 379

Lerner, Alan Jay
Brigadoon, 134
Camelot, 193
Love Life, 138
My Fair Lady, 168
On a Clear Day You Can See Forever, 213
Paint Your Wagon, 152

Lewine, Richard
Make Mine Manhattan, 137

Lindsay-Abaire, David
Shrek: The Musical, 363

Lippa, Andrew
Addams Family, The, 374

Lloyd Webber, Andrew
Aspects of Love, 283
Cats, 263
Evita, 254
Jesus Christ Superstar, 233
Joseph and the Amazing Technicolor
Dreamcoat, 260
Phantom of the Opera, The, 278
Song and Dance, 271
Starlight Express, 276
Sunset Boulevard, 300

Loesser, Frank
Greenwillow, 187
Guys and Dolls, 148 & 290
How to Succeed in Business Without Really
Trying, 196, 302
Most Happy Fella, The, 170 & 293
Where's Charley, 138

Loewe, Frederick
Brigadoon, 134
Camelot, 193
My Fair Lady, 168
Paint Your Wagon, 152

Lopez, Robert
Avenue Q, 330

Lorick, Robert
Tap Dance Kid, The, 268

Lynne, Jeff
Xanadu, 352

M, Lebo
Lion King, The, 310

MacDermot, Galt
Hair, 224, 365
Two Gentlemen of Verona, 234

MacDonough, Glen
Babes in Toyland, 8

Maltby Jr., Richard
Miss Saigon, 285
Song and Dance, 271

Mancina, Mark
Lion King, The, 310

Mancini, Henry
Victor/Victoria, 303

Mark, Zane
Bring In 'Da Noise, Bring In 'Da Funk, 306

Martin, Hugh
Best Foot Forward, 114
High Spirits, 208

Marvin, Mel
Dr. Seuss' How the Grinch Stole Christmas, 348

Marx, Jeff
Avenue Q, 330

Mason, Timothy
Dr. Seuss' How the Grinch Stole Christmas, 348

McCarthy, Joseph
Irene, 32, 238
Rio Rita, 55

McCartney, Paul
Rain—A Tribute to the Beatles on Broadway,
379

McHugh, Jimmy
As the Girls Go, 139
Blackbirds of 1928, 63
Sugar Babies, 255

McLellan, C. M. S.
Pink Lady, The, 18

Menken, Alan
Beauty and the Beast, 297
Little Mermaid, The, 355
Little Shop of Horrors, 262

Mercer, Johnny
Li'l Abner, 171
St. Louis Woman, 129

Merrill, Bob
Carnival, 195
Funny Girl, 207
New Girl in Town, 173
Sugar, 235
Take Me Along, 183

Miller, Robin
Dames at Sea, 226

Miller, Roger
Big River, 270

Miranda, Lin-Manuel
In the Heights, 357

Monnot, Marguerite
Irma la Douce, 190

More, Julian
Irma la Douce, 190

Moross, Jerome
Golden Apple, The, 160

Morrison, Greg
Drowsy Chaperone, The, 342

Morton, Jelly Roll
Jelly's Last Jam, 292

Nash, Ogden
One Touch of Venus, 120

Newley, Anthony
Roar of the Greasepaint—The Smell of the
Crowd, The, 212
Stop the World—I Want To Get Off, 199

Norman, Marsha
The Secret Garden, 286

Norman, Monty
Irma la Douce, 190

O'Keefe, Laurence
Legally Blonde, 351

Pascal, Milton
Follow the Girls, 124

Pitchford, Dean
Footloose, 313

Porter, Cole
Anything Goes, 88, 277
Can-Can, 156
DuBarry Was a Lady, 109
Fifty Million Frenchmen, 69
Gay Divorce, 82
Jubilee, 92
Kiss Me, Kate, 141 & 315
Leave It to Me!, 105
Let's Face It!, 115
Mexican Hayride, 122
New Yorkers, The, 74
Panama Hattie, 111
Red, Hot and Blue!, 96
Silk Stockings, 166

Rado, James
Hair, 224, 365

Ragni, Gerome
Hair, 224, 365

Reynolds, Herbert
Blue Paradise, The, 21

Rice, Edward E.
Evangeline, 4

Rice, Tim
Aida, 316
Beauty and the Beast, 297
Chess, 279
Evita, 254
Jesus Christ Superstar, 233
Joseph and the Amazing Technicolor
Dreamcoat, 260
Lion King, The, 310

Rifkin, Jay
Lion King, The, 310

Robin, Leo
Gentlemen Prefer Blondes, 146
Hit the Deck!, 56

Rodgers, Mary
Once Upon a Mattress, 18

Rodgers, Richard
Allegro, 136
Babes in Arms, 98

Boys from Syracuse, The, 107
By Jupiter, 116
Carousel, 127, 296
Connecticut Yankee, A, 58
Dearest Enemy, 48
Do I Hear a Waltz?, 210
Flower Drum Song, 178, 327
Garrick Gaieties, The, 46
I Married an Angel, 102
I'd Rather Be Right, 98
Jumbo, 93
King and I, The, 151, 248, 303
Me and Juliet, 157
No Strings, 197
Oklahoma!, 119, 255, 325
On Your Toes, 94, 264
Pal Joey, 112, 153
Peggy-Ann, 54
Sound of Music, The, 184
South Pacific, 143, 358
Too Many Girls, 108

Romberg, Sigmund
Blossom Time, 38
Blue Paradise, The, 21
Desert Song, The, 54
Maytime, 24
New Moon, The, 64
Rosalie, 62
Sinbad, 29
Student Prince in Heidelberg, The, 45
Up in Central Park, 126

Rome, Harold
Call Me Mister, 129
Destry Rides Again, 180
Fanny, 164
Pins and Needles, 100
Wish You Were Here, 154

Ross, Adrian
Merry Widow, The, 15, 120

Ross, Jerry
Damn Yankees, 167
Pajama Game, The, 161, 341

Rubens, Paul
Florodora, 6

Russell, Brenda
Color Purple, The, 340

Sager, Carole Bayer
They're Playing Our Song, 252

Samuels, Arthur
Poppy, 40

Santoriello, Jill
Tale of Two Cities, A, 360

Sater, Steven
Spring Awakening, 345

Scanlan, Dick
Thoroughly Modern Millie, 325

Schmidt, Harvey
Fantasticks, The, 189, 343
I Do! I Do!, 220
110 in the Shade, 203, 352

Schönberg, Claude-Michel
Les Misérables, 275, 349
Miss Saigon, 285

Schwartz, Arthur
At Home Abroad, 89
Band Wagon, The, 74
Flying Colors, 80
Inside U.S.A., 137
Little Show, The, 67
Three's a Crowd, 73
Tree Grows in Brooklyn, A, 152

Schwartz, Stephen
Godspell, 233
Magic Show, The, 240
Pippin, 236
Wicked, 332

Shaiman, Marc
Hairspray, 326

Shapiro, Dan
Follow the Girls, 124

Sheik, Duncan
Spring Awakening, 345

Sherman, Richard M.
Mary Poppins, 344

Sherman, Robert B.
Mary Poppins, 344

Simon, Lucy
The Secret Garden, 286

Sissle, Noble
Shuffle Along, 34

Sklar, Matthew
Wedding Singer, The, 346

Slater, Glenn
Little Mermaid, The, 355

Sloane, A. Baldwin
Wizard of Oz, The, 8

Smalls, Charlie
Wiz, The, 241

Smith, Harry B.
Countess Maritza, 53
Fortune Teller, The, 6
Girl from Utah, The, 19
Robin Hood, 5

Composer/Lyricist Index

Smith, Robert B.
Sweethearts, 19, 134

Snow, Tim
Footloose, 313

Sondheim, Stephen
Company, 229, 344
Do I Hear a Waltz?, 210
Follies, 232, 320
Funny Thing Happened on the Way to the Forum, A, 198, 304
Gypsy, 182, 282, 329, 359
Into the Woods, 277, 326
Little Night Music, A, 237 & 373
Pacific Overtures, 245, 333
Passion, 298
Sunday in the Park With George, 269, 356
Sweeney Todd, 253, 338
West Side Story, 175, 364

Stamper, David
Ziegfeld Follies, 38

Stange, Stanislaus
Chocolate Soldier, The, 16

Stewart, Michael
Barnum, 256
I Love My Wife, 245

Stiles, George,
Mary Poppins, 344

Stilgoe, Richard
Phantom of the Opera, The, 278
Starlight Express, 275

Stothart, Herbert
Rose-Marie, 43

Straus, Oscar
Chocolate Soldier, The, 16

Strauss Jr., Johann
Great Waltz, The, 87

Strouse, Charles
Annie, 247
Applause, 228
Bye Bye Birdie, 188
Golden Boy, 210

Stuart, Leslie
Florodora, 6

Styne, Jule
Bells Are Ringing, 171
Do Re Mi, 194
Funny Girl, 207
Gentlemen Prefer Blondes, 146
Gypsy, 182, 282, 329, 359
High Button Shoes, 136, 163
Peter Pan, 254
Sugar, 235

Sullivan, Arthur
Pirates of Penzance, The, 258

Swift, Kay
Fine and Dandy, 72

Taymor, Julie
Lion King, The, 310

Tesori, Jeanine
Shrek: The Musical, 363
Thoroughly Modern Millie, 325

Tierney, Harry
Irene, 32, 238
Rio Rita, 55

Tietjens, Paul
Wizard of Oz, The, 8

Tobias, Charles
Hellzapoppin, 103

Townshend, Pete
Tommy, 294

Udell, Peter
Purlie, 228
Shenandoah, 242

Waller, Fats
Ain't Misbehavin', 251

Ulvaeus, Bjorn
Chess, 279
Mamma Mia!, 323

Warren, Harry
42nd Street, 257, 322

Waters, Darryl
Bring In 'Da Noise, Bring In 'Da Funk, 306

Weill, Kurt
Knickerbocker Holiday, 104
Lady in the Dark, 113
Lost in the Stars, 144
Love Life, 138
One Touch of Venus, 120
Street Scene, 132
Threepenny Opera, The, 159

Whiting, Richard A.
Take a Chance, 82

Wilbur, Richard
Candide, 172, 239

Wildhorn, Frank
Jekyll and Hyde, 308
Scarlet Pimpernel, The, 309
Victor/Victoria, 303

Willis, Allee,
Color Purple, The, 340

Willson, Meredith
Music Man, The, 177, 319
Unsinkable Molly Brown, The, 191

Wilson, Sandy
Boy Friend, The, 162

Wise, Jim
Dames at Sea, 226

Wittman, Scott
Hairspray, 326

Wodehouse, P. G.
Leave It to Jane, 26
Oh, Boy!, 24
Oh, Lady! Lady!!, 26
Rosalie, 62

Woldin, Judd
Raisin, 239

Wolfe, George C.
Bring In 'Da Noise, Bring In 'Da Funk, 306

Wright, Robert
Grand Hotel, 281
Kismet, 158
Song of Norway, 124

Yazbeck, David
Dirty Rotten Scoundrels, 334
Full Monty, The, 319

Yeston, Maury
Nine, 262, 329
Grand Hotel, 281
Titanic, 307

Yorkey, Brian
Next to Normal, 368

Youmans, Vincent
Hit the Deck!, 56
No, No, Nanette, 47, 231
Take a Chance, 82

Young, Rida Johnson
Maytime, 24
Naughty Marietta, 17

Zippel, David
City of Angels, 282

Zimmer, Hans
Lion King, The, 310

Librettist Index

Abbott, George
Boys from Syracuse, The, 107
Damn Yankees, 167
Fiorello!, 186
High Button Shoes, 136
New Girl in Town, 173
On Your Toes, 94, 264
Pajama Game, The, 161, 341
Pal Joey, 112, 153
Tree Grows in Brooklyn, A, 152
Where's Charley?, 138

Ackerman, Peter
Pajama Game, The (2006), 341

Ahrens, Lynn
Once on This Island, 284

Allers, Roger
Lion King, The, 310

Anderson, Maxwell
Knickerbocker Holiday, 104
Lost in the Stars, 144

Appell, Don
Milk and Honey, 195

Armstrong, Billie Joe
American Idiot, 377

Ashman, Howard
Little Mermaid, The, 355
Little Shop of Horrors, 262

Atteridge, Harold
Sinbad, 29

Barer, Marshall
Once Upon a Mattress, 181

Barras, Charles M.
Black Crook, The, 3

Barrett, James Lee
Shenandoah, 242

Bart, Lionel
Oliver!, 201

Bartholomae, Philip
Very Good Eddie, 23

Baum, L. Frank
Wizard of Oz, The, 8

Beane, Douglas Carter
Xanadu, 352

Behrman, S. N.
Fanny, 164

Bequelin, Chad
Wedding Singer, The, 346

Besoyan, Rick
Little Mary Sunshine, 186

Bissell, Richard
Damn Yankees, 167
Pajama Game, The, 161, 341

Black, Don
Sunset Boulevard, 300

Blackwell, Charles
Tap Dance Kid, The, 268

Blake, Paul
Irving Berlin's White Christmas, 362

Blitzstein, Marc
Cradle Will Rock, The, 101
Threepenny Opera, The, 159

Blossom, Henry
Mlle. Modiste, 10
Red Mill, The, 13

Bobbie, Walter
Footloose, 313

Bock, Jerry
Apple Tree, The, 218

Bolton, Guy
Anything Goes, 88
Follow the Girls, 124
Girl Crazy, 72
Lady, Be Good!, 44
Leave It to Jane, 26
Oh, Boy!, 24
Oh, Kay!, 53
Oh, Lady! Lady!!, 26
Rio Rita, 55
Rosalie, 62
Sally, 33
Tip-Toes, 52
Very Good Eddie, 23

Bond, Christopher
Sweeney Todd (2005), 338

Bontemps, Arna
St. Louis Woman, 129

Bramble, Mark
Barnum, 256
42nd Street, 257, 322

Brickman, Marshall
Jersey Boys, 339
Addams, Family, The, 374

Bricusse, Leslie
Jekyll and Hyde, 308
Roar of the Greasepaint—The Smell of the
Crowd, The, 212
Stop the World—I Want to Get Off, 199

Brooks, Mel
Producers, The, 321
Young Frankenstein, 353

Brown, Lew
Flying High, 71

Brown, William F.
Wiz, The, 241

Burrows, Abe
Can-Can, 156
Guys and Dolls, 148, 290
How to Succeed in Business
Without Really Trying, 196, 302
Silk Stockings, 166

Capote, Truman
House of Flowers, 165

Casey, Warren
Grease, 234, 298, 354

Chodorov, Jerome
Wonderful Town, 155, 332

Cohan, George M.
Forty-five Minutes from Broadway, 13
Little Johnny Jones, 10

Comden, Betty
Applause, 228
Bells Are Ringing, 171
On the Town, 126
On the Twentieth Century, 249

Cook, Joe
Fine and Dandy, 72

Coopersmith, Jerome
Apple Tree, The, 218

Coward, Noel
Bitter Sweet, 68

Cross, Beverly
Half a Sixpence, 211

Crouse, Russel
Anything Goes, 88
Call Me Madam, 147
Hooray for What!, 100
Red, Hot and Blue!, 96
Sound of Music, The, 184

Crouse, Timothy
Anything Goes, 277

Cryer, Gretchen
I'm Getting My Act Together and Taking It on
the Road, 252

Cullen, Countee
St. Louis Woman, 129

Dante, Nicholas
Chorus Line, A, 243, 343

D'Arienzo, Chris
Rock of Ages, 366

Davis, Eddie
Follow the Girls, 124

Davis, Luther
Grand Hotel, 281
Kismet, 158

Davis, Ossie
Purlie, 228

De Gresac, Fred
Sweethearts, 19

DeSylva, B. G.
DuBarry Was a Lady, 109
Flying High, 71
Follow Thru, 67
Good News!, 56
Hold Everything!, 65
Louisiana Purchase, 110
Panama Hattie, 111
Take a Chance, 82

Dietz, Howard
Poppy, 40

DiPietro, Joe
Memphis, 369

Donnelly, Dorothy
Blossom Time, 38
Poppy 40
Student Prince in Heidelberg, The, 45

Driver, Donald
Your Own Thing, 222

Ebb, Fred
Chicago, 244, 307

Edwards, Blake
Victor/Victoria, 303

Elice, Rick
Jersey Boys, 339
Addams Family, The, 374

Escott, Colin
Million Dollar Quartet, 375

Eyen, Tom
Dreamgirls, 261

Falls, Robert
Aida, 316

Feldman, Rebecca
25th Annual Putnam County Spelling Bee, The,
337

Fellowes, Julian
Mary Poppins, 344

Fields, Dorothy
Annie Get Your Gun, 130, 315
Let's Face It!, 115
Mexican Hayride, 122
Redhead, 179
Up in Central Park, 126

Fields, Herbert
Annie Get Your Gun, 130, 315
Connecticut Yankee, A, 58
Dearest Enemy, 48
DuBarry Was a Lady, 109
Fifty Million Frenchmen, 69
Hit the Deck!, 56
Let's Face It!, 115
Mexican Hayride, 122
New Yorkers, The, 74
Panama Hattie, 111
Peggy-Ann, 54
Redhead, 179
Up in Central Park, 126

Fields, Joseph
Flower Drum Song, 178
Wonderful Town, 155, 332

Fields, W. C.
Poppy, 40

Fierstein, Harvey
La Cage aux Folles, 266, 333, 376

Finn, William
Falsettos, 293

Flaherty, Stephen
Once on This Island, 284

Fosse, Bob
Chicago, 244, 307
Pippin, 236

Frank, Melvin
Li'l Abner, 171

Fratti, Mario
Nine, 262 , 329

Fry, Stephen
Me and My Girl, 273

Fuller, Dean
Once Upon a Mattress, 181

Furber, Douglas
Me and My Girl, 273

Furth, George
Company, 229, 344

Gaines, Reg E.
Bring In 'Da Noise, Bring In 'Da Funk, 306

Gelbart, Larry
City of Angels, 282
Funny Thing Happened on the
Way to the Forum, A, 198, 304

Gershe, Leonard
Destry Rides Again, 180

Gesner, Clark
You're a Good Man, Charlie Brown, 221

Gibson, William
Golden Boy, 210

Gilbert, William S.
Pirates of Penzance, The, 258

Gilbert, Willie
How to Succeed in Business Without
Really Trying, 302

Glickman, Will
Plain and Fancy, 166

Goldman, James
Follies, 232, 320

Goodwin, J. Cheever
Evangeline, 4

Gray, Timothy
High Spirits, 208

Green, Adolph
Applause, 228
Bells Are Ringing, 171
On the Town, 126
On the Twentieth Century, 249

Guare, John
Two Gentlemen of Verona, 234

Hach, Heather
Legally Blonde, 351

Haimsohn, George
Dames at Sea, 226

Hall, Lee
Billy Elliot: The Musical, 361

Hall, Owen
Florodora, 6

Hammerstein II, Oscar
Allegro, 136
Carmen Jones, 122
Carousel, 127, 296
Desert Song, The, 54
Flower Drum Song, 178, 327

King and I, The, 151, 248, 303
Me and Juliet, 157
Music in the Air, 81
New Moon, The, 64
Oklahoma!, 119, 255, 325
Rose-Marie, 43
Show Boat, 60, 128, 299
South Pacific, 143, 358
Sunny, 50
Sweet Adeline, 68

Hampton, Christopher
Sunset Boulevard, 300

Harbach, Otto
Cat and the Fiddle, The, 77
Desert Song, The, 54
Firefly, The, 18
Madame Sherry, 17
No, No, Nanette, 47
Roberta, 84
Rose-Marie, 43
Sunny, 50

Harburg, E. Y.
Finian's Rainbow, 133, 370
Jamaica, 176

Harnick, Sheldon
Apple Tree, The, 218

Harrigan, Edward
Mulligan Guard Ball, The, 4

Hart, Lorenz
Babes in Arms, 98
By Jupiter, 116
I Married an Angel, 102
On Your Toes, 94, 264

Hart, Moss
Face the Music, 79
Great Waltz, The, 87
I'd Rather Be Right, 98
Jubilee, 92
Lady in the Dark, 113

Hauptman, William
Big River, 270

Hecht, Ben
Jumbo, 93

Hellman, Lillian
Candide, 172

Heneker, David
Irma la Douce, 190

Herlihy, Tim
Wedding Singer, The, 346

Herzig, Sig
Bloomer Girl, 125

Heyward, DuBose
Porgy and Bess, 91, 156

Hirson, Roger O.
Pippin, 236

Holm, John Cecil
Best Foot Forward, 114
Sweethearts, 134

Holmes, Rupert
Curtains, 350
Mystery of Edwin Drood, The, 271

Holzman, Winnie
Wicked, 332

Hood, Basil
Merry Widow, The, 15

Hooker, Brian
Vagabond King, The, 48

Hoyt, Charles H.
Trip to Chinatown, A, 5

Hudes, Quiara Alegria
In the Heights, 357

Hwang, David Henry
Aida, 316
Flower Drum Song, 327
Tarzan, 347

Idle, Eric
Monty Python's Spamalot, 336

Ives, David
Irving Berlin's White Christmas, 362

Jacobs, Jim
Grease, 234, 298, 354

Janney, Russell
Vagabond King, The, 48

Johnson, Catherine
Mamma Mia!, 324

Jones, Bill T.
Fela!, 372

Jones, Tom
Fantasticks, The, 189, 343

Kanin, Garson
Do Re Mi, 194

Kaufman, George S.
Cocoanuts, The, 51
I'd Rather Be Right, 98
Of Thee I Sing, 78
Silk Stockings, 166

King, Larry L.
Best Little Whorehouse in Texas, The, 250

Kirkwood, James
Chorus Line, A, 243, 343

Knighton, Nan
Scarlet Pimpernel, The, 309

Kober, Arthur
Wish You Were Here, 154

Kopit, Arthur
Nine, 262, 329

Kotis, Greg
Urinetown, 323

Lacey, Franklin
Music Man, The, (2000), 319

Lane, Jeffrey
Dirty Rotten Scoundrels, 334

Lapine, James
Falsettos, 293
Into the Woods, 277, 326
Passion, 298
Sunday in the Park With George, 269, 356

Larson, Jonathan
Rent, 305

Latouche, John
Golden Apple, The, 160

Laurents, Arthur
Do I Hear a Waltz?, 210
Gypsy, 182, 329, 359
West Side Story, 175

Lawrence, Jerome
Mame, 217

Lazarus, Milton
Song of Norway, 124

Lederer, Charles
Kismet, 158

Lee, Robert E.
Mame, 217

Lennart, Isobel
Funny Girl, 207

Lerner, Alan Jay
Brigadoon, 134
Camelot, 193
Love Life, 138
My Fair Lady, 168
On a Clear Day You Can See Forever, 213
Paint Your Wagon, 152

Lewis, Jim
Fela!, 372

Lindsay, Howard
Anything Goes, 88
Call Me Madam, 147

Hooray for What!, 100
Red, Hot and Blue!, 96
Sound of Music, The, 184

Lindsay-Abaire, David
Shrek: The Musical, 363

Lloyd Webber, Andrew
Aspects of Love, 283
Phantom of the Opera, The, 278

Loesser, Frank
Greenwillow, 187
Most Happy Fella, The, 170, 293

Logan, Joshua
Fanny, 164
South Pacific, 143, 358
Wish You Were Here, 154

Longstreet, Stephen
High Button Shoes, 136

Loos, Anita
Gentlemen Prefer Blondes, 146

Lucas, Craig
Light in the Piazza, The, 338

Ludwig, Ken
Crazy for You, 288

Lyles, Aubrey
Shuffle Along, 34

MacArthur, Charles
Jumbo, 93

MacDonough, Glen
Babes in Toyland, 8

Mandel, Frank
Desert Song, The, 54
New Moon, The, 64
No, No, Nanette, 47

Marion Jr., George
Too Many Girls, 108

Martin, Bob
Drowsy Chaperone, The, 342

Martin, Hugh
High Spirits, 208

Mason, Timothy
Dr. Seuss' How the Grinch Stole Christmas, 348

Masteroff, Joe
Cabaret, 219 & 312
She Loves Me, 202, 296

Masterson, Peter
Best Little Whorehouse in Texas, The, 250

Mayer, Michael
American Idiot, 377

McAnuff, Des
Tommy 294

McGowan, John
Flying High, 71
Girl Crazy, 72
Hold Everything!, 65

McGrath, Leueen
Silk Stockings, 166

McGuire, William Anthony
Rosalie, 62
Three Musketeers, The, 63
Whoopee, 66

McKellar, Don
Drowsy Chaperone, The, 342

McLellan, C. M. S.
Pink Lady, The, 18

McNally, Terrence
Full Monty, The, 319
Kiss of the Spider Woman—The Musical, 295
Ragtime, 311, 371

Mecchi, Irene,
Lion King, The, 310

Meehan, Thomas
Annie, 247
Hairspray, 326
Producers, The, 321
Young Frankenstein, 353

Meyer, Timothy S.
My One and Only, 264

Miller, Flournoy
Shuffle Along, 34

Miller, Robin
Dames at Sea, 226

Montgomery, James
Irene, 32

More, Julian
Irma la Douce, 190

Morris, Richard
Thoroughly Modern Millie, 325
Unsinkable Molly Brown, The, 191

Mutrux, Floyd
Million Dollar Quartet, 375

Nash, N. Richard
Happy Time, The, 222
110 in the Shade, 203, 352

Nash, Ogden
One Touch of Venus, 120

Nelson, Richard
Chess, 279

Nemiroff, Robert
Raisin, 239

Newley, Anthony
Roar of the Greasepaint—The Smell of the
Crowd, The, 212
Stop the World—I Want to Get Off, 199

Norman, Marsha
Color Purple, The, 340
Secret Garden, The, 286

Norman, Monty
Irma la Douce, 190

O'Hara, John
Pal Joey, 112, 153

Odets, Clifford
Golden Boy, 210

O'Donnell, Mark
Hairspray, 326
Young Frankenstein, 349

Panama, Norman
Li'l Abner, 171

Pascal, Fran
George M!, 223

Pascal, John
George M!, 223

Perelman, S. J.
One Touch of Venus, 120

Peters, Clark
Five Guys Named Moe, 289

Pitchford, Dean
Footloose, 313

Post, W. H.
Vagabond King, The, 48

Rado, James
Hair, 224, 365

Ragni, Gerome
Hair, 224, 365

Randall, Bob
Magic Show, The, 240

Reiss, Jay
25th Annual Putnam County Spelling Bee, The,
337

Rice, Elmer
Street Scene, 132

Rigby, Harry
Irene, 238

Roberts, Ben
Merry Widow, The, 120

Rodgers, Richard
Babes in Arms, 98
By Jupiter, 116
I Married an Angel, 102
On Your Toes, 94, 264

Roos, William
As the Girls Go, 139

Root, Lynn
Cabin in the Sky, 111

Rose, L. Arthur
Me and My Girl, 273

Rose, Philip
Purlie, 228
Shenandoah, 242

Russell, Robert
Take Me Along, 183

Ryskind, Morrie
Cocoanuts, The, 51
Louisiana Purchase, 110
Of Thee I Sing, 78
Strike Up the Band, 70

Saidy, Fred
Bloomer Girl, 125
Finian's Rainbow, 133, 370
Jamaica, 176

Samuels, Lesser
Greenwillow, 187

Santoriello, Jill
Tale of Two Cities, A, 360

Sater, Steven
Spring Awakening, 345

Scanlan, Dick
Thoroughly Modern Millie, 325

Schulberg, Budd
What Makes Sammy Run?, 206

Schulberg, Stuart
What Makes Sammy Run?, 206

Schwab, Laurence
Follow Thru, 67
Good News!, 56
New Moon, The, 64
Take a Chance, 82

Shapiro, Mel
Two Gentlemen of Verona, 234

Shaw, David
Redhead, 179

Sheinkin, Rachel
25th Annual Putnam County Spelling Bee,
The, 337

Sheldon, Sidney
Merry Widow, The, 120
Redhead, 179

Sherwood, Robert E.
Miss Liberty, 144

Shevelove, Burt
Funny Thing Happened on the
Way to the Forum, A, 198, 304
No, No, Nanette, 231

Silvers, Sid
Take a Chance, 82

Silvers, Phil
High Button Shoes, 136

Simon, Neil
Little Me, 200
Promises, Promises, 226, 378
Sweet Charity, 216, 272
They're Playing Our Song, 252

Slater, Glenn
Little Mermaid, The, 355

Smith, Betty
Tree Grows in Brooklyn, A, 152

Smith, Edgar
Blue Paradise, The, 21

Smith, Harry B.
Countess Maritza, 53
Fortune Teller, The, 6
Girl from Utah, The, 19
Robin Hood, 5
Sweethearts, 19
Watch Your Step, 20

Smith, Paul Gerard
Funny Face, 59

Spewack, Bella
Kiss Me, Kate, 141, 315
Leave It to Me!, 105

Spewack, Samuel
Kiss Me, Kate, 141, 315
Leave It to Me!, 105

Stange, Stanislaus
Chocolate Soldier, The, 16

Stein, Joseph
Fiddler on the Roof, 209, 333
Gentlemen Prefer Blondes, 146
Irene, 238
Jamaica, 176
Plain and Fancy, 166
Raisin, 239
Take Me Along, 183
Zorba, 225, 268

Stewart, Donald Ogden
Fine and Dandy, 72

Stewart, Michael
Bye Bye Birdie, 188
Carnival, 195
42nd Street, 257, 322
George M!, 223
Hello, Dolly!, 204
I Love My Wife, 245

Stilgoe, Richard
Phantom of the Opera, The, 278

Stone, Peter
Annie Get Your Gun, 315
Curtains, 350
My One and Only, 264
1776, 227
Sugar, 235
Titanic, 307
Will Rogers Follies, The, 287
Woman of the Year, 260

Swerling, Jo
Guys and Dolls, 290

Tanner, James T.
Girl from Utah, The, 19

Taylor, Dwight
Gay Divorce, 82

Taylor, Samuel
No Strings, 197

Tebelak, John-Michael
Godspell, 233

Thompson, Fred
Follow the Girls, 124
Funny Face, 59
Lady, Be Good!, 44
Rio Rita, 55
Tip-Toes, 52

Thompson, Jay
Once Upon a Mattress, 181

Townshend, Peter
Tommy, 294

Udell, Peter
Purlie, 228
Shenandoah, 242

Wallop, Douglass
Damn Yankees, 167

Wasserman, Dale
Man of La Mancha, 215, 329

Weidman, Jerome
Fiorello!, 186

Weidman, John
Anything Goes, 277
Contact, 318
Pacific Overtures, 245, 333

Weinstock, Jack
How to Succeed in Business Without
Really Trying, 302

Wheeler, Hugh
Candide, 239
Irene, 238
Little Night Music, A, 237, 373
Pacific Overtures (2004), 333
Sweeney Todd, 253, 338

Whitty, Jeff
Avenue Q, 330

Willson, Meredith
Music Man, The, 177, 319

Wilson, Sandy
Boy Friend, The, 162

Wodehouse, P. G.
Anything Goes, 88
Leave It to Jane, 26
Oh, Boy!, 24
Oh, Kay!, 53
Oh, Lady! Lady!!, 26

Wolfe, George C.
Jelly's Last Jam, 292

Wolverton, Linda
Aida, 316
Beauty and the Beast, 297

Yellen, Sherman
Rothschilds, The, 230

Yorkey, Brian
Next to Normal, 368

Young, Rida Johnson
Maytime, 24
Naughty Marietta, 17

Zaltzberg, Charlotte
Raisin, 239

Director Index

Abbott, George
Best Foot Forward, 114
Boys from Syracuse, The, 107
Call Me Madam, 147
Damn Yankees, 167
Fiorello!, 186
Funny Thing Happened on the Way to the
  Forum, A, 198
High Button Shoes, 136
Jumbo, 93
Me and Juliet, 157
New Girl in Town, 173
On the Town, 126
On Your Toes, 94, 264
Once Upon a Mattress, 181
Pajama Game, The, 161
Pal Joey, 112
Too Many Girls, 108
Tree Grows in Brooklyn, A, 152
Where's Charley?, 138
Wonderful Town, 155

Alexander, David
Pal Joey, 153

Alton, Robert
Pal Joey, 153

Anderson, John Murray
Dearest Enemy, 48
Greenwich Village Follies, 31
Jumbo, 93
Life Begins at 8:40, 87
New Faces of 1952, 154
Ziegfeld Follies, 85, 93

Anthony, Joseph
Most Happy Fella, The, 170
110 in the Shade, 203

Ashford, Rob
Promises, Promises, 378

Ashley, Christopher
Memphis, 369
Xanadu, 352

Ashman, Howard
Little Shop of Horrors, 262

Augins, Charles
Five Guys Named Moe, 289

August, Matt
Dr. Seuss' How the Grinch Stole Christmas, 348

Avian, Bob
Chorus Line, A, 343

Baker, Word
Fantasticks, The, 189
I'm Getting My Act Together and
  Taking It on the Road, 252

Balanchine, George
Cabin in the Sky, 111

Bay, Howard
As the Girls Go, 139

Beal, John
New Faces of 1952, 154

Bennett, Michael
Chorus Line, A, 243
Dreamgirls, 261
Follies, 232
My One and Only, 264

Benrimo, J. H.
Blue Paradise, The, 21

Besoyan, Rick
Little Mary Sunshine, 186

Blakemore, Michael
City of Angels, 282
Kiss Me, Kate, 315

Bobbie, Walter
Chicago, 307
Footloose, 313
Irving Berlin's White Christmas, 362

Boleslawsky, Richard
Three Musketeers, The, 63

Bramble, Mark
42nd Street, 322

Breen, Robert
Porgy and Bess, 156

Brentano, Felix
Merry Widow, The, 120

Brook, Peter
House of Flowers, 165
Irma la Douce, 190

Brooks, Walter
Shuffle Along, 34

Buntrock, Sam
Sunday in the Park With George, 356

Burnside, R. H.
Watch Your Step, 20

Burrows, Abe
Can-Can, 156
How to Succeed in Business Without Really
Trying, 196
What Makes Sammy Run?, 206

Cacoyannis, Michael
Zorba, 268

Caird, John
Les Misérables, 275, 349

Calhoun, Jeff
Grease, 293

Capalbo, Carmen
Threepenny Opera, The, 159

Carlyle, Warren
Finian's Rainbow, 370
Tale of Two Cities, A, 360

Carroll, Earl
Earl Carroll Vanities, 76

Carroll, Vinnette
Don't Bother Me, I Can't Cope, 235

Champion, Gower
Bye Bye Birdie, 188
Carnival, 195
42nd Street, 257
Happy Time, The, 222
Hello, Dolly!, 204
High Spirits, 208
I Do! I Do!, 220
Irene, 238
Lend an Ear, 139
Sugar, 235

Charlot, Andre
Andre Charlot's Revue of 1924, 42

Charnin, Martin
Annie, 247

Coe, Peter
Oliver!, 201

Cohan, George M.
Forty-five Minutes from Broadway, 13
Little Johnny Jones, 10

Coini, Jacques
Naughty Marietta, 17

Collier, William
Music Box Revue, 37

Colvan, Zeke
Show Boat, 60

Connolly, Bobby
Ziegfeld Follies, 85

Coward, Noel
Bitter Sweet, 68
High Spirits, 208

Crouch, Julian
Addams Family, The, 374

Crowley, Bob
Tarzan, 347

Da Costa, Morton
Music Man, The, 177
Plain and Fancy, 166

Daldry, Stephen
Billy Elliot: The Musical, 361

Dale, Grover
Magic Show, The, 240

Daniele, Graciela
Annie Get Your Gun, 315
Once on This Island, 284

Delmar, Harry
Follow the Girls, 124

de Mille, Agnes
Allegro, 136

Dexter, John
Do I Hear a Waltz?, 210

Dickey, Paul
Rose-Marie, 43

Dietz, Howard
Flying Colors, 80

Dixon, Harry
Robin Hood, 5

Dodge, Marcia Milgrom
Ragtime, 371

Donehue, Vincent J.
Sound of Music, The, 184

Donnelly, Dorothy
Poppy, 40

Dowling, Edward Duryea
Hellzapoppin, 103

Doyle, John
Company, 344
Sweeney Todd, 338

Driver, Donald
Your Own Thing, 222

Eagle, Oscar
Cocoanuts, The, 51

Edouin, Willie
Florodora, 6

Director Index

Edwardes, Felix
Lady, Be Good!, 44

Edwards, Blake
Victor/Victoria, 303

Ellis, Scott
Curtains, 350
She Loves Me, 296

Errol, Leon
Ziegfeld Follies, 20

Eyre, Richard
Mary Poppins, 344

Falls, Robert,
Aida, 316

Feuer, Cy
Boy Friend, The, 162
Little Me, 200
Silk Stockings, 166

Field, Ron
Applause, 228

Figman, Max
Vagabond King, The, 48

Flatt, Ernest
Sugar Babies, 255

Ford, Harry
Dearest Enemy, 48

Fosse, Bob
Chicago, 244
Dancin', 250
Little Me, 200
Pippin, 236
Redhead, 179
Sweet Charity, 216, 272

Frazee, H. H.
No, No, Nanette, 47

Freeman, Charles K.
Song of Norway, 124

Friedman, Charles
Carmen Jones, 122
Pins and Needles, 100
Street Scene, 132

Galati, Frank
Ragtime, 311

Gerson, Hal
Lend an Ear, 139

Gilbert, Bill
Red Mill, The, 128

Glenville, Peter
Take Me Along, 183

Gordon, Robert H.
Call Me Mister, 129
Inside U.S.A., 137

Green, Morris
Fine and Dandy, 72

Greif, Michael
Next to Normal, 368
Rent, 305

Gresham, Herbert
Follies of 1907, 14
Pink Lady, The, 18

Griffin, Gary
Color Purple, The, 340

Guthrie, Tyrone
Candide, 172

Gutierrez, Gerald
Most Happy Fella, The, 293

Hammerstein II, Oscar
Allegro, 136
Music in the Air, 81
Show Boat, 60, 128

Hammerstein, Reginald
Sweet Adeline, 68

Hammerstein, William
Oklahoma!, 255

Hanggi, Kristin
Rock of Ages, 366

Harburg, E. Y.
Bloomer Girl, 125

Hardy, Joseph
You're a Good Man, Charlie Brown, 221

Harrigan, Edward
Mulligan Guard Ball, The, 4

Harrison, Ray
Little Mary Sunshine, 186

Hart, Moss
Camelot, 193
Lady in the Dark, 113
Miss Liberty, 144
My Fair Lady, 168

Harwood, John
Oh, Kay!, 53
Rio Rita, 55
Tip-Toes, 52

Hill, George Roy
Greenwillow, 187

Holder, Geoffrey
Wiz, The, 241

Hope, Vida
Boy Friend, The, 162

Hopper, Lewis
Florodora, 6

Hoyt, Charles H.
Trip to Chinatown, A, 5

Huffman, J. C.
Blossom Time, 38
Countess Maritza, 53
Sinbad, 29
Student Prince in Heidelberg, The, 45

Hunt, Peter
Scarlet Pimpernel, The, 309
1776, 227

Hurley, Arthur
Desert Song, The, 54

Hytner, Nicholas
Carousel, 296
Miss Saigon, 285

Iscove, Rob
Peter Pan, 254

Johnson, Terry
La Cage aux Folles, 376

Jones, Bill T.
Fela!, 372

Jones, Richard
Titanic, 307

Jones, Tom
Fantasticks, The, 343

Kail, Thomas
In the Heights, 357

Kanin, Garson
Do Re Mi, 194
Funny Girl, 207

Kaufman, George S.
Face the Music, 79
Guys and Dolls, 148
I'd Rather Be Right, 98
Of Thee I Sing, 78

Kazan, Elia
Love Life, 138
One Touch of Venus, 120

Kelly, Gene
Flower Drum Song, 178

Kennedy, John
Mexican Hayride, 122
Sweethearts, 134
Up in Central Park, 126

Kent, Jonathan
Man of La Mancha, 329

Kenyon, Neal
Dames at Sea, 226

Kern, Jerome
Music in the Air, 81

Kidd, Michael
Destry Rides Again, 180
Li'l Abner, 171
Rothschilds, The, 230

Lapine, James
Falsettos, 293
Into the Woods, 277, 326
Passion, 298
Sunday in the Park With George, 269
25th Annual Putnam County Spelling Bee, The,
337

Latham, Fred
Firefly, The, 18
Mlle. Modiste, 10
Red Mill, The, 13
Sweethearts, 19

Laurents, Arthur
Gypsy, 282, 359
La Cage aux Folles, 266
West Side Story, 364

Layton, Joe
Barnum, 256
George M!, 223
No Strings, 197

Leach, Wilford
Mystery of Edwin Drood, The, 271
Pirates of Penzance, The, 258

Lederer, George
Madame Sherry, 17

Leftwich, Alexander
Connecticut Yankee, A, 58
Girl Crazy, 72
Hit the Deck!, 56
Little Show, The, 67
Strike Up the Band, 70

Lerner, Alan Jay
Camelot, 193

Leslie, Lew
Blackbirds of 1928, 63

Lester, Edwin
Song of Norway, 124

Leveaux, David
Fiddler on the Roof, 333
Nine, 329

Lewis, Albert
Cabin in the Sky, 111

Lewis, Robert
Brigadoon, 134
Jamaica, 176
On a Clear Day You Can See Forever, 213

Liebman, Max
Make Mine Manhattan, 137

Lilley, Edward Clark
Flying High, 71
Show Is On, The, 97
Ziegfeld Follies, 85, 93

Lindsay, Howard
Anything Goes, 88
Gay Divorce, 82
Hooray for What!, 100
Red, Hot and Blue!, 96

Lloyd, Norman
Golden Apple, The, 160

Lloyd, Phyllida
Mamma Mia!, 324

Loeb, Philip
Garrick Gaieties, The, 46
Life Begins at 8:40, 87

Logan, Joshua
Annie Get Your Gun, 130
By Jupiter, 116
Fanny, 164
I Married an Angel, 102
Knickerbocker Holiday, 104
South Pacific, 143
This Is the Army, 117
Wish You Were Here, 154

Longbottom, Robert
Flower Drum Song, 327

Lynne, Gillian
Cats, 263

MacGregor, Edgar
DuBarry Was a Lady, 109
Follow Thru, 67
Funny Face, 59
Good News!, 56
Let's Face It!, 115
Louisiana Purchase, 110
New Moon, The, 64
Panama Hattie, 111
Take a Chance, 82

Malone, J. A. E.
Girl from Utah, The, 19

Maltby Jr., Richard
Ain't Misbehavin', 251
Fosse, 314
Song and Dance, 271

Mamoulian, Rouben
Carousel, 127
Lost in the Stars, 144
Oklahoma!, 119
Porgy and Bess, 91
St. Louis Woman, 129

Mann, Daniel
Paint Your Wagon, 152

Mantello, Joe
Wicked, 332

Marion, George
Merry Widow, The, 15
Ziegfeld Follies, 34

Marre, Albert
Kismet, 158
Man of La Mancha, 215
Milk and Honey, 195

Marshall, Kathleen
Grease, 354
Pajama Game, The, 341
Wonderful Town, 332

Masterson, Peter
Best Little Whorehouse in Texas, The, 250

Matalon, Vivian
Tap Dance Kid, The, 268

Mayer, Michael
American Idiot, 377
Spring Awakening, 345
Thoroughly Modern Millie, 325

McAnuff, Des
Big River, 270
How to Succeed in Business Without
Really Trying, 302
Jersey Boys, 339
Tommy, 294

McCoy, Frank
Fine and Dandy, 72

McDermott, Phelim
Addams Family, The, 374

McGuire, William Anthony
Rosalie, 62
Three Musketeers, The, 63
Whoopee, 66

McKayle, Donald
Raisin, 239

Mendes, Sam
Cabaret, 312
Gypsy, 329

Miyamoto, Amon
Pacific Overtures, 333

Milton, Robert
Oh, Boy!, 24
Oh, Lady! Lady!!, 26
Peggy-Ann, 54

Miner, Worthington
On Your Toes, 94

Minnelli, Vincente
At Home Abroad, 89
Hooray for What!, 100
Show Is On, The, 97

Mitchell, Jerry
Legally Blonde, 351

Mitchell, Julian
Babes in Toyland, 8
Fortune Teller, The, 6
Trip to Chinatown, A, 5
Wizard of Oz, The, 8
Ziegfeld Follies, 20

Mitchell, Thomas
At Home Abroad, 89

Moore, Jason
Avenue Q, 330
Shrek: The Musical, 363

Moore, Robert
Promises, Promises, 226
They're Playing Our Song, 252
Woman of the Year, 260

Moore, Tom
Grease, 234

Moses, Gilbert
Wiz, The, 241

Newley, Anthony
Roar of the Greasepaint—The Smell of the
Crowd, The, 212
Stop the World—I Want to Get Off, 199

Nicholaw, Casey
Drowsy Chaperone, The, 342

Nichols, Mike
Apple Tree, The, 218
Monty Python's Spamalot, 336
My One and Only, 264

Nunn, Trevor
Aspects of Love, 283
Cats, 263
Chess, 279
Les Misérables, 275, 349
Little Night Music, A, 373
Oklahoma!, 325
Starlight Express, 276
Sunset Boulevard, 300

O'Brien, Jack
Dirty Rotten Scoundrels, 334
Full Monty, The, 319
Hairspray, 326

Ockrent, Mike
Crazy for You, 288
Me and My Girl, 273

O'Horgan, Tom
Hair, 224
Jesus Christ Superstar, 233

Paulus, Diane
Hair, 365

Penn, Arthur
Golden Boy, 210

Phillips, Robin
Jekyll and Hyde, 308

Price, Lonny
110 in the Shade, 352

Prince, Harold
Cabaret, 219
Candide, 239
Company, 229
Evita, 254
Follies, 232
Kiss of the Spider Woman— The Musical, 295
Little Night Music, A, 237
On the Twentieth Century, 249
Pacific Overtures, 245
Phantom of the Opera, The, 278
She Loves Me, 202
Show Boat, 299
Sweeney Todd, 253
Zorba, 225

Rando, John
Urinetown, 323
Wedding Singer, The, 346

Renshaw, Christopher
The King and I, 303

Rice, Edward B.
Evangeline, 4

Robbins, Jerome
Bells Are Ringing, 171
Fiddler on the Roof, 209
Funny Girl, 207
Funny Thing Happened on the Way to the
Forum, A, 198
Gypsy, 182
Jerome Robbins' Broadway, 279
Pajama Game, The, 161
Peter Pan, 163
West Side Story, 175
Wonderful Town, 155

Director Index

Rose, Philip
Purlie, 228
Shenandoah, 242

Roth, Robert Jess
Beauty and the Beast, 297

Royce, Edward
Irene, 32
Leave It to Jane, 26
Oh, Boy!, 24
Oh, Lady! Lady!!, 26
Sally, 33
Ziegfeld Follies, 34

Ruben, José
Cat and the Fiddle, The, 77

Saks, Gene
Half a Sixpence, 211
I Love My Wife, 245
Mame, 217

Schaeffer, Eric
Million Dollar Quartet, 375

Schary, Dore
Unsinkable Molly Brown, The, 191

Schorr, William
Bloomer Girl, 125

Schulman, Susan H.
Secret Garden, The, 286

Shapiro, Mel
Two Gentlemen of Verona, 234

Sher, Bartlett
Light in the Piazza, The, 338
South Pacific, 358

Shevelove, Burt
No, No, Nanette, 231

Short, Hassard
As Thousands Cheer, 83
Band Wagon, The, 74
Carmen Jones, 122
Face the Music, 79
Great Waltz, The, 87
Jubilee, 92
Lady in the Dark, 113
Make Mine Manhattan, 137
Mexican Hayride, 122
Music Box Revue, 37
Roberta, 84
Show Boat, 128
Sunny, 50
Three's a Crowd, 73

Sillman, Leonard
New Faces, 86

Sinclair, Charles
Dearest Enemy, 48

Sinclair, Robert
Babes in Arms, 98

Smuin, Michael
Sophisticated Ladies, 259

Spewack, Samuel
Leave It to Me!, 105

Stange, Stanislaus
Chocolate Soldier, The, 16

Stone, Ezra
This Is the Army, 117

Stroman, Susan
Contact, 318
Music Man, The, 319
Producers, The, 321
Young Frankenstein, 353

Tanner, Tony
Joseph and the Amazing Technicolor
Dreamcoat, 260

Taymor, Julie
Lion King, The, 310

Tebelak, John-Michael
Godspell, 233

Temple, Edward
Maytime, 24

Tharp, Twyla
Movin' Out, 328

Thompson, Fred
Follow the Girls, 124

Tronto, Rudy
Sugar Babies, 255

Tune, Tommy
Best Little Whorehouse in Texas, The, 250
Grand Hotel, 281
My One and Only, 264
Nine, 262
Will Rogers Follies, The, 287

van Druten, John
King and I, The, 151

Vincent, Leon
Black Crook, The, 3

Walsh, Thommie
My One and Only, 264

Warchus, Matthew
Follies, 320

Wayburn, Ned
Ziegfeld Follies, 29, 31, 38

Welles, Orson
Cradle Will Rock, The, 101

Wheatley, William
Black Crook, The, 3

White, George
Flying High, 71
George White's Scandals, 40, 52, 76

Wilson, John C.
Gentlemen Prefer Blondes, 146
Kiss Me, Kate, 141

Wiman, Dwight Deere
Little Show, The, 67

Windust, Bretaigne
Finian's Rainbow, 133

Wolfe, George C.
Bring In 'Da Noise, Bring In 'Da Funk, 306
Jelly's Last Jam, 292

Woolley, Monty
Fifty Million Frenchmen, 6
Jubilee, 92
New Yorkers, The, 74

Zaks, Jerry
Anything Goes, 277
Funny Thing Happened on the Way to the
Forum, A, 304
Guys and Dolls, 290
La Cage aux Folles, 333

Zambello, Francesca
Little Mermaid, The, 355

Choreographer Index

Adolphus, Theodore
Sweethearts, 134

Albertieri, Signor
Firefly, The, 18

Alfred, Julian
Poppy, 40
Vagabond King, The, 48

Alton, Robert
Anything Goes, 88
By Jupiter, 116
DuBarry Was a Lady, 109
Hooray for What!, 100
Leave It to Me!, 105
Life Begins at 8:40, 87
Me and Juliet, 157
Pal Joey, 112, 153
Panama Hattie, 111
Show Is On, The, 97
Too Many Girls, 108
Ziegfeld Follies, 85, 93

Arenal, Julie
Hair, 224

Armitage, Karole
Hair, 365

Ashford, Rob
Curtains, 350
Promises, Promises, 378
Thoroughly Modern Millie, 325
Wedding Singer, The, 346

Astaire, Fred
Sunny, 50

Augins, Charles
Five Guys Named Moe, 289

Avian, Bob
Chorus Line, A, 243
Miss Saigon, 285
Sunset Boulevard, 300

Balanchine, George
Babes in Arms, 98
Boys from Syracuse, The, 107
Cabin in the Sky, 111
I Married an Angel, 102
Louisiana Purchase, 110
Merry Widow, The, 120
On Your Toes, 94, 264
Song of Norway, 124
Where's Charley?, 138
Ziegfeld Follies, 93

Barclift, Nelson
This Is the Army, 117

Barstow, Richard
New Faces of 1952, 154

Bennett, David
Andre Charlot's Revue of 1924, 42
Rose-Marie, 43
Sunny, 50
Very Good Eddie, 23

Bennett, Michael
Chorus Line, A, 243, 343
Company, 229
Dreamgirls, 261
Follies, 232
My One and Only, 264
Promises, Promises, 226

Berkeley, Busby
Connecticut Yankee, A, 58

Birch, Patricia
Candide, 239
Grease, 234
Little Night Music, A, 237
Pacific Overtures, 245
They're Playing Our Song, 252
You're a Good Man, Charlie Brown, 221

Blankenbuehler, Andy
In the Heights, 357

Bourne, Matthew
Mary Poppins, 344

Breaux, Marc
Do Re Mi, 194

Broadbent, Aida
Red Mill, The, 128

Broome, John
Stop the World—I Want to Get Off, 199

Butterell, Jonathan
Fiddler on the Roof, 333
Light in the Piazza, The, 338
Nine, 329

Byrd, Donald
Color Purple, The, 340

Calhoun, Jeff
Annie Get Your Gun, 315
Grease, 298

Carlyle, Warren
Finian's Rainbow, 370
Tale of Two Cities, A, 360

Carrafa, John
Urinetown, 323
Into The Woods, 326

Ceballos, Larry
Fifty Million Frenchmen, 69

Chadman, Christopher
Guys and Dolls, 290

Champion, Gower
Bye Bye Birdie, 188
Carnival, 195
42nd Street, 257, 322
Happy Time, The, 222
Hello, Dolly!, 204
Lend an Ear, 139
Sugar, 235

Charmoli, Tony
Woman of the Year, 260

Cilento, Wayne
Aida, 316
How to Succeed in Business Without Really
  Trying, 302
Tommy, 294
Wicked, 332

Ciulla, A. C.
Footloose, 313

Clarke, Hope
Jelly's Last Jam, 292

Cole, Jack
Funny Thing Happened on the Way to the
  Forum, A, 198
Jamaica, 176
Kismet, 158
Man of La Mancha, 215

Connolly, Bobby
Desert Song, The, 54
Flying High, 71
Follow Thru, 67
Funny Face, 59
Good News!, 56
New Moon, The, 64
Take a Chance, 82
Ziegfeld Follies, 85

Costa, David
Black Crook, The, 3

Cowan, Edie
Little Shop of Horrors, 262

Dale, Grover
Magic Show, The, 240

Daniele, Graciela
Annie Get Your Gun, 315
Mystery of Edwin Drood, The, 271
Once on This Island, 284
Pirates of Penzance, The, 258
Ragtime, 311
Zorba, 268

Daniels, Danny
High Spirits, 208
Little Show, The, 67
Sweet Adeline, 68
Tap Dance Kid, The, 268

Darling, Peter
Billy Elliot: The Musical, 361

Deas, Lawrence
Shuffle Along, 34

DeLuca, John
Dr. Seuss' How the Grinch Stole Christmas, 348

de Mille, Agnes
Allegro, 136
Bloomer Girl, 125
Brigadoon, 134
Carousel, 127
Gentlemen Prefer Blondes, 146
Hooray for What!, 100
Oklahoma!, 119, 255
110 in the Shade, 203
One Touch of Venus, 120
Paint Your Wagon, 152

Denby, Edwin
Knickerbocker Holiday, 104

Devine, Kelly
Rock of Ages, 366

Dodge, Marcia Milgrom
Ragtime, 371

Doyle, John
Company, 344
Sweeney Todd, 338

Erdman, Jean
Two Gentlemen of Verona, 234

Fagan, Garth
Lion King, The, 310

Faison, George
Don't Bother Me, I Can't Cope, 235
Wiz, The, 241

Faria, Arthur
Ain't Misbehavin', 251

Felix, Seymour
Hit the Deck!, 56
Peggy-Ann, 54
Rosalie, 62
Whoopee, 66

Choreographer Index

Field, Ron
Applause, 228
Cabaret, 219
Zorba, 225

Fields, Herbert
Garrick Gaieties, The, 46

Flatt, Ernest
Sugar Babies, 255

Flatt, Kate
Les Misérables, 275, 349

Fokine, Michel
Rosalie, 62
Ziegfeld Follies, 38

Fosse, Bob
Bells Are Ringing, 171
Chicago, 244
Damn Yankees, 167
Dancin', 250
Fosse, 314
How to Succeed in Business Without Really
    Trying, 196
Little Me, 200
New Girl in Town, 173
Pajama Game, The, 161
Pippin, 236
Redhead, 179
Sweet Charity, 216, 272

Foster, Allan K.
Jumbo, 93
Maytime, 24

French, Bert
Music Box Revue, 37

Fuller, Larry
Evita, 254
On the Twentieth Century, 249
Sweeney Todd, 253

Gennaro, Liza
Most Happy Fella, The, 293

Gennaro, Peter
Annie, 247
Fiorello!, 186
Irene, 238
Unsinkable Molly Brown, The, 191
West Side Story, 175

Geva, Tamara
Whoopee, 66

Gillespie, F. M.
Blossom Time, 38

Glover, Savion
Bring In 'Da Noise, Bring In 'Da Funk, 306

Gould, David
Fine and Dandy, 72

Gregory, Gillian
Me and My Girl, 273

Haakon, Paul
Mexican Hayride, 122

Hale, George
Earl Carroll Vanities, 76
Girl Crazy, 72
New Yorkers, The, 74
Of Thee I Sing, 78
Red, Hot and Blue!, 96
Strike Up the Band, 70

Haney, Carol
Flower Drum Song, 178
Funny Girl, 207
She Loves Me, 202

Harrison, Ray
Little Mary Sunshine, 186

Haskell, Jack
Hold Everything!, 65

Heawood, John
Boy Friend, The, 162

Hemmer, Carl
Dearest Enemy, 48

Hines, Gregory
Jelly's Last Jam, 292

Hoggett, Stephen
American Idiot, 377

Holbrook, Al
Chocolate Soldier, The, 16

Holm, Hanya
Camelot, 193
Golden Apple, The, 160
Kiss Me, Kate, 141
My Fair Lady, 168

Hutchinson, Ed
Blue Paradise, The, 21

Iscove, Rob
Peter Pan, 254

Johnson, Louis
Purlie, 228

Jones, Bill T.
Fela!, 372
Spring Awakening, 345

Kelly, Gene
Best Foot Forward, 114

Kenyon, Neal
Dames at Sea, 226

Kidd, Michael
Can-Can, 1 56
Destry Rides Again, 180
Finian's Rainbow, 133
Guys and Dolls, 148
Li'l Abner, 171
Love Life, 138
Rothschilds, The, 230

Knechtges, Dan
110 in the Shade, 352
25th Annual Putnam County Spelling Bee, The, 337
Xanadu, 352

Kosloff, Alexis
Sinbad, 29
Sunny, 50

Krupska, Dania
Most Happy Fella, The, 170

Lambert, Hugh
How to Succeed in Business Without Really Trying, 196

Layton, Joe
Barnum, 256
George M!, 223
Greenwillow, 187
No Strings, 197
Once Upon a Mattress, 181
Sound of Music, The, 184

Lee, Baayork
Chorus Line, A, 343

Lee, Sammy
Cocoanuts, The, 51
Firefly, The, 18
Lady, Be Good!, 44
No, No, Nanette, 47
Oh, Kay!, 53
Rio Rita, 55
Show Boat, 60
Tip-Toes, 52

LeTang, Henry
Sophisticated Ladies, 259

Levy, Ted L.
Jelly's Last Jam, 292

Lichtefeld, Michael
The Secret Garden, 286

Limon, Jose
Roberta, 84

Littlefield, Catherine
Follow the Girls, 124
Sweethearts, 134

Logan, Joshua
Wish You Were Here, 154

Lonergan, John
Roberta, 84

Longbottom, Robert
Flower Drum Song, 327

Loring, Eugene
Carmen Jones, 122
Silk Stockings, 166

Losch, Tilly
Bitter Sweet, 68

Losee, Harry
At Home Abroad, 89
Show Is On, The, 97

Lynne, Gillian
Aspects of Love, 283
Cats, 263
Phantom of the Opera, The, 278
Roar of the Greasepaint—The Smell of the Crowd, The, 212

MacMillan, Sir Kenneth
Carousel, 296

Marshall, Kathleen
Follies, 320
Grease, 354
Kiss Me, Kate, 315
Pajama Game, The, 341
Wonderful Town, 332

Marshall, Rob
Cabaret, 312
Funny Thing Happened on the Way to the Forum, A, 304
She Loves Me, 296
Victor/Victoria, 303

Martins, Peter
On Your Toes, 264
Song and Dance, 271

Mason, Jack
Countess Maritza, 53
Sinbad, 29

Mason, Virginia
Stop the World—I Want to Get Off, 199

Mattox, Matt
What Makes Sammy Run?, 206

McGurn, Ned
I'd Rather Be Right, 98

McKayle, Donald
Golden Boy, 210
Raisin, 239
Sophisticated Ladies, 259

McKneely, Joey
West Side Story, 364

Choreographer Index

Mear, Stephen
Little Mermaid, The, 355

Mitchell, Jerry
Dirty Rotten Scoundrels, 334
Full Monty, The, 319
Gypsy, 329
Hairspray, 326
La Cage aux Folles, 333
Legally Blonde, 351

Mitchell, Julian
Babes in Toyland, 8
Follies of 1907, 14
Pink Lady, The, 18
Sunny, 50
Wizard of Oz, The, 8
Ziegfeld Follies, 20

Miyamoto, Amon
Pacific Overtures, 333

Morgan Jr., Charles
Sweethearts, 19

Newberry, Barbara
Gay Divorce, 82

Nicholaw, Casey
Drowsy Chaperone, The, 342
Monty Python's Spamalot, 336

Nip, Tom
Fine and Dandy, 72

O'Neil, John
Follies of 1907, 14

Page, Lynne
Little Night Music, A, 373

Painter, Walter
City of Angels, 282

Pan, Hermes
As the Girls Go, 139

Paterson, Vincent
Kiss of the Spider Woman—
The Musical, 295

Pelty, Adam
Scarlet Pimpernel, The, 309

Perez, Luis
Man of La Mancha, 329

Peters, Michael
Dreamgirls, 261

Phillips, Arlene
Starlight Express, 276

Pizzi, Joey
Jekyll and Hyde, 308

Prince, Josh
Shrek: The Musical, 363

Randall, Carl
Countess Maritza, 53
Gay Divorce, 82
Knickerbocker Holiday, 104

Rasch, Albertina
Band Wagon, The, 74
Cat and the Fiddle, The, 77
Face the Music, 79
Flying Colors, 80
Great Waltz, The, 87
Jubilee, 92
Lady in the Dark, 113
Rio Rita, 55
Three Musketeers, The, 63
Three's a Crowd, 73

Reinking, Ann
Chicago, 307

Roberson, Ken
Avenue Q, 330

Robbins, Jerome
Bells Are Ringing, 171
Call Me Madam, 147
Fiddler on the Roof, 209, 333
Gypsy, 182, 282, 329, 359
High Button Shoes, 136
Jerome Robbins' Broadway, 279
King and I, The, 151, 248, 303
Miss Liberty, 144
On the Town, 126
Peter Pan, 163
West Side Story, 175, 364
Wish You Were Here, 154

Rose, Sam
Hold Everything!, 65

Ross, Herbert
Apple Tree, The, 218
Do I Hear a Waltz?, 210
House of Flowers, 165
On a Clear Day You Can See Forever, 213
Tree Grows in Brooklyn, A, 152

Royce, Edward
Irene, 32
Leave It to Jane, 26
Oh, Boy!, 24
Oh, Lady! Lady!!, 26
Sally, 33
Ziegfeld Follies, 34

Saddler, Donald
Milk and Honey, 195
No, No, Nanette, 231
On Your Toes, 264
Wonderful Town, 155

Salmon, Scott
La Cage aux Folles, 266

Sandor, Gluck
Earl Carroll Vanities, 76
Pins and Needles, 100

Scheck, Max
Student Prince in Heidelberg, The, 45

Sherman, Lee
Make Mine Manhattan, 137

Sidney, Robert
This Is the Army, 117

Sillman, Leonard
New Faces, 86

Skinner, Randy
42nd Street, 322
Irving Berlin's White Christmas, 362

Smith, Joe
Follies of 1907, 14

Smuin, Michael
Anything Goes, 277
Sophisticated Ladies, 259

Snyder, Gene
At Home Abroad, 89

Sokolow, Anna
Street Scene, 132

Stapleton, Leonora
Tarzan, 347

Stroman, Susan
Contact, 318
Crazy for You, 288
Music Man, The, 319
Oklahoma!, 325
Producers, The, 321
Show Boat, 299
Young Frankenstein, 353

Taylor-Corbett, Lynne
Chess, 279

Tamiris, Helen
Annie Get Your Gun, 130
Fanny, 164
Inside U.S.A., 137
Plain and Fancy, 166
Show Boat, 128
Up in Central Park, 126

Tanner, Tony
Joseph and the Amazing Technicolor
Dreamcoat, 260

Tarasoff, I.
Music Box Revue, 37

Taylor-Corbett, Lynne
Titanic, 307

Tharp, Twyla
Movin' Out, 328

Theodore, Lee
Apple Tree, The, 218

Tiller, John
Sunny, 50

Trujillo, Sergio
Addams Family, The, 374
Jersey Boys, 339
Memphis, 369

Tucker, Robert
Shenandoah, 242

Tune, Tommy
Best Little Whorehouse in Texas, The, 250
Grand Hotel, 281
My One and Only, 264
Nine, 262
Will Rogers Follies, The, 287

Van Laast, Anthony
Mamma Mia!, 324

Walker, Bonnie
Gypsy, 359

Walker, Chet
Fosse, 314

Walsh, Thommie
My One and Only, 264
Nine, 262

Walters, Charles
Let's Face It!, 115
St. Louis Woman, 129

Watson, Janet
Big River, 270
Fantasticks, The, 343

Wayburn, Ned
Ziegfeld Follies, 29, 31, 38

Weidman, Charles
As Thousands Cheer, 83
I'd Rather Be Right, 98
Life Begins at 8:40, 87

West, Matt
Beauty and the Beast, 297

Watson, Janet
Fantasticks, The, 343

White, George
George White's Scandals, 40, 52, 76

White, Onna
Half a Sixpence, 211
I Love My Wife, 245
Irma la Douce, 190

Mame, 217
Music Man, The, 177
1776, 227
Take Me Along, 183

Wood, DeeDee
Do Re Mi, 194

White, George
George White's Scandals, 40, 52, 76

Yearby, Marlies
Rent, 305

Major Cast Members Index

Abarbanell, Lina
Madame Sherry, 17

Abeles, Edward
Oh, Lady! Lady!!, 26

Aberlin, Betty
I'm Getting My Act Together and Taking It on the Road, 252

Ackerman, Loni
George M!, 223
No, No, Nanette, 231

Adair, Yvonne
Gentlemen Prefer Blondes, 146
Lend an Ear, 139

Adam, Noelle
No Strings, 197

Adams, Edie
Li'l Abner, 171
Wonderful Town, 155

Adams, Joe
Jamaica, 176

Adams, Leslie
As Thousands Cheer, 83

Adams, Margaret
Jubilee, 92

Adams, Nick
La Cage aux Folles, 376

Adler, Bruce
Crazy for You, 288
Oklahoma!, 255

Adler, Larry
Flying Colors, 80

Adrian, Max
Candide, 172

Agress, Ted
Shenandoah, 242

Ailey, Alvin
House of Flowers, 165
Jamaica, 176

Akers, Karen
Grand Hotel, 281
Nine, 262

Akram, George
West Side Story, 364

Alberghetti, Anna Maria
Carnival, 195

Albert, Eddie
Boys from Syracuse, The, 107
Miss Liberty, 144

Alda, Alan
Apple Tree, The, 218

Alda, Delyle
Ziegfeld Follies, 31

Alda, Robert
Guys and Dolls, 148
What Makes Sammy Run?, 206

Aldredge, Tom
Into the Woods, 277
Passion, 295

Alexander, Cris
On the Town, 126

Alexander, Jason
Jerome Robbins' Broadway, 279

Alford, Lamar
Godspell, 233

Allard, Martine
Tap Dance Kid, The, 268

Allen, Debbie
Raisin, 239
Sweet Charity, 272

Allen, Elizabeth
Do I Hear a Waltz?, 210

Allen, Fred
Little Show, The, 67
Three's a Crowd, 73

Allen, Jonelle
Two Gentlemen of Verona, 234

Allen, Lester
George White's Scandals, 40
Three Musketeers, The, 63

Allen, Rae
Damn Yankees, 167
On a Clear Day You Can See Forever, 213

Allen, Sasha
Hair, 365

Allen, Vera
At Home Abroad, 89
Show Is On, The, 97

Allmon, Clint
Best Little Whorehouse in Texas, The, 250

Alloway, Jacqueline
George M!, 223

Allworth, Frank
Hold Everything!, 65

Allyson, June
Best Foot Forward, 114
Panama Hattie, 111

Altman, Ruth
Boy Friend, The, 162

Alvarez, Anita
Finian's Rainbow, 133
Gentlemen Prefer Blondes, 146

Alvarez, Carmen
Apple Tree, The, 218
Irene, 238
Zorba, 225

Alvarez, David
Billy Elliot: The Musical, 361

Ameche, Don
Silk Stockings, 166

Ames, Florenz
Of Thee I Sing, 78

Andre, Ann
Red Mill, The, 128

Andreas, Christine
La Cage aux Folles, 376
Oklahoma!, 255
On Your Toes, 264
Scarlet Pimpernel, The, 309

Andrews, George Lee
Little Night Music, A, 237
On the Twentieth Century, 249
Phantom of the Opera, The, 278

Andrews, Julie
Boy Friend, The, 162
Camelot, 193
My Fair Lady, 168
Victor/Victoria, 303

Andrews, Nancy
Little Me, 200
Plain and Fancy, 166

Angela, June
King and I, The, 248

Angelus, Muriel
Boys from Syracuse, The, 107

Anker, Helen
Promises, Promises, 378

Antoon, Jason
Contact, 318

Anzell, Hy
Little Shop of Horrors, 262

Apolinar, Danny
Your Own Thing, 222

Applegate, Fred
La Cage aux Folles, 376

Arcaro, Flavia
Chocolate Soldier, The, 16
Dearest Enemy, 48

Archer, Cheryl
Love Life, 138

Ard, Ken
Starlight Express, 276

Arden, Eve
Let's Face It!, 115
Ziegfeld Follies, 85, 93

Ardeo, David
Joseph and the Amazing Technicolor
Dreamcoat, 260

Arkin, Juki
Milk and Honey, 195

Armus, Sidney
Wish You Were Here, 154

Arnaz, Desi
Too Many Girls, 108

Arnaz, Lucie
Dirty Rotten Scoundrels, 334
They're Playing Our Song, 252

Arno, Sig
Song of Norway, 124

Arnst, Bobbe
Rosalie, 62

Arthur, Beatrice
Fiddler on the Roof, 209
Mame, 217
Threepenny Opera, The, 159

Ashmanskas, Brooks
Gypsy, 329
Promises, Promises, 378

Asro, Alexander
Leave It to Me!, 105

Astaire, Adele
Band Wagon, The, 74
Funny Face, 59
Lady, Be Good!, 44

Astaire, Fred
Band Wagon, The, 74
Funny Face, 59
Gay Divorce, 82
Lady, Be Good!, 44

Astin, John
Threepenny Opera, The, 159

Ates, Nejla
Fanny, 164

Atkins, Cholly
Gentlemen Prefer Blondes, 146

Atwell, Roy
Firefly, The, 18

Auberjonois, Rene
Big River, 270
City of Angels, 282

Azaria, Hank
Monty Python's Spamalot, 336

Azito, Tony
Pirates of Penzance, The, 258

Babatunde, Obba
Dreamgirls, 261

Babcock, John
The Secret Garden, 286

Bacall, Lauren
Applause, 228
Woman of the Year, 260

Bach, Sebastian
Jekyll and Hyde, 308

Bailey, Pearl
House of Flowers, 165
St. Louis Woman, 129

Bain, Conrad
Candide, 172

Baker, Benny
DuBarry Was a Lady, 109
Let's Face It!, 115

Baker, Jennifer
Stop the World—I Want to Get Off, 199

Baker, Josephine
Ziegfeld Follies, 93

Baker, Kenny
One Touch of Venus, 120

Baker, Lenny
I Love My Wife, 245

Baker, Mark
Candide, 239

Baker, Susan
Stop the World—I Want to Get Off, 199

Balaban, Bob
You're A Good Man, Charlie Brown, 221

Baldwin, Kate
Finian's Rainbow, 370

Ball, Michael
Aspects of Love, 283

Ballard, Kaye
Carnival, 195
Golden Apple, The, 160

Banderas, Antonio
Nine, 329

Bane, Paula
Call Me Mister, 129

Banks, Leslie
Lost in the Stars, 144

Bannerman, Margaret
By Jupiter, 116

Barbeau, Adrienne
Grease, 234

Barbour, James
Tale of Two Cities, A, 360

Barclift, Nelson
This Is the Army, 117

Barker, John
Band Wagon, The, 74
Cocoanuts, The, 51
Follow Thru, 67
No, No, Nanette, 47

Barnabee, Henry Clay
Robin Hood, 5

Baronova, Irina
Follow the Girls, 124

Barr, Lillian
Trip to Chinatown, A, 5

Barrett, Brent
Annie Get Your Gun, 315

Barrie, Barbara
Company, 229

Barrie, Gracie
Show Is On, The, 97

Barrie, Leslie
Anything Goes, 88

Barrile, Anthony
Tommy, 294

Barrison, Mabel
Babes in Toyland, 8

Barry, Gene
La Cage aux Folles, 266
Merry Widow, The, 120

Bart, Roger
Producers, The, 321
Young Frankenstein, 353

Bartlett, Josephine
Mlle. Modiste, 10

Bartlett, Michael
Follies, 232

Barto & Mann
Hellzapoppin, 103

Barto, Betty Lou
As the Girls Go, 139

Barton, James
Paint Your Wagon, 152

Barton, Steve
Phantom of the Opera, The, 278

Baskerville, Priscilla
Sophisticated Ladies, 259

Baskin, Derrick
Little Mermaid, The, 355
Memphis, 369

Battle, Hinton
Miss Saigon, 285
Sophisticated Ladies, 259
Tap Dance Kid, The, 268
Wiz, The, 241

Battles, John
Allegro, 136
On the Town, 126

Bavaar, Tony
Paint Your Wagon, 152

Baxley, Barbara
She Loves Me, 202

Bayes, Nora
Follies of 1907, 14

Bayes, Nora
Follies of 1907, 14

Beach, Gary
Beauty and the Beast, 297
La Cage Au Folles, 333
Les Misérables, 349
Producers, The, 321

Beane Jr., George
Trip to Chinatown, A, 5

Berresse, Michael
Kiss Me, Kate, 315

Beatty, Roberta
Student Prince in Heidelberg, The, 45

Beatty, Talley
Inside U.S.A., 137
Show Boat, 128

Beechman, Laurie
Annie, 247
Joseph and the Amazing Technicolor
Dreamcoat, 260

Beery, Noah
Up in Central Park, 126

Begley, Edward
Red Mill, The, 13

Belasco, Leon
Silk Stockings, 166

Belaver, Harry
Annie Get Your Gun, 130

Bell, Marion
Brigadoon, 134

Bell, Michael
Show Boat, 299

Belmore, Bertha
By Jupiter, 116

Benanti, Laura
Gypsy, 359
Into the Woods, 326
Nine, 329
Wedding Singer, The, 346

Benedict, Paul
Music Man, The, 319

Beniades, Ted
Golden Boy, 210

Benjamin, P. J.
Sophisticated Ladies, 259

Bennett, Craig
Tale of Two Cities, A, 360

Bennett, Wilda
Music Box Revue, 37

Benson, Jodi
Crazy for You, 288

Benson, Peter
Promises, Promises, 378

Benzell, Mimi
Milk and Honey, 195

Bergen, Polly
Follies, 320

Berghof, Herbert
Miss Liberty, 144

Bergman, Sandahl
Dancin', 250

Berlin, Irving
Music Box Revue, 37
This Is the Army, 117

Bernal, Barry K.
Miss Saigon, 285

Bernard, Crystal
Annie Get Your Gun, 315

Bernard, Sam
Music Box Revue, 37

Bernardi, Herschel
Zorba, 225

Berresse, Michael
Chorus, Line, A, 343
Light in the Piazza, The, 338

Berry, Eric
Boy Friend, The, 162
Pippin, 236

Beruh, Joseph
Threepenny Opera, The, 159

Bettis, Valerie
Inside U.S.A., 137

Beyer, Mark
Rain—A Tribute to the Beatles on Broadway,
379

Bickel, George
Follies of 1907, 14

Bierko, Craig
Music Man, The, 319

Bigley, Isabel
Guys and Dolls 148
Me and Juliet, i57

Bikel, Theodore
Sound of Music, The, 184

Binder, Ryan Patrick
Grease, 354

Binney, Constance
Oh, Lady! Lady!!, 26

Birch, Peter
Carousel, 127

Bishop, Kelly
Chorus Line, A, 243

Bithorn, Joe
Rain—A Tribute to the Beatles on Broadway,
379

Blaine, Vivian
Guys and Dolls, 148

Blair, Betsy
Panama Hattie, 111

Blair, Pamela
Best Little Whorehouse in Texas, The, 250
Chorus Line, A, 243
Sugar, 235

Blaisdell, J. W.
Black Crook, The, 3

Blake, Eubie
Shuffle Along, 34

Blake, Richard H.
Wedding Singer, The, 346

Blakely, Michelle
Grease, 298

Blanchard, Tammy
Gypsy, 329

Blane, Ralph
Hooray for What!, 100
Louisiana Purchase, 110

Blankenbuehler, Andy
Fosse, 314

Blazer, Judith
Titanic, 307

Bledsoe, Jules
Show Boat, 60

Bliss, Helena
Song of Norway, 124

Blitzstein, Marc
Cradle Will Rock, The, 101

Blore, Eric
Gay Divorce, 82

Blum, Joel
Show Boat, 299

Blumenkrantz, Jeff
How to Succeed in Business Without Really Trying, 302

Blyden, Larry
Apple Tree, The, 218
Flower Drum Song, 178
Wish You Were Here, 154

Bobbie, Walter
Guys and Dolls, 290

Bocchi, Nicole
Dr. Seuss' How the Grinch Stole Christmas, 348

Boerers, Jessica
Funny Thing Happened on the Way to the Forum, A, 304

Bogardus, Stephen
Falsettos, 293
Irving Berlin's White Christmas, 362
Man of La Mancha, 329

Boggess, Sierra
Little Mermaid, The, 355

Bohmer, Ron
Ragtime, 371

Boland, Mary
Face the Music, 79
Jubilee, 92

Boles, John
One Touch of Venus, 120

Boley, May
Fortune Teller, The, 6
Jubilee, 92

Bolger, Ray
By Jupiter, 116
George White's Scandals, 76
Life Begins at 8:40, 87
On Your Toes, 94
Where's Charley?, 138

Bolin, Shannon
Damn Yankees, 167
Golden Apple, The, 160

Bologna, David
Billy Elliot: The Musical, 361

Bond, Ruth
One Touch of Venus, 120

Bond, Sheila
Make Mine Manhattan, 137
Street Scene, 132
Wish You Were Here, 154

Bonfanti, Marie
Black Crook, The, 3

Boniface, George
Black Crook, The, 3

Booth, Shirley
Tree Grows in Brooklyn, A, 152

Bordoni, Irene
Louisiana Purchase, 110

Boris, Ruthanna
Hooray for What!, 100
Song of Norway, 124

Borle, Christian
Legally Blonde, 351
Monty Python's Spamalot, 336

Borstelmann, Jim
Young Frankenstein, 353

Bosley, Tom
Beauty and the Beast, 297
Fiorello!, 186

Boston, Gretha
Show Boat, 299

Bostwick, Barry
Grease, 234

Bottoms, John
Two Gentlemen of Verona, 234

Boulden, Alice
Fine and Dandy, 72

Bourneuf, Philip
Miss Liberty, 144

Bova, Joseph
42nd Street, 257
Once Upon a Mattress, 181

Bowers, Kenny
Annie Get Your Gun, 130
Best Foot Forward, 114

Bowler, Annie Kemp
Black Crook, The, 3

Bowman, Patricia
Ziegfeld Follies, 85

Boyd, Anna
Trip to Chinatown, A, 5

Bracken, Eddie
Too Many Girls, 108

Bradbury, Lane
Gypsy, 182

Bradford, Alex
Don't Bother Me, I Can't Cope, 235

Bradley, Brian
Grease, 298

Brady, Scott
Destry Rides Again, 180

Braswell, Charles
Company, 229
Mame, 217

Braun, Trevor
Little Mermaid, The, 355

Breaker, Daniel
Shrek: The Musical, 363

Breaux, Marc
Destry Rides Again, 180
Kiss Me, Kate, 141

Bremer, Lucille
Panama Hattie, 111

Brennan, Eileen
Hello, Dolly!, 204
Little Mary Sunshine, 186

Brennan, Maureen
Candide, 239

Brent, Romney
Garrick Gaieties, The, 46
Little Show, The, 67

Breuler, Robert
Carousel, 296

Brian, Donald
Forty-five Minutes from Broadway, 13
Girl from Utah, The, 19
Little Johnny Jones, 10
Merry Widow, The, 15

Brice, Elizabeth
Watch Your Step, 20

Brice, Fanny
Ziegfeld Follies, 34, 85, 93

Bridgewater, DeeDee
Wiz, The, 241

Briggs, Matt
Bloomer Girl, 125

Brightman, Sarah
Phantom of the Opera, The, 278

Brinkley, Grace
Flying High, 71
Of Thee I Sing, 78

Brisebois, Danielle
Annie, 247

Britton, Pamela
Brigadoon, 134

Broderick, Helen
As Thousands Cheer, 83
Band Wagon, The, 74
Fifty Million Frenchmen, 69
Follies of 1907, 14

Broderick, Matthew
How to Succeed in Business Without Really
Trying, 302
Producers, The, 321

Brooks, David
Bloomer Girl, 125
Brigadoon, 134

Brooks, Lawrence
Song of Norway, 124

Brooks, Phyllis
Panama Hattie, 111

Brotherson, Eric
Gentlemen Prefer Blondes, 146

Brown, Anne
Porgy and Bess, 91

Brown, Ashley
Mary Poppins, 344

Brown, Georgia
Oliver!, 201

Brown, Jeb
Grease, 354

Brown, Russ
Damn Yankees, 167
Flying High, 71

Brown, Sandra
Carousel, 296

Browne, Harry C.
Oh, Lady! Lady!!, 26

Browne, Roscoe Lee
My One and Only, 264

Browning, Susan
Big River, 270
Company, 229

Brox Sisters
Cocoanuts, The, 51
Music Box Revue, 37

Bruce, Betty
Boys from Syracuse, The, 107
Up in Central Park, 126

Bruce, Carol
Do I Hear a Waltz?, 210
Louisiana Purchase, 110
Show Boat, 128

Bruce, Shelley
Annie, 247

Bruce, Vince
Will Rogers Follies, The, 287

Bryant, David
Les Misérables, 275

Bryant, Glenn
Carmen Jones, 122

Bryant, Nana
Connecticut Yankee, A, 58

Bryne, Barbara
Into the Woods, 277
Sunday in the Park With George, 269

Brynner, Yul
King and I, The, 151, 248

Bubbles, John W.
Porgy and Bess, 91

Buchanan, Jack
Andre Charlot's Revue of 1924, 42

Buckley, Betty
Cats, 263
Mystery of Edwin Drood, The, 271
1776, 227

Buddeke, Kate
Carousel, 296
Gypsy, 329

Buell, Bill
Titanic, 307

Buffalo Bills, The
Music Man, The, 177

Buloff, Joseph
Oklahoma!, 119

Bundy, Laura Bell
Hairspray, 326
Legally Blonde, 351

Buntrock, Stephen R.
Grease, 354

Burch, Shelly
Nine, 262

Burge, Gregg
Song and Dance, 271
Sophisticated Ladies, 259

Burgess, Tituss
Little Mermaid, The, 355

Burghoff, Gary
You're a Good Man, Charlie Brown, 221

Burke, Georgia
Porgy and Bess, 156

Burke, Ione
Evangeline, 4

Burke, Marie
Great Waltz, The, 87

Burke, Maurice
Up in Central Park, 126

Burkhardt, Brandi
Tale of Two Cities, A, 360

Burmester, Leo
Fantasticks, The, 343
Les Misérables, 275

Burnett, Carol
Once Upon a Mattress, 181

Burns, Andréa
In the Heights, 357

Burns, David
Do Re Mi, 194
Face the Music, 79
Funny Thing Happened on the Way to the
Forum, A, 198
Hello, Dolly!, 204
Make Mine Manhattan, 137
Music Man, The, 177

Burrell, Deborah
Dreamgirls, 261

Burstein, Danny
Drowsy Chaperone, The, 342
South Pacific, 358

Burtka, David
Gypsy, 329

Burton, Haven
Shrek: The Musical, 363

Burton, Richard
Camelot, 193

Butler, Kerry
Hairspray, 326
Xanadu, 352

Butt, Jennifer
Les Misérables, 275

Butterworth, Charles
Flying Colors, 80
Sweet Adeline, 68

Butz, Norbert Leo
Dirty Rotten Scoundrels, 334
Wicked, 332

Buzzell, Eddie
Desert Song, The, 54

Buzzi, Ruth
Sweet Charity, 216

Byron, Lorna
Red Mill, The, 128

Caesar, Sid
Little Me, 200
Make Mine Manhattan, 137

Cahill, Marie
New Yorkers, The, 74

Cahoon, Kevin
Lion King, The, 310

Calin, Mickey
West Side Story, 175

Callahan, Bill
As the Girls Go, 139
Call Me Mister, 129
Mexican Hayride, 122

Callaway, Liz
Miss Saigon, 285

Calloway, Cab
Porgy and Bess, 156

Calloway, J. Bernard
Memphis, 369

Calvin, Henry
Kismet, 158

Cameron, Madeline
Follow Thru, 67
Hit the Deck!, 56

Campbell, Alan
Sunset Boulevard, 300

Campbell, Craig
Firefly, The, 18

Campbell, Nell
Nine, 329

Cannon, Maureen
Best Foot Forward, 114
Up in Central Park, 126

Canova, Judy
Ziegfeld Follies, 93

Cantor, Eddie
Whoopee, 66
Ziegfeld Follies, 29, 31
Capers, Virginia
Raisin, 239

Carder, Tom
Joseph and the Amazing Technicolor
Dreamcoat, 260

Carey, Macdonald
Lady in the Dark, 113

Cariou, Len
Applause, 228
Little Night Music, A, 237
Sweeney Todd, 253

Carle, Richard
New Yorkers, The, 74

Carlson, Violet
Sweet Adeline, 68

Carmello, Carolee
Addams Family, The, 374
Falsettos, 293

Carminati, Tullio
Music in the Air, 81

Carmon, Sean A.
La Cage aux Folles, 376

Carnahan, Kristi
Kiss of the Spider Woman—The Musical, 295

Carney, Alan
Fanny, 164

Carpenter, Constance
Andre Charlot's Revue of 1924, 42
Connecticut Yankee, A, 58
Oh, Kay!, 53

Carpenter, John
Guys and Dolls, 290

Carpenter, Thelma
Inside U.S.A., 137

Carpinello, James
Rock of Ages, 366

Carr, Larry
Make Mine Manhattan, 137

Carradine, John
Funny Thing Happened on the Way to the
Forum, A, 198

Carradine, Keith
Dirty Rotten Scoundrels, 334
Will Rogers Follies, The, 287

Carrington, Katherine
Face the Music, 79
Music in the Air, 81

Carroll, Barbara
Me and Juliet, 157

Carroll, David
Chess, 279
Grand Hotel, 281

Carroll, Diahann
House of Flowers, 165
No Strings, 197

Carroll, Joan
Panama Hattie, 111

Carroll, June
New Faces of 1952, 154

Carroll, Marie
Oh, Boy!, 24

Carroll, Ronn
Annie Get Your Gun, 315
How to Succeed in Business Without Really
Trying, 302
Oklahoma, 325

Carson, Doris
Cat and the Fiddle, The, 77
On Your Toes, 94
Strike Up the Band, 70

Carter, Nell
Ain't Misbehavin', 251

Carter, Ralph
Raisin, 239

Carus, Emma
Follies of 1907, 14

Carver, Brent
Kiss of the Spider Woman—The Musical, 295

Case, Allen
Once Upon a Mattress, 181

Case, Allison
Hair, 365

Casella, Max
Lion King, The, 310
Music Man, The, 319

Caskey, Marilyn
Gypsy, 359

Casnoff, Philip
Chess, 279

Cassidy, Jack
Inside U.S.A., 137
She Loves Me, 202
Wish You Were Here, 154

Castelli, Ralph
Rain—A Tribute to the Beatles on Broadway,
379

Castle, Irene
Watch Your Step, 20

Castle, Vernon
Watch Your Step, 20

Casto, Jean
Pal Joey, 112

Castree, Paul
Grease, 298

Catania, Claudia
Most Happy Fella, The, 293

Catlen, Walter
Lady, Be Good!, 44
Sally, 33

Cavanaugh, Hobart
As the Girls Go, 139
Irene, 32

Cavenaugh, Matt
Movin' Out, 328
West Side Story, 364

Cawthorn, Joseph
Fortune Teller, The, 6
Girl from Utah, The, 19
Sunny, 50

Ceballos, Rene
Dancin', 250

Cerveris, Michael
Sweeney Todd, 338
Titanic, 307
Tommy, 294

Chadman, Christopher
Dancin', 250

Chaisson, Gilles
Rent, 305

Chamberlin, Kevin
Addams Family, The, 374

Chandler, Jamie Beth
Starlight Express, 276

Chang, John
King and I, The, 303

Channing, Carol
Gentlemen Prefer Blondes, 146
Hello, Dolly!, 204
Lend an Ear, 139

Channing, Stockard
Two Gentlemen of Verona, 234

Champion, Marge
Follies, 320

Champlin, Donna Lynne
Sweeney Todd, 338

Chanler-Berat, Adam
Next to Normal, 368

Chaplin, Sydney
Bells Are Ringing, 171
Funny Girl, 207

Chapman, William
Greenwillow, 187

Charles, Walter
Aspects of Love, 283

Charnin, Martin
West Side Story, 175

Chasen, Dave
Fine and Dandy, 72

Chastain, Don
No Strings, 197

Cheng, Kam
Miss Saigon, 285

Chenoweth, Kristin
Promises, Promises, 378
Wicked, 332

Ching, William
Allegro, 136

Chisholm, Robert
Sweet Adeline, 68

Choi, Hye-Young
King and I, The, 248

Choi, Joohee
King and I, The, 303

Christie, Audrey
I Married an Angel, 102

Christmas, David
Dames at Sea, 226

Chryst, Gary
Guys and Dolls, 290

Church, George
Oklahoma!, 119
On Your Toes, 94

Church, Sandra
Gypsy, 182

Churchill, Stuart
This Is the Army, 117

Ciannelli, Eduardo
Rose-Marie, 43

Cilento, Wayne
Chorus Line, A, 243
Dancin', 250

Claire, Ina
Ziegfeld Follies, 20

Claire, Marion
Great Waltz, The, 87

Claire, Stella
Boy Friend, The, 162

Clark, Bobby
As the Girls Go, 139
Mexican Hayride, 122
Strike Up the Band, 70
Sweethearts, 134

Clark, Dort
Bells Are Ringing, 171
Wonderful Town, 155

Clark, Harry
Kiss Me, Kate, 141
One Touch of Venus, 120
Wish You Were Here, 154

Clark, Victoria
Titanic, 307
How to Succeed in Business
Without Really Trying, 302
Light in the Piazza, The, 338

Clarke, Hope
Don't Bother Me, I Can't Cope, 235

Clary, Robert
New Faces of 1952, 154

Clayburgh, Jill
Pippin, 236
Rothschilds, The, 230

Clayton, Lou
New Yorkers, The, 74

Clayton, Jan
Carousel, 127
Show Boat, 128

Cleese, John
Half a Sixpence, 211
Monty Python's Spamalot, 336

Clemente, Rene
Cats, 263

Clements, Dudley
Of Thee I Sing, 78
Strike Up the Band, 70

Clendening, Eddie
Million Dollar Quartet, 375

Clift, Montgomery
Jubilee, 92

Close, Glenn
Barnum, 256
Sunset Boulevard, 300

Major Cast Members Index

Clyde, June
Hooray for What!, 100

Coca, Imogene
Flying Colors, 80
New Faces, 86
On the Twentieth Century, 249

Cochrane, June
Connecticut Yankee, A, 58
Garrick Gaieties, The, 46

Cody, Jennifer
Shrek: The Musical, 363

Coe, George
On the Twentieth Century, 249

Coffman, Kyle
West Side Story, 364

Cohan, George M.
I'd Rather Be Right, 98
Little Johnny Jones, 10

Cohan, Helen
Little Johnny Jones, 10

Cohan, Jerry
Little Johnny Jones, 10

Cohenour, Patti
Big River, 270
Light in the Piazza, The, 338
Mystery of Edwin Drood, The, 271

Colbert, Helen
Porgy and Bess, 156

Cole, Cozy
Carmen Jones, 122

Cole, Kay
Chorus Line, A, 243

Cole, Lester
Peggy-Ann, 54

Coleman, Herbert
Lost in the Stars, 144

Coleman, Warren
Lost in the Stars, 144
Porgy and Bess, 91

Coles, Charles îHoniî
Gentlemen Prefer Blondes, 146
My One and Only, 264

Collier, William
Music Box Revue, 37

Collins, Charles
Red Mill, The, 128

Collins, Dorothy
Follies, 232

Colson, Kevin
Aspects of Love, 283

Colt, Ethel Barrymore
Follies, 232
George White's Scandals, 76

Comden, Betty
On the Town, 126

Compton, Betty
Fifty Million Frenchmen, 69
Funny Face, 59
Hold Everything!, 65
Oh, Kay!, 53

Condos, Steve
Sugar, 235

Conkey, Thomas
Sweethearts, 19

Conklin, Peggy
Little Show, The, 67

Conlow, Peter
Take Me Along, 183

Connell, Gordon
Big River, 270
Hello, Dolly!, 204

Connell, Jane
Crazy for You, 288
Mame, 217
Me and My Girl, 273

Connick, Harry Jr.
Pajama Game, The, 341

Conor, Harry
Trip to Chinatown, A, 5

Conried, Hans
Can-Can, 156

Conte, John
Allegro, 136

Convy, Bert
Cabaret, 219
Fiddler on the Roof, 209

Conway, Shirl
Plain and Fancy, 166

Cook, Barbara
Candide, 172
Music Man, The, 177
Plain and Fancy, 166
She Loves Me, 202

Cook, Carole
42nd Street, 257

Cook, Joe
Fine and Dandy, 72

Cook, Olga
Blossom Time, 38

Cook, Roderick
Woman of the Year, 260

Cookson, Peter
Can-Can, 156

Cooper, Chuck
Finian's Rainbow, 370

Cooper, Horace
Where's Charley?, 138

Cooper, Marilyn
Woman of the Year, 260

Cooper, Melville
Jubilee, 92
Merry Widow, The, 120

Coote, Robert
Camelot, 193
My Fair Lady, 168

Cordon, Norman
Street Scene, 132

Corthell, Herbert
Vagabond King, The, 48

Cossart, Ernest
Great Waltz, The, 87

Costello, Diosa
Too Many Girls, 108

Costello, Dolores
George White's Scandals, 40

Courtney, Inez
Good News!, 56

Cowan, Jerome
As Thousands Cheer, 83

Cowles, Eugene
Fortune Teller, The, 6
Robin Hood, 5

Cox, Christopher
Ragtime, 371

Cox, Veanne
La Cage aux Folles, 376

Crane, W. H.
Evangeline, 4

Crater, Allene
Red Mill, The, 13

Crawford, Kathryn
New Yorkers, The, 74

Crawford, Michael
Phantom of the Opera, The, 278

Creel, Gavin
Hair, 365
La Cage aux Folles, 333
Thoroughly Modern Millie, 325

Cripe, Michael
Victor/Victoria, 303

Crivello, Anthony
Kiss of the Spider Woman—The Musical, 295

Crofoot, Leonard John
Barnum, 256

Cropper, Roy
Blossom Time, 38

Crosby, Kim
Into the Woods, 277

Cross, Wellington
No, No, Nanette, 47

Crumb, Ann
Aspects of Love, 283

Crumm, Max
Grease, 354

Crutchfield, Buddy
Most Happy Fella, The, 293

Cryer, Gretchen
I'm Getting My Act Together and Taking It on the
Road, 252
Little Me, 200
110 in the Shade, 203

Cuccioli, Robert
Jekyll and Hyde, 308

Cuervo, Alma
Titanic, 307

Cullen, Sean
South Pacific, 358

Cullum, John
Camelot, 193
Dr. Seuss' How the Grinch Stole Christmas, 348
On a Clear Day You Can See Forever, 213
On the Twentieth Century, 249
110 in the Shade, 352
Shenandoah, 242
Urinetown, 323

Cumming, Alan
Cabaret, 312

Cummings, Constance
Little Show, The, 67

Cummings, Robert
Ziegfeld Follies, 85

Cumpsty, Michael
42nd Street, 322
Sunday in the Park With George, 356

Cunningham, Cecil
Greenwich Village Follies, 31

Cunningham, John
Company, 229
Titanic, 307
Zorba, 225

Cunningham, Nicholas
La Cage aux Folles, 376

Curatolo, Joey
Rain—A Tribute to the Beatles on Broadway, 379

Curless, John
King and I, The, 303

Curley, George
Fantasticks, The, 189

Curry, Steve
Hair, 224

Curry, Tim
Monty Python's Spamalot, 336

Curtis, Keene
Rothschilds, The, 230

Cypher, Jon
Man of La Mancha, 215

Dailey, Dan
Babes in Arms, 98

D'Abruzzio, Stepahnie
Avenue Q, 330

Dacal, Janet
In the Heights, 357

Dale, Grover
Greenwillow, 187
Half a Sixpence, 211
Li'l Abner, 171

Dale, Jim
Barnum, 256

Dale, Margaret
Lady in the Dark, 113
Oh, Lady! Lady!!, 26
Rosalie, 62

Daley, Tyne
Gypsy, 282

Dalmes, Mony
Unsinkable Molly Brown, The, 191

d'Amboise, Charlotte
Chorus Line, A, 343
Jerome Robbins' Broadway, 279

d'Amboise, Christopher
Song and Dance, 271

Damiano, Jennifer
Next to Normal, 368

Damon, Stuart
Do I Hear a Waltz?, 210
Irma la Douce, 190

Dana, Dick
As the Girls Go, 139

Dandridge, Merle
Tarzan, 347

Daniel, Billy
Let's Face It!, 115

Daniele, Graciela
Chicago, 244

Daniels, Billy
Golden Boy, 210

Daniels, Danny
Best Foot Forward, 114
Make Mine Manhattan, 137
Street Scene, 132

Daniels, David
Plain and Fancy, 166

Daniels, William
On a Clear Day You Can See Forever, 213
1776, 227

Danilova, Alexandra
Great Waltz, The, 87
Song of Norway, 124

Danner, Blythe
Follies, 320

Danner, Braden
Les Misérables, 275

Dannheisser, Adam
Rock of Ages, 366

D'Antonakis, Fleury
Do I Hear a Waltz?, 210

D'Arcy James, Brian
Shrek: The Musical, 363

D'Arle, Yvonne
Countess Maritza, 53
Three Musketeers, The, 63

Darling, Jean
Carousel, 127

Darrington, Earl
Ragtime, 371

Da Silva, Howard
Cradle Will Rock, The, 101
Fiorello!, 186
Oklahoma!, 119
1776, 227

David, Clifford
On a Clear Day You Can See Forever, 213
1776, 227

David, Keith
Jelly's Last Jam, 292

Davie, Erin
Little Night Music, A, 373

Davies, Brian
Funny Thing Happened on the Way to the
    Forum, A, 198
Sound of Music, The, 184

Davies, Marion
Oh, Boy!, 24

Davila, Diana
Two Gentlemen of Verona, 234

Davis, Bessie McCoy
Greenwich Village Follies, 31

Davis, Clifton
Two Gentlemen of Verona, 234

Davis, Daniel
La Cage aux Folles, 333

Davis, Guy
Finian's Rainbow, 370

Davis, Jessie Bartlett
Robin Hood, 5

Davis, Mary Bond
Jelly's Last Jam, 292

Davis, Ossie
Jamaica, 176

Davis Jr., Sammy
Golden Boy, 210

Dawn, Eleanor
No, No, Nanette, 47

Dawn, Hazel
Pink Lady, The, 18

Dawson, Mark
Fiorello!, 186
High Button Shoes, 136
Me and Juliet, 157
New Girl in Town, 173
Sweethearts, 134

Day, Edith
Irene, 32

Daye, Bobby
Shrek: The Musical, 363

Dazie, Mlle.
Follies of 1907, 14

Deagon, Arthur
Rose-Marie, 43

Dean, Bradley
Little Night Music, A, 373

Dean, Charles
Irving Berlin's White Christmas, 362

Deane, Sydney
Florodora, 6

Deas, Lawrence
Shuffle Along, 34

DeCarlo, Yvonne
Follies, 232

Deems, Mickey
Little Me, 200

de Guzman, Josie
Guys and Dolls, 290

De Jesús, Robin
In the Heights, 357
La Cage aux Folles, 376

DeKoven, Roger
Funny Girl, 207

de la Pe—a, George
On Your Toes, 264

de Lappe, Gemze
King and I, The, 151
Paint Your Wagon, 152

De Lavallade, Carmen
House of Flowers, 165

Delroy, Irene
Follow Thru, 67

de Luce, Virginia
New Faces of 1952, 154

DeMarco, Antonio
Girl Crazy, 72

DeMarco, Renee
Girl Crazy, 72

Demarest, Frances
Blue Paradise, The 21
Madame Sherry, 17

Demarest, William
Earl Carroll Vanities, 76

Demas, Carole
Grease, 234

Dempsey, Jerome
Mystery of Edwin Drood, The, 271

Dench, Judi
Into the Woods, 326

Denham, George
Babes in Toyland, 8

Denman, Jeffry
Irving Berlin's White Christmas, 362

Dennen, Barry
Jesus Christ Superstar, 233

deRosa, Stephen
Into the Woods, 326

Derr, Richard
Plain and Fancy, 166

Derricks, Cleavant
Dreamgirls, 261

Derwent, Clarence
Three Musketeers, The, 63

De Shields, Andre
Ain't Misbehavin', 251
Full Monty, The, 319
Wiz, The, 241

Devine, Loretta
Dreamgirls, 261

Diamond, Jack
Kiss Me, Kate, 141

Dickey, Annamary
Allegro, 136

Dickson, Dorothy
Oh, Boy!, 24

Diener, Joan
Kismet, 158
Man of La Mancha, 215

Diggs, Taye
Rent, 305

Dillon, Denny
My One and Only, 264

Dilly, Erin
Follies, 320

DiLuca, Dino
House of Flowers, 165

Dingle, Charles
Miss Liberty, 144

Dittman, Dean
On the Twentieth Century, 249

Dix, Tommy
Best Foot Forward, 114

Dixon, Jerry
Five Guys Named Moe, 289
Once on This Island, 284

Dixon, Harland
Oh, Kay!, 53
Tree Grows in Brooklyn, A, 152

Dixon, Lee
Oklahoma!, 119

Dixon, MacIntyre
Gypsy, 329

Dodge, Jerry
George M!, 223
Hello, Dolly!, 204

Dokuchitz, Jonathan
Tommy, 294

Dolce, Frank
Billy Elliot: The Musical, 361

Dolores
Sally, 33

Donahue, Jack
Rosalie, 62
Sunny, 50

Donath, Ludwig
She Loves Me, 202

Donen, Stanley
Pal Joey, 112

Doner, Kitty
Sinbad, 29

Donlevy, Brian
Hit the Deck!, 56
Life Begins at 8:40, 87

Donnelly, Jamie
George M!, 223

Dooley, Johnny
Ziegfeld Follies, 31

Dooley, Ray
Ziegfeld Follies, 31, 34

D'Orsay, Fifi
Follies, 232

Dossett, John
Gypsy, 329

Douglas, Larry
King and I, The, 151

Douglass, Margaret
Bloomer Girl, 125

Douglass, Stephen
Damn Yankees, 167
Golden Apple, The, 160
110 in the Shade, 203

Dovey, Alice
Pink Lady, The, 18
Very Good Eddie, 23

Dowd, M'el
Camelot, 193

Dowdy, Helen
Porgy and Bess, 91, 156

Dowling, Eddie
Ziegfeld Follies, 31

Doyle, Sean Patrick
La Cage aux Folles, 376

Drake, Alfred
Babes in Arms, 98
Kismet, 158
Kiss Me, Kate, 141
Oklahoma!, 119

Duchene, Marie
Naughty Marietta, 17

Du Clos, Danielle
Aspects of Love, 283

Duell, William
Funny Thing Happened on the Way to the
Forum, A, 304

Dulaline, Pierre
Grand Hotel, 281

Dumbrille, Douglass
Three Musketeers, The, 63

Dumke, Ralph
By Jupiter, 116
Merry Widow, The, 120
Show Boat, 128

Dumont, Margaret
Cocoanuts, The, 51

Dunbar, Dixie
Life Begins at 8:40, 87

Duncan, Ryan
Shrek: The Musical, 363

Duncan, Sandy
Peter Pan, 254

Duncan, Todd
Cabin in the Sky, 111
Lost in the Stars, 144
Porgy and Bess, 91

Duncan-Gibbs, Mamie
Jelly's Last Jam, 292

Dunham, Katherine
Cabin in the Sky, 111

Dunn, James
Evangeline, 4
Panama Hattie, 111

Dunn, Ralph
Pajama Game, The, 161

Dunn, Vera
Anything Goes, 88

Duquesnay, Ann
Bring In 'Da Noise, Bring In 'Da Funk, 306
Jelly's Last Jam, 292

Durant, Jack
Earl Carroll Vanities, 76
Pal Joey, 112

Durante, Jimmy
Jumbo, 93
New Yorkers, The, 74
Red, Hot and Blue!, 96

Durning, Charles
Happy Time, The, 222

Dussault, Nancy
Do Re Mi, 194

Dyson, Ronald
Hair, 224

Eagan, Daisy
Secret Garden, The, 286

Earley, Kevin
Tale of Two Cities, A, 360

Eastham, Richard
South Pacific, 143

Eaton, Mary
Ziegfeld Follies, 34, 38

Eaton, Sally
Hair, 224

Ebersole, Christine
42nd Street, 322
Oklahoma!, 255

Ebsen, Buddy
Flying Colors, 80
Show Boat, 128
Whoopee, 66
Ziegfeld Follies, 85

Ebsen, Vilma
Flying Colors, 80
Ziegfeld Follies, 85

Edelman, Gregg
City of Angels, 282
Into the Woods, 326
Passion, 298
Tale of Two Cities, A, 360
Wonderful Town, 332

Edens, Roger
Girl Crazy, 72

Eder, Linda
Jekyll and Hyde, 308

Edmonds, Louis
Candide, 172

Edouin, May
Florodora, 6

Edouin, Willie
Florodora, 6

Edwards, Alan
Lady, Be Good!, 44
Poppy, 40

Edwards, Cliff
Lady, Be Good!, 44
Sunny, 50

Edwards, Maurice
Fiddler on the Roof, 209

Egan, Susan
Beauty and the Beast, 297

Eggerth, Marta
Merry Widow, The, 120

Elg, Taina
Nine, 262

Elias, Alix
Two Gentlemen of Verona, 234

Elliman, Yvonne
Jesus Christ Superstar, 233

Ellington, Mercedes
Sophisticated Ladies, 259

Elliott, Patricia
Little Night Music, A, 237

Elliott, William
Pink Lady, The, 18

Ellis, Anita
Flower Drum Song, 178

Ellis, Charles
Show Boat, 60

Ellis, Mary
Rose-Marie, 43

Elmore, Steve
Company, 229
Dames at Sea, 226

Elzy, Ruby
Porgy and Bess, 91

Emerson, Hope
Street Scene, 132

Engel, Georgia
Drowsy Chaperone, The, 342

England, Paul
Where's Charley?, 138

Epstein, Alvin
No Strings, 197

Ernst, Leila
Pal Joey, 112
Too Many Girls, 108

Errol, Leon
Sally, 33
Ziegfeld Follies, 20

Erwin, Barbara
Annie, 247

Eskew, Doug
Five Guys Named Moe, 289

Esparza, Raul
Company, 344

Esper, Michael
American Idiot, 377

Estabrook, Christine
Spring Awakening, 345

Etting, Ruth
Whoopee, 66

Evan, Robert
Jekyll and Hyde, 308

Evans, Daniel
Sunday in the Park With George, 356

Evans, Greek
Student Prince in Heidelberg, The, 45

Evans, Rex
Gentlemen Prefer Blondes, 146

Evans, Wilbur
Mexican Hayride, 122
Up in Central Park, 126

Evelyn, John
Bitter Sweet, 68

Everett, Tanya
Fiddler on the Roof, 209

Everhart, Rex
Anything Goes, 277
Woman of the Year, 260

Everidge, Daniel
Grease, 354

Ewell, Lois
Forty-five Minutes from Broadway, 13
Merry Widow, The, 15

Ewoldt, Ali
Les Misérables, 349

Eythe, William
Lend an Ear, 139

Fabiani, Joel
I'm Getting My Act Together and Taking It on the
Road, 252

Faber, Mary
American Idiot, 377

Fabray, Nanette
High Button Shoes, 136
Let's Face It!, 115
Love Life, 138

Fairbanks Twins
George White's Scandals, 52
Oh, Kay!, 53
Ziegfeld Follies, 29

Faison, George
Purlie, 228

Faison, Sandy
Annie, 247

Falana, Lola
Golden Boy, 210

Falk, Willy
Miss Saigon, 285

Fantasia
Color Purple, The, 340

Faye, Alice
George White's Scandals, 76

Faye, Alina
Finian's Rainbow, 370

Faye, Joey
High Button Shoes, 136
Little Me, 200

Fenholt, Jeff
Jesus Christ Superstar, 233

Ferguson, Jesse Tyler
25th Annual Putnam County Spelling Bee, The,
337

Ferland, Danielle
Into the Woods, 277

Field, Ron
Lady in the Dark, 113

Fields, W. C.
George White's Scandals, 40
Poppy, 40
Ziegfeld Follies, 20, 29, 34

Fierstein Harvey,
Hairspray, 326

Figman, Max
New Moon, The, 64
Vagabond King, The, 48

Finley, Felicia
Wedding Singer, The, 346

Finneran, Katie
Promises, Promises, 378

Fischer, Allison
Grease, 354

Fisher, Irving
Sally, 33

Fisher, Nelle
Make Mine Manhattan, 137

Fitch, Robert
Annie, 247

Fitzgerald, Christopher
Finian's Rainbow, 370
Wicked, 332
Young Frankenstein, 353

Fitzhugh, Venita
Girl from Utah, The, 19

Fletcher, Jack
Sugar Babies, 255

Fletcher, Susann
Jerome Robbins' Broadway, 279

Foard, Merwin
Kiss Me, Kate, 315
La Cage aux Folles, 333

Fogler, Dan
25th Annual Putnam County Spelling Bee, The,
337

Fonda, Henry
New Faces, 86

Fontana, Santino
Billy Elliot: The Musical, 361
Sunday in the Park With George, 356

Ford, Chip
Shenandoah, 242

Major Cast Members Index

Ford, Helen
Dearest Enemy, 48
Peggy-Ann, 54

Forde, Hal
As Thousands Cheer, 83
Oh, Boy!, 24

Forsythe, Henderson
Best Little Whorehouse in Texas, The, 250

Fortier, Robert
Pal Joey, 153

Foster, Hunter
Footloose, 313
Grease, 298
Million Dollar Quartet, 375
Urinetown, 323

Foster, Sutton
Drowsy Chaperone, The, 342
Shrek: The Musical, 363
Thoroughly Modern Millie, 325
Young Frankenstein, 353

Fowler, Beth
Beauty and the Beast, 297
Peter Pan, 254

Fowler, Steve
Starlight Express, 276

Foy Jr., Eddie
At Home Abroad, 89
Cat and the Fiddle, The, 77
Pajama Game, The, 161
Red Mill, The, 128

Franchi, Sergio
Do I Hear a Waltz?, 210

Francine, Anne
Anything Goes, 277

Francis, Dorothy
Sunny, 50

Franklin, Bonnie
Applause, 228

Franklin, Irene
Sweet Adeline, 68

Franklin, Lidija
Brigadoon, 134

Franz, Joy
Into the Woods, 277

Franzell, Carlotta
Carmen Jones, 122

Fraser, Alison
Gypsy, 359
Secret Garden, The, 286

Fratantoni, Diane
Tommy, 296

Frawley, Paul
Music Box Revue, 37
Sunny, 50

Frear, Fred
Merry Widow, The, 15

Frederick, Vicki
Dancin', 250

Fredericks, Charles
Show Boat, 128

Freed, Sam
Candide, 239

Freeman, Cheryl
Tommy, 294

Freeman, Howard
Knickerbocker Holiday, 104

Freeman, Jonathan
42nd Street, 322
How to Succeed in Business Without Really
Trying, 302
She Loves Me, 296

Freeman, Kathleen
Full Monty, The, 319

Frey, Leonard
Fiddler on the Roof, 209

Frey, Nathaniel
Call Me Madam, 147
Damn Yankees, 167
Fiorello!, 186
High Button Shoes, 136
She Loves Me, 202
Tree Grows in Brooklyn, A, 152
Wonderful Town, 155

Friedman, Peter
Ragtime, 311

Frierson, Andrea
Once on This Island, 284

Froman, Jane
Ziegfeld Follies, 85

Frothingham, George
Robin Hood, 5

Fuller, Larry
Funny Girl, 207

Fuller, Lorenzo
Kiss Me, Kate, 141
St. Louis Woman, 129

Fuller, Penny
Applause, 228

Furber, Douglas
Andre Charlot's Revue of 1924, 42

Gable, June
Candide, 239

Gaines, Boyd
Contact, 318
Gypsy, 359
She Loves Me, 296

Gallagher & Shean
Ziegfeld Follies, 38

Gallagher, Helen
Brigadoon, 134
High Button Shoes, 136
No, No, Nanette, 231
Pal Joey, 153
Sweet Charity, 216

Gallagher, John Jr.
American Idiot, 377
Spring Awakening, 345

Gallagher, Peter
Guys and Dolls, 290

Galloway, Jenny
Les Misérables, 349

Galloway, Leata
Hair, 224

Gambatese, Jenn
Tarzan, 347

Garber, Victor
Sweeney Todd, 253

Garde, Betty
Oklahoma!, 119

Gardella, Tess
Show Boat, 60

Gardiner, Reginald
At Home Abroad, 89
Show Is On, The, 97

Gardner, J. E.
Chocolate Soldier, The, 16

Gardner, Jack
Madame Sherry, 17

Gardner, Rita
Fantasticks, The, 189

Garland, Patricia
Chorus Line, A, 243

Garner, Jay
Best Little Whorehouse in Texas, The, 250
La Cage aux Folles, 266

Garrett, Betty
Call Me Mister, 129
Follies, 320

Garrison, David
Titanic, 307

Gateson, Marjorie
Sweethearts, 134

Gautier, Dick
Bye Bye Birdie, 188

Gavon, Igors
Hello, Dolly!, 204

Gaxton, William
Anything Goes, 88
Connecticut Yankee, A, 58
Fifty Million Frenchmen, 69
Leave It to Me!, 105
Louisiana Purchase, 110
Of Thee I Sing, 78

Gaynes, George
Wonderful Town, 155

Gear, Luella
Gay Divorce, 82
Life Begins at 8:40, 87
On Your Toes, 94
Poppy, 40

Gee, Lonie
Shuffle Along, 34

Geer, Will
Cradle Will Rock, The, 101
110 in the Shade, 203

Gemignani, Alexander
Les Misérables, 349
Sunday in the Park With George, 356
Sweeney Todd, 338

Gennaro, Peter
Bells Are Ringing, 171
Guys and Dolls, 148
Pajama Game, The 161

Gettlefinger, Sara
Dirty Rotten Scoundrels, 334

Getze, Tilda
Jumbo, 93
Pal Joey, 112

Geva, Tamara
Flying Colors, 80
On Your Toes, 94
Three's a Crowd, 73
Whoopee, 66

Ghostley, Alice
New Faces of 1952, 154

Gibbs, Sheila
Once on This Island, 284

Gilford, Jack
Cabaret, 219
Funny Thing Happened on the Way to the
Forum, A, 198
No, No, Nanette, 231
Once Upon a Mattress, 181

Gillette, Anita
Carnival, 195

Gillette, Priscilla
Golden Apple, The, 160

Gillingwater, Claude
Mlle. Modiste, 10

Gillmore, Margalo
Peter Pan, 163

Gingold, Hermione
Little Night Music, A, 237

Givot, George
Do Re Mi, 194
Mexican Hayride, 122

Gleason, Jackie
Follow the Girls, 124
Take Me Along, 183

Gleason, Joanna
Dirty Rotten Scoundrels, 334
I Love My Wife, 245
Into the Woods, 277

Gleckler, Robert
Take a Chance, 82

Glockner, Eleanor
Beauty and the Beast, 297

Glover, John
Drowsy Chaperone, The, 342

Glover, Montego
Memphis, 369

Glover, Savion
Bring In 'Da Noise, Bring In 'Da Funk, 306
Jelly's Last Jam, 292

Glynn, Carlin
Best Little Whorehouse in Texas, The, 250

Goddard, Willoughby
Oliver!, 201

Godkin, Paul
High Button Shoes, 136

Goff, Jerry
Strike Up the Band, 70

Golden, Annie
Full Monty, The, 319

Goldin, Ricky Paull
Grease, 298

Goldsberry, Renee Elise
Color Purple, The, 340

Goldwyn, Tony
Promises, Promises, 378

Gomez, Carlos
In the Heights, 357

Gonzalez, Mandy
In the Heights, 357

Goodman, Dody
Miss Liberty, 144
Wonderful Town, 155

Goodman, Henry
Producers, The, 321

Goodwin, Deidre,
Chorus, Line, A, 343
Nine, 329

Gordon, Hayes
Brigadoon, 134

Gossett, Louis
Golden Boy, 210

Gottschell, Ruth
Mary Poppins, 344

Gould, Elliott
Irma la Douce, 190

Goulet, Robert
Camelot, 193
Happy Time, The, 22

Goz, Harry
Chess, 279

Grable, Betty
DuBarry Was a Lady, 109

Graff, Ilene
I Love My Wife, 245

Graff, Randy
City of Angels, 282
Fiddler on the Roof, 333
Les Misérables, 275

Grafton, Gloria
Jumbo, 93

Graham, R. E.
Florodora, 6
Merry Widow, The, 15

Graham, Ronald
Boys from Syracuse, The, 107
By Jupiter, 116
DuBarry Was a Lady, 109

Graham, Ronny
New Faces of 1952, 154

Graham, William
Little Mary Sunshine, 186

Grammer, Kelsey
La Cage aux Folles, 376

Granger, Michael
Fiddler on the Roof, 209

Grant, Micki
Don't Bother Me, I Can't Cope, 235

Granville, Bernard
Ziegfeld Follies, 20

Gray, Alexander
Ziegfeld Follies, 38

Gray, Dolores
Destry Rides Again, 180

Gray, Gilda
Ziegfeld Follies, 38

Green, Adolph
On the Town, 126

Green, Cody
West Side Story, 364

Green, Marion
I'd Rather Be Right, 98

Green, Mitzi
Babes in Arms, 98

Greene, Ellen
Little Shop of Horrors, 262

Greenleaf, Augusta
Red Mill, The, 13

Greenstreet, Sydney
Roberta, 84

Gregg, Julie
Happy Time, The, 222

Gregg, Mitchell
No Strings, 197
Unsinkable Molly Brown, The, 191

Gregory II, Chester
Tarzan, 347

Gregory, Paul
Whoopee, 66

Grey, Joel
Cabaret, 219
Chicago, 307
George M!, 223
Wicked, 332

Griffies, Ethel
Miss Liberty, 144

Griffith, Andy
Destry Rides Again, 180

Grimes, Tammy
42nd Street, 257
High Spirits, 208
Unsinkable Molly Brown, The, 191

Groenendaal, Cris
Funny Thing Happened on the Way to the
Forum, A, 304
Phantom of the Opera, The, 278

Groener, Harry
Cats, 263
Crazy for You, 288
Oklahoma!, 255

Groff, Jonathan
Spring Awakening, 345

Groody, Louise
Hit the Deck!, 56
No, No, Nanette, 47

Grossmith, Lawrence
Cat and the Fiddle, The, 77

Grout, James
Half a Sixpence, 211

Grove, Betty Ann
George M!, 223
On Your Toes, 264

Guest, Lance
Million Dollar Quartet, 375

Guittard, Laurence
Little Night Music, A, 237
Oklahoma!, 255

Gunton, Bob
Big River, 270
Evita, 254

Guyse, Sheila
Lost in the Stars, 144

Gwynne, Fred
Irma la Douce, 190

Gwynne, Haydn
Billy Elliot: The Musical, 361

Haakon, Paul
At Home Abroad, 89
Hooray for What!, 100

Mexican Hayride, 122
Show Is On, The, 97

Hackett, Albert
Whoopee, 66

Hadary, Jonathan
Gypsy, 282

Haines, A. Larry
Promises, Promises, 226

Hale, Chester
Music Box Revue, 37

Hale, George
Cocoanuts, The, 51

Haley, Jack
Follow Thru, 67
Inside U.S.A., 137
Take a Chance, 82

Hall, Adelaide
Blackbirds of 1928, 63
Jamaica, 176

Hall, Bettina
Anything Goes, 88
Cat and the Fiddle, The, 77
Little Show, The, 67

Hall, Delores
Best Little Whorehouse in Texas, The, 250

Hall, Juanita
Flower Drum Song, 178
House of Flowers, 165
South Pacific, 143
St. Louis Woman, 129
Street Scene, 132

Hall, Natalie
Music in the Air, 81

Hall, Thurston
Fifty Million Frenchmen, 69

Halliday, Gordon
Shenandoah, 242

Halliday, Robert
Desert Song, The, 54
New Moon, The, 64
Tip-Toes, 52

Hallor, Edith
Leave It to Jane, 26

Halston, Julie
Gypsy, 329

Hamilton, Caroline
Robin Hood, 5

Hamilton, Gloria
Lend an Ear, 139

Hamilton, Nancy
New Faces, 86

Hamilton, Thomas
As Thousands Cheer, 83

Hammond, Jonathan
Ragtime, 371

Hanan, Stephen
Cats, 263

Haney, Carol
Pajama Game, The, 161

Hanley, Ellen
Annie Get Your Gun, 130
Fiorello!, 186

Hanneford, Poodles
Jumbo, 93

Hansen, William
Brigadoon, 134

Hanson, Alexander
Little Night Music, A, 373

Harada, Ann
Avenue Q, 330

Harman, Paul
Chess, 279

Harney, Ben
Dreamgirls, 261

Haro, Joey
West Side Story, 364

Harper, Valerie
Take Me Along, 183

Harrigan, Edward
Mulligan Guard Ball, The, 4

Harrington, Pat
Call Me Madam, 147
Panama Hattie, 111

Harrington, Robert
Peter Pan, 163

Harris, Barbara
Apple Tree, The, 218
On a Clear Day You Can See Forever, 213

Harris, Harriet
Thoroughly Modern Millie, 325

Harris, Sam
Grease, 298

Harrison, Gregory
Follies, 320

Harrison, Ray
Make Mine Manhattan, 137

Harrison, Rex
My Fair Lady, 168

Harrold, Orville
Naughty Marietta, 17

Hart, Linda
Anything Goes, 277

Hart, Teddy
Boys from Syracuse, The, 107
One Touch of Venus, 120

Hart, Tony
Mulligan Guard Ball, The, 4

Hart, Vivian
Countess Maritza, 53

Hartman, David
Hello, Dolly!, 204

Hartman, Grace
Red, Hot and Blue!, 96

Hartman, Paul
Red, Hot and Blue!, 96

Harum, Eivind
Woman of the Year, 260

Harvey, Georgette
Porgy and Bess, 91

Haskell, David
Godspell, 233

Hassell, George
Countess Maritza, 53
Student Prince in Heidelberg, The, 45

Hasselhoff, David
Jekyll and Hyde, 308

Havoc, June
Mexican Hayride, 122
Pal Joey, 112

Hawkins, June
Carmen Jones, 122
St. Louis Woman, 129

Hawks, Victor W.
South Pacific, 358

Haworth, Jill
Cabaret, 219

Hay, Mary
Sally, 33
Sunny, 50

Hayden, Michael
Carousel, 296

Hayden, Sophie
Most Happy Fella, The, 293

Hayes, Bill
Me and Juliet, 157

Hayes, Sean
Promises, Promises, 378

Haynes, Tiger
Wiz, The, 241

Hazzard, John E.
Very Good Eddie, 23

Headley, Heather
Aida, 316
Lion King, The, 310

Heald, Anthony
Anything Goes, 277

Hearn, George
La Cage aux Folles, 266
Sunset Boulevard, 300

Heatherton, Joey
Sound of Music, The, 184

Heatherton, Ray
Babes in Arms, 98

Hecht, Paul
Rothschilds, The, 230
1776, 227

Heffernan, John
Purlie, 228

Heinsohn, Elisa
Phantom of the Opera, The, 278

Hemsley, Sherman
Purlie, 228

Henderson, Florence
Fanny, 164
Wish You Were Here, 154

Henning, Doug
Magic Show, The, 240

Hensley, Shuler
Oklahoma, 325
Tarzan, 347
Young Frankenstein, 353

Herbert, Evelyn
New Moon, The, 64

Herbert, Joseph
Fortune Teller, The, 6

Herbert, Ralph
Maytime, 24

Major Cast Members Index

Herbert, Tim
Follow the Girls, 124

Herdlicka, Hunter Ryan
Little Night Music, A, 373

Heredia, Wilson Jermaine
Rent, 305

Herlie, Eileen
Take Me Along, 183

Herrera, John
Mystery of Edwin Drood, The, 271

Herz, Ralph
Madame Sherry, 17

Hewer, John
Boy Friend, The, 162

Hewen, Christopher
My Fair Lady, 168
Unsinkable Molly Brown, The, 191

Hewitt, Alan
Call Me Madam, 147

Heywood, Billie
New Faces, 86

Hibbert, Edward
Curtains, 350
Drowsy Chaperone, The, 342

Hickey, John Benjamin
Cabaret, 312

Hicks, Rodney
Rent, 305

Higgins, Joel
Shenandoah, 242

Hill, Annabelle
Kiss Me, Kate, 141

Hill, Arthur
Wizard of Oz, The, 8

Hill, Bobby
Don't Bother Me, I Can't Cope, 235

Hill, Ruby
St. Louis Woman, 129

Hillner, John
Crazy for You, 288

Hines, Gregory
Jelly's Last Jam, 292
Sophisticated Ladies, 259

Hingston, Seán Martin
Promises, Promises, 378

Hinnant, Bill
You're a Good Man, Charlie Brown, 221

Hinnant, Skip
You're a Good Man, Charlie Brown, 221

Hitchcock, Raymond
Ziegfeld Follies, 34

Hobson, Louis
Next to Normal, 368

Hoch, Chris
La Cage aux Folles, 376

Hoctor, Harriet
Three Musketeers, The, 63
Ziegfeld Follies, 93

Hodge, Douglas
La Cage aux Folles, 376

Hodges, Eddie
Music Man, The, 177

Hodges, Joy
I'd Rather Be Right, 98

Hoey, Evelyn
Fifty Million Frenchmen, 69

Hoff, Christian
Jersey Boys, 339

Hoffa, Portland
George White's Scandals, 52
Little Show, The, 67
Three's a Crowd, 73

Hoffman, Jackie
Addams Family, The, 374
Hairspray, 326
Xanadu, 352

Hoffman Jr., Max
Sweet Adeline, 68

Holbrook, Curtis
West Side Story, 364
Xanadu, 352

Holder, Geoffrey
House of Flowers, 165

Holgate, Ronald
Annie Get Your Gun, 315
Funny Thing Happened on the Way to the
Forum, A, 198
1776, 227

Holliday, Jennifer
Dreamgirls, 261

Holliday, Judy
Bells Are Ringing, 171

Hollis, Melody
Irving Berlin's White Christmas, 362

Holloway, Stanley
My Fair Lady, 168

Holloway, Sterling
Garrick Gaieties, The, 46

Holm, Celeste
Bloomer Girl, 125
Oklahoma!, 119

Holman, Libby
Garrick Gaieties, The, 46
Little Show, The, 67
Three's a Crowd, 73

Holmes, E. B.
Black Crook, The, 3

Holmes, Taylor
I'd Rather Be Right, 98

Hong, Arabella
Flower Drum Song, 178

Hope, Bob
Red, Hot and Blue!, 96
Roberta, 84
Ziegfeld Follies, 93

Hopkins, Miriam
Music Box Revue, 37

Hopkins, Ryan
King and I, The, 303

Hopper, Edna Wallace
Florodora, 6

Horne, Lena
Jamaica, 176

Horton, Robert
110 in the Shade, 203

Hoty, Dee
City of Angels, 282
Footloose, 313
Will Rogers Follies, The, 287

Houston, Ethel Du Fre
Sweethearts, 19

Howard, Esther
Sunny, 50

Howard, Eugene
George White's Scandals, 52, 76
Ziegfeld Follies, 85

Howard, Ken
Promises, Promises, 226
1776, 227

Howard, Willie
George White's Scandals, 52, 76
Girl Crazy, 72
Ziegfeld Follies, 85

Howes, Sally Ann
What Makes Sammy Run?, 206

Howland, Beth
Company, 229

Hoysradt, John
Cradle Will Rock, The, 101
Ziegfeld Follies, 93

Huey, Richard
Bloomer Girl, 125

Huff, Forrest
Sinbad, 29

Huffman, Cady
Producers, The, 321
Will Rogers Follies, The 287

Hunt, Ida Brooks
Chocolate Soldier, The, 16

Huntley Jr., G. P.
Gay Divorce, 82

Hurst, David
Camelot, 193

Husmann, Ron
Fiorello, 186

Huston, Walter
Knickerbocker Holiday, 104

Hutcherson, LaVern
Porgy and Bess, 156

Hutton, Betty
Panama Hattie, 111

Hutton, Bill
Joseph and the Amazing Technicolor
Dreamcoat, 260

Hutton, Ina Ray
Ziegfeld Follies, 85

Hyers, Frank
Panama Hattie, 111

Hyman, Phyllis
Sophisticated Ladies, 259

Hyson, Carl
Oh, Boy!, 24

Ide, Letitia
As Thousands Cheer, 83

Major Cast Members Index

Iglehart, James Monroe
Memphis, 369

Ing, Alvin
Flower Drum Song, 327
Pacific Overtures, 333

Ingham, Barrie
Jekyll and Hyde, 308

Ingram, Rex
Cabin in the Sky, 111
St. Louis Woman, 129

Ingram, Tad
Most Happy Fella, The, 293

Irving, George S.
Bells Are Ringing, 171
Call Me Mister, 129
Gentlemen Prefer Blondes, 146
Happy Time, The, 222
Irene, 238
Irma la Douce, 190
Me and Juliet, 157
Me and My Girl, 273
Oklahoma!, 119
On Your Toes, 264

Irwin, Charles
Up in Central Park, 126

Ives, Burl
Boys from Syracuse, The, 107
This Is the Army, 117

Ivey, Dana
Sunday in the Park With George, 269

Ivey, Judith
Follies, 320

Jabara, Paul
Hair, 224

Jackman, Hope
Oliver!, 201

Jackson, Cheyenne
Finian's Rainbow, 370
Xanadu, 352

Jackson, Christopher
In the Heights, 357

Jackson, Eddie
New Yorkers, The, 74

Jackson, Ernestine
Raisin, 239

Jackson, Ethel
Merry Widow, The, 15

Jackson, Robert
Raisin, 239

Jacobs, Adam
Les Misérables, 349

Jacobson, Irving
Man of La Mancha, 215

Jacoby, Mark
Man of La Mancha, 329
Ragtime, 311
Show Boat, 299
Sweeney Todd, 338
Sweet Charity, 272

James, Brian d'Arcy,
Dirty Rotten Scoundrels, 334
Titanic, 307

James, Polly
Half a Sixpence, 211

James, Zachary
Addams Family, The, 374

Jamin-Bartlett, D.
Little Night Music, A, 237

Jamison, Judith
Sophisticated Ladies, 259

Jardon, Dorothy
Madame Sherry, 17

Jarvis, Mitchell
Rock of Ages, 366

Jbara, Gregory
Billy Elliot: The Musical, 361
Dirty Rotten Scoundrels, 334
Victor/Victoria, 303

Jeffreys, Anne
Street Scene, 132

Jenkins, Daniel H.
Big River, 270

Jennings, Ken
Sweeney Todd, 253
Urinetown, 323

Jerome, Timothy
Grand Hotel, 281
Me and My Girl, 273

Jeter, Michael
Grand Hotel, 281

Jillian, Ann
Sugar Babies, 255

Jillson, Joyce
Roar of the Greasepaint—The Smell of the
Crowd, The, 212

Johns, Glynis
Little Night Music, A, 237

Johnson, Chic
Hellzapoppin, 103

Johnson, Christine
Carousel, 127

Johnson, Hall
Blackbirds of 1928, 63

Johnson, J. Rosamond
Cabin in the Sky, 111
Porgy and Bess, 91

Johnson, Karen
You're a Good Man, Charlie Brown, 221

Johnson, Susan
Most Happy Fella, The, 170

Johnson, Van
Pal Joey, 112
Too Many Girls, 108

Johnston, Fannie
Florodora, 6

Johnston, Johnny
Tree Grows in Brooklyn, A, 152

Johnston, Justine
Follies, 232
Me and My Girl, 273

Johnstone, Justine
Oh, Boy!, 24
Watch Your Step, 20
Ziegfeld Follies, 20

Jolson, Al
Sinbad, 29

Jonas, Johanne
Godspell, 233

Jonay, Roberta
Allegro, 136

Jones, Anne
Once Upon a Mattress, 181

Jones, Candy
Mexican Hayride, 122

Jones, David
Oliver!, 201

Jones, Dean
Company, 229

Jones, John Price
Good News!, 56

Jones, Leilani
Little Shop of Horrors, 262

Jones, Nellie
Mulligan Guard Ball, The, 4

Jones, Rebecca Naomi
American Idiot, 377

Jones, Reed
Cats, 263

Jones, Tom
Fantasticks, The, 189

Jordan, Dorothy
Funny Face, 59

Joy, Nicholas
Music in the Air, 81

Joyce, Elaine
Sugar, 235

Jue, Francis
Pacific Overtures, 333

Julia, Raul
Nine, 262
Two Gentlemen of Verona, 234

Kahn, Madeline
On the Twentieth Century, 249

Kain, Luka
South Pacific, 358

Kandel, Paul
Tommy, 294

Kane, Brad
She Loves Me, 296

Kaplan, Jonathan
Falsettos, 293

Karl, Andy
Legally Blonde, 351

Karl, Tom
Robin Hood, 5

Karnilova, Maria
Call Me Mister, 129
Fiddler on the Roof, 209
Gypsy, 182
Miss Liberty, 144
Zorba, 225

Kasznar, Kurt
Sound of Music, The, 184

Kavanaugh, Stan
Ziegfeld Follies, 93

Kayden, Spencer
Urinetown, 323

Kaye, A. P.
Jumbo, 93

Kaye, Danny
Lady in the Dark, 113
Let's Face It!, 115

Kaye, Judy
On the Twentieth Century, 249
Mamma Mia!, 324
Phantom of the Opera, The, 278
Ragtime, 311

Kaye, Stubby
Guys and Dolls, 148
Li'l Abner, 171

Kazan, Lainie
Funny Girl, 207

Kazee, Steve
110 in the Shade, 352

Keagy, Grace
Woman of the Year, 260

Keane, George
Brigadoon, 134

Kearns, Allen
Funny Face, 59
Girl Crazy, 72
Tip-Toes, 52

Keaton, Diane
Hair, 224

Kedrova, Lila
Zorba, 268

Keeler, Ruby
No, No, Nanette, 231

Keenan-Bolger, Celia
Les Misérables, 349

Keith, Larry
Titanic, 307

Kellogg, Lynn
Hair, 224

Kellaway, Cecil
Greenwillow, 187

Kelly, Gene
Leave It to Me!, 105
Pal Joey, 112

Kelly, Harry
Watch Your Step, 20
Ziegfeld Follies, 29

Kelly, Kristen Lee
Rent, 305

Kelly, Patsy
Flying Colors, 80
Irene, 238
No, No, Nanette, 231

Kelton, Pert
Greenwillow, 187
Music Man, The, 177
Sunny, 50

Kennedy, Madge
Poppy, 40

Kennedy, Sandy
King and I, The, 151

Kenney, Ed
Flower Drum Song, 178

Kent, William
Funny Face, 59
Girl Crazy, 72
Rose-Marie, 43

Kermoyan, Michael
Camelot, 193
King and I, The, 248

Kert, Larry
West Side Story, 175

Khan, Chaka
Color Purple, The, 340

Kiepura, Jan
Merry Widow, The, 120

Kikuchi, Susan
Jerome Robbins' Broadway, 279
King and I, The, 248

Kiley, Richard
Kismet, 158
Man of La Mancha, 215
No Strings, 197
Redhead, 179

Kilty, Jack
Make Mine Manhattan, 137

Kim, Randall Duk
Flower Drum Song, 327
King and I, The, 303

Kim, Taewon
The King and I, 303

Kimball, Chad
Memphis, 369

Kimball, Grace
Wizard of Oz, The, 8

Kimbrough, Charles
Company, 229
Sunday in the Park With George, 269

King, Charles
Hit the Deck!, 56
New Yorkers, The, 74
Watch Your Step, 20

King, Dennis
I Married an Angel, 102
Rose-Marie, 43
Three Musketeers, The, 63
Vagabond King, The, 48

King, John Michael
King and I, The, 248
My Fair Lady, 168

King, Mabel
Wiz, The, 241

Kinney, Ray
Hellzapoppin, 103

Kirby, Max
Bitter Sweet, 68

Kirk, Lisa
Allegro, 136
Kiss Me, Kate, 141

Kitt, Eartha
New Faces of 1952, 154

Klausner, Terri
Sophisticated Ladies, 259

Klavun, Walter
What Makes Sammy Run?, 206

Klein, Robert
Apple Tree, The, 218
They're Playing Our Song, 252

Kline, Kevin
On the Twentieth Century, 249
Pirates of Penzance, The, 258

Klugman, Jack
Gypsy, 182

Knight, June
Jubilee, 92
Sweethearts, 134
Take a Chance, 82

Kobart, Ruth
Funny Thing Happened on the Way to the Forum, A, 198
How to Succeed in Business Without Really Trying, 196

Kober, Andrew
Hair, 365

Kollmar, Richard
Knickerbocker Holiday, 104
Too Many Girls, 108

Korbich, Eddie
Carousel, 296
Drowsy Chaperone, The, 342

Kosloff, Alexis
Sinbad, 29

Kouyaté, Ismael
Fela!, 372

Kowalik, Trent
Billy Elliot: The Musical, 361

Kraft, Beatrice
Kismet, 158

Krakowski, Jane
Grand Hotel, 281
Nine, 329
Starlight Express, 276

Kramer, Marsha
Peter Pan, 254

Kreis, Levi
Million Dollar Quartet, 375

Kritzer, Leslie
Legally Blonde, 351

Krupska, Dania
Can-Can, 156

Kubala, Michael
Jerome Robbins' Broadway, 279

Kudisch, Mark
Thoroughly Modern Millie, 325

Kuhn, Judy
Chess, 279
Les Misérables, 275

Kuhner, John
Your Own Thing, 222

Kulish, Kiril
Billy Elliot: The Musical, 361

Kushnier, Jeremy
Footloose, 313

La Chanze
Color Purple, The, 340
Once on This Island, 284

LaBrecque, Doug
Show Boat, 299

Lackey, Herndon
Kiss of the Spider Woman—The Musical, 295

Ladd, Cheryl
Annie Get Your Gun, 315

LaFosse, Robert
Jerome Robbins' Broadway, 279

Lahr, Bert
DuBarry Was a Lady, 109
Flying High, 71
Hold Everything!, 65
Life Begins at 8:40, 87
Show Is On, The, 97

Laine, Cleo
Mystery of Edwin Drood, The, 271

Lalor, Frank
Pink Lady, The, 18

Lambert, Gelan
Fela!, 372

Lambert, Mark
Little Night Music, A, 237

Lambert, Robert
Gypsy, 282

Lamberts, Heath
Beauty and the Beast, 297

Lamont, Robin
Godspell, 233

Land, Ken
Promises, Promises, 378

Landes, Steve
Rain—A Tribute to the Beatles on Broadway,
389

Lane, Nathan
Addams Family, The, 374
Funny Thing Happened on the Way to the
Forum, A, 304
Guys and Dolls, 290
Producers, The, 321

Lane, Rosemary
Best Foot Forward, 114

Lang, Harold
Kiss Me, Kate, 141
Pal Joey, 153

Lang, Pearl
Carousel, 127
One Touch of Venus, 120

Langner, Christine
Cats, 263

Lanier, Jane
Jerome Robbins' Broadway, 279

Lanning, Jerry
Mame, 217

Lansbury, Angela
Little Night Music, A, 373
Mame, 217
Sweeney Todd, 253

Larkin, Leigh Ann
Gypsy, 359
Little Night Music, A, 373

Larner, Elizabeth
Me and My Girl, 273

Larsen, Liz
Most Happy Fella, The, 293

Larson, William
Fantasticks, The, 189

LaRue, Grace
Follies of 1907, 14

Lascoe, Henry
Carnival, 195
Silk Stockings, 166
Wonderful Town, 155

Latessa, Dick
Hairspray, 326
Promises, Promises, 378
Will Rogers Follies, The, 287

Latham, Cynthia
Redhead, 179

Laughlin, Anna
Wizard of Oz, The, 8

Laurence, Paula
One Touch of Venus, 120

Law, Evelyn
Ziegfeld Follies, 38

Law, Jennie Lou
Lend an Ear, 139

Lawlor, Mary
Good News!, 56
No, No, Nanette, 47

Lawrence, Carol
New Faces of 1952, 154
West Side Story, 175

Lawrence, Eddie
Bells Are Ringing, 171

Lawrence, Gertrude
Andre Charlot's Revue of 1924, 42
King and I, The, 151
Lady in the Dark, 113
Oh, Kay!, 53

Lawrence, Jane
Where's Charley?, 138

Lawrence, Megan
Hair, 365

Lawrence, Steve
What Makes Sammy Run?, 206

Lay, Dilys
Boy Friend, The, 162

Laye, Evelyn
Bitter Sweet, 68

Layton, Joe
Wonderful Town, 155

Lazar, Aaron
Les Misérables, 349
Little Night Music, A, 373
Tale of Two Cities, A, 360

Lean, Cecil
Blue Paradise, The, 21

Leavel, Beth
Crazy for You, 288
Drowsy Chaperone, The, 342

Lee, Baayork
Chorus Line, A, 243
King and I, The, 151

Lee, Gavin
Mary Poppins, 344

Lee, Irving Allen
Sweet Charity, 272

Lee, Kathryn
As the Girls Go, 139

Lee, Lois
High Button Shoes, 136

Lee, Sammy
Firefly, The, 18

Lee, Sondra
Hello, Dolly!, 204
High Button Shoes, 136
Peter Pan, 163

Leeds, Andrew Harrison
Falsettos, 293

Leeds, Phil
Can-Can, 156

Lenox, Adriane
Kiss Me, Kate, 315

Lenya, Lotte
Cabaret, 219
Threepenny Opera, The, 159

LeRoy, Hal
Too Many Girls, 108

LeRoy, Ken
West Side Story, 175

Levene, Sam
Guys and Dolls, 148

Levering, Kate
42nd Street, 322
Music Man, The, 319

Levy, Caissie
Hair, 365

Levey, Ethel
Little Johnny Jones, 10

Lewis, Ada
Very Good Eddie, 23

Lewis, Marcia
Chicago, 307
Grease, 298

Lewis, Mary
Ziegfeld Follies, 34, 38

Lewis, Norm
Les Misérables, 349
Little Mermaid, The, 355

Lewis, Tom
Little Johnny Jones, 10

Lewis, Ted
Greenwich Village Follies, 31

Lewis-Evans, Kecia
Once on This Island, 284

Li, Li Jun
South Pacific, 358

Lightner, Winnie
George White's Scandals, 40

Ligon, Tom
Your Own Thing, 222

Lillie, Beatrice
Andre Charlot's Revue of 1924, 42
At Home Abroad, 89
High Spirits, 208
Inside U.S.A., 137
Show Is On, The, 97

Lilo
Can-Can, 156

Limon, Jose
As Thousands Cheer, 83

Linden, Hal
Rothschilds, The, 230

Lindsay, Robert
Me and My Girl, 273

Linn, Bambi
Carousel, 127
Oklahoma!, 119

Linn-Baker, Mark
Funny Thing Happened on the Way to the Forum, A, 304

Lishner, Leon
Threepenny Opera, The, 159

Litel, John
Irene, 32

Lithgow, John
Dirty Rotten Scoundrels, 334

Little, Cleavon
Purlie, 228

Llana, Jose
Flower Drum Song, 327
King and I, The, 303
25th Annual Putnam County Spelling Bee, The, 337

Loeb, Philip
Band Wagon, The, 74
Flying Colors, 80
Garrick Gaieties, The, 46

Logan, Ella
Finian's Rainbow, 133

Logan, Stacey
Beauty and the Beast, 297

London, Caroline
Dr. Seuss' How the Grinch Stole Christmas, 348

Long, Shorty
Most Happy Fella, The, 170

Long, Tamara
Dames at Sea, 226

Long Jr., Nick
Louisiana Purchase, 110

Lopez, Carlos
Grease, 298

Lopez, Priscilla
Chorus Line, A, 243
In the Heights, 357

Loring, Estelle
Inside U.S.A., 137

Lorraine, Lillian
Ziegfeld Follies, 29

Lorraine, Ted
Blue Paradise, The, 21

Losch, Tilly
Band Wagon, The, 74

Lotito, Mark
Most Happy Fella, The, 293

Loudon, Dorothy
Annie, 247

Louise, Merle
Company, 229
Into the Woods, 277
Kiss of the Spider Woman—The Musical, 295
La Cage aux Folles, 266
Sweeney Todd, 253

Louise, Tina
Li'l Abner, 171

Love, Edward
Dancin', 250

Lowe, Jackie
Tap Dance Kid, The, 268

Lucas, Jonathan
Golden Apple, The, 160

Lucci, Susan
Annie Get Your Gun, 315

Luce, Claire
Gay Divorce, 82

Luckey, Susan
Take Me Along, 183

Luisi, James
Sweet Charity, 216
Zorba, 225

Lukas, Paul
Call Me Madam, 147

Luke, Keye
Flower Drum Song, 178

Luker, Rebecca
Music Man, The, 319
Mary Poppins, 344
Secret Garden, The , 286
Show Boat, 299

Lumb, Geoffrey
Oliver!, 201

Lund, Art
Most Happy Fella, The, 170

LuPone, Patti
Anything Goes, 277
Evita, 254
Gypsy, 359
Sweeney Todd, 338

LuPone, Robert
Chorus Line, A, 243

Luz, Franc
Little Shop of Horrors, 262

Lyles, Aubrey
Shuffle Along, 34

Lynch, Stephen
Wedding Singer, The, 346

Lynch, Teddy
New Faces, 86

Lynde, Paul
Bye Bye Birdie, 188
New Faces of 1952, 154

Lyndeck, Edmund
Into the Woods, 277
Sweeney Todd, 253

Lyon, Rick
Avenue Q, 330

Lyons, Colette
Show Boat, 128

Lyons, Rob
Million Dollar Quartet, 375

Lytell, Bert
Lady in the Dark, 113

Macalush, Crysta
Tommy, 294

Macaulay, Joseph
Funny Girl, 207
Three Musketeers, The, 63

MacDonald, Christie
Sweethearts, 19

MacDonald, Jeanette
Tip-Toes, 52

MacDonald, W.H.
Robin Hood, 5

Mack, Annie
Mulligan Guard Ball, The, 4

Mack, Cecil
Blackbirds of 1928, 63

Mack, George E.
Anything Goes, 88
Of Thee I Sing, 78

Mackaye, Dorothy
Rose-Marie, 43

Mackenzie, Will
Half a Sixpence, 211

MacLaine, Shirley
Me and Juliet, 157
Pajama Game, The, 161

MacMurray, Fred
Roberta, 84
Three's a Crowd, 73

MacNeil, Cornell
Sweethearts, 134
Where's Charley?, 138

MacRae, Heather
Falsettos, 293

Madden, Jeanne
Knickerbocker Holiday, 104

Maggart, Brandon
Applause, 228

Maguire, Michael
Les Misérables, 275

Mahoney, Francis X.
Show Boat, 60

Mahoney, Will
Earl Carroll Vanities, 76

Mahony-Bennett, Kathleen
Anything Goes, 277

Main, Marjorie
Music in the Air, 81

Mais, Michele
Rock of Ages, 366

Makarova, Natalia
On Your Toes, 264

Mako
Pacific Overtures, 245

Mala, Spiro
Most Happy Fella, The, 293

Malina, Luba
Mexican Hayride, 122

Mallory, Ramona
Little Night Music, A, 373

Mallory, Victoria
Follies, 232
Little Night Music, A, 237

Mambo, Kevin
Fela!, 372

Mandan, Robert
Applause, 228

Mandavi, Aasif
Oklahoma, 325

Mann, Terrence
Addams Family, The, 374
Beauty and the Beast, 297
Cats, 263
Les Misérables, 275
Scarlet Pimpernel, The, 309

Manning, Jack
Do I Hear a Waltz?, 210

Manson, Alan
This Is the Army, 117

Mansur, Susan
Irving Berlin's White Christmas, 362

Manzano, Sonia
Godspell, 233

Maple, Audrey
Firefly, The, 18

Marand, Patricia
Wish You Were Here, 154

Marceau, Yvonne
Grand Hotel, 281

Margulies, David
Wonderful Town, 332

Maricle, Marijane
Paint Your Wagon, 152

Marie, Julienne
Do I Hear a Waltz?, 210

Marker, Preshy
Funny Thing Happened on the Way to the Forum, A, 198

Markham, Monte
Irene, 238

Marks, Joe E.
Li'l Abner, 171
Peter Pan, 163

Marlowe, Gloria
Plain and Fancy, 166

Marlowe, Marion
Sound of Music, The, 184

Maroulis, Constantine
Rock of Ages, 366

Marsh, Howard
Blossom Time, 38
Show Boat, 60
Student Prince In Heidelberg, The, 45

Marshall, Austin
I'd Rather Be Right, 98

Marshall, Everett
George White's Scandals, 76
Ziegfeld Follies, 85

Marshall, Jay
Love Life, 138

Marshall, Mort
Gentlemen Prefer Blondes, 146
Little Me, 200

Martin, Andrea
Oklahoma, 325
Young Frankenstein, 353

Martin, Barney
Chicago, 244

Martin, Hugh
Hooray for What!, 100
Louisiana Purchase, 110

Martin, Jesse L.
Rent, 305

Martin, Leila
Phantom of the Opera, The, 278
Rothschilds, The, 230

Martin, Mary
I Do! I Do!, 220
Leave It to Me!, 105
One Touch of Venus, 120
Peter Pan, 163
Sound of Music, The, 184
South Pacific, 143

Martin, Millicent
Boy Friend, The, 162

Martin, Virginia
How to Succeed in Business Without Really Trying, 196
Little Me, 200

Martindel, Edward
Naughty Marietta, 17

Martyn, Kathlene
Lady, Be Good!, 44

Marvenga, Ilse
Student Prince in Heidelberg, The, 45

Marx Brothers
Cocoanuts, The, 51

Mason, Karen
Mamma Mia!, 324

Mason, Luba
How to Succeed in Business Without Really Trying, 302

Massey, Daniel
She Loves Me, 202

Massi, Bernice
No Strings, 197
What Makes Sammy Run?, 206

Mastrantonio, Elizabeth
Man of La Mancha, 329

Mathews, George
Do Re Mi, 194

Mathis, Stanley Wayne
Jelly's Last Jam, 292

Matlock, Norman
Two Gentlemen of Verona, 234

Matteson, Ruth
Merry Widow, The, 120

Matthews, Edward
Porgy and Bess, 91

Matthews, Inez
Carmen Jones, 122
Lost in the Stars, 144

Matthews, Jessie
Andre Charlot's Revue of 1924, 42

Matthews, Roger
Shuffle Along, 34

Mattox, Matt
Once Upon a Mattress, 181

Mattson, Eric
Carousel, 127

Mature, Victor
Lady in the Dark, 113

May, Ada
Rio Rita, 55

May, Marty
Annie Get Your Gun, 130
Best Foot Forward, 114

Mayes, Sally
She Loves Me, 296

Mayfair, Mitzi
Show Is On, The, 97
Take a Chance, 82

Mayfield, Cleo
Blue Paradise, The, 21

Mayfield, Julian
Lost in the Stars, 144

Mayhew, Stella
Hit the Deck!, 56

Maynard, Tyler
Little Mermaid, The, 355

Mayro, Jacqueline
Gypsy, 182

Mazzie, Marin
Kiss Me, Kate, 315
Passion, 298
Ragtime, 311

McAllen, Kathleen Rowe
Aspects of Love, 283

McArdle, Andrea
Annie, 247
Starlight Express, 276

McCarthy, Jeff
Urinetown, 323

McCarthy Sisters
George White's Scandals, 52

McCarty, Mary
Chicago, 244
Follies, 232
Miss Liberty, 144

McCarty, Michael
Mary Poppins, 344

McCauley, Jack
Gentlemen Prefer Blondes, 146
High Button Shoes, 136
Hit the Deck!, 56
Little Show, The, 67
Show Is On, The, 97

McClelland, Kay
City of Angels, 282
Into the Woods, 277

McClendon, Afi
Once on This Island, 284

McComas, Carroll
Oh, Lady!, Lady!!, 26

McConnell, Lulu
Peggy-Ann, 54
Ziegfeld Follies, 38

McCormick, Myron
South Pacific, 143

McCourt, Sean
Mary Poppins, 344
Wicked, 332

McCown, Ellen
Greenwillow, 187

McCracken, Joan
Bloomer Girl, 125
Me and Juliet, 157
Oklahoma!, 119

McCullough, Paul
Strike Up the Band, 70

McCurry, John
Porgy and Bess, 156

McCutcheon, Bill
Anything Goes, 277

McDonald, Audra Ann
Carousel, 296
110 in the Shade, 352
Ragtime, 311

McDonald, Gertrude
Tip-Toes, 52

McDonald, Grace
Babes in Arms, 98

McDonald, Ray
Babes in Arms, 98

McDonnell, Kyle
Make Mine Manhattan, 137

McDowall, Roddy
Camelot, 193

McElroy, Michael
Tommy, 294

McEntire, Reba
Annie Get Your Gun, 315

McFarland, Nan
Sound of Music, The, 184

McGill, Bruce
My One and Only, 264

McGillin, Howard
Anything Goes, 277
Mystery of Edwin Drood, The, 271
She Loves Me, 296

McGowan, Jack
George White's Scandals, 40

McGrath, Katherine
Tale of Two Cities, A, 360

McGrath, Michael
Monty Python's Spamalot, 336

McHale, Duke
Babes in Arms, 98

McIntyre, Gerry
Once on This Island, 284

McKean, Michael
Pajama Game, The, 341

McKechnie, Donna
Chorus Line, A, 243
Company, 229
How To Succeed in Business Without Really
Trying, 196
Promises, Promises, 226

McKee, Lonette
Show Boat, 299

McKneely, Joey
Jerome Robbins' Broadway, 279

McLennan, Oliver
Rosalie, 62

McLerie, Allyn Ann
Miss Liberty, 144
On the Town, 126
One Touch of Venus, 120
Where's Charley?, 138

McMartin, John
Follies, 232
Into the Woods, 326
Little Mary Sunshine, 186
Show Boat, 299
Sweet Charity, 216

McNaughton, Tom
Sweethearts, 19

McNeely, Anna
Cats, 263

McQueen, Armelia
Ain't Misbehavin', 251

Meader, George
Cat and the Fiddle, The, 77

Medford, Kay
Bye Bye Birdie, 188
Funny Girl, 207
Paint Your Wagon, 152

Meehan, Danny
Funny Girl, 207

Meiser, Edith
Garrick Gaieties, The, 46
Let's Face It!, 115
Mexican Hayride, 122
Peggy-Ann, 54
Unsinkable Molly Brown, The, 191

Meisner, Sanford
Garrick Gaieties, The, 46

Menzel, Idina
Rent, 305
Wicked, 332

Mercer, Marian
Promises, Promises, 226
Your Own Thing, 222

Merediz, Olga
In the Heights, 357

Merkel, Una
Take Me Along, 183

Merlin, Joanna
Fiddler on the Roof, 209

Merman, Ethel
Annie Get Your Gun, 130
Anything Goes, 88
Call Me Madam, 147
DuBarry Was a Lady, 109
George White's Scandals, 76
Girl Crazy, 72
Gypsy, 182
Panama Hattie, 111
Red, Hot and Blue!, 96
Take a Chance, 82

Merrill, Dina
On Your Toes, 264

Merrill, Gary
This Is the Army, 117

Merrill, Scott
Threepenny Opera, The, 159

Metaxa, Georges
Cat and the Fiddle, The, 77

Meyers, Timothy
Grease, 234

Michaels, Frankie
Mame, 217

Michele, Lea
Spring Awakening, 345

Michelena, Vera
Ziegfeld Follies, 34

Michell, Keith
Irma la Douce, 190

Michener, Dean
Golden Apple, The, 160

Middleton, Ray
Annie Get Your Gun, 130
Knickerbocker Holiday, 104
Love Life, 138
Man of La Mancha, 215
Roberta, 84

Migenes, Julia
Fiddler on the Roof, 209

Migliaccio, Donna
Ragtime, 371

Miguel, Mayumi
Promises, Promises, 378

Milburn, Mary
Ziegfeld Follies, 34

Milford, Penelope
Shenandoah, 242

Miller, Ann
Sugar Babies, 255

Miller, Buzz
Funny Girl, 207

Miller, Flournoy
Shuffle Along, 34

Miller, Marilyn
As Thousands Cheer, 83
Rosalie, 62
Sally, 33
Sunny, 50
Ziegfeld Follies, 29, 31

Mills, Stephanie
Wiz, The, 241

Minski, Les
Tale of Two Cities, A, 360

Miranda, Lin-Manuel
In the Heights, 357

Mireille
Bitter Sweet, 68

Mitchell, Abbie
Porgy and Bess, 91

Mitchell, Arthur
House of Flowers, 165

Mitchell, Brian Stokes
Kiss Me, Kate, 315
Man of La Mancha, 329
Ragtime, 311

Mitchell, Frank
Earl Carroll Vanities, 76

Mitchell, James
Brigadoon, 134
Carnival, 195
Paint Your Wagon, 152

Mitchell, John Cameron
Secret Garden, The, 286

Mitchell, Lauren
Into the Woods, 277

Mitty, Nomi
Tree Grows in Brooklyn, A, 152

Mitzman, Marcia
Chess, 279
Tommy, 294

Mladova, Milada
Merry Widow, The, 120

Molaskey, Jessica
Sunday in the Park With George, 356

Molina, Alfred
Fiddler on the Roof, 333

Molina, Lauren
Rock of Ages, 366

Monk, Debra
Curtains, 350

Montalban, Ricardo
Jamaica, 176

Montevecchi, Lilianne
Grand Hotel, 281
Nine, 262

Montgomery, David
Red Mill, The, 13
Wizard of Oz, The, 8

Moore, Constance
By Jupiter, 116

Moore, Crista
Gypsy, 282

Moore, Florence
Music Box Revue, 37

Moore, Karen
Gypsy, 182

Moore, Melba
Hair, 224
Purlie, 228

Moore, Monette
Flying Colors, 80

Moore, Tim
Blackbirds of 1928, 63

Moore, Victor
Anything Goes, 88
Forty-five Minutes from Broadway, 13
Funny Face, 59
Hold Everything!, 65
Leave It to Me!, 105
Louisiana Purchase, 110
Of Thee I Sing, 78
Oh, Kay!, 53

Moran, Lois
Of Thee I Sing, 78

Mordente, Tony
West Side Story, 175

Moreland, Mantan
Blackbirds of 1928, 63

Morgan, Cass
Memphis, 369

Morgan, Frank
Band Wagon, The, 74
Rosalie, 62

Morgan, Helen
Show Boat, 60
Sweet Adeline, 68

Morgan, Lee
Tommy, 294

Morison, Patricia
Kiss Me, Kate, 141

Morris, Anita
Jesus Christ Superstar, 233
Magic Show, The, 240
Nine, 262

Morris, David
On Your Toes, 94

Morris, Howard
Gentlemen Prefer Blondes, 146

Morrison, Matthew
Hairspray, 326
Light in the Piazza, The, 338
South Pacific, 358

Morrow, Doretta
King and I, The, 151
Kismet, 158
Where's Charley?, 138

Morse, Robert
How to Succeed in Business Without Really
Trying, 196
Sugar, 235
Take Me Along, 183

Morton, Charles
Black Crook, The, 3

Morton, Harry K.
Countess Maritza, 53
Greenwich Village Follies, 31

Morton, Joe
Raisin, 239

Moses, Burke
Beauty and the Beast, 297
Fantasticks, The, 343

Moss, Arnold
Follies, 232

Moss, Kathi
Nine, 262

Moss & Fontana
Sunny, 50

Mostel, Zero
Fiddler on the Roof, 209
Funny Thing Happened on the Way to the
Forum, A, 198

Mowry, Greg
Starlight Express, 276

Mugleston, Linda
Wonderful Town, 332
Young Frankenstein, 353

Mulheren, Michael
Kiss Me, Kate, 315
La Cage aux Folles, 333

Mullally, Megan
Grease, 298
How to Succeed in Business Without
Really Trying, 302
Young Frankenstein, 353

Mundin, Herbert
Andre Charlot's Revue of 1924, 42

Mundy, Meg
Hooray for What!, 100

Munshin, Jules
Call Me Mister, 129

Munson, Ona
Hold Everything!, 65

Mura, Corinna
Mexican Hayride, 122

Murphy, Donna
King and I, The, 303
Passion, 298
Wonderful Town, 332

Murphy, George
Of Thee I Sing, 78
Roberta, 84

Murphy, Sally
Carousel, 296

Murray, Elizabeth
Madame Sherry, 17
Watch Your Step, 20

Murray, J. Harold
Face the Music, 79
Rio Rita, 55

Murray, Mae
Ziegfeld Follies, 20

Murray, Peg
Cabaret, 219

Murray, Wynn
Babes in Arms, 98
Boys from Syracuse, The, 107

Myers, Pamela
Company, 229
Into the Woods, 326

Mylett, Jeffrey
Godspell, 233

Myrtil, Odette
Cat and the Fiddle, The, 77
Countess Maritza, 53
Red Mill, The, 128

Nabel, Bill
Most Happy Fella, The, 293

Nagrin, Daniel
Annie Get Your Gun, 130

Nakasone, Aiko
Rent, 305

Nathan, Stephen
Godspell, 233

Naughton, James
Chicago, 307
City of Angels, 282
I Love My Wife, 245

Nealy, Milton Craig
Five Guys Named Moe, 289
Once on This Island, 284

Neff, Hildegarde
Silk Stockings, 166

Nelson, Gene
Follies, 232
Lend an Ear, 139

Nelson, Kenneth
Fantasticks, The, 189

Nelson, Novella
Purlie, 228

Nelson, Portia
Golden Apple, The, 160

Nemitz, Lenora
Gypsy, 359

Nervo & Knox
Ziegfeld Follies, 38

Nesbitt, Cathleen
My Fair Lady, 168

Neuberger, Jan
Dr. Seuss' How the Grinch Stole Christmas, 348

Neuwirth, Bebe
Addams Family, The, 374
Chicago, 307
Sweet Charity, 272

Neway, Patricia
Sound of Music, The, 184

Newley, Anthony
Roar of the Greasepaint—The Smell of the Crowd, The, 212
Stop the World—I Want to Get Off, 199

Newman, Barry
What Makes Sammy Run?, 206

Newman, Phyllis
Wish You Were Here, 154

Newmar, Julie
Li'l Abner, 171
Silk Stockings, 166

Ngaujah, Sahr
Fela!, 372

Nicholas, Fayard & Harold
Babes in Arms, 98
St. Louis Woman, 129
Ziegfeld Follies, 93

Nichols, Darius
Hair, 365
110 in the Shade, 352

Nichols, Barbara
Pal Joey, 153

Nichols, Red
Girl Crazy, 72
Strike Up the Band, 70

Nielsen, Alice
Fortune Teller, The, 6

Niesen, Gertrude
Follow the Girls, 124
Ziegfeld Follies, 93

Nodin, Gerald
Bitter Sweet, 68

Nolan, Kathy
Peter Pan, 163

Noll, Christiane
Jekyll and Hyde, 308
Ragtime, 371

Nordstrom, Clarence
Knickerbocker Holiday, 104

Norris, William
Babes in Toyland, 8
Connecticut, Yankee, A, 58
Maytime, 24

Northrop, Patricia
Pal Joey, 153

Norton, Jim
Finian's Rainbow, 370

Nouri, Michael
Victor/Victoria, 303

Novis, Donald
Jumbo, 93

Nye, Carrie
Half a Sixpence, 211

Nye, Lewis
Inside U.S.A., 137

Nyman, Betty Anne
Annie Get Your Gun, 130

Nype, Russell
Call Me Madam, 147

O'Connell, Hugh
Face the Music, 79
Ziegfeld Follies, 93

O'Day, Nell
Fine and Dandy, 72

O'Dea, June
Of Thee I Sing, 78

O'Denishawn, Florence
Ziegfeld Follies, 34, 38

O'Donnell, Rosie
Grease, 298

O'Hara, Jill
George M!, 223
Promises, Promises, 226

O'Hara, Kelli
Follies, 320
Light in the Piazza, The, 338
Pajama Game, The, 341
South Pacific, 358

O'Hare, Denis
Cabaret, 312

O'Haughey, M.
Chicago, 244

O'Malley, Kerry
Irving Berlin's White Christmas, 362

O'Malley, Muriel
Allegro, 136

O'Neal, Frederick
House of Flowers, 165

O'Neal, William
Annie Get Your Gun, 130
Desert Song, The, 54
New Moon, The, 64

O'Neal, Zelma
Follow Thru, 67
Good News!, 56

O'Ramey, Georgia
Leave It to Jane, 26
No, No, Nanette, 47

Orfeh
Legally Blonde, 351

O'Shea, Michael
Red Mill, The, 128

Oh, Soon-Teck
Pacific Overtures, 245

Ohringer, Jane
Evita, 254

Olaf, Pierre
Carnival, 195

Oliver, Edna May
Oh, Boy!, 24
Show Boat, 60

Oliver, Thelma
Sweet Charity, 216

Olivette, Nina
Hold Everything!, 65

Olivo, Karen
West Side Story, 364

Olsen, Ole
Hellzapoppin, 103

Olsen, George
Good News!, 56
Sunny, 50
Whoopee, 66

Olvis, William
Candide, 172

Onrubia, Cynthia
Song and Dance, 271

Osnes, Laura
Grease, 354

Opatoshu, David
Silk Stockings, 166

Opel, Nancy
Fiddler on the Roof, 333
Urinetown, 323

Oppenheimer, Alan
Sunset Boulevard, 300

Opsahl, Jason
Grease, 298

Orbach, Jerry
Carnival, 195
Chicago, 244
Fantasticks, The, 189
42nd Street, 257
Promises, Promises, 226

Osato, Sono
On the Town, 126
One Touch of Venus, 120

Osborne, Vivienne
Three Musketeers, The, 63

Oscar, Brad
Producers, The, 321

Osgood, Pearl
Flying High, 71

Oshins, Julie
This Is the Army, 117

Osterwald, Bibi
Golden Apple, The, 160

Owen, Reginald
Three Musketeers, The, 63

Oxford, Earl
Life Begins at 8:40, 87
This Is the Army, 117
Three's a Crowd, 73

Page, Ken
Ain't Misbehavin', 251
Cats, 263

Page, Patrick
Dr. Seuss' How the Grinch Stole Christmas, 348

Paige, Janis
Pajama Game, The, 161

Palmer, Byron
Where's Charley?, 138

Palmer, Leland
Pippin, 236
Your Own Thing, 222

Palmer, Peter
Li'l Abner, 171

Palmer, Sean
Little Mermaid, The, 355

Parker, Frank
Follow the Girls, 124

Parker, John Eric
Memphis, 369

Parker, Lew
Girl Crazy, 72
Red, Hot and Blue!, 96

Parker, Mary
Let's Face It!, 115

Parker, Timothy Britten
Rent, 305

Parkinson, Elizabeth
Movin' Out, 328

Parlato, Dennis
Chess, 279

Parrish, Elizabeth
La Cage aux Folles, 266

Parry, William
Gypsy, 329
Sunday in the Park With George, 269

Parsons, Estelle
Pirates of Penzance, The, 258

Pascal, Adam
Aida, 316
Rent, 305

Patinkin, Mandy
Evita, 254
Secret Garden, The, 286
Sunday in the Park With George, 269

Patricola, Tom
George White's Scandals, 52

Patterson, Meredith
Irving Berlin's White Christmas, 362

Paul, Guy
King and I, The, 303

Paulee, Mona
Most Happy Fella, The, 170

Pawk, Irene
Crazy for You, 288

Pawk, Michele
Cabaret, 312

Payne, John
At Home Abroad, 89

Peacock, Bertram
Blossom Time, 38

Pearce, Alice
Gentlemen Prefer Blondes, 146
On the Town, 126

Pedi, Tom
Guys and Dolls, 148

Peil, Mary Beth
Nine, 329
Sunday in the Park With George, 356

Pendleton, Austin
Fiddler on the Roof, 209

Penman, Lea
Annie Get Your Gun, 130

Pennington, Ann
George White's Scandals, 52
New Yorkers, The, 74
Ziegfeld Follies, 20, 29

Percival, Walter
Mlle. Modiste, 10

Perez, Luis
Jerome Robbins' Broadway, 279

Perkins, Anthony
Greenwillow, 187

Peters, Bernadette
Annie Get Your Gun, 315
Dames at Sea, 226
George M!, 223
Gypsy, 329
Into the Woods, 277
Song and Dance, 271
Sunday in the Park With George, 269

Peters, Lauri
Sound of Music, The, 184

Peterson, Kurt
Follies, 232

Petina, Irra
Candide, 172
Song of Norway, 124

Petkoff, Robert
Ragtime, 371

Pettiford, Valerie
Fosse, 314

Phillips, Eddie
Funny Thing Happened on the
Way To the Forum, A, 198

Phillips, Lou Diamond
King and I, The, 303

Picon, Molly
Milk and Honey, 195

Pidgeon, Walter
Take Me Along, 183

Pierce, David Hyde
Curtains, 350
Monty Python's Spamalot, 336

Pinkins, Tonya
Jelly's Last Jam, 292

Pistone, Charles
Most Happy Fella, The, 293

Pitkin, Robert
Blue Paradise, The, 21
Finian's Rainbow, 133
Leave It to Jane, 26

Pitre, Louise
Mamma Mia!, 324

Plant, Mark
Jubilee, 92

Platt, Marc
Oklahoma!, 119

Playten, Alice
Hello, Dolly!, 204

Plimpton, Shelley
Hair, 224

Plunkett, Maryann
Me and My Girl, 273

Pollard, Michael J.
Bye Bye Birdie, 188

Pollock, Channing
Ziegfeld Follies, 34

Pope, Stephanie
Jelly's Last Jam, 292

Poppen, Detmar
Dearest Enemy, 48
Three Musketeers, The, 63

Porter, Billy
Grease, 298

Powell, Eleanor
At Home Abroad, 89
Fine and Dandy, 72
Follow Thru, 67

Powers, Jenny
Grease, 354

Powers, Tom
Oh, Boy!, 24

Prager, Stanley
Pajama Game, The, 161

Preisser, Cherry & June
Ziegfeld Follies, 85, 93

Premice, Josephine
Jamaica, 176

Presnell, Harve
Unsinkable Molly Brown, The, 191

Press, Brian
Beauty and the Beast, 297

Preston, Robert
I Do! I Do!, 220
Music Man, The, 177

Price, Gerald
Fanny, 164
Threepenny Opera, The, 159

Price, Gilbert
Roar of the Greasepaint—The Smell of the
Crowd, The, 212

Price, Leontyne
Porgy and Bess, 156

Primus, Pearl
Show Boat, 128

Prince, Faith
Guys and Dolls, 290
Jerome Robbins' Broadway, 279

Prince, Jack
Destry Rides Again, 180

Prochnik, Bruce
Oliver!, 201

Profanato, Gene
King and I, The, 248

Prouty, Jed
Pink Lady, The, 18

Prud'homme, Cameron
New Girl in Town, 173
Unsinkable Molly Brown, The, 191

Pruette, William
Chocolate Soldier, The, 16
Mlle. Modiste, 10

Pryce, Jonathan
Dirty Rotten Scoundrels, 334
Miss Saigon, 285

Puck, Eva
Irene, 32
Show Boat, 60

Pully, B. S.
Guys and Dolls, 148

Purcell, Charles
Dearest Enemy, 48
Maytime, 24

Purpuro, Sandra
Grease, 298

Quayle, Anna
Stop the World—I Want to Get Off, 199

Quinn, Anthony
Zorba, 268

Racey, Noah
Curtains, 346

Radio Rogues
Hellzapoppin, 103

Rado, James
Hair, 224

Rae, Charlotte
Li'l Abner, 171
Threepenny Opera, The, 159

Ragland, Oscar
New Yorkers, The, 74
Take a Chance, 82

Ragland, Rags
Panama Hattie, 111

Ragni, Gerome
Hair, 224

Raitt, John
Carousel, 127
Pajama Game, The, 161

Rall, Tommy
Call Me Madam, 147
Milk and Honey, 195
Miss Liberty, 144

Ralph, Sheryl Lee
Dreamgirls, 261
Thoroughly Modern Millie, 325

Ramirez, Sara
Monty Python's Spamalot, 336

Ramsey, Kevin
Five Guys Named Moe, 289

Randall, Carl
Countess Maritza, 53
Oh, Lady! Lady!!, 26
Ziegfeld Follies, 20

Randolph, John
Sound of Music, The, 184

Raphael, Gerrianne
Man of La Mancha, 215
Threepenny Opera, The, 159

Rapp, Anthony
Rent, 305

Raskin, Kenny
Beauty and the Beast, 297

Rathburn, Roger
No, No, Nanette, 231

Ratliff, Joseph
Red Mill, The 13

Raymond, Helen
Anything Goes, 88
Music Man, The, 177
One Touch of Venus, 120
Very Good Eddie, 23

Reams, Lee Roy
Applause, 228
42nd Street, 257

Reardon, John
Do Re Mi, 194

Reeder, George
Destry Rides Again, 180
Funny Girl, 207

Reeves, Steve
Kismet, 158

Reeves-Smith, H.
Great Waltz, The, 87

Regan, Walter
Irene, 32

Regay, Pearl
Desert Song, The, 54
George White's Scandals, 40
Rose-Marie, 43

Reichard, Daniel J.
Jersey Boys, 339

Reilly, Charles Nelson
Bye Bye Birdie, 188
Hello, Dolly!, 204
How to Succeed in Business Without Really
Trying, 196

Reinders, Kate
Gypsy, 329

Reiner, Carl
Inside U.S.A., 137

Reinking, Ann
Chicago, 307
Dancin', 250
Pippin, 236

Remme, John
Gypsy, 282

Rene, Nikki
Once on This Island, 284

Revill, Clive
Irma la Douce, 190
Oliver!, 201

Reynolds, Debbie
Irene, 238

Rhodes, Erik
Can-Can, 156
Gay Divorce, 82
Jamaica, 176

Ribeiro, Alfonso
Tap Dance Kid, The, 268

Rice, Reva
Starlight Express, 276

Rice, Sarah
Sweeney Todd, 253

Rich, Doris
Redhead, 179

Rich, Irene
As the Girls Go, 139

Richards, Donald
Finian's Rainbow, 133

Richards, Houston
Anything Goes, 88
Let's Face It!, 115

Richardson, Desmond
Fosse, 314

Richardson, Natasha
Cabaret, 312

Richardson, Ron
Big River, 270

Richert, Wanda
42nd Street, 257

Richman, Harry
George White's Scandals, 52

Ridges, Stanley
Sally, 33

Riegler, Adam
Addams Family, The, 374

Rifkin, Ron
Cabaret, 312

Riggs, Ralph
Of Thee I Sing, 78
Oklahoma!, 119

Riley, Eric
Once on This Island, 284

Ring, Blanche
Strike Up the Band, 70

Ripley, Alice
Next to Normal, 368
Sunset Boulevard, 300

Ritchard, Cyril
Peter Pan, 163
Roar of the Greasepaint—The Smell of the
Crowd, The, 212
Sugar, 235

Ritter, Thelma
New Girl in Town, 173

Rivera, Chita
Bye Bye Birdie, 188
Chicago, 244
Kiss of the Spider Woman—The Musical, 295
Nine, 329
West Side Story, 175

Roane, Frank
Lost in the Stars, 144

Roberti, Lyda
Roberta, 84

Roberts, Joan
Follies, 320
Oklahoma!, 119

Roberts, Tony
Sugar, 235
Victor/Victoria, 303
Xanadu, 352

Robertson, Guy
Great Waltz, The, 87

Robins, A.
Jumbo, 93

Robins, Edward H.
Leave It to Me!, 105
Louisiana Purchase, 110
Of Thee I Sing, 78

Robinson, Bill
Blackbirds of 1928, 63

Rodgers, Eileen
Fiorello!, 186

Rodriguez, Krysta
Addams Family, The, 374

Rogers, Ginger
Girl Crazy, 72

Rogers, Jaime
Golden Boy, 210

Rogers, Will
Ziegfeld Follies, 29, 38

Roland, Steve
110 in the Shade, 203

Roll, Eddie
West Side Story, 175

Rolph, Marti
Follies, 232

Romano, David
Phantom of the Opera, The, 278

Ronstadt, Linda
Pirates of Penzance, The, 258

Rooney, Mickey
Sugar Babies, 255

Rooney Sr., Pat
Guys and Dolls, 148

Rose, George
Mystery of Edwin Drood, The, 271
Peter Pan, 254
Pirates of Penzance, The, 258

Rose, Reva
You're a Good Man, Charlie Brown, 221

Rosenblat, Barbara
Secret Garden, The, 286

Ross, Herbert
Bloomer Girl, 125

Ross, Jamie
Woman of the Year, 260

Ross, Rusty
Dr. Seuss' How the Grinch Stole Christmas, 348

Ross, Ted
Raisin, 239
Wiz, The, 241

Major Cast Members Index

Roth, Lillian
Earl Carroll Vanities, 76

Roudenko, Lubov
Annie Get Your Gun, 130
Merry Widow, The, 120

Rounseville, Robert
Candide, 172
Knickerbocker Holiday, 104
Man of La Mancha, 215
Merry Widow, The, 120
Up in Central Park, 126

Rowles, Polly
No Strings, 197

Ruben, Jose
Cat and the Fiddle, The, 77

Rubin—Vega, Daphne
Les Misérables, 349
Rent, 305

Rubinstein, John
Pippin, 236

Ruffelle, Frances
Les Misérables, 275

Ruivivar, Francis
Passion, 298

Rule, Janice
Miss Liberty, 144

Rupert, Michael
Falsettos, 293
Happy Time, The, 222
Legally Blonde, 351
Sweet Charity, 272

Rushworth, Frank
Fortune Teller, The, 6

Russell, Jenna
Sunday in the Park With George, 356

Russell, Rosalind
Wonderful Town, 155

Ruysdael, Basil
Cocoanuts, The, 51

Ryan, Irene
Pippin, 236

Ryan, Steve
Guys and Dolls, 290

Ryness, Bryce
Hair, 365

Sabella, Ernie
Curtains, 350
Funny Thing Happened on the Way to the Forum, A, 304

Guys and Dolls, 290
Man of La Mancha, 329

Saddler, Donald
Follies, 320

Sadoff, Fred
South Pacific, 143

Saget, Bob
Drowsy Chaperone, The, 342

St. Darr, Deborah
Candide, 239

St. John, Betta
South Pacific, 143

St. John, Howard
Li'l Abner, 171

Sajous, Christina
American Idiot, 377

Saldivar, Matthew
Grease, 354

Salonga, Lea
Flower Drum Song, 327
Miss Saigon, 285

Sams, Jeffrey D.
Five Guys Named Moe, 289

San Juan, Olga
Paint Your Wagon, 152

Sanderson, Julia
Girl from Utah, The, 19

Sandifur, Virginia
Follies, 232

Sands, Stark
American Idiot, 377

Santiago-Hudson, Ruben
Jelly's Last Jam, 292

Santley, Joseph
Music Box Revue, 37

Sappington, Margo
Promises, Promises, 226

Sarandon, Chris
Rothschilds, The, 230

Sarnoff, Dorothy
King and I, The, 151

Sato, Isao
Pacific Overtures, 245

Saunders, Gertrude
Shuffle Along, 34

Saunders, Lanna
Milk and Honey, 195

Savage, Archie
South Pacific, 143

Savo, Jimmy
Boys from Syracuse, The, 107

Savoy & Brennan
Ziegfeld Follies, 29

Sawyer, Ivy
Music Box Revue, 37

Saxon, Don
Street Scene, 132

Saxon, Luther
Carmen Jones, 122

Sayre, Loretta Ables
South Pacific, 358

Scaglione, Josefina
West Side Story, 364

Scardino, Don
I'm Getting My Act Together and Taking It on the
  Road, 252

Scheerer, Bob
Boy Friend, The, 162
Lend an Ear, 139

Scheff, Fritzi
Mlle. Modiste, 10

Schilling, Gus
Hold Everything!, 65

Schnabel, Stefan
Plain and Fancy, 166

Schneider, Jana
Mystery of Edwin Drood, The, 271

Schoeffler, Paul
Rock of Ages, 366

Schools, Victoria
Best Foot Forward, 114

Schramm, David
Finian's Rainbow, 370

Schwab, Buddy
As the Girls Go, 139
Boy Friend, The, 162
Guys and Dolls, 148

Scott, Bonnie
How to Succeed in Business Without Really
  Trying, 196

Scott, Sherie Rene
Aida, 316
Dirty Rotten Scoundrels, 334
Little Mermaid, The, 355
Tommy, 294

Scott, Timothy
Cats, 263

Seal, Elizabeth
Irma la Douce, 190

Segal, Vivienne
Blue Paradise, The, 21
Desert Song, The 54
I Married an Angel, 102
Oh, Lady! Lady!!, 26
Pal Joey, 112, 153
Three Musketeers, The, 63

Sell, Janie
Irene, 238

Sellars, Lee
West Side Story, 364

Selya, John
Movin' Out, 328

Sengbloh, Saycon
Fela!, 372

Serabian, Lorraine
Zorba, 225

Sergava, Katharine
Oklahoma!, 119

Serrano, Vincent
Rio Rita, 55

Sewell, Danny
Oliver!, 201

Shackleton, Robert
Sweethearts, 134

Shaddow, Elena
La Cage aux Folles, 376

Shafer, Robert
Damn Yankees, 167
Song of Norway, 124

Shapiro, Debbie
Jerome Robbins' Broadway, 279
Zorba, 268

Sharma, Barbara
Sweet Charity, 216

Sharp, Jon Marshall
Carousel, 296

Sharpe, Albert
Finian's Rainbow, 133

Shaw, Oscar
Flying High, 71
Leave It to Jane, 26
Oh, Kay!, 53
Very Good Eddie, 23

Shaw, Reta
Pajama Game, The, 161

Shaw, Tro
West Side Story, 364

Shea, Jere
Passion, 298

Shean, Al
Music in the Air, 81

Sheik, Kacie
Hair, 365

Shelley, Carole
Billy Elliot: The Musical, 361
Wicked, 332

Shelley, Joshua
Make Mine Manhattan, 137

Shelly, Norman
Promises, Promises, 226

Shelton, James
New Faces, 86

Shelton, Reid
Annie, 247
My Fair Lady, 168
Wish You Were Here, 154

Sherman, Hal
Hellzapoppin, 103

Sherman, Hiram
Cradle Will Rock, The, 101

Sherwood, Gregg
As the Girls Go, 139

Sherwood, Madeline
Do I Hear a Waltz?, 210

Shields, Brooke,
Wonderful Town, 332

Shimoda, Yuki
Pacific Overtures, 245

Shimono, Sab
Pacific Overtures, 245

Shindle, Kate
Legally Blonde, 351

Shirley, Florence
Oh, Lady! Lady!!, 26

Shively, A. J.
La Cage aux Folles, 376

Shoemaker, Ann
Half a Sixpence, 211

Shriner, Herb
Inside U.S.A., 137

Shull, Robert B.
Victor/Victoria, 303

Shutta, Ethel
Follies, 232
Whoopee, 66

Shy, Gus
Good News!, 56
New Moon, The, 64

Sidney, Robert
This Is the Army, 117

Sieber, Christoher
Into the Woods, 326
Monty Python's Spamalot, 336
Shrek: The Musical, 363

Sikora, Megan
Curtains, 350

Sillman, Leonard
New Faces, 86

Sills, Douglas
Scarlet Pimpernel, The 309

Silva, Marguerite
Fortune Teller, The, 6

Silver, Joe
Gypsy, 182

Silver, Johnny
Guys and Dolls, 148

Silvers, Phil
Do Re Mi, 194
High Button Shoes, 136

Silvers, Sid
Take a Chance, 82

Simmons, J.K.
Guys and Dolls, 290

Sissle, Noble
Shuffle Along, 34

Skinner, Emily
Full Monty, The, 319

Slate, Henry
South Pacific, 143

Slezak, Walter
Fanny, 164
I Married an Angel, 102
Music in the Air, 81

Slutsker, Peter
On Your Toes, 264

Smith, Alexis
Follies, 232

Smith, Art
West Side Story, 175

Smith, Gerald Oliver
Oh, Kay!, 53

Smith, Buddy
Tommy, 294

Smith, Kate
Flying High, 71

Smith, Muriel
Carmen Jones, 122

Smith, Queenie
Tip-Toes, 52

Smith, Rex
Pirates of Penzance, The, 258
Scarlet Pimpernel, The, 309

Smith, Sally
Roar of the Greasepaint—The Smell of the
Crowd, The, 212

Smith, Sammy
How to Succeed in Business Without Really
Trying, 196

Smith, Sheila
Follies, 232
Sugar, 235

Snow, Harry
Once Upon a Mattress, 181

Soboloff, Arnold
Peter Pan, 254

Soo, Jack
Flower Drum Song, 178

Soules, Dale
Magic Show, The, 240

Spanger, Amy
Kiss Me, Kate, 315
Rock of Ages, 366

Sparber, Herschel
Guys and Dolls, 282

Spearman, Rawn
House of Flowers, 165

Spencer, J. Robert
Next to Normal, 368

Spencer, Kenneth
Show Boat, 128

Spinella, Stephen
Spring Awakening, 345

Stadlen, Lewis J.
Candide, 239
Funny Thing Happened on the Way
to the Forum, A, 304
Producers, The, 321

Stafford, Joseph
Peter Pan, 163

Stander, Lionel
Pal Joey, 153

Stanek, Jim
Funny Thing Happened on the Way
to the Forum, A, 304

Stanley, Dorothy
Show Boat, 299

Stanley, Elizabeth
Million Dollar Quartet, 375

Stanley, Pat
Fiorello!, 186

Stanton, Olive
Cradle Will Rock, The, 101

Stapleton, Jean
Bells Are Ringing, 171
Damn Yankees, 167
Funny Girl, 207

Starbuck, Betty
Garrick Gaieties, The, 46
Gay Divorce, 82
Peggy-Ann, 54

Stauffer, Richard
Fantasticks, The, 189

Steel, John
Ziegfeld Follies, 31

Steele, Ryan
West Side Story, 364

Steele, Tommy
Half a Sixpence, 211

Steggert, Bobby
Ragtime, 371

Steinborn, Carly Jane
Tommy, 294

Stephens, Harvey
South Pacific, 143

Stevens, Fisher
Carousel, 296

Stevens, Leslie
La Cage aux Folles, 266

Stewart, Gwen
Rent, 305

Stewart, Johnny
High Button Shoes, 136
King and I, The, 151
Love Life, 138

Stewart, Melville
Firefly, The, 18
Ziegfeld Follies, 20

Stewart, Scot
Sugar Babies, 255

Stiers, David Ogden
Magic Show, The, 240

Stiller, Jerry
Golden Apple, The 160

Stockwell, Harry
As Thousands Cheer, 83

Stokes, Heather
Grease, 298

Stone, Dorothy
Red Mill, The 128

Stone, Ezra
This Is the Army, 117

Stone, Fred
Red Mill, The, 13
Wizard of Oz, The, 8

Stone, Jessica
Grease, 298

Stone, Leonard
Redhead, 179

Stone, Sid
Sugar Babies, 255

Story, Gloria
Sweethearts, 134

Stoska, Polyna
Street Scene, 132

Strasberg, Lee
Garrick Gaieties, The, 46

Stratton Jr., Gil
Best Foot Forward, 114

Streisand, Barbra
Funny Girl, 207

Strickland, Josh
Tarzan, 347

Stritch, Billy
42nd Street, 322

Stritch, Elaine
Company, 229
Pal Joey, 153
Show Boat, 299

Stuart, Michel
Chorus Line, A, 243

Sullivan, Brian
Street Scene, 132

Sullivan, Elliott
Brigadoon, 134

Sullivan, Jo
As the Girls Go, 139
Most Happy Fella, The, 170
Threepenny Opera, The, 159

Sullivan, Lee
Brigadoon, 134

Summerhays, Jane
Me and My Girl, 273

Sunshine, Marion
Follies of 1907, 14

Sutton, Kay
DuBarry Was a Lady, 109

Suzuki, Pat
Flower Drum Song, 178

Swenson, Inga
110 in the Shade, 203

Swenson, Swen
Destry Rides Again, 180
Little Me, 200

Swenson, Will
Hair, 365

Syers, Mark
Evita, 254

Szot, Paulo
South Pacific, 358

Tabbert, William
Fanny, 164
Follow the Girls, 124
South Pacific, 143

Taliaferro, Mabel
Bloomer Girl, 125

Tallchief, Maria
Song of Norway, 124

Talva, Galina
Call Me Madam, 147

Tamara
Leave It to Me!, 105
Roberta, 84

Tartaglia, John
Avenue Q, 330
Shrek: The Musical, 363

Tatum, Marianne
Barnum, 256
King and I, The, 248

Taylor, Clarice
Wiz, The, 241

Taylor, Wesley
Addams Family, The, 374
Rock of Ages, 366

Teague, Anthony
110 in the Shade, 203

Teeter, Lara
On Your Toes, 264

Temperley, Stephen
Crazy for You, 288

Tempest, Florence
Follies of 1907, 14

Templeton, Fay
Forty-five Minutes from Broadway, 13
Roberta, 84

Terris, Norma
Show Boat, 60

Terry, Ethelind
Rio Rita, 55

Testa, Mary
42nd Street, 322
Funny Thing Happened on the Way
to the Forum, A, 304
Xanadu, 352

Thacker, Rusty
Your Own Thing, 222

Theodore, Donna
Shenandoah, 242

Theodore, Lee Becker
King and I, The, 151
West Side Story, 175

Thigpen, Helen
Porgy and Bess, 156

Thoman, J. W.
Evangeline, 4

Thomas, Hugh
Fantasticks, The, 189

Thomas, Tasha
Wiz, The, 241

Thomas Jr., William
La Cage aux Folles, 266

Thompson, Connie
Evangeline, 4

Thompson, Jack
Connecticut Yankee, A, 58
Fifty Million Frenchmen, 69

Thomson, Carolyn
Vagabond King, The, 48

Thorne, Raymond
Annie, 247

Tinney, Frank
Watch Your Step, 20

Tobey, Kenneth
Golden Boy, 210

Tobias, George
Leave It to Me!, 105
Silk Stockings, 166

Tobin, Genevieve
Fifty Million Frenchmen, 69

Tokio, Prince
Follies of 1907, 14

Tombes, Andrew
Face the Music, 79
Tip-Toes, 52
Ziegfeld Follies, 38

Toner, Thomas
Me and My Girl, 273
Secret Garden, The, 286

Toro, Natalie
Tale of Two Cities, A, 360

Torti, Robert
Starlight Express, 276

Towers, Constance
King and I, The, 248

Treacher, Arthur
Panama Hattie, 111

Trentini, Emma
Firefly, The, 18
Naughty Marietta, 17

Troy, Louise
High Spirits, 208

Major Cast Members Index

Truex, Ernest
Very Good Eddie, 23

Truex, Philip
This Is the Army, 117

Tryon, Tom
Wish You Were Here, 154

Tucker, Sophie
Leave It to Me!, 105

Tumeo, Vincent
Sunset Boulevard, 300

Tune, Tommy
My One and Only, 264

Turgeon, Peter
Little Me, 200

Turner, Glen
Five Guys Named Moe, 289

Tuttle, Ashley,
Movin' Out, 328

Tveit, Aaron
Next to Normal, 368

Twiggy
My One and Only, 264

Tyers, John
Inside U.S.A., 137

Ukena Jr., Paul
Will Rogers Follies, The, 287

Ullett, Nick
Me and My Girl, 273

Umeki, Miyoshi
Flower Drum Song, 178

Umoh, Stephanie
Ragtime, 371

Upton, Frances
Whoopee, 66

Utley, Byron
Rent, 305

Valenti, Michael
Your Own Thing, 222

Valentine, Paul
Wish You Were Here, 154

Vallee, Rudy
George White's Scandals, 76
How to Succeed in Business Without Really
Trying, 196

Van, Bobby
No, No, Nanette, 231

Van & Schenck
Ziegfeld Follies, 31, 34

Van Dyke, Dick
Bye Bye Birdie, 188

Van Dyke, Marcia
Tree Grows in Brooklyn, A, 152

Vance, Vivian
Anything Goes, 88
Hooray for What!, 100
Let's Face It!, 115
Red, Hot and Blue!, 96

Vanderbilt, Gertrude
Maytime, 24

Vandis, Titos
On a Clear Day You Can See Forever, 213

Vassar, Queenie
Girl from Utah, The, 19

Venner, Tracy
Gypsy, 282

Venuta, Benay
By Jupiter, 116

Vera-Ellen
By Jupiter, 116
Panama Hattie, 111

Verdon, Gwen
Can-Can, 156
Chicago, 244
Damn Yankees, 167
New Girl in Town, 173
Redhead, 179
Sweet Charity, 216

Vereen, Ben
Jesus Christ Superstar, 233
Pippin, 236

Verrett, Shirley
Carousel, 296

Vestoff, Virginia
1776, 227

Vickery, John
Lion King, The, 310

Vichi, Gerry
How to Succeed in Business Without
Really Trying, 302

Victor, Eric
Inside U.S.A., 137

Vidnovic, Martin
Fantasticks, The, 343
King and I, The, 248
Oklahoma!, 255

Vilan, Demetrios
On Your Toes, 94

Vincent, Tony
American Idiot, 377

Vinkler, Greg
West Side Story, 364

Vita, Michael
On Your Toes, 264

Vye, Murvyn
Carousel, 127

Waara, Scott
Most Happy Fella, The, 293

Wagner, Jack
Jekyll and Hyde, 308

Wagstaff, Joe
Fine and Dandy, 72

Wakefield, Ann
Boy Friend, The, 162

Walburn, Raymond
Funny Thing Happened on the Way to the
Forum, A, 198

Waldron, Jack
Pal Joey, 153

Walker, Fredi
Rent, 305

Walker, Nancy
Best Foot Forward, 114
Do Re Mi, 194
On the Town, 126

Wallace, George
New Girl in Town, 173

Wallace, Paul
Gypsy, 182

Walsh, Barbara
Company, 344
Falsettos, 293

Walsh, Mary Jane
I'd Rather Be Right, 98
Let's Face It!, 115
Too Many Girls, 108

Walsh, Thommie
Chorus Line, A, 243

Walston, Ray
Damn Yankees, 167
House of Flowers, 165
Me and Juliet, 157

Walters, Charles
DuBarry Was a Lady, 109
I Married an Angel, 102
Jubilee, 92
New Faces, 86
Show Is On, The, 97

Walters, Dorothy
Irene, 32

Walters, Polly
Red, Hot and Blue!, 96

Ward, Aida
Blackbirds of 1928, 63

Ward, Charles
Dancin', 250

Waring, Fred
New Yorkers, The, 74

Warren, Lesley Ann
110 in the Shade, 203

Warrick, Ruth
Irene, 238

Washburn, Grace
Sinbad, 29

Washington, Lamont
Hair, 224

Waterman, Willard
Mame, 217

Waters, Ethel
As Thousands Cheer, 83
At Home Abroad, 89
Cabin in the Sky, 111

Watson, Betty Jane
As the Girls Go, 139

Watson, Bobbie
Irene, 32

Watson Jr., Harry
Follies of 1907, 14
Tip-Toes, 52

Watson, Milton
Earl Carroll Vanities, 76

Watson, Susan
Bye Bye Birdie, 188
No, No, Nanette, 231

Wayne, David
Finian's Rainbow, 133
Happy Time, The, 222
Merry Widow, The, 120

Wayne, Paula
Golden Boy, 210

Webb, Clifton
As Thousands Cheer, 83
Flying Colors, 80
Little Show, The, 67
Sunny, 50
Three's a Crowd, 73

Webb, Teddy
Blue Paradise, The, 21

Weber, Steven
Producers, The, 321

Weede, Robert
Milk and Honey, 195
Most Happy Fella, The, 170

Weedon, William
Merry Widow, The, 15

Weeks, Alan
Tap Dance Kid, The, 268

Weiner, John
La Cage aux Folles, 266

Weiss, Jeff
Carousel, 296

Welch, Elizabeth
Blackbirds of 1928, 63

Wendel, Elmarie
Little Mary Sunshine, 186

Werrenrath, Reinald
Music in the Air, 81

Wescott, Marcy
Boys from Syracuse, The, 107
Too Many Girls, 108

West, Bernie
Bells Are Ringing, 171

West, Buster
Follow the Girls, 124
George White's Scandals, 52

West, Will
Ziegfeld Follies, 20

Westenberg, Robert
Into the Woods, 277
Secret Garden, The, 286
Sunday in the Park With George, 269
Zorba, 268

Westfeldt, Jennifer
Wonderful Town, 332

Wheaton, Anna
Oh, Boy!, 24

Wheeler, Bert
Rio Rita, 55

White, Amelia
Crazy for You, 288

White, George
George White's Scandals, 40
Ziegfeld Follies, 20

White, Jane
Follies, 320
Once Upon a Mattress, 181

White, Lillias
Fela!, 372
How to Succeed in Business Without Really Trying, 302

White, Onna
Guys and Dolls, 148
Silk Stockings, 166

White, Sammy
Show Boat, 60

White, Terri
Barnum, 256

Whiteman, Paul
George White's Scandals, 40
Jumbo, 93

Whiting, Jack
Golden Apple, The, 160
Hold Everything!, 65
Hooray for What!, 100
Take a Chance 82
Ziegfeld Follies 38

Whittell, Josephine
No, No, Nanette, 47

Wickes, Mary
Oklahoma!, 255

Wilkerson, Arnold
Don't Bother Me, I Can't Cope, 235

Wilkinson, Colm
Les Misérables, 275

Wilkof, Lee
Kiss Me, Kate, 315
Little Shop of Horrors, 262
She Loves Me, 296
Sweet Charity, 272

Willard, John
Very Good Eddie, 23

Williams, Allison
Jelly's Last Jam, 292
Sweet Charity, 272

Williams, Ann
Applause, 228

Williams, Bert
Ziegfeld Follies, 20, 31

Williams, Bob
Sugar Babies, 255

Williams, Derek
Jubilee, 92

Williams, Ellis E.
Once on This Island, 284

Williams, Frances
Cocoanuts, The, 51
George White's Scandals, 52
Life Begins at 8:40, 87
New Yorkers, The, 74

Williams, Herb
At Home Abroad, 89

Willams, Hope
New Yorkers, The, 74

Williams, Jack
Let's Face It!, 115

Williams, Ralph
She Loves Me, 202

Williams, Sammy
Chorus Line, A, 243

Williams, Treat
Follies, 320

Williams, Vanessa
Into the Woods, 326

Williamson, Ruth
La Cage aux Folles, 333
Music Man, The, 319

Wills Jr., Lou
One Touch of Venus, 120
Tree Grows in Brooklyn, A, 152

Wilson, Billy
Jamaica, 176

Wilson, Dooley
Bloomer Girl, 125
Cabin in the Sky, 111

Wilson, Edwin
Sweethearts, 19

Wilson, Lloyd
Trip to Chinatown, A, 5

Wilson, Mary Louise
Cabaret, 312

Wilson, Patrick
Full Monty, The, 319
Oklahoma, 325

Wilson, Patricia
Fiorello!, 186

Winninger, Charles
No, No, Nanette, 47
Show Boat, 60

Winokur, Marissa Jaret
Hairspray, 326

Winston, Hattie
Tap Dance Kid, The, 268

Winter, Edward
Cabaret, 219
Promises, Promises, 226

Winters, David
West Side Story, 175

Winters, Lawrence
Call Me Mister, 129

Wise, Savannah
Ragtime, 371

Wise, Scott
Fosse, 314
Guys and Dolls, 290
Jerome Robbins' Broadway, 279
Movin' Out, 328
Song and Dance, 271

Withee, Mabel
Cocoanuts, The, 51
Sinbad, 29

Witter, William C.
Barnum, 256

Wolfington, Iggie
Music Man, The, 177

Wolfson, Martin
South Pacific, 143

Wolpe, Lenny
Drowsy Chaperone, The, 342

Wong, B. D.
Pacific Overtures, 333

Wood, DeeDee
Can-Can, 156

Wood, Helen
Pal Joey, 153

Wood, Peggy
Maytime, 24
Naughty Marietta, 17

Wood, Susan
Grease, 298

Woodard, Charlaine
Ain't Misbehavin', 251

Major Cast Members Index

Woods, Carol
Follies, 320

Woodward, Edward
High Spirits, 208

Woolf, Walter
Countess Maritza, 53

Woolley, Monty
On Your Toes, 94

Woolsey, Robert
Poppy, 40
Rio Rita, 55

Wopat, Tom
Annie Get Your Gun, 315

Wright, Ben
Into the Woods, 277

Wright, Jeffrey
Bring In 'Da Noise, Bring In 'Da Funk, 306

Wright, Samuel E.
Lion King, The, 310
Tap Dance Kid, The, 268

Wyatt, Kirsten
Grease, 354

Wyckoff, Evelyn
Lady in the Dark, 113

Wyler, Gretchen
Silk Stockings, 166

Wylie, John
Grand Hotel, 281

Wyman, Nicholas
Phantom of the Opera, The, 278
Tale of Two Cities, A, 360

Wynn, Bessie
Babes in Toyland, 8
Wizard of Oz, The, 8

Wynn, Ed
Hooray for What!, 100
Ziegfeld Follies, 20

Yarnell, Bruce
Camelot, 193

Yates, Deborah
Contact, 318

Yeamans, Annie
Mulligan Guard Ball, The, 4

York, Rachel
Dirty Rotten Scoundrels, 334
Scarlet Pimpernel, The, 309
Victor/Victoria, 303

Young, Eric Jordan
Ragtime, 371

Young, John Lloyd
Jersey Boys, 339

Yuriko
King and I, The, 151

Zeta-Jones, Catherine
Little Night Music, A, 373

Zien, Chip
Falsettos, 293
Into the Woods, 277

Ziemba, Karen
Contact, 318
Curtains, 350

Zimmerman, Leigh
Funny Thing Happened on the Way
to the Forum, A, 304

Zorich, Louis
Follies, 320
She Loves Me, 296

Zorina, Vera
I Married an Angel, 102
Louisiana Purchase, 110

Theatre Index

Adelphi Theatre
On the Town, 126
Street Scene, 132

Alvin Theatre (later Neil Simon)
Annie, 247
Anything Goes, 88
Boys from Syracuse, The, 107
Company, 229
Funny Face, 59
Funny Thing Happened on the Way to the
    Forum, A, 198
Girl Crazy, 72
Greenwillow, 187
High Spirits, 208
House of Flowers, 165
I'd Rather Be Right, 98
Lady in the Dark, 113
Music in the Air, 81
Porgy and Bess, 91
Red, Hot and Blue!, 96
Shenandoah, 242
Tree Grows in Brooklyn, A, 152

Ambassador Theatre
Blossom Time, 38
Bring In 'Da Noise, Bring In 'Da Funk, 306

American Airlines Theatre
Pajama Game, The, 341

Apollo Theatre
Flying High, 71
George White's Scandals, 52, 76
Poppy, 40
Take a Chance, 82

Brooks Atkinson Theatre
Grease, 354
Rock of Ages, 366
She Loves Me, 296

Ethel Barrymore Theatre
Best Foot Forward, 114
Company, 344
Gay Divorce, 82
I Love My Wife, 245
Knickerbocker Holiday, 104
Pal Joey, 112

Vivian Beaumont Theatre
Anything Goes, 277
Carousel, 296
Contact, 318
Light in the Piazza, The, 338
South Pacific, 358

Martin Beck Theatre (later Al Hirschfeld)
Bye Bye Birdie, 188
Cabin in the Sky, 111
Candide, 172
Grand Hotel, 281
Guys and Dolls, 290
Into the Woods, 277
Kiss Me, Kate, 315
Man of La Mancha, 329
Milk and Honey, 195
St. Louis Woman, 129

Belasco Theatre
Follies, 320
Hit the Deck!, 56

Biltmore Theatre
Hair, 224

Booth Theatre
Most Happy Fella, The, 293
Next to Normal, 368
Once on This Island, 284
Sunday in the Park With George, 269

Bouwerie Lane Theatre
Dames at Sea, 226

Broadhurst Theatre
Aspects of Love, 283
Cabaret, 219
Dancin', 250
Fiorello!, 186
Fosse, 314
Half a Sixpence, 211
Hold Everything!, 65
Into the Woods, 326
Les Misérables, 349
Kiss of the Spider Woman—The Musical, 295
Make Mine Manhattan, 137
110 in the Shade, 203
Pal Joey, 153
Tap Dance Kid, The, 268

Broadway Theatre
Candide, 239
Carmen Jones, 122
Color Purple, The, 340
Evita 254
Gypsy, 182
Happy Time, The, 222
Les Misérables, 275
Miss Saigon, 285
New Yorkers, The 74
Promises, Promises, 378
Purlie, 228
Shrek: The Musical, 363
This Is the Army, 117
Zorba, 268

Theatre Index

Earl Carroll Theatre
Earl Carroll Vanities, 76

Casino Theatre
Blue Paradise, The, 21
Desert Song, The 54
Florodora, 6
Vagabond King, The, 48

Center Theatre
Great Waltz, The, 87

Cherry Lane Theatre
Godspell, 233

Circle in the Square Theatre
25th Annual Putnam County Spelling Bee, The, 337

Cort Theatre
Magic Show, The, 240

Eden Theatre (former Phoenix)
Grease, 234

Entermedia Theatre
Best Little Whorehouse in Texas, The, 250
Joseph and the Amazing Technicolor
Dreamcoat, 260

Erlanger's Theatre
Fine and Dandy, 72

54th Street Theatre
No Strings, 197
What Makes Sammy Run?, 206

Ford Center for the Performing Arts (later
Hilton)
Ragtime, 311
42nd Street, 322

46th Street Theatre (later Richard Rodgers)
Chicago, 244
Damn Yankees, 167
Do I Hear a Waltz?, 210
DuBarry Was a Lady, 109
Finian's Rainbow, 133
Follow Thru, 67
Good News!, 56
Guys and Dolls, 148
Hellzapoppin, 103
How to Succeed in Business Without Really
Trying, 196
I Do! I Do!, 220
Love Life, 138
New Girl in Town, 173
Nine, 262
No, No, Nanette, 231
Panama Hattie, 111
Raisin, 239
Redhead, 179
1776, 227

Fulton Theatre
New Faces, 86

Garrick Theatre
Garrick Gaieties, The, 46

Gershwin Theatre (former Uris)
Show Boat, 299
Starlight Express, 276
Oklahoma!, 325
Wicked, 332

Globe Theatre (later Lunt-Fontanne)
Cat and the Fiddle, The, 77
George White's Scandals, 40
No, No, Nanette, 47
Ziegfeld Follies, 34

John Golden Theatre
Avenue Q, 330
Falsettos, 293

Greenwich Village Theatre
Greenwich Village Follies, 31

Hammerstein's Theatre
Sweet Adeline, 68

Helen Hayes Theatre (former Little)
Xanadu, 352

Mark Hellinger Theatre
Jesus Christ Superstar, 233
My Fair Lady, 168
On a Clear Day You Can See Forever, 213
Plain and Fancy, 166
Sugar Babies, 255

Hilton Theatre (former Ford Center)
Dr. Seuss' How the Grinch Stole Christmas, 348
Young Frankenstein, 353

Hippodrome
Jumbo, 93

Al Hirschfeld Theatre (former Martin Beck)
Curtains, 350
Hair, 365
Tale of Two Cities, A, 360
Wedding Singer, The, 346
Wonderful Town, 332

Imperial Theatre
Annie Get Your Gun, 130
Billy Elliot: The Musical, 361
Call Me Madam, 147
Carnival, 195
Chess, 279
Destry Rides Again, 180
Dirty Rotten Scoundrels, 334
Dreamgirls, 261
Fiddler on the Roof, 209
Flying Colors, 80
Jamaica, 176
Jerome Robbins' Broadway, 279
Jubilee, 92
Leave It to Me!, 105
Let's Face It!, 115
Louisiana Purchase, 110

Miss Liberty, 144
Most Happy Fella, The, 170
Mystery of Edwin Drood, The, 271
New Moon, The, 64
Oh, Kay!, 53
Oliver!, 201
On Your Toes, 94
One Touch of Venus, 120
Pippin, 236
Rose-Marie, 43
Silk Stockings, 166
Song of Norway, 124
They're Playing Our Song, 252
Too Many Girls, 108
Wish You Were Here, 154
Zorba, 225

Jardin de Paris
Follies of 1907, 14

Jolson's 59th Street Theatre (later New Century)
Student Prince in Heidelberg, The, 45

Walter Kerr Theatre (former Ritz)
Little Night Music, A, 373

Knickerbocker Theatre
Dearest Enemy, 48
Girl from Utah, The, 19
Mlle. Modiste, 10
Red Mill, The, 13

Labor Stage (former Princess)
Pins and Needles, 100

Liberty Theatre
Blackbirds of 1928, 63
Lady, Be Good!, 44
Little Johnny Jones, 10
Tip-Toes, 52

Longacre Theatre
Ain't Misbehavin', 251
La Cage aux Folles, 376
Leave It to Jane, 26

Lunt-Fontanne Theatre (former Globe)
Addams Family, The, 374
Little Me, 200
Little Mermaid, The, 355
Peter Pan, 254
Rothschilds, The, 230
Sophisticated Ladies, 259
Sound of Music, The, 184
Titanic, 307

Lyric Theatre
Chocolate Soldier, The, 16
Cocoanuts, The, 51
Fifty Million Frenchmen, 69
Firefly, The, 18
Three Musketeers, The 63

Madison Square Garden Theatre
Trip to Chinatown, A, 5

Majestic Theatre (Columbus Circle)
Babes in Toyland, 8
Wizard of Oz, The, 8

Majestic Theatre (W. 44th St.)
Allegro, 136
Camelot, 193
Carousel, 127
Fanny, 164
Golden Boy, 210
Me and Juliet, 157
Merry Widow, The, 120
Music Man, The, 177
Phantom of the Opera, The, 278
South Pacific, 143
Sugar, 235
Wiz, The, 241

Marquis Theatre
Annie Get Your Gun, 315
Drowsy Chaperone, The, 342
Irving Berlin's White Christmas, 362
La Cage aux Folles, 333
Me and My Girl, 273
Thoroughly Modern Millie, 325
Victor/Victoria, 303

Henry Miller Theatre
Cabaret, 312
Urinetown, 323

Minskoff Theatre
Fiddler On the Roof, 333
Irene, 238
Scarlet Pimpernel, The, 309
Sunset Boulevard, 300
Sweet Charity, 272

Music Box
As Thousands Cheer, 83
Little Show, The, 67
Lost in the Stars, 144
Music Box Revue, 37
Of Thee I Sing, 78

National Theatre (later Billy Rose, then Trafalgar, then Nederlander)
Call Me Mister, 129
Lend an Ear, 139

Nederlander Theatre
Million Dollar Quartet, 375
Rent, 305

New Amsterdam Theatre
Band Wagon, The, 74
Face the Music, 79
Forty-five Minutes from Broadway, 13
Lion King, The, 310
Madame Sherry, 17
Mary Poppins, 344
Merry Widow, The 15
Pink Lady, The, 18
Roberta, 84
Rosalie, 62
Sally, 33

Sunny, 50
Sweethearts, 19
Watch Your Step, 20
Whoopee, 66
Ziegfeld Follies, 20, 29, 31, 38

New Century Theatre (former Jolson's)
Follow the Girls, 124
High Button Shoes, 136
Inside U.S.A., 137
Kiss Me, Kate, 141
Up in Central Park, 126

New York Theatre
Naughty Marietta, 17

Niblo's Garden
Black Crook, The, 3
Evangeline, 4

Eugene O'Neill Theatre
Big River, 270
Fela!, 372
Five Guys Named Moe, 289
Full Monty, The, 319
Grease, 298
Nine, 329
She Loves Me, 202
Spring Awakening, 345
Sweeney Todd, 338

Orpheum Theatre
Little Mary Sunshine, 186
Little Shop of Horrors, 262
Your Own Thing, 222

Palace Theatre
Aida, 316
Applause, 228
Beauty and the Beast, 297
George M!, 223
Legally Blonde, 351
La Cage aux Folles, 266
Oklahoma!, 255
Sweet Charity, 216
West Side Story, 364
Will Rogers Follies, The, 287
Woman of the Year, 260

Phoenix Theatre (later Eden)
Golden Apple, The, 160
Once Upon a Mattress, 181

Playhouse Theatre
Don't Bother Me, I Can't Cope, 235

Plymouth Theatre (later Gerald Schoenfeld)
Irma la Douce, 190
Jekyll and Hyde, 308
Passion, 298

Princess Theatre
Oh, Boy!, 24
Oh, Lady! Lady!!, 26
Very Good Eddie, 23

Public Theatre
Chorus Line, A, 243
I'm Getting My Act Together and Taking It on the
Road, 252

Richard Rodgers Theatre
Chicago, 307
Footloose, 313
How to Succeed in Business Without Really
Trying, 302
In the Heights, 357
Movin' Out, 328
Tarzan, 347

Royale Theatre (later Bernard Jacobs)
Boy Friend, The, 162
New Faces of 1952, 154
Song and Dance, 271

St. James Theatre
American Idiot, 377
Barnum, 256
Do Re Mi, 194
Finian's Rainbow, 370
Flower Drum Song, 178
Funny Thing Happened on the Way to the
Forum, A, 304
Gypsy, 282, 359
Hello, Dolly!, 204
King and I, The, 151
Li'l Abner, 171
My One and Only, 264
Oklahoma!, 119
On the Twentieth Century, 249
Pajama Game, The, 161
Producers, The
Secret Garden, The, 286
Tommy, 294
Two Gentlemen of Verona, 234
Where's Charley?, 138

Selwyn Theatre
Three's a Crowd, 73

Gerald Schoenfeld Theatre (former Plymouth)
A Chorus Line, 343

Shubert Theatre
Apple Tree, The, 218
Babes in Arms, 98
Bells Are Ringing, 171
Bloomer Girl, 125
By Jupiter, 116
Can-Can, 156
Chorus Line, A, 243
Countess Maritza, 53
Crazy for You, 288
Gypsy, 329
I Married an Angel, 102
Little Night Music, A, 237
Maytime, 24
Memphis, 369
Monty Python's Spamalot, 336
Paint Your Wagon, 152
Promises, Promises, 226

Roar of the Greasepaint—The Smell of the
Crowd, The, 212
Stop the World—I Want to Get Off, 199
Sweethearts, 134
Take Me Along, 183

63rd St. Music Hall
Shuffle Along, 34

Neil Simon Theatre (former Alvin**)**
Hairspray, 326
King and I, The, 303
Music Man, The, 319
Ragtime, 371
Rain—A Tribute to the Beatles on Broadway,
379

Snapple Theatre Center/Jerry Orbach Theatre
Fantasticks, The, 343

Standard Theatre
Robin Hood, 5

Studio 54
110 in the Shade, 352
Pacific Overtures, 333
Sunday in the Park With George, 356

Sullivan Street Playhouse
Fantasticks, The, 189

Theatre Comique
Mulligan Guard Ball, The, 4

Theatre de Lys
Threepenny Opera, The, 159

Theatre 80 St. Marks
You're a Good Man, Charlie Brown, 221

Times Square Theatre
Andre Charlot's Revue of 1924, 42
Strike Up the Band, 70

Uris Theatre (later Gershwin)
King and I, The, 248
Pirates of Penzance, The 258
Sweeney Todd, 253

Vanderbilt Theatre
Connecticut Yankee, A, 58
Irene, 32
Peggy-Ann, 54

Virginia Theatre (former ANTA, later August
Wilson)
City of Angels, 282
Flower Drum Song, 327
Jelly's Last Jam, 292
On Your Toes, 264

Wallack's Theatre
Fortune Teller, The, 6

Washington Square Theatre
Man of La Mancha, 215

August Wilson Theatre (former Virginia)
Jersey Boys, 339

Windsor Theatre
Cradle Will Rock, The, 101

Winter Garden
As the Girls Go, 139
At Home Abroad, 89
Cats, 263
Follies, 232
42nd Street, 257
Funny Girl, 207
Hooray for What!, 100
Life Begins at 8:40, 87
Mame, 217
Mamma Mia!, 324
Mexican Hayride, 122
Pacific Overtures, 245
Peter Pan, 163
Show Is On, The, 97
Sinbad, 29
Unsinkable Molly Brown, The, 191
West Side Story, 175
Wonderful Town, 155
Ziegfeld Follies, 85, 93

Ziegfeld Theatre
Bitter Sweet, 68
Brigadoon, 134
Gentlemen Prefer Blondes, 146
Kismet, 158
Porgy and Bess, 156
Red Mill, The, 128
Rio Rita, 55
Show Boat, 60, 128